THIRD EDITION

# MANAGERIAL ECONOMICS

## Economic Tools for Today's Decision Makers

**Paul G. Keat**

*Thunderbird, The American Graduate School
of International Management*

**Philip K. Y. Young**

*Pace University*

Prentice Hall, Upper Saddle River, New Jersey 07458

## PRENTICE HALL SERIES IN ECONOMICS

*To my wife, Sheilah, and my children, Diana and Andrew*
*P.G.K.*

*To my wife, Ilse, and my children, Christopher and Adriana*
*P.K.Y.Y.*

Senior Editor:  *Rod Banister*
Editor-in-Chief:  *PJ Boardman*
VP/Editorial Director:  *James C. Boyd*
Associate Editor:  *Gladys Soto*
Editorial Assistant:  *Marie McHale*
Senior Marketing Manager:  *Lori Braumberger*
Director of Production:  *Michael Weinstein*
Production Manager:  *Gail Steier de Acevedo*
Production Coordinator:  *Maureen Wilson*
Permissions Coordinator:  *Monica Stipanov*
Manufacturing Buyer:  *Natacha St. Hill Moore*
Senior Manufacturing Manager:  *Vincent Scelta*
Cover Design:  *Kiwi Design*
Cover Art/Photo:  *Alexandra Maldonado/Stock Illustration Source, Inc.*
Full Service Composition:  *Carlisle Publishers Services*

Copyright © 2000, 1996 by Prentice-Hall, Inc.
Upper Saddle River, New Jersey 07458

**Library of Congress Cataloging-in-Publication Data**
Keat, Paul G.
    Managerial economics : economic tools for today's decision makers / Paul G. Keat,
Philip K.Y. Young.—3rd ed.
      p.  cm.
    Includes bibliographical references and index.
    **ISBN 0-13-013538-0**
    1. Managerial economics.  I. Title.  II. Young, Philip K. Y.
HD30.22 .K39 2000
338.5'024'658 21—dc21                              99-045707

Prentice-Hall International (UK) Limited, London
Prentice-Hall of Australia Pty. Limited, Sydney
Prentice-Hall Canada, Inc., Toronto
Prentice-Hall Hispanoamericana, S.A., Mexico
Prentice-Hall of India Private Limited, New Delhi
Prentice-Hall of Japan, Inc., Tokyo
Prentice-Hall (Singapore) Pte Ltd.
Editora Prentice-Hall do Brasil, Ltda., Rio de Janeiro

Printed in the United States of America

10 9 8 7 6 5 4 3 2

# Brief Contents

# Contents

# Preface

One day after class, a student in one of our courses commented on the managerial economics text then being used: "This book is very dry. What it needs is a plot!" To a large extent, the idea for this text stemmed from this remark. This is a text that we believe will excite readers about managerial economics as well as inform them about this vital part of management education. Each chapter begins with a "Situation," in which managers in a fictional company, Global Foods, Inc., must make certain key decisions about their products in the beverage industry. After the relevant economic concepts or tools of analysis are presented, each chapter ends with a "Solution," a suggested way in which these concepts or tools can be used to help managers make the best decision. In the first and second editions of the text, Global Foods competed in the soft drinks segment of the beverage industry. In fact, chapter 1 opens with Global CEO Bob Burns considering the decision for Global Foods to enter the soft drink market. In this third edition, as readers will see reading chapter 2, Bob is recommending that his company also enter the rapidly growing bottled water segment of the industry.

The heart of managerial economics is the microeconomic theory of the firm. Much of this theory was formalized in a textbook written over 100 years ago by Professor Alfred Marshall of Cambridge University. Indeed, if readers were to refer to his *Principles of Economics* (1890), they would find many of the diagrams and equations presented in this text as well as all other texts in managerial economics. To be sure, the world has changed greatly since Marshall's ideas were developed. Market structures other than the "perfectly competitive model" are now much more important. Technology moves at such a rapid pace that the rate of obsolescence of products is now often measured in months rather than years. Competition among firms is frequently conducted on a global scale rather than a local or national one. Multinational firms invest, manufacture, and sell around the world. In so doing, they sometimes buy out their global competitors or form alliances or joint ventures with them. In the few years since the publication of the second edition, the Internet and e-commerce have become critical elements of most businesses.

Yet through all of these changes, basic microeconomic principles such as supply and demand, elasticity, short-run and long-run shifts in resource allocation, diminishing returns, economies of scale, and pricing according to marginal revenue and marginal cost continue to be important tools of analysis for managerial decision makers. In fact, the overall objective of this text is to demonstrate to our readers that the application of microeconomic theory has stood the test of time and continues to be relevant to many facets of modern business decision making.

One of the key lessons for managers to learn in studying economic analysis is the importance of understanding shifts in market demand and supply. In the first edition (1992), we cited Sun Microsystems as a good example of a company that was able to succeed in a market known for its rapidly changing supply and demand. At the time, we pointed out Sun's leadership in production and marketing of workstations as evidence of this. In our second edition (1996), we observed how Campbell Soup and Grand Met, two leading global food manufacturers, were trying to take advantage of the growing demand for salsa and Mexican foods by buying food companies that produced these products. As we were writing this third edition, we noted that two dominant industry leaders, Levi's and Kellogg's, are being seriously challenged in their respective markets because of their inability to keep up with changes in market supply and demand. Ten years ago, Levi's was the leader in the U.S. market for blue jeans. Today, it has fallen to second place behind Lee's. In addition to Lee's, much of Levi's share was lost to private-label jeans sold by such retail chains as J.C. Penney and Sears and to designer-label jeans such as Calvin Klein. Kellogg's is still the leader in the American market for breakfast cereal, but its market share has declined by several percentage points.

So we can see that for these two giants and household brand names, both changing consumer tastes (demand) and increased competition (supply) have seriously hurt their businesses. Younger consumers of "Generation X" and especially of "Generation Y" (those 19 years and younger) look on plain blue jeans as something for their parents (the aging baby boomers). The changing lifestyles of many Americans leave them with little time to sit down for an "ideal" breakfast that includes cereal, toast, and orange juice. Instead, many will grab a bagel and a beverage at a convenience store on their way to work or school. (What passenger vehicle made today does not have cup holders?)

Our text contains numerous examples of companies facing the challenges of changing market conditions. We point out a few here simply to give readers some introductory examples of just how relevant and fresh economic analysis can be. We are well aware of the reputation that economics courses have among some business students of being "too theoretical and not practical enough for the real world." In our opinion, nothing could be further from the truth. We know that the instructors in managerial economics will agree with us on this matter. We hope that this text will serve as a solid supplement to their classroom efforts to demonstrate to their students the importance and utility of economic theory for business decision making.

This text is designed for upper-level undergraduate courses and first-year MBA courses in managerial economics and applied economics. Very often, we have found that MBA students enter the managerial economics course with varying degrees of preparation for the subject. The first two chapters are a general introduction to economics and economic reasoning, and chapter 3 reviews the basic elements of supply and demand theory. The appendix to chapter 2 reviews the mathematics that can be used to help explain the material in selected chapters. We have purposely limited the use of calculus in this text. Thus, this appendix is intended primarily for those instructors and students who desire the economy of expression gained by using calculus and who want a general review of this mathematical technique. In addition, we have included brief mathematical appendices at the end of as well as within selected chapters.

In addition to discussing the applications of economic theory to the firm, our text (as is the custom with all texts in managerial economics) includes chapters on various tools of analysis that are helpful to business decision makers but that are not part of the core of traditional microeconomic theory. They are demand, production and cost estimation using regression analysis, forecasting, linear programming, capital budgeting, and risk analysis. Another subject, the role of government, can often be found in microeconomics texts under the heading of "market externalities." We are able to treat all of these subjects only in an introductory fashion. However, we hope that we have provided enough discussion and explanation on these topics to give readers a solid understanding of how they can be used in managerial decision making.

## Improvements in the Third Edition

In this third edition, we have sought to improve on the two previous editions by incorporating what we continue to learn from using the book in our classes. In addition, we received a number of useful comments from the faculty selected by Prentice Hall to review this edition's draft. One way in which we have tried to keep the material fresh and current is to incorporate many recent business examples from the popular press in this edition. This is particularly noticeable in the section, "International Applications," found at the end of most chapters.

We recognize that with the ease of accessing library data bases and informative Web sites on the Internet, any new example that we cite, no matter how recent, can be easily supplemented with still more current data during the semester in which this text is used. Our hope is that our discussion in the text will motivate readers to do so.

The following major changes and additions have been made in this third edition:

- Chapter 15, on the role of government, has been almost entirely rewritten. The section on regulation has been replaced with a new section on doing business with the government, written by a member of the staff of Booz-Allen & Hamilton's office in Washington, DC. The importance of the Coase Theorem in dealing with externalities has also been added. Many of the previously regulated companies in such industries as telecommunications, airlines, commercial banks, and electric utilities have started to consider mergers and acquisitions as a way of dealing with their new competitive environment. Hence, a section on mergers has essentially replaced the second edition's coverage of regulated industries.
- Chapter 7, on production, now combines both the theory and the estimation of the production function. Based on recommendations by various reviewers, we have moved the section on isoquants and isocosts to an appendix. The application of production theory to service companies is demonstrated by the use of an extended example of call centers.
- Linear programming is now treated in Appendix A at the end of the book. It was written by a professor of management science and focuses on establishing the important concepts without resorting to the use of graphs and numerical examples based on the simplex method. Instead, it shows how Solver, an additional software program that works with Microsoft Excel, can very quickly determine the optimal solution to any linear programming problem.
- In chapter 2, on the goals of the firm, the section on transaction costs has been considerably expanded with new examples. Also, a discussion of

Economic Value Added (EVA®) and Market Value Added (MVA®), measures of wealth creation, has been added.

- In chapter 10, on monopolistic competition and oligopoly, the section on industrial organization has been rewritten and expanded. For example, it now includes a definition of the concentration index and the HH index. A very important change is the expanded discussion of Michael Porter's strategic approach. Particular attention was paid to linking the structure-conduct-performance (SCP) approach to industrial organization to the ideas on strategy advanced by Professor Porter.

- An appendix to chapter 6, on forecasting, provides a descriptive review of new software packages for forecasting.

- Chapter 16, a new integrative chapter on economic concepts and tools, provides students with an analysis of the semiconductor industry and the competitive challenges of a company within that industry. It shows students the immediate practicality of many of the most basic but critically important concepts in managerial economics.

- In addition to these major changes, there are a number of smaller, yet significant, improvements. Game theory and its application in pricing and strategy are discussed at greater length in chapter 10. There is a brief new section on multinational transfer pricing in chapter 12. A section on how to calculate the market value of a firm has been added to chapter 13. Chapter 14 introduces the concept of "real options," which shows how a company can increase the value of a capital investment project when the company has the flexibility to increase, decrease, postpone, shut down, or even abandon a project.

- Key terms found in the "Important Concepts" section at the end of each chapter are now in **boldface** when used for the first time in the chapter.

## Ancillary Materials

 **Excel® Spreadsheets:** More than two dozen spreadsheet templates accompany the text and are intended to help students solve many of the questions raised in text discussions. An index of the applications is printed on the inside of the front cover of this book. This student aid can be downloaded from the Companion Web site for this book, which can be accessed at *http://www.prenhall.com/keatyoung.*

 **Interactive Study Guide:** On-line self-assessment, offering multiple-choice and essay questions for every chapter, is available to students at no cost at *http://www.prenhall.com/keat.* Graded by Prentice Hall's server, these quizzes provide students with immediate feedback, including additional help and section references linked to the text. Results for these activities can be sent to as many as four e-mail addresses.

**Instructor's Manual and Test Bank:** This volume provides answers to all of the questions and problems found in the text, as well as a group of multiple-choice and short-answer questions.

## Acknowledgments

We wish to thank our colleagues at Thunderbird, The American Graduate School of International Management, Pace University, and former colleagues at IBM for their assistance and encouragement in our work on this and the previous two editions of this text. We are particularly grateful to Dr. Jack Yurkiewicz, professor of management science at Pace University, and Sylvia Von Bostel, of Booz-Allen & Hamilton, for their contributions to the third edition. We also wish to thank Joseph Di Giorno, Divisional Technology Manager at Ernst & Young LLP, for providing the Web site list which can be found on the inside of the back cover.

We also thank Michael E. Waggy, of University of North Carolina, Charlotte, for writing the Interactive Study Guide.

Our appreciation also goes to the reviewers of all three editions of this text: Michael J. Applegate, Oklahoma State University; Robert Britt, West Virginia University; Peter Brust, University of Tampa; Charles Callahan, III, State University of New York, College at Brockport; John Conant, Indiana State University; Lewis Freiberg, Northeastern Illinois University; Edward H. Heinze, Valparaiso University; George Hoffer, Virginia Commonwealth University; Al Holtmann, University of Miami; Richard A. Jenner, San Francisco State University; Douglas Lamdin, University of Maryland, Baltimore County; Jerry Manahan, Midwestern State University; Cynthia McCarty, Jacksonville State University; Yale L. Meltzer, College of Staten Island; L. W. (Bill) Murray, University of San Francisco; Jan Palmer, Ohio University–Athens; Leila J. Pratt, The University of Tennessee at Chattanooga; L. B. Pulley, University of Virginia; Mathew Roelofs, Western Washington University; Roy Savoian, Lynchburg College; Frederica Shockley, California State University–Chico; William Doyle Smith, University of Texas at El Paso; James Tallant, Cape Fear Community College; Mo-Yin Tam, University of Illinois at Chicago; Yien-I Tu, University of Arkansas; Daryl N. Winn, University of Colorado; Richard Winkelman, Arizona State University; Richard Zuber, University of North Carolina at Charlotte; Habib Zuberi, Central Michigan University.

In closing, we would like to express our appreciation to the helpful, encouraging, and patient team at Prentice Hall including Rod Banister, senior editor; William Becher, editorial assistant; Gladys Soto, associate editor; and Maureen Wilson, project editor. Thanks also go to Terry Routley, our editor at Carlisle Publishers Services, and freelance copyeditor Robert L. Marcum.

# About the Authors

**Paul G. Keat** has been a member of the World Business Faculty at Thunderbird, American Graduate School of International Management, for the past twelve years. Presently he is a Lecturer in the Department of World Business and Director of Research at the International Trade Finance Center at Thunderbird. Prior to his coming to Thunderbird he was for many years associated with the International Business Machines Corporation in professional and managerial capacities.

His education includes a B.B.A. in accounting from the Baruch School of the City University of New York, an M.A. from Washington University, and a Ph.D. in economics from the University of Chicago.

Dr. Keat began his IBM career in the department of economic research and then moved into the long-range planning area. Later, as a member of the finance function, he spent several years at IBM's European headquarters in Paris, as manager in the financial planning area, and then as the financial manager for the company's European software business. After his return to the United States, Dr. Keat served as manager in the pricing area of one of the company's manufacturing groups. Before leaving IBM in 1987 he was associated with the company's International Finance, Planning and Administration School (IFPA), where he taught managerial economics, lectured on finance in a number of company-related courses, and managed academic courses. He also taught at IBM's IFPA school at La Hulpe, Belgium.

Dr. Keat has taught at several U.S. universities, including Washington University, CUNY, and Iona College. He was an adjunct professor of finance at the Lubin Graduate School of Business at Pace University, and he also taught in Pace's Executive MBA program.

**Philip K. Y. Young** is Professor of Economics at the Lubin School of Business at Pace University. His experiences at Pace include serving as executive director of Corporate Programs. In this capacity, he was responsible for the management and development of Pace's executive MBA program and all of its corporate educational and training programs. He is also the recipient of Pace University's outstanding teacher award.

Dr. Young served as the first visiting professor at the International Finance, Planning and Administration School of the IBM Corporation, where he developed and taught courses for IBM in both the United States and La Hulpe, Belgium. His areas of research and publication include ethnic entrepreneurship and doing business in the Asia-Pacific region.

Dr. Young is also an active participant in training and education programs for major corporations in a variety of industries such as information technology, telecommunications, packaged consumer goods, financial services, and consulting. His current clients include IBM, Bell Atlantic, British Telecom, Avon, and Booz-Allen & Hamilton. He teaches these courses in the United States, Western and Central Europe, Latin America, and Asia. He has a B.A. from the University of Hawaii, a master's in international affairs from Columbia University, and a Ph.D. in economics from New York University.

# CHAPTER 1

# Introduction

## THE SITUATION

The last of the color slides was barely off the screen when Bob Burns, the CEO of Global Foods, Inc., turned to his board of directors to raise the question that he  had been waiting all week to ask. "Well, ladies and gentlemen, are you with me in this new venture? Is it a 'go'? Shall we get into the soft drink business?"

"It's not that easy, Bob. We need some time to think it over. You're asking us to endorse a very major *decision,* one that will have a long-term impact on the direction of the company."

"I appreciate your wish to deliberate further, Dr. Breakstone," Bob responded, "but I would like to reach a decision today. As the president of a major university, you have been especially valuable in advising this company in matters relating to social and governmental policies. But we must diversify our business very soon in order to maintain the steady growth in profits that we have achieved in recent years. As my presentation showed, the manufacturing and marketing of our own brand of soft drink is one of the best ways to do this. It represents a significant diversification, yet it is very closely related to our core business: food.

"The *economics* of the soft drink market tell us that we would be foolish to pass up the kind of *investment return* that the market offers to those newcomers willing to take the *risk.* The food business is generally a mature one. On the other hand, our *forecast* indicates that there is still a lot of room for growth in the soft drink market. To be sure, there is a tremendous amount of *competition* from the 'red team' and the 'blue team.' But we already have expertise in the food business, and it should carry over into the beverage market."

"That's just it, Bob," interjected another board member. "Are we prepared to take this risk? You yourself acknowledged that the *market power* wielded by the two dominant companies in this business is not to be taken lightly. Others have tried to take market share from them and have failed miserably. Moreover, the projections that you have shown for a growing soft
*(Continued)*

1

drink market are based on the *assumption* that the growth rate will remain the same as it has been in the past ten years or so. As we all know, the soft drink market has been growing, but it has also been very fickle. Only recently, Americans were on a health kick, and fruit juices and bottled waters along with health foods were in fashion. Now it seems that soft drinks are back in style again. Who knows what people will want in the future? Maybe we'll all go back to drinking five cups of coffee a day. And what about all the money that we're going to have to spend up front to *differentiate* our product? As you well know, in the processed-food business, establishing brand recognition—not to mention brand loyalty—can be extremely difficult and costly."

"Well, ladies and gentlemen, all your concerns are certainly legitimate ones, and believe me, I have given much thought to these drawbacks. This is one of the biggest decisions that I will have made since becoming CEO. My staff has spent hundreds of hours analyzing all available data to arrive at a judgment. Our findings indicate a strong probability of earning an above-average return on an investment in the soft drink business, a return commensurate with the kind of risk we know exists in that market. But if we could make all our decisions with 100 percent certainty simply by feeding numbers into a computer, we'd all be out of a job. To be sure, details on production, cost, pricing, distribution, advertising, financing, and organizational structure remain to be ironed out. However, if we wait until all these details are worked out, we may be missing a window of opportunity that might not appear again in this market for a long time. I say that we should go ahead with this project as soon as possible. And unanimity among the board members will give me greater confidence in this endeavor."

# Introduction: Economics and Managerial Decision Making

Managerial Economics is one of the most important and useful courses in your curriculum of studies. It will provide you with a foundation for studying other courses in finance, marketing, operations research, and managerial accounting. It will also provide you with a theoretical framework for tying together courses in the entire curriculum so that you can have a cross-functional view of your studies.

**Economics** is "the study of the behavior of human beings in producing, distributing and consuming material goods and services in a world of scarce resources."[1] *Management* is the discipline of organizing and allocating a firm's scarce resources to achieve its desired objectives.[2] These two definitions clearly point to the relationship between economics and managerial decision making. In fact, we can combine these two terms and define **managerial economics** as the use of economic analysis to make business decisions involving the best use of an organization's scarce resources.

---

[1]Campbell McConnell, *Economics,* New York: McGraw-Hill, 1993, p. 1.
[2]For books supporting this definition, see Peter Drucker, *Management,* New York: Harper & Row, 1973.

Joel Dean, the author of the first managerial economics textbook, defines managerial economics as "the use of economic analysis in the formulation of business policies." He also notes a "big gap between the problems of logic that intrigue economic theorists and the problems of policy that plague practical management [which] needs to be bridged in order to give executives access to the practical contributions that economic thinking can make to top-management policies."[3]

William Baumol, a highly respected economist and industry consultant, stated that an economist can use his ability to build theoretical models and apply them to any business problem, no matter how complex, break it down into essential components, and describe the relationship among the components, thereby facilitating a systematic search for an optimal solution. In his extensive experience as a consultant to both industry and government, he found that every problem that he worked on was helped in some way by "the method of reasoning involved in the derivation of some economic theorem."[4]

William H. Meckling, the former dean of the Graduate School of Management at the University of Rochester, expressed a similar sentiment in an interview conducted by *The Wall Street Journal.* In his view, "economics is a discipline that can help students solve the sort of problems they meet within the firm." Recalling his experience as the director of naval warfare analysis at the Center for Naval Analysis and as an economic analyst at the Rand Corporation, one of the nation's most prominent think tanks, Mecklin stated that these institutions are "dominated by physical scientist types, really brilliant people." But he went on to say that "the economists knew how to structure the problems . . . the rest of the people knew a lot about technical things but they had never thought about how you structure big issues."[5]

As it has evolved in undergraduate and graduate programs over the past half century, managerial economics is essentially a course in applied microeconomics that includes selected quantitative techniques common to other disciplines such as linear programming (management science), regression analysis (statistics, econometrics, and management science), capital budgeting (finance), and cost analysis (managerial and cost accounting). Looked at from our perspective as economists, we see that in fact many disciplines in business studies have drawn from the core of microeconomics for concepts and theoretical support. For example, the economic analysis of demand and price elasticity can be found in most marketing texts. The division of markets into four types—perfect competition, pure monopoly, monopolistic competition, and oligopoly—is generally the basis for the analysis of the competitive environment presented in books on corporate strategy and marketing strategy.[6]

There are a number of other examples to be found. The economic concept of opportunity cost serves as the foundation for the analysis of relevant cost in managerial

[3]Joel Dean, *Managerial Economics,* Englewood Cliffs, NJ: Prentice-Hall, 1951, p. vii.
[4]William Baumol, "What Can Economic Theory Contribute to Managerial Economics?" *American Economic Review,* 51, 2 (May 1961), p. 114.
[5]"Economics Has Much to Teach the Businessman," *The Wall Street Journal,* May 3, 1983.
[6]Professor Michael Porter, whose books on strategy have greatly influenced this field of study, is himself a Ph.D. in economics.

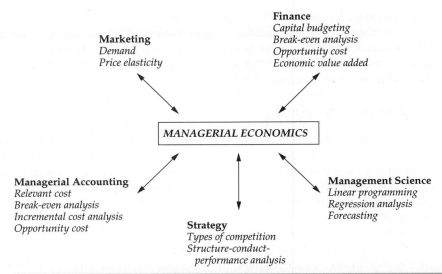

**Marketing**
*Demand*
*Price elasticity*

**Finance**
*Capital budgeting*
*Break-even analysis*
*Opportunity cost*
*Economic value added*

*MANAGERIAL ECONOMICS*

**Managerial Accounting**
*Relevant cost*
*Break-even analysis*
*Incremental cost analysis*
*Opportunity cost*

**Strategy**
*Types of competition*
*Structure-conduct-*
  *performance analysis*

**Management Science**
*Linear programming*
*Regression analysis*
*Forecasting*

**FIGURE 1.1** Managerial Economics and Other Business Disciplines

accounting and for the use of the "hurdle rate"[7] in finance. As you will see in the next chapter, opportunity cost also plays an important part in understanding how firms create "economic value" for their shareholders. Finally, in recent years, certain authors have linked their managerial economics texts thematically with strategy and human resources.[8] Figure 1.1 illustrates our view that managerial economics is closely linked with many other disciplines in a business curriculum.

Our approach in this text is to show the linkages of economics with other business functions, while maintaining a focus on the heart of managerial economics: the microeconomic theory of the behavior of consumers and firms in competitive markets. When clearly understood and exemplified in actual business examples, this theory provides managers with a basic framework for making key business decisions about the allocation of their firm's scarce resources. Perhaps the most important of these decisions is whether to compete in a particular market for a good or service; in other words, the need to answer the fundamental question: "What business should we be in?" This is the very question addressed by Bob Burns and the rest of the board of directors of Global Foods in this chapter's "Situation."

In seeking an answer to this question, Bob and the board had to take into account a number of critical economic factors covered in this text. For example, they had to consider (1) the anticipated market demand for soft drinks, (2) the degree of competition

---

[7]Essentially, this is a company's cost of funds expressed as a percentage (e.g., 15%). Any project funded by the company should have a rate of return that is greater than this level.
[8]See for example, David Besanko et. al., *Economics of Strategy,* New York: John Wiley & Sons, 1996, and James A. Brickley et al., *Managerial Economics and Organizational Architecture,* New York, Irwin, McGraw-Hill, 1997.

in the market, (3) the extent of the market power held by existing firms, and (4) the importance of establishing product differentiation in order to compete with other firms in the market. In addition, one of the board members strongly felt that much of the success of this venture hinged on the validity of the assumption made about the future tastes and preferences of consumers.

## The Economics of a Business

Another way to appreciate the study of managerial economics in a business curriculum is to consider how the material covered in this text relates to what we call the **economics of a business.** By this we mean "the key factors that affect the ability of a firm to earn an acceptable rate of return on its owners' investment." (See chapter 2 for a discussion of financial goals of a firm such as return on investment, profit maximization, and economic value added.) The most important of these factors are competition, technology, and customers.

The impact of changing economics on well-established companies can be better understood and appreciated within the framework of a 'four-stage model' of change. This model is shown in Figure 1.2.

Stage I can be called "the good old days" for companies such as IBM, Kodak, Sears, and any number of other solid, blue-chip companies whose dominance of the market allowed them to achieve high profit margins by simply marking up their costs to provide them with a suitable level of profit. Then changes in technology, competition, and customers put pressures on their profit margins as well as market share and forced them into Stage II, where they sought refuge through cost cutting, downsizing, restructuring, and reengineering. In the United States, this began to occur in the 1980s and continued on to the early 1990s, when consultants such as Michael Hammer touted the benefits of "reengineering" as a means of dealing with these changes.[9]

From the mid 1990s on, companies sought to enter Stage III when they realized that the continual focus on cost had its limits insofar as its ability to increase profits. After all, there is only so much money that a company can save by reducing its workforce or by becoming more efficient. Therefore, in Stage III "top-line growth" became the major focus.[10] Although companies may have reaffirmed their ability to grow their top line, Wall Street analysts questioned their ability to grow in a *profitable* manner. Thus Stage IV becomes a necessary part of a company's full recovery from the impact of changing economics.[11]

Avon is a good example of a well-established company that has gone through the first three stages and is seeking a firm footing in Stage IV. Stage I for Avon lasted until the latter part of the 1970s. As more and more women began to enter the workforce on a full-time basis, the effectiveness of Avon's vaunted sales force (the "Avon ladies") began to decline. In the 1980s, Avon chose to deal with this change by diversifying rather than taking the full brunt of cost cutting implied in Stage II. In the late 1980s, they were actually faced with the threat of a hostile take over by Amway. By the early 1990s, Avon

[9]Michael Hammer and James Champy, *Reengineering the Corporation,* New York: Harper Collins, 1993.
[10]See for example Robert G. Cross, *Revenue Management,* New York: Broadway Books, 1997.
[11]For a recent book on "profitable growth," see Ram Charan and Noel M. Tichy, *Every Business Is a Growth Business,* New York: Random House, 1998.

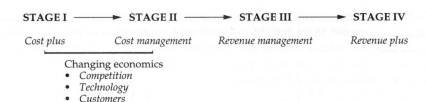

**FIGURE 1.2** Four Stages of Change

divested itself of its acquisitions and started its way through Stage II by consolidating its manufacturing facilities and call centers worldwide. In 1997, it embarked on a substantial reengineering program that is supposed to save hundreds of millions of dollars for the company. Because Avon had to make up for lost time due to its excursions into diversification, its entry into Stage III overlapped that of Stage II. The mid 1990s marked the beginning of Stage III when Avon expanded aggressively into emerging markets such as China, India, Central Europe, and Russia. It also continued to grow in Latin America, a region of the world in which it had already developed a considerable amount of business. In their U.S. and Western European markets, Avon is spending more on marketing to improve and modernize the image of Avon products. For example, it recently opened "Avon Centre" in the fashionable Trump Tower building on Fifth Avenue in New York City.[12]

In the previous edition of this text, published in 1996, we noted a number of well-established companies that were thrust from Stage I into Stage II because of the changing economics of their business. Among them were IBM, Sears, and Kodak. Since that time, we see that IBM has moved into stages III and IV by aggressively building up its Global Services business (computer operations, service bureau and consulting) and by rejuvenating its mainframe computer as a network server. It is also counting on its "e-commerce" business to grow its revenue and profit in the future. However, some of its hardware business is still subject to considerable economic pressures. In 1998, IBM reported an operating loss of close to $1 billion in its personal computers division.

Sears, too, seems to now be on the road to recovery with its repositioning as a women's clothing store (e.g., "Come see the softer side of Sears"). However, in 1998, it unfortunately encountered a serious scandal involving the unethical collection of funds from former Sears credit card holders who had declared bankruptcy and were therefore not legally obligated to Sears for any past-due monies.

Kodak is still struggling to some extent, having had to announce in late 1998 intended layoffs of more than 10,000 regular employees. However, it has become much more aggressive in reducing the prices of its lower-speed films to match Fuji and private-label film manufacturers and has concentrated on marketing the higher-margin high-speed and specialty films. More important, it has increased its resources and efforts in the digital imaging business.

---

[12]The Asian currency crisis and the economic problems in Russia and key countries in Latin America such as Brazil have caused the company's dollar denominated sales and profit to decline. However, unit volume and sales denominated in local currencies have continued to increase in high single digit figures in these areas of the world despite their economic woes. (Avon Annual Report, 1998).

There are numerous other current examples of companies whose changing economics have thrust them into Stage II or who are fighting to get into Stage III or IV. At the time this edition was being prepared, two well-known companies—Levi's and Kellogg's—had both announced major layoffs and plant closings because of falling sales and profits. No doubt readers will witness more such changes during the course of reading this text. But the four stages of change model provides more than just a framework to judge current business events. The model also underscores the importance of various topics covered in this text. For example, in Stage I when the company dominates the market, the monopoly model whereby firms are free to price their products using the "MR = MC rule" (you will learn about this in chapter 9) would be particularly useful. In Stage II, when the company must engage in cost cutting in response to changing competition, customers, and technology, the material in chapters 7 and 8 on cost and production and in chapter 9's section on highly competitive markets become vital to understand. In Stage III, when the company tries to grow its way out of its decline, chapters 4, 5, and 6 provide critical information. These chapters cover the qualitative and quantitative analysis of demand, the keys to growing revenue. Finally in Stage IV, when the company strives for profitable growth, just about all the material in this text can prove helpful.

## A Brief Review of Important Economic Terms and Concepts

For purposes of study and teaching, economics is divided into two broad categories, microeconomics and macroeconomics. The former concerns the study of individual consumers and producers in specific markets, and the latter deals with the aggregate economy. Topics in microeconomics include supply and demand in individual markets, the pricing of specific outputs and inputs (also called factors of production, or resources), production and cost structures for individual goods and services, and the distribution of income and output in the population. Topics in macroeconomics include analysis of the gross domestic product (also referred to as "national income analysis"), unemployment, inflation, fiscal and monetary policy, and the trade and financial relationships among nations.

Microeconomics is the category that is most utilized in managerial economics. However, certain aspects of macroeconomics must also be included because decisions by managers of firms are influenced by their views of the current and future conditions of the macroeconomy. For example, we can well imagine that the management of a company producing capital equipment (e.g., computers, machine tools, trucks, or robotic instruments) would indeed be remiss if they did not factor into their sales forecast some consideration of the macroeconomic outlook. For these and other companies whose businesses are particularly sensitive to the business cycle, a recession would have a very unfavorable effect on their sales, whereas a robust period of economic expansion would be beneficial. But for the most part, managerial economics is based on the variables, models, and concepts that embody microeconomic theory.

As defined in the previous section, economics is the study of how choices are made regarding the use of scarce resources in the production, consumption, and distribution of goods and services. The key term is *scarce resources*. **Scarcity** can be defined as a condition in which resources are not available to satisfy all the needs and wants of a specified group of people. Although scarcity refers to the supply of a **resource,** it makes sense only in relation to the demand for the resource. For example, there is only one

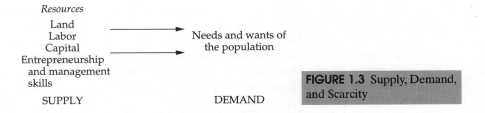

*Resources*
Land
Labor
Capital
Entrepreneurship
and management
skills

Needs and wants of
the population

SUPPLY                                    DEMAND

**FIGURE 1.3** Supply, Demand, and Scarcity

Mona Lisa. Therefore, we can safely say that the supply of this particular work of art by da Vinci is limited. Nevertheless, if for some strange reason no one wanted this magnificent work of art, then in purely economic terms it would not be considered scarce. Let us take a less extreme and certainly more mundane example: broken glass on the streets of New York City. Here we have a case of a "resource" that is not scarce not only because there is a lot of broken glass to be found, but also because nobody wants it! Now suppose there were a new art movement inspired by the use of materials retrieved from the streets of urban areas, with broken glass from the streets of New York being particularly desirable. The once-plentiful resource would fast become a "scarce" commodity.

The relative nature of scarcity is represented in Figure 1.3. As can be seen in the figure, the supply of resources is used to meet the demand for these resources by the population. Because the population's needs and wants exceed the ability of the resources to satisfy all the demands, scarcity exists.

In an introductory economics course, the concept of scarcity is usually discussed in relation to an entire country and its people. For example, you will probably recall from your first course in economics the classic example of "guns" (representing a country's devotion of resources to national defense) versus "butter" (representing the use of resources for peacetime goods and services). To be sure, scarcity is a condition individual consumers and producers must also deal with. This text is primarily concerned with the way in which managers of the producing organizations contend with scarcity. But before discussing this particular aspect of the problem, let us review the condition of scarcity from the perspective of an entire country.

The intent of the "guns versus butter" example is to illustrate that scarcity forces a country to choose the amounts of resources that it wishes to allocate between defense and peacetime goods and services. In so doing, its people must reckon with the **opportunity cost** of their decision. This type of cost can be defined as the amount or subjective value that must be sacrificed in choosing one activity over the next best alternative. In the "guns versus butter" example, one activity involves the production of war goods and services, and the other pertains to peacetime goods and services. Because of the scarcity of resources, the more that the country allocates to guns, the less it will have to produce butter, and vice versa. The opportunity cost of additional units of guns are the units of butter that the country must forgo in the resource allocation process. The opposite would apply as resources are allocated more for the production of butter than for guns.

In the presence of a limited supply relative to demand, countries must decide how to allocate their scarce resources. This decision is central to the study of economics. In fact, economics has been defined as "the science which studies human behavior as a relationship between ends and scarce means which have alternative uses."[13] Essentially, the allocation decision can be viewed as comprising three separate choices:

1. *What* goods and services should be produced and in what quantities?
2. *How* should these goods and services be produced?
3. *For whom* should these goods and services be produced?

These are the well-known *what, how,* and *for whom* questions found in the introductory chapter of all economic principles textbooks.

The first question incorporates the "guns versus butter" decision. Should a country with scarce resources produce guns? Should it produce butter? If so, how much butter and how many guns? The same applies to the countless other goods and services or product groups that a country is capable of producing.

The second question involves the allocation of a country's resources in the production of a particular good or service. Suppose a country decides to produce a certain amount of butter. What amounts of land, labor, capital, and entrepreneurial efforts should it devote to this end? Should it use more workers than machinery (a labor-intensive process) or vice versa (a capital-intensive process)? The important point to remember about this question is that it is an economic and not a technical one. It is not asking which formula or recipe should be used to make butter; it is asking what combination of the factors of production should be used in producing a given amount of the product.

The meaning of the third question should be readily apparent. It is a decision that must be made about the distribution of a country's output of goods and services among the members of its population.

All countries must deal with these three basic questions because all have scarce resources. Scarcity is a more serious problem in some countries than in others, but all have needs and wants that cannot be completely met by their existing resources. Precisely how these countries go about making allocation decisions is the question to which we now turn.

There are essentially three ways a country can answer the questions of what, how, and for whom. These ways, referred to as *processes,* are as follows:

1. **Market process:** The use of supply, demand, and material incentives to answer the questions of what, how, and for whom.
2. **Command process:** The use of the government or some central authority to answer the three basic questions. (This process is sometimes referred to as the *political process.*)
3. **Traditional process:** The use of customs and traditions to answer the three basic questions.

Countries generally employ a combination of these three processes to allocate their scarce resources. The market process is predominant in the United States, although the command process plays an important role. Hence, the United States is said to have a mixed economy. Based on the levels of spending by the federal, state, and

---

[13]Lionel Robbins, *An Essay on the Nature and Significance of Economic Science,* 2nd ed., London: Macmillan and Co., Ltd., 1935, p. 16.

local governments, we can state that approximately one-fifth of the goods and services produced in the United States are influenced by the command process. The command process does not necessarily mean that a government literally orders the production of certain amounts of guns, butter, or other goods or services; rather, a government may use the material incentives of the market process to allocate resources in certain ways, a process often referred to as *indirect command*. For example, the government offers defense contractors the opportunity to earn a profit by producing military goods and services. In addition, the government can control the allocation of resources in a more direct way through various laws governing the actions of both consumers and producers. For example, the government controls manufacturing and distribution through such agencies as the Food and Drug Administration. It attempts to control consumer use of certain foods and drugs through various laws and regulations. A simple but important example of this pertains to the tobacco industry. Over the past several decades, the U.S. government has made determined efforts to convince people to stop smoking. These efforts range from warnings on cigarette packages to the banning of smoking on airline flights. Prohibition during the 1920s offers another example of the government's efforts to stop the consumption of certain goods or services.

In addition to using rules and regulations and its fiscal power, the government can also influence the allocation of scarce resources through subsidies, tariffs, and quotas. Further discussion of these aspects of the command process in the U.S. economy is found in other sections of this chapter and throughout the rest of the text. In fact, chapter 15 is devoted to a discussion of the role of government in the market economy.

The traditional process is also at work in the U.S. economy, but this process can be better understood by considering its impact on different countries throughout the world, particularly those whose economies are still developing. Examples of the traditional process are found in the eating habits, and in the patterns of work and social interaction in such countries. Two examples of how the traditional process influences the allocation of scarce resources are religious restrictions on certain foods, such as beef and pork, and hiring practices based primarily on familial relationships. A branch of anthropology called economic anthropology is particularly concerned with the impact of customs and traditions on the economic questions of what, how, and for whom. In the business curriculum, students will find this subject of particular importance in courses on international business.

Because of the predominance of the market process in the U.S. economy, our discussion of the allocation of scarce resources is based on the assumption that managers operate primarily through the mechanisms of supply, demand, and material incentive (i.e., the profit motive). Their decisions about what goods to produce, how they should be produced, and for whom they should be produced are essentially market oriented. That is, firms choose to produce certain goods and services because, given the demand for these products and the cost of using scarce resources, they can earn sufficient profit to justify their particular use of these resources. Moreover, they combine their scarce resources to produce maximum output in the least costly way. Finally, they supply these goods and services to those segments of the population expected to provide the most material reward for their efforts.

**TABLE 1.1 The Three Basic Economic Questions**

| *From the Standpoint of a Country* | *From the Standpoint of a Company* |
|---|---|
| 1. What goods and services should be produced? | 1. The product decision |
| 2. How should these goods and services be produced? | 2. The hiring, staffing, procurement, and capital-budgeting decisions |
| 3. For whom should these goods and services be produced? | 3. The market segmentation decision |

Table 1.1 compares the three basic questions from the standpoint of a country and from the standpoint of a company, where they form the basis of the **economic decisions for the firm.** From the firm's point of view, question 1 is the product decision. At some particular time, a firm may decide to provide new or different goods or services or to stop providing a particular good or service. For example, Gateway 2000, the seller of personal computers through direct mail, decided in 1997 to expand its range of product offerings to include servers as well as PCs. Also in that year, Mercedes began selling its version of a sports utility vehicle to compete in the high end of this market. As an example of new services, consider the wireless companies' offering of digital services (as opposed to the older analog services), typical of the many product introductions taking place in the information technology and communications industry. And as you will see in the next chapter, Global Foods decides to sell bottled water in addition to carbonated soft drinks. Bottled water actually represents the fastest growing segment of the nonalcoholic beverage market, and certainly our fictional company does not want to get left behind.

Question 2 is a basic part of a manager's responsibility. It involves personnel practices such as hiring and firing as well as questions concerning the purchase of items ranging from raw materials to capital equipment. For example, the decision to automate certain clerical activities using a network of personal computers results in a more capital-intensive mode of production. The resolution to use more supplementary, part-time workers in place of full-time workers is another example of a management decision concerning how goods and services should be produced. A third example involves the selection of materials in the production of a certain item (e.g., the combination of steel, aluminum, and plastic used in an automobile).

The firm's decision concerning question 3 is not completely analogous to that of a country. Actually, a firm's decision regarding *market segmentation* (a term used in the marketing field) is closely related to question 1 for a country. In deciding what segment of the market to focus on, the firm is not literally deciding who gets the good or service. For example, suppose a firm decides to target a certain demographic segment by selling only a "high-end" or premium version of a product. In a free-market economy, this would not prevent anyone from buying the product. However, the way in which a company markets the product (which includes its pricing and distribution policies) makes certain segments of the market more likely to purchase the product.

Perhaps one of the best ways to link the economic problem of making choices under conditions of scarcity with the tasks of a manager is to consider the view put forth by Professor Robert Anthony that a manager is essentially a person who is responsible for the allocation of a firm's scarce resources.[14]

It is interesting to note that "managers" or "management skills" was not delineated as a separate factor of production by early economic theorists. The four traditional categories of resources are land, labor, capital, and entrepreneurship. The last category can be treated as broad enough to include management, but the two classifications do involve different characteristics or skills.

The term *entrepreneurship* is generally associated with the ownership of the means of production. But in addition, it implies willingness to take certain risks in the pursuit of goals (e.g., starting a new business, producing a new product, or providing a different kind of service). Management, on the other hand, involves the ability to organize and administer various tasks in pursuit of certain objectives. An important part of a manager's job is to monitor and guide people in an organization. In the words of Peter Drucker, who has been called "the founding father of the science of management,"

> It is "management" that determines what is needed and what has to be achieved [in an organization]. . . . Management is work. Indeed, it is the specific work of a modern society, the work that distinguishes our society from all earlier ones. . . . As work, management has its own skills, its own tools, its own techniques.[15]

Part of being a good manager involves taking risks, so experts have advised managers to become more "entrepreneurial." By the same token, entrepreneurs may require professional management expertise to run their venture more effectively. Michael Dell, founder of Dell Computer Corporation, is perhaps one of the best examples of an entrepreneur who required professional management at some point in the development of his company. Back in the mid 1990s, Dell's rapid growth created serious process and control problems. To his credit, Michael Dell brought in seasoned executives from large corporations to help the company deal with these problems. The success of his company today indicates the importance of professional management in rapidly growing start-ups.

Some economists cite management skills as a separate factor of production. Others include them in the general category of entrepreneurship. Still others combine entrepreneurship and management skills into one category, as we have done. An interesting treatment of the subject was given by Alfred Marshall, whose work in economic theory about 100 years ago still provides much of the foundation for modern microeconomics. Marshall used the building trade to illustrate certain differences between managerial and entrepreneurial skills and activities. According to Marshall, individuals may well be able to manage the construction of their own homes even though they are less efficient than a professional contractor would be. However, it is another matter when housing construction is carried out on a large scale.

---

[14]Actually, Anthony divided the planning and control process in a firm into three activities: strategic planning (i.e., setting the firm's overall objectives), management control (i.e., making sure that scarce resources are obtained and used effectively and efficiently in the firm's accomplishment of its objectives), and operational control (i.e., making sure that specific tasks are carried out effectively and efficiently). These ideas were first put forth in R. N. Anthony, *Planning and Control Systems: A Framework for Analysis,* Boston: Harvard Business School, Division of Research, 1965.

[15]Drucker, *Management,* p. xi.

> When this [housing construction] is done on a large scale, as for instance in opening a new suburb, the stakes at issue are so large as to offer an attractive field to powerful capitalists with a very high order of general business ability, but perhaps with not much technical knowledge of the building trade. They rely on their own judgment for the decision as to what are likely to be the coming relations of demand and supply for different kinds of houses; but they entrust to others the *management of details* [emphasis added]. They employ architects and surveyors to make plans in accordance with their general directions, and then enter into contracts with professional builders for carrying them out. But they themselves *undertake the chief risks of the business* [emphasis added], and control its general direction.[16]

You may be somewhat surprised at the freshness of observations made a century ago. You may also feel that Marshall was referring simply to management tasks and responsibilities at different levels. Putting Marshall's ideas in terms of today's large corporation, what he refers to as "the decision as to what are likely to be the coming relations of demand and supply" most likely involves strategic decisions made by upper management. What he terms "the management of details" is usually carried out by lower levels of management (e.g., by first-line supervisors).

Regardless of how the classification is handled, it is important to be aware of the distinction between the two factors. Obviously, the content of this text is devoted to developing management skills. Nonetheless, a mastery of the economic principles presented in this book could well lead to a sharpening of one's entrepreneurial skills by helping to assess the market conditions and risks involved in a particular venture.

## The Case of Global Foods, Inc.: Situations and Solutions

Prior sections of this chapter cited various reasons why an understanding of economics is important to managerial decision making. An effective way of demonstrating this importance is to cite real-world examples gleaned from the popular press and distilled from the findings of research studies on the use of economics in managerial decision making. All other texts in managerial economics do this, and this book is no exception. But in addition, we hope to show how economic terms and concepts can be applied to managerial decision making through the use of a series of hypothetical situations such as the one presented at the beginning of this chapter. In fact, each chapter will begin with a *situation* requiring some sort of decision or action relating directly to the subject matter of the chapter. For example, in this chapter, a decision must be made about whether to enter the soft drink market. This is a fundamental business decision involving the allocation of a firm's scarce resources, a major theme of this chapter.

At the end of each chapter, a *solution* for the situation will be presented based on the knowledge gained from reading the chapter. We use the term *solution* rather loosely because it may not involve a specific answer, as one might expect in the solution to a mathematical problem. In our view, the ambiguity of a solution is very

---

[16]Alfred Marshall, *Principles of Economics,* 8th ed., Philadelphia: Porcupine Press, 1920, reprinted 1982, pp. 245–46. (First edition published in 1890.)

much in keeping with conditions in the real world. Very often in an actual business problem, there is no unique formula that one can use to compute the answer. Either the formula does not exist or is not entirely applicable to the problem, or the problem itself is not amenable to a straightforward quantitative solution technique. And even when a specific numerical solution is arrived at—as is the case in chapter 13 on capital budgeting—there may be other considerations of a qualitative nature that temper the acceptability of the solution. Therefore, the solutions offered at the end of the chapters are only suggested outcomes of the situations. (You may wish to consider alternative ways for the managers depicted in the situations to deal with their tasks or problems.)

The situations used throughout the book are based on one industry and one firm in that industry. As you have already learned, we will be using the soft drink industry. Moreover, we will be following the trials and tribulations of the managers of Global Foods, Inc., and, in certain cases, the managers of firms that do business with Global. This will help to tie together the disparate aspects of economic analysis. Also, we felt that a focus on one firm in one industry will create added interest in the events depicted in the situations, further motivating mastery of each chapter's material.

A number of industries were initially considered. We chose the soft drink industry based on the following criteria:

1. The industry should be one that all readers can relate to as consumers.
2. The goods or services sold in the industry should be essentially nontechnical, and the means of production should be relatively easy for the layperson to understand.
3. The competitive environment should be very intense.
4. Information about the industry should be readily available (e.g., from trade journals and research monographs), and news about current activities in this industry should be frequently reported in the popular media.

The soft drink industry closely meets all of these criteria. Just about everyone consumes this product, and the product itself is rather simple: carbonated water, sweeteners, and various flavorings. The packaging is also uncomplicated. Soft drinks are sold today in 12-ounce aluminum cans, in 1- and 2-liter plastic bottles, and in glass bottles. The making of the syrup and the bottling of the beverage involve various manufacturing processes that are relatively easy to understand. The two most important trade publications in the soft drink industry are *Beverage World* and *Beverage Digest*. We found them to be excellent sources of background information on the industry. Moreover, the major soft drink companies are constantly reported on in major periodicals. Recent articles from these sources will be cited throughout the text.

The situations used in each chapter, along with the characters portrayed at Global, are entirely fictitious. However, the features of each situation closely resemble actual business problems or circumstances with which managers must often deal. The verity of the issues involved in each situation is based on the authors' experiences in private industry as well as on extensive interviews with managers from various companies in the soft drink business. The following section gives a summary of the situations and solutions presented in the chapters. The main decisions to be made by the characters portrayed in the situations are included under the heading "Key Question."

## Summary of the Situations and Solutions

### 1 INTRODUCTION

**Situation:** Bob Burns, CEO of Global Foods, Inc., asks the board of directors to approve a decision to enter the soft drink business.

**Key Question:** "Should we enter the soft drink business?"

**Solution:** The Board approves the decision, and Global Foods enters the soft drink business.

### 2 THE FIRM AND ITS GOALS

**Situation:** In an effort to increase the company's revenues, Bob Burns considers entry into the bottled water market, the fastest-growing segment of the nonalcoholic beverage industry.

**Key Question:** "How can we improve the value of our company when the Wall Street analysts are judging us primarily on our ability to grow our revenue and profit?"

**Solution:** Bob decides to take Global Foods into the bottled water business.

### 3 SUPPLY AND DEMAND

**Situation:** Ross Harris, senior purchasing agent for Global Foods, and Kathy Martinez, staff associate for a major producer of high-fructose corn syrup (HFCS), must prepare studies for their respective companies as a prelude to a major contract negotiation between the suppliers and users of HFCS.

**Key Question:** "What is the best time period within which to lock in the price of HFCS?"

**Solution:** The suppliers and users of HFCS agree to a compromise in which the price of HFCS is to be established every 3 months instead of every 12 months.

### 4 DEMAND ELASTICITY

**Situation:** Henry Caulfield, the proprietor of a "Gas 'n Go" convenience store, must evaluate the desirability of various pricing schedules for soft drinks set by the major beverage companies.

**Key Question:** "For what price should I sell this new soft drink?"

**Solution:** He decides that the relative inelasticity of the products in question makes it difficult to increase sales by lowering the price.

### 5 DEMAND ESTIMATION

**Situation:** Jennifer Harrah, senior research associate of a market research firm, is assigned the task of producing a statistical model that will help to explain the determinants of soft drink consumption. Her firm's client is Global Foods, Inc.

**Key Question:** "What are the key determinants of demand for soft drinks, and what are their quantitative impacts on sales?"

**Solution:** Jennifer estimates the quantitative impacts of a selected number of factors on soft drink sales with the use of multiple regression analysis.

## 6 FORECASTING

**Situation:** Frank Robinson, newly appointed head of Global's forecasting department, is asked to estimate the next year's sales of Citronade, the company's lemon-lime soda.

**Key Question:** "What will next year's sales for Citronade be?"

**Solution:** Frank uses a trend analysis, adjusted seasonally as well as cyclically, to forecast the coming year's sales.

## 7 THE THEORY AND ESTIMATION OF PRODUCTION

**Situation:** Christopher Lim, production manager, is concerned about the best way to bottle the water that the company now intends to sell. To differentiate Global Food's product in a highly competitive market, the marketing people want to use glass bottles. In Chris' view, this may help in the marketing of the product, but may well increase production costs significantly.

**Key Question:** "Should we package the water in glass bottles?"

**Solution:** Chris recommends that plastic bottles should be used to package both the carbonated soft drink and the bottled water products.

## 8 THE THEORY AND ESTIMATION OF COST

**Situation:** Maria Hernandez, newly hired MBA, is assigned the task of identifying ways in which the company can become the low-cost producer of bottled water.

**Key Question:** "What is the least costly way to produce and distribute bottled water?"

**Solution:** Maria identifies various short- and long-run measures to reduce the firm's cost of production. This involves partially outsourcing certain bottling activities and selling a certain type of bottled water.

## 9 PRICING AND OUTPUT DECISIONS: PERFECT COMPETITION AND MONOPOLY

**Situation:** Frank Robinson is appointed product manager of the new bottled water product. One of his first tasks is to recommend a price for the product.

**Key Question:** "What price should we charge for our new product?"

**Solution:** After analyzing the demand elasticity and short-run cost structure of the product, Frank recommends a price based on the MR = MC rule.

## 10 PRICING AND OUTPUT DECISIONS: MONOPOLISTIC COMPETITION AND OLIGOPOLY

**Situation:** The Management Committee of Global Foods asks Frank to reconsider his pricing recommendation because his analysis did not take into account certain competitive and market issues.

**Key Question:**    "What is the best price for a product, given its demand, cost, and competition?"

**Solution:**    After much debate, the management committee, with Frank's additional help, decides to set the price of its product slightly lower than the premium-priced competitors but slightly higher than the "value brands."

## 11   BREAK-EVEN ANALYSIS (VOLUME-COST-PROFIT)

**Situation:**    Suzanne Prescott, a senior analyst for the new bottled water division, is asked to prepare a profit plan for the coming year.

**Key Question:**    "What is the profit outlook for the coming year for our new bottled water product, Waterpure?"

**Solution:**    She uses break-even analysis to forecast the coming year's profit for this new product. She also uses sensitivity analysis to provide best-case and worst-case scenarios.

## 12   SPECIAL PRICING PRACTICES

**Situation:**    Rebecca James must decide what price bid she should submit to a large airport caterer that wishes to award a contract to a single supplier.

**Key Question:**    "How should the bid price be set to give Global Foods a good shot at obtaining the large caterer's contract?"

**Solution:**    Since demand elasticities differ in different markets, the price offered in this price-sensitive market will have to be sufficiently low to give Global a good chance of winning the contract.

## 13   CAPITAL BUDGETING

**Situation:**    George Kline, the manager of Global's capital planning department, is considering two new project proposals. One involves the expansion of company activities into a new geographical region, and the other involves the purchase of a new depalletizing machine to replace the one currently in use.

**Key Questions:**    "Should we expand into a new geographical area? Should we replace one of our depalletizers?"

**Solution:**    Using capital budgeting techniques involving the calculation of net present value and internal rates of return, George recommends that the firm accept the first project proposal and reject the second one.

## 14   RISK AND UNCERTAINTY

**Situation:**    George is asked by the firm's treasurer to consider the risk involved in going ahead with the project to expand into a new geographical area.

**Key Question:**    "What is the extent of our risk in expanding our geographic area?"

**Solution:**    After considering various acceptable ways to adjust a capital project for risk, George decides to rely primarily on sensitivity analysis. In addition to his original findings, George presents the treasurer with an optimistic and a pessimistic set of results.

## 15 THE ROLE OF GOVERNMENT IN THE MARKET ECONOMY

**Situation:** Bill Adams, the chief information officer (CIO) of Global Foods, Inc., is told by CEO Bob Burns that Global Foods must outsource its telecommunications network. Although Bill does not agree, he tries to make the best of it by trying to find the best company to handle Global Foods telecommunications requirements.

**Key Question:** "Which telecommunications company is best equipped to handle Global Foods' voice and data communications requirements?"

**Solution:** No specific solution is offered, but the main point of this situation is that increasing deregulation in industries such as telecommunications has given companies such as Global Foods many more options in running their business operations.

## 16 MANAGERIAL ECONOMICS IN ACTION: COMPETING IN THE SEMICONDUCTOR INDUSTRY

This chapter is new for this edition. It will link many of the concepts discussed throughout the book with other areas of business studies including strategy, marketing, finance, international business, industrial organization, and organizational development. All the material is factual. Therefore, no situation or solution for a fictional company such as Global Foods will be needed.

---

### THE SOLUTION

After about an hour of heated debate, Bob had a suggestion to make to the board. "Look, we've been discussing this to such an extent that perhaps the key arguments I made in my presentation have gotten lost or confused. Let me summarize the seven key reasons why we want to enter the soft drink business, and then let's vote on this matter.

"1. *Outlook for the industry:* Prospects for growth in the industry continue to be strong. Therefore, we can expect the demand for our products to be a part of this positive industry trend.

"2. *Market size and structure:* Although the industry is dominated by Coca-Cola and Pepsi-Cola, we believe there is still room for the entry of niche marketers. A number of regional and spe-

cialty companies have emerged over the past few years, particularly those offering sparkling fruit juices. We believe we can be as successful, if not more successful, than these new entrants.

"3. *Manufacturing, packaging, and distribution:* Our experience in the manufacturing of food products will give us a significant head start when we enter the soft drink business. Moreover, we do not plan to build bottling facilities from scratch. Instead, we look to purchase and consolidate existing bottling plants currently owned and operated by independent firms or by multiple franchise operations. We are also encouraged by the number of new cost-reducing technologies that have been introduced and the fact that the cost of the artificial sweetener aspartame should decline now that Monsanto's patent has expired.

*(Continued)*

"4   *Transportation and distribution:* We already have a well-managed fleet of vehicles that deliver our food products. We also have important influence and contacts in the retail food business. These will be essential in establishing a presence on the shelves of supermarkets and convenience stores throughout the country.

"5.   *Pricing, advertising, and promotion:* As the 'new kid on the block,' we recognize that we will have to enter the market as a price follower. However, in time, as our products are developed and marketed, we should be able to establish some independence either to raise or lower our prices in comparison with the rest of the industry. As far as advertising and promotion are concerned, we have an excellent advertising agency that has served us well with our current product line. However, we shall be flexible enough to consider other agencies if the need arises. Moreover, our experience with various promotional programs (e.g., discount coupons through direct mail and magazine inserts) should be transferable to the soft drink industry. Most important, all advertising and promotional efforts should be greatly aided by the fact that our company name—Global Foods—enjoys a high degree of consumer recognition (along with the specific brand names of our products).

"6.   *New products:* As you have seen in the detailed report, we have exciting plans for several new products as well as a full line of naturally and artificially sweetened carbonated drinks. Through an independent market research company, we have tested consumer preferences for our new offerings. The results have been most satisfactory.

"7.   *Financial considerations:* As stated at the very beginning of this presentation, our main goal is to create value for our shareholders. We must continue to grow in a profitable manner if we are to continue satisfying the financial expectations of our shareholders. We compete in a mature industry that enables us to generate a considerable amount of cash from our current line of products with well-entrenched brand names. We believe that we should use this cash to expand into the soft drink business. As all our financial projections and analysis indicate, this effort should yield a rate of return that is more than enough to compensate us for the investment and its associated risk."

After giving this executive summary, Bob Burns asked the board for a final decision. "All right, let's vote. All those in favor of entering the soft drink market? Opposed? Great, it's unanimous. Ladies and gentlemen, we're going into the soft drink business."

## Summary

Managerial economics is a discipline that combines microeconomic theory with management practice. Microeconomics is the study of how choices are made to allocate scarce resources with competing uses. An important function of a manager is to decide how to allocate a firm's scarce resources. Examples of such decisions are the selection of a firm's products or services, the hiring of personnel, the assigning of personnel to particular functions or tasks, the purchase of materials and equipment, and the pricing of products and services. This text will show how the application of economic theory and concepts helps managers to make allocation decisions that are in the best economic interests of their firms.

Throughout the text, numerous examples will be cited to illustrate how economic theory and concepts can be applied to management decision making. References will also be made to business cases and economic events that have been reported in the popular press. However, a unique feature of this book is a unifying case study of a food and beverage company, Global Foods, Inc. Each chapter begins with a situation in which the managers of this firm have to make key economic decisions. The solutions that end the chapters suggest ways that economic analysis can assist in the decision-making process.

## Important Concepts

**Command process:** The use of central planning and the directives of government authorities to answer the questions of *what, how,* and *for whom.* (p. 9)

**Economic decisions for the firm:** "What goods and services should be produced?"—the product decision. "How should these goods and services be produced?"—the hiring, staffing, and capital-budgeting decision. "For whom should these goods and services be produced?"—the market segmentation decision. (p. 11)

**Economics:** The study of how choices are made under conditions of scarcity. The basic economic problem can be defined as: "What goods and services should be produced and in what quantities?" "How should these goods and services be produced?" "For whom should these goods and services be produced?" (p. 2)

**Economics of a business:** The key factors that affect the ability of a firm to earn an acceptable rate of return on its owners' investment. The most important of these factors are competition, technology, and customers. (p. 5)

**Managerial economics:** The use of economic analysis to make business decisions involving the best use of a firm's scarce resources. (p. 2)

**Market process:** The use of supply, demand, and material incentives to answer the questions of *what, how,* and *for whom.* (p. 9)

**Opportunity cost:** The amount or subjective value forgone in choosing one activity over the next best alternative. This cost must be considered whenever decisions are made under conditions of scarcity. (p. 8)

**Resources:** Also referred to as *factors of production* or *inputs,* economic analysis usually includes four basic types: land, labor, capital, and entrepreneurship. This chapter also includes managerial skills as well as entrepreneurship. (p. 7)

**Scarcity:** A condition that exists when resources are limited relative to the demand for their use. In the market process, the extent of this condition is reflected in the price of resources or the goods and services they produce. (p. 7)

**Traditional process:** The use of customs and traditions to answer the questions of *what, how,* and *for whom.* (p. 9)

## Questions

1. Define *scarcity* and *opportunity cost.* What role do these two concepts play in the making of management decisions?
2. Elaborate on the basic economic questions of *what, how,* and *for whom.* Provide specific examples of these questions with respect to the use of a *country's* scarce resources.
3. Following are examples of typical economic decisions made by the managers of a firm. Determine whether each is an example of *what, how,* or *for whom.*
   a. Should the company make its own spare parts or buy them from an outside vendor?
   b. Should the company continue to service the equipment that it sells or ask customers to use independent repair companies?

   **c.** Should a company expand its business to international markets or concentrate on the domestic market?

   **d.** Should the company replace its own communications network with a "virtual private network" that is owned and operated by another company?

   **e.** Should the company buy or lease the fleet of trucks that it uses to transport its products to market?

**4.** Define the market process, the command process, and the traditional process. How does each process deal with the basic questions of *what, how,* and *for whom?*

**5.** Discuss the importance of the command process and the traditional process in the making of management decisions. Illustrate specific ways in which managers must take these two processes into account.

**6.** Explain the differences between management skills and entrepreneurship. Discuss how each factor contributes to the economic success of a business.

**7.** Compare and contrast microeconomics with macroeconomics. Although managerial economics is based primarily on microeconomics, explain why it is also important for managers to understand macroeconomics.

**8.** What do you think is the key to success in the soft drink industry? What chance do you think Global Foods has in succeeding in its new venture into the soft drink market? Explain. (Answer these questions on the basis of the information provided in the chapter as well as any other knowledge you might have about the food and beverage business.)

**9.** Essentially, what do you think are the changing aspects of the economics (i.e., customers, technology, and competition) of the following industries?

   **a.** telecommunications

   **b.** retail merchandising

   **c.** higher education

   **d.** aerospace and defense

**10.** (Optional) Have you been personally involved in the making of a decision for a business concerning *what, how,* or *for whom?* If so, explain your rationale for making such decisions. Were these decisions guided by the market process, the command process, or the traditional process? Explain.

## Take It to the Net

We invite you to visit the Keat/Young page on the Prentice Hall Web site at:

**http://www.prenhall.com/keat**

for additional resources.

# CHAPTER 2

# The Firm and Its Goals

## THE SITUATION

Bob Burns looked over the last few numbers provided to him in a consultant's report on the soft drink industry, closed the binder and turned to Ellen Fisher, Global Foods' vice president of marketing. "Looking back, our decision to get into the soft drink industry was a good one, but who would have thought that an industry that showed such strong growth in the early 1990s would start to peak so soon? And also, we should have known that the two leading brands wouldn't stand still while we tried to increase our market share. Coke has been very successful with its Sprite® against Cadbury-Schweppes' 7-Up®, and it seems that they will launch a rival brand to Cadbury's Dr Pepper®. I think we need to get into a growing market.

"An idea occurred to me recently when I was watching the Yankees-Mets baseball game on television. When one of the Yankee players returned to the dugout after hitting a home run, he didn't go to the water cooler, but instead picked up a bottle of water. I already knew that bottled water was the fastest-growing segment of the beverage industry, and statistics I've seen since rein-

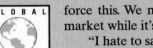

force this. We must get into this market while it's still growing."

"I hate to say this, Bob, but it may be a case of 'too little, too late,'" said Ellen. "Established companies such as Perrier have been around for a long time; Perrier also owns strong American brands such as Poland Spring, Deer Park, and Calistoga. Evian, which is owned by the French company, Danone, has also been quite successful in the United States. I am afraid that if we entered the market we would start way behind."

"I'm not prepared to give up so easily, Ellen," replied Bob. "We have good distribution channels, bottling know-how and marketing savvy. This business is close to our core competency and it is still growing. We have told analysts that we expect to grow at a 10 percent rate in revenue and even more in profits, given our tight cost controls. At our upcoming shareholder meeting, our shareholders as well as the analysts will be expecting to hear our plans for further business expansion. In the past, we did it with the help of soft drinks, and now is the time to grow our beverage division with bottled water."

# Introduction

Chapter 1 explained that managerial economics deals primarily with the problem of deciding how best to allocate a firm's scarce resources among competing uses. The best or optimal decision is the one that enables the firm to meet its desired objectives most closely. This chapter will elaborate on the process of making decisions under conditions of scarcity by discussing the goals of a firm and the economic significance of the optimal decision. The appendix to this chapter explains the role of marginal analysis in economic decision making. This appendix also presents a review of the mathematics used in this text to illustrate key economic concepts and methods of analysis.

The major portion of this chapter will be devoted to a discussion of the goals of the firm. However, in order to carry on this discussion sensibly, we must first define and explain the term, *the firm.*

# The Firm

The traditional (neoclassical) theory of economics defined the **firm** as a collection of resources that is transformed into products demanded by consumers. The costs at which the firm produces are governed by the available technology, and the amount it produces and the prices at which it sells are influenced by the structure of the markets in which it operates. The difference between the revenue it receives and the costs it incurs is *profit.* It is the aim of the firm to maximize its profit.

The preceding theory assumes the existence of the firm. But this leaves the reason for its existence unanswered. Why does a firm perform certain functions internally while it conducts other actions through the market? It appears that the size of the firm is not determined strictly by technological considerations. Then why are some firms very small and others large?

Answers to the preceding questions began to appear in 1937 when Ronald Coase postulated that a company compares costs of organizing an activity internally with the cost of using the market system for its transactions.[1]

If there were no costs of dealing with the outside market, a firm would be organized so that all of its transactions would be with the outside. However, it is incorrect to assume that the marketplace does not involve any costs. In dealing through the market, the firm incurs **transaction costs.**

Transaction costs are incurred when a company enters into a contract with other entities. These costs include the original investigation to find the outside firm, followed by the cost of negotiating a contract, and later yet, enforcing the contract. Transaction costs are influenced by uncertainty, frequency of recurrence, and asset-specificity.[2]

Uncertainty, the inability to know the future perfectly, increases transaction costs because it is not possible to include all contingencies in a contract, particularly a long-term contract. Frequent transactions also tend to make it necessary for explicit contracts to exist.

---

[1]The seminal work in this area was by Ronald H. Coase in "The Nature of the Firm," *Economica,* 4 (1937), pp. 386–405, reprinted in R. H. Coase, *The Firm, the Market and the Law,* Chicago: University of Chicago Press, 1988, pp. 33–55. Coase was awarded the Nobel Prize in Economics in 1991.
[2]Much of this discussion is based on Oliver E. Williamson, "Transaction-Cost Economics: The Governance of Contractual Relations," *Journal of Law and Economics,* vol. 22 (October 1979), pp. 233–61.

But probably the most important of these characteristics is asset-specificity. If a buyer contracts for a specialized product with just one seller, and furthermore, if the product necessitates the use of some specialized machinery, the two parties become tied to one another. In this case, future changes in market conditions (or in production technology) may lead to **opportunistic behavior,** where one of the parties seeks to take advantage of the other. In such cases, transaction costs will be very high.

When transaction costs are high, a company may choose to provide the service or product itself. However, carrying out operations internally creates its own costs. A major cost is that, in hiring workers to do the work within the firm, the firm incurs monitoring and supervision costs to insure that the work is done efficiently. Quite possibly, employees who work for a fixed wage or salary may have less incentive to work efficiently than an outside contractor.

Employers will try to decrease monitoring costs by using incentives to increase employees' output. Among such incentives are bonuses, benefits, and perquisites ("perks"). Another popular incentive is to provide workers with the possibility of stock ownership, using stock options and employee stock plans. Stock ownership is also used to attract new employees. Such employees will, of course, benefit when the company is profitable and its stock increases in value. However, incentives come with a price tag.

The trade-off between external transaction costs and the cost of internal operations can be shown on the simple graph in Figure 2.1. When a company operates at the vertical axis, all of its operations are conducted with the outside. As we move to the right on this graph, the firm substitutes internal for external operations. The cost of external transactions decreases, while the cost of internal operations increases. The total cost is the vertical summation of the two costs, and decreases at first as the company finds that internalizing some operations is efficient. However, as more of the operations are internalized, some efficiency is lost, and the total cost begins to rise again. The company will choose to allocate its resources between external transactions and internal opera-

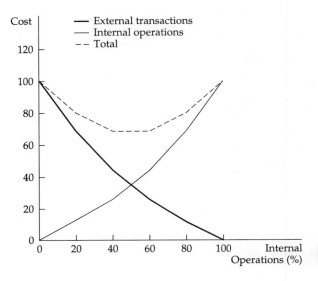

**FIGURE 2.1** Firm Costs

tions so that the total cost is at a minimum, which in this case will occur about midway between the two extremes.

If transaction costs for a specific product or service are higher than the costs of carrying on the activity internally, then a company benefits from performing this particular task inhouse. An independent firm may not find it profitable to produce a product if only one or few customers demand it. However, as markets expand, the demand for a product or service, which may have been limited in the past, now expands. This will permit new firms to specialize in activities that previously had to be performed by the firm that needed this task to be performed. Thus new companies and industries come into existence. This is true not only in the case of products, where outsourcing has existed for some time and is still growing, but also for services that at one time were performed by the firm itself and are now produced by independent firms—for example, cleaning services, security services, and cafeterias are often now run by specialized firms. Another example would be the college bookstore that is operated by one of the large companies in the book industry. This idea is actually rather old. It really started with Adam Smith, who stated that "the division of labor is limited by the extent of the market." George Stigler discussed this point in a 1951 article, and concluded that as industries expand, companies that previously had produced everything internally will tend to experience "vertical disintegration."[3] What has happened, of course, is that transaction costs have decreased and that the possibility of "opportunistic behavior" has diminished as well.

In the manufacturing sector especially, outsourcing is not new. In seeking to reduce their costs, particularly during what we have described in chapter 1 as Stage II in our four-stage model of change, many companies have, over the past decade, resorted to outsourcing a number of their business functions. For example, taking a cue from Toyota and other Japanese auto manufacturers, Ford and Chrysler have gained considerable cost efficiencies by outsourcing the manufacturing of up to half of the parts that go into the making of their vehicles. The bitter and costly labor strike at General Motors during the summer of 1998 was largely about the issue of outsourcing. To be cost competitive, GM realized that it had to increase its outsourcing activities, and obviously the union was trying to resist this move. However, outsourcing has recently moved into areas not previously covered. For example, companies have begun to outsource their entire information systems operations and human resource functions. Companies such as EDS, Andersen Consulting, and IBM have become major suppliers of these functions.

More will be said about outsourcing in chapters 7 and 8, concerning production and cost. At this point, however, it is worthwhile to mention just two recent examples. During the summer of 1998, British Airways was about to order 100 short-haul jetliners. As reported in *The Wall Street Journal,* in deciding between two potential suppliers, the airline "wants as little as possible to do with the planes.... Instead it is seeking to be the first international carrier to lease such a large new fleet by the month—and their engines by the hour...." It also wanted the winning bidder to "supply everything from spare parts to routine maintenance to flight training." The two companies bidding for

---

[3]George J. Stigler, "The Division of Labor is Limited by the Extent of the Market," *Journal of Political Economy,* vol. 59 (June 1951), pp. 185–93.

BA's business, Boeing Co. and Airbus Industrie, were even talking about the possibility of ready-to-go flight crews. While aircraft and engine leasing as well as maintenance contracts with service companies are not new in the airline industry, the British Airways plan was seen "by many as a watershed." The reason behind this plan is to decrease costs in a constantly increasing competitive environment.[4]

In our second example, United Technologies Corporation recently chose the IBM Corporation to develop and manage a procurement system. Although in the past IBM has taken on outsourcing business, it usually took over only a client's computer system. Under this new arrangement, IBM will use its software and hardware to create UT's procurement system, but it will also negotiate and handle contracts with suppliers from office supplies to temporary staff. UT expects to trim its annual purchasing cost by $750 million within two years. Again, it must be emphasized that although outsourcing business process management is not new, this is a relatively new endeavor for IBM, which has been mainly known for being the world's largest information technology and computer services company.[5]

We end this discussion with the conclusion that a firm will trade off costs incurred in conducting transactions with the outside market with the costs of internalizing such transactions in order to minimize the combination of the two. This is consistent with the overall economic goals of the firm, the subject to which we turn next.

## The Economic Goal of the Firm and Optimal Decision Making

Every business has a goal. Most students would assert that the primary goal of a business is to earn a certain amount of profit (i.e., to "make money"), and, in fact, the economic theory of the firm—the foundation on which much of managerial economics rests—assumes that the principal objective of a firm is to maximize its profits (or minimize its losses).[6] Thus, throughout this text, unless otherwise stated, we will assume this same objective, known among economists as the **profit-maximization hypothesis.**

To be sure, there are other goals that a firm can pursue, relating to market share, revenue growth, profit margin, return on investment, technology, customer satisfaction, and shareholder value (i.e., maximizing the price of its stock). It is crucial to be aware of precisely what a firm's goals are. Different goals can lead to very different managerial decisions given the same limited amount of resources. For example, if the main goal of the firm is to maximize market share rather than profit, the firm might decide to reduce its prices. If the main goal is to provide the most technologically advanced products, the firm might well decide to allocate more resources to research and development. The added research and development expenses would most likely reduce the amount of profit the firm earns in the short run but may result in increased profits over

---

[4]Frederic M. Biddle, "British Airways Moves Closer to Being 'Virtual Airline,' " *The Wall Street Journal,* June 25, 1998.

[5]Raju Narisetti, "IBM Picked to Develop, Run a System for United Technologies Procurement," *The Wall Street Journal,* June 29, 1998.

[6]As we will see in Chapter 9, a firm may lose money in the short run and still be better off than it would be if it were to shut down operations, as long as its losses are less than its fixed costs. However, if it is going to lose money, from an economic standpoint it is optimal to minimize its losses.

time as the company increases its technological lead over its competitors. If the main goal of the firm is to carry a complete line of products and services, it may choose to sell certain products even though they might not be earning a profit.

Given the goal (or goals) that the firm is pursuing, we can say that the **optimal decision** in managerial economics is one that brings the firm closest to this goal. For example, as you will see in chapter 9, to maximize its profit (or minimize its loss), a firm should price its product at a level where the revenue earned on the last unit of a product sold (called *marginal revenue*) is equal to the additional cost of making this last unit (called *marginal cost*). In other words, the optimal price equates the firm's marginal revenue with its marginal cost.

One additional concept should be presented in our discussion of a firm's goals. In economics, a distinction is made between the "short-run" time period and the "long-run" time period. As explained in greater detail in later sections of this text (see chapters 3, 7, and 8), these time periods actually have nothing directly to do with calendar time. During the short run, we assume that a firm can vary the amount of certain resources (e.g., labor hours) but must operate with a fixed amount of at least one of its resources (e.g., factory space). Theoretically, in the long run, a firm is able to vary the quantities of all resources being utilized. In this text, we will look at both short-run and long-run decisions made by the firm. We will assume that a company's goal is to maximize profits both in the short and long run. However, it must be understood that a business will, at times, sacrifice profitability in the short run with the anticipation of maximized long-run profits.

# Goals Other Than Profit

## ECONOMIC GOALS

The concept of profit maximization has been attacked as incomplete by many writers. They point out that companies may have other economic objectives, such as those mentioned previously.

For the time being, we will omit discussion of the objective of "value" or "shareholder wealth" maximization and consider some of the other alternatives concerning a company's activity during a single period of time (such as a year). It is readily admitted that profit maximization is a rather vague term. How does a company know that its profits in a given period are the largest they can be? Or, more correctly (from an ex ante, or planning, viewpoint), how does a company know that the actions it is taking in this time frame will result, if all goes as expected, in the greatest possible profit?

Let us look at the objectives set out by a company's chief executive officer (or a committee representing the company's top management). It is not unusual for the CEO or his representatives, having decided on the achievable results for the next fiscal period, to distribute objectives to the various operating heads at the beginning of the planning cycle. Now imagine this memorandum from the firm's CEO to the general manager of one of the company's operating units:

Dear Joe:

We have had a pretty good year in 1999, and we believe that 2000 should be even better.

I am therefore issuing the following objective for your unit in 2000. Take any and all actions that will ensure that your profit is maximized.

Corporate management is confident that you will not disappoint us. We know that the objective we have given you is challenging. We also are convinced that it is achievable.

John, CEO

This memorandum is obviously an extreme simplification, but what is Joe to do with his marching orders to maximize profit? What resources does he have to do this? And how can his performance be measured at the end of the year? What is his maximum profit?

Now let us look at another "objective" memorandum:

Dear Joe,

We have had a pretty good year in 1999, and we expect that 2000 should be even better. We are assigning specific objectives to each of our operating units in such a way that the total result will be a financial posture consistent with our economic and industry forecasts, our available resources, and good increases in productivity. With this in mind, we want you to build your 2000 plan to correspond to the following objectives for your unit:

1. Your revenue should increase by 10 percent from 1999.
2. The profit margin of your unit should increase from 8 percent to 9 percent, and your return on assets should be 10 percent.
3. Your division will receive $10 million of company funds for expansion projects whose minimum internal rate of return should be 12 percent.
4. The head count of your unit can increase by no more than 2 percent.

Corporate management is confident that you will not disappoint us. We know that the objective we have given you is challenging. We also are convinced that it is achievable.

John, CEO

Assuming that this memorandum makes more sense (which it certainly should, for otherwise our point has been lost), does this mean that the company's objective is not really profit maximization at all, but rather a growth rate, a profit margin, or a return on its assets? This is what many writers on this subject say.

Such a conclusion is, however, misleading. Any of these measures in itself is incomplete, and each should be seen as a realistic target consistent with the ultimate objective of maximizing the firm's overall profits. Management, in this example, advised by its expert staff regarding the company's economic environment, competition, technological advances, and market potential, has come to the conclusion that maximum profits can be achieved by the combination of growth and profit measures included in its memorandum.

Thus, the specific objectives assigned to an operating unit are really proxies for the overall objective of profit maximization. The achievement of these proxies is also measurable at the end of the fiscal period; the division executive's performance and contribution toward the company's profits can be evaluated, and rewards in terms of bonuses or incentive plans can then be determined.

## NONECONOMIC OBJECTIVES

In this complex world, companies may have objectives that are not strictly economic or at least do not appear to be governed by economic thinking. Indeed, some large companies have published statements of principles that, if accepted at face value, would indicate that making profits is the last thing they strive for. Profits may be mentioned as only one of several objectives, and they may actually be listed last. Furthermore, the statements do not mention any maximum but rather concentrate on such measures as "adequate" or "reasonable" return to stockholders. Such modesty is certainly more palatable to the public. What, then, are some of the guiding principles such companies publish?

1. Provide a good place for our employees to work.
2. Provide good products/services to our customers.
3. Act as a good citizen in our society.

These actions are costly, and at first glance may seem to interfere with profit maximization. However, consider the following: Satisfied employees not only tend to be more productive, but will remain with the company longer, thus decreasing expensive labor turnover. Without satisfied customers, a company will not remain in business. Supporting good causes, such as charitable and other nonprofit organizations, will create goodwill and ultimately potential sales. Therefore, it would be worthwhile for a company to spend resources on such **noneconomic objectives** consistent with increases in revenues and profit. If this is the case, then attaining these objectives is not incompatible with profit maximization, and, indeed, these objectives could be classified as economic.

We could enlarge this discussion of so-called noneconomic objectives, but the point has been made. Today's markets and institutions constrain companies in many ways that did not exist in the past. Therefore, companies must concern themselves with creating employee and customer satisfaction and maintaining social responsibility to a much higher degree than in the past. But these considerations do not contradict the profit maximization principle. If companies were maximizers in the past, under less restrictive conditions, they are still maximizers today but have to operate within the requirements imposed by current standards and the costs that accompany them.

# Once Again—Do Companies Maximize Profits?

We have discussed some possible alternative objectives to profit maximization and concluded that none of these objectives is necessarily inconsistent with our basic principle. Now let us look at another criticism that has recently been leveled at the view of profit maximization as the primary objective.

The argument is that today's corporations do not maximize at all. Instead, their aim is to "satisfice." To understand this argument, we have to consider two parts of this idea:

1. The position and power of stockholders in today's corporation.
2. The position and power of professional management in today's corporation.

Years ago the owner or owners of a business also managed it. Businesses were predominantly quite small and lent themselves to being operated as individual proprietorships, partnerships, or small, closely held corporations. Modern businesses, particularly medium-sized or large corporations, of course, cannot be managed by the owners, who are the shareholders and number in the thousands or even hundreds of thousands. Many stockholders own only minute pieces of a corporation. Further, stockholders tend to diversify their holdings; thus, they may hold small interests in many different corporations. The argument asserts that most stockholders are not well informed on how well a corporation can do and will be satisfied with an adequate dividend and some reasonable growth. And since they own different stocks, poor performance on one of their holdings may be offset by some of their other assets: the stockholder is more concerned with the portfolio of stocks than with any individual stock. Shareholders may not be capable of knowing whether corporate management is doing its best for them and they actually may not be very concerned as long as they receive what they consider a satisfactory return on their investment—hence **"satisficing."**

Second, in a modern corporation professional managers—the chairman of the board, the president, a group of vice presidents, and other high-level managers—direct the operations of a company. Although they are overseen by a board of directors (which usually includes a large number of insiders), they are responsible for major decision making. It is claimed by a number of writers that managers (who commonly hold a relatively small number of shares) have their own objectives, which do not include maximization of shareholder earnings. Indeed, it is often said that managers tend to be much more conservative—that is, risk averse—than stockholders would be, since their jobs will most likely be safer if they turn in a competent and steady, if unspectacular, performance. They could probably benefit stockholders in the long run by taking some well-calculated risks. However, they may be too cautious to do so, and thus they miss out on opportunities. They fear that they may not survive the reverses that could result from risk taking. If stockholders need only be satisfied, this may be the appropriate way for management to go.

Further, management's interests may actually be contrary to those of stockholders. For instance, management may be more interested in revenue growth than profits. Why? It has been claimed that management remuneration tends to be a function of revenue size rather than profits. Several studies have been made on this subject, but the evidence is considerably less than overwhelming. Also, company management may be more interested in maximizing its own income, may indulge in various perquisites, and in general may not act in the best interest of the widely dispersed, somewhat disinterested and lethargic stockholder population.[7]

The two sides in this relationship tend to complement one another. The owners of the corporation—the stockholders—are not interested in maximization, or even if they are, they are not well enough informed and have too little power. The corporation's management, whose selfish motives lead them to act in their own favor when stockholder and management goals differ, will manage in a way that serves their interest while keeping the stockholder satisfied with adequate return and moderate growth.

Like all ideas presented by intelligent people, this one probably contains a certain amount of truth. Each of the points seems eminently reasonable and, for all we know,

---

[7]A formal theory dealing with the potential conflicts between shareholders and management has been developed by Michael C. Jensen and William H. Meckling in their article "Theory of the Firm: Managerial Behavior. Agency Costs and Ownership Structure" (*Journal of Financial Economics,* October 1976, pp. 350–60). These conflicts arise whenever managers own less than 100 percent of the stock, which is, of course, the predominant situation in today's large corporation. To ensure that managers act on behalf of the stockholder, the latter will have to incur "agency costs," which are expenditures to monitor managers' actions, to structure the organization in such a way as to limit management's action, and so forth.

could be valid over limited periods of time. But let us look at some of the realities of life and also some recent events in the business world that tend to contradict this argument.

You, the reader of this book, may be among that group of far-flung stockholders owning a hundred shares in a company with millions of shares outstanding. However, particularly in the case of large corporations, much of the outstanding stock is held by institutions and in professionally managed accounts. Among these are banks that manage large pension funds, insurance companies with their extensive portfolios, and mutual funds. These organizations employ expert analysts (who are only human and therefore, at least occasionally, make mistakes) who study companies and pass judgment on the quality of their management and their promise for the future. Of course, they deal mostly with stock prices, but after all, stock prices are a reflection of a company's profitability.[8] These analysts make recommendations to their management on which stocks to buy and which to sell. Companies that underperform would be weeded out of these institutional portfolios, with a consequent drop in their stock prices.

Now, what happens when certain stocks tend to underperform in the market? They become targets for takeovers by others. We really do not have to belabor this point, since anyone reading the business sections of daily newspapers or other business publications is very much aware of recent events in the takeover and buyout arenas. In addition to the accumulation of stock and subsequent tender offers by outside financiers, we have also witnessed the existence of proxy fights by dissident large stockholders. Thus, it appears that management in today's corporation is not insulated from outside pressures. Management is constrained to act in agreement with stockholders, who look for increases in stock values and returns and who act to "punish" the managements of those companies that appear to underperform.

Another argument leads to a similar conclusion. Competitive pressures also act to stimulate management to performance. If a company's results lag behind those of competitors, those lethargic stockholders who do not challenge the company directly will tend to sell its shares and turn to those companies providing better returns and better prospects of returns. The price of the company's stock will suffer relative to prices of the others; such a scenario will not go unnoticed in financial markets. Company management will come under the gun to improve performance, and ultimately management may be replaced because of pressure by outside board members, a successful proxy fight, or even a takeover. General Motors, International Business Machines, and Eastman Kodak are just a few examples of companies that recently replaced their chief executive officers. A very vocal and sometimes effective advocate of shareholder rights has been the California Public Employees' Retirement System (Calpers).[9] With more than $150 billion in assets, it has demonstrated that changes in corporate governance can be accomplished.

Management has another, more direct, motivation to act in concert with the objectives of stockholders. Parts—frequently large parts—of an executive's remuneration

---

[8]The connection between profits and stock prices will be examined in the next section, when we expand the maximization principle to include the wealth of stockholders.
[9]See, for instance, Stuart Silverstein, "Calpers Raps Big Business for Neglecting Shareholders," *Los Angeles Times,* March 21, 1992; Susan Pulliam, "Calpers Goes Over CEO's Heads in Its Quest for Higher Returns," *The Wall Street Journal,* January 22, 1993; Martha Groves, "Calpers Puts New Pressure on Companies," *Los Angeles Times,* January 23, 1993.

are tied to performance in terms of operating profits for the corporation or for units supervised by the particular executive.[10] Furthermore, an executive's compensation package is usually enhanced by the issuance of stock options. Since the value of stock options depends on the price of the company's stock, which in turn is a function of the company's profit performance, self-serving company managers may find that their objectives (less than miraculously) coincide with those of the stockholders.

Thus, there appears to be a strong convergence of management and stockholder objectives, contrary to the claims of some well-known writers.

### PROFIT MAXIMIZATION, RESTATED

It is readily agreed that the existence of the profit-maximization objective can never be proven conclusively. We must note, however, that lack of financial success by a company is not necessarily a contravention of the principle. The best of plans may go awry, and management's judgment certainly is not error-proof. Under certain circumstances, the aim for loss minimization may replace the goal of profit maximization, but this too supports our basic premise. As difficult as it is to point to acts of profit maximization by management, none of the alternative constructions lends itself as well as a yardstick by which to measure business activity. As long as a corporation strives to do better, that is, prefers higher profits to lower profits and lower costs to higher costs, and acts consistently in those directions, the assumption of profit maximization serves as a better basis for judging a company's decisions than any of the other purported objectives. And, incidentally, this "striving to do better" can include a multitude of decisions, including those that lead to a revenue increase greater than a cost increase, a revenue decrease smaller than a cost decrease, or a constant revenue with decreased costs. All of these decisions involve an increase in profits.

However, maximizing profits in the very short term (e.g., one year) can always be accomplished by management. If, for instance, revenue in the coming year is expected to decline, a company can keep up its profits by cutting expenses. If management seeks to do this without an immediate further reaction on revenue, it can eliminate some development projects. The effect of a lack of new products will not be felt right away, but the shortsightedness of this management decision will come home to roost only a few years hence. This is the decision area in which the objective of period profit maximization can be attacked more logically. Profit maximization for one period is an incomplete measure from the viewpoint of a business organization that is expected to operate into the infinite—or at least the foreseeable—future.

## Maximizing the Wealth of Stockholders

Because period profit maximization is an extremely useful way to look at day-to-day decision making in the firm, we will use it as our model throughout most of this book. However, there is another view of maximization that is usually adopted in finance textbooks and that takes into consideration a stream of earnings over time. This concept includes not only the evaluation of a stream of cash flows; it also considers the

---

[10]The fact that these performance incentives may be tied to near-term profits can create a problem, since the executive's horizon may be shortened. More about this will be discussed later.

all-important idea of the time value of money.[11] Since it is an obvious fact that a dollar earned in the future is worth less than a dollar earned today, the future streams must be discounted to the present. Both the shape of these streams through time and the interest rate at which they are discounted affect the value of the stockholders' wealth today. The discount rate in particular is affected by risk, so risk becomes another component of the valuation of the business. Financial theorists differentiate various types of risk, with the two major types commonly identified as business risk and financial risk.

**Business risk** involves variation in returns due to the ups and downs of the economy, the industry, and the firm. This is the kind of risk that attends all business organizations, although to varying degrees. Some businesses are relatively stable from period to period, whereas others incur extreme fluctuations in their financial returns. For instance, public utilities (i.e., suppliers of electricity and gas as well as the operating telephone companies) tend to have more stable earnings over time than do industrial companies, particularly those in industries that are highly cyclical (e.g., steel, automobiles, and capital goods), or companies in high-tech fields.

**Financial risk** concerns the variation in returns that is induced by leverage. *Leverage* signifies the proportion of a company financed by debt. Given a certain degree of leverage, the earnings accruing to stockholders will fluctuate with total profits (before the deduction of interest and taxes). The higher the leverage, the greater the potential fluctuations in stockholder earnings. Thus, financial risk moves directly with a company's leverage.

How do we obtain a measure of stockholders' wealth? By discounting to the present the cash streams that stockholders expect to receive out into the future. Since we know today's price of a company's stock, we can—given the expected dividends to be received by the stockholders—determine the discount rate the investment community applies to the particular stock. This discount rate includes the pure time value of money as well as the premiums for the two categories of risk. The dividend stream is used to represent the receipts of stockholders because that is all they really receive from the company. Of course, a stockholder also looks for a capital gain, but selling the stock at some point involves someone else buying it; thus, this payment represents only a trade, an exchange of funds. However, dividends represent the returns on the stock generated by the corporation. In equation form, we have the following:

$$P = \frac{D_1}{(1 + k)} + \frac{D_2}{(1 + k)^2} + \frac{D_3}{(1 + k)^3} + \cdots + \frac{D_n}{(1 + k)^n}$$

where $P$ = Present price of the stock
$D$ = Dividends received per year (in year 1, year 2, . . . year $n$)
$k$ = Discount rate applied by the financial community, often referred to as the cost of equity capital of the company

If it is assumed that the corporation will have an infinitely long life, and if dividends will remain the same year after year, then the price of each share of stock can be calculated as a perpetuity with the following formula:

$$P = D/k$$

[11]Time value of money and discounting of flows will be discussed in much greater detail in the appendix to chapter 13.

Investors, however, will usually expect dividends to rise. In the case where dividends grow at a constant rate each year, the formula for share price becomes

$$P = D_1/(k - g)$$

where $D_1$ = the dividend to be paid during the coming year
$g$ = the annual constant growth rate of the dividend expressed as a percentage[12]

Multiplying $P$ by the number of shares outstanding gives the total value of the company's common equity.[13]

A simple example will help clarify the above equation. Assume that a company expects to pay a dividend of $4 in the coming year, and expects dividends to grow at 5 percent each year. The rate at which stockholders discount their cash flows (which is really the rate of return stockholders require to earn from this stock) is 12 percent. There are 1 million shares outstanding. We would expect the price of each share to be:

$$P = 4/(.12 - .05) = 4/.07 = \$57.14$$

The value of the company's stock would be $57.14 million. This is the expected market value given the variables that we have assumed. However, this may not be the maximum value the company could achieve. The variables in the equation may have to change. Since $k$ is a function of the company's level of risk (both business and financial), the company may be able to decrease $k$ by lowering the riskiness of its operations or by changing its leverage. It can affect $g$ and $D$ by retaining more or less of its earnings. By retaining a larger portion of its earnings and devoting a smaller portion of its earnings to dividends, the company may be able to increase its growth rate $g$.

Thus, under this construction, maximizing the wealth of the shareholder means that a company tries to manage its business in such a way that the dividends over time paid from its earnings and the risk incurred to bring about the stream of dividends always create the highest price and thereby the maximum value for the company's stock.

This **wealth maximization** hypothesis tends to weaken even further the management-versus-stockholder argument. Corporate executives, for whom stock options represent a significant portion of remuneration, now have an even greater incentive to aim at results that conform to the objectives of the stockholders.

This is a rather complex if quite obvious development of the maximization principle. As stated previously, we will work primarily with the profit maximization hypothesis because it is quite sufficient for most of our purposes. We will return to the wealth maximization rule in chapter 13 when we discuss a company's investment and replacement decisions involving expenditures for which the resulting payoffs flow into the corporation over a considerable period of time. In that chapter we will also briefly discuss how the market tends to determine the rate of return it requires from a company (and

---

[12]The derivation of these formulas is discussed in greater detail in chapter 13.
[13]The value of a company's equity can also be obtained by calculating the present value of the expected stream of "free cash flows." However, when free cash flow is correctly constructed, it is essentially equal to dividends paid. This subject will be discussed at greater length in chapter 13 when the calculation of the value of corporation is presented.

thus sets the discount rate $k$, the company's cost of capital). In chapter 14 we will examine the question of risk and uncertainty and attempts to find ways to deal with it.

## MARKET VALUE ADDED AND ECONOMIC VALUE ADDED

Various publications have measured the wealth of stockholders by taking the price per share quoted in the stock market pages and multiplying it by the number of shares outstanding.[14] The product is, of course, the current value of the shares, and thus reflects the value of the company accorded to it by the market. But such a measure does not show the wealth that has been created by the company. After all, suppose that the stockholders had contributed more capital than the stock was worth currently. Then, actually, the company would have "destroyed" some of the stockholders' wealth. What is really important is how much the stockholders' investment is worth today relative to what they have contributed to the corporation in originally buying the stock and then having earnings retained by the corporation for reinvestment.

A relatively new measure has become very popular with the financial community as well as many corporations themselves. It is called **Market Value Added (MVA®)** and has been developed by the consulting firm of Stern Stewart.[15] MVA represents the difference between the market value of the company and the capital that investors have paid into the company.

The market value of the company includes the value of both equity and debt. The capital includes the book value of debt and equity on the company's balance sheet plus a number of adjustments that increase the basic number. Among these adjustments is the inclusion of research and development (R&D) expense (which accountants treat as expense). Prior years' R&D is cumulated and amortized over a number of years. Another item that is included is the amortization of goodwill. Thus, in the end, the contributed capital of the corporation will turn out to be larger than merely the book value of equity and debt. While the market value of a corporation will always be positive, the Market Value Added may be positive or negative, depending on whether the market value of the company is greater than the capital which investors contributed. Where a corporation's market value is less than the contributed capital, investors' wealth has actually been "destroyed."

Stern Stewart publishes an annual ranking of 1,000 corporations and their MVA. The most recent data available (for year-end 1997) rank General Electric first and Coca-Cola second, the former having created over $196 billion in value for its investors, and the latter $158 billion. On the other end of the scale (ranking at 1,000) is General Motors, whose MVA was a negative $14 billion.[16]

Basically, MVA is a forward-looking measure. If market value reflects the financial markets' appraisal of a company's future cash streams, then MVA represents the financial markets' assessment of the company's future net cash flows (i.e., after subtracting the investments the company must make to achieve those cash streams).

---

[14]See, for instance, *Business Week,* July 13, 1998, pp. 51–91.
[15]This concept was originally introduced in 1990. See G. Bennett Stewart III, "Announcing the Stern Stewart Performance 1,000: A New Way of Viewing Corporate America," *Journal of Applied Corporate Finance,* summer 1990, pp. 38–59.
[16]S. Tully, "America's Greatest Wealth Creators," *Fortune,* November 9, 1998, pp. 193–204. The same article also published an update of MVA's as of September 30, 1998. Microsoft, which had been third at the end of 1997, leapfrogged over both G.E. and Coca-Cola with an MVA of $259 billion. G.E.'s MVA grew to $215 billion on this date.

Another measurement developed by Stern Stewart is **Economic Value Added (EVA®)**. EVA is calculated as follows:

$$\text{EVA} = (\text{Return on Total Capital} - \text{Cost of Capital}) \times \text{Total Capital}$$

Actually, the calculation of return on capital (profit divided by capital) is nothing new. However, EVA subtracts an estimated cost of capital from return. If the resulting number is positive, then the company has earned more than its investors require, and thus will add to investors' wealth. On the other hand, if cost is greater than return, then value is being destroyed.

To avoid distortions created by accounting conventions, Stern Stewart makes numerous adjustments to the return and capital numbers. Actually, EVA could be said to be very much like "economic profits," which are mentioned briefly in the next section of this chapter and are discussed thoroughly in chapter 9. However, when these numbers are calculated they are generally based on past results, and do not necessarily say anything about a company's future profitability. Still, "Stern Stewart says that there is a close correlation between EVA and MVA—if managers improve EVA, the company's MVA is highly likely to improve too."[17]

Over the last few years, many companies have begun emphasizing the EVA measure over more traditional measures such as earnings per share and return on equity, as have money managers such as Oppenheimer, Calpers, and others.[18]

## Economic Profits

Throughout this chapter we have been using the term *profit* and assumed that it has some kind of meaning. But we have not defined it. We only said that profit—and its maximization—is uppermost in the company owner's and manager's minds. In a way, profit is easy to define. Every company that closes its books annually and whose accountants construct a statement of earnings (whether this company is public, so that everybody can see the published statement and its "bottom line," or whether it is private) knows what its profits are. The accountants report the level of profits, and they also affirm that everything in the financial statements has been done in conformance with generally accepted accounting principles (GAAP).

Unfortunately, things are not quite that simple. Profits, as reported on an earnings statement, are not necessarily definitive. Accountants have certain amounts of freedom in recording items leading to the "bottom line."[19] A few examples will suffice:

1. There are different ways of recording depreciation. In the past the straight-line method, the sum-of-the-years'-digits method, the declining balance method, and probably others have been used. Under present tax law the Accelerated Cost Recovery System (ACRS) is most frequently employed.

---

[17]"A Star to Sail By?" *The Economist,* August 2, 1997, p. 54.
[18]Tully, "America's Greatest Wealth Creators," p. 195. The following articles discuss how companies use the EVA concept: "Stern Stewart EVA™ Roundtable," *Journal of Applied Corporate Finance,* summer 1994, pp. 46–70; S. Milunovich and A. Tsuei, "EVA® in the Computer Industry," *Journal of Applied Corporate Finance,* spring 1996, pp. 104–15: A. Jackson, "The How and Why of EVA® at CS First Boston," *Journal of Applied Corporate Finance,* spring 1996, pp. 98–103.
[19]Some writers in this field have said that accountants take too many liberties. Professor Abraham Briloff has written a number of books and articles on this subject.

2. There are various ways of recording inventories, the famous FIFO (first-in, first-out) and LIFO (last-in, first-out) being just two alternatives.
3. Amortization of such items as goodwill and patents can be recorded differently.

This is just a small sample of the better-known alternative treatments by accountants, and any of these are in conformance with GAAP. Moreover, the tax return that a company completes and sends to the IRS may be quite different from the published statement of a public company.

As if the question of what accounting profits really are were not enough, the economist compounds this problem even further. Everybody agrees that profit equals revenue minus costs (and expenses). But economists do not agree with accountants on the concept of costs. An accountant reports costs on a historical basis. The economist, however, is concerned with the costs that a business considers in making decisions, that is, future costs. We will concern ourselves with this concept more thoroughly later in this book, but we must touch on the subject now, albeit briefly. Basically, economists deal with something they call *opportunity costs* or *alternative costs:* this means that the cost of a resource is what a business must pay for it to attract it into its employ or, put differently, what a business must pay to keep this resource from finding employment elsewhere. To get down to specific examples, we can mention the following:

1. *Historical costs versus replacement costs.* To an economist, the replacement cost of a piece of machinery (and, therefore, the level of periodic depreciation on the replacement cost) is important, whereas an accountant measures cost—and depreciation—on a historical basis.
2. *Implicit costs and normal profits.*
   a. The owners' time and interest on the capital they contribute are usually counted as profit in a partnership or a single proprietorship. But the owners could work for someone else instead and invest their funds elsewhere. So these two items are really costs to the business and not profit.
   b. The preceding item is not relevant in the case of a corporation, since even top executives are salaried employees, and interest on corporate debt is deducted as an expense before profits are arrived at. However, the payments made to the owners/stockholders—dividends—are not part of cost; they are recorded as a distribution of profits. But surely a part of the shareholders' return is similar to the interest on debt, since stockholders could have invested their funds elsewhere and require a certain return in order to leave the investment with the corporation. Thus, on this account, corporate profits as recorded by accountants tend to be overstated.

It appears, therefore, that an economist includes costs that would be excluded by an accountant. Indeed, the economist refers to the second category of costs—which are essential to obtain and keep the owners' resources in the business—as **normal profits,** which represent the return that these resources demand to remain committed to a particular firm.

Thus **economic costs** include not only the historical costs and explicit costs recorded by the accountants, but also the replacement costs and implicit costs (normal profits) that must be earned on the owners' resources. In the rest of this book, profits are considered to be **economic profits,** which are defined as total revenue minus all the economic costs we have described in this section.

# International Application

The model of a firm's goals discussed in this chapter applies predominantly to firms operating in the United States and possibly the United Kingdom. However, one must ask whether profit maximization or shareholder wealth maximization is also valid for other countries. It is often said that for many reasons (e.g., political, cultural, legal, and institutional), firms in other countries pursue goals that include the interests of other groups, such as labor, community, government, and so on, in addition to interests of stockholders. In some countries, for instance, labor unions are represented on the board of directors. Thus, it may be necessary to consider such interests in our discussions. However, even if such considerations are important, it is possible for us to treat them as constraints on the actions of a firm. Even if profit or shareholder wealth maximization is not the only objective, as long as firms attempt to take actions that will improve their earnings—within specific constraints—our maximization model can still be used. It is important to recognize, however, that multinational firms (e.g., a U.S. parent corporation operating in many different countries through subsidiaries or branches) will encounter restrictions and complications, which they must consider in doing business abroad. We list these and explain them briefly:

1. Foreign currencies and their exchange rates must be considered. Thus, revenues, costs, and other cash flows that are denominated in other currencies must be translated into domestic currencies, and their potential changes must be analyzed for their impact on the business. Under certain circumstances, a profitable activity abroad can become unprofitable from the viewpoint of the domestic parent corporation.

2. Legal differences must be taken into account. Dissimilarities in tax laws can have important consequences on results of transactions between the domestic parent corporation and its foreign subsidiary. Differences in legal systems make the tasks of executives considerably more complex.

3. Most Americans have in the past mastered only their own language and, thus, are often at a disadvantage when dealing with their multilingual counterparts in other countries.

4. The differences in cultural environments influence the defining of business goals and attitudes toward risk. Thus, such differences can greatly affect the way business is conducted.

5. The role of government in defining the rules under which companies operate varies from country to country. While in some countries market competition prevails, in others the political process dictates the behavior of firms in much greater detail.

6. Corporations operating in different countries may be restricted from transferring corporate resources out of the country and may even face the danger of expropriation. This is political risk, which must be included in any economic analysis of a company's prospects.[20]

The points just discussed as well as others must always be considered by companies doing business abroad. While some of the differences may have adverse effects on a company, participation in a global market is a necessity for most large (and even small) firms

---

[20]The preceding points can be found in Eugene F. Brigham and Louis C. Gapenski, *Intermediate Financial Management,* 5th ed., Fort Worth, TX: The Dryden Press, 1996.

today. Profitability, and even survival, can depend on a company's entering global markets and competing worldwide.

## THE SOLUTION

It was a lively stockholder meeting. Bob Burns thought to himself that it was a good thing that the speech he prepared with the help of his assistants was short, since the stockholders were eager to enjoy the rest of the day with other activities that Global Foods had arranged. After covering the results for the most recent fiscal year, Bob continued:

"Over the past decade, American-based global companies have experienced heightened competition necessitating a restructuring of their operations, and more recently the economic crises in the economies of Asia as well as other areas in the world.

"Throughout this period, your management has maintained as its primary objective to continue to increase the value of your investment in the company. We are well aware that, recently, the price of our stock has not been increasing at the rate it did earlier in this decade. However, throughout this period we have remained committed to a long-run increase in the price of our stock. To accomplish this goal, we need to return to a double-digit annual increase in revenue as well as profits.

"As a part of this growth strategy, we are entering the growing market for bottled water. In the past 10 years, sales of bottled water in the United States have increased by 144 percent, and annual per capita consumption has more than doubled.[21] This is not a fad, but a trend. The quality of the water we drink has become increasingly important, as the confidence of Americans in their tap water is eroding.

"In order to maintain and increase our profits we have, over the last few years, been extremely diligent and successful in decreasing our production, marketing and administrative costs. But there is a limit to such endeavors. In the long run, we must find new ways and growing markets to increase our profitability and thus discharge our responsibility to you, our stockholders—increase the value of your investment. Entering the market for bottled water is one of the directions which will bring this about."

## Summary

In this text we will generally assume that a firm's short-run and long-run objective is the maximization of its profit or the minimization of its loss. Although a firm can select from a number of other goals, both in the short run and the long run, the assumption of profit maximization provides us with a clear-cut model for explaining how firms can use economic concepts and tools of analysis to make optimal decisions. In presenting these concepts and tools

---

[21]Corby Kummer, "Carried Away," *New York Times Magazine,* August 30, 1998, p. 40.

of analysis, a certain amount of mathematics will be employed. Thus, before proceeding to the next chapter, we believe that a brief review of the mathematics used in this text will be helpful. This review is contained in the appendix following this chapter.

## Important Concepts

**Business risk:** The variability of returns (or profits) due to fluctuations in general economic conditions or conditions specifically affecting the firm. (p. 33)

**Economic cost:** All cost incurred to attract resources into a company's employ. Such cost includes explicit cost usually recognized on accounting records as well as opportunity cost. (p. 37)

**Economic profit:** Total revenue minus total economic cost. An amount of profit earned in a particular endeavor above the amount of profit that the firm could be earning in its next best alternative activity. Also referred to as *abnormal profit* or *above-normal profit.* (p. 37)

**Economic Value Added (EVA):** The difference between a company's return on total capital and its cost of capital. (p. 36)

**Financial risk:** The variability of returns (or profits) induced by leverage (the proportion of a company financed by debt). The higher the leverage, the greater the potential fluctuation in stockholder earnings for a given change in total profits. (p. 33)

**Firm:** An organization that transforms resources into products demanded by consumers. The firm chooses to organize resources internally or to obtain them through the market. (p. 23)

**Market Value Added (MVA):** The difference between the market value (equity plus debt) of a company and the amount of capital investors have paid into the company. (p. 35)

**Noneconomic objectives:** A company's objectives that do not appear to be governed by economic thinking but rather define how a business should act. "Acting as a good corporate citizen" is an example of a noneconomic objective. (p. 29)

**Normal profit:** An amount of profit earned in a particular endeavor that is just equal to the profit that could be earned in a firm's next best alternative activity. When a firm earns normal profit, its revenue is just enough to cover both its accounting cost and its opportunity cost. It can also be considered as the return to capital and management necessary to keep resources engaged in a particular activity. (p. 37)

**Opportunistic behavior:** One party to a contract seeks to take advantage of the other. (p. 24)

**Optimal decision:** The decision that enables the firm to meet its desired objective most closely. (p. 27)

**Profit-maximization hypothesis:** One of the central themes in economics, the claim that a company will strive to attain the highest economic profit in each period. (p. 26)

**Satisficing:** A concept in economics based on the principle that owners of a firm (especially stockholders in a large corporation) may be content with adequate return and growth since they really cannot judge when profits are maximized. (p. 30)

**Transaction costs:** Cost incurred by a firm in dealing with another firm, and include the cost of investigation, negotiation, and enforcement of contracts. (p. 23)

**Wealth maximization:** A company's management of its business in such a manner that the cash flows over time to the company, discounted at an appropriate discount rate, will cause the value of the company's stock to be at a maximum. (p. 34)

## Questions

1. The following is a quote from a *New York Times* article: "If a company makes product donations to the school—computers for instance—then the image of a company goes up as graduate students use the company's products." Does such action square with a company's objective of profit maximization? Discuss.

2. Is the maximization of profit margin (profit as a percent of total sales) a valid financial objective of a corporation? Discuss.

3. "The growth of consumer information organizations, legal requirements, and warranty requirements has caused significant increases in the cost of customer satisfaction. Thus it is no longer useful to talk about profit maximization as a company objective." Comment on this quote.

4. Discuss the difference between profit maximization and shareholder wealth maximization. Which of these is a more comprehensive statement of a company's economic objectives?

5. Explain the term *satisfice* as it relates to the operations of a large corporation.

6. Why may corporate managers not specifically aim at profit (or wealth) maximization for their companies?

7. What are some of the forces that cause managers to act in the interest of shareholders?

8. Do you believe that profit (or shareholder wealth) maximization still represents the best overall economic objective for today's corporation?

9. Because of inflation, a company must replace one of its (fully depreciated) machines at twice the nominal price paid for a similar machine eight years ago. Based on present accounting rules, will the company have covered the entire cost of the new machine through depreciation charges? Explain by contrasting accounting and economic costs.

10. How do implicit costs lead to a difference between accounting and economic profits?

11. You have a choice of opening your own business or being employed by someone else in a similar type of business. What are some of the considerations in terms of opportunity costs that you would have to include in arriving at your decision?

12. Various depreciation methods can be used to arrive at an accounting profit number. From the viewpoint of the economist, how should annual depreciation be determined?

13. Do you believe that the profit-maximization model can be applied to the activities of a multinational corporation? Explain.

14. Recently many companies have discontinued performing certain activities internally and have contracted these activities to outside suppliers. Some examples of these actions are plant security, operation of company cafeterias, document copying, and travel services. How would you explain these changes?

15. What are some reasons for companies internalizing transaction costs?

16. A company has 2 million shares outstanding. It paid a dividend of $2 during the past year, and expects that dividends will grow at 6 percent annually in the future. Stockholders require a rate of return of 13 percent. What would you expect the price of each share to be today, and what is the value of the company's common stock?

17. Discuss the difference between the calculation of shareholder wealth and the concept of Market Value Added. Which of the two would appear to be more meaningful from the viewpoint of a shareholder?

## Take It to the Net

We invite you to visit the Keat/Young page on the Prentice Hall Web site at:

**http://www.prenhall.com/keat**

for additional resources.

## Appendix 2A

### Review of Mathematical Concepts Used in Managerial Economics

Economics is the most mathematical of all the social sciences. Indeed, to the uninitiated reader, many academic journals in economics resemble a mathematics or physics journal. Because this text is intended to show the practical applications of economic theory, this presents something of a dilemma. On one hand, the economic theory of managerial decision making has evolved along with the rest of economics to a point where it can be (and usually is) profusely expressed in mathematical terms. On the other hand, industry experience indicates that managers seldom use the more advanced mathematical expressions of economic theory. They do, nonetheless, rely quite often on many of the concepts, graphs, and relatively simple numerical examples that are used throughout this text to assist them in their decision making.

But the dilemma does not end here. Regardless of the role of mathematics in managerial decision making, it certainly serves as an important instructional vehicle for economics professors. Using calculus enables the very concise expression of complex functional relationships and the quick solution of problems involving the optimal allocation of scarce resources. Moreover, students with extensive academic backgrounds or work experience in applied mathematics (i.e., engineers and scientists) often find that they are able to discern the essential nature of an economic problem more easily with equations and calculus than with narratives and tabular examples.

We have resolved the dilemma in the following way. The explanations of economic terms, concepts, and methods of analysis rely primarily on verbal definitions, numerical tables, and graphs. As appropriate, chapter appendixes will present the same material using algebra and calculus. At times, algebra and calculus will be employed in the main body of a chapter. Moreover, problems and exercises at the end of the chapter will give students ample opportunity to reinforce their understanding of the material with the use of algebra and calculus, as well as with tables and graphs.

The authors' experience as teachers indicates that many students have already learned the mathematics employed in this text, both in the main body and in the appendixes. However, some students may have studied this material some time ago and may therefore benefit from a review. Such a review is offered in the balance of this appendix. It is intended only as a brief refresher. For a more comprehensive review readers should consult any of the many texts and review books on this subject.[22] In fact, any college algebra or calculus text would be just as suitable as a reference.

# Variables, Functions, and Slopes: The Heart of Economic Analysis

A *variable* is any entity that can assume different values. Each academic discipline focuses attention on its own set of variables. For example, in the social sciences, political scientists may study power and authority, sociologists may study group cohesiveness, and psychologists may study paranoia. Economists study such variables as price, output, rev-

---

[22]See, for example, Bodh R. Gulati, *College Mathematics with Applications to the Business and Social Sciences,* New York: Harper & Row, 1978; and Donald and Mildred Stanel, *Applications of College Mathematics,* Lexington, MA: D.C. Heath, 1983.

| TABLE 2A.1 Tabular Expression of the TR Function | |
|---|---|
| *Units Sold* *(Q)* | *Total Revenue* *(TR)* |
| 0 | $ 0 |
| 1 | 5 |
| 2 | 10 |
| 3 | 15 |
| 4 | 20 |
| 5 | 25 |

enue, cost, and profit. The advantage that economics has over the other social sciences is that most of its variables can be measured in a relatively unambiguous manner.[23]

Once the variables of interest have been identified and measured, economists try to understand how and why the values of these variables change. They also try to determine what conditions will lead to optimal values. Here the term *optimal* refers to the best possible value in a particular situation. *Optimal* may refer to the maximum value (as in the case of profit), or it may refer to the minimum value (as in the case of cost). In any event, the analysis of the changes in a variable's value, often referred to as a variable's "behavior," is almost always carried out in relation to other variables. In mathematics, the relationship of one variable's value to the values of other variables is expressed in terms of a function. Formally stated in mathematical terms, $Y$ is said to be a function of $X$ (i.e., $Y = f(x)$, where $f$ represents "function" if for any value that might be assigned to $X$ a value of $Y$ can be determined). For example, the demand function indicates the quantity of a good or service that people are willing to buy, given the values of price, tastes and preferences, prices of related products, number of buyers, and future expectations. A functional relationship can be expressed using tables, graphs, or algebraic equations.

To illustrate the different ways of expressing a function, let us use the total revenue function. Total revenue (or sales) is defined as the unit price of a product ($P$) multiplied by the number of units sold ($Q$). That is, TR = $P \times Q$. In economics the general functional relationship for total revenue is that its value is dependent on the number of units sold. That is, TR = $f(Q)$. Total revenue, or TR, is called the *dependent variable* because its value depends on the value of $Q$. $Q$ is called the *independent variable* because its value may vary independently of the value of TR. For example, suppose a product is sold for $5 per unit. Table 2A.1 shows the relationship between total revenue and quantity over a selected range of units sold.

Figure 2A.1 shows a graph of the values in Table 2A.1. As you can see in this figure, we have related total revenue to quantity in a linear fashion. There does not always have to be a linear relationship between total revenue and quantity. As you will see in the next section, this function, as well as many other functions of interest to economists, may assume different nonlinear forms.

---

[23]To be sure, variables in the other social sciences are measurable, but in many instances, the measurement standards themselves are subject to discussion and controversy. For example, psychologists may use the result of some type of IQ test as a measure of intelligence. But there is an ongoing debate as to whether this result is reflective of one's native intelligence or socioeconomic background.

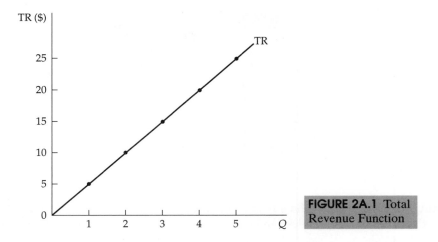

**FIGURE 2A.1** Total Revenue Function

We can also express the relation depicted in Table 2A.1 and Figure 2A.1 in the following equation:

$$TR = 5Q \qquad \text{(2A.1)}$$

where  TR = Dependent variable (total revenue)
   $Q$ = Independent variable (quantity)
   5 = Coefficient showing the relationship between changes in TR relative to changes in $Q$

This equation can also be expressed in the general form:

$$Y = a + bX \qquad \text{(2A.2)}$$

where   $Y$ = Dependent variable (i.e., TR)
    $X$ = Independent variable (i.e., $Q$)
    $b$ = Coefficient of $X$ (i.e., the given $P$ of $5)
    $a$ = Intercept term (in this case, 0)

In a linear equation, the coefficient $b$ (which takes the value of 5 in our total revenue function) can also be thought of as the change in $Y$ over the change in $X$, (i.e., $(\Delta Y)/(\Delta X)$). In other words, it represents the slope of the line plotted on the basis of Equation (2A.2). The slope of a line is a measure of its steepness. This can be seen in Figure 2A.1, which, for purposes of discussion, we have reproduced in Figure 2A.2. In this figure, the steepness of the line between points $A$ and $B$ can be seen as $BC/AC$.

The slope of a function is critical to economic analysis because it shows the change in a dependent variable relative to a change in a designated independent variable. As explained in the next section of this appendix, this is the essence of *marginal analysis.*

## The Importance of Marginal Analysis in Economic Analysis

One of the most important contributions that economic theory has made to managerial decision making is the application of what economists call *marginal analysis.* Essentially, marginal analysis involves the consideration of changes in the values of variables

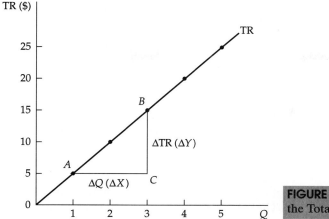

**FIGURE 2A.2** The Slope of the Total Revenue Line

from some given starting point. Stated in a more formal mathematical manner, marginal analysis can be defined as the amount of change in a dependent variable that results from a unit change in an independent variable. If the functional relationship between the dependent and independent variables is linear, this change is represented by the slope of the line. In the case of our total revenue function, $TR = 5Q$, we can readily see that the coefficient, 5, indicates the marginal relationship between TR, the dependent variable, and $Q$, the independent variable. That is, total revenue is expected to change by \$5 for every unit change in $Q$.

Most economic decisions made by managers involve some sort of change in one variable relative to a change in other variables. For example, a firm might want to consider raising or lowering the price from \$5 per unit. Whether or not it is desirable to do so would depend on the resulting change in revenues or profits. Changes in these variables would in turn depend on the change in the number of units sold as a result of the change in price. Using the usual symbol for change, $\Delta$ (delta), this pricing decision can be summarized via the following illustration:

The top line shows that a firm's price affects its profit. The dashed arrows indicate that changes in price will change profit via changes in the number of units sold ($\Delta Q$), in revenue, and in cost. Actually, each of the dashed lines represents a key function used in economic analysis. $\Delta P$ to $\Delta Q$ represents the demand function. $\Delta Q$ to $\Delta$Revenue is the total revenue function, $\Delta Q$ to $\Delta$Cost is the cost function, and $\Delta Q$ to $\Delta$Profit is the profit function. Of course, the particular behavior or pattern of profit change relative to changes in quantity depends on how revenue and cost change relative to changes in $Q$.

Marginal analysis comes into play even if a product is new and being priced in the market for the first time. When there is no starting or reference point, different values of a variable may be evaluated in a form of sensitivity or what-if analysis. For example, the decision makers in a company such as IBM may price the company's new workstations by charting a list of hypothetical prices and then forecasting how many units the company will be able to sell at each price. By shifting from price to price, the decision makers would be engaging in a form of marginal analysis.[24]

Many other economic decisions rely on marginal analysis, including the hiring of additional personnel, the purchase of additional equipment, or a venture into a new line of business. In each of these cases, it is the change in some variable (e.g., profit, cash flow, productivity, or cost) associated with the change in a firm's resource allocation that is of importance to the decision maker. Consideration of changes in relation to some reference point is also referred to as *incremental analysis*. A common distinction made between incremental and marginal analysis is that the former simply considers the change in the dependent variable whereas the latter considers the change in the dependent variable relative to a one-unit change in the independent variable. For example, suppose lowering the price of a product results in a sales increase of 1,000 units and a revenue increase of $2,000. The incremental revenue would be $2,000, and the marginal revenue would be $2 ($2,000/1,000).

## Functional Forms: A Variation on a Theme

For purposes of illustration, we will often rely on a linear function to express the relationship among variables. This is particularly the case in chapter 3, on supply and demand. But there are many instances when a linear function is not the proper expression for changes in the value of a dependent variable relative to changes in some independent variable. For example, if a firm's total revenue does not increase at the same rate as additional units of its product are sold, a linear function is clearly not appropriate. To illustrate this phenomenon, let us assume that a firm has the power to set its price at different levels and that its customers respond to different prices on the basis of the following schedule:

| $P$ | $Q$ |
|-----|-----|
| $7 | 0 |
| 6 | 100 |
| 5 | 200 |
| 4 | 300 |
| 3 | 400 |
| 2 | 500 |
| 1 | 600 |
| 0 | 700 |

The algebraic and graphical expressions of this relationship are shown in Figure 2A.3. As implied in the schedule and as shown explicitly in Figure 2A.3, we have assumed a linear relationship between price and quantity demanded.

Based on the definition of total revenue as TR $= P \times Q$, we can create a total revenue schedule as well as a total revenue equation and graph. These are all shown in Figure 2A.4.

---

[24]One of the authors was a member of the pricing department of IBM for a number of years. This type of sensitivity analysis involving marginal relationships is indeed an important part of the pricing process. Much more about pricing will be said in later chapters.

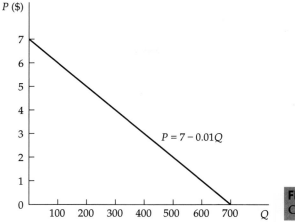

**FIGURE 2A.3** Demand Curve

Since we know that the demand curve is $Q = 700 - 100P$ and TR $= P \times Q$, we can arrive at the values of the coefficient and intercept terms as well as the functional form in a very straightforward manner. First, we need to express $P$ in terms of $Q$ so that we can substitute this relationship into the total revenue equation:

$$Q = 700 - 100P \qquad \text{(2A.3)}$$

or

$$P = 7 - 0.01Q \qquad \text{(2A.4)}$$

Substituting the Equation (2A.4) into the total revenue equation gives

$$\begin{aligned}
\text{TR} &= P \times Q \qquad \text{(2A.5)} \\
&= (7 - 0.01Q)Q \\
&= 7Q - 0.01Q^2
\end{aligned}$$

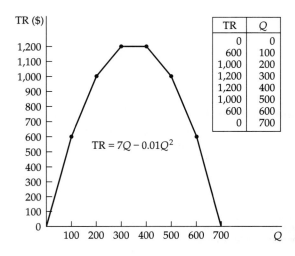

| TR | Q |
|---|---|
| 0 | 0 |
| 600 | 100 |
| 1,000 | 200 |
| 1,200 | 300 |
| 1,200 | 400 |
| 1,000 | 500 |
| 600 | 600 |
| 0 | 700 |

$$\text{TR} = 7Q - 0.01Q^2$$

**FIGURE 2A.4** Total Revenue

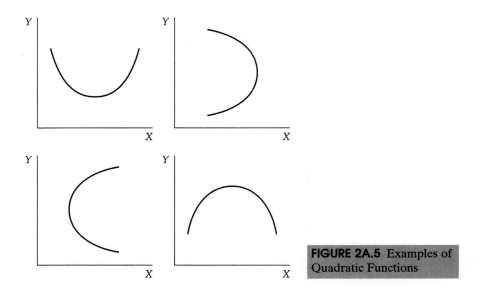

**FIGURE 2A.5** Examples of Quadratic Functions

As can be seen, a linear demand function results in a nonlinear total revenue function. More precisely, the functional relationship between total revenue and quantity seen here is expressed as a quadratic equation. Basically, this particular functional relationship is obtained whenever the independent variable is raised to the second power (i.e., squared) as well as to the first power. Graphically, quadratic equations are easily recognized by their parabolic shape. The parabola's actual shape and placement on the graph depend on the values and signs of the coefficient and intercept terms. Figure 2A.5 shows four different quadratic functions.

If, in addition to being squared, the independent variable is raised to the third power (i.e., cubed), the relationship between the dependent and independent variables is called a cubic function. Figure 2A.6 illustrates different cubic functions. As in the case of quadratic equations, the pattern and placement of these curves depend on the values and signs of the coefficients and intercept terms.

The independent variable can also be raised beyond the third power. However, anything more complex than a cubic equation is generally not useful for describing the relationship among variables in managerial economics. Certainly, there is no need to go beyond the cubic equation for purposes of this text. As readers will see in ensuing chapters, the most commonly used forms of key functions are (1) linear demand function, (2) linear or quadratic total revenue function, (3) cubic production function, (4) cubic cost function, and (5) cubic profit function. Some variations to these relationships will also be used, depending on the specifics of the examples being discussed.

There are other nonlinear forms used in economic analysis besides those just listed. These forms involve the use of exponents, logarithms, and reciprocals of the independent variables. Simple examples of these types of nonlinear form are shown in Figure 2A.7. These forms are generally used in the statistical estimation of economic functions, such as the demand, production, and cost functions, and in the forecasting of variables based on some trend over time (i.e., time series analysis). More will be said about these particular functional forms in chapters 5, 6, 9, and 10.

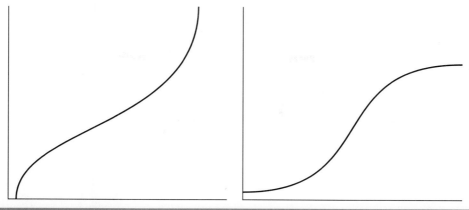

**FIGURE 2A.6** Examples of Cubic Functions

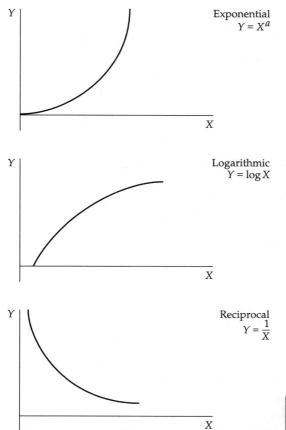

Exponential
$Y = X^a$

Logarithmic
$Y = \log X$

Reciprocal
$Y = \dfrac{1}{X}$

**FIGURE 2A.7** Examples of
Selected Nonlinear Functions

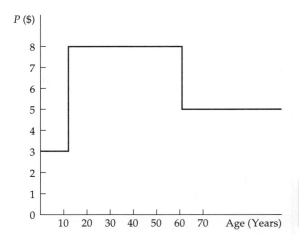

**FIGURE 2A.8** Example of a Step Function: Age Groups and Admission Price

## CONTINUOUS FUNCTIONAL RELATIONSHIPS

In plotting a functional relationship on a graph, we have assumed that changes in the value of the dependent variable are related in a continuous manner to changes in the independent variable. Intuitively, a function can be said to be continuous if it can be drawn on a graph without taking the pencil off the paper.[25] Perhaps the best way to understand a continuous function is to observe its opposite, a function with discontinuity. Suppose the admission price to an amusement park is established as follows: Ages 1 through 12 must pay $3, ages 13 through 60 must pay $8, and ages 61 and above must pay $5. A graph of the relationship between admission price and age is shown in Figure 2A.8. Notice that there is a jump or break in the graph at the level separating children from adults and the level separating adults from senior citizens. Because of these breaks in the relationship between the independent and dependent variables, this discontinuous relationship is also referred to as a *step function.*

Unless otherwise specified, the functional relationships analyzed in this text are considered to be continuous. Looking back at our example of the demand and total revenue functions, we can see that they indeed indicate a continuous relationship between price and quantity and between total revenue and quantity (see Figures 2A.1 and 2A.4). However, a closer look at the intervals used in the examples might lead you to question the applicability of a continuous function in actual business situations. For instance, let us observe again in Figure 2A.9 the relationship between total revenue and quantity first shown in Figure 2A.4.

The inquiring reader might ask whether or not this relationship, $TR = 7Q - 0.01Q^2$, is in fact valid for points *within* each of the given intervals. For example, if the firm sold 150 units, would it earn $825? Even if the answer is affirmative, to be a truly continuous function, the relationship would have to hold no matter how small the in-

---

[25]This particular way of explaining a continuous function is taken from Gulati, *College Mathematics.* To be sure, the author provides a much more rigorous definition of this concept.

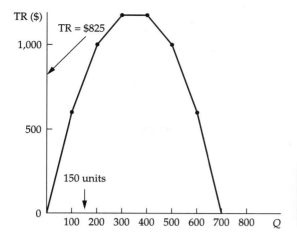

**FIGURE 2A.9** Discrete Intervals in a Continuous Function: The Example of Total Revenue

tervals of quantity considered.[26] For example, if the firm sold 150.567 units, its revenue would be $827.265.

But at this point, an adjustment to strict mathematics must be tempered with common sense. There are many instances in economic analysis in which continuous functions are assumed to represent relationships among variables, even though the variables themselves are subject to limitations in how finely they can be subdivided. For example, a firm may only be able to sell its product in lots of 100 or, at the very least, in single units. A firm might not want to consider price changes in terms of cents, but only in terms of dollars. In other cases, it might not be a matter of a firm's choice but of what resources are available. For example, suppose we have a function relating persons hired to the output they produce. (In chapter 7, this is referred to as the short-run production function.) Let us further suppose that labor resources are measured in terms of units of people (as opposed to hours, minutes, or even seconds of work time). Many economic activities in business involve variables that must be measured in discrete intervals (e.g., people, units of output, monetary units, machines, factories). For purposes of analysis, we will assume that all the economic variables are related to each other in a continuous fashion but are valid only at stated discrete intervals.

## Using Calculus

Calculus is a mathematical technique that enables one to find instantaneous rates of change of a continuous function. That is, instead of finding the rate of change between two points on a plotted line, as shown in Figure 2A.2, calculus enables us to find the rate of change in the dependent variable relative to the independent variable at a particular point on the function. However, calculus can be so applied *only* if a function is

---

[26]According to mathematicians, "A function is said to be continuous over an open interval if it is continuous at *every* point in that interval" (Gulati, *College Mathematics,* p. 505).

continuous. Thus, we needed to establish firmly the validity of using continuous functions to represent the relationships among economic variables.

Our brief introduction to calculus and its role in economic analysis begins with the statement that if all functional relationships in economics were linear, there would be no need for calculus! This point may be made clearer by referring to an intuitive definition of calculus. To quote the author of an extremely helpful and readable book on this subject:

> Calculus, first of all, is wrongly named. It should never have been given that name. A far truer and more meaningful name is "SLOPE-FINDING."[27]

It is not difficult to find the slope of a linear function. We simply take any two points on the line and find the change in $Y$ relative to the change in $X$. The relative change is, of course, represented by the $b$ coefficient in the linear equation. Moreover, because it is linear, the slope or rate of change remains the same between any two points over the entire range of intervals one wishes to consider for the function. This is shown in the algebraic expression of the linear function by the constancy of the $b$ coefficient.

However, finding the slope of a nonlinear function poses a problem. Let us arbitrarily take two points on the curve shown in Figure 2A.10 and label them $A$ and $D$. The slope or rate of change of $Y$ relative to the change in $X$ can be seen as $DL/AL$. Now, on this same curve let us find the slope of a point closer to point $D$ and call it $C$. Notice that the slope of the line between these two points is less than the slope between $D$ and $A$. (The measure of this slope is $DM/CM$.) The same holds true if we consider point $B$, a point that is still closer to $D$; the slope between $B$ and $D$ is less than the two slopes already considered. In general, we can state that in reference to the curve shown in Figure 2A.10, the slope between point $D$ and a point to the left decreases as the point moves closer to $D$. Obviously, this is not the case for a linear equation because the slope is constant.

To understand how calculus enables us to find the slope or rate of change of a nonlinear function, let us resume the experiment. Suppose we keep on measuring changes in $Y$ relative to smaller and smaller changes in $X$. Graphically, this can be represented in Figure 2A.10 by moving point $B$ toward point $D$. As smaller and smaller changes in $X$ are considered, point $B$ moves closer and closer to point $D$ until the limit at which it appears to become one and the same with point $D$. When this occurs, the slope or rate of change of $Y$ relative to $X$ can be represented as point $D$ itself. Graphically, this is represented by the slope of a line tangent to point $D$. In effect, this slope is a measure of the change in $Y$ relative to a very small (i.e., infinitesimally small) change in $X$. To find the magnitude of the slope of tangency to any point on a line, we need to employ calculus, or more specifically, a concept used in calculus called the *derivative*.

In mathematics, a derivative is a measure of the change in $Y$ relative to a very small change in $X$. Using formal mathematical notation, we can define the derivative as

$$\frac{dY}{dX} = \lim_{\Delta X \to 0} \frac{\Delta Y}{\Delta X}$$

---

[27]Eli S. Pine, *How to Enjoy Calculus,* Hasbrouck Heights, NJ: Steinlitz-Hammacher, 1983. Pine's definition is, of course, a simplification since it leaves out integral calculus. Nevertheless, we recommend this book highly for those who wish a "user-friendly" review of differential calculus.

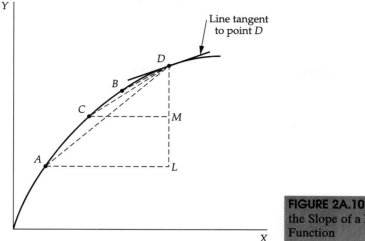

**FIGURE 2A.10** Finding the Slope of a Nonlinear Function

This notation can be expressed as, "The derivative of $Y$ with respect to $X$ equals the limit (if such a limit exists) of the change in $Y$ relative to the change in $X$ as the change in $X$ approaches zero.[28] As you can see from the discussion in the previous two paragraphs, the derivative turns out to be the slope of a line that is tangent to some given point on a curve. By convention, mathematicians use $d$ to represent very small changes in a variable. Hence, $dY/dX$ means "changes in $Y$ relative to very small changes in $X$." For changes between two distinct points, the delta sign ($\Delta$) is used.

## FINDING THE DERIVATIVES OF A FUNCTION

There are certain rules for finding the derivatives of a function. We shall present in some detail two rules that will be used extensively in this text. The other rules and their use in economic analysis will be only briefly mentioned. Formal proofs of all of these rules are not provided. Interested students may consult any introductory calculus text for this information.

***Constants.***    The derivative of a constant must always be zero. Derivatives involve rates of change, and a constant, by definition, never changes in value. Expressed formally, if $Y$ equals some constant, (e.g., $Y = 100$), then

$$\frac{dY}{dX} = 0$$

The null value of the derivative of a constant is illustrated in Figure 2A.11. Here we have assumed $Y$ to have a constant value of 100. Clearly, this constant value of $Y$ is unaffected by changes in the value of $X$. Thus, $dY/dX = 0$.

---

[28]The concept of *limit* is critical to understanding the derivative. We have tried to present an intuitive explanation of this concept by considering the movement of point $B$ in Figure 2A.10 closer and closer to point $D$, so that in effect the changes in $X$ become smaller and smaller. *At the limit*, $B$ becomes so close to $D$ that, for all intents and purposes, it is the same as $D$. This situation would represent the smallest possible change in $X$. For a more formal explanation of *limit*, readers should consult any introductory calculus text.

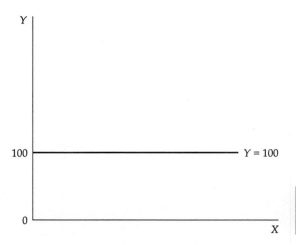

**FIGURE 2A.11** The Derivative of a Constant Equals Zero

**Power Functions.**   A *power function* is one in which the independent variable, *X*, is raised to the power of one or more. This type of function can be expressed in general terms as

$$Y = bX^n \qquad \text{(2A.6)}$$

where  $Y$  = Dependent variable
       $b$  = Coefficient of the dependent variable
       $X$  = Independent variable
       $n$  = Power to which the independent variable is raised

The rule for finding the derivative of this type of function is

$$\frac{dY}{dX} = nbX^{(n-1)} \qquad \text{(2A.7)}$$

Thus, suppose we have the equation

$$Y = 10X^3 \qquad \text{(2A.8)}$$

The derivative of this equation according to this rule is

$$\frac{dY}{dX} = 3 \times 10X^{(3-1)}$$

$$= 30X^2 \qquad \text{(2A.9)}$$

Thus, at the point where $X = 5$, the "instantaneous" rate of change of $Y$ with respect to $X$ is $30(5)^2$, or 750.

**Sums and Differences.**   For convenience in presenting the rules in the remainder of this appendix, we will use the following notations:

$U = g(X)$, where $U$ is an unspecified function, $g$, of $X$
$V = h(X)$, where $V$ is an unspecified function, $h$, of $X$

Given the function $Y = U + V$, the derivative of the sum (difference) is equal to the sum (difference) of the derivatives of the individual terms. In notational form,

$$\frac{dY}{dX} = \frac{dU}{dX} + \frac{dV}{dX}$$

For example, if $U = g(X) = 3X^2$, $V = h(X) = 4X^3$ and $Y = U + V = 3X^2 + 4X^3$, then

$$\frac{dY}{dX} = 6X \times 12X^2$$

***Products.***   Given the function $Y = UV$, its derivative can be expressed as follows:

$$\frac{dY}{dX} = U\frac{dV}{dX} + V\frac{dU}{dX}$$

This rule states that the derivative of the product of two expressions ($U$ and $V$) is equal to the first term multiplied by the derivative of the second, plus the second term times the derivative of the first. For example, let $Y = 5X^2(7 - X)$. By letting $U = 5X^2$ and $V = (7 - X)$, we obtain

$$\frac{dY}{dX} = 5X^2\frac{dV}{dX} + (7 - X)\frac{dU}{dX}$$

$$= 5X^2(-1) + (7 - X)10X$$

$$= -5X^2 + 70X - 10X^2$$

$$= 70X - 15X^2$$

***Quotients.***   Given the function $Y = U/V$, its derivative can be expressed as follows:

$$\frac{dY}{dX} = \frac{V(dU/dX) - U(dV/dX)}{V^2}$$

For example, suppose we have the following function:

$$Y = \frac{5X - 9}{10X^2}$$

Using the formula and letting $U = 5X - 9$ and $V = 10X^2$, we obtain the following:

$$\frac{dY}{dX} = \frac{10X^2 \times 5 - (5X - 9)\,20X}{100X^4}$$

$$= \frac{50X^2 - 100X^2 + 180X}{100X^4}$$

$$= \frac{180X - 50X^2}{100X^4}$$

$$= \frac{18 - 5X}{10X^3}$$

***Applying the Rules to an Economic Problem and a Preview of Other Rules for Differentiating a Function.***   There are several other rules for differentiating a function that are used in economic analysis. These involve differentiating a logarithmic function and the "function of a function" (often referred to in mathematics as the *chain rule*). We will present these rules as they are needed in the appropriate chapters. In fact, almost all of the mathematical examples involving calculus will require only the rules for constants, powers, and sums and differences. As an example of how these three rules are applied, we return to the total revenue and demand functions presented earlier in this appendix. Recall that

$$\text{TR} = 7Q - 0.01Q^2 \qquad \text{(2A.10)}$$

Using the rules for powers and for sums and differences, we find that the derivative of this *function* is

$$\frac{d\text{TR}}{dQ} = 7 - 0.02Q \qquad \text{(2A.11)}$$

The derivative of the total revenue function is also called the *marginal revenue function* and plays a very important part in many aspects of economic analysis. (See chapter 4 for a complete discussion of the definition and uses of marginal revenue.)

Turning now to the demand function first presented in Figure 2A.3, we recall that

$$Q = 700 - 100P \qquad \text{(2A.12)}$$

Using the rules for constants, powers, and sums and differences, we see that the derivative of this function is:

$$\frac{dQ}{dP} = 0 - 1(100)P^{(1-1)} \qquad \text{(2A.13)}$$

$$= -100P^0$$

$$= -100$$

Notice that, by the conventions of mathematical notation, variables such as $P$ that have no stated exponent are assumed to be raised to the first power (i.e., $n = 1$). Thus, based on the rule for the derivative of a power function, $(n - 1)$ becomes $(1 - 1)$, or zero.[29] Therefore, $dQ/dP$ is equal to the constant value 100. Recall our initial statement that there is no need for calculus if only linear functions are considered. This is supported by the results shown in Equation (2A.13). Here we can see that the first derivative of the linear demand equation is simply the value of the $b$ coefficient, 100. That is, no matter what the value of $P$, the change in $Q$ with respect to a change in $P$ is 100 (i.e., the slope of the linear function, or the $b$ coefficient in the linear equation). Another way to express this is that for a linear function, there is no need to take the derivative $dY/dX$. Instead, we can use the slope of the line represented by $\Delta Y/\Delta X$.

***Partial Derivatives.***   Many functional relationships in this text will entail a number of independent variables. For example, let us assume that a firm has a demand function represented by the following equation:

$$Q = -100P + 50I + P_s + 2N \qquad \text{(2A.14)}$$

where   $Q$ = Quantity demanded
$P$ = Price of the product
$I$ = Income of customers
$P_s$ = Price of a substitute product
N = Number of customers

If we want to know the change in $Q$ with respect to a change in a particular independent variable, we can take the partial derivative of $Q$ with respect to that variable. For

---

[29]The rule in algebra is that any value raised to the zeroth power is equal to unity.

example, the impact of a change in $P$ on $Q$, with other factors held constant, would be expressed as

$$\frac{\delta Q}{\delta P} = -100 \qquad \textbf{(2A.15)}$$

The conventional symbol used in mathematics for the partial derivative is the lowercase Greek letter delta, $\delta$. Notice that all we did was use the rule for the derivative of a power function on the $P$ variable. Because the other independent variables, $I$, $P_s$, and $N$, are held constant, they are treated as constants in taking the partial derivative. (As you recall, the derivative of a constant is zero.) Thus, the other terms in the equation drop out, leaving us with the instantaneous impact of the change in $P$ on $Q$. This procedure applies regardless of the powers to which the independent variables are raised. It just so happens that in this equation, all the independent variables are raised only to the first power.[30]

## FINDING THE MAXIMUM AND MINIMUM VALUES OF A FUNCTION

A primary objective of managerial economics is to find the optimal values of key variables. This means finding "the best" possible amount or value under certain circumstances. Marginal analysis and the concept of the derivative are very helpful in finding optimal values. For example, given a total revenue function, a firm might want to find the number of units it must sell to maximize its revenue. Taking the total revenue function first shown in Equation (2A.5), we have

$$\text{TR} = 7Q - 0.01Q^2 \qquad \textbf{(2A.16)}$$

The derivative of this function (i.e., marginal revenue) is

$$\frac{d\text{TR}}{dQ} = 7 - 0.02Q \qquad \textbf{(2A.17)}$$

Setting the first derivative of the total revenue function (or the marginal revenue function) equal to zero and solving for the revenue-maximizing quantity, $Q^*$, gives us[31]

$$7 - 0.02Q = 0 \qquad \textbf{(2A.18)}$$
$$Q^* = 350$$

Thus, the firm should sell 350 units of its product if it wants to maximize its total revenue. In addition, if the managers wish to know the price that the firm should charge to sell the "revenue-maximizing" number of units, they can go back to the demand equation from which the total revenue function was derived, that is,

$$P = 7 - 0.01Q \qquad \textbf{(2A.19)}$$

By substituting the value of $Q^*$ into this equation, we obtain

$$P^* = 7 - 0.01(350) \qquad \textbf{(2A.20)}$$
$$= \$3.50$$

---

[30]An expression such as this is referred to in mathematics as a *linear additive equation.*
[31]Henceforth, all optimal values for $Q$ and $P$ (e.g., values that maximize revenue or profit or minimize cost) will be designated with an asterisk.

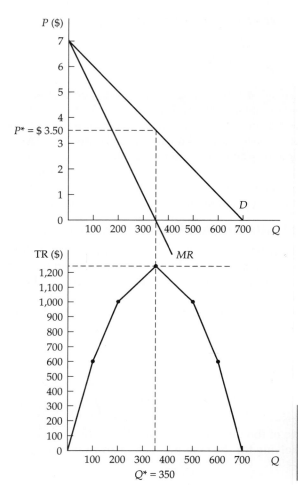

**FIGURE 2A.12** Demand Function, Total Revenue Function, and Revenue-Maximizing Price and Quantity

The demand function, the total revenue function, and the revenue-maximizing price and quantity are all illustrated in Figure 2A.12.

To further illustrate the use of the derivative in finding the optimum, let us use an example that will play an important part in chapters 9 and 10. Suppose a firm wishes to find the price and output levels that will maximize its profit. If the firm's revenue and cost functions are known, it is a relatively simple matter to use the derivative of these functions to find the optimal price and quantity. To begin with, let us assume the following demand, revenue, and cost functions:

$$Q = 17.2 - 0.1P \qquad \text{(2A.21)}$$

or

$$P = 172 - 10Q \qquad \text{(2A.22)}$$

$$TR = 172Q - 10Q^2 \qquad \text{(2A.23)}$$

$$TC = 100 + 65Q + Q^2 \qquad \text{(2A.24)}$$

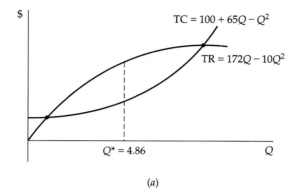

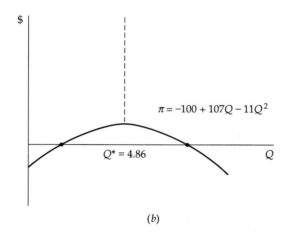

FIGURE 2A.13 Total Revenue, Total Cost, and Total Profit Functions

By definition, profit ($\pi$) is equal to total revenue minus total cost. That is,

$$\pi = TR - TC \tag{2A.25}$$

Substituting Equations (2A.23) and (2A.24) into (2A.25) gives us:

$$\pi = 172Q - 10Q^2 - 100 - 65Q - Q^2 \tag{2A.26}$$
$$= -100 + 107Q - 11Q^2$$

To find the profit-maximizing output level, we simply follow the same procedure used to find the revenue-maximizing output level. We take the derivative of the total profit function, set it equal to zero, and solve for $Q^*$:

$$\frac{d\pi}{dQ} = 107 - 22Q = 0$$

$$22Q = 107 \tag{2A.27}$$

$$Q^* = 4.86 \tag{2A.28}$$

The total revenue and cost functions and the total profit function are illustrated in Figure 2A.13a and b, respectively.

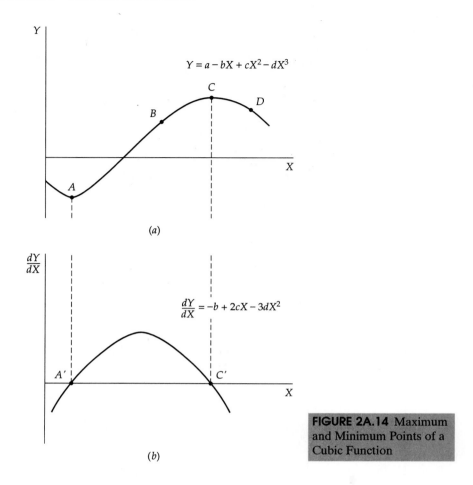

$$Y = a - bX + cX^2 - dX^3$$

(a)

$$\frac{dY}{dX} = -b + 2cX - 3dX^2$$

(b)

**FIGURE 2A.14** Maximum and Minimum Points of a Cubic Function

***Distinguishing Maximum and Minimum Values in the Optimization Problem.*** In economic analysis, finding the optimum generally means finding either the maximum or minimum value of a variable, depending on what type of function is being considered. For example, if the profit or total revenue function is the focus, the maximum value is obviously of interest. If a cost function is being analyzed, its minimum value would be the main concern. Taking the derivative of a function, setting it equal to zero, and then solving for the value of the independent variable enables us to find the maximum or minimum value of the function.

However, there may be instances in which a function has both a maximum and a minimum value. When this occurs, the method described previously cannot tell us whether the optimum is a maximum or a minimum. This situation of indeterminacy can be seen in Figure 2A.14a. The graph in this figure represents a cubic function of the general form $Y = a - bX + cX^2 - dX^3$. Clearly, this function has both a minimum (point A) and a maximum (point C). As a generalization, if we took the first derivative at the four points designated in Figure 2A.14a, we would find that

At point *A, dY/dX* = 0.
At point *B, dY/dX* > 0.
At point *C, dY/dX* = 0.
At point *D, dY/dX* < 0.

As expected, the first derivatives of points *A* and *C* are equal to zero, reflecting the fact that their lines of tangency are horizontal (i.e., have zero slope). The positive and negative values of the derivatives at points *B* and *D* are reflective of their respective upward and downward lines of tangency. However, because *both* points *A* and *C* have first derivatives equal to zero, a problem arises if we wish to know whether these points indicate maximum or minimum values of *Y*. Of course, in Figure 2A.14 we can plainly see that point *A* is the minimum value and point *C* is the maximum value. However, there is a formal mathematical procedure for distinguishing a function's maximum and minimum values. This procedure requires the use of a function's *second derivative.*

The second derivative of a function is the derivative of its first derivative. The procedure for finding the second derivative of a function is quite simple. All the rules for finding the first derivative apply to obtaining the second derivative. Conceptually, we can consider the second derivative of a function as a measure of the rate of change of the first derivative. In other words, it is a measure of "the rate of change of the rate of change."[32]

Let us illustrate precisely how the second derivative is used to determine the maximum and minimum values by presenting a graph of the function's first derivative in Figure 2A.14*b*. As a check on your understanding of this figure, notice that, as expected, the second derivative has a negative value when the original function decreases in value and a positive value when the original function increases in value. But now consider another aspect of this figure. Recall that the second derivative is a measure of the rate of change of the first derivative. Thus, graphically, we can find the second derivative by evaluating the slopes of lines tangent to points on the graph of the *first derivative*. See points *A'* and *C'* in Figure 2A.14*b*. By inspection of this figure, it should be quite clear that the slope of the line tangent to point *A'* is positive and the slope of the line tangent to point *C'* is negative. This enables us to conclude the following: At the minimum point of a function, the second derivative is *positive*. At the maximum point of a function, the second derivative is *negative.*[33]

---

[32]Mathematics and physics texts often use the example of a moving automobile to help distinguish the first and second derivatives. To begin with, the function can be expressed as $M = f(T)$, or miles traveled is a function of the time elapsed. The first derivative of this function describes the automobile's velocity. As an example of this, imagine a car moving at the rate of speed of 45 miles per hour. Now suppose this car has just entered a freeway, starts to accelerate, and then reaches a speed of 75 mph. The measure of this acceleration as the car goes from 45 mph to 75 mph is the second derivative of the function. Because the car is accelerating (i.e., going faster and faster), the second derivative is some positive value. In other words, the distance (measured in miles) that the car is traveling is increasing at *an increasing* rate. To extend this example a bit further, suppose the driver of the car, realizing that this section of the freeway is closely monitored by radar, begins to slow down to the legal speed limit of 60 mph. As the driver slows down, or decelerates, the speed at which the car is traveling is reduced. In other words, the distance (in miles) that the car is traveling is increasing at a *decreasing rate.* Deceleration, being the opposite of acceleration, implies that the second derivative in this case is negative.
[33]Let us return to the automobile example for an alternative explanation of the second-order condition for determining a function's maximum value. Let us imagine that, at the very moment the car reached 75 mph, the driver started to slow down. This means that at the precise moment the accelerating car started to decelerate, it had reached its *maximum* speed. In mathematical terms, if a function is increasing at an *increasing* rate (i.e., its second derivative is positive), then the moment it starts to increase at a *decreasing* rate (i.e., its second derivative becomes negative), it has reached its maximum value. Similar reasoning can be used to explain the second-order condition for determining the minimum value of a function.

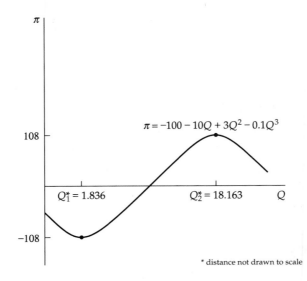

$\pi = -100 - 10Q + 3Q^2 - 0.1Q^3$

108

$Q_1^* = 1.836$

$Q_2^* = 18.163$

$Q$

$\pi$

−108

* distance not drawn to scale

**FIGURE 2A.15** Cubic Profit Function

Using mathematical notation, we can now state the *first-* and *second-order conditions* for determining the maximum or minimum values of a function.

Maximum value:  $dY/dX = 0$ (first-order condition)
$d^2/dx^2 < 0$ (second-order condition)

Minimum value:  $dY/dX = 0$ (first-order condition)
$d^2/dx^2 > 0$ (second-order condition)

We will now illustrate how the first- and second-order conditions are used to find the profit-maximizing level of output for a firm. Suppose this firm has the following revenue and total cost functions:

$$TR = 50Q \qquad (2A.29)$$

$$TC = 100 + 60Q - 3Q^2 + 0.1Q^3 \qquad (2A.30)$$

Based on these equations the firm's total profit function is

$$\pi = 50Q - (100 + 60Q - 3Q^2 + 0.1Q^3) \qquad (2A.31)$$
$$= 50Q - 100 - 60Q + 3Q^2 - 0.1Q^3$$
$$= -100 - 10Q + 3Q^2 - 0.1Q^3$$

Notice that this firm's profit function contains a term that is raised to the third power because its cost function is also raised to the third power. In other words, the firm is assumed to have a cubic cost function, and therefore it has a cubic profit function. Plotting this cubic profit function gives us the graph in Figure 2A.15. We can observe in this figure that the level of output that maximizes the firm's profit is about 18.2 units, and the level of output that minimizes its profit (i.e., maximizes its loss) is about 1.8 units.

Let us employ calculus along with the first- and second-order conditions to determine the point at which the firm maximizes its profit. We begin as before by finding the first derivative of the profit function, setting it equal to zero, and solving for the value of $Q$ that satisfies this condition.

$$\pi = -100 - 10Q + 3Q^2 - 0.1Q^3 \qquad \textbf{(2A.32)}$$

$$\frac{d\pi}{dQ} = -10 + 6Q - 0.3Q^2$$

$$= -0.3Q^2 + 6Q - 10 = 0 \qquad \textbf{(2A.33)}$$

Note that Equation (2A.33) has been rearranged to conform to the general expression for a quadratic equation. Because the first derivative of the profit function is quadratic, there are two possible values of $Q$ that satisfy the equation.[34]

$$Q_1^* = 1.836 \qquad Q_2^* = 18.163$$

As expected $Q_1^*$ and $Q_2^*$ coincide with the two points shown in Figure 2A.13. Although both $Q_1^*$ and $Q_2^*$ fulfill the first-order condition, only one satisfies the second-order condition. To see this, let us find the second derivative of the function by taking the derivative of the marginal profit function expressed in Equation (2A.33):

$$\frac{d^2\pi}{dQ^2} = -0.6Q + 6$$

By substitution, we see that at output level 1.836 the value of the second derivative is a positive number:

$$\frac{d^2\pi}{dQ^2} = -0.6(1.836) + 6 = 4.89$$

On the other hand, we see that at output level 18.163 the value of the second derivative is a negative number:

$$\frac{d^2\pi}{dQ^2} = -0.6(18.163) + 6 = -4.89$$

Thus, we see that only $Q_2^*$ enables us to adhere to the second-order condition that $d^2\pi/dQ^2 < 0$. This confirms in a formal, mathematical manner what we already knew from plotting and evaluating the graph of the firm's total profit function: $Q_2$ is the firm's profit-maximizing level of output.

## Five Key Functions Used in This Text

Five key functions will be used in this text: (1) demand, (2) total revenue, (3) production, (4) total cost, and (5) profit. The following diagrams show the algebraic and graphical

---

[34]The economic rationale for cost functions of different degrees is explained in chapter 8. The first derivative of a cubic function is a quadratic function. Such a function can be expressed in the general form

$$Y = aX^2 + bX + c$$

Perhaps you recall from your previous studies of algebra that the values of $X$ that set the quadratic function equal to zero can be found by using the formula for the "roots" of a quadratic equation:

$$X = \frac{-b \pm \sqrt{b^2 - 4ac}}{2a}$$

By substituting the values of the coefficients in Equation (2A.33) (i.e., $a = -0.3$, $b = 6$, $c = -10$) we obtain the answers shown.

expressions for these functions. As can be seen, the demand function is linear, the total revenue function is quadratic, and the production, cost, and profit functions are cubic. Note that the last three functions all refer to economic conditions in the short run.

**1.** Demand

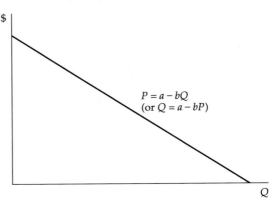

$P = a - bQ$
(or $Q = a - bP$)

**2.** Total revenue

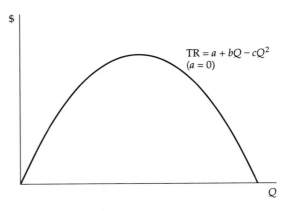

$TR = a + bQ - cQ^2$
($a = 0$)

**3.** Production (short run)

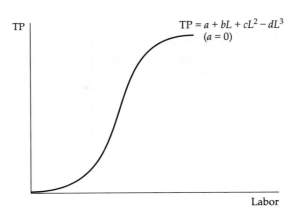

$TP = a + bL + cL^2 - dL^3$
($a = 0$)

**4.** Cost (short run)

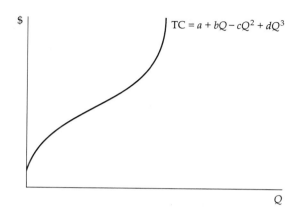

$$TC = a + bQ - cQ^2 + dQ^3$$

**5.** Profit (short run)

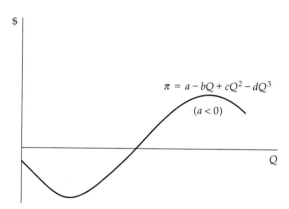

$$\pi = a - bQ + cQ^2 - dQ^3$$
$$(a < 0)$$

## Summary

As you proceed with your study of managerial economics and the reading of this text, you will find that the essence of economic analysis is the study of functional relationships between certain dependent variables (e.g., quantity demanded, revenue, cost, profit) and one or more independent variables (e.g., price, income, quantity sold). Mathematics is a tool that can greatly facilitate the analysis of these functional relationships. For example, rather than simply saying that "the quantity of a product sold depends on its price," we can use an algebraic equation to state precisely how many units of a product a firm can expect to sell at a particular price. Moreover, when we engage in a marginal analysis of the impact of price on quantity demanded, we can use the first derivative of this equation to measure the change in quantity demanded relative to changes in price.[35] Furthermore, as shown in this appendix, the precise

---

[35]In chapter 4, you will see how this first derivative is incorporated into a formula for *elasticity*, a value indicating the percentage change in a dependent variable, such as units sold, with a percentage change in an independent variable, such as price.

algebraic expression of the demand function enables us to derive a firm's total revenue and marginal revenue functions. And with the help of calculus, the optimal price and quantity (e.g., the price and quantity that maximize revenue) can be quickly found.

The more data a firm is able to obtain about its key economic functions (i.e., demand, revenue, production, cost, and profit), the more mathematics can be employed in the analysis. The more that mathematics can be utilized, the more precise a manager can be about such key decisions as the best price to charge, the best markets to compete in, and the most desirable levels of resource allocation. Unfortunately, in the real world firms do not often have the luxury of accurate or complete data with which to work. This is another aspect of decision making and will be discussed in chapters 5 and 6.

## Questions

1. Define the following terms: *function, variable, independent variable, dependent variable, functional form.*
2. Briefly describe how a function is represented in tabular form, in graphical form, and in an equation. Illustrate using the relationship between price and quantity expressed in a demand function.
3. Express in formal mathematical terms the following functional relationships. You may use the general form $Y = f(X)$. However, in each case be as specific as possible about what variables are represented by $Y$ and $X$. (For example, in the first relation, advertising is the $X$ variable and could be measured in terms of the amount of advertising dollars spent annually by a firm.)
   a. The effectiveness of advertising.
   b. The impact on output resulting from increasing the number of employees.
   c. The impact on labor productivity resulting from increasing automation.
   d. The impact on sales and profits resulting from price reductions.
   e. The impact on sales and profits resulting from a recession.
   f. The impact on sales and profits resulting from changes in the financial sector (e.g., the stock market or the bond market).
   g. The impact on cost resulting from the use of outside vendors to supply certain components in the manufacturing process.
4. What is a continuous function? Does the use of continuous functions to express economic relationships present any difficulties in analyzing real-world business problems? Explain.
5. Define in mathematical terms the slope of a line. Why is the slope considered to be so important in the quantitative analysis of economic problems?
6. Define *marginal analysis.* Give examples of how this type of analysis can help a managerial decision maker. Are there any limitations to using this type of analysis in actual business situations? Explain.
7. Explain why the first derivative of a function is an important part of marginal analysis.
8. Explain how an analysis of the first derivative of the function $Y = f(X)$ enables one to find the point at which the $Y$ variable is at its maximum or minimum.
9. (Optional) Explain how an analysis of the second derivative of a function enables one to determine whether the variable is a maximum or a minimum.
10. Briefly explain the difference between $\Delta Y/\Delta X$ and $dY/dX$. Explain why in a linear equation, there is no difference between the two terms.

## Problems

1. Answer the following questions on the basis of the accompanying demand schedule.

| Price | Quantity |
|-------|----------|
| $100  | 25       |
| 80    | 35       |
| 60    | 45       |
| 40    | 55       |
| 20    | 65       |
| 0     | 75       |

   a. Express the schedule as an algebraic equation in which $Q$ is the dependent variable. Plot this on a graph.
   b. Express the schedule as an algebraic equation in which $P$ is the dependent variable. Plot this on a graph.
2. You are given the following demand equations:

$$Q = 450 - 16P$$

$$Q = 360 - 80P$$

$$Q = 1,500 - 500P$$

   a. Determine each equation's total revenue and marginal revenue equations.
   b. Plot the demand equation and the marginal and total revenue equations on a graph.
   c. Use calculus to determine the prices and quantities that maximize the revenue for each equation. Show the points of revenue maximization on the graphs that you have constructed.
3. You are given the following cost equations:

$$TC = 1,500 + 300Q - 25Q^2 + 1.5Q^3$$

$$TC = 1,500 + 300Q + 25Q^2$$

$$TC = 1,500 + 300Q$$

   a. Determine each equation's average variable cost, average cost, and marginal cost.
   b. Plot each equation on a graph. On separate graphs, plot each equation's average variable cost, average cost, and marginal cost.
   c. Use calculus to determine the minimum point on the marginal cost curve.
4. Given the demand equation shown, perform the following tasks:

$$Q = 10 - .004P$$

   a. Combine this equation with each of the cost equations listed in question 3. Use calculus to find the price that will maximize the short-run profit for each of the cost equations.
   b. Plot the profit curve for each of the cost equations.

# CHAPTER 3

# Supply and Demand

## THE SITUATION

Ross Harris, as a senior purchasing agent responsible for the sweetener used in Global Foods' soft drink product, reported directly to the vice president in charge of purchasing for the entire firm. In two weeks, Ross's firm would be sitting down with the major producers of high-fructose corn syrup (HFCS) to set the price of HFCS for the coming year. Other major soft drink companies would also begin their annual negotiations. Ever since HFCS began replacing sugar (or sucrose) as a sweetener in soft drinks, the major soft drink firms had been negotiating annually with the largest refiners of HFCS on the coming year's price. On balance, the arrangement had worked well for the soft drink industry. Once the price had been determined, soft drink makers were protected from any increase in the spot price for HFCS. Of course, if the price of HFCS fell below the fixed price, the soft drink firms would end up paying more for the product than if they had relied primarily on the spot market for their supply.

This year, however, the major HFCS refiners wanted to change one of the key terms of the pricing agreement. Instead of setting the price on an annual basis, the refiners wanted it to be set every 90 days. "They [the refiners] say they want a more 'market-sensitive' price for their product," Ross's boss explained. "And from the way the spot price of HFCS has been fluctuating in recent years, I don't blame them for this request. As it so happens, most of the agreements have protected us against price increases and have hurt the refiners by preventing them from selling at the higher spot prices."

"Needless to say, this change from an annual to a quarterly agreement puts us in a potentially riskier situation, since we would be able to protect ourselves from possible increases in the price of HFCS for only three months. The management committee does not know whether it is worth 'going to the mat' with the refiners to keep the arrangement on an annual basis. The proposed arrangement may turn out to be beneficial or at least no

*(Continued)*

different from the current one. Ross, I want you and your staff to do a quick but thorough analysis of the situation. Basically, tell us the pros and cons of a quarterly contract."

Meanwhile, Kathy Martinez, whose company was one of the major refiners that processed corn into the HFCS, was given the assignment of preparing a market analysis for corn, the major ingredient of HFCS. This was to be combined with an analysis of the cost of processing the corn into HFCS. The combined report would then be used by her company's negotiating team as supporting material in the firm's efforts to change the contract pricing period from an annual to a quarterly basis. Kathy had only 10 more days in which to complete her portion of the report.

# Introduction

In this chapter, we introduce the basic elements of supply and demand. Although for some of you, this chapter will serve as a review of material covered in an economics principles course, it has been included because it is essential that every reader have a thorough grounding in supply and demand before proceeding to the particulars of managerial economics. There may be situations—such as those described for Ross and Kathy—in which you may be required to conduct or evaluate a study with a considerable use of supply-and-demand analysis. But regardless of how directly this chapter's material may apply to your work, most of the material covered in this book will relate in some way to supply or demand. Indeed, supply and demand can be considered the conceptual framework within which the specifics of managerial economics are discussed.

# Market Demand

The **demand** for a good or service is defined as

> *Quantities* of a good or service that people are ready to *buy* at various *prices* within some given *time period, other factors* besides price held constant.

Note that in this definition "ready" implies that consumers are prepared to buy a good or service both because they are willing (i.e., they have a preference for it) and they are able (i.e., they have the income to support this preference).

Demand can first be illustrated with an example in which we imagine that you, the reader, are part of a simple market experiment. Suppose you were asked to respond to the following survey question: "In a one-week period, how many slices of pizza would you be prepared to buy at the following prices: $2.00, $1.50, $1.00, $.50, and $.05?" Every reader would obviously have their own pattern of response. Let us assume that a sample of three readers responds in the following way:

| Price (per slice) | $Q_{D1}$ | $Q_{D2}$ | $Q_{D3}$ | $Q_{DM}$ |
|---|---|---|---|---|
| $2.00 | 0 | 2 | 3 | 5 |
| 1.50 | 1 | 2 | 5 | 8 |
| 1.00 | 2 | 2 | 8 | 12 |
| 0.50 | 3 | 3 | 10 | 16 |
| 0.05 | 4 | 4 | 12 | 20 |

As you can see, the combined responses of the three individuals make up the total **market demand** ($Q_{DM}$) for pizza, the sum of all the individual demands.

Market demand is illustrated with a simple numerical function, as shown in Table 3.1. This table shows a hypothetical demand for pizza. As the price of a slice of pizza falls from $7.00 to zero, the amount that consumers in this market are willing to buy increases from zero to 700 slices. This inverse relationship between price and the **quantity demanded** of pizza is called the **Law of Demand.** There may be instances in which consumers behave in an "irrational" manner by buying more as the price rises and less as the price falls because they associate price with quality. But in the economic analysis of demand, it is assumed that buyers do not associate price with quality and will therefore follow the Law of Demand.

The Law of Demand can be observed in the curve shown in Figure 3.1, derived from the schedule of numbers in Table 3.1. Notice that the curve in this figure slopes downward and to the right, indicating that the quantity of pizza demanded increases as the price falls and vice versa.

A change in the demand for pizza or any other product is indicated by a change in the entire schedule of quantities demanded at a list of prices or a shift in the demand curve either to the left or to the right. We see these changes in Table 3.2 and Figure 3.2.

To summarize, we can say the following:

Changes in price result in **changes in the quantity demanded** (i.e., movements *along* the demand curve).

Changes in the nonprice determinants result in **changes in demand** (i.e., *shifts* in the demand curve).

**TABLE 3.1  Market Demand for Pizza**

| Price (per slice) | $Q_D$ |
|---|---|
| $7.00 | 0 |
| 6.00 | 100 |
| 5.00 | 200 |
| 4.00 | 300 |
| 3.00 | 400 |
| 2.00 | 500 |
| 1.00 | 600 |
| 0 | 700 |

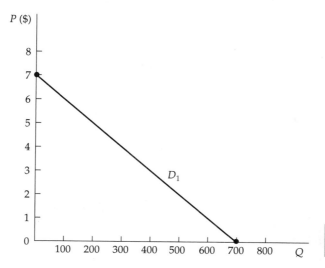

**FIGURE 3.1** Market Demand Curve for Pizza

This difference can be seen in Table 3.2 in the following manner. At the price of $5 the quantity demanded in the first list of responses ($Q_{D1}$) is 200. If the price drops to $4, then the *quantity demanded* increases to 300. However, if the *demand* increases to $Q_{D2}$, then at the price of $5 the quantity increases to 300 and in fact increases by 100 units at each of the prices being offered.

Factors that can cause demand to change are called **nonprice determinants of demand.** Following is a list of these determinants and a brief elaboration of their impact on demand.

1. *Tastes and preferences.* Why do people buy things? Marketing professors, corporate market researchers, and advertising executives spend their careers trying to answer this question. Economists use a general-purpose category in their list of nonprice determinants called *tastes and preferences* to account for the personal

**TABLE 3.2   Different Levels of Market Demand for Pizza**

| Price (per slice) | $Q_{D1}$ | $Q_{D2}$ | $Q_{D3}$ |
|---|---|---|---|
| $7.00 | 0 | 100 | 0 |
| 6.00 | 100 | 200 | 0 |
| 5.00 | 200 | 300 | 100 |
| 4.00 | 300 | 400 | 200 |
| 3.00 | 400 | 500 | 300 |
| 2.00 | 500 | 600 | 400 |
| 1.00 | 600 | 700 | 500 |
| 0 | 700 | 800 | 600 |

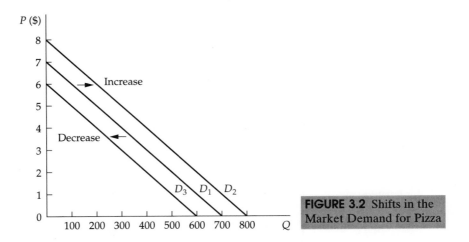

**FIGURE 3.2** Shifts in the Market Demand for Pizza

likes and dislikes of consumers for various goods and services. These tastes and preferences may themselves be affected by other factors. Advertising, promotions, and even government reports can have profound effects on demand via their impacts on people's tastes and preferences for a particular good or service.

2. *Income.* As people's incomes rise, it is reasonable to expect their demand for a product to increase and vice versa. In the next chapter, the possibility of demand moving in the *opposite direction* to changes in income will be discussed.

3. *Prices of related products.* A good or service can be related to another by being a substitute or by being a complement. If the price of a substitute product changes, we expect the demand for the good under consideration to change in the *same direction* as the change in the substitute's price. Consider, for example what would happen to the demand for software if the price of computer hardware falls, or to the demand for compact discs if the price of CD players falls. It is reasonable to expect that the demand for the two items would *rise* as a result of a *fall* in the price of their respective *complementary* products.

4. *Future expectations.* If enough buyers expect the price of a good or service to rise (fall) in the future, it may cause the current demand to increase (decrease). In markets for various financial instruments (e.g., stocks, bonds, negotiable certificates of deposit, U.S. Treasury bills, etc.) as well as for agricultural commodities and precious metals, expectations of future price changes among both buyers and sellers play an important part in determining the market demand. In most of these types of markets, speculation among buyers and sellers is an important factor to consider. Buyers and sellers act on a current price of a product not for its immediate consumption but because of the possibility of gaining from some future transaction. (Recall the old adage "buy low and sell high.") In fact, for most of these products, a sizable and growing *futures* market has emerged, in which buyers and sellers conduct transactions for these products at some agreed-upon future date. Naturally, expectations of future price movements have an impact on

the supply and demand for the future delivery of a commodity. In turn, movements of futures prices could have an impact on the current (also called "spot") supply and demand for the commodity.

This factor can also affect the demand for consumer and commercial products. For example, the demand for DVD recorders, digital cameras, home entertainment systems, laptop computers, and personal digital assistants was probably not as high as sellers expected when these products were first introduced, because buyers were waiting for their prices to come down at a later time.

5. *Number of buyers.* The impact of the number of buyers on demand should be apparent; as far as sellers are concerned, the more the merrier. What is interesting, nonetheless, is how changing demographics and tastes and preferences within demographic groups can affect the pool of potential buyers for a particular good or service. In other words, sheer numbers (i.e., population) may not be as important as differences within the population. For example, the tracking of the baby boom generation from childhood to adulthood and eventually to retirement age has proven to be a fascinating study for market researchers. One can plainly see the impact on the demand for such items as children's apparel, furniture, and toys during the 1950s and 1960s, when this group was growing up.

As the baby boomers grew into their teen years, the demand for such items as records, stereos, certain types of cars, and admissions to movie theaters went up accordingly. Market researchers are now busy contemplating the impact on the demand for an assortment of goods and services—from health care to retirement condominiums—that will stem from the "graying" of this segment of the population.

We will discuss further how changes in these factors change demand and market price. But first we must introduce the concept of supply. By combining supply with demand, we can conduct a complete analysis of the market, both in the short run and in the long run.

## Market Supply

The **supply** of a good or service is defined as

> *Quantities* of a good or service that people are ready to *sell* at various *prices* within some given *time period, other factors* besides price held constant.

Notice that the only difference between this definition and that of demand is that in this case the word *sell* is used instead of *buy*. Just as in the case of demand, supply is based on an assumed length of time within which price and the other factors can affect the **quantity supplied.**

Recall that the law of demand states that the quantity demanded is related inversely to price, other factors held constant. On the other hand, the law of supply states that quantity supplied is related *directly* to price, other factors held constant. Thus, any schedule of numbers representing a relationship between price and quantity supplied would show a *decrease* in the quantity supplied as price falls.

| TABLE 3.3 | Market Supply for Pizza | | |
|---|---|---|---|
| **P** | **$Q_{S1}$** | **$Q_{S2}$** | **$Q_{S3}$** |
| $7 | 600 | 700 | 500 |
| 6 | 500 | 600 | 400 |
| 5 | 400 | 500 | 300 |
| 4 | 300 | 400 | 200 |
| 3 | 200 | 300 | 100 |
| 2 | 100 | 200 | 0 |
| 1 | 0 | 100 | 0 |
| 0 | 0 | 0 | 0 |

Table 3.3 shows a hypothetical supply schedule. Also shown are two additional supply schedules, one indicating a greater supply and the other showing a reduced supply. These schedules are shown as supply curves in Figure 3.3. The supply curve has a positive slope, reflecting the direct relationship between price and quantity supplied.

In analyzing the supply side of the market, it is important to make the distinction between *quantity supplied* and *supply*. The distinction between these two terms is the same as that used for the demand side of the market:

Changes in *price* result in **changes in the quantity supplied** (i.e., movements along the supply curve).
Changes in *nonprice determinants* result in **changes in the supply** (i.e., shifts of the supply curve).

Just as there are nonprice determinants of demand, there are **nonprice determinants of supply.** A change in any one or a combination of these factors will change market supply (i.e., cause the supply line to shift to the right or the left). Let us briefly discuss each factor to understand why this is expected to happen.

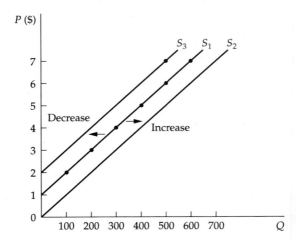

**FIGURE 3.3** Supply Curves for Pizza

1. *Costs and technology.* The two factors of costs and technology can be treated as one because they are so closely related. *Costs* refer to the usual costs of production, such as labor costs, costs of materials, rent, interest payments, depreciation charges, and general and administrative expenses—in other words, all of the items usually found in a firm's income statement. *Technology* refers to technological innovations or improvements introduced to reduce the unit cost of production (e.g., automation, robotics, and computer hardware and software utilization). Technological changes that result in entirely new products for final consumption are not considered part of this category. These new products would have to be considered in an entirely different market analysis. In any event, unit cost reductions, whether from technological innovations or simply management decisions, will result in an increase in market supply. Increases in the unit cost of production will have the opposite effect.

2. *Prices of other goods or services offered by the seller.* From the consumer's standpoint, any good or service has other goods or services related to it either as substitutes or as complements. From the producer's standpoint, there can also be substitutes or complements for a particular good or service offered in the market. For example, suppose the sellers of pizza notice that the price of hot dogs increases substantially. In the extreme case, they may drop their line of pizza and substitute hot dogs. Or they may at least reduce the amount of resources (e.g., labor and store space) devoted to the selling of pizza in favor of hot dogs. In either case, the market supply of pizza would decrease. If the sellers were already selling two (or more) products, the change in market conditions would prompt them to reallocate their resources toward the more profitable products. (Given this possibility, it may be more appropriate to say that the sellers consider pizza and hot dogs as "competing" products rather than as "substitute" products.)

3. *Future expectations.* This factor has a similar impact on sellers as on buyers; the only difference is the direction of the change. For example, if sellers anticipate a rise in price, they may choose to hold back the current supply to take advantage of the higher future price, thus decreasing market supply. As we discussed in the section on demand, an expected rise in price will increase the current demand for a product.

4. *Number of sellers.* Clearly, the number of sellers has a direct impact on supply. The more sellers, the greater the market supply.

5. *Weather conditions.* Bad weather (e.g., floods, droughts, unusual seasonal temperatures) will reduce the supply of an agricultural commodity. Good weather will have the opposite impact.

With this discussion of supply, we are now able to combine supply with demand into a complete analysis of the market.

## Market Equilibrium

Now that we have reviewed the definitions and mechanics of demand and supply, we are ready to examine their interaction in the market. Market demand and supply are compared in Table 3.4 and Figure 3.4.

You can see in both the table and the graph that at the price of $4, the market is cleared in the sense that the quantity demanded (300) is equal to the quantity supplied

| TABLE 3.4 | Supply and Demand for Pizza | |
|---|---|---|
| *P* | $Q_D$ | $Q_S$ |
| $ 7 | 0 | 600 |
| 6 | 100 | 500 |
| 5 | 200 | 400 |
| →4 | 300 | 300 |
| 3 | 400 | 200 |
| 2 | 500 | 100 |
| 1 | 600 | 0 |
| 0 | 700 | 0 |

(300). Thus, $4 is called the **equilibrium price,** and 300 is referred to as the **equilibrium quantity.** Another way to view this market situation is to imagine what would happen if the price were not at the equilibrium level. For example, suppose the price were at a higher level, say $5. At this price, as you can see in Table 3.4 the quantity supplied would exceed the quantity demanded, a condition called a **surplus.** At a lower price, say $3, the situation is reversed: The quantity demanded exceeds the quantity supplied. This situation is called a **shortage.** Both the surplus and the shortage conditions are indicated in Figure 3.4.

In the event of a surplus or a shortage, various competitive pressures cause the price to change (decrease in the case of a surplus, and increase in the event of a shortage). The price thus serves to clear the market of the imbalance. The clearing process continues until equilibrium (i.e., quantity demanded equals quantity supplied) is arrived at. In the case of a surplus, sellers wishing to rid themselves of the extra items offer the product at a lower price to induce people to buy more. At the same time, as the price falls, suppliers are discouraged from offering as much as before. In the case of a market

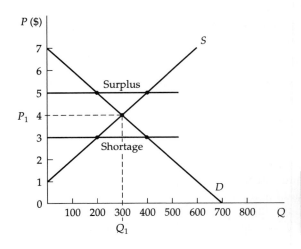

**FIGURE 3.4** Supply and Demand Curves for Pizza, Indicating Market Equilibrium

shortage, as the price rises toward the equilibrium level, the market is cleared because the quantity demanded decreases while the quantity supplied increases. In the event of a shortage, sellers try to take advantage of the situation by raising their prices, and people are thus discouraged from buying as much as before. Also, sellers are induced to offer a greater number of items in the market. Both actions serve to clear the market of a shortage.

To summarize the material in this section, remember the following definitions:

*Equilibrium price:* The price that equates the quantity demanded with the quantity supplied; (i.e., the price that clears the market of a surplus or shortage).

*Equilibrium quantity:* The amount that people are willing to buy and sellers are willing to offer at the equilibrium price level.

*Shortage:* A market situation in which the quantity demanded exceeds the quantity supplied, *at a price below the equilibrium level.*

*Surplus:* A market situation in which the quantity supplied exceeds the quantity demanded, *at a price above the equilibrium level.*

# Comparative Statics Analysis

The model of market demand, supply, and equilibrium price and quantity developed in the preceding sections can now be used to analyze the market. The particular method of analysis we will use is called *comparative statics analysis.* This is a commonly used method in economic analysis and will be used throughout the text. In general, this method of analysis proceeds as follows:

1. State all the assumptions needed to construct the model.
2. Begin by assuming that the model is in equilibrium.
3. Introduce a change in the model. In so doing, a condition of disequilibrium is created.
4. Find the new point at which equilibrium is restored.
5. Compare the new equilibrium point with the original one.

In effect, comparative statics analysis is a form of sensitivity analysis, or what business people often refer to as *what-if* analysis. For example, if we were doing a what-if analysis of a company's cash flow, we would start with a given pro forma income statement adjusted to provide the cash flow for a given period of time. We would then conduct sensitivity analysis by supposing that certain factors changed, such as revenue, cost, or the rate of depreciation. We would then inspect how changes in these factors would change the cash flow of the firm over time. In the same manner, economists conduct a what-if analysis of their models.

The term *statics* alludes to the theoretically stable point of equilibrium, and *comparative* refers to the comparison of the various points of equilibrium. The ensuing sections will explain exactly how comparative statics analysis is used in the analysis of the market.

### SHORT-RUN MARKET CHANGES: THE "RATIONING FUNCTION" OF PRICE

**MODULE 3A**

Let us continue with our analysis of pizza. Following the steps involved in comparative statics analysis, we start by assuming that all factors except the price of pizza are held constant, and the various patterns of response to price among buyers and sellers are

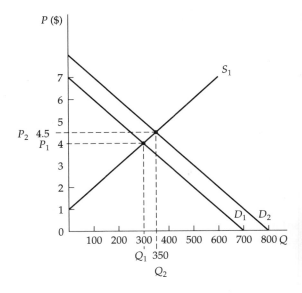

**FIGURE 3.5** Increase in Demand for Pizza and Resulting Impact on Market Equilibrium

represented by the supply and demand lines in Figure 3.4. We make a fresh start by redrawing this graph in Figure 3.5. It would also be useful to recall all of the nonprice determinants that could affect the demand or supply for a product. They are listed for you in Table 3.5.

As noted in step 2 in the previous section, we begin this analysis in the condition of equilibrium. This is denoted in Figure 3.5 as the point where the supply line intersects with the $D_1$ demand line (i.e., the price level where quantity supplied is equal to quantity demanded).

Based on step 3 we introduce a change in one or more of the assumptions made when the model was constructed. Any one or more of the factors shown in Table 3.5 can cause this change. Let us assume that a new government study shows pizza to be the most nutritious of all fast foods and that consumers substantially increase their demand for pizza as a result of this study. In Figure 3.5, this increase is represented by a shift in the demand curve from $D_1$ to $D_2$. As you can see, this shift results in a new, higher equi-

| TABLE 3.5   Nonprice Determinants of Demand and Supply | |
| --- | --- |
| **Demand** | **Supply** |
| 1. Tastes and preferences | 1. Costs and technology |
| 2. Income | 2. Prices of other products offered |
| 3. Prices of related products | 3. Future expectations among sellers |
| 4. Future expectations among buyers | 4. Number of sellers |
| 5. Number of buyers | 5. Weather conditions (particularly for agricultural products) |

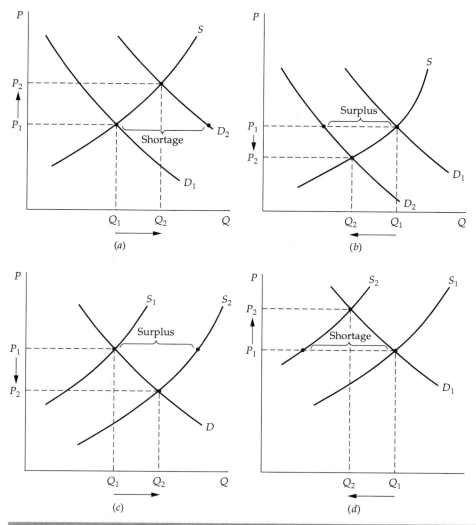

**FIGURE 3.6** Changes in Supply and Demand and Their Short-Run Impact on Market Equilibrium (the Rationing Function of Price)

librium price of $4.50. Notice also that the new equilibrium quantity is greater than the original equilibrium quantity.

The comparison of the new equilibrium point with the original one (step 5 in comparative statics analysis) leads us to conclude that, as a result of a change in tastes and preferences, the price of pizza rises, and so does the quantity bought and sold.

This analysis can be repeated using other possible changes in market conditions (e.g., the price of cheese rises, the price of soft drinks falls). Each time, the same procedure should be followed. If we consider only one possible change at a time, the effects on equilibrium price and quantity can be illustrated as in Figure 3.6. Instead of using specific numbers, we have designated the prices and quantities with the symbols $P$ and $Q$ along with appropriate subscripts. We can summarize the effects shown in the graphs as follows:

> An increase in demand causes equilibrium price and quantity to rise. (See Figure 3.6*a*.)
> A decrease in demand causes equilibrium price and quantity to fall. (See Figure 3.6*b*.)
> An increase in supply causes equilibrium price to fall and quantity to rise. (See Figure 3.6*c*.)
> A decrease in supply causes equilibrium price to rise and quantity to fall. (See Figure 3.6*d*.)

In Figure 3.6 we observe that the shift in demand or supply has in effect created either a shortage or a surplus at the original price $P_1$. Thus, the equilibrium price has to rise or fall to clear the market. When the market price changes to eliminate the imbalance between quantities supplied and demanded, it is serving what economists call the **rationing function of price.** The term *rationing* is often associated with shortages, but we have defined it to include a surplus situation as well.

### LONG-RUN MARKET ANALYSIS: THE "GUIDING" OR "ALLOCATING FUNCTION" OF PRICE

The comparative statics analysis presented earlier required only that you consider the response of equilibrium price and quantity to a given change in supply or demand. This response was dubbed the "rationing function" of price. Let us consider what might happen as a result of this change in market price. To illustrate this, we shall examine the market for hot dogs, a presumed substitute for pizza. The two markets are represented by the supply and demand diagrams in Figure 3.7.

Now let us assume that at the same time people's tastes and preferences change in favor of pizza, their tastes and preferences become more adverse to hot dogs (e.g., for health reasons). The changes in the demand for the two products are shown in Figure 3.7 by a downward shift in the demand for hot dogs and an upward shift in the demand for pizza ($D_1$ to $D_2$). This would cause a shortage in the pizza market and a surplus in the hot dog market. But as we know, the rationing function of price will immediately start to correct these market imbalances. As the price of hot dogs falls, the surplus is eliminated; as the price of pizza rises, the shortage is eliminated. (For the purpose of the analysis, it really does not matter where the price of pizza stands in relation to the price of hot dogs. To simplify matters, we have assumed that the two prices were about equal before the change in tastes and preferences occurred. The point is that after price performs its rationing function, the equilibrium price of pizza will be higher than the equilibrium price of hot dogs in relative terms.)

Now suppose that the prices have indeed changed, and the two markets are once again in equilibrium. What do you suppose will happen next? As you might well imagine, the depressed price of hot dogs will cause the sellers to begin allocating less of their resources to this market. Some may even go out of the business of making or selling hot dogs. On the other hand, the higher price of pizza will induce the allocation of more resources into this market. New pizza stands and restaurants may be opened. Food companies may build new plants to produce frozen pizza for distribution through supermarkets. The effect of these follow-on adjustments to the initial change in equilibrium

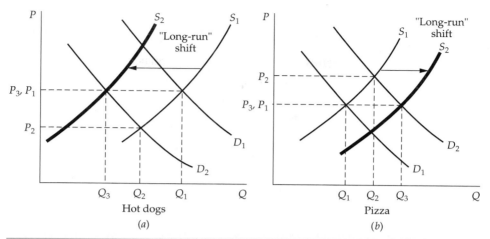

**FIGURE 3.7** Short-Run and Long-Run Changes in Supply (in Response to an Initial Change in Demand)

prices can be seen in the figure as a rightward shift in the supply of pizza and a leftward shift in the supply of hot dogs.

After this "long-run" adjustment is made, equilibrium price and quantity may well return to the levels at which they were before the initial changes in demand took place (i.e., $P_3$ in each market may be close to or equal to $P_1$). But the main point is that $Q_3$ is considerably less than $Q_1$ in the hot dog market and considerably more than $Q_1$ in the pizza market. These differences represent the shifting of resources out of the hot dog market and into the pizza market. Several centuries ago, Adam Smith referred to this shifting of resources into and out of markets in response to price changes as the "invisible hand."[1] Another way to express these shifts in supply is that they represent a response to "price signals" sent to the owners of the factors of production. In any event, when resources have been shifted out of the market for hot dogs and into the market for pizza, price is fulfilling its **guiding** or **allocating function.** Defined in a more formal manner, the guiding or allocating function of price is the movement of resources into or out of markets in response to a change in the equilibrium price of a good or service.

The preceding example illustrates a basic distinction made in economic analysis between the "short run" and the "long run." This distinction has nothing to do directly with a specific calendar time. Instead, it refers to the amount of time it takes for sellers and buyers to react to changes in the market equilibrium price. The following descriptions of the short run and the long run will help readers distinguish the two time periods.

1. **Short run**
   a. Period of time in which sellers already in the market respond to a change in equilibrium price by adjusting the amount of certain resources, which economists call *variable inputs*. Examples of such inputs are labor hours and raw

---

[1]For Smith, the "visible" hand was that of the government, which might try to dictate the allocation of resources among different markets by the command process rather than by the market process.

materials. A short-run adjustment by sellers can be envisioned as a movement along a particular supply curve.

**b.** Period of time in which buyers already in the market respond to changes in equilibrium price by adjusting the quantity demanded for a particular good or service. A short-run adjustment by buyers can be envisioned as a movement along a particular demand curve.

**2. Long run**

**a.** Period of time in which new sellers may enter a market or the original sellers may exit from a market. This period is long enough for existing sellers to either increase or decrease their *fixed factors* of production. Examples of fixed factors include property, plant, and equipment. A long-run adjustment by sellers can be seen graphically as a shift in a given supply curve.

**b.** Period of time in which buyers may react to a change in equilibrium price by changing their tastes and preferences or buying patterns. (*The Wall Street Journal* and other sources of business news may refer to this as a "structural change" in demand.) A long-run adjustment by buyers can be seen graphically as a shift in a given demand curve.

Another good way of distinguishing the short run from the long run is to note that the rationing function of price is a short-run phenomenon, whereas the guiding function is a long-run phenomenon.

Let us summarize the short-run "rationing function" and the long run "guiding function" of price in terms of our example involving pizza and hot dogs:

**1.** Changing tastes and preferences cause the demand for pizza to increase and the demand for hot dogs to decrease.

**2.** The changing demand for the two products causes a shortage in the pizza market and a surplus in the hot dog market.

**3.** In response to the surplus and shortage in the two markets, price serves as a *rationing* agent by decreasing in the hot dog market and increasing in the pizza market. That is, the short-run response by suppliers of the two products is to change their variable inputs (i.e., movement downward along the supply line in the market for hot dogs, and movement upward along the supply line in the market for pizza).

**4.** In the *long run,* price fulfills its *guiding* function by causing sellers and potential sellers to respond by increasing capacity or entering the market for pizza and by decreasing capacity or leaving the market for hot dogs (i.e., rightward shift in the supply line for pizza and leftward shift in the supply line for hot dogs).

**5.** As a result of the shifts in supply, new equilibrium levels of price and quantity are established. The new quantities bought and sold represent shifts in resources out of one market and into the other.

The distinction between short- and long-run changes in the market can also be made in cases that begin with changes in supply rather than in demand. One of the best examples is the case of the Organization of Petroleum Exporting Countries (OPEC) and the world oil market. A complete analysis of this case is beyond the scope of this text. However, the headline of an article in *Newsweek* perhaps best sums up the

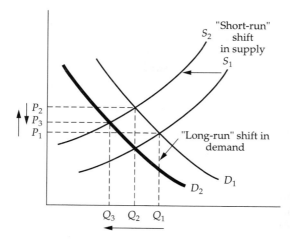

**FIGURE 3.8** Short-Run and Long-Run Changes in Demand (in Response to an Initial Change in Supply)

activities in this market in the decade following the OPEC's major price hike in late 1973: "OPEC, Meet Adam Smith."[2] This reference to the great classical economist Adam Smith pertained to his concept of the "invisible hand," or the guiding function of price.

OPEC conspired to raise the price of oil by limiting production to an amount that would support a price above the current level. The supply-and-demand diagram shown in Figure 3.8 illustrates this action. As we can see, limiting the production of oil can be envisioned as a leftward shift in the supply line to the level where it intersects the demand curve for oil at some designated point above the current market price (i.e., $P_2$ rather than $P_1$). The short-run response by consumers to the increase in oil prices was to cut back their consumption of oil. But in the terms specific to our analysis, this reduction can be seen as a decrease in the *quantity demanded* for oil. In other words, the decrease in the supply of oil (i.e., the shift of supply line to the left) prompted a *movement back along the demand curve* for oil.

However, over time consumers began to change their pattern of consumption of oil. They formed car pools, they bought more fuel-efficient cars, they turned their thermostats down in their homes, and they even tried to follow the new 55 mph speed limit established on highways throughout the country. Industrial users of oil responded by substituting more fuel-efficient machinery as soon as it became cost-efficient to make these changes. The effect of this *long-run* change in the pattern of oil usage was to cause the demand for oil to gradually fall. Graphically, this is represented by a leftward shift of the demand curve for oil from $D_1$ to $D_2$. Notice that as a result of this long-run shift in demand, the equilibrium price and quantity fell. As seen in Figure 3.8, the long-run quantity that is bought and sold (i.e., $Q_3$) was now even less than it was before this decrease in demand took place. This indicates a further shift of resources out of this market.

---

[2]*Newsweek,* October 29, 1984, p. 93.

As in the case of pizza and hot dogs, price fulfilled its short-run rationing function as well as its long-run guiding function. When the supply line for oil first shifted to the left—in large part due to the OPEC conspiracy—a shortage was created. This imbalance forced the market price up to clear the market of this shortage. The higher price served as a signal to buyers to change their consumption pattern for oil, that is, to become more economical in their use of oil.

Thus, price served to reallocate an economy's resources in the sense that the buyer's long-run response was to rely more on resources other than those in the oil market. In fact, a sizable portion of these alternative resources involved the production of goods and services that helped people to reduce their consumption of oil. For example, resources were shifted into the production of fuel-efficient cars and machinery, wood-burning stoves, kerosene heaters, firewood, sweaters, and flannel pajamas.

An additional facet of this long-run, guiding function of price can be observed. In retrospect, OPEC's efforts to raise the world price of oil by deliberately reducing the supply made it possible for non-OPEC oil producers to justify such projects as drilling for oil in the North Sea and Alaska. Moreover, the oil-producing efforts of Mexico were encouraged by the rising oil prices. Over the long run, these additional sources increased the world's supply of oil, putting further pressures on OPEC to limit their supply to keep oil prices from falling.[3]

Because the distinction between short- and the long-run changes in the market is such an essential part of manager's understanding of the workings of the market process, we present one last review of these changes in Table 3.6.

## USING SUPPLY-AND-DEMAND ANALYSIS TO FORECAST MARKET PRICES: THE LODGING INDUSTRY'S PERFORMANCE OVER THE PAST DECADE

An important practical application of supply-and-demand analysis involves the qualitative forecasting of market prices. This involves the forecasting of the direction and relative strengths of changes in supply and demand in order to then forecast the direction and relative strength of changes in market prices. For example, typical questions asked in qualitative forecasting are: (1) Will the supply of a product rise or fall? (2) If both supply and demand are expected to rise, which one rises further? (3) As a result of these changes, will price rise or fall? Quantitative forecasting involves the precise magnitudes of these changes. We shall look at how economists attempt to do this in chapters 5 and 6. For now, let us provide a good example of how analysts use their knowledge of supply and demand to help them in qualitative forecasting.

In the first edition of our text, we showed how Wall Street analysts used the evaluation of supply and demand to forecast the prospects in the hotel business. At the beginning of 1989, three analysts had this to say about the outlook for the year in the hotel business:

> Analyst #1: "Look for continuing problems due to supply exceeding demand and an increase in the cost of capturing occupancy as the industry remains competitive."

---

[3]The Gulf crisis in 1990 caused a temporary rise in oil prices. As the situation stabilized, oil prices fell to their precrisis level.

**TABLE 3.6 Short-Run and Long-Run Changes in the Market**

| *Initial Change*<br>*(Short-Run Time Period)* | *Follow-on Change*<br>*(Long-Run Time Period)* |
|---|---|
| Increase in demand causes<br>*price to rise* | *Supply increases* as new sellers enter the market<br>and original sellers increase production capacity |
| Decrease in demand causes<br>*price to fall* | *Supply decreases* as less profitable firms or those<br>experiencing losses exit the market or decrease<br>production capacity |
| Increase in supply causes<br>*price to fall* | *Demand increases* as tastes and preferences of<br>consumers eventually change in favor of the product<br>relative to substitutes |
| Decrease in supply causes<br>*price to rise* | *Demand decreases* as tastes and preferences of<br>consumers eventually change away from the product<br>and toward the substitutes |

Analyst #2: "There will be a reasonably healthy, modest room rate increase of 3–4 percent and flat to slightly higher occupancy levels."

Analyst #3: "Supply and demand are roughly in equilibrium. While the rate of new construction has slowed dramatically since the mid-1980s, this in all likelihood will be offset by a slowdown in the growth of the economy.[4]

As you can see, the three analysts were not in agreement with each other because each had a different set of assumptions about the factors influencing supply and demand in this industry.

In the second edition, we had the benefit of hindsight to judge which analyst's prognosis was most accurate. According to *Lodging Outlook,* a newsletter published by Smith Travel Research, the demand for U.S. rooms increased 5.4 percent in 1989, while supply increased 3.0 percent. As would be expected, this put upward pressures on room rates. On the average, room rates rose 3.5 percent in 1989 according to this same source. Occupancy rates increased slightly from 62.3 percent in 1988 to 63.8 percent. Overall, the hotel industry did fairly well as the U.S. economy completed what we know today as the final year of the economic expansion that had begun in 1982.

Given these results, it appears that Analyst #2's forecast was the most accurate. This is most impressive because he had also ventured forth with a quantitative (i.e., a 3 to 4 percent rise in room rates) as well as a qualitative forecast. Note that Analyst #3 was correct in anticipating a slowdown in the growth of the economy, although his forecast was a bit premature. The U.S. economy did not experience a recession until July 1990. However, as we can easily see looking back, none of the analysts could have possibly foreseen the attack on Kuwait by Iraq and the subsequent outbreak of the Gulf War in 1991. This war severely hurt the hospitality and travel industries throughout the early 1990s.[5]

---

[4]"Analysts Examine Key Market Indicators," special section on business travel, *The Wall Street Journal,* January 9, 1989.
[5]All of the figures on the hotel industry including those reported by Smith Travel Research are reported in Standard and Poor's Industry Surveys, March 15, 1990.

As the second edition of this text was being prepared, the lodging industry was starting to benefit from the expansion of the U.S. economy. As a matter of fact, 1995 was considered to be the most profitable year in the history of the industry.[6] However, as we prepare this third edition, the U.S. economy, having completed over 90 consecutive months of expansion, is faced with the possibility that the recession in the Asian countries and the economic crisis in Russia will spill over into the rest of the world. Already, hotel and airline bookings have dropped substantially in the Asian countries. If the recession in Asia takes on global proportions, the lodging industry in the United States and Europe will undoubtedly suffer. Because this industry is so sensitive to changes in the macroeconomy, any forecast of this industry's domestic sales will ultimately depend on the accuracy of forecasting American and global economic performance.

## Supply, Demand, and Managerial Decision Making

The forces of supply and demand affect the business decisions of all firms in a competitive market economy. In the extreme case, these forces are the sole determinants of the market price. More will be said about this type of market in chapter 9. But for now, readers should realize that managers operating in this type of market earn a profit by making decisions about the allocation of resources based on their short- and long-run assessment of the movements of supply, demand, and prices. Examples of managers who must make decisions in this market environment are Ross Harris in our "Situation" and the actual managers who must purchase sugar on the world market (see "International Application: The World Sugar Market," later in this chapter).

There are other types of competitive markets in which firms exercise varying degrees of control over the price of their product. Economists refer to this type of control as **market power.** While supply and demand establish the overall framework in which prices are established, individual firms can exert market power over their price, because of their dominant size in the market or because of their ability to differentiate their product through advertising, brand names, and special features.

When firms do exercise market power, it is important for their managers to understand market demand on two levels. First, there is the overall demand for the product that is offered by all sellers in the market. This is what we have been calling *market demand* throughout this chapter. Second, there is the demand by buyers for the product that is being offered by a particular firm. We can call this the *firm* or *company demand*. Up to this point in the chapter the focus has been primarily on market demand. In this section, we offer several examples of why it is important for managers to understand the firm-specific demand for their product as well as the overall market demand.

In the early 1990s, Gerber, then the leading manufacturer of baby food in the United States, invested about $25 million in the purchase and renovation of a juice plant in Rzeszow, an out-of-the-way town in southern Poland, in order to produce baby food for a market that *The New York Times* described as a "sheer dream." This was because "Polish babies had never sampled the even consistency of specially processed food from a jar." Gerber also spent a considerable amount of time and money training Polish workers to achieve American standards of food quality. (For example, Polish workers

---

[6]See *U.S. Industry and Trade Outlook,* "The Lodging Industry," 1998.

had to be constantly monitored for smoking on the factory floor.) But once the manufacturing capacity was in place and the product quality had been established, consumers were not responding as expected.

As it turned out, Polish mothers perceived store-bought baby food as inferior to what they could prepare themselves for their babies. Several women who were interviewed expressed the sentiment that their mothers took the time and trouble to prepare the food for them and they could not conceive of doing anything less for their babies. The statistics tell the story. The annual per baby consumption of prepared food in the United States is 622 jars. In Poland it is 12.[7] Given this unfortunate experience in Poland, it was not surprising to learn that in 1994, Gerber agreed to be purchased by Sandoz, a large Swiss multinational pharmaceutical company.

Another good example of a company failing to understand the demand for its product is Schwinn. In the prosperous 1950s and 1960s, Schwinn dominated the bicycle market in the United States. However, starting in the late 1970s, mountain bikes became increasingly more popular. Schwinn completely missed this trend. Besides being unresponsive to this change in demand, Schwinn also did not adequately prepare for changes in the supply side of this market. During this same period of time, lower-priced bikes made in Asian countries began to appear in increasing numbers in bicycle shops and toy stores throughout the United States. This failure to understand and respond to changes in demand and supply led to Schwinn's filing for bankruptcy in 1992. A year later, buoyed by a new management and the protection of Chapter 11, it began to offer a rejuvenated line of bikes, including the popular mountain bike.[8]

In the latter half of the 1990s the new owners of Schwinn repositioned the company as a fitness and recreation company, calling itself "Schwinn Cycling and Fitness, Inc.," In so doing, it adjusted to a number of changes in demand and supply in the marketplace. First, there is continuing strength in the demand for fitness and exercise. In the decade of the 1990s, "working out" for people in their 20s and 30s has become an integral part of their lives starting from college and continuing on to the workplace. Furthermore, aging baby boomers, with their increased discretionary incomes and desire to remain healthy and fit, are a large part of the demand for health club services as well as for exercise equipment that they can use at home.

But at the same time, supply has also increased relative to the demand. There are many more fitness centers and makers of exercise equipment than there were in the past. In an effort to differentiate themselves, manufacturers such as Schwinn are constantly trying to find new types of equipment and exercise routines to offer customers. In addition to its line of road and mountain bikes, the company now produces one of the more popular lines of indoor-stationary cycles. A visit to a typical health club on a Saturday morning will find the "spinning classes"[9] full of stationary bike enthusiasts imagining that they are somewhere on a leg of the Tour de France who are being encouraged to "burn" by a trained leader who is probably also an aerobics instructor.

Recently, Schwinn has made another business decision in response to the aging baby boomer market. To commemorate 100 years of technical innovation, the company

---

[7]"In Poland, Gerber Learns the Lesson of Tradition," *The New York Times,* November 8, 1993.
[8]"Pump, Pump, Pump at Schwinn," *Business Week,* August 23, 1993, p. 79.
[9]"Spinning" is a registered trademark of Schwinn so other terms are used when other manufacturers' equipment are involved.

decided to produce the original "Black Phantom," first sold in 1949. This is what the company's Web site had to say about this product:

> Before we could build a single Phantom, we had to build just over a million bucks worth of tools. . . . With their gleaming chrome, integrated headlight, frame mounted horn tank, wide leather saddle and Schwinn Typhoon balloon tires, the original Phantoms represent the emergence of style and sophistication that had never been seen before.[10]

The retail price of this tribute to nostalgia is about $2,500.

One of the lessons learned from the Schwinn case is the need for suppliers to assess the supply and demand conditions in the market, particularly in the long run. Referring back to our supply and demand diagrams, it is one thing to increase the quantity supplied in response to higher demand and prices. It is quite another to commit resources over the long term, thereby causing the supply curve itself to shift. If the higher demand is not sustained, or if too many others enter or add capacity, a company's growth strategy could fail. Already there are at least three other makers of stationary bikes, including sneaker manufacturer Reebok, although Schwinn still has the lead in market share.

In Schwinn's case, going from a nearly bankrupt condition in the early 1990s to one of the most dominant producers of bicycles in the world in less than 10 years required a strong belief that the long-run demand for mountain bikes and exercise equipment would be sustained. It also required management's willingness to spend enough money on research and development and plant and equipment to capture a large part of this growing demand. Because it is a privately held company, it is difficult to find figures to show the extent of their financial success, but in 1997 the company purchased its arch rival, GT, for $90 million. This should be an indication of how well the company is doing.[11]

A third case that illustrates the importance of understanding supply and demand conditions concerns the market for long-distance air travel.[12] In the fall of 1998, Singapore Airlines and Delta Airlines announced new strategies to compete in this market. Singapore Airlines had planned to invest about $300 million to upgrade its first, business, and economy class. On the other hand, Delta had planned to eliminate entirely its first-class service, while upgrading its business-class service. Essentially, this is what the two airlines had planned:

**Singapore Airlines**
1. First class will have a special lounge and a redesigned cabin with 12 "minisuites," equipped with seat-beds, power outlets for computers, retractable desks and 14-inch video monitors. Previously, there were 14 first-class seats in their 37 Boeing 747-400s.
2. Business class will have seats that are based on the frame of the first class, privacy dividers, and power outlets. The number of seats will be reduced from 65 to 58.

---

[10]Retrieved October 2, 1998, from the Schwinn corporate Web site: www.schwinn.com/collector/bphantom.html.
[11]Some of the details of Schwinn's turnaround strategy were learned in an interview with a Schwinn retail distributor in Brewster, NY, September 1998.
[12]Jane L. Levere, "Business Travel," *New York Times,* September 16, 1998.

3. Economy class will have upgraded seats and champagne served throughout the flight.
4. The entire project will take 18 months to complete.

**Delta Airlines**
1. Business class will have new seats, upgraded wine and food, and a modern entertainment system.
2. The change will take about 8 to 10 months to complete.

The rationale for the two companies' investment decisions is largely based on their assessment of supply and demand. Dr. Choong Kong Cheong, deputy chairman and chief executive officer of Singapore Airlines, said the decision was made because "Singapore's passengers always expect the best from us [and] we're determined to stay ahead of the competition." In spite of the Asian economic crisis, he said his company was going to make this investment because "We're continuing to upgrade our product and service because we can't afford to be left behind."

Delta officials said their decision to eliminate first class was because "the demand for business class far exceeded that for first class." Their data indicates that in 1997 intercontinental business demand grew four times faster than that for first class. It also showed that the number of business class passengers was seven times the number of those in first class.

It will be interesting to see what prices the two airlines will charge for their respective services. The response by business travelers to their prices will be a key factor in determining which investment strategy is the most economically sound. This reaction of consumers to different prices and price changes is the principal subject of our next chapter.

# International Application: The World Sugar Market[13]

While our "Situation" indicates the importance of high fructose corn syrup as a sweetener of carbonated soft drinks in the United States, sugar is still the primary sweetener of soft drinks bottled around the world.[14] And world sugar prices, like world corn prices, are governed primarily by the forces of supply and demand. In 1998, world sugar prices were trading at their lowest levels in a decade. This is obviously beneficial to soft drink companies, but has hurt sugar suppliers. Let us look at the nonprice determinants of supply and demand that have caused the low prices.

**Nonprice Determinants of Supply**
1. There have been favorable weather conditions in primary sugar growing countries such as Brazil, Thailand, and Australia.
2. Brazil (the world's third-largest supplier of sugar after the European Union and India) has shifted an increased amount of its supply of cane crop to the sugar market because of the lower demand and prices for alcohol made from sugar.

---

[13]Information in this section is based on Paul Solman, "Outlook for Sugar Less Than Sweet," *Financial Times,* September 17, 1998, p. 28.
[14]Readers may find it interesting to know that there are about 8 to 10 teaspoons of sugar (or its HFCS equivalent) in a 12-oz. can of a carbonated soft drink.

**WORLD SUGAR**

Liffe white sugar price ($ per tonne)

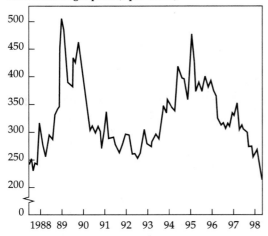

World production & consumption (in tonnes, raw value)*

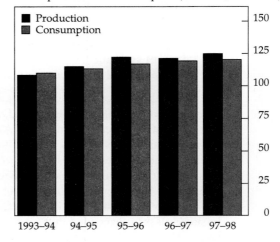

*\*Oct-Sept*

**FIGURE 3.9** World Supply, Demand, and Price for Sugar, 1988–1998

*Source:* From Paul Solman, "Outlook for Sugar Less Than Sweet," *Financial Times,* September 17, 1998.

### Nonprice Determinants of Demand

1. The economic crisis in Asia has reduced the demand for sugar by countries in this region.
2. There has been a substantial increase in domestic sugar output in China and India. This has greatly reduced their demand for imported sugar in the world sugar market.
3. On August 1, 1998, substantial tariffs were imposed in Russia, another major sugar importing country (from 1 percent to 75 percent on raw sugar and from 25 percent to 45 percent on white sugar).

If the supply of sugar produced in China and India continues to grow, these two countries could eventually become net exporters rather than importers of sugar and their supply on world markets would put further pressures on international sugar prices.

All of these nonprice determinants combined to cause a world surplus of one to two million tons of sugar in 1998. Analysts believe that this surplus could increase to as much as five million in the next year. World sugar prices, once as high as $500 per ton in the late 1980s, were slightly over $215 per ton in 1998. The graphs shown in Figure 3.9 summarize world supply and demand conditions and prices for sugar over the past 10 years.

## THE SOLUTION

In his presentation to the management committee, Ross Harris recommended that Global Foods, Inc., acquiesce to the HFCS manufacturers' request to negotiate a pricing and delivery contract on a quarterly basis. "Based on our current projections of demand and supply, we believe that there will be a slight upward trend in HFCS prices in the short run," Ross began. "This means that if we negotiate on a quarterly basis, we may have to pay a bit more for the product, because the negotiated price will reflect the underlying supply and demand conditions in the market. However, if we bought the product in the spot market, we would be operating in an extremely volatile environment. In our business, I strongly believe that continuity of supply and the quality of the product are just as important as the price. By negotiating a contract with the suppliers, we are assured of at least a minimum amount of high-quality product at the contracted price. If we order too much, we can always sell the surplus to other companies in the food industry. If we do not order enough, we can always meet the shortage by purchasing product in the spot market. As you all know, we currently handle our surpluses and shortages of HFCS in this manner. In fact, this is how we know that the product in the spot market is not always of top quality.

In talking to purchasing agents in the rest of the industry and with some of my contacts in the HFCS manufacturing business," Ross continued, "I am convinced that the HFCS compa-

nies are very adamant about setting the price on a quarterly basis. The volatility of supply-and-demand conditions in the market for corn has hurt their profit margins in the past, and they want greater flexibility in pricing the final product in order to compensate for the upward movements in the price of corn."

Ross made a final point. "I stated that our projections call for some upward trend in the price of HFCS in the near term. However, if we continue the present arrangement of negotiating the price with our suppliers—even if it is done on a quarterly rather than a yearly basis—we will be helping to preserve a relatively stable market environment in which they can project with greater certainty the future demand for HFCS. This will enable them to better plan for their manufacturing capacity requirements. In *the long run,* this should mean fewer chances of supply bottlenecks, shortages, and higher prices."

The report by Kathy Martinez was short and to the point. The market for corn was found to be typical of markets in which agricultural commodities were bought and sold. She presented a chart showing that these markets are characterized by *price volatility* brought on by frequent changes in supply and demand conditions (see Figure 3.10).

Kathy went on to explain that in the market for corn in the United States, the major factors affecting supply are weather conditions, the output of corn in other countries, and the U.S. government's acreage control program.

*(Continued)*

Another factor is the market for alternative uses for corn. The supply available for the HFCS market depends on the supply and demand conditions for these alternative uses.

As far as the demand for HFCS is concerned, she noted that the major factor has been the soft drink industry's increasing use of the sweetener as a substitute for sugar. However, soft drink demand is subject to seasonal fluctuations, being the highest in the summer and lowest in the winter. Pricing on a yearly basis does not allow the flexibility to price according to these seasonal fluctuations. In particular, it does not allow prices to be raised in response to the increase in the summer demand for HFCS.

Kathy's report summarized the situation as follows. On the supply side, the price of corn, the major ingredient of HFCS, is very volatile. On the demand side, the major buyers of HFCS are the soft drink manufacturers, the makers of a product that has seen steady long-term growth, subject to seasonal fluctuations. Thus, HFCS manufacturers must try to protect themselves from adverse corn price fluctuations by establishing greater pricing flexibility vis-à-vis the customers responsible for the major part of the demand.[15]

**FIGURE 3.10** Monthly Average Corn Cash Prices, Chicago

*Source:* Economic Research Service, USDA

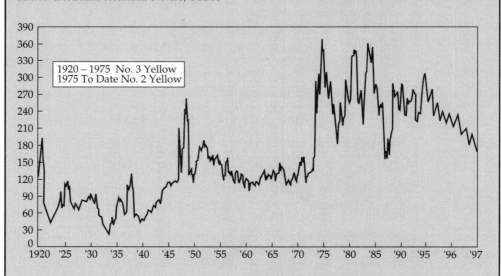

1920 – 1975  No. 3 Yellow
1975 To Date No. 2 Yellow

[16]This "solution" is based on an actual change in the industry that occurred in 1986. Prior to that time, the price of HFCS was established between HFCS manufacturers and the major soft drink companies once a year. The reasons that the HFCS manufacturers wanted to shift to quarterly negotiations are essentially those discussed here. The actual reasons the soft drink companies agreed to go along with the change are not known. (For a detailed account of this, see *Chemical Marketing Reporter*, March 24, 1986.)

# Summary

This chapter has presented the basic elements of supply and demand. We began by introducing the *law of demand* and the *law of supply* and the nonprice factors that affect demand and supply. The law of demand states that, other factors held constant, the quantity demanded is inversely related to price. The law of supply states that, other factors held constant, the quantity supplied is directly related to price. Other factors that affect demand are (1) tastes and preferences, (2) income, (3) prices of related products, (4) number of buyers, and (5) future expectations. Other factors that affect supply are (1) costs, (2) technology, (3) prices of other products that sellers can supply, (4) number of sellers, (5) future expectations, and (6) weather conditions. Both numerical and graphical examples of supply and demand and how they interrelate to determine the equilibrium price and quantity were presented. The appendix to this chapter presents the same material in algebraic terms.

We studied how price serves a short-run rationing function and a long-run guiding function in the marketplace. Price serves a rationing function when it increases or decreases to clear the market of a shortage or surplus caused by a change in market conditions (i.e., a shifting of the supply or demand curve). Price changes serve as a guiding function signaling producers or consumers to put more or less of their resources in the affected markets.

In explaining the rationing and guiding functions of price, we noted the particular way in which economists define the short run and the long run. We also discussed how comparative statics analysis is used to explain the rationing and guiding functions of the price. This technique, involving the comparison of equilibrium points before and after changes in the market have occurred, is a standard way of analyzing problems and will be used throughout this text.

# Important Concepts

**Change in demand:** The result of a change in one or more of the nonprice determinants of demand, graphically represented by a *shift* in the demand curve (rightward for an increase in demand and leftward for a decrease in demand). (p. 70)

**Change in supply** The result of a change in one or more of the nonprice determinants of supply, graphically represented by a *shift* in the supply curve (rightward for an increase and leftward for a decrease). (p. 74)

**Change in the quantity demanded:** The result of a change in the price of a good or service, graphically represented by a *movement along* a particular demand curve. (p. 70)

**Change in the quantity supplied:** The result of a change in the price of a good or service, graphically represented by a *movement along* a particular supply curve. (p. 74)

**Demand:** Quantities of a good or service that people are ready to buy at various prices, other factors besides the price held constant. Demand can be expressed as a numerical sched- ule, as a demand curve on a graph, or as an algebraic equation. (p. 69)

**Equilibrium price:** The price that equates the quantity demanded with the quantity supplied; the price that clears the market of any shortage or surplus. (p. 76)

**Equilibrium quantity:** The amount that people are ready to buy and sell at the equilibrium price level. (p. 76)

**Guiding function of price:** Also referred to as the *allocating function of price,* the movement of resources into or out of markets as a result of changes in the equilibrium market price. This is considered to be a long-run function. On the supply side of the market, sellers may enter or leave the market or may vary all of their factors of production. On the demand side, consumers may change their tastes or preferences or find long-lasting alternatives to a particular good or service. (p. 81)

**Law of Demand:** The quantity demanded depends *inversely* on price. (p. 70)

**Long run:** A time period in which new sellers may enter a market or sellers already in a market may leave. This time period is sufficient for both old and new sellers to vary *all* of their factors of production. From the standpoint of consumers, the long run provides time enough to respond to price changes by actually changing their tastes or preferences or their use of alternative goods and services. For example, suppose bad weather in Brazil results in an increase in the price of coffee. In the short run, people are expected to buy less coffee because of the higher price. However, in the long run, they may buy even less coffee because the higher price will have prompted them to drink more tea on a regular basis. (p. 82)

**Market demand:** The sum of all individual demands for a good or service. (p. 70)

**Market power:** The power to set the market price. (p. 86)

**Nonprice determinants of demand:** (1) Tastes and preferences, (2) income, (3) prices of related products (i.e., substitutes or complements), (4) future expectations, (5) number of buyers. (p. 71)

**Nonprice determinants of supply:** (1) Costs, (2) technology, (3) prices of other products that may be produced by a firm, (4) future expectations, (5) number of sellers, (6) weather conditions. (p. 74)

**Quantity demanded:** The amount that people are ready to buy at a given price. (p. 70)

**Quantity supplied:** The amount that people are ready to sell at a given price. (p. 73)

**Rationing function of price:** The increase or decrease in price to clear the market of any shortage or surplus. This is considered to be a short-run function because both buyers and sellers are expected to respond only to price changes. (p. 80)

**Shortage:** A condition that exists in the market when the quantity demanded exceeds the quantity supplied at a price *below* the equilibrium or market-clearing price. (p. 76)

**Short run:** A time period in which only those sellers already in the market may respond to a change in market price by using more or less of their variable resources. From the standpoint of consumers, the short run is a period in which they respond only to price changes. As a result of a change in price, consumers may change their tastes or preferences or their use of alternative goods or services. However, in economic analysis, these related changes are considered long-run phenomena. (p. 81)

**Supply:** Quantities of a good or service that people are ready to *sell* at various prices, other factors besides price held constant. Supply can be expressed as a numerical schedule, as a supply curve on a graph, or as an algebraic equation. (p. 73)

**Surplus:** A condition that exists in the market when the quantity supplied exceeds the quantity demanded at a price that lies *above* the equilibrium or market-clearing price. (p. 76)

## Questions

1. Define *demand*. Define *supply*. In your answers, explain the difference between *demand* and *quantity demanded* and between *supply* and *quantity supplied*.
2. List the key nonprice factors that influence demand and supply.
3. In defining demand and supply, why do you think economists focus on price while holding constant other factors that might have an impact on the behavior of buyers and sellers?
4. Define comparative statics analysis. How does it compare with sensitivity analysis or what-if analysis used in finance, accounting, and statistics?
5. Define the *rationing function* of price. Why is it necessary for price to serve this function in the market economy?
6. Define the *guiding* or *allocating function* of price.
7. Discuss the differences between the short run and the long run from the perspective of producers and from the perspective of consumers.

8. Explain the difference between shortages and scarcity. In answering this question, you should consider the difference between the short run and the long run in economic analysis.

9. Why do you think it is important for managers to understand the mechanics of supply and demand both in the short run and in the long run? Give examples of companies whose business was either helped or hurt by changes in supply or demand in the markets in which they were competing.

10. "If Congress levies an additional tax on luxury items, the prices of these items will rise. However, this will cause demand to decrease, and as a result the prices will fall back down, perhaps even to their original levels." Do you agree with this statement? Explain.

11. Overheard at the water cooler in the corporate headquarters of a large manufacturing concern: "The competition is really threatening us with their new product line. I think we should consider offering discounts on our current line in order to stimulate demand." In this statement, is the term *demand* being used in a manner consistent with economic theory? Explain. Illustrate your answer using a line drawn to represent the demand for this firm's product line.

12. Briefly list and elaborate on the factors that will be affecting the demand for the following products in the next several years. Do you think these factors will cause the demand to increase or decrease?
    a. convenience foods (sold in food shops and supermarkets)
    b. products purchased on the Internet
    c. fax machines
    d. film and cameras
    e. videos rented from retail outlets
    f. pay-per-view televison programing
    g. airline travel within the United States; airline travel within Europe
    h. gasoline

13. Briefly list and elaborate on the factors that will be affecting the supply of the following products in the next several years. Do you think these factors will cause the supply to increase or decrease?
    a. crude oil
    b. beef
    c. computer memory chips
    d. hotel rooms
    e. fast food outlets in emerging markets
    f. credit cards issued by financial institutions
    g. laptop computers
    h. PC servers

## Problems

1. The following function describes the demand condition for a company that makes caps featuring names of college and professional teams in a variety of sports.

$$Q = 2,000 - 100\,P$$

where $Q$ is cap sales and $P$ is price.
    a. How many caps could be sold at $12 each?
    b. What should the price be in order for the company to sell 1,000 caps?
    c. At what price would cap sales equal zero?

2. Consider the following supply and demand curves for a certain product.

$$Q_S = 25,000\,P$$

$$Q_D = 50,000 - 10,000\,P$$

    **a.** Plot the demand and supply curves.

    **b.** What are the equilibrium price and equilibrium quantity for the industry? Determine the answer both algebraically and graphically. (Round to the nearest cent.)

**3.** The following relations describe the supply and demand for posters.

$$Q_D = 65{,}000 - 10{,}000\,P$$

$$Q_S = -35{,}000 + 15{,}000\,P$$

where $Q$ is the quantity and $P$ is the price of a poster, in dollars.

    **a.** Complete the following table.

| Price | $Q_S$ | $Q_D$ | Surplus or Shortage |
|-------|-------|-------|---------------------|
| $6.00 | | | |
| 5.00 | | | |
| 4.00 | | | |
| 3.00 | | | |
| 2.00 | | | |
| 1.00 | | | |

    **b.** What is the equilibrium price?

**4.** The following relations describe monthly demand and supply for a computer support service catering to small businesses.

$$Q_D = 3{,}000 - 10\,P$$

$$Q_S = -1{,}000 + 10\,P$$

where $Q$ is the number of businesses that need services and $P$ is the monthly fee, in dollars.

    **a.** At what average monthly fee would demand equal zero?

    **b.** At what average monthly fee would supply equal zero?

    **c.** Plot the supply and demand curves.

    **d.** What is the equilibrium price/output level?

    **e.** Suppose demand increases and leads to a new demand curve:

$$Q_D = 3{,}500 - 10\,P$$

    What is the effect on supply? What are the new equilibrium $P$ and $Q$?

    **f.** Suppose new suppliers enter the market due to the increase in demand, so that the new supply curve is $Q = -500 + 10\,P$.

    What are the new equilibrium price and equilibrium quantity?

    **g.** Show these changes on the graph.

**5.** The ABC marketing consulting firm found that a particular brand of portable stereo has the following demand curve for a certain region:

$$Q = 10{,}000 - 200\,P + 0.03\,\text{Pop} + 0.6I + 0.2A$$

where $Q$ is the quantity per month, $P$ is price ($\$$), Pop is population, $I$ is disposable income per household ($\$$), and $A$ is advertising expenditure ($\$$).

**a.** Determine the demand curve for the company in a market in which $P = 300$, Pop $= 1,000,000$, $I = 30,000$, and $A = 15,000$.

**b.** Calculate the quantity demanded at prices of $200, $175, $150, and $125.

**c.** Calculate the price necessary to sell 45,000 units.

**6.** Joy's Frozen Yogurt shops have enjoyed rapid growth in northeastern states in recent years. From the analysis of Joy's various outlets, it was found that the demand curve follows this pattern:

$$Q = 200 - 300\,P + 120\,I + 65\,T - 250\,A_c + 400\,A_j$$

where $Q$ = Number of cups served per week
$P$ = Average price paid for each cup
$I$ = Per capita income in the given market (thousands)
$T$ = Average outdoor temperature
$A_c$ = Competition's monthly advertising expenditures (thousands)
$A_j$ = Joy's own monthly advertising expenditures (thousands)

One of the outlets has the following conditions: $P = 1.50, I = 10, T = 60, A_c = 15, A_j = 10$.

**a.** Estimate the number of cups served per week by this outlet. Also determine the outlet's demand curve.

**b.** What would be the effect of a $5,000 increase in the competitor's advertising expenditure? Illustrate the effect on the outlet's demand curve.

**c.** What would Joy's advertising expenditure have to be to counteract this effect?

**7.** Illustrate the example of the world sugar market with supply and demand diagrams. Be sure to show how the relative shifts in supply and demand have led to the reduction in the world price of sugar.

**8.** Over the past decade, the demand for compact discs (CDs) has dramatically increased. What are some of the causes of this increase in demand? According to supply-and-demand theory, price should rise when demand increases. However, in recent years the average price of a CD has actually fallen. Explain this apparent contradiction between the theory and fact.

**9.** Suppose a firm has the following demand equation:

$$Q = 1,000 - 3,000P + 10A$$

where $Q$ = quantity demanded
$P$ = product price (in dollars)
$A$ = advertising expenditure (in dollars)

Assume for the questions below that $P = \$3$ and $A = \$2,000$.

**a.** Suppose the firm dropped the price to $2.50. Would this be beneficial? Explain. Illustrate your answer with the use of a demand schedule and demand curve.

**b.** Suppose the firm raised the price to $4.00 while increasing its advertising expenditure by $100. Would this be beneficial? Explain. Illustrate your answer with the use of a demand schedule and a demand curve.

(Hint: First construct the schedule and the curve assuming $A = \$2,000$. Then construct the new schedule and curve assuming $A = \$2,100$.)

**10.** A travel company has hired a management consulting company to analyze demand in 26 regional markets for one of its major products: a guided tour to a particular country. The consultant uses data to estimate the following equation (the estimation technique is discussed in detail in chapter 5):

$$Q = 1,500 - 4P + 5A + 10I + 3PX$$

where  $Q$  =  amount of the product demanded
$P$  =  price of the product in dollars
$A$  =  advertising expenditures in **thousands** of dollars
$I$  =  income in **thousands** of dollars
$PX$  =  price of some other travel products offered by a competing travel company

**a.** Calculate the amount demanded for this product using the following data:

$P$  =  $400
$A$  =  $20,000
$I$  =  $15,000
$PX$  =  $500

**b.** Suppose the competitor reduced the price of its travel product to $400 to match the price of this firm's product. How much would this firm have to increase its advertising in order to counteract the drop in its competitor's price? Would it be worth it for them to do so? Explain.

**c.** What other variables might be important in helping to estimate the demand for this travel product?

**11.** Following are three sample demand equations. Plot them on a graph in which $Q$ is on the vertical axis and $P$ is on the horizontal axis. Then transform these equations so that $P$ is expressed in terms of $Q$ and plot these transformed equations on a graph in which $P$ is on the vertical axis and $Q$ is on the horizontal axis.

**a.** $Q = 250 - 10\,P$
**b.** $Q = 1,300 - 140\,P$
**c.** $Q = 45 - 0.5\,P$

**12.** Use the following equation to derive a demand schedule and a demand curve. What types of products might exhibit this type of nonlinear demand curve? Explain?

$$Q = 100P^{-0.3}$$

# Take It to the Net

We invite you to visit the Keat/Young page on the Prentice Hall Web site at:

**http://www.prenhall.com/keat**

for additional resources.

# Appendix 3A

## The Mathematics of Supply and Demand

This appendix presents the short-run analysis of supply and demand using algebraic equations and graphs. As you will see, the mechanics of supply and demand can be very concisely expressed in algebraic equations. Furthermore, viewing the demand function in terms of an equation will better prepare you for the next two chapters on demand elasticity and estimation.

The demand function for a good or service can be expressed mathematically as:

$$Q_D = f(P, X_1, ..., X_n)$$

where $Q_D$ = Quantity demanded
$P$ = Price
$X_1, ..., X_n$ = Other factors believed to affect the quantity demanded

Using pizza once again as our example, let us assume that price and the nonprice factors affect the demand for pizza in the following way:

$$Q_D = -100\,P + 1.5\,P_{hd} - 5\,P_{sd} + 20\,A + 15\,\text{Pop} \tag{3A.1}$$

where $Q_D$ = Quantity demanded for pizza (pies)
$P_{hd}$ = Price of hot dogs (cents)
$P_{sd}$ = Price of soft drinks (cents)
$A$ = Advertising expenditures (thousands of dollars)
Pop = Percentage of the population aged 10 to 35

Suppose we hold constant all factors affecting the quantity demanded for pizza except price by assuming the values of these nonprice factors to be

$P_{hd}$ = 100 ($1.00 or 100 cents)
$P_{sd}$ = 75 ($.75 or 75 cents)
$A$ = 20 ($20,000)
Pop = 35 (35 percent)

Substituting these values into Equation (3A.1) gives us

$$
\begin{aligned}
Q_D &= -100\,P + 1.5\,(100) - 5\,(75) + 20\,(20) + 15\,(35) \\
&= 700 - 100\,P
\end{aligned}
\tag{3A.2}
$$

All of the values of the nonprice variables are now included in the constant term, 700. Plotting this equation gives us the demand curve shown in Figure 3A.1.

Those familiar with the graphical presentation of algebraic equations may be puzzled about the way in which economists present the supply and demand equations in graphical form. As a rule, the dependent variable is placed on the vertical or $Y$ axis, and the independent variable is placed on the horizontal or $X$ axis. Given this format, one would expect $Q$, the dependent variable, to be placed on the vertical axis and $P$, the independent variable, to be placed on the horizontal axis. However, in this chapter, as well as in the next, $Q$ is placed on the horizontal axis, and $P$ on the vertical axis. It seems that the originator of these diagrams, Professor Alfred Marshall, first presented them in this

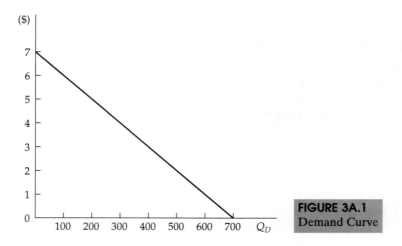

**FIGURE 3A.1**
Demand Curve

manner.[17] Since then economists have followed this way of presenting supply and demand in graphical form.

Regardless of Marshall's original reasons for reversing the axes, let us simply state that in the analysis of cost, revenue, and profit, the quantity of output is the independent variable. Thus, placing $Q$ on the horizontal axis in the analysis of supply and demand simply prepares us for its subsequent designation as an independent variable.

In the meantime, an adjustment must be made in linking the supply and demand equations to their graphs in order to conform to mathematical convention. In supply-and-demand analysis, whenever an equation such as $Q_D = 700 - 100\,P$ is plotted on a graph, we must do one of two things. If we wish to be consistent with mathematical convention, we must place $Q_D$ on the vertical axis and the $P$ on the horizontal axis. This is shown in Figure 3A.2a. If we wish to follow the usual format in economics, we must re-arrange the terms in the equation so that $P$ is expressed in terms of $Q_D$.

$$Q_D = 700 - 100P$$

$$100\,P = 700 - Q_D$$

$$P = \frac{700 - QD}{100}$$

$$P = 7 - 0.01\,QD$$

As such, $P$ is now the dependent variable and can be plotted on the vertical axis. $Q_D$ is now the independent variable and can be plotted on the horizontal axis. This is illustrated in Figure 3A.2b.

Let us review this point by assuming that one of the nonprice factors affecting the quantity demanded for pizza has changed. In particular, suppose the price of hot dogs

[17]Alfred Marshall, *Principles of Economics,* 8th ed., Philadelphia: Porcupine Press, 1920, reprinted 1982, p. 288.

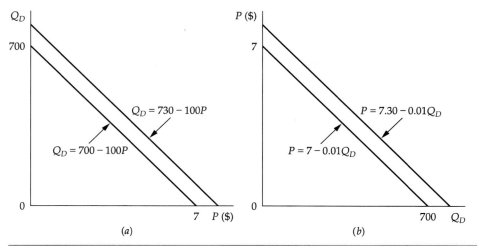

**FIGURE 3A.2** Transforming the Demand Curve

increases to $1.20. In Equation (3A.2), this would increase the constant or "$Y$ intercept" term from 700 to ⁻30. This, in effect, would cause the demand curve to shift from its original position to the new one shown in Figure 3A.2*a*. Figure 3A.2*b* shows the effect of an increase in the price of hot dogs on the transformed demand equation. In this case, the constant term or "$Y$ intercept" increases from 7 to 7.3 and is also shown by a rightward shift in the demand curve.

We now focus on the supply by assuming that the supply equation is the same as the curve used in Table 3.4 and Figure 3.3. This equation can be expressed as:

$$Q_s = -100 + 100\,P \qquad (3A.3)$$

Once the supply and demand equations are given, there are several ways to find the equilibrium price and quantity. One way is to solve for the supply and demand equations simultaneously. This is done by first setting up the two equations in the following way:

$$Q_D = 700 - 100\,P$$
$$Q_S = -100 + 100\,P$$

We can then eliminate $P$ by adding the equations together. This gives us

$$2\,Q = 700 - 100 \qquad (3A.4)$$
$$= 600$$
$$Q^* = 300$$

To find the equilibrium price ($P^*$), we simply return to either the demand or the supply equation, insert the value for the equilibrium quantity, (300), and solve for $P$. Using Equation (3A.2), this would give us

$$300 = 700 - 100\ P$$

$$100\ P = 700 - 300$$

$$P* = 4$$

Notice that when we added the supply and demand equations together, we no longer made the distinction between $Q_S$ and $Q_D$, because in equilibrium $Q_S = Q_D$. In fact, this brings us to the other way in which the supply and demand equations can be used to determine the equilibrium price and quantity. By definition, market equilibrium occurs when the quantity supplied is equal to the quantity demanded. Thus, we can set Equation (3A.2) equal to Equation (3A.3) and solve for the unknown $P$. That is,

$$700 - 100\ P = -100 + 100\ P$$

$$200P = 800$$

$$P* = 4$$

And by inserting the value of 4 into either equation, we obtain the equilibrium quantity, 300.

You now have three ways to view the basic elements of supply and demand. First, there are supply and demand schedules, as shown in Tables 3.1, 3.2, 3.3, and 3.4, in which the equilibrium price is found by matching the quantity supplied with the quantity demanded. Second, there are supply and demand diagrams, as presented in most of the figures in this chapter, in which price and quantity are determined by the intersection of the supply and demand curves. Finally, there are supply and demand equations, which enable one to find equilibrium price and quantity by solving for the unknowns in the two equations. For teaching purposes, the use of graphs is favored. But regardless of the manner in which the concepts of supply and demand are presented, there remains the challenge for business decision makers to ascertain the actual supply and demand data for their particular industries and organizations.

# CHAPTER 4

# Demand Elasticity

## THE SITUATION

Henry Caulfield is the owner-operator of a local "Gas 'n Go" gas station and convenience store. Henry chose to locate his store in an area at least ten minutes away by car from the nearest supermarket or grocery store. For the most part, Henry's business has been quite successful.

Then one day he noticed that a new grocery store was opening just one block away. A month later he noticed that a new convenience store had opened for business less than a three-minute drive away. Henry realized that to maintain the status quo in the face of this new competition, he would have to make some tough decisions about his pricing and promotion policies and the mix of items carried in his store.

The items that he carried were typical of those found in retail establishments of this type, with beer, cigarettes, hot coffee, and soft drinks accounting for about 75 percent of total sales. Soft drinks were by far the best-selling item in his store. Essentially, the retail price of soft drinks was based on the wholesale price plus a mark-up of about 400 percent. Henry recognized that this mark-up was considerably higher than the one used by a supermarket, but he believed that people were willing to pay more for the convenience.

On certain occasions, Henry would offer a particular brand of soft drink at a substantial discount. Regardless of whether he lost or made money on soft drinks by this action, he found that it helped to attract additional customers into his store, and gasoline sales actually increased. Several people from an adjacent town told him that they waited until they were in the vicinity of his station to fill their tanks because of his discount on soda. Given the public's responsiveness to special discounts on soft drinks and the ability of this product to promote other products, Henry decided to use the pricing of soft drinks as his main weapon against his new competition. Instead of offering a temporary discount, he decided to reduce the price of soft drinks permanently. However, after a month, despite the lower soft drink prices, there was a noticeable decline in his revenue from soft drinks. Henry realized that he would have to reassess his competitive tactic.

## The Economic Concept of Elasticity

In the previous chapter we studied the idea of demand and discussed the movement along a demand curve (i.e., change in quantity demanded). We found the demand curve to slope downward to the right; this means, of course, that the lower the price, the greater the quantity of the product consumed. We are now going to discuss the question of how sensitive the change in quantity demanded is to a change in price. The measurement of this sensitivity in percentage terms is called the **price elasticity of demand.** Henry Caulfield made implicit use of this concept when he decided to lower his soft drink prices to compete with the new stores in his area. But this is only one of the elasticity measures with which we will concern ourselves in this chapter. We will also cover the concepts of income elasticity, cross-elasticity, and supply elasticity.

In most general terms, we can define **elasticity** as a percentage relationship between two variables, that is, the percentage change in one variable relative to a percentage change in another. In different terms, we divide one percentage by the other:

$$\text{Coefficient of elasticity} = \frac{\text{Percent change in A}}{\text{Percent change in B}}$$

The result of this division is the **coefficient of elasticity.** It is then our task to interpret the coefficient and to determine the effects of the change. The meaning of the size as well as the sign of the coefficient (the coefficient may be negative or positive) will be the focus of our inquiry for the remainder of this chapter. Let us first turn to the most frequently encountered elasticity concept, the price elasticity of demand.

## The Price Elasticity of Demand

When Henry Caulfield contemplated lowering his price to counteract his new competition, he was dealing with price elasticity of demand. He was determining whether by lowering his prices he would raise his unit sales sufficiently to increase his total revenue.[1]

When we speak of the price elasticity of demand, we are dealing with the sensitivity of quantities bought to a change in the producer's price. Thus, this concept describes an action that is within the producer's (or, in this case, the dealer's) control. Other elasticities to be discussed later are outside the producer's control and may evoke other actions on the producer's part to counteract them.

Demand price elasticity is defined as a percentage change in quantity demanded caused by a one percent change in price. Let us develop this concept mathematically. We can write the expression, "percentage change in quantity demanded" as

$$\frac{\Delta \ Quantity \ demanded}{Initial \ quantity \ demanded}$$

where $\Delta$ (delta) signifies an absolute change. The second part of this relationship, "percentage change in price," can be written as

---

[1]More important, he was wondering whether he would actually increase his profits with this action. However, we are not yet in a position to deal with this question.

$$\frac{\Delta \ Price}{Initial \ price}$$

Dividing the first expression by the second, we arrive at the expression for the price elasticity of demand:

$$\frac{\Delta \ Quantity}{Quantity} \div \frac{\Delta \ Price}{Price} = \frac{\% \Delta \ Quantity}{\% \Delta \ Price}$$

This is the general expression. We turn now to the actual computation of elasticities, and we will describe two methods of obtaining the price elasticity of demand.

**MODULE 4A**

## MEASUREMENT OF PRICE ELASTICITY

Let us begin with **arc elasticity,** the method most commonly used in economics textbooks. The formula for this indicator is

$$E_p = \frac{Q_2 - Q_1}{(Q_1 + Q_2)/2} \div \frac{P_2 - P_1}{(P_1 + P_2)/2}$$

where $E_p$ = Coefficient of arc price elasticity
$Q_1$ = Original quantity demanded
$Q_2$ = New quantity demanded
$P_1$ = Original price
$P_2$ = New price

The numerator of this coefficient, $(Q_2 - Q_1)/[(Q_1 + Q_2)/2]$, indicates the percentage change in the quantity demanded. The denominator, $(P_2 - P_1)/[(P_1 + P_2)/2]$, indicates the percentage change in the price.

Notice that the change in each variable is divided by the *average* of its beginning and ending values. For example, if the price of a product rises from $11 to $12, causing a fall in the quantity demanded from 7 to 6, the formula gives the following price elasticity coefficient:

$$E_p = \frac{6-7}{(7+6)/2} \div \frac{12-11}{(11+12)/2}$$

$$= \frac{-1}{6.5} \div \frac{1}{11.5}$$

$$= \frac{-1}{6.5} \times \frac{11.5}{1}$$

$$= \frac{-11.5}{6.5}$$

$$= -1.77$$

The reason the arc elasticity formula employs the average of the beginning and ending values can be clearly seen. If we had used the beginning values, the coefficient would be

$$Ep = \frac{6-7}{7} \div \frac{12-11}{11}$$

$$= \frac{-1}{7} \div \frac{1}{11}$$

$$= \frac{-1}{7} \times \frac{11}{1}$$

$$= \frac{-11}{7}$$

$$= -1.57$$

However, suppose the price fell from \$12 to \$11, causing the quantity demanded to rise from 6 to 7 units. Using the beginning values would result in a coefficient of $-2$ (readers can make this calculation themselves to obtain the answer). Thus, the *same* unit change in price and quantity gives *different* values of elasticity, depending on whether the price increases or decreases.[2] By using the average of the beginning and ending values, we avoid this ambiguity. The price elasticity coefficient is the same whether price increases or decreases.

An additional source of ambiguity arises in the computation of elasticity when we consider changes over different ranges of price and quantity. For example, suppose that the values of price and quantity provided in the preceding analysis are part of the hypothetical demand schedule shown in Table 4.1.

The numbers in this schedule indicate a linear relationship between quantity demanded and price, with a unit change in price resulting in a unit change in quantity over the entire range of the schedule.[3] Suppose we compute the arc elasticity for a price change from \$12 to \$10 rather than between \$12 and \$11. Using the arc elasticity formula gives

$$Ep = \frac{6-8}{(8+6)/2} \div \frac{12-10}{(10+12)/2}$$

$$= \frac{-2}{7} \div \frac{2}{11}$$

$$= \frac{-2}{7} \times \frac{11}{2}$$

$$= \frac{-22}{14}$$

$$= -1.57$$

---

[2]The reason for this ambiguity is simply that the base number differs between a percentage increase and a decrease between two numbers. A good example of this can be found in the retail trade. Suppose a company buys a dress wholesale for \$100 and marks it up 100 percent, thereby establishing the retail price at \$200. Suppose in a clearance sale it decides to sell it at cost. This would represent a 50 percent markdown (i.e., from \$200 down to \$100).

[3]The algebraic expression of this demand equation is $P = 18 - Q$, or $Q = 18 - P$.

| TABLE 4.1 | Hypothetical Demand Schedule | |
| --- | --- |
| *Price* | *Quantity* |
| 18 | 0 |
| 17 | 1 |
| 16 | 2 |
| 15 | 3 |
| 14 | 4 |
| 13 | 5 |
| 12 | 6 |
| 11 | 7 |
| 10 | 8 |
| 9 | 9 |
| 8 | 10 |
| 7 | 11 |
| 6 | 12 |
| 5 | 13 |

Notice that the coefficient is different from the previously computed value. In fact, for any given value of price, the arc elasticity coefficient will vary depending on the new price's distance from the original price.[4]

To adjust for the ambiguity inherent in the use of the arc formula, economists recommend the use of **point elasticity,** the second of the two ways to compute the elasticity coefficient. This method of computation is expressed as follows (we shall use the Greek letter $\epsilon$ when we are referring specifically to point elasticity):

$$\epsilon_p = \frac{dQ}{dP} \times \frac{P_1}{Q_1}$$

To compute point elasticity, we employ one of the economist's favorite mathematical devices, the derivative. Students familiar with elementary calculus, or who learned about it in the appendix to chapter 2, will have no difficulty with this expression. The key is that by assuming very small changes (actually, in calculus the change is "infinitesimally small") in price and quantity around some given level, we avoid the problem of the measure of elasticity differing based on the amount of change.

To find the derivative of $Q$ with respect to $P$ (i.e., $dQ/dP$), we need the algebraic expression of the demand equation. The equation implied in Table 4.1 is $Q = 18 - P$. The derivative of $Q$ with respect to $P$ is $-1$. Thus, the point elasticity coefficient at \$12 and 6 units is:

$$\epsilon_p = -1 \times \frac{12}{6}$$

$$= -2$$

---

[4]Interested readers should try computing the arc elasticity for changes between \$12 and \$9, between \$12 and \$8, and so on. They will find that the arc elasticity coefficient decreases as the change in price increases.

Actually, whenever the demand equation is linear, the point elasticity formula appears almost too simple because the first derivative of this equation with respect to $P$ is a constant. From a practical standpoint, there is really no need to use calculus for finding the point elasticity of a linear demand function. The first derivative $dQ/dP$ is the same as the (constant) slope of the demand line, $\Delta Q/\Delta P$. Thus, the point elasticity of a linear demand function can be expressed as:

$$\epsilon_p = \frac{\Delta Q}{\Delta P} \times \frac{P_1}{Q_1}$$

Of course, in cases where the demand curve is nonlinear, calculus must be employed to compute point elasticity. For example, consider the following demand curve.

$$Q = 100 - P^2$$

Assuming $P_1 = 5$, then $Q = 75$. Then the point elasticity is

$$\epsilon_p = -2P \times \frac{5}{75}$$

$$= -2(5) \times \frac{5}{75}$$

$$= \frac{-50}{75}$$

$$= -0.67$$

While it is very convenient to use linear demand curves, in reality the shape of the demand curve may be different. In the preceding illustration, price decreases will bring forth smaller increases in quantity. Such a demand curve would take on a concave shape. On the other hand, the demand curve may be convex. (The equation for such a curve would be, for instance, $Q = 10/p^2$.) An example of such a demand curve would occur when, for instance, some quantities would be purchased even at a very high price; in such a case, the demand curve would become almost vertical near the price axis.

So far we have discussed both linear and nonlinear demand curves whose elasticity changes as we move along the curve. However, we could encounter a demand curve whose elasticity is constant over its relevant range. Such a curve would be described by the following equation:

$$Q = aP^{-b}$$

a being a constant, and $-b$ representing the elasticity coefficient. This nonlinear equation can be converted to linear by expressing it in logarithms:

$$\log Q = \log a - b(\log P)$$

Such a demand curve would plot as a straight line on double log (or log-log) graph paper, and its elasticity $(-b)$ would be the same at any point on the curve. For example, let the demand equation be $Q = 100P^{-1.7}$. From this equation we can generate the following demand schedule:

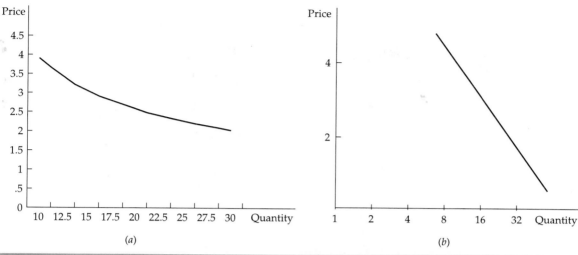

(a)    (b)

**FIGURE 4.1** Constant Elasticity

| Quantity | 10 | 12.5 | 15 | 17.5 | 20 | 22.5 | 25 | 27.5 | 30 |
|---|---|---|---|---|---|---|---|---|---|
| Price | 3.875 | 3.398 | 3.052 | 2.788 | 2.577 | 2.405 | 2.260 | 2.137 | 2.030 |

The two graphs in Figure 4.1 illustrate this demand curve. Figure 4.1a shows the curve using the normal arithmetic scales. In Figure 4.1b the scales are transformed into logarithms, and the demand curve plots as a straight line, signifying that the elasticity is constant throughout.[5]

The concept of point elasticity, as well as the use of calculus, will be found to be of particular importance in the next chapter, when the estimation of demand equations will be discussed. However, for now, using discrete changes and the arc elasticity coefficient would appear to be the more realistic thing for Henry Caulfield (and most other practical businesspeople) to do. He may not be familiar with calculus, but this certainly does not detract from his business acumen. He is dealing with a concrete problem: how much he will sell if he lowers his price by a discrete quantity (i.e., a certain number of cents). Arc elasticity is perfectly suitable for this problem.

We must realize, however, that in actual business situations, the effects of elasticity may be calculated in simple percentage terms, using the starting price and quantity as base numbers. For instance, a businessperson may state that it is expected that a 10 percent decrease in price will result in a 20 percent increase in quantity, implying that elasticity is −2; as an example, a decrease in price from $10 to $9 will increase quantity sold from 1,000 to 1,200 units. Of course, this would suggest that raising the price from $9 to $10 (an 11.1 percent

---

[5]We will encounter constant elasticity again in chapter 7 when we discuss the Cobb-Douglas production function.

increase) would decrease quantity from 1,200 to 1,000 units (a decrease of 16.7 percent). The elasticity in this case is $-1.5$. This asymmetry creates the same problem that we discussed earlier, which was solved by employing arc elasticity. In actual situations, however, we must be realistic and understand that a movement down along the demand curve may not bring about the same results as a movement up along the demand curve. And even more important, we should remember that mathematical refinement may not be the most essential. What is critical to the businessperson faced with a decision is whether a decrease in price will create sufficiently more quantity to improve profits.

Economists, in their neat way, have created categories of elasticity:

1. *Relative elasticity of demand:*

$$E_p > 1 \text{ (in absolute terms)}^6$$

This occurs when a 1 percent change in price causes a change in quantity demanded greater than 1 percent. The coefficient calculated earlier, 1.77, is a case of relatively elastic demand.

2. *Relative inelasticity of demand:*

$$0 < E_p < 1 \text{ (in absolute terms)}$$

Here the percentage change in price is greater than the corresponding change in quantity. For example, in Table 4.1 as price is lowered from 8 to 7, quantity rises from 10 to 11, giving a coefficient of 0.71.

3. *Unitary elasticity of demand:*

$$E_p = 1 \text{ (in absolute terms)}$$

A 1 percent change in price results in a 1 percent change in quantity in the opposite direction.

These are three common measures of elasticity. But there are also two limiting cases at the extremes of the elasticity scale:

1. *Perfect elasticity:*

$$E_p = \infty \text{ (in absolute terms)}$$

In this case, there is only one possible price, and at that price an unlimited quantity can be sold. The demand curve for $E_p = \infty$ is a horizontal line. We will encounter a demand curve with this shape later, when we discuss perfect competition.

2. *Perfect inelasticity:*

$$E_p = 0$$

Under this condition, the quantity demanded remains the same regardless of price. Such a demand curve may exist for certain products within a particular price range. An example may be the case of salt. Today's price of salt is about 39 cents per pound. If this price were to rise to 49 cents (a significant percentage increase),

---

[6]Since a demand curve has a negative slope, the coefficient of price elasticity will be negative. However, it is often more efficient to ignore the minus sign and to discuss the elasticity coefficient in absolute terms.

or fall to 29 cents (a significant percentage decrease), it is very doubtful that the consumption of salt would change at all.

Both of these extreme cases, although possible under certain conditions, will seldom be observed in real life. Still, the two limits should be well understood by every student of economics.

## THE DETERMINANTS OF ELASTICITY

Now that we have described what elasticity is, let us look into the reasons that the demand for some goods and services is elastic, whereas for others it is inelastic. In other words, what determines elasticity? As we look into this question, we must remember that the elasticity for a particular product may differ at different prices. Thus, although the demand elasticity for salt is very low—possibly zero—in the vicinity of its current price, it may not be so inelastic at $5 or $10 per pound.

It is often said—and many use this as a rule of thumb—that demand is inelastic for goods considered to be necessities, and it is elastic for luxury products. For example, the demand for furs, gems, and expensive automobiles is probably more elastic than the demand for milk, shoes, and electricity.

Unfortunately, the luxury/necessity dichotomy is ambiguous. Demand for expensive automobiles may be elastic, but if we consider the demand for Mercedes autos, we will probably find that within the prevailing price range, a movement up or down of several thousand dollars would make relatively little difference to those people who are in the market for this particular kind of car. The probable reason for such inconsistencies is relatively simple: One person's luxury is another person's necessity.

Several important factors that influence demand elasticity are outlined in Figure 4.2, and are discussed in the course of the next few pages.

Probably the most important determinant of elasticity is ease of substitution. This argument cuts both ways: If there are many good substitutes for the product in question, elasticity will be high; conversely, if this commodity is a good substitute for others, its demand elasticity will also be high. The broader the definition of a commodity, the lower its price elasticity will tend to be, since there is less opportunity for substitution. For instance, the demand elasticity for beer or bread will tend to be less than that for a particular brand of beer or for white bread. There are fewer substitutes for bread in general (particularly if we include in this definition other baked products, such as rolls and bagels) than there are for white bread or, even further, a specific brand of white bread. If the price of bread rises (relative to other products), we may consume somewhat less

> ► Ease of substitution
> ► Proportion of total expenditures
> ► Durability of product
>     ■ Possibility of postponing purchase
>     ■ Possibility of repair
>     ■ Used product market
> ► Length of time period

**FIGURE 4.2** Factors Affecting Demand Elasticity

bread than before. However, if the price of brand A white bread rises, while other white bread prices remain the same, then one would expect the quantity of brand A demanded to drop significantly as consumers switch to other brands.

Henry's convenience store was once the only game in town, so to speak. His nearest competitor was relatively distant. Now customers can substitute for Henry's merchandise by walking one block to the grocery store. And since Henry was most likely selling the same soft drink brands as his close competitor, the substitution effect is extremely strong.

Another major determinant of demand elasticity is the proportion of total expenditures spent on a product. Here we can go back to our salt example. The reason for the low elasticity of demand for salt is that the proportion of a consumer unit's (e.g., an individual, a family, and so on) income spent on salt is extremely small. A hefty price increase (e.g., from 39 cents to 49 cents per pound) would probably cause a shrug of the shoulder but would affect consumption of salt very little.

The spending on soft drinks by a typical individual or a family constitutes a larger portion of income than spending on salt. However, in most circumstances, spending on soda still represents a relatively small percentage of a family's income. Thus, we would not expect a change in price to affect the quantity of demand significantly. Still, in households where large quantities of soft drinks are consumed, a price change could have some effect on quantities sold, although it would probably require a substantial change in price to affect purchases significantly.

However, for a product such as a large appliance, the situation may be entirely different. To most families, a clothes washer represents more than a trivial expense, and a price change could have an important impact on purchases. Thus, we expect the demand elasticity for a clothes washer to be considerably greater than that for salt or soft drinks. There is another possible reason for the relatively high demand elasticity of a clothes washer. An appliance purchase may be postponable, since there is commonly a choice between buying and repairing. Faced with a higher purchase price, a consumer may choose to repair the old appliance.[7]

Despite the entry of new firms into Henry's market, the geographical size of the market is limited to a relatively small local area. As markets broaden, more and more product substitution becomes possible. Advances in modes of transportation and communication and decreases in their cost have increased the size of markets over time. Thus, the number of substitutes competing for consumers' dollars have increased. Markets have not only widened within national borders, they have more frequently crossed borders, increasing the importance of international trade. Although advances in transportation and communications have been instrumental, an extremely important trend toward freer trade through international trade agreements has undermined artificial barriers (tariffs and quotas). This has increased competition globally and, thus, has increased demand elasticities facing firms. The consumer is the ultimate beneficiary of such trends.

---

[7]The choice between buying and maintaining becomes even more pronounced for the purchase of an automobile. Here, of course, the price and the proportion of a person's income are considerably higher. In this case, there is a third possibility for the consumer: the purchase of a used car. Thus, recalling what we said about substitutability, we can say that the elasticity of demand for cars in general is lower than the demand elasticity for new cars. Of course, it is also possible to purchase a used washing machine, but there is no organized market for these as there is for cars.

## THE ELASTICITY OF DERIVED DEMAND

This section of the elasticity discussion represents a small digression, albeit an important one. So far we have discussed demand elasticity for a final product, that is, a product purchased for consumption, such as soft drinks, a clothes washer, salt, white bread or beer.

We are now going to look briefly at the demand for items that go into the production of a final commodity, such as materials, machinery, and labor. The demand for such components of a final product is called **derived demand.** In other words, these components are not demanded for their own sake but because there is a demand for the final product requiring them.

The great British economist Alfred Marshall, about whom previous references were made, described four principles governing the elasticity of the derived demand curve.[8] According to Marshall, the derived demand curve will be more inelastic:

1. The more essential is the component in question
2. The more inelastic is the demand curve for the final product
3. The smaller is the fraction of total cost going to this component
4. The more inelastic is the supply curve of cooperating factors

An example will illustrate this concept. Let us consider demand for residential housing (the final product) and the derived demand for one class of labor employed in construction, electricians. After all, the demand for electricians does not exist for its own sake but is due to the demand for housing. Probably all of Marshall's principles apply in this case, but two of them are particularly important. The first is essentiality: You just cannot build a house without employing electricians. Second, the cost of electrical work is probably a relatively small percentage of the entire cost of the house.

Suppose the electricians demand and obtain a substantial wage increase. A contractor may try to cut a few corners with regard to electrical work, but most of it must still be done. Thus, the employment of electricians will not decrease much. The implication here is that the elasticity of demand for electricians is low. Assume that the work of electricians involves 10 percent of the total cost of construction (this cost is probably overstated). A 10 percent wage increase for electricians represents a 1 percent increase in the total cost of construction. This small addition to the total cost will most likely not trigger a price increase and thus will not affect the employment of electricians to any significant extent. If we also consider the probability that the demand for housing is somewhat inelastic and that the supply elasticity of cooperating factors (i.e., other crafts employed on the project) is rather low, we can conclude that the demand elasticity for electricians is relatively low.

These conclusions tend to hold in the short run much more than in the long run. Over a short period of time, employment of electricians will not drop very much. However, given a longer adjustment period, elasticity of demand will rise as people find ways to substitute for the expensive factor, both on the production side and on the consumption side.[9]

---

[8]Alfred Marshall, *Principles of Economics,* 8th ed., Philadelphia: Porcupine Press, reprinted 1982, pp. 319–20.

[9]A very interesting analysis of short- and long-run elasticity effects on the economic power of labor unions can be found in Milton Friedman, *Price Theory: A Provisional Text,* Hawthorne, NY: Aldine, 1962, pp. 155–59.

## ELASTICITY IN THE SHORT RUN AND IN THE LONG RUN

A long-run demand curve will generally be more elastic than a short-run curve. Here "short run" is defined as an amount of time that does not permit a full adjustment by consumers to a price change. In the shortest of runs, no adjustment at all may be possible, and the demand curve over the relevant range may be almost perfectly inelastic. As the time period lengthens, consumers will find ways to adjust to the price change by using substitutes (if the price has risen), by substituting the good in question for another (if the price has fallen), or by shifting consumption to or from this particular product (i.e., by consuming more or less of other commodities).

A good example is the case of energy costs. When heating oil prices shot up in the 1970s, the immediate response by consumers was not great. As time passed, however, consumers adjusted their oil consumption. They became used to lower temperatures around the house and at work. They began to dress more warmly indoors. (Would this result in a higher demand for sweaters? We will look at this particular idea, known as cross-elasticity, later in this chapter.) Over a still longer period, consumers (including one of the authors) converted their homes from oil heat to gas heat. Not only was there conversion, but more newly built homes were equipped with gas heat. In addition, homes up for resale would advertise gas heating to attract potential buyers, and gas-heated homes commanded a premium price. How can we demonstrate this phenomenon graphically?

We can represent this relationship between the short run and the long run using a series of short-run demand curves intersected by the long-run demand curve, as illustrated in Figure 4.3. Each of the short-run demand curves ($D_{S1}$ to $D_{S5}$) is rather inelastic. Assume that the original position is point $a$, which represents a price of $P_1$ and a quantity of $Q_1$. If the price rises to $P_2$, consumers will, in the short run, decrease the quantity demanded to point $b$, at quantity $Q_2$, a relatively small difference in quantity. As time passes, during which consumers adjust to using substitutes, a new short-run demand curve, $D_{S2}$, will result, and demand will take place at point $c$, at $Q_3$, which represents a much larger decrease in quantity. Thus, we can connect points $a$ and $c$ to illus-

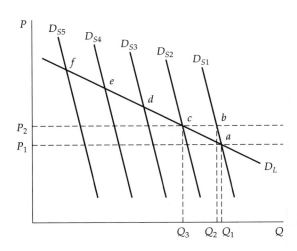

**FIGURE 4.3** Short-Run versus Long-Run Elasticity

trate the change in quantity demanded in the long run. Then, for constantly increasing prices, we can generate new short-run demand curves, $D_{S3}$, $D_{S4}$, and $D_{S5}$, and connect points *d, e,* and *f* to create a long-run demand curve.

In other words, in the short run, price changes increase or decrease the quantity demanded very little, up or down each of the short-run curves. However, over time, adjustment permits movement to another short-run curve, and a long-run demand curve is created. And the long-run demand curve formed from a point on each short-run curve is obviously far more elastic.

The lengths of the short run and the long run depend on how quickly an adjustment can be made. In the case of heating oil, the long run represented several years. But let us return to the case of Henry Caulfield. Once Henry cuts his price (if he decides to do so), the news will probably spread quite quickly around the community. The adjustment from the short run to the long run will probably be a matter of days, or weeks at most.

**MODULE 4B**
**MODULE 4C**

## DEMAND ELASTICITY AND REVENUE

Demand elasticity in itself is a rather interesting concept. However, if all it meant was the responsiveness of quantity to price change, it could be easily dismissed. But there is an aspect of demand elasticity that is terribly important to Henry Caulfield or any other businessperson in the throes of a pricing decision (in either direction).

There is a relationship between the price elasticity of demand and revenue received. A decrease in price would decrease revenue if nothing else were to happen. But since demand curves tend to be downward sloping, a decrease in price will increase the quantity purchased, and this will increase receipts. Which of the two tendencies is stronger? Remember that elasticity is defined as the percentage change in quantity divided by percentage change in price. If the former is larger (and, therefore, the coefficient will be greater than 1 in absolute terms), then the quantity effect is stronger and will more than offset the opposite price effect.

What does that entail for revenue? If price decreases and, in percentage terms, quantity rises more than price has dropped, then total revenue will increase. We summarize the rules describing the relationship between elasticity and total revenue (TR) in Table 4.2.

Let us return to the example of a straight-line demand curve and see what happens to revenue. You will remember that elasticity on such a curve decreases as we move

**TABLE 4.2  The Relationship between Price Elasticity and Total Revenue (TR)**

|  | Demand | | |
|---|---|---|---|
|  | *Elastic* | *Unitary Elastic* | *Inelastic* |
| Price increase | TR↓ | $\overline{\text{TR}}$ | TR↑ |
| Price decrease | TR↑ | $\overline{\text{TR}}$ | TR↓ |

| TABLE 4.3 | Demand Schedule Showing Total Revenue and Elasticity Values | | |
|---|---|---|---|
| *Price* | *Quantity* | *Arc Elasticity* | *Revenue* |
| 18 | 0 | | 0 |
| 17 | 1 | −35.0 | 17 |
| 16 | 2 | −11.0 | 32 |
| 15 | 3 | −6.2 | 45 |
| 14 | 4 | −4.1 | 56 |
| 13 | 5 | −3.0 | 65 |
| 12 | 6 | −2.3 | 72 |
| 11 | 7 | −1.8 | 77 |
| 10 | 8 | −1.4 | 80 |
| 9 | 9 | −1.1 | 81 |
| 8 | 10 | −0.9 | 80 |
| 7 | 11 | −0.7 | 77 |
| 6 | 12 | −0.6 | 72 |
| 5 | 13 | −0.4 | 65 |
| 4 | 14 | −0.3 | 56 |
| 3 | 15 | −0.2 | 45 |
| 2 | 16 | −0.2 | 32 |
| 1 | 17 | −0.1 | 17 |
| 0 | 18 | 0 | 0 |

down and to the right. Total revenue and arc elasticity at each price interval are calculated in Table 4.3. Figures 4.4 and 4.5 show graphically the relationship between elasticity and revenue. It is obvious that as price decreases, revenue rises when demand is elastic, falls when it is inelastic, and reaches its peak (i.e., is level) when elasticity of demand equals 1.

At this point we can formally introduce a term we will use a great deal throughout this book: **marginal revenue.** This concept can be defined as the change in total revenue as quantity changes by one unit.[10]

$$\Delta TR \div \Delta Q$$

Now we can add to the previous table a *marginal revenue* column. This is shown in Table 4.4.[11] Marginal revenue is positive as total revenue rises (and the demand curve is elastic). When total revenue reaches its peak (elasticity equals 1), marginal revenue reaches zero.[12]

---

[10]Readers with knowledge of calculus will see that we are dealing again with a derivative, $dTR/dQ$, the derivative of total revenue with respect to quantity.

[11]In this table only a subset of the prices and quantities is shown. This should be sufficient for an understanding of the concept of marginal revenue.

[12]Again, elementary calculus will be of help. As was shown in the appendix to chapter 2, where the mathematics of managerial economics was explained, if $dTR/dQ$ equals zero, we can solve for the maximum revenue.

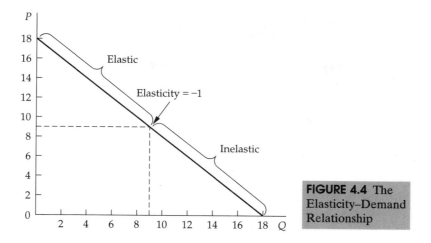

**FIGURE 4.4** The Elasticity–Demand Relationship

Figure 4.6 shows the mathematical and graphic relationship between the demand curve and marginal revenue (MR). It turns out that when the demand curve is described by a straight line, the marginal revenue curve is twice as steep as the demand curve. Under these circumstances, the marginal revenue curve can be drawn by bisecting the distance between the *Y*-axis (vertical axis) and the demand curve. Of course, at the point where marginal revenue crosses the *X*-axis (horizontal axis), the demand curve is unitarily elastic (and total revenue reaches its maximum).[13]

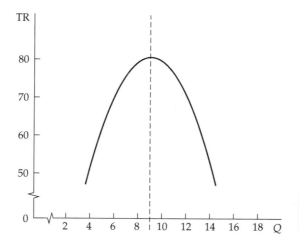

**FIGURE 4.5** The Effect of Elasticity on Total Revenue

---

[13]In mathematical terms, the path from the demand curve to the marginal revenue curve can be traced as follows:

| | |
|---|---|
| Demand curve: | $P = a - bQ$ |
| Total revenue: | $PQ = aQ - bQ^2$ |
| Marginal revenue: | $d\text{TR}/dQ = a - 2bQ$ |

| TABLE 4.4 | Demand Schedule with Marginal Revenue Added | | | |
|---|---|---|---|---|
| Price | Quantity | Total Revenue | Marginal Revenue | Arc Elasticity |
| 13 | 5 | 65 | 9 | −3.0 |
| 12 | 6 | 72 | 7 | −2.3 |
| 11 | 7 | 77 | 5 | −1.8 |
| 10 | 8 | 80 | 3 | −1.4 |
| 9 | 9 | 81 | 1 | −1.1 |
| 8 | 10 | 80 | −1 | −0.9 |
| - | 11 | 77 | −3 | −0.7 |

All of this is going through Henry's mind as he is deciding how to counteract his competition. For him to benefit at all from decreasing his price, the demand curve for soft drinks from his store must be elastic. A price cut leading to a decrease in revenue would be self-defeating (or even disastrous). But this is not his only concern. If Henry is a profit maximizer, then it is profit, not revenue, that concerns him. If the demand for his product is elastic, revenue will increase. But as he sells more units, his total cost will, of course, rise. Will the increase in revenue more than offset the additional cost? That is the question uppermost in Henry's mind. Unfortunately, we are not ready to answer at this point. We first have to study production functions and cost functions, and then link demand and cost in chapters 9 and 10.

## THE MATHEMATICS OF ELASTICITY

It is now time to apply some of the calculus you have learned. Point elasticity was mentioned earlier in this chapter and was said to require the use of differential calculus. The formula for point elasticity was given as

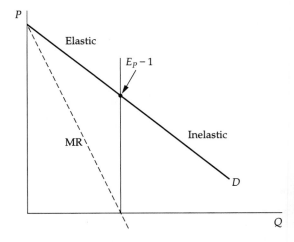

**FIGURE 4.6** The Relationship between Demand and Marginal Revenue

$$dQ/dP \times P/Q$$

For this formula to be employed, the demand curve has to be stated in the form of an equation. The equation for the demand curve represented in Table 4.1 is

$$Q = 18 - P$$

Therefore, $dQ/dP$ equals $-1$. This is the slope of the straight-line demand curve.

As stated in the discussion of arc elasticity, elasticity changes along the demand curve (except in the case of constant elasticity discussed previously). So does point elasticity, of course. Thus, the point at which elasticity is measured must be specified. For example, the point elasticity at $Q = 5$ and $P = 13$ is

$$-1 \times 13 \div 5 = -2.6$$

In Table 4.3 the arc elasticity was shown to be $-3$ in the interval between $P = 13$ and $P = 14$ and between $Q = 4$ and $Q = 5$, and $-2.3$ in the next interval. Point elasticity, as should be expected, is somewhere between the two arc elasticities. At $Q = 10$ and $P = 8$, the result is

$$-1 \times 8 \div 10 = -0.8$$

We are now in the inelastic section of the demand curve.

We also mentioned the use of calculus in reference to marginal revenue, which was defined as $d\text{TR}/dQ$. For this purpose, we will reverse our demand function so that quantity becomes the independent variable.

| Demand: | $P = 18 - Q$ |
|---|---|
| Total revenue: | $\text{TR} = PQ = 18Q - Q^2$ |
| Marginal revenue: | $d\text{TR}/dQ = 18 - 2Q$ |

At $Q = 5$ and $\text{TR} = 65$, marginal revenue is

$$18 - (2 \times 5) = 8$$

Again, since we are measuring TR at a point rather than over an interval, the result (MR $= 8$) will be somewhat different from the marginal revenue obtained in Table 4.4, where discrete differences were used in the calculation.

At $Q = 10$, $\text{MR} = 18 - (2 \times 10) = -2$. We are now in the area of negative marginal revenue (relative inelasticity on the demand curve), or at a quantity higher than the one that produces maximum revenue.

If we wish to find the point where revenue is maximized, we look for the point at which $\text{MR} = 0$. Thus,

$$18 - 2Q = 0$$
$$18 = 2Q$$
$$9 = Q$$

This result, again, is not the same but is very similar to the number found in Table 4.4, where discrete intervals rather than infinitely small differences were used.

## EMPIRICAL ELASTICITIES

In the next chapter we will explain how economists estimate demand curves and elasticities from industry and product data. But it may be of interest at this point to reinforce the meaning of price elasticity by mentioning briefly the results of some studies published in recent years.

A recent study of the demand for coffee estimated the price elasticity to be −0.2 in the short run and −0.33 in the long run.

A study of the demand for kitchen and other household appliances stated that the elasticity was −0.63. There is sensitivity to price change, but for a 1 percent change in price, quantity demanded will change only 0.63 percent. Demand is inelastic.

Meals (excluding alcoholic beverages) purchased at restaurants have a high demand elasticity of −2.27.

During the 1960s, Gregory Chow studied the demand for computers and concluded that price elasticity was −1.44. Here demand is relatively elastic, and quantity demanded will rise 1.44 percent for every 1 percent decrease in price.

A study of air-travel demand over the North Atlantic found price elasticity to be −1.2. Furthermore, the elasticity for first-class travel was, as one would expect, considerably lower than that for economy travel, −0.4 and −1.8, respectively.

The U.S. Department of Agriculture estimated the price elasticity of a number of farm products. Among them were potatoes at −0.27, butter at −0.62, and peaches at −1.49.

The price elasticity of beer has been estimated at −0.84 and of wine at −0.55.[14]

# The Cross-Elasticity of Demand

The previous discussion dealt with the influence of a price change on the quantity demanded of the product subject to the price change. **Cross-elasticity** deals with the impact (again, in percentage terms) on the quantity demanded of a particular product created by a price change in a related product (while everything else remains constant). What is the meaning of "related" products? In economics we talk of two types of relationships: **substitutes** and **complements.**

[14]A. A. Okunade, "Functional Forms and Habit Effects in the U.S. Demand for Coffee," *Applied Economics,* 24, (1992), pp. 1203–12; H. S. Houthakker and L. D. Taylor, *Consumer Demand in the United States: Analysis and Projections,* 2nd ed., Cambridge, MA: Harvard University Press, 1970, pp. 63, 81; G. C. Chow, "Technological Change and Demand for Computers," *American Economic Review,* December 1967, pp. 1117–30; J. M. Cigliano, "Price and Income Elasticities for Airline Travel," *Business Economics,* September 1980, pp. 17–21; Daniel B. Suits, "Agriculture," in Walter Adams and James Brock, *The Structure of American Industry,* 9th ed., Englewood Cliffs, N.J.: Prentice-Hall, 1994, p. 5; D. Heien and G. Pompelli, "The Demand for Alcoholic Beverages: Economic and Demographic Effects," *Southern Economic Journal,* January 1989, pp. 759–69.

In Henry Caulfield's case, we are dealing with substitutes. The sodas sold by the new grocery store are substitutes for those sold by Henry. They probably are the same products (same brands) but are sold by different suppliers, and one supplier can be considered a substitute for the other. Of course, there are also substitutes on Henry's own shelves—he stocks different brands of cola, for example.

Much of the time when we consider cross-elasticity we are dealing with similar products (not just different brands of the same product) in a more general sense. Thus, chicken and beef can be considered to be substitutes; a change in the price of chicken will have an effect on the consumption of beef. Other instances of substitutes come to mind easily: coffee and tea, butter and oleomargarine, aluminum and steel, and glass and plastic.

Complements are products that are consumed or used together. Henry sells potato chips, pretzels, and other "munchies" that are consumed together with soft drinks. Other cases of complementary products are peanut butter and jam, stereo sets and CD's, tennis rackets and tennis balls, and personal computers and floppy disks.

The definition of cross-elasticity is a measure of the percentage change in quantity demanded of product A resulting from a 1 percent change in the price of product B. The general equation can be written as

$$E_X = \frac{\Delta Q_A}{Q_A} \div \frac{\Delta P_B}{P_B}$$

Again, we run into a little problem regarding the denominator in this expression, and arc elasticity comes to the rescue:[15]

$$E_X = \frac{(Q_{2A} - Q_{1A})}{(Q_{2A} + Q_{1A})/2} \div \frac{(P_{2B} - P_{1B})}{(P_{2B} + P_{1B})/2}$$

What about cross-elasticity coefficients? First, let us look at the sign. A decrease in the price of the supermarket's soft drinks will cause the quantity of soft drinks sold by Caulfield to decrease. And, of course, if the supermarket raises prices, Caulfield's sales will rise. Thus, the sign of cross-elasticity for substitutes is positive. On the other hand, the coefficient sign for cross-elasticity of complements is negative. For instance, a decrease in the price of CD's could lead to increased purchases of stereo systems.

To measure the strength of the elasticity coefficient, we employ a more arbitrary definition than for demand elasticity. As a rule of thumb in business, two products are considered good substitutes or complements when the coefficient is larger than 0.5 (in absolute terms, since the coefficient for complements is negative).

---

[15]The following equation, obtained by arithmetic manipulation, may be easier for some readers:

$$E_X = \frac{(Q_{2A} - Q_{1A})}{(P_{2B} - P_{1B})} \times \frac{(P_{2B} + P_{1B})/2}{(Q_{2A} + Q_{2A})/2}$$

Or, if point elasticity is of interest, the use of calculus gives

$$\frac{dQ_A}{dP_B} \times \frac{P_B}{Q_A}$$

The calculations would proceed similarly to those for demand elasticity.

### EMPIRICAL ELASTICITIES

Again, it should be useful to briefly mention some study results:

> The cross-elasticity of Florida Indian River oranges and Florida interior oranges was shown to be between +1.16 and +1.56 in a study conducted in supermarkets in Grand Rapids, Michigan. The coefficients are very high and positive, signifying strong substitutability. On the other hand, the cross-elasticities between the two Florida oranges and California oranges were between +0.01 and +0.19; obviously, California oranges are not good substitutes for Florida oranges, and vice versa.

> A study of the residential demand for electric energy found the cross-elasticity with respect to prices of gas energy to be low, about +0.13.

> Aluminum's cross-elasticity of demand with respect to prices of steel was estimated at about +2.0, and even somewhat higher with respect to copper.

> The cross-elasticity of demand for beef with respect to pork prices was calculated to be about +0.25. With respect to prices of chicken, it was about +0.12. Both numbers indicate that the products are substitutes, but in this study, the elasticity coefficients were relatively low.[16]

## Income Elasticity

Before the arrival of his competitors, Henry Caulfield saw his sales grow, not only as the number of households in the area increased, but also as the household income level in the area rose. This represents quantity of sales as a function of (i.e., influenced by) consumers' income. As a measure of the sensitivity of this relationship, economists use the term **income elasticity of demand.** The general expression for this elasticity is

$$E_Y = \%\Delta Q \div \%\Delta Y$$

where $Y$ represents income.[17] The definition of income elasticity is a measure of the percentage change in quantity consumed resulting from a 1 percent change in income.

As before, we shall turn to arc elasticity for the actual calculation of income elasticity.[18]

---

[16]M. B. Goodwin, W. F. Chapman, Jr., and W. T. Hanley, *Competition between Florida and California Valencia Oranges in the Fruit Market,* Bulletin 704, Agricultural Station, Institute of Food and Agriculture Services, University of Florida, December 1965; R. Halvorsen, "Residential Demand for Electric Energy," *Review of Economics and Statistics,* 57 (February 1975), pp. 12–18; Merton J. Peck, *Market Control in the Aluminum Industry,* Cambridge, MA: Harvard University Press, 1961, pp. 31–34; Daniel B. Suits, "Agriculture," in Walter Adams, *The Structure of American Industry,* 8th ed., New York: Macmillan, 1990, p. 11.

[17]Again, in terms of calculus, this expression could be written as

$$\epsilon_y = \partial Q / \partial Y \times Y \div Q$$

This, of course, expresses the point elasticity. Also, as the reader can see partial derivatives have been used. As in all other cases of elasticity, the assumption is that only the effect of income on quantity is being measured, with all other possible variables in the demand relationship, (e.g., price, price of related products, interest rates, advertising) held constant.

[18]As in the case of the other elasticities, the equation can be rewritten in several different forms. The student can select the equation that is most convenient:

$$E_Y = [(Q_2 - Q_1) \div (Q_2 + Q_1)] \div [(Y_2 - Y_1) \div (Y_2 + Y_1)]$$
$$E_Y = [(Q_2 - Q_1) \div (Q_2 + Q_1)] \times [(Y_2 + Y_1) \div (Y_2 - Y_1)]$$
$$E_Y = [(Q_2 - Q_1) \div (Y_2 - Y_1)] \times [(Y_2 + Y_1) \div (Q_2 + Q_1)]$$

$$E_Y = \frac{(Q_2 - Q_1)}{(Q_2 + Q_1)/2} \div \frac{(Y_2 - Y_1)}{(Y_2 + Y_1)/2}$$

In the case of income elasticity, the coefficient can be either positive or negative. For most products, one would expect income elasticity to be positive. After all, given a rise in income, a person will spend more. Thus, when the coefficient is positive, we refer to the income elasticity as normal. (Later, this definition will be refined in relation to elasticities for "superior" commodities.)

The coefficient of +1 represents another dividing line. As income rises, people can increase consumption of products (and services) proportionally, less than proportionally, or more than proportionally to the income rise. If the expenditure on product A goes up by 10 percent when income goes up by 10 percent, then the income elasticity coefficient equals 1. That is, the proportion of the consumer's income spent on this commodity remains the same before and after the change in income.[19] Suppose a consumer's annual income is $30,000 and spending on clothing is $2,700 per year. If this person's income rises by 10 percent to $33,000, and he or she then spends $2,970 annually on clothing—also a 10 percent increase—the proportion of total income spent on clothing remains at 9 percent.

If the income elasticity coefficient is greater or less than 1, the fraction of income spent on the product in question changes more or less than proportionally with income. Products whose income elasticities exceed +1, taking larger portions of consumers' income as incomes increase, are often referred to as "superior" commodities.

Again, a brief review of empirical studies that have estimated income elasticities will illustrate this concept:

Short-run income elasticity for food expenditure has been estimated to be about 0.5 and the elasticity of restaurant meals 1.6. The results show that as incomes rise, spending for food eaten at home increases at a slower rate than income and, thus, takes up a smaller portion of income. On the other hand, the expenditure on restaurant meals rises substantially more rapidly as incomes rise, thus becoming a higher proportion of income.

The short-run income elasticity for jewelry and watches appeared to be 1.0; however, the elasticity in the long run was estimated at 1.6. Apparently, consumers take some time to adjust their demand.

The income elasticity of beer has been calculated at a relatively low 0.4.

The U.S. Department of Agriculture has estimated income elasticities for a group of farm products, among them eggs at 0.57, butter at 0.37, peaches at 1.43, and peas at 1.05.

The income elasticity for air travel between the United States and Europe was a relatively high 1.9.[20]

---

[19]Remember that, by definition, the price of the product remains the same. Thus, it does not matter whether we measure an increase in quantity of the product or in expenditures on the product.

[20]Houthakker and Taylor, *Consumer Demand in the United States,* pp. 62–63, 72. Actually, this study measured the relationship between spending on food and total expenditures, rather than income. Since the proportion of total expenses to income is relatively stable, this substitution does not significantly change results. Kenneth G. Elzinga, "The Beer Industry," in Walter Adams and James Brock, *The Structure of American Industry,* p. 146; Daniel B. Suits, "Agriculture," in Walter Adams and James Brock, *The Structure of American Industry,* p. 5; J. M. Cigliano, "Price and Income Elasticities for Airline Travel," *Business Economics,* September 1980, pp. 17–21.

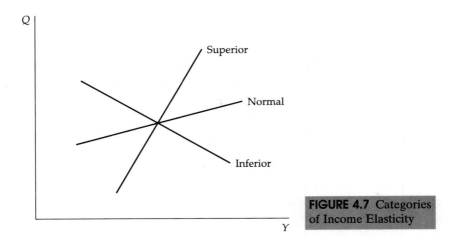

**FIGURE 4.7** Categories of Income Elasticity

It is possible that the income elasticity coefficient will be less than zero. This would occur if the quantity bought of (or the expenditure on) a product were to decrease absolutely as the result of an increase in income. Although such a result may at first seem implausible, a little reflection will show that such a condition may very well exist. Some products will be demanded by consumers whose incomes are low: but as incomes rise, and consumers feel "better off," they will shift consumption to goods more commensurate with their new economic status. What types of products would be disfavored? The usual examples that economists use are potatoes, pork and beans, and canned luncheon meat.[21] Commodities of this type are usually referred to as **inferior goods.**

So, let us now recapitulate the concept of income elasticity by specifying three categories:

Income elasticity $> 1$: superior goods
Income elasticity $\geq 0$, and $\leq 1$: normal goods
Income elasticity $< 0$: inferior goods

We can depict these situations graphically as shown in Figure 4.7.

## Other Elasticity Measures

We have covered the three most common elasticity measures, but there are others. Elasticity is encountered every time a change in some variable affects quantities. For instance, one thing that Henry could do to counteract his competition is to advertise his

---

[21]With apologies to consumers at all income levels who happen to like these particular items.

products. He might speculate how an increase in advertising expenses would affect his total sales. Thus, **advertising elasticity** can be defined as the percentage change in quantity relative to a 1 percent change in advertising expenses.

Another variable that could have a significant impact on demand—particularly for durable goods—is the interest rate. No one would deny that shifts in mortgage interest rates can cause significant changes in the demand for residential (or nonresidential) construction. Also, the special loan rates offered by automobile manufacturers to customers beginning in the 1980s appear to stimulate car sales, and sales tend to sag when the low rates are terminated.

Elasticity could also be calculated in relation to population size. What is the effect on sales of changes in population? For instance, we could calculate the elasticity of demand for baby carriages as a result of population increases due to the baby boom (and the children of the baby boomers). Or we could investigate the effect of a change in the number of adults (population above the age of 18) on the annual purchases of automobiles (again, as always, holding all other variables constant). And, of course, in Henry Caulfield's case, changes in his community's population will affect his sales. The degree to which sales will be affected is measured by elasticity.

These are just a few examples of possible elasticity calculations. In the next chapter, when we discuss demand estimation, we will see that economists use many variables to explain changes in demand. Although price elasticity, cross-elasticity, and income elasticity are the ones most frequently measured, elasticities can be obtained for a large variety of variables.

## Elasticity of Supply

Before we close this chapter, it will be useful to devote a little space to the **price elasticity of supply.** The price elasticity of supply measures the percentage change in quantity supplied as a result of a 1 percent change in price. In other words, this elasticity is a measure of the responsiveness of quantities produced by suppliers to a change in price. In the previous chapter, we developed a supply schedule and a supply curve, and we found that the curve slopes upward and to the right. Thus, the arc coefficient of supply elasticity,

$$E_S = \frac{(Q_2 - Q_1)}{(Q_2 + Q_1)/2} \div \frac{(P_2 - P_1)}{(P_2 + P_1)/2}$$

is a positive number: quantity and price move in the same direction.

The interpretation of the coefficient is the same as for the case of demand elasticity. The higher the coefficient, the more quantity supplied will change (in percentage terms) in response to a change in price.

## THE SOLUTION

Henry Caulfield is no stranger to the economic concept of price elasticity. He has a bachelor's degree in business administration and was doing well as the regional manager of a large supermarket chain when he decided to leave his job and open his own business. Indeed, it was his understanding of price elasticity that prompted him to reduce the soft drink prices as a way of competing against the two new stores in his area. When he had offered special discounts on soft drinks in the past, he noticed that people were very responsive. In fact, Henry had kept a record of the relationship between price and sales, a part of which is shown in Table 4.5. The "special" price was offered as part of the store's "Fourth of July Celebration" sale.

The data indicate an elastic demand for soft drinks at Henry's store. When demand is price elastic, a reduction in price causes total revenue to increase. This was exactly what had happened when Henry had offered his "Fourth of July" celebration special. He was now puzzled because the permanent price reduction did not seem to be having the same positive effect on his total revenue.

**TABLE 4.5   Sales Data for 2-Liter Bottles of Soft Drinks**

| Average Price | Average Weekly Sales | Total Revenue |
|---|---|---|
| Regular Price: $1.89 | 1,050 | $1,985 |
| Special Price: $.89 | 2,450 | 2,181 |

Then, in a flash, it dawned on him. One of the most important aspects of demand elasticity—and, for that matter, of any aspect of economic analysis—is the assumption that certain factors are held constant in the examination of the impact of one variable on another. In this case, it was assumed that other factors besides price did not have an impact (or at least not much of an impact) on quantity when Henry had offered the special holiday price for his soft drink. What other factors besides price might now be taken into account?

To begin with, last summer Henry did not have any close competitors. Therefore, when he offered his discount, there was no other store nearby to match this price reduction. Obviously, the two new stores were not going to stand by idly watching potential customers go to Henry because he had the lowest price for soft drinks. Therefore, the demand for soft drinks at Henry's store was much less elastic than he thought because he was unable to take away their business. To make matters worse, this "price war" among the three stores might have actually reduced their total soft drink revenues. This is because when all three stores dropped their price, they might well have brought the quantity demanded into the inelastic range of their combined demand curves. (We assume here that the three stores constitute the entire local market for soft drinks.)

But regardless of the reaction of his competitors and the possible impact that all of their price cuts might

*(Continued)*

have had on the degree of price elasticity, there was one simple fact that Henry had completely overlooked. Last year's discount took place in summer, a time when the seasonal demand for this product increases anyway. Thus, when Henry cut the price, the demand for his product had already started to increase and his increased revenue may have been caused by the fact that during this time the demand curve was moving to the right.

One final factor had to be considered. In the past, all of his discounts on soft drinks were "specials" and, therefore, temporary in nature. Consumers knew that they had to take advantage of these specials during a designated period. Since they now realized that the price of soft drinks in Henry's store was permanently lowered, they were in no hurry to buy the product. In other words, Henry had failed to take "future expectations" into account.

Thus, to be able to measure elasticity, Henry would have to separate the effects on unit sales of price from all the other nonprice determinants of demand. Since he had not done this, he had overestimated the degree of responsiveness by his customers to his price reduction. As a result, unfortunately, the reduction in soft drink

prices did not provide a solution for Henry. But at least he now understood why it did not.[22] In addition, this analysis reminded Henry never to take for granted that "other factors remain constant." In the real world, conditions are changing all the time, and it is important to factor these changes into the analysis. As a small consolation, Henry realized that the entry of additional suppliers into the market was all part of the economics of running a successful business. After all, if people did not think he was making any money, they would probably not be as willing to start a competing enterprise.

_____

[22]Our example may help you to understand an apparent paradox in the pricing of soft drinks in supermarkets. Very often, substantial discounts on soft drinks are offered at all supermarkets during the summer (i.e., "summer specials"). These discounts either may be offered by the soft drink companies to the supermarkets, which then pass them on to customers, or they may be initiated by the supermarkets themselves. Why should they do this at a time when demand is high? After all, economic theory states that an increase in demand causes prices to rise, other factors held constant. What probably happens is that one of the major soft drink companies decides to take market share away from the other major producers by cutting its price. The others quickly follow. The same is true among supermarkets. These price wars can and do occur at any time during the year. It is just that a "summer special" is a good reason to have a sale.

## Summary

This chapter has dealt with the important concept of elasticity. In the most general terms, elasticity is defined as the sensitivity of one variable to another or, more specifically, the percentage change in one variable caused by a 1 percent change in another. Several forms of elasticity connected with the demand curve were discussed.

The first was price elasticity of demand: the percentage change in the quantity demanded of a product caused by a percentage change in its own price. Since demand curves slope downward and to the right, the coefficient of price elasticity is negative. If the coefficient is less than $-1$ (or greater than 1 in absolute terms), demand is said to be elastic. On the other hand, the elasticity coefficient can indicate inelasticity or unitary elasticity.

Elasticity is also tied to total revenue. When demand is elastic, revenue rises as quantity demanded increases; revenue reaches its peak at the point of unitary elasticity and descends as quantity rises on the demand curve's inelastic sector. From the concept of revenue, we developed marginal revenue as the change in revenue when quantity changes by one unit. Marginal revenue is positive at quantities where demand is elastic and becomes negative when the demand curve becomes inelastic.

Next, we explained cross-elasticity, the relationship between the demand for one product and the price of another. Products can be substitutes, and their cross-elasticity is then positive; cross-elasticity is negative for products that are complements.

The third major elasticity concept, income elasticity, measures the sensitivity of demand for a product to changes in the income of the population. Goods and services were defined as superior, normal, and inferior, depending on the responsiveness of spending on a product relative to percentage changes in income.

The examples calculated in the chapter used the method of arc elasticity, which measures changes in both variables over discrete intervals, rather than point elasticity, which deals with change over an infinitely small interval and consequently may require knowledge of elementary calculus.

Several other subtopics appeared in this chapter:

Other elasticities, such as advertising and interest elasticity.

Derived demand, which is the demand for inputs to a final product, and the price elasticity of derived demand.

Supply elasticity, the measure of the sensitivity of quantities produced to the price charged by the producers.

In the next chapter, which discusses methods of estimating demand functions, elasticity concepts will be employed again, and they will reappear in various guises in many of the chapters that follow.

## Important Concepts

**Advertising elasticity:** The percentage change in quantity demanded caused by a 1 percent change in advertising expenses. (p. 125)

**Arc elasticity:** Elasticity which is measured over a discrete interval of a demand (or a supply) curve. (p. 105)

**Coefficient of elasticity:** The percentage change in one variable divided by the percentage change in the other variable. (p. 104)

**Complementary good:** A product consumed in conjunction with another. Two goods are complementary if the quantity demanded of one increases when the price of the other decreases. (p. 120)

**Cross-elasticity:** The percentage change in the quantity consumed of one product as a result of a 1 percent change in the price of a related product. (p. 120)

**Derived demand:** The demand for products or factors that are not directly consumed but go into the production of a final product. The demand for such a product or factor exists because there is demand for the final product. (p. 113)

**Elasticity:** The sensitivity of one variable to another or, more precisely, the percentage change in one variable relative to a percentage change in another. (p. 104)

**Income elasticity:** The percentage change in quantity demanded caused by a 1 percent change in income. (p. 122)

**Inferior good:** A product whose consumption decreases as income increases (i.e., its income elasticity is negative). (p. 124)

**Marginal revenue:** The change in total revenue resulting from changing quantity by one unit. (p. 116)

**Point elasticity:** Elasticity measured at a given point of a demand (or a supply) curve. (p. 107)

**Price elasticity of demand:** The percentage change in quantity demanded caused by a 1 percent change in price. (p. 104)

**Price elasticity of supply:** The percentage change in quantity supplied as a result of a 1 percent change in price. (p. 125)

**Substitute good:** A product that is similar to another and can be consumed in place of it. Two goods are substitutes if the quantity consumed of one increases when the price of the other increases. (p. 120)

## Questions

1. State the general meaning of *elasticity* as it applies to economics. Define the *price elasticity of demand*.
2. Explain the difference between *point elasticity* and *arc elasticity*. What problem can arise in the calculation of the latter, and how is it usually dealt with? In actual business situations, would you expect arc elasticity to be the more useful concept? Why or why not?
3. It has often been said that craft unions (electricians, carpenters, etc.) possess considerably greater power to raise wages than do industrial unions (automobile workers, steel workers, and so on). How would you explain this phenomenon in terms of demand elasticity?
4. Discuss the relative price elasticity of the following products:
   a. Mayonnaise
   b. A specific brand of mayonnaise
   c. Chevrolet automobiles
   d. Jaguar automobiles
   e. Washing machines
   f. Air travel (vacation)
   g. Beer
   h. Diamond rings
5. What would you expect to happen to spending on food at home and spending on food in restaurants during a decline in economic activity? How would income elasticity of demand help explain these changes?
6. Would you expect the cross-elasticity coefficients between each of the following pairs of products to be positive or negative? Why?
   a. Personal computers and software
   b. Electricity and natural gas
   c. Apples and oranges
   d. Bread and VCRs
7. Why is it unlikely that a firm would sell at a price and quantity where its demand curve is price inelastic?
8. Which products would exhibit a higher elasticity with respect to interest rates, automobiles or small appliances? Why?
9. The immediate effect of gasoline price increases in the aftermath of the Persian Gulf crisis in August 1990 on gasoline consumption was not very significant. Would you expect the consumption of gasoline to be more severely affected if these higher prices remained in effect for a year or more? Why or why not?
10. In December 1990, the federal tax on gasoline increased by 5 cents per gallon. Do you think that such an increase, reflected in the price of gasoline, would have a significant impact on gasoline consumption?

11. Why do you think that whenever governments (federal and state) wish to increase revenues, they usually propose an increase in taxes on cigarettes and alcohol?
12. Could a straight-line demand curve ever have the same elasticity on all of its points?
13. If a demand curve facing a firm is horizontal or nearly so, what does it say about this firm's competition?
14. A company faced by an elastic demand curve will always benefit by decreasing price. True or false? Explain.
15. Discuss the income elasticities of the following consumer products:
    a. Margarine
    b. Fine jewelry
    c. Living room furniture
    d. Whole lobsters
16. If the income elasticity of tomatoes is estimated to approximate +.25, what would you expect to happen to the consumption of tomatoes as personal income rises?

## Problems

1. The Acme Paper Company lowers its price of envelopes (1,000 count) from $6 to $5.40. If its sales increase by 20 percent following the price decrease, what is the elasticity coefficient?
2. The demand function for a cola-type soft drink in general is $Q = 20 - 2P$, where $Q$ stands for quantity and $P$ stands for price.
    a. Calculate point elasticities at prices of 5 and 9. Is the demand curve elastic or inelastic at these points?
    b. Calculate arc elasticity at the interval between $P = 5$ and $P = 6$.
    c. At which price would a change in price and quantity result in approximately no change in total revenue? Why?
3. The equation for a demand curve has been estimated to be $Q = 100 - 10P + 0.5Y$ where $Q$ is quantity, $P$ is price, and $Y$ is income. Assume that $P = 7$ and $Y = 50$.
    a. Interpret the equation.
    b. At a price of 7, what is price elasticity?
    c. At an income level of 50, what is income elasticity?
    d. Now assume that income is 70. What is the price elasticity at $P = 8$?
4. Mr. Smith has the following demand equation for a certain product: $Q = 30 - 2P$.
    a. At a price of $7, what is the point elasticity?
    b. Between prices of $5 and $6, what is the arc elasticity?
    c. If the market is made up of 100 individuals with demand curves identical to Mr. Smith's, what will be the point and arc elasticity for the conditions specified in parts *a* and *b?*
5. The Teenager Company makes and sells skateboards at an average price of $70 each. Over the past year they sold 4,000 of these skateboards. The company believes that the price elasticity for this product is about −2.5. If it decreases the price to $63, what should be the quantity sold? Will revenue increase? Why?
6. The ABC Company manufactures AM/FM clock radios and sells on average 3,000 units monthly at $25 each to retail stores. Its closest competitor produces a similar type of radio that sells for $28.
    a. If the demand for ABC's product has an elasticity coefficient of −3, how much will it sell per month if the price is lowered to $22?
    b. The competitor decreases its price to $24. If cross-elasticity between the two radios is 0.3, what will ABC's monthly sales be?

7. The Mesa Redbirds football team plays in a stadium with a seating capacity of 80,000. However, during the past season, attendance averaged only 50,000. The average ticket price was $30. If price elasticity is $-4$, what price would the team have to charge in order to fill the stadium? If the price were to be decreased to $27 and the average attendance increased to 60,000, what is the price elasticity?

8. The Efficient Software Store had been selling a spreadsheet program at a rate of 100 per month and a graphics program at the rate of 50 per month. In September 1990, Efficient's supplier lowered the price for the spreadsheet program, and Efficient passed on the savings to customers by lowering its retail price from $400 to $350. The store manager then noticed that not only had sales of the spreadsheet program risen to 120, but the sales of the graphics program increased to 56 per month. Explain what has happened. Use both arc price elasticity and arc cross-elasticity measures in your answer.

9. Given the demand equation $Q = 1,500 - 200P$, calculate all the numbers necessary to fill in the following table:

| P | Q | Elasticity Point | Elasticity Arc | Total Revenue | Marginal Revenue |
|---|---|---|---|---|---|
| $7.00 | | | | | |
| 6.50 | | | | | |
| 6.00 | | | | | |
| 5.50 | | | | | |
| 5.00 | | | | | |
| 4.50 | | | | | |
| 4.00 | | | | | |
| 3.50 | | | | | |
| 3.00 | | | | | |
| 2.50 | | | | | |

10. Would you expect cross-elasticity between the following pairs of products to be positive, negative, or zero?
    a. Television sets and VCRs
    b. Rye bread and whole-wheat bread
    c. Construction of residential housing and furniture
    d. Breakfast cereal and men's shirts
    Explain the relationship between each pair of products.

11. According to Houthakker and Taylor, the price elasticity of shoes in the United States is 0.7, and the income elasticity is 0.9.
    a. Would you suggest that the Brown Shoe Company cut its prices to increase its revenue?
    b. What would be expected to happen to the total quantity of shoes sold in the United States if incomes rise by 10 percent?

12. A book store opens across the street from the University Book Store (UBS). The new store carries the same textbooks but offers a price 20 percent lower than UBS. If the cross-elasticity is estimated to be 1.5, and UBS does not respond to its competition, how much of its sales is it going to lose?

13. A local supermarket lowers the price of its vanilla ice cream from $3.50 per half gallon to $3. Vanilla ice cream (unit) sales increase by 20 percent. The store manager notices that the (unit) sales of chocolate syrup increase by 10 percent.
    a. What is the price elasticity coefficient of vanilla ice cream?
    b. Why have the sales of chocolate syrup increased, and how would you measure the effect?
    c. Overall, do you think that the new pricing policy was beneficial for the supermarket?

14. The Compute Company store has been selling its special word processing software, Aceword, during the last ten months. Below are shown monthly sales and the price for Aceword. Also shown are the prices for a competitive software, Goodwrite, and estimates of monthly family income. Calculate all the appropriate elasticities, keeping in mind that you can calculate an elasticity measure only when all other factors do not change.

| Month | Price Aceword | Quantity Aceword | Family Income | Price Goodwrite |
|-------|---------------|------------------|---------------|-----------------|
| 1     | 120           | 200              | 4000          | 130             |
| 2     | 120           | 210              | 4000          | 145             |
| 3     | 120           | 220              | 4200          | 145             |
| 4     | 110           | 240              | 4200          | 145             |
| 5     | 114           | 230              | 4200          | 145             |
| 6     | 115           | 215              | 4200          | 125             |
| 7     | 115           | 220              | 4400          | 125             |
| 8     | 105           | 230              | 4400          | 125             |
| 9     | 105           | 235              | 4600          | 125             |
| 10    | 105           | 220              | 4600          | 115             |

15. The demand curve for product $X$ is given as $Q = 2000 - 20P$.
    a. How many units will be sold at $10?
    b. At what price would 2,000 units be sold? 0 units? 1,500?
    c. Write equations for total revenue and marginal revenue (in terms of $Q$).
    d. What will be the total revenue at a price of $70? What will be the marginal revenue?
    e. What is the point elasticity at a price of $70?
    f. If price were to decrease to $60, what would total revenue, marginal revenue, and point elasticity be now?
    g. At what price would elasticity be unitary?

# Take It to the Net

We invite you to visit the Keat/Young page on the Prentice Hall Web site at:

**http://www.prenhall.com/keat**

for additional resources.

## Appendix 4A

## Applications of Supply and Demand

The last two chapters laid the foundation for the student's knowledge of supply and demand and elasticity. Knowing these elements is essential for any further study of economics and is a necessary prerequisite for all the chapters that follow.

Before we discuss the various building blocks that will complete the study of managerial economics, this appendix will endeavor to reinforce the concepts of supply and demand and of elasticity in two ways:

1. Some specific applications of supply and demand will be discussed, including the effects of price controls, excise taxes, and agricultural policies.
2. Various actual situations as reported in the press will be introduced and discussed, and it will be shown that the materials we have just learned can be applied to analyze these situations.

# Interference with the Price Mechanism

In chapter 3, we discussed the movement toward equilibrium in both the short and long run. A change in demand or supply will call forth actions that will cause equilibrium to occur at a new supply-demand intersection. It was shown that in the short run, price changes will eliminate shortages or surpluses. In the long run, resources in the economy shift from the production of one product to another in response to changes in demand. The shift away from one equilibrium and the move to a new equilibrium will proceed when these movements are permitted to occur freely and are not impeded by any outside interference. Thus, when the supply of corn decreased and price rose so the market cleared at this new price—that is, at the new intersection of supply and demand—there was nothing inhibiting this change from taking place.

However, with present economic institutions, free movement of prices is not always allowed. At least three times in the last 50 years,[23] price controls were imposed in the United States. Prices on various products were set (or fixed at existing levels), and these products could not be sold at prices higher than those prescribed by government. Such a policy is usually referred to as setting a *price ceiling.* If the price ceiling for a product is set at the prevailing equilibrium level, then the ceiling will have no effect (until a change in circumstances dictated a higher price). But if the price were set below the equilibrium price,[24] then, as explained in chapter 3, a shortage would result. In Figure 4A.1, the equilibrium price is $P_0$, and the quantity sold (and clearing the market) at this price is $Q_0$. If for some reason the price winds up at $P_1$ under free-market conditions (i.e., no price controls), the price will rise until the equilibrium price ($P_0$) is again reached. But if the price is prescribed to be no higher than $P_1$,[25] the

---

[23]During World War II, the Korean War, and again in 1971.

[24]It is obvious that a ceiling set above the equilibrium price would be meaningless.

[25]Price ceilings can be enforced by the government imposing fines or even prison sentences on violators. Such punishment would have appeared rather lenient to some of our ancestors. During the times of price controls in ancient Egypt, Greece, and Rome, the death sentence was the penalty for breaking price control laws. The edict of Diocletian in A.D. 301 imposed the death sentence on those selling at prices higher than decreed, as well as on those buying at such prices (Robert L. Schuettinger and Eamonn F. Butler, *Forty Centuries of Wage and Price Controls,* Washington, DC: Heritage Foundation 1979, p. 23).

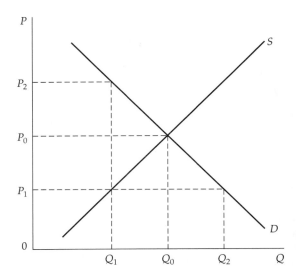

**FIGURE 4A.1** The Effect of a Price Ceiling on Supply and Demand

movement toward equilibrium will not take place. Only $Q_1$ will be supplied while $Q_2$ is demanded at the lower price, so a shortage of magnitude $Q_1 - Q_2$ will be established. Thus, only the consumers in the interval $0 - Q_1$ will be able to buy this particular product. What will be the result of this forced disequilibrium? Possibly consumers will try to shift their demand to other products, causing a pressure on the other products' prices. And if these products are also price controlled, shortages of these other goods will occur.

There is another possible result. Since only $Q_1$ units of the product will be supplied at price $P_1$, these units could be purchased at price $P_2$ along the demand curve. Consumers would be willing to pay $P_2$, a price higher than the equilibrium price, $P_0$, for the limited quantity $Q_1$. Thus, a strong pressure on the price will be exerted, and somewhere in this process the difference between $P_1$ and $P_2$ will be paid to the suppliers.

An example of such a case was the price of automobiles after World War II. A ceiling price below the price level that would have cleared the market was imposed on new cars. This low price caused automobile manufacturers to limit their production. However, consumers were paying high prices for these cars in the way of a dealer's premium. They may also have received lower trade-in prices on their old automobiles or may have bought their new car as a "used" one, since second-hand cars were not price controlled. The price they actually paid was indeed higher than it could have been if the manufacturers had charged a higher list price.[26] Similarly, where rent ceilings have been imposed many people end up paying a bonus to the superintendent or to a rental agent.

Another example precedes those just discussed by more than 150 years. During the Revolutionary War, the legislature of Pennsylvania imposed limits on prices of goods

---

[26]Milton Friedman, *Price Theory: A Provisional Text,* Hawthorne, NY: Aldine 1962, p. 18.

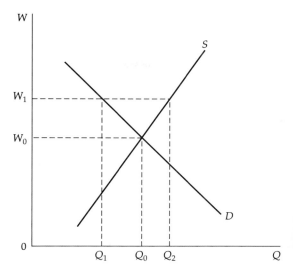

**FIGURE 4A.2** The Effect of a Price Floor on Supply and Demand

sold to the military and was thus instrumental in creating extreme shortages of food for George Washington's army at Valley Forge.[27]

On the other side of the price control coin are price floors. In such cases, a price is established below which the product or service may not be sold. An excellent example of a price floor is the legal minimum wage. Employers are not allowed to pay their workers less than the established minimum, and must, therefore, deal with the disturbance to a price equilibrium.[28]

If the equilibrium wage (e.g., per hour) for some unskilled work were to be at level $W_0$ as shown in Figure 4A.2, but the law stated that a wage lower than $W_1$ is illegal, then a surplus of labor $Q_1 - Q_2$ would exist. In the absence of the minimum wage law, wages would drop to $W_0$, and the quantity supplied and demanded of labor would meet at $Q_0$. Thus, all workers offering themselves for employment at that wage would be hired.

But if the wage cannot fall below $W_1$, what will happen? The unemployed will look for work elsewhere. If the minimum wage prevails in all types of employment, they would not be able to find work. However, there are still some forms of employment in the United States that are not covered by law. And, a person can become self-employed, in which case minimum wages do not apply.[29]

The effect of increases in minimum wages on employment has been widely studied by economists for many years. In the past, most economists agreed that increases in minimum wages had a negative effect on employment, especially in the case of young and unskilled workers. Unemployment has generally been the highest among teenage

---

[27]Schuettinger and Butler, *Forty Centuries,* p. 41.
[28]Wages are, of course, the price of labor, so it is quite correct to discuss minimum wages under the topic of price floors.
[29]And, at the risk of sounding facetious, the extreme case of self-employment is unemployment.

workers, many of whom have dropped out of school and acquired few if any skills.[30] However, several recent studies have questioned the traditional findings, concluding that minimum wage increases have not necessarily led to decreased employment.[31] While the new studies cast doubt on the traditional hypothesis, it is much too early to dismiss it. Much additional research is necessary to clarify the effect that increases in minimum wages have on employment.[32]

Several additional points should be made regarding the impact of minimum wages. Even if an increase in the minimum does have a negative effect on employment, workers who remain employed at the higher wage will benefit. The workers can be found in the interval $0 - Q_1$.[33] Second, the short-run effects of an increased legal minimum are probably stronger than the long-run effects. As time passes, the wage levels in the economy will rise (either due to inflation or in real terms), and at some point the minimum wage may approach the free-market equilibrium wage. A third point also appears worth mentioning. Because an increase in the minimum wage must be passed by the legislature (the U.S. Congress in the case of a federal minimum), it is a part of the political process. Legislators may be reluctant to enact a minimum wage increase if it would increase unemployment. Thus, such legislation may be passed only if it would appear to have a minimal effect.

Another example of government controls is in the area of agriculture. We will discuss this subject later.

## The Incidence of Taxes

From the viewpoint of the economics of the firm, one important example of applied analysis using supply and demand curves and elasticities is in the area of the incidence or effect of excise taxes on the prices and quantities of products.

An excise tax is a tax imposed as a specific amount per unit of product. It is also sometimes referred to as a specific tax, as compared to a sales tax, which is levied as a percent of the price of the product or service. The federal excise tax on gasoline as of

---

[30]Among many studies, see, for instance, C. Brown, C. Gilroy, and A. Kohen, "The Effect of the Minimum Wage on Employment and Unemployment," *Journal of Economic Literature,* 20 (June 1982), pp. 487–528; B. S. Frey, W. Pommerehne, F. Schneider, and G. Gilbert, "Consensus and Dissension among Economists: An Empirical Inquiry," *American Economic Review,* 74 (December 1984), pp. 986–94; T. G. Moore, "The Effect of Minimum Wages on Teenage Unemployment Rates," *Journal of Political Economy,* July/August 1971, pp. 897–902. A more recent study that finds negative effects on employment is D. Deere, K. M. Murphy, and F. Welch, "Employment and the 1990–1991 Minimum Wage Hike," *American Economic Review Papers and Proceedings,* 85 (May 1995), pp. 232–37.

[31]See, for instance, D. Card, and A. B. Krueger, "Minimum Wages and Employment: A Case Study of the Fast-Food Industry in New Jersey and Pennsylvania," *American Economic Review,* 84 (September 1994), pp. 772–84; D. Card, "Do Minimum Wages Reduce Employment? A Case Study of California, 1987–89," *Industrial and Labor Relations Review,* 46 (October 1992), pp. 38–54; L. F. Katz and A. B. Krueger, "The Effect of the Minimum Wage on the Fast-Food Industry, *Industrial and Labor Relations Review,* 46 (October 1992), pp. 6–21.

[32]A good summary of the recent research and an analysis of various hypotheses regarding the effect of minimum wages on employment is M. Zavodny, "Why Minimum Wage Hikes May Not Reduce Employment," *Economic Review,* Federal Reserve Bank of Atlanta, 83, 2 (second quarter 1998), pp. 18–28.

[33]It is an interesting decision, implicitly made by the U.S. Congress when it passes a law increasing the minimum wage, whether the overall welfare of the country will be increased if some part of the labor force has its wages improved while another part has its income lowered.

**TABLE 4A.1  Demand and Supply and Tax Incidence**

| Unit Price | Quantity Demanded | Quantity Supplied | |
|:---:|:---:|:---:|:---:|
| | | *Without Tax* | *With Tax* |
| $6 | 5 | 25 | 20 |
| 5 | 10 | 20 | 15 |
| 4 | 15 | 15 | 10 |
| 3 | 20 | 10 | 5 |
| 2 | 25 | 5 | 0 |
| 1 | 30 | 0 | |

this writing is 18.3 cents per gallon. The sales tax, which is usually collected by states and local communities, in the city of Phoenix, Arizona, for example, is 7.0% of the price of a product. Sales taxes are often referred to as ad valorem taxes. We could discuss the incidence of either ad valorem or specific taxes, but we will choose the latter for our analysis. The principles and applications are similar, but a specific tax provides a simpler and more straightforward illustration.

A numerical example will aid in this exposition. Table 4A.1 shows the demand and supply schedules for a particular product. The equilibrium price is $4. At this price, 15 units will be demanded, and 15 units will be supplied, thus clearing the market.[34] The demand and supply curves are shown in Figure 4A.3a, where an equilibrium at $P = 4$ and $Q = 15$ can be observed.

Now suppose the government imposes an excise tax of $1 per unit, which it will collect from the sellers. The effect is to shift the supply curve up by the unit tax. The shift can be thought of in the following way: Before the enactment of the tax, suppliers offered to sell 20 units at $5. But now, for the producers to obtain $5 per unit, these products will have to be sold at $6 apiece (of which $1 will be remitted to the government).[35] In effect, the production cost for this good has risen by $1 per unit. The last column in Table 4A.1 shows the new supply schedule.

The important question to be asked is what will be the market-clearing price and quantity after the imposition of the new excise tax. An easy answer would be, $1 more than before, or $5. Certainly, the suppliers would prefer not to receive less per unit than they had been getting before the tax. But this is not the correct answer, except in very rare cases.[36] The new intersection will be at $4.50, and the quantity will be 12.5 units.[37]

---

[34]An arithmetic solution can be obtained as follows: the equation of the demand curve for the schedule shown in Table 4A.1 is $Q_D = 35 - 5P$, and the equation for the supply curve is $Q_S = -5 + 5P$. Solving for $Q_D = Q_S$, we obtain

$$35 - 5P = -5 + 5P$$
$$40 = 10P$$
$$4 = P$$

[35]The equation of this new supply curve is $Q_S = -10 + 5P$.
[36]This will occur where the demand curve is perfectly inelastic.
[37] Using our equations,

$$35 - 5P = -10 + 5P$$
$$45 = 10P$$
$$4.5 = P$$

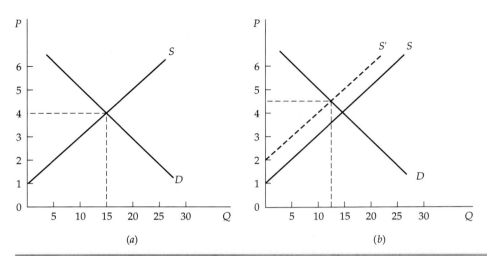

**FIGURE 4A.3** The Influence of an Excise Tax on Supply and Demand

Thus, sellers will receive only $3.50 per unit after the imposition of the tax, and consumers will be paying 50 cents more than before. In economic jargon, 50 cents of the tax has been shifted forward to consumers, and 50 cents has been shifted back to the producers. This new equilibrium is shown in Figure 4A.3b.

How the incidence of the tax is distributed between the two parties to the transaction depends on the elasticity of the supply and demand curves. The more elastic the demand curve, the larger will be the portion of the tax that the supplier has to bear. In Figure 4A.4a, we repeat the demand and supply curves previously shown and add a second demand curve, which (before the tax) also intersects the supply curve at $4 and 15 units but at all other points is flatter (more elastic) than the original demand function. In Fig-

**FIGURE 4A.4** Effect of Demand Elasticity on Equilibrium

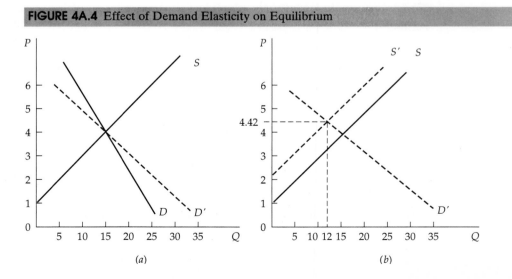

ure 4A.4*b,* the tax is added on to the supply curve. With the new demand curve, the equilibrium price is $4.42, and the quantity demanded is just above 12 units.[38]

The effect of the tax on the equilibrium quantity is of significance to the government unit levying the tax. It is obvious that a government setting a new (or increasing an old) excise tax is taking such action to increase its revenue. However, if the demand curve for the particular product is very elastic, the erosion of the revenue base will cut short the amount of revenue the government expects to collect. In the present case, the government would have collected $12.50 in revenue with the original demand curve and only $12.08 for the more elastic demand curve. Had the demand curve been perfectly inelastic (vertical), then not only would the entire tax have been shifted to the consumer, but government revenue would have been $15 because the number of units sold would have remained at 15. Thus, a government would prefer to enact an excise tax on a product with low demand elasticity.[39]

Some of the more familiar excise taxes are those on tobacco and alcohol. Because the consumption of these products is not considered desirable by today's standards, tobacco and alcohol are very frequently among the first to be selected when additional taxes are contemplated. All states as well as the federal government impose an excise tax on these two products. In some cases, the amount of the tax on each unit is greater than 50 percent of the total price of the product. Because of the low esteem in which these products are held by a large segment of the population, opposition to the imposition of a tax (or an additional tax) is generally not great (except by the two industries involved). These taxes are often referred to as "sin" taxes. But would it have been attractive to levy such high excise taxes on these two products had the demand curve for them been very elastic? Probably not, because the tax base would have eroded significantly. Therefore, the government unit that wants to achieve what is popularly known as a "revenue enhancement" will find it considerably more favorable to enact an excise tax on products whose demand elasticity in the range of the tax increase is relatively low. Tobacco and alcohol seem to fit this category well. Thus, a government unit can claim to be taxing "undesirable" commodities and at the same time help to maximize its revenue.

Among the many proposals to fight the large federal deficits of the late 1980s is the imposition of a very large tax (as much as 30 to 50 cents per gallon) on gasoline. The popular estimate has been that each cent of tax would decrease the deficit by about $1 billion. However, such calculations may not consider what would happen to the consumption of gasoline over time. The experience with OPEC's price increases in the

---

[38] The equation for the more elastic demand curve is $Q_D = 43 - 7P$ and the equilibrium price is

$$43 - 7P = -10 + 5P$$
$$53 = 12P$$
$$4.4167 = P$$

[39]You have certainly been subjected to a tax increase in some product you consume, whether it was tobacco, gasoline, or alcohol, to mention just three products on which excise taxes are levied by both federal and local governments. You will probably recall that on the day the tax was increased, the price of say, gasoline, rose by the precise amount of the tax. This is because, first of all, the increase may have been relatively small in comparison to the total price, so that the demand curve may be quite inelastic in this relatively narrow price range. Second, as we have already learned, demand elasticity tends to be lowest in the very short run, so, the tax may be completely (or almost completely) shifted to the consumer at first. But as time passes, there may be a series of small price decreases, or—and this is the more likely scenario in an inflationary environment—prices may not rise as quickly as they otherwise would have.

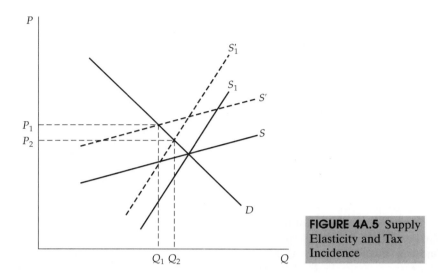

**FIGURE 4A.5** Supply Elasticity and Tax Incidence

1970s and early 1980s shows that the long-run demand curve for gasoline is by no means inelastic.

The elasticity of supply is also important from the viewpoint of tax incidence. From Figure 4A.5, we can see that the effect on the price and quantity is greater the higher the elasticity of supply. If supply elasticity is relatively low, the producer will bear the greater burden of the tax.[40]

## Interference with the Price Mechanism II: Agriculture

It may seem out of place to discuss agriculture in a textbook on managerial economics. But business decisions are not made only in manufacturing or service industries. Farming is a business also, and farmers, whether they own large or small properties, must make decisions that will affect their future. However, owners of agricultural enterprises make their decisions under circumstances quite different from those of other business-people. In the United States, for many decades, the federal government has had in place a body of laws designed to help farmers. We will not discuss the philosophy or merits of these long-entrenched policies. Instead, our interest lies in the effect these policies have on prices and the production of agricultural commodities.

Farm incomes in this country, as well as elsewhere, are rather unstable. Both the short-run demand curves and supply curves for food are quite inelastic. Thus, if, for example, some natural disaster decreases the crop of wheat in a given year (i.e., moves the supply curve to the left), the price of wheat will soar. An unexpectedly large crop will drive prices down (and, since the demand curve is inelastic, will bring about a decrease

---

[40]Again, as in the case of demand, chances are that in the very short run, supply curves will be rather inelastic, as suppliers cannot immediately remove resources from this industry to another pursuit. As time progresses, however, and resources shift out of the affected industry, the supply curve will become more elastic, and both price and production will be affected to a more significant degree.

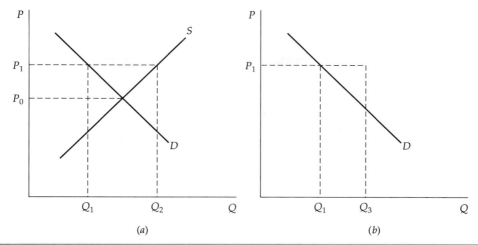

**FIGURE 4A.6** The Use of Price Supports

in farm income). On the other side of the coin, since supply curves in agriculture also are inelastic in the short run, a small change in demand will create a significant price response. To protect farmers,[41] the U.S. government has enacted various types of controls.

One of the techniques that has been used is price supports. The government in effect guarantees the farmer that if the entire crop cannot be sold at a stipulated price, the government will buy the unsold (surplus) portion from the farmer. Figure 4A.6a illustrates this situation.

You will recognize this situation to be almost identical to the price floor discussed earlier. In this case, of course, to relieve the downward pressure on the price of the product, the government takes care of the surplus by buying it up. Assume that the support price is fixed at $P_1$, whereas the free-market price would have been $P_0$. Farmers will then be able to sell quantity $Q_1$ to consumers; however, given the support price, they will produce quantity $Q_2$, and thus a surplus $Q_2 - Q_1$ will be created. This surplus will be purchased by the government at the support price. The cost to the government is $P_1 \times (Q_2 - Q_1)$, and the farmers' total revenue is $P_1 \times Q_2$. This, of course, is also the total cost to consumers and to the government combined.[42]

To reduce the amounts that have to be paid to the farmers, a policy of production controls was instituted. Let us assume that a production quota is at $Q_3$, as shown on Figure 4A.6b: then, the government expenditure will decrease from $P_1 \times (Q_2 - Q_1)$ to $P_1 \times (Q_3 - Q_1)$, and the farmers' income will be $P_1 \times Q_3$.[43]

---

[41]In the longer run, farm productivity has been rising substantially, moving the supply curve to the right and creating a long-run decrease in farm prices.
[42]The payments to farmers by the government must be obtained through tax revenues: thus, the consumers as well as business pay for that part of the total food bill.
[43]Actually, to draw the production quota line vertically from the X-axis is not quite correct. At some point, the supply curve drawn in Figure 4A.6a will cross the production quota line. Only above that intersection point will the vertical line be effective.

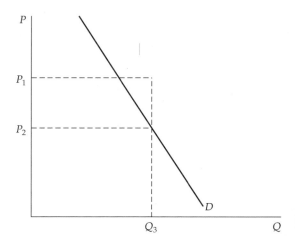

**FIGURE 4A.7** The Effect of Target Prices

Another type of policy is the establishment of target prices guaranteed by the government. Such a policy will protect the farmer in the same way as the price support policy; however, instead of selling the product at the supported prices, the producers sell their crops at market prices and collect the difference between the market and target prices for each unit sold from the U.S. government. If we assume the existence of production controls in this case as well. Figure 4A.7 illustrates the results. The price prevailing in the market is now $P_2$,[44] and the quantity sold is $Q_3$. Price $P_2$ is, however, less than the target price $P_1$, and the government will reimburse the farmer the difference between $P_2$ and $P_1$ for each of the units sold, or $Q_3$. Thus, the cost to the government (actually, the taxpayers) is $Q_3 \times (P_1 - P_2)$. In this case, the consumers bought quantities at a lower price than under the price support system of Figure 4A.6*b*, and the government is not forced to become the owner of these farm products and to bear the cost of the storage.

If the target price in Figure 4A.7 is the same as the support price in Figure 4A.6*b*, then the total amount going to the farmers and paid out by the combined forces of consumers and government (not counting storage costs) will be the same, $P_1 \times Q_3$. But the distribution of the total costs between the government and the consumer will be different, depending on the elasticity of the demand curve. We learned that when total revenue rises in response to a price increase, the demand curve is inelastic. If we concentrate on the total amount paid by the consumer directly for the farm product, we see that with price supports (Figure 4A.6*b*), the total consumer expenditure is $P_1 \times Q_1$, and with target prices it is $P_2 \times Q_3$. Because $P_1$ is higher than $P_2$, then if the area $P_1 \times Q_1$ is larger than the area $P_2 \times Q_3$, the demand curve (in this interval) must be inelastic. To recap, if the demand curve is inelastic, the consumer will pay more under the price support program than under the target price policy. And since the total combined expenditures (government and consumer) are the same under both systems, the government

[44]This is not the free-market price, since $Q_3$ represents the quantity that would be sold under conditions of production controls, a quantity presumably less than would have been produced and sold in the absence of controls.

portion of this total cost is larger under the target price system. Since most economists agree that demand curves for most agricultural commodities are inelastic, the target price system would tend to be more expensive for the government.[45]

After many decades of providing financial aid, the U.S. government began, in 1996, to phase out agricultural subsidies, while still providing declining payments during a period of transition ending in 2002. However, several events occurred in 1998 to create severe financial difficulties for farmers, among these being the Asian economic crisis and very ample crops. Prices of wheat, soybeans, and corn, as well as prices of hogs and cattle, declined sharply, causing expectations of considerably lower farm incomes and resulting in an exodus from the farming industry. In the meantime, pressure has been rising in the U.S. Congress to roll back the "Freedom to Farm" law, which enacted the end of farm supports.[46]

# Actual Situations

We will now turn to some actual events, reported in newspapers and journals, that can easily be explained using supply-and-demand analysis. Some of these items describe events that took place a number of years ago. These older examples are included because they teach us lessons regarding supply–demand analysis that are really timeless. Together with these, a number of recent examples illustrate how the subjects discussed in the previous two chapters have current applications.

### VOLUNTARY EXPORT RESTRAINTS

In 1981 the United States and Japan agreed that Japan would limit its exports of cars to the United States to 1,680,000 annually. The limit was later increased but was still considerably below the number that would have been sold in the United States in the absence of this quota. What was the result? The price of Japanese vehicles rose. The effect of such a limitation can be seen in Figure 4A.8a. The original quantity and price of Japanese cars sold in the United States are shown as $Q_0$ and $P_0$. The imposition of the "voluntary" export quota on Japan at a limit less than the equilibrium quantity changed the shape of the supply curve. At the level of exports, $Q_1$, the supply curve becomes vertical, and the demand curve now intersects the supply curve at $P_1$—a new, higher price.

Given the restriction, the Japanese began to ship their higher-priced models to the United States to satisfy the upper portion of the market. Since the demand for Japanese cars now could not be satisfied, American consumers sought to purchase domestic or other imported automobiles. Such action shifted the demand curve for the rest of the automobile market to the right, as illustrated in Figure 4A.8b, thus increasing the number and the price of vehicles purchased. It was estimated by one economist that new car prices in 1984 were $1,500 higher than they would have been had quotas not been in effect. The additional cost to American consumers was $13 billion. The beneficiaries of this increased cost were the big three automobile manufacturers (to the tune of about

[45]Storage costs are not being considered in this conclusion. On the other hand, the government may be able at some time to sell some of the stored products and thus recover a part of its original expenditures.
[46]S. Kilman, "On the Northern Plains, Free-Market Farming Yields Pain, Upheaval," *The Wall Street Journal,* May 5, 1998; S. Kilman, "U.S. Slices Forecasts for Many Farm Prices," *The Wall Street Journal,* August 13, 1998.

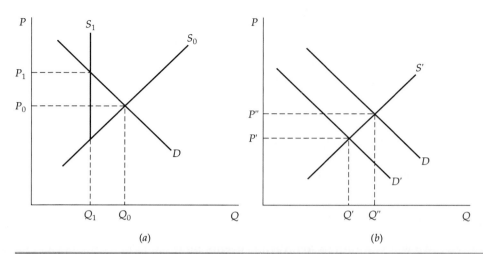

**FIGURE 4A.8** Imposition of Voluntary Export Restraints

$6 billion in higher profits), the autoworkers (about $3 billion in overtime payments), and the American dealers of Japanese cars and the Japanese manufacturers themselves (about $4 billion).[47] Subsequently, Japanese automobile manufacturers began to produce their cars in the United States. In 1985 and thereafter, the U.S. dollar weakened considerably against the Japanese yen. The prices of Japanese cars in the United States rose significantly, permitting U.S. manufacturers to continue to increase their prices and enjoy higher profits.[48] But in 1998, with the Japanese yen displaying substantial weakness, it is Japanese cars which appear to have a price advantage.

## ECONOMIC CONSEQUENCES OF OTHER IMPORT RESTRICTIONS

A 1973 study calculated that the loss to American consumers due to import restrictions on sugar was $586 million per year. Ilse Mintz estimated that the restrictions raised the price of sugar by 2.57 cents per pound and decreased consumption from 23.2 to 22.4 billion pounds per year. Figure 4A.9 shows this situation. The shaded area representing consumer loss can be calculated as follows:

| | |
|---|---|
| $0.0257 \times 22.4$ billion | $575.7 million |
| $0.0257 \times (23.2 - 22.4 \text{ bill.}) \times 0.5$ | 10.3 million |
| | $586.0 million |

A similar type of study performed in 1977 looked at the consequences of the imposition of import quotas on steel. The study showed that a price increase of $11 per ton of steel and a resulting decrease in steel consumption of 0.9 million tons per year would have cost the consumer over $1 billion per year and would have created a gain of about $870 million for U.S. steel producers. Thus, consumers lose more than U.S. producers gain. A

---

[47]Yoshi Tsurumi, "They're Merely a Subsidy for Detroit," *The New York Times,* December 16, 1984.
[48]"Schools Brief," *Economist,* October 25, 1986, pp. 84–85.

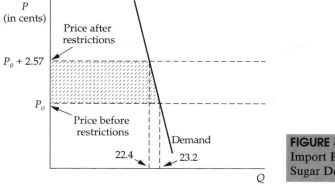

FIGURE 4A.9 Effect of Import Restrictions on Sugar Demand

part of the difference would accrue to foreign producers. Another part is due to the decrease in steel consumption, and another results due to the substitution of high-cost U.S. steel for cheaper foreign steel.[49]

## THE DEMAND FOR BEEF

Recently there has been a shift away from beef demand. The result has been an increase in the consumption of seafood, but the main beneficiary of this shift in demand appears to be chicken. Table 4A.2 shows data for these consumption changes over 12 years.

Demand for beef was very high into the early 1970s, and prices kept rising. However, the concern raised about the link between red meat and cholesterol levels was instrumental in putting a check on beef demand. Also, around this same time, chicken producers developed new and convenient chicken products that appealed to the public. Table 4A.2 shows that beef consumption per capita dropped 16 percent from 1975 to 1987, while chicken consumption rose 57 percent. Fish consumption also rose significantly, 26 percent, but considerably less than chicken.

| TABLE 4A.2 U.S. Consumption per Capita, in Pounds | | |
|---|---|---|
| | *1975* | *1987* |
| Beef | 88.0 | 73.4 |
| Chicken | 39.9 | 62.7 |
| Fish | 12.2 | 15.4 |

*Source:* Reprinted by permission of *The Wall Street Journal,* © 1989 Dow Jones and Company, Inc. All rights reserved worldwide.

---

[49]Ilse Mintz, *U.S. Import Quotas: Costs and Consequences,* Washington, DC: American Enterprise Institute, 1973; Federal Trade Commission, *Staff Report on the United States Steel Industry and Its International Rivals,* November 1977. Both of these studies are discussed in Edwin Mansfield, *Microeconomics,* 5th ed., New York: W. W. Norton, 1985, pp. 100–103, 509–12.

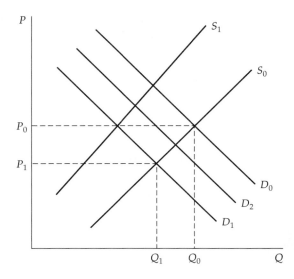

**FIGURE 4A.10** The Downward Shift in Beef Demand

During this period, the U.S. cattle population decreased substantially. As discussed previously, a change in supply is a long-run reaction to changes in demand.[50] More recently, however, the beef industry has begun to take steps that appear to have stopped the demand slide. Actually, there has been some increase in the demand for beef, as the industry has had some limited success with advertising campaigns. In 1987 cattle growers voted to establish a $1-per-animal fund for product and nutritional research and a national advertising campaign. One possible way to combat the demand for chicken is to offer branded merchandise, a method chicken producers have been using for years. The beef industry appears to be rather slow in emulating some of the marketing techniques of the chicken producers, but, according to the research director of the beef council, "there is a sense of emergency that we have to become marketers."[51] These trends are graphically depicted in Figure 4A.10. The original equilibrium of beef prices and production was at the intersection of $P_0$ and $Q_0$. As consumer preferences shifted from beef to chicken and fish, the demand curve for beef moved to the left, from $D_0$ to $D_1$. Quantities produced were less, and prices declined relatively.[52]

Over time, resources shifted out of beef production. According to the National Cattlemen's Association, the number of beef cattle decreased from 130 million in 1975 to about 110 million in 1985.[53] The shift of resources is shown on Figure 4A.10 as a movement of the supply curve from $S_0$ to $S_1$. This action tended to stabilize beef prices dur-

---

[50]The discussion in this section is based on the following articles: Marj Charlier, "Beef's Drop in Appeal Pushes Some Packers to Try New Products," *The Wall Street Journal,* August 8, 1985; Marj Charlier, "The U.S. Beef Industry Just Can't Seem to Get the Hang of Marketing," *The Wall Street Journal,* January 4, 1989.
[51]Charlier. "U.S. Beef Industry."
[52]Absolute prices of both chicken and beef may have risen due to inflationary factors, which were very strong in the 1970s and early 1980s.
[53]Charlier, "Beef's Drop in Appeal."

ing the period.[54] In the last few years, as just described, beef producers have begun to fight back, if not always effectively. The various campaigns mounted by the industry to convince consumers of beef's beneficial qualities are intended to move the demand curve to the right, from $D_1$ and $D_2$. Whether the new demand curve will be between $D_1$ and $D_0$ or even to the right of $D_0$ cannot be foreseen. The danger lurking in this effort to increase beef demand is that, given the present low level of beef herds,[55] beef prices may soar, thus discouraging consumers. If the supply curve for beef in the short run is rather inelastic, this is what could happen.

## THE EUROPEAN COMMUNITY AND WINE CONSUMPTION

Excess supplies of wine have created a problem for the European Community (EC). In the mid 1980s, members of the EC collectively produced 16.5 billion liters of wine. However, only 13.5 billion liters were consumed.

To protect the almost 2 million wine growers in the area, the EC has offered financial incentives to decrease the amount of land under production. There has been a 10 percent decrease in land used for producing wine in the past decade, but production has continued to grow. Therefore, the EC has been purchasing the surplus. In 1985 these purchases totaled about $872 million.[56]

This situation is nearly identical to our discussion of U.S. agricultural policies, which is illustrated in Figure 4A.6.

## DEMAND FOR VARIOUS CONSUMER PRODUCTS

It is a well-known fact that women have significantly increased their participation in the labor force since the end of World War II. After the war, men returned from the armed services, and women, who had taken the men's place in the work force, returned to their traditional pursuits. In 1947, women made up about 28 percent of total employment. Women then began to enter the labor force again, and the proportion of female employment rose to 35 percent by 1965 and to 45 percent by 1987. With the change in women's functions, a change in U.S. living patterns and consumption habits followed. According to a *Wall Street Journal* article, homes in the United States are not quite as clean as they were in the past.[57] Whereas women once spent much of their time as housewives, their acceptance into the labor force has changed this traditional role. "Sales of scouring powder, mildew removers, floor wax and dishwashing liquid slipped again last year, continuing a 10-year trend," according to Selling Areas Marketing, Inc., a New York-based research company.[58] On the other hand, sales of paper plates and aluminum baking pans have risen significantly. In addition, new time-saving household products have come to the market, and a new service business—maid services—has sprung up.

---

[54]Similarly, increases in chicken-producing resources dampened the price effect of the increased chicken demand.

[55]Beef supplies were further depleted in 1988 because of the severe drought.

[56]Ivo Downey, "Hard to Swallow," *Sphere,* October 1986, p. 19. When this article was written, Spain and Portugal were about to become full EC members. The wine production of these two countries was expected to add about 25 percent to the EC's total output.

[57]Betsy Morris, "Homes Get Dirtier as Women Seek Jobs and Men Volunteer for the Easy Chores," *The Wall Street Journal,* February 12, 1985.

[58]Morris, "Homes Get Dirtier."

Another recent shift in consumer demand has occurred in the market for coffee. The major producers of regular brands (e.g., Procter & Gamble, Kraft General Foods, and Nestlé) have seen their supermarket sales decline. A part of this decrease has been due to a shift in shopping habits to warehouse club stores. However, another major reason lies in an increase in the popularity of whole-bean coffees and gourmet brands. According to an officer of Brother Gourmet Coffees, Inc., one of the largest companies in the specialty coffee business, "Sales of specialty beans to grocery chains are rising about 25% annually." This shift in coffee drinkers' tastes has also been instrumental in creating a vast market for specialty coffee houses. While the number of these cafés is still on the rise, in some cities the field is becoming quite crowded.[59]

Recently, there has been another trend that has created problems for U.S. supermarkets and packaged goods manufacturers. With the economy thriving and a significant number of households with working couples, there has been a vast increase in spending on restaurant and take-away meals at the expense of at-home eating. In 1997, it was estimated that away-from-home eating accounted for about 45 percent of total spending on food. The profits of packaged goods manufacturers have been slipping in 1998. Supermarkets are actually being hit not only by increased restaurant eating but also by competition from discount stores such as Wal-Mart. Many supermarket chains are now trying to compete by having special sections that prepare both hot and cold meals packaged for consumers who do not want to cook meals at home. Usually the profit margin on such meals is greater than on the usual items on grocery shelves, which offsets the decreases in sales of supermarkets' regular merchandise.[60]

## COLLEGE TUITION PRICING

The administration of a graduate school with which one of the authors is familiar decided to increase tuition fees by a large percentage over two years in the early 1990s. This increase was significantly steeper than the usual considerable annual rise at most schools. The new tuition schedule raised the cost substantially above that incurred by students at state-run universities (which were originally lower anyway), coming close to, but still below, some of the so-called "elite" schools. It turned out that this strategy was very successful, increasing tuition revenues substantially with no significant decline in applications for admission. The administration had found a niche somewhere on the inelastic portion of the demand curve.

## A FRENCH NEWSPAPER AND ITS DEMAND ELASTICITY

In July 1994, the French daily newspaper, *Le Quotidien,* suspended publication. In order to boost its revenue in the face of increasing competition and France's recession, *Le Quotidien* slashed its price from FF6 to FF4. Its circulation increased from 30,000 units to 40,000. But this resulted in a decrease of its revenue from FF180,000 per day to FF160,000. The demand curve turned out to have an arc elasticity of −0.71. A similar action involved a decrease in the price of the *London Times* in September 1993. The price was dropped from

---

[59]Kathleen Deveny, "For Coffee's Big Three, a Gourmet-Brew Boom Proves Embarrassing Bust," *The Wall Street Journal,* November 4, 1993; Patrick M. Reilly, "Coffeehouse Craze Scalds Some Owners," *The Wall Street Journal,* November 4, 1993.
[60]Richard Tomkins, "Home Truths for U.S. Grocers," *Financial Times,* August 11, 1998.

45 to 30 pence, while the daily prices of its competitors remained unchanged. Between August 1993 and May 1994, the *Times'* daily circulation rose from 355,000 to only 518,000, resulting in a decrease in revenue. Again, the demand curve appears to have been inelastic.[61]

## CONTROLLING TRAFFIC IN CITY CENTERS

In 1998, Singapore began a new system of controlling traffic in its city center. Motorists must purchase prepaid cash cards and tolls are deducted electronically from this card (which is placed on the car's dashboard). The tolls differ depending on the time of the day a car enters the city. If a car enters the central area without this card, its registration plate will be photographed and a violation notice mailed. The program appears to have been successful. Traffic has decreased by 17 percent during the enforcement period, and the speed at which cars pass through the city center has increased. Singapore is not the only city using this procedure; among others, several Norwegian cities use such cards.[62] A different method to decrease traffic is used in Minneapolis. Here, one of the largest employers, American Express Financial Advisors, is subsidizing the area's bus systems in return for greatly reduced monthly bus tickets for its employees.[63]

Although actions in both Singapore and Minneapolis aim at decreasing rush hour traffic, the two methods have very different effects on the demand for the use of automobiles. In the case of Singapore, the action has increased the cost of travel into the city center, and has caused a movement up along the demand curve, a decrease in the quantity demanded. On the other hand, in Minneapolis, the result is to lower the cost of bus travel, a substitute for car commuting. The demand curve for auto travel will now shift to the left, a decrease in demand.

The effect of these two actions can be illustrated by simple graphs. Assume that the demand for automobile traffic in Singapore is as shown on Figure 4A.11*a*. If the quantity demanded before the imposition of the toll is at $P_0$ and $Q_0$, then after the toll is implemented, the new equilibrium will be at the intersection of $P_1$ and $Q_1$. This, of course, as we saw in chapter 3, is a decrease in quantity demanded. Now, let us take a look at the Minneapolis situation. In this case, Figure 4A.11*a* represents the demand for bus travel. The decrease in bus fares resulting from the financial aid given to the bus systems, will cause a move on the demand curve from $P_0$ (the price of fares before the decrease) to $P_2$; this is an increase in quantity demanded from $Q_0$ to $Q_2$. Figure 4A.11*b* depicts the demand for automobile traffic into downtown. Demand curve $D_0$ represented the demand before the bus fare cuts went into effect. With the decrease in bus fares, the substitution effect will result in a new demand curve $D_1$, and the demand for automobile travel will decrease from point $Q_0$ to $Q_1$.

## SPONSORING THE OLYMPIC GAMES

In August 1998, the IBM Corporation announced that it would no longer be a sponsor of the Olympic Games after the year 2000. IBM had spent more than $100 million on the 1998 Winter Olympics, providing much technology free of charge. Abby Kohnstamm,

---

[61]Alice Rawsthorn, "Crisis in French Press May See More Casualties," *Financial Times,* July 6, 1994; R. W. Stevenson, "A Cheaper Times of London Wins Readers," *New York Times,* June 13, 1994.
[62]Sheila McNulty and John Parker, "How to Stop Traffic Jams," *Financial Times,* May 9, 1998.
[63]*The Wall Street Journal,* August 27, 1998.

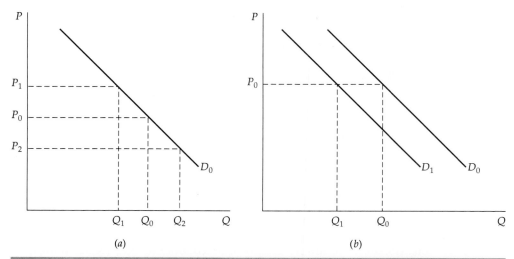

**FIGURE 4A.11** The Effect of Two Different Policies on Automobile Travel

IBM's vice president of corporate marketing was quoted in an internal memorandum that IBM "could not justify the investment based on the marketing return we could reasonably expect." Here is a case where revenues from the advertising of IBM's name and technology did not rise sufficiently to offset the expenditure. Or we may say that advertising elasticity was not high enough to warrant this significant expense.[64]

## Summary

As the preceding examples show, it is extremely important that a manager or entrepreneur understand such cause-and-effect relationships. Demand and supply curves move continually in an economic society. It is management's task to identify such movements, to understand their consequences, and to design strategies and tactics to minimize adverse results and take advantage of new opportunities. Knowledge of economic interrelationships is a tool that will assist decision makers in taking these important actions.

---

[64]Raju Narisetti, "IBM is Ending Olympics Deal in Cost Dispute," *The Wall Street Journal,* August 7, 1998.

# CHAPTER 5

# Demand Estimation

## THE SITUATION

Jennifer Harrah was assigned the task of developing and testing a statistical model that would help to explain consumer demand for soft drinks. Jennifer  worked for a major market research firm that had a worldwide reputation for its work in the "FMCG" (fast-moving consumer goods) sector of the economy. Her firm had just been hired by Global Foods, Inc., to conduct preliminary research into the soft drink market.

As a regular consumer of soft drinks, Jennifer often wondered what affected people's demand for these beverages. Moreover, she had done a case study on Global Foods in graduate school and was looking forward to working with the very company she recalled as very interesting to study at the time. In the study, Global Foods was portrayed as the classic example of a large, multinational company that faced declining profit margins and demand for its products because of the maturity of the markets in which they were being sold. Her class had reached the conclusion that the best way for

this company to energize itself was to go into markets where growth in unit sales and profit margins was very high, and that also related to food, its core business.

However, Jennifer was surprised that the company chose soft drinks as its new product line. Her class had decided that microwavable frozen gourmet meals were a logical candidate for the firm's expansion efforts.

In a meeting with the senior partner of her firm and a representative of Global Foods, Inc., Jennifer's assignment was spelled out in greater detail. The partner opened the meeting by saying, "Jennifer, I'm going to put you in charge of the entire project. You decide on the best way to obtain the data, the statistical technique to use to analyze the data, and the most effective way to present the results to our client. Global will give you as much assistance as possible. They have their own internal market research group, but the CEO felt that the use of an outside consultant would give the study more objectivity and credibility.

*(Continued)*

Your only constraint is time. This is a top-priority project for our client. In fact, the CEO wants you to produce the results in three weeks, give or take a few days. Can you do it?"

"This is an assignment made in heaven," Jennifer thought. "An inter-

esting subject, a large, well-known client, an opportunity for interaction with top management, and a major contract for our firm." She waited a bit so as not to seem too eager and then replied, "No problem. The report will be ready in 20 days."

# Introduction

In the previous chapters, we analyzed the demand function from a theoretical standpoint. We showed how each of the determinants of demand—price and the nonprice factors, such as tastes and preferences and income—affects the amount people are willing to purchase of a particular good or service. Hypothetical numerical examples were devised to illustrate the concept of elasticity, a key way in which economists measure the sensitivity of quantity demanded to changes in price and the nonprice determinants of demand. The use of hypothetical data is a convenient way to illustrate the theory. But to put the theory into practice, managers of a firm need to know the true quantitative relationship between demand and the factors that affect it.

What would consumers be willing to pay for a particular good or service? How can we produce a good or service to enable us to sell enough at a certain price to receive an acceptable return on our investment? What impact does advertising have on sales? Can we expect different segments of the market (e.g., by region, income level, occupational category) to react in different ways to our marketing efforts? In short, "*what do consumers really want?*"

For business decision makers, the answer to this question is crucial. We can anticipate that they would be willing to pay considerable sums of money to obtain this information, and, in fact, they do. Many firms have their own market research departments as well as economic research departments. Others hire independent consulting firms, and still others rely on the research arms of their advertising agencies. The leading providers of market research services in the United States are ACNielsen and IRI. ACNielsen also has a strong global presence, while IRI is just starting to expand outside of the United States.

There are a number of ways in which market researchers seek out the "truth" of consumer behavior. They might use the direct approach of a **consumer survey,** either face to face (e.g., stopping people in shopping centers) or by telephone. Perhaps some of you have at some time been a participant in this type of data gathering.

Another direct approach used by market researchers is the focus group. Consumers are asked to attend a group meeting conducted by the researcher, at which various questions are asked regarding a company's goods and services. Company representatives may be present or may choose to observe the proceedings from behind a two-way mirror. The major problem with such direct methods is that consumers often cannot be realistic about how they would act in actual market situations.

To get a more accurate view of the "true" behavior of consumers, market research firms such as ACNielsen also gather data by getting people to participate in consumer panel surveys. Volunteers in this activity are provided with a scanner, which enables them to record all their consumer purchases by reading the bar codes of every item they buy from retail stores. The survey participants then transmit the scanned data to the market research firm on a regular basis via a special modem attached to their home phones.

Technology is making it possible for companies to accumulate, store, and process large amounts of data about consumer behavior. The data are primarily collected with the aid of scanning technology (e.g., bar code readers and point-of-sale [POS] terminals) used at the checkout counters of stores and supermarkets throughout the United States and Western Europe. In most other parts of the world, data on consumer purchases are still done by actual on-site "audits" by market research personnel. However, eventually, it is expected that many more countries, particularly the so-called "Big Emerging Markets" will be using scanning technology. (We know of one company in Argentina that owns both a MasterCard franchise and a chain of supermarkets. Because there are fewer restrictions on the use of databases in Argentina, this company is able to merge their credit card and shopping files to create a much more detailed portrait of their consumers and their shopping preferences.)

Companies such as NCR specialize in providing storage capacity that is measured in "terabits" or trillions of bits of information. IBM recently developed a storage technology that enables the entire contents of the Library of Congress to be stored on a device approximately the size of the head of a pin. Wal-Mart has built a data warehouse of information about what every single one of its customers purchases in every one of its stores every day of the year. The amount of data stored in this warehouse is allegedly second only to that stored by the U.S. government. All of these developments enable statistical analysts to draw on a much richer set of data to estimate consumer demand.

The procedure commonly used by economists to estimate consumer demand is **regression analysis.** Besides its application in demand estimation, it is used to estimate production and cost functions (see chapters 7 and 8). It is also used in macroeconomic studies of consumption, investment, international trade, and interest rates. The first section following is an abridged version of the entire chapter's contents, in which we briefly explain what regression analysis is, how to interpret its results, and how to apply the results to management decisions. A more detailed presentation of regression analysis in managerial decision making follows the summary. However, for a comprehensive discussion of this topic, consult a statistics or econometrics text.

# A Summary of Regression Analysis

### SPECIFYING THE REGRESSION EQUATION AND OBTAINING THE DATA

In estimating the demand for a particular good or service, first determine all the factors that might influence this demand. Suppose we wanted to estimate the demand for pizza by college students in the United States. What variables would most likely affect their demand for pizza? We could start to answer this question by using price and all of the non-price determinants listed in chapter 3 (i.e., tastes and preferences, income, prices of related goods, future expectations, number of buyers). But it is not always possible or appropriate to include all of these variables in a particular demand analysis. As an example of this, in the demand for pizza, one would not think that "future expectations" would play an important role. Moreover, there may be other variables not specifically considered in the economic theory of demand that may have an impact on pizza purchases. For instance, in this chapter's "solution" we include the average annual temperature as a determinant of the demand for soft drinks.[1]

Ideally, all variables that are believed to have an impact on demand should be included in the regression analysis. In reality, the variables used in regression analysis are based on the availability of data and the cost of generating new data. The two types of data used in regression analysis are **cross-sectional** and **time series.** Cross-sectional data provide information on variables for a given period of time. Time series data give information about the variables over a number of periods of time. For the purpose of illustration, let us assume that we have obtained cross-sectional data on college students by conducting a survey of 30 randomly selected college campuses in the United States during a particular month.

Suppose that we have gathered the following information for each campus from this survey: (1) average number of slices consumed per month by students, (2) average price of a slice of pizza in places selling pizza in and around the campus, (3) annual tuition cost, (4) average price of a soft drink sold in the pizza places, and (5) location of the campus (urban versus suburban or rural). The data obtained from our hypothetical survey are presented in Table 5.1.

The reasons for selecting these variables are based on the economic theory of demand. Therefore, it should be clear why the price of pizza and the price of its complementary product, a soft drink, were selected for this study. But sometimes a researcher may have to use some creativity in coming up with variables that represent such factors as income and tastes and preferences. Because of the difficulty of finding out the average income of the students (or their families) who attend a particular college, tuition was used as a proxy variable. The location dummy variable is included to find out whether the demand for pizza is affected by the number of available substitutes for pizza. The assumption behind this is that colleges in urban areas may have more eating establishments from which to choose and this might adversely affect the students' demand for pizza.

Using these data, we then express the regression equation to be estimated in the following linear, additive fashion:

$$Y = a + b_1X_1 + b_2X_2 + b_3X_3 + b_4X_4$$

where $Y$ = Quantity of pizza demanded (average number of slices per capita per month)

$a$ = The constant value or $Y$ intercept

$X_1$ = Average price of a slice of pizza (in cents)

$X_2$ = Annual tuition (in thousands of dollars)

$X_3$ = Average price of a 12-ounce can of soft drink (in cents)

$X_4$ = Location of campus (1 if located in a concentrated urban area, 0 if otherwise)

$b_1, b_2, b_3, b_4$ = The coefficients of the $X$ variables measuring the impact of the variables on the demand for pizza

---

[1]However, it could be argued that the climate affects demand via its impact on the "tastes and preferences" of consumers.

| TABLE 5.1 | Sample Data: The Demand for Pizza | | | | |
|:---:|:---:|:---:|:---:|:---:|:---:|
| *College* | *Y* | *X₁* | *X₂* | *X₃* | *X₄* |
| 1 | 10 | 100 | 14 | 100 | 1 |
| 2 | 12 | 100 | 16 | 95 | 1 |
| 3 | 13 | 90 | 8 | 110 | 1 |
| 4 | 14 | 95 | 7 | 90 | 1 |
| 5 | 9 | 110 | 11 | 100 | 0 |
| 6 | 8 | 125 | 5 | 100 | 0 |
| 7 | 4 | 125 | 12 | 125 | 1 |
| 8 | 3 | 150 | 10 | 150 | 0 |
| 9 | 15 | 80 | 18 | 100 | 1 |
| 10 | 12 | 80 | 12 | 90 | 1 |
| 11 | 13 | 90 | 6 | 80 | 1 |
| 12 | 14 | 100 | 5 | 75 | 1 |
| 13 | 12 | 100 | 12 | 100 | 1 |
| 14 | 10 | 110 | 10 | 125 | 0 |
| 15 | 10 | 125 | 14 | 130 | 0 |
| 16 | 12 | 110 | 15 | 80 | 1 |
| 17 | 11 | 150 | 16 | 90 | 0 |
| 18 | 12 | 100 | 12 | 95 | 1 |
| 19 | 10 | 150 | 12 | 100 | 0 |
| 20 | 8 | 150 | 10 | 90 | 0 |
| 21 | 9 | 150 | 13 | 95 | 0 |
| 22 | 10 | 125 | 15 | 100 | 1 |
| 23 | 11 | 125 | 16 | 95 | 1 |
| 24 | 12 | 100 | 17 | 100 | 0 |
| 25 | 13 | 75 | 10 | 100 | 1 |
| 26 | 10 | 100 | 12 | 110 | 1 |
| 27 | 9 | 110 | 6 | 125 | 0 |
| 28 | 8 | 125 | 10 | 90 | 0 |
| 29 | 8 | 150 | 8 | 80 | 0 |
| 30 | 5 | 150 | 10 | 95 | 0 |

$Y$ = Quantity
$X_1$ = Price of pizza
$X_2$ = Tuition
$X_3$ = Price of soft drinks
$X_4$ = Location

$Y$, or the quantity demanded, is called the dependent variable. The $X$ variables are referred to as the independent or explanatory variables. It is important to note the unit of measurement used for each of the variables. The researcher may choose how to record the data for use in regression analysis. Here we are measuring the prices of pizza and soft drinks in cents and tuition in thousands of dollars. Notice, too, that the unit of measurement for the location variable is quite different from the others. It takes the value of "1" if the campus is located in an urban area and "0" otherwise. By measuring location in this way, the location variable is considered to be a *binary* or *dummy variable*. Given this particular setup of the regression equation and measurement scheme for the variables, we can now estimate the values of the *b* coefficients of the independent variables as well as the *a* intercept term by using any one of the many available software packages containing regression analysis.

## ESTIMATING AND INTERPRETING THE REGRESSION COEFFICIENTS

Among the software packages used by economists to conduct a regression analysis of the demand for a good or service are SPSS, SAS, and Micro TSP. To estimate the demand for pizza, we employed the regression function contained in Excel. Although it only contains the basic elements of regression (for example, it does not provide a Durbin-Watson test), we believe it is perfectly suitable for many types of regression analysis that would be conducted in business research. Besides, Excel (and Lotus 1-2-3) is more available in both businesses and colleges and universities than are statistical software packages.

Using the regression function in Excel, we obtained the following estimates for our pizza-demand regression equation:

$$Y = 26.67 - 0.088X_1 + 0.138X_2 - 0.076X_3 - 0.544X_4$$

$$(0.018) \quad (0.087) \quad (0.020) \quad (0.884)$$

$$R^2 = 0.717 \qquad \text{Standard error of } Y \text{ estimate} = 1.64$$

$$\bar{R}^2 = 0.67 \qquad F = 15.8$$

(Standard errors of the coefficients are listed in parentheses.)

Before interpreting these results, we should first think about what direction of impact changes in the explanatory variables are expected to have on the demand for pizza as evidenced by the signs of the estimated regression coefficients. To put it more formally, we can state the following hypotheses about the anticipated relationship between each of the explanatory variables and the demand for pizza:

Hypothesis 1: The price of pizza $(X_1)$ is an inverse determinant of the quantity of pizza demanded (i.e., the sign of the coefficient is expected to be negative).
Hypothesis 2: Assuming tuition to be a proxy for income, pizza could be either a "normal" or an "inferior." Therefore, we hypothesize that tuition $(X_2)$ is a determinant of the demand for pizza, but we cannot say beforehand whether it is an inverse or a direct determinant (i.e., the sign of the coefficient could be either positive or negative).
Hypothesis 3: The price of a soft drink $(X_3)$ is an inverse determinant of the demand for pizza (i.e., the sign of the coefficient is expected to be negative).
Hypothesis 4: Location in an urban setting $(X_4)$ is expected to be an inverse determinant of the demand for pizza.

Turning now to the regression results, we observe that the $X_1$ coefficient has a negative sign, and this is exactly what we would expect because of the law of demand. As the price of pizza $(X_1)$ changes, the quantity demanded for pizza will change in the op-posite direction. This is what a negative coefficient tells us. The positive sign of the tu-ition coefficient tells us that tuition costs and quantity of pizza demanded are directly related to each other. Higher tuition costs are associated with a greater demand for pizza, and vice versa. Thus, pizza appears to be a "normal" product. The negative sign of the soft drink price confirms the complementarity between soft drinks and pizza. As the price of a soft drink goes up, college students tend to buy less pizza. The opposite would hold true for a reduction in the price of a soft drink. Finally, the negative sign of the dummy location variable tells us that those students who attend colleges in urban areas will buy about half a slice of pizza per month (i.e., 0.544) less than their counter-parts in the suburbs or rural areas.

An interpretation of the magnitudes of the estimated regression coefficients is a bit more involved. Each estimated coefficient tells us how much the demand for pizza will change relative to a unit change in each of the explanatory variables. For example, a $b_1$ of $-0.088$ indicates that a unit change in price will result in a change in the de-mand for pizza of 0.088 in the opposite direction. Price, as you will recall, was mea-sured in cents. Therefore, according to our regression estimates, a 100-cent (or $1.00) increase will result in a decrease in the quantity demanded for pizza of 8.8 ($100 \times 0.088$). A tuition increase of one unit (in this case $1,000) results in an increase in the quantity demanded for pizza of 0.138. Are these changes and those associated with changes in the price of soft drinks and the location of the college campus substantial or inconsequential?

Researchers who are constantly estimating the demand for a particular good or ser-vice will have a fairly accurate idea whether the magnitudes of the coefficients esti-mated in a particular study are high or low relative to their other work. But if there are no other studies available for comparison, then researchers can at least use the elastic-ities of demand in order to gauge the relative impact that the explanatory variables have on the quantity demanded.

From our discussion of elasticity in chapter 4, you can see that regression analysis results are ideal for point-elasticity estimation. Recall that the formula for computing point elasticity is

$$\epsilon_x = \frac{dQ}{dX} \cdot \frac{X}{Q}$$

where $Q$ = quantity demanded and $X$ = any variable that affects $Q$ (e.g., price or in-come). In the case of our estimated demand for pizza, let us assume that the explana-tory variables have the following values:

Price of pizza $(X_1)$ = 100 (i.e., $1.00)
Annual college tuition $(X_2)$ = 14 (i.e., $14,000)
Price of a soft drink $(X_3)$ = 110 (i.e., $1.10)
Location of campus $(X_4)$ = Urban area (i.e., $X_4$ = 1)

Therefore, inserting these values into the estimated equation gives us

$$Y = 26.67 - 0.088\,(100) + 0.138\,(14) - 0.076\,(110) - 0.544\,(1)$$
$$= 10.898 \text{ or } 11 \text{ (rounded to the nearest slice)}$$

To compute the point elasticities for each of the variables assuming the preceding values, we simply plug in the appropriate numbers into the point-elasticity formula. The partial derivative of $Y$ with respect to changes in each of the variables (i.e., $\delta Y/\delta X$) is simply the estimated coefficient of each of the variables.

$$\text{Price elasticity: } -0.088 \times \frac{100}{10.898} = -0.807$$

$$\text{Tuition elasticity: } 0.138 \times \frac{14}{10.898} = 0.177$$

$$\text{Cross-price elasticity: } -0.076 \times \frac{110}{10.898} = -0.767$$

With these estimates, we can say that the demand for pizza is somewhat price inelastic and that there is some degree of cross-price elasticity between soft drinks and pizza. Judging from the rather low elasticity coefficient of 0.177, tuition does not appear to have that great an impact on the demand for pizza.

## STATISTICAL EVALUATION OF THE REGRESSION RESULTS

Our regression results are based on a *sample* of colleges across the country. How confident are we that these results are truly reflective of the *population* of college students? The basic test of the statistical significance of each of the estimated regression coefficients is called the **t-test.** Essentially, this test is conducted by computing a *t*-value or *t*-statistic for each of the estimated coefficients. This is done by dividing the estimated coefficient by its **standard error.**[2] That is:

$$t = \frac{\hat{b}}{\text{standard error of } \hat{b}}$$

As is the common practice in presentations of regression results, the standard errors in our pizza regression are presented in parentheses under the estimated coefficients. Using the **rule of 2,** we can say that an estimated coefficient is statistically significant if the absolute value of the coefficient divided by its standard error is greater than or equal to 2.[3]

It is evident from the preceding regression equation that $X_1$ (price of pizza) and $X_3$ (price of soft drinks) are statistically significant because the absolute values of their *t*-statistics are 4.89 and 3.80, respectively. The other two variables, $X_2$ (tuition) and $X_4$ (location), are not statistically significant because the absolute values of their *t*-statistics are less than 2.

If the estimated coefficient of a variable passes the *t*-test, we can be very confident that the variable truly has an impact on demand. If it does not pass the *t*-test, then in all likelihood, the variable does not truly have an impact for the whole population of college students. In other words, the regression coefficients are nonzero numbers simply because of a fluke in the sample of students that we took from the population.

---

[2]In the following equation, the little "hat" (circumflex) over the b is a commonly used notation by statistical analysts to denote a value estimated from sample data.
[3]Readers are reminded that this is only a summary description of the *t*-test. For more details, see the fuller discussion later in this chapter.

In statistical analysis, the best we can hope for is to be very confident that our sample results are truly reflective of the population that they represent. However, we can never be absolutely sure. Therefore, statistical analysts set up degrees of uncertainty. As explained in greater detail later in this chapter, using the rule of 2 generally implies a 5 percent level of significance. In other words, by declaring a coefficient that passes the rule-of-2 version of the *t*-test to be statistically significant, we leave ourselves open to a 5 percent chance that we may be mistaken.

Another important statistical indicator used to evaluate the regression results is the **coefficient of determination** or $R^2$. This measure shows the percentage of the variation in a dependent variable accounted for by the variation in all of the explanatory variables in the regression equation. This measure can be as low as 0 (indicating that the variations in the dependent variable are not accounted for at all by the variation in the explanatory variables) and as high as 1.0 (indicating that all of the variation in the dependent variable can be accounted for by the explanatory variables). For statistical analysts, the closer $R^2$ is to 1.0, the greater the explanatory power of the regression equation.

In our pizza regression, $R^2 = 0.717$. This means that about 72 percent of the variation in the demand for pizza by college students can be accounted for by the variation in the price of pizza, the cost of tuition, the price of a soft drink, and the location of the college. As explained later in this chapter, $R^2$ increases as more independent variables are added to a regression equation. Therefore, most analysts prefer to use a measure that adjusts for the number of independent variables used so that equations with different numbers of independent variables can be more fairly compared. This alternative measure is called the adjusted $R^2$. As it turns out, the adjusted $R^2$ for this equation is 0.67. Another test, called the **F-test,** is often used in conjunction with the $R^2$. Interested readers should refer to "The *F*-Test," later in this chapter for an explanation of this test.

## REVIEW OF KEY STEPS FOR ANALYZING REGRESSION RESULTS

We will now review all of the key steps discussed so far in the regression analysis of a demand equation using the following equation:

$$Q = 70 - 10P + 4P_X + 50I$$

$$(3) \quad (2) \quad (30) \quad \text{(standard errors of the estimated coefficients are noted in parentheses)}$$

$n = 56$

$R^2 = .47$

where $Q$ = the quantity of a product demanded
  $P$ = the price of the product (in cents)
  $P_X$ = the price of a related product (in cents)
  $I$ = per capita income (in dollars)
  $n$ = sample size
  $R^2$ = adjusted multiple coefficient of determination

### Step 1: Check Signs and Magnitudes

The negative sign for the $P$ variable indicates an inverse relationship between price and the quantity demanded for the product. A unit *increase* in price (i.e., 1 cent) will cause the quantity to *decrease* by 10 units. A unit *decrease* in price will cause the quantity to *increase* by 10 units. So for example, if price was decreased by $1.00, quantity would increase by 1,000 units.

The positive sign for the $P_X$ variable indicates a direct relationship between the price of a related product and the quantity demanded. This indicates that the related product is a *substitute* for the product in question. For example, if the price of the related product changes by one unit (i.e., 1 cent), then the quantity demanded of the product in question will change by 4 units in the *same direction*.

The positive sign for the *I* variable indicates that the product is *normal* or perhaps *superior*, depending on the magnitude of the income elasticity coefficient. A unit change in per capita income (i.e., $1,000) will cause the quantity to change by 50 units in the *same direction*.

### Step 2: Compute Elasticity Coefficients

To compute elasticity coefficients, we need to assume certain levels of the independent variables $P$, $P_X$, and $I$. Let us say they are as follows:

$P = 100$ (remember, this is 100 cents or $1.00)

$P_X = 120$ (also in cents)

$I = 25$ (this represents $25,000)

Inserting these values into the previous equation gives us

$$Q = 70 - 10(100) + 4(120) + 50(25)$$

$$Q = 800$$

We now use the formula for point elasticity to obtain the elasticity coefficients. Recall that

$$\epsilon_x = \frac{\delta Q}{\delta X} \cdot \frac{X}{Q}$$

Using this formula, we obtain

$$\epsilon_p = -10 \cdot \frac{100}{800}$$

$$= -1.25$$

$$\epsilon_{p_x} = 4 \cdot \frac{120}{800}$$

$$= .6$$

$$\epsilon_I = 50 \cdot \frac{25}{800}$$

$$= 1.56$$

### Step 3: Determine Statistical Significance

Using the "rule of 2" as an approximation for the .05 level of significance, we can say that $P$ and $P_X$ are statistically significant because their $t$ values are both greater than

2 (e.g., 3.3 and 2, respectively). $I$ is not statistically significant at the .05 level because its $t$ value is only 1.67.

As an added consideration, we note that the $R^2$ of .47 indicates that 47 percent of the variation in quantity can be accounted for by variations in the three independent variables $P$, $P_X$, and $I$. While this is not actually an indication of statistical significance, it does show the explanatory power of the regression equation. For cross-section data, this $R^2$ level can be interpreted as being moderately high.

## IMPLICATIONS OF THE REGRESSION ANALYSIS FOR MANAGEMENT DECISIONS

In our experience, the "proof of the pudding" in the business world of any statistical analysis, including regression analysis, is the extent to which the results can help managers to make good decisions. In our pizza example, the results indicate that the price of pizza and the price of its complementary product, the soft drink, are key factors influencing the demand for pizza. Their elasticity coefficients are both less than 1 and both variables' coefficients passed the $t$-test. What does this mean for those in the pizza business? First, it means that they can expect price decreases to lead to decreases in revenue, other factors remaining constant. Therefore, they would probably not want to try lowering price in an effort to increase sales. But they could try lowering the price of soft drinks, with the anticipation that the lower price of the soft drink will attract people to buy the pizza.

In statistical analysis, it is often as important to find out what does *not* pass the $t$-test as much as it is to find out what passes. In our example, we learned that tuition and location do not have statistically significant impacts on pizza demand. Moreover, the magnitudes of their coefficients were relatively small. For managers of national chains such as Pizza Hut or Domino's, this would indicate that they would not have to be very concerned about the type of college (private or public) or its location (urban or rural) in deciding where to open pizza franchises.

We hope that this summary is sufficient for those instructors and readers who simply want a general idea of how regression analysis can be used in business analysis and decision making. For a more detailed discussion, continue with the rest of this chapter.

# Regression Analysis

The basic intent of regression analysis is to estimate a quantitative relationship among variables. The first step in this statistical procedure is to specify the regression model (also referred to as the regression equation). The second is to obtain data on the variables specified in the model. The third is to estimate the quantitative impact each of the independent variables has on the dependent variable. The fourth step is to test the statistical significance of the regression results. Finally, the results of the regression analysis may be used as supporting material in the making of business policies and decisions.

Regression analysis involves two basic types of variables: the dependent variable and the independent variables. The latter are also called the *explanatory* variables. As evidenced by its name, the dependent variable is the one whose value depends on the value of some other variable or variables. The dependent variable is the central focus of any regression study and is the variable that researchers try to explain and predict. In the regression analysis of demand, the dependent variable is the quantity demanded of a particular good or service. If only one independent variable is employed in the analysis, we use the term *simple regression.* If more than one independent variable is involved, we use the term *multiple regression.* As you would expect, the independent variables most commonly used in the regression analysis of demand are price, price of related products, tastes and preferences, income, and the number of buyers. For purposes of explanation and illustration, it is much easier to focus on simple regression. After the simple regression model has been developed and explained, we will present the multiple regression model.

## THE SIMPLE REGRESSION MODEL

Our discussion of simple regression begins with a formal statement of the relationship we hypothesize to exist between the dependent variable and the independent variable. Stated as a mathematical equation, this relationship is as follows:

$$Y = a + bX + u \tag{5.1}$$

where $Y$ = Dependent variable
$X$ = Independent variable
$a$ = Intercept
$b$ = Slope
$u$ = Random factor

Notice that regression analysis seeks the best *linear* relationship between the dependent variable and the independent variable.[4] Thus, $a$ denotes the intercept of the line and $b$ the slope of the line. Note that another term, $u$, is included in the formal statement of the regression model. It is usually referred to as the "random" or "error" term. Although its value is not actually a part of the estimated impact of $X$ on $Y$, its inclusion in the formal regression equation is essential. To understand why, allow us to deviate from the main topic to a brief discussion about the difference between *deterministic* and *probabilistic* models in statistical analysis.

Suppose that you want to develop a simple model of the gasoline consumption of your car, with the dependent variable being the amount of gasoline used and the independent variable being the number of miles traveled. If you knew the number of miles per gallon that your car is able to obtain, it would be a matter of simple arithmetic to quantify this relationship. For example, if your car's gas mileage is 20 miles per gallon and you traveled 100 miles, your consumption would be 5 gallons of gasoline. This relationship can be generalized as $Y = 0.05X$. Figure 5.1a shows the deterministic relationship between $X$ and $Y.$

Now suppose that you decide to measure the relationship between miles traveled and gasoline consumed by recording this information for five separate trips, each 100 miles longer than the last, beginning with a 100-mile trip. As you can imagine, the actual amount of gasoline consumed relative to miles traveled would not conform exactly to what is predicted in the deterministic model. Suppose the actual recorded data are

---

[4]The application of regression to economic problems generally assumes a linear relationship between the dependent variable and the independent variable(s). In fact, the term linear regression analysis is often used in economic studies. There are more advanced, nonlinear regression techniques that can be used. However, as shown later, economists frequently transform nonlinear relations into equations suitable for linear regression analysis.

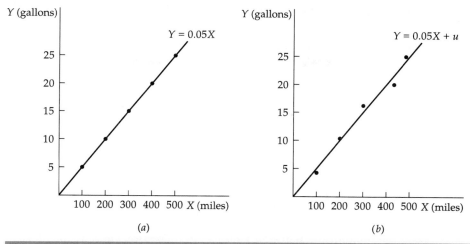

**FIGURE 5.1** Gasoline Consumption Model

those shown in Figure 5.1b. As you can see, the plotting of each trip's mileage along with gasoline consumption actually results in a scattering of points rather than a path of points along a straight line. This implies that other factors besides miles traveled (e.g., weather conditions, traffic patterns, and driving habits) affect gasoline consumption. Our model of gasoline mileage must therefore be restated as $Y = 0.05X + u$, where the value of $u$ accounts for the deviation of the points from the straight line representing $Y = 0.05X$. The variable $u$ represents the factors other than the independent variable that can affect the value of the dependent variable.

We assume in statistical theory that this $u$ factor has a random rather than a systematic impact on the dependent variable. In statistical theory, randomly occurring events are described in terms of the probability of their occurrence. Hence, the term *probabilistic* is used to describe an equation that contains the random $u$ element. You will see why it is important to understand the nature of a probabilistic model when we arrive at the section discussing the statistical significance of the regression results.

## DATA USED IN REGRESSION ANALYSIS

The data used in regression analysis are divided into two types: cross-sectional and time series. Cross-sectional data provide information on a variable at a given point in time. The different values of the variable represent a cross section of observations of such entities as individuals, groups of individuals, and locations (e.g., county, city, metropolitan area, state, or country). Time series data provide information on one entity over time (e.g., the annual per capita income of a state over a period of 20 years). The pizza examples cited earlier involved cross-sectional data, since information was gathered on a cross section of individuals on campuses at a given point in time (actually, a one-week period). Information on a time series basis might involve tracking the per-capita purchase of pizza in a given region of the country relative to its price over a period of time. For example, we could look at the annual per-capita consumption of pizza in the United States.

## ESTIMATING THE REGRESSION EQUATION

The estimation of the regression equation involves a search for the best linear relationship between the dependent and the independent variable. Thus, the regression equation we seek to estimate can be expressed as

$$Y = a + bX \qquad (5.2)$$

where  $Y$ = Dependent variable
$X$ = Independent variable
$a$ = Intercept of the line with the $Y$-axis
$b$ = Slope of the line

The intercept and slope are usually referred to as the *parameters* or **coefficients of the regression equation.**

Figure 5.2 shows a scatter plot of hypothetical data for $Y$ and $X$. As indicated in part *a* of this figure, any number of lines could be drawn through the scatter plot to represent the relationship between $Y$ and $X$. In regression analysis, the most common way to estimate the relationship is called the **method of ordinary least squares (OLS).** Essentially, this method requires that a line be drawn through the scatter of points in such a way that the *sum of the squared deviations of each of the points from the line is minimized.* The least squares line is shown in Figure 5.2*b*. An illustration of the least squares method is shown in Figure 5.3.

The actual estimation of the regression line is a relatively simple matter, given the availability of computers and software packages. Many hand-held calculators contain programs or special function keys for estimating simple regression equations. However, when more than one independent variable is used (i.e., multiple regression analysis), the processing power of a computer is required. In any event, those wishing to review the formulas for estimating the equations as well as the mathematical derivations of these formulas may consult a statistics or econometrics text. Using the method of least squares, we arrive at the regression line indicated in Figure 5.2*b*.

**FIGURE 5.2** Linear Representations of Scatter Plots

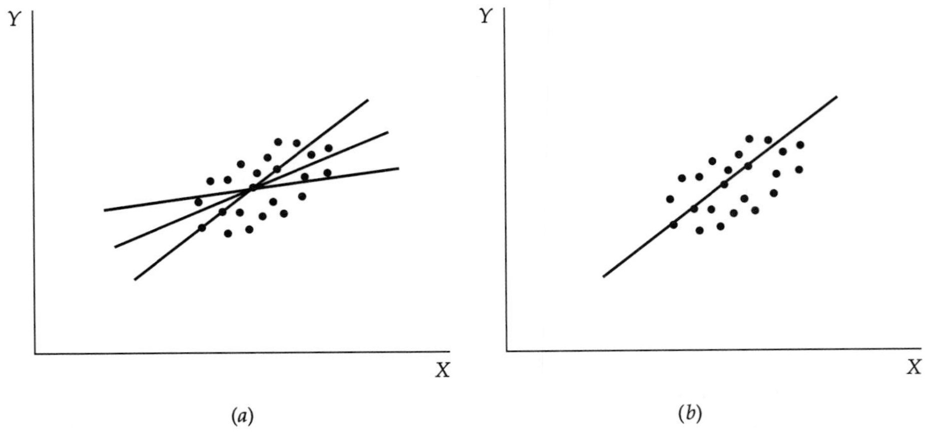

(a)

(b)

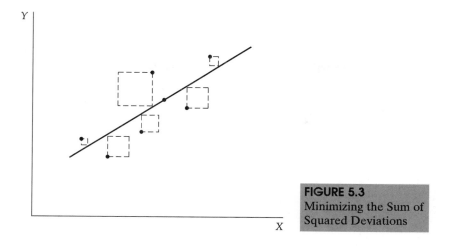

**FIGURE 5.3**
Minimizing the Sum of
Squared Deviations

Although the method of least squares provides a good linear representation of the scatter of points, there is clearly a difference in fit of the least squares lines shown in Figure 5.4a and b. Mere observation indicates that Figure 5.4b represents a better fit of the regression line through the scatter of points. This is obviously because of the nature of the scatter of points and not because of the way in which the lines were constructed. Both regression lines were drawn in a manner satisfying the least squares criterion. Thus, it would be useful to have some measure of how well a regression line fits the scatter of points.

## The Coefficient of Determination: A Measure of the Explanatory Power of the Estimated Regression Equation[5]

To explain the meaning of the coefficient of determination, we need to introduce a few concepts and notations used in standard statistics and econometrics texts. Whenever regression results based on sample data are presented, a "hat" (circumflex) is placed over the estimated values:

$$\hat{Y} = \hat{a} + \hat{b}X \tag{5.3}$$

The hats over $Y$, $a$, and $b$ signify that their values are estimated using a sample data set. A reasonable approach to measuring how well this estimated regression equation does in determining the value of $Y$ given the value of $X$ is to compare the values of $\hat{Y}$ with the actual $Y$ values found in the sample.

The scatter plot shown in Figure 5.5 will help to explain this approach. Equation (5.3) represents the estimated regression line through the scatter of points. Let us take one of these points, point $A$, for purposes of illustration. You can see that the deviation of this point from the regression line is indicated by the distance between $A$ and $B$ in

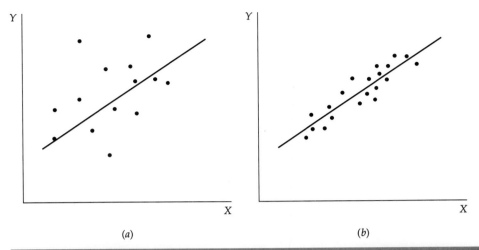

**FIGURE 5.4** Regression Lines with Different Fits Through the Scattering of Points

Figure 5.5. If we added up the squared deviations of each of the points from the regression line, we would obtain the smallest possible sum, because the method of least squares was used to estimate the regression line. Thus, in evaluating the fit of this regression line to the scatter plot of actual data, we need some standard of comparison.

Suppose you were asked to predict the amount of pizza demanded by consumers without the help of a regression equation. Would it not be reasonable to use the mean value (i.e., the arithmetic average) of quantity demanded as the predicted value? Statistical theorists, in fact, use the mean value of the dependent variable ($Y$) as the basis for comparing the relative "goodness of fit" of the regression line to the scatter of actual data points. In effect, this particular measure answers the question: How much better off are we in using a regression line to predict the value of $Y$ than we are in simply using the mean of $Y$?

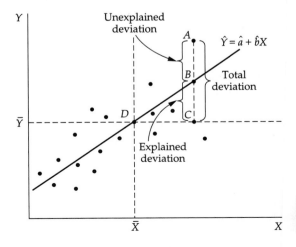

**FIGURE 5.5** Explained and Unexplained Deviations

In Figure 5.5, the mean of $Y$ (i.e., $\bar{Y}$) is indicated by the dotted line. The deviation of the regression line from the mean value of $Y$ is indicated by the distance between points $B$ and $C$. Note that the regression line always passes through the point representing the mean of $X$ and the mean of $Y$.[6] This is indicated by point $D$ in Figure 5.5. Thus, we observe in Figure 5.5 that the deviation of a sample value of $Y$ from its mean can be divided into two separate components: $AB$ and $BC$. More formally, we can state the following:

$AC = (Y_i - \bar{Y})$ = Total deviation of the $i$th sample value of $Y$ from the sample mean

$BC = (\hat{Y}_i - \bar{Y})$ = Explained deviation of $Y_i$ from $Y$

$AB = (Y_i - \hat{Y}_i)$ = Unexplained deviation of $Y_i$ from $\bar{Y}$

$BC$ is the "explained" deviation of the sample value of $Y$ from its mean because it can be accounted for by the regression line. $AB$ is the "unexplained" portion of the total deviation because its value differs from that estimated by the regression line. If the breakdown between the explained and unexplained components is measured for every observation, and the resulting values are squared (to compensate for positive and negative deviations) and then added together, we arrive at the following relationships:

$\text{TSS} = \sum(Y_i - \bar{Y})^2$ = Total sum of squares
(sum of the squared deviations of the sample values of $Y$ from the mean)

$\text{RSS} = \sum(\hat{Y}_i - \bar{Y})^2$ = Regression sum of squares
(sum of the squared deviations of the estimated values from the mean)

$\text{ESS} = \sum(Y_i - \hat{Y}_i)^2$ = Error sum of squares
(sum of the squared deviations of the sample values from the estimated values)

The abbreviations TSS, RSS, and ESS are commonly used in econometrics books for these relationships, so we will use them here in reference to the total, explained, and unexplained components, respectively, of the variation of the sample values from their mean. To summarize, we can simply say that TSS = RSS + ESS. From these relationships, we can construct a measure of the explanatory power of the regression equation.

The most commonly used measure of the explanatory power of the regression equation is called the *coefficient of determination*. The symbol used for this measure is $R^2$. We define this measure in the following way:

$$R^2 = \frac{\text{RSS}}{\text{TSS}} = 1 - \frac{ESS}{TSS} \tag{5.4}$$

If RSS is equal to TSS, this means that the total deviation of $Y$ from its sample mean can be "explained" or accounted for by the equation. This also implies that $R^2$ is equal to 1. Another way to view this situation is to look at the alternative expression of $R^2$,

---

[6]For the proof of why this always is the case when the method of least squares is used, consult a statistics or econometrics text.

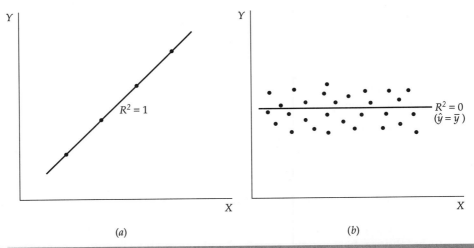

**FIGURE 5.6** The Coefficient of Determination

$1 - \text{ESS/TSS}$. If the regression line accounts for the total deviation of $Y$ from its mean, there would be no error sum of squares (i.e., ESS = 0). This means ESS/TSS = 0, and therefore $R^2 = 1$. Figure 5.6*a* illustrates a situation in which $R^2 = 1$. You can see in this figure that $R^2 = 1$ means that every point on the scatter plot lies on the regression line.

At the other extreme, if the regression line does not account for any of the variation of $Y$ from its mean, $R^2$ assumes the value of 0. As you can see from the formula, $R^2 = 0$ means that RSS/TSS = 0. Using the alternative formula for $R^2$, we see that this means ESS = TSS (i.e., ESS/TSS = 1). Such a case would indicate that the mean value of $Y$ is just as useful as the least squares regression line in predicting the value of $Y$ (i.e., $\hat{Y} = \bar{Y}$). Figure 5.6*b* illustrates this case.

In actuality, $R^2$ will assume some value between the two extremes of 0 and 1. Clearly, the closer $R^2$ is to unity, the greater the explanatory power of the regression equation. For example, an $R^2$ of 0.93 indicates a very good fit of the regression line to the scatter of points (see Figure 5.7*a*). This statistic indicates that 93 percent of the variation in $Y$ from its mean can be accounted for by the regression equation. An $R^2$ close to 0 indicates a regression equation with very little explanatory power. For example, $R^2 = .15$ (i.e., only 15 percent of the variation in $Y$ from its mean is explained) is shown in Figure 5.7*b*.

Whether a given value of $R^2$ is considered "high" or "low," or "acceptable" or "unacceptable" in statistical analysis depends on the type of data being used (cross-sectional versus time series), the particular standards of the researcher, and the typical $R^2$ computed in studies of a similar nature. Studies employing cross-sectional data generally have a lower $R^2$ than those using time series data. This is because time series data—as would be expected—have a built-in trend element that usually causes the $Y$ and $X$ variables to move closely together over time. It is not uncommon for the estimation of demand using time series data to produce an $R^2$ of 0.90 or above. Macroeconomic studies of the consumption function usually have an $R^2$ of 0.95 or more. Ordi-

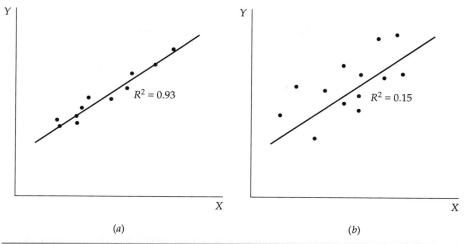

**FIGURE 5.7** Indicator of Regression Line Fit

narily, if a researcher estimates a regression equation with $R^2 = 0.75$, it means that the regression model has rather strong explanatory power. However, since most consumption function studies produce $R^2$ values of 0.95 or above, a consumption equation with an $R^2$ value of 0.75 would have to be considered relatively low.

One further point should be mentioned about $R^2$. As additional variables are added to the regression equation (i.e., as we move from simple regression to multiple regression), the regression equation, naturally, will "explain" more of the variation in the dependent variable. In fact, it can be shown that the addition of some random number or a variable completely unrelated to the regression model will improve the goodness of fit of the regression equation (i.e., will increase the magnitude of $R^2$). To compensate for the fact that regression equations with more independent variables tend to have higher $R^2$ values, we can use a measure called the "corrected" or "adjusted" coefficient of determination, $\bar{R}^2$. This measure is defined as

$$\bar{R}^2 = R^2 - \frac{k}{n - k - 1}(1 - R^2)$$

where $k$ = Number of independent variables

$n$ = Sample size

By observation, you can deduce that in multiple regression $R^2$ will always exceed $\bar{R}^2$. The difference between the two measures will depend, of course, on the size of the sample ($n$) and the number of independent variables ($k$). For a given sample size, $\bar{R}^2$ will show an increasing adjustment downward from $R^2$ as the number of independent variables increases. Regardless of the number of independent variables in the equation, the amount of downward adjustment from $R^2$ will decrease as the sample size increases. At any rate, almost all regression software packages automatically compute $\bar{R}^2$ along with $R^2$.

## Evaluating the Regression Coefficients

Up to this point, we have discussed regression analysis in reference to what is called *descriptive statistics*. Data are gathered on two variables, one dependent and the other independent; a line is fitted through the scatter of points representing the values of the two variables; and a measure of how well the line fits the scatter is developed. But to evaluate the usefulness of the results of the regression analysis for making business decisions, we need to enter the realm of *inferential statistics*.

A researcher seeking certain information about some population can attempt to obtain data either on the entire population or on some sample of the population. In just about all cases, a sample from the population is used because of the prohibitive cost of obtaining information on the whole population. Moreover, in many cases it is simply impossible to obtain complete population data. But if a sample is used instead of the population, the researcher must assess the degree to which the results of the sample reflect the population. In other words, it becomes necessary to *make inferences* about the population based on what is known about the sample and to make a judgment about how good these inferences are.

Suppose we are conducting a study of the demand for pizza on a university campus with a student population of 4,500. The variables under study are income and average quantity of pizza slices demanded per month. Suppose further that we are able to obtain information on the entire population of students. This is shown in Table 5.2, where consumers have been divided into 10 groups according to weekly after-tax income, starting with $100 per week and increasing by $20 intervals to $280. The average number of pizza slices purchased per month is shown in the matrix of numbers. To make this illustration as simple as possible, we have assumed that there are 450 student consumers in each of the 10 income categories. For example, reading *down* in the $100 column, we see that 10 students (i.e., one-tenth of 100) buy an average of 10 slices of pizza per month, 30 students (i.e., one-tenth of 300) buy an average of 10.5 slices per month, and so on. (Note the vertical arrow in Table 5.2.) By reading *across* each row, we can observe the number of pizza slices demanded for the nine frequency categories. (Note the horizontal arrow in Table 5.2.) We observe that the number of pizza slices demanded in-

**TABLE 5.2  Number of Pizza Slices Consumed per Month, by Weekly Income**

|  | f | $100 | $120 | $140 | $160 | $180 | $200 | $220 | $240 | $260 | $280 |
|---|---|---|---|---|---|---|---|---|---|---|---|---|
| (1) | 100 | 10.0 | 11.5 | 13.0 | 14.5 | 16.0 | 17.5 | 19.0 | 20.5 | 22.0 | 23.5 |
| (2) | 300 | 10.5 | 12.0 | 13.5 | 15.0 | 16.5 | 18.0 | 19.5 | 21.0 | 22.5 | 24.0 |
| (3) | 600 | 10.8 | 12.3 | 13.8 | 15.3 | 16.8 | 18.3 | 19.8 | 21.3 | 22.8 | 24.3 |
| (4) | 800 | 11.2 | 12.7 | 14.2 | 15.7 | 17.2 | 18.7 | 20.2 | 21.7 | 23.2 | 24.7 |
| (5) | 900 | 11.5 | 13.0 | 14.5 | 16.0 | 17.5 | 19.0 | 20.5 | 22.0 | 23.5 | 25.0 |
| (6) | 800 | 11.8 | 13.3 | 14.8 | 16.3 | 17.8 | 19.3 | 20.8 | 22.3 | 23.8 | 25.3 |
| (7) | 600 | 12.2 | 13.7 | 15.2 | 16.7 | 18.2 | 19.7 | 21.2 | 22.7 | 24.2 | 25.7 |
| (8) | 300 | 12.5 | 14.0 | 15.5 | 17.0 | 18.5 | 20.0 | 21.5 | 23.0 | 24.5 | 26.0 |
| (9) | 100 | 13.0 | 14.3 | 16.0 | 17.5 | 19.0 | 20.5 | 22.0 | 23.5 | 25.0 | 26.5 |
|  | 4,500 | | | | | | | | | | |

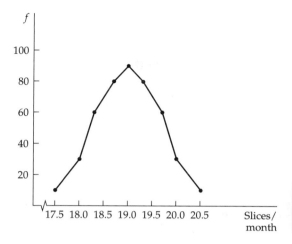

**FIGURE 5.8** Pizza Demand: Distribution of Consumers Earning $200 per Week

creases as weekly income increases. For example, in the second row, frequency 300, we see that the 30 individuals (i.e., one-tenth of 300) who have an average weekly income of $100 buy 10.5 slices of pizza per month; the 30 who earn an average of $120 per month buy 12 pizza slices per month, and so on. The most frequently occurring average number of slices for each income category is seen by reading across the row indicated by the frequency of 900. As it turns out, this row also represents the average number of slices of pizza for each income category.

Figure 5.8 shows the distribution of those consumers who earn $200 per week. The entire data set in Table 5.2 is illustrated in Figure 5.9. Notice that we assume that there is a normal, continuous distribution for each income level. Each distribution has a different mean or expected value, but all have the same variance.

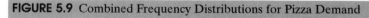

**FIGURE 5.9** Combined Frequency Distributions for Pizza Demand

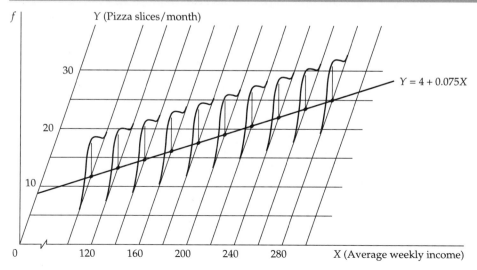

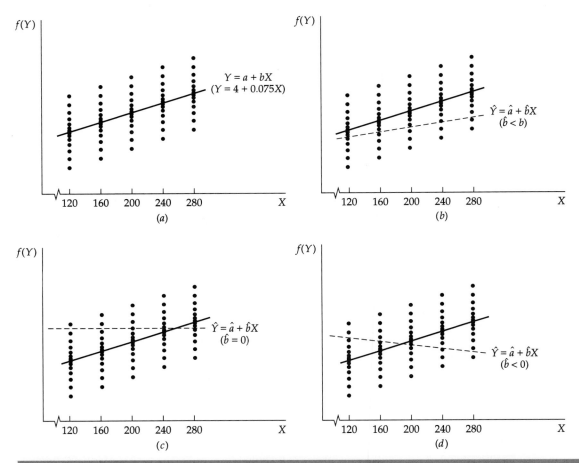

**FIGURE 5.10** Population Regression Line and Three Sample Regression Lines

For such population data, the regression line would be

$$Y = 4 + 0.075X \qquad\qquad (5.5)$$

Now suppose that we select a sample of pizza buyers from this population. As you can well imagine, this sample might indicate a different relationship between income and quantity demanded of pizza. To demonstrate this point, we have drawn a "bird's-eye view" of a portion of Figure 5.9 in Figure 5.10a. Notice that the dense cluster of population points symmetrically placed around the mean of each distribution reflects the normal, bell-shaped distribution that we have assumed to exist for each income level.

The solid line drawn through the scatter of points in Figure 5.10 indicates the true regression line for the population. However, the sample of points selected for a regression study is different from the scatter of points for the population. This would cause the regression equation estimated for the sample to be different from the one for the population. Examples of possible differences between the sample and population regression equations are shown in Figure 5.10b, c, and d. The sample regression equations are represented by the broken lines.

As you can see, a least squares regression line fitted through the sample points in Figure 5.10b would show a positive relationship between income and the demand for pizza. However, because the slope is not as steep as the slope for the population regression line, the magnitude of this relationship is smaller. The sample shown in Figure 5.10c indicates that no relationship exists between income and the demand for pizza. The sample Figure 5.10d actually shows a negative relationship between income and pizza demand, implying that pizza is an "inferior" product.

In reality, data on the population such as those shown in Table 5.2 are unknown to researchers. All they have to work with are sample data of the type illustrated in Figure 5.10b, c, and d. How confident can a researcher be about the extent to which the regression equation for the sample truly represents the unknown regression equation for the population? The answer to this question is presented in the following section.

## A TEST FOR THE STATISTICAL SIGNIFICANCE
## OF THE ESTIMATED REGRESSION COEFFICIENTS

The test used to establish, with a certain degree of confidence, that the regression coefficients estimated from sample data are truly reflective of the population is called the test of *statistical significance*. Because this test involves what are called *t*-values, it is commonly referred to as the *t*-test.

Our explanation of this test begins with a review of the error term, *u*, introduced at the beginning of this chapter. In statistical theory, it is assumed that this term is randomly distributed about the population regression line in a normal fashion, with its mean being the value of *Y* given the value of *X* and with some amount of variance.[7]

As illustrated in Figure 5.10, a random sample taken from the population may produce regression results that are quite different from a regression line fitted through the population. If we repeatedly selected a random sample of a given size from this population and estimated a regression line for each one of these samples, we would generate a large number of sample regression lines (see Figure 5.11). Each of these sample regression lines has its own intercept and slope coefficients, $\hat{a}$ and $\hat{b}$. In statistical theory, it can be shown that if the error term of the population is normally distributed about its regression line with some constant variance $(\sigma_u^2)$, then repeated sampling will produce a distribution of estimated regression coefficients, $\hat{a}$ and $\hat{b}$, *that are themselves normally distributed with a mean or expected value equal to the population's regression coefficients, and with a variance equal to a number related to the variance of the error term in some systematic fashion.* The following equations express this statement in notational form. Because we are primarily interested in the slope coefficient, we shall focus our attention on *b*. However, the same statements can be made about the intercept term, *a*.

---

[7]Recall that a normal distribution is the symmetric, bell-shaped curve so often used in statistics. As such, it can be defined by two values, its mean and its variance (or standard deviation, the square root of the variance). The larger the variance, the more "spread out" the normal distribution becomes.

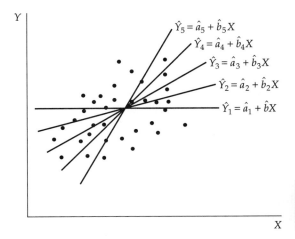

**FIGURE 5.11** Regression Lines Produced from Repeated Sampling

$$E(\hat{b}) = b \tag{5.6}$$

$$var(\hat{b}) = \sigma_{\hat{b}}^2 = \frac{\sigma_u^2}{\sum (X_1 - \bar{X})^2} \tag{5.7}$$

Equation (5.6) is fairly straightforward. It states that the mean or expected value of the estimated coefficient $\hat{b}$ is equal to $b$, the true (but unknown) regression coefficient for the entire population. Equation (5.7) states that the variance of the distribution of regression coefficients estimated from a repeated sampling of the population is equal to the variance of the population's error term, $u$, divided by the sum of the squared deviations of each observed value of $X$ from the mean of $X$. The verbalization of Equation (5.7) is rather cumbersome, to be sure. But the important thing to keep in mind is that we need to know the variance of the distribution of sample $\hat{b}$ terms to determine the probability of the occurrence of any one particular $\hat{b}$.

Because information about the variance of the population's error term is generally unknown, we resort to the use of an *estimator* of the population variance. In statistical theory, it can be shown that an unbiased estimator of the variance of the distribution of error terms $(\hat{\sigma}_u^2)$ is equal to the *sum of the squared residuals of each of the sample points from the estimated regression line, divided by the sample size minus 2* (i.e., $n - 2$). *Residuals* are the differences between the actual values of $Y$ and those estimated from the regression equation (i.e., $Y_i$ minus $\hat{Y}_i$). Expressed in notational form,

$$\hat{\sigma}_u^2 = \frac{\sum (Yi - \hat{Y}i)^2}{n - 2}$$

In turn, the unbiased estimator of the variance of the sample $b$ term $(\hat{\sigma}_{\hat{b}}^2)$ is equal to the estimator of the variance of the error terms divided by the sum of the squared deviations of each observed value of $X$ from the mean of $X$. In notational form,

$$\hat{\sigma}_{\hat{b}}^2 = \frac{\hat{\sigma}_u^2}{\sum (X_i - \bar{X})^2}$$

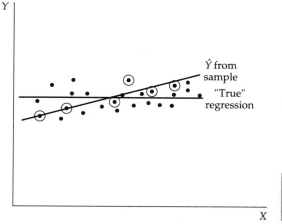

FIGURE 5.12 False Relationship Indicated by Sample Regression

$\hat\sigma$

We obtain the standard deviation of the distribution of sample $\hat b$ coefficients simply by taking the square root of the estimated variance of this distribution. That is,

$$SE_{\hat b} = \sqrt{\hat\sigma^2_{\hat b}}$$

As is the custom, we shall refer to standard deviation of the sample regression coefficient as the standard error of the coefficient ($SE_{\hat b}$). And, as we are about to show, $SE_{\hat b}$ plays a central role in the *t*-test.

In conducting the *t*-test, we start by hypothesizing that the true (but unknown) regression coefficient for the population is a certain value. In statistical analysis, this is called the **null hypothesis.** Typically in economic research, we hypothesize the population's regression coefficient to be 0; that is, there is no relationship between $X$ and $Y$ in the population. The **alternative hypothesis** is that there is indeed a relationship between $X$ and $Y$. Using conventional statistical notation, we can state the null and alternative hypotheses as:

$$H_0 : b = 0$$

$$H_a : b \neq 0$$

If the $b$ or slope coefficient is truly 0, as the null hypothesis states, then for the entire population, changes in $X$ would have no impact on $Y$.

Suppose the true value of $b$ were indeed 0. Would it still be possible to select a sample that showed a relationship between $Y$ and $X$? Most certainly it would, and Figure 5.12 shows exactly how this could happen. Notice in this figure that the scatter plot of the population is such that a regression line fitted through the points is horizontal (i.e., has zero slope). But suppose the sample that we selected—indicated by the circled points in Figure 5.12—happened to show a positive relationship when a least squares line is fitted through the sample scatter. Based on the results of the regression analysis of the sample data, we would conclude that for the entire population a direct relationship exists between $X$ and $Y$, when there really is none. This kind of error would be of obvious concern to decision makers. For example, suppose a regression analysis of sales on advertising expenditures mistakenly showed a positive relationship between the two variables and prompted a firm to increase substantially the size of its advertising

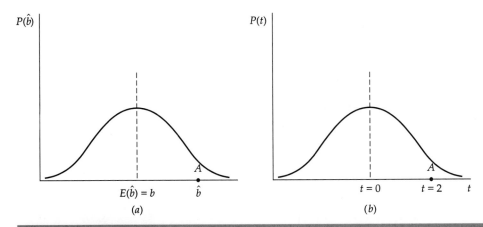

**FIGURE 5.13** The *t*-Distribution

budget. Since in reality there is no impact of advertising on sales, this decision would lead to a waste of the firm's financial resources.

Earlier, we stated that if the error term of the population regression equation is normally distributed, it can be shown that the estimated sample coefficients are also normally distributed. It can also be demonstrated mathematically that the *standardized deviation* of each sample's estimate from the actual population value has a *t*-distribution.[8] Figure 5.13 illustrates this point. In Figure 5.13*a,* we see a normal distribution of estimated $\hat{b}$ coefficients with its midpoint designating the mean or expected value. The vertical axis of the graph measures the probability of the occurrence of the different values of the estimate $\hat{b}$. Obviously, the mean or expected value of $\hat{b}$ has the greatest probability of occurring. Suppose that the estimated sample coefficient $\hat{b}$ is the one shown by point *A* in Figure 5.13*a*. What is the probability of such a point occurring? To find the answer to this question, we standardize the differences between any point in the distribution and its expected value. This is done using the following equation:

$$t = \frac{\hat{b} - E(\hat{b})}{SE_{\hat{b}}} \tag{5.8}$$

This value shows how many *t*-units away from the expected value is the estimated coefficient $\hat{b}$. To interpret this *t*-value, we also need to know the number of **degrees of freedom** (d.f.) involved in this case. For any given sample, d.f. is defined as $n - k - 1$, where *n, k,* and 1 represent the sample size, the number of independent variables, and the intercept term, respectively. For example, in a regression equation with a sample of 62 observations, there would be 60 degrees of freedom. The probability of the occurrence of value *A* (converted into 2 units) can now be found with the help of a *t***-table,** as shown in Table B.4 in Appendix B at the end of the text. In this table, we see that for 60 d.f.,

[8]The *t*-distribution is a symmetric, bell-shaped distribution that closely resembles the normal distribution. Its precise shape depends on a measure called *degrees of freedom*. In simple regression, there are $n - 2$ degrees of freedom. As the sample size (*n*) increases, the *t*-distribution tends toward the standard normal distribution. In the limit, the two become identical.

the probability that *t* will have a value of 1.671 or more is about 5 percent. (See column for "one-tail, *a* = 0.05.") Therefore, the probability that *t* will have a value of 2 or more would clearly be less than 5 percent.

After finding the *t*-value for the estimated regression coefficient $\hat{b}$, the researcher must then decide whether to reject the null hypothesis that there is no relationship between *X* and *Y* in the population. The standard procedure is to establish what is called the *critical t-value* based on a predetermined point on the *t*-distribution. Usually this point is set at the 0.05 *level of significance.* We can then turn to the *t*-table to find the critical value of *t* corresponding to this level of significance. For example, the table shows that for 60 degrees of freedom, the range between 2.0 and −2.0 includes about 95 percent of the values of *t*. Another way of saying this is that the chance of obtaining a *t*-value greater than 2.0 or less than −2.0 is about 5 percent or less. Figure 5.14 illustrates the 0.05 level of significance on a *t*-distribution with 60 degrees of freedom. Notice that the values of *t* that are greater or less than the critical *t*-value lie on the two ends or "tails" of the distribution.

The preceding conclusion helps us to understand the rationale for the "rule of 2" often employed by economists in their evaluation of the *t*-test. This rule states that the null hypothesis that *b* = 0 can be rejected if the *t*-value is less than or equal to −2 or greater than or equal to 2. Using the absolute value of *t*, we can state that the null hypothesis can be rejected if

$$|t^*| > 2$$

The implication of this rule of thumb is that the 0.05 level of significance is being used to select the critical *t*-value, *t**. As you can see in the *t*-table at the 0.05 level of significance, 2 serves as a useful approximation of the critical *t*-value for about 20 degrees of freedom and above.

## A Suggested Classroom Exercise to Illustrate the Use of the *t*-Test

At this point, you may still be a bit puzzled about the notion of a *t*-value and its use in testing the relationship between the sample *b* and the unknown population *b*, particularly if you are unfamiliar with statistical theory. We will, therefore, present a simple exercise that you may wish to try yourselves or along with your classmates and instructor. This exercise deals with the pizza demand example used earlier.

Cut 45 cardboard squares of equal size. According to Table 5.2, there are nine possible levels of demand for pizza for each income category. Thus, each of the squares is to be given a value ranging from 1 to 9. As shown in the first column of Table 5.2, there

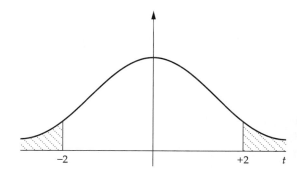

**FIGURE 5.14** Critical *t*-Values for Two-Tail Test, 5 Percent Level of Significance, 60 Degrees of Freedom

should be one square labeled 1, three squares labeled 2, six squares labeled 3, and so on. (Note that we have divided the frequencies in each income category by 100. There are 4,500 observations in the population, but we have reduced the number of squares used to 45 simply for convenience. As long as the relative frequencies are the same, it should not matter whether 45 or 4,500 squares are used in this exercise.)

Place all 45 squares in an envelope. Then select one square for each income category. Be sure to put the square back into the envelope after each selection. By doing this, you are generating a random sample of 10 observations, one for each income category. Because the number 5 occurs most frequently (9 times in this exercise and 900 times in the hypothetical population of student consumers) it is clear that the probability of drawing this number from the envelope is the greatest. In fact, each time a square is selected, there is a 20 percent chance (i.e., 9/45) that the number 5 will be selected. Then combine the number drawn with its income category to determine the corresponding pizza consumption.

Suppose one of these exercises produces the following table of numbers. As a reference to the exercise, the number that was drawn from the envelope is included in parentheses to the quantities demanded for pizza.

| Average Quantity of Pizza Slices Demanded (Y) | Weekly Income (X) |
|---|---|
| 10.0 (1) | $100 |
| 13.0 (5) | 120 |
| 15.2 (7) | 140 |
| 16.0 (5) | 160 |
| 16.0 (1) | 180 |
| 18.7 (4) | 200 |
| 21.2 (7) | 220 |
| 22.3 (6) | 240 |
| 22.0 (1) | 260 |
| 26.0 (8) | 280 |

A scatter plot of these data is presented in Figure 5.15. The regression equation estimated for this sample is

$$Y = 3.27 + 0.078X \tag{5.9}$$

$$(0.86) \quad (0.004)$$

Let us now conduct a *t*-test for the significance of the estimated sample coefficient, $\hat{b}$. Recall that the null and alternative hypotheses can be expressed in the following manner:

$$H_0 : b = 0$$

$$H_a : b \neq 0$$

Clearly, our sample $\hat{b}$ coefficient of 0.078 is greater than zero. Therefore, we must determine the probability of encountering such a sample value from a population whose true value is really zero. We begin by subtracting zero (the hypothesized population value of $b$) from 0.078 (the estimated sample value, $\hat{b}$), and then we divide this

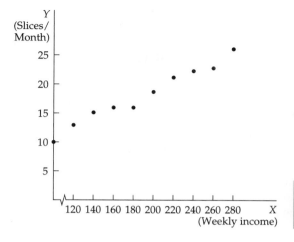

**FIGURE 5.15** Scatter Plot of Sample Data for Pizza Experiment

difference by the standard error of $\hat{b}$. By convention, the standard error of an estimated regression coefficient is presented in parentheses under the coefficient. As you can see in Equation (5.9), the standard error of $\hat{b}$ is 0.004, and the standard error of the intercept is 0.86. This procedure is summarized here.

$$t = \frac{0.078 - 0}{0.004}$$

$$t = 19.5 \tag{5.10}$$

Equation (5.10) is referred to as the *t*-ratio or the *t*-value.

From the results of the equation, you can see that if the population coefficient, *b*, were truly zero, then 0.078 would lie 19.5 *t*-units away from the mean. Turning to Table B.4 in Appendix B of this text, we see that the probability of encountering such a value is so remote that it is not even included in the chart. However, this table does show that the probability of obtaining a *t*-value (with 8 degrees of freedom) greater than 3.355 or less than −3.355 from a distribution whose mean is zero is one out of one hundred (i.e., 0.01). This implies that the probability of obtaining a value of 19.5 is virtually nil. And so we come to the rather obvious conclusion that the true value of the population coefficient is, in all likelihood, not equal to zero. In terms of statistical theory, we reject the null hypothesis.

In using regression analysis, economists almost always hypothesize the population coefficient to be equal to zero (i.e., $H_0 : b = 0$). However, the value of the unknown population coefficient can be hypothesized to be any value that the researcher desires. For example, suppose that a number of previous studies on the demand for pizza estimated the value of the coefficient of the income variable to be about 0.073. We might then use these previous studies as the justification for hypothesizing that the unknown coefficient is equal to this value:

$$H_0 : b = 0.73$$

$$H_a : b \neq 0.73$$

We find the corresponding $t$-ratio to be

$$t = \frac{0.078 - 0.073}{0.004}$$

$$t = 1.25$$

Suppose we test this hypothesis using the 0.05 level of significance, two-tail test. Turning again to the $t$-table in the appendix, we find a critical $t$-value of 2.306 for a regression with 8 degrees of freedom. Since the $t$-value of 1.25 is not greater than 2.306, we are *not* able to reject the null hypothesis. Once again, this does not mean that we can now say that the population coefficient is indeed 0.073. However, this failure to pass the $t$-test means that we are unable to say with a high degree of certainty that the population value is *not* 0.073. Until future studies indicate otherwise, researchers may want to assume the working hypothesis that the unknown population coefficient is around 0.073.

### The $t$-Distribution and the One-Tail and Two-Tail Tests

In using regression analysis for economic and business research, it is standard for the null hypothesis to state that there is no relationship between a particular independent variable and the dependent variable (e.g., $b = 0$). However, researchers usually have a choice as to whether the alternative hypothesis states that the independent variable simply has some impact on the dependent variable (a **two-tail test**) or whether it indicates a positive or a negative impact (a **one-tail test**). In the evaluation of the relationship between income and the quantity demanded for pizza, our alternative hypothesis was that changes in income had an effect on the quantity demanded for pizza; it did not state whether this effect was positive or negative. If we had some *a priori* reason for believing that the effect of income on quantity demanded was either positive or negative, it would be reflected in the alternative hypothesis. For example, if we hypothesized that pizza is a "normal" good, the alternative hypothesis would be that changes in income have a direct relation to changes in quantity demanded. If we hypothesized that pizza is an "inferior" good, the alternative hypothesis would claim an inverse relationship between the two variables. Using the notation we have developed:

If pizza is hypothesized to be a "normal good" (i.e., the income variable's coefficient is positive), then

$$H_0 : b \leq 0$$

$$H_a : b > 0$$

If pizza is hypothesized to be an "inferior good" (i.e., the income variable's coefficient is negative), then

$$H_0 : b \geq 0$$

$$H_a : b < 0$$

If income is hypothesized simply to have an impact (either positive or negative) on the demand for pizza, then

$$H_0 : b = 0$$

$$H_a : b \neq 0$$

### Summary: Steps in Conducting the *t*-Test of the Statistical Significance of Estimated Regression Coefficients

This has been a rather lengthy discussion of the *t*-test, so it might be helpful to summarize each of the steps involved in carrying out this test.

Step 1: State the hypothesis.

For example, "Pizza is a normal good." (In other words, income is hypothesized to have a direct relation to the demand for pizza.)

Step 2: Restate the hypothesis in terms suitable for statistical testing.

With respect to the preceding hypothesis about income and the pizza,

$$H_0 : b \leq 0$$
$$H_a : b > 0$$

Step 3: Establish a critical level of rejection, and find the *t*-value that corresponds to this level.

For example, for a one-tail test, the 0.05 level, and 8 degrees of freedom (the number we assumed for the pizza analysis), $t^* = 1.86$. Thus, if the *t*-statistic is greater than 1.86, we can reject the null hypothesis at the 0.05 level of significance.

Step 4: Find the *t*-statistic by transforming the difference between the estimated *b* and its hypothesized value, 0.

For example, suppose the estimated coefficient is 2.5 and the standard error of the coefficient is 1.3. Then

$$t = \frac{2.5 - 0}{1.3}$$
$$= 1.92$$

Step 5: Compare the resulting *t*-value with the critical value. Then decide whether to reject the null hypothesis.

In our example, 1.92 is greater than the critical *t*-value of 1.86 for a one-tail test with 8 degrees of freedom. Therefore, we can reject the null hypothesis and state that income has a statistically significant direct impact on the demand for pizza.

## Multiple Regression Analysis

Let us begin our explanation of multiple regression by specifying the following *linear; additive regression model* for the demand for pizza:

$$Y = a + b_1X_1 + b_2X_2 + b_3X_3 + b_4X_4 \tag{5.11}$$

where  $Y$ = Quantity of pizza demanded (average number of slices per capita per month)
$X_1$ = Average price of a slice of pizza (in cents)
$X_2$ = Annual tuition (in thousands of dollars)
$X_3$ = Average price of a 12-ounce can of soft drink (in cents)
$X_4$ = Location of campus (1 if campus is located in a concentrated urban area, 0 otherwise)

Assume as we did in our opening section of this chapter that a regression analysis of cross-sectional data of 30 college campuses yields the following estimated relationship between the quantity demanded for pizza and our selection of independent variables:

$$Y = 26.67 - 0.088^*X_1 + 0.138X_2 - 0.076^*X_3 - 0.544X_4$$

$$(0.018) \qquad (0.087) \qquad (0.020) \qquad (0.884) \qquad \textbf{(5.12)}$$

$$R^2 = 0.71 \qquad F = 15.8 \quad n = 30$$

$$\bar{R}^2 = 0.67 \qquad \text{Standard error of } Y = 1.64$$

The asterisks indicate statistical significance at the 0.05 level.

In evaluating this equation, we first look at the signs of the estimated coefficients of the independent variables. (We usually ignore the intercept term because by itself this term does not have any economic meaning.) Note that, as expected, the sign of the price variable is negative. The sign of the variable $X_2$ is positive, indicating that the higher the college tuition, the more pizza is purchased by the students. The sign of $X_3$, the variable for the price of soft drinks, is negative, indicating that pizza and soft drinks are complementary products.

There is one variable in the equation, $X_4$, that may seem a bit odd. This is called a *binary* or *dummy variable.* It assumes the value of 1 if the campus is located in a concentrated urban area and a value of 0 otherwise. This type of variable will be explained in greater detail in a later section. However, at this point we can point out that the coefficient of this variable measures the difference in the demand for pizza by students attending colleges or universities in urban areas versus students in institutions located outside of urban areas. As you can see by the magnitude and sign of the $X_4$ coefficient, the former group is estimated to eat 0.544 less slices of pizza per month than the latter group.

The magnitudes of the coefficients indicate the change in the quantity of pizza demanded relative to a unit change in a particular independent variable *assuming the values of the other variables are unchanged.* This feature of multiple regression analysis is extremely useful in economic and business research because, as you can see, it follows the comparative statics approach to the analysis of problems so commonly used in economic theory. Thus, the equation tells us that, all other factors held constant, a unit (i.e., a one-cent) decrease in the price of pizza will cause the quantity demanded of pizza to rise by 0.088 units. Unless one has actual experience in or prior knowledge about the retail pizza business, it is difficult to judge whether or not the magnitudes of the regression coefficients represent typical patterns of demand for pizza relative to changes in the independent variables. However, as noted earlier, one way to assess these magnitudes is to compute the elasticities of demand with respect to these independent variables. To compute these elasticities, we have to assume a certain starting point for the values of the independent variables. Let us assume the following values:

> Price of pizza ($X_1$) = 100 (i.e., $1.00)
> Annual college tuition ($X_2$) = 14 (i.e., $14,000)
> Price of a soft drink ($X_3$) = 110 (i.e., $1.10)
> Location of campus ($X_4$) = Urban area (i.e., $X_4 = 1$)

Given these values, we then compute the monthly per-capita demand for pizza to be

$$Y = 26.67 - 0.088 \,(100) + 0.138 \,(14) \tag{5.13}$$

$$-0.076 \,(110) - 0.544 \,(1)$$

$$= 10.898 \text{ or } 11 \text{ (rounded to nearest whole slice)}$$

Recall the general formula for point elasticity to be:

$$\frac{\delta Y}{\delta X} \times \frac{X}{Y}$$

We now use this formula to compute the various demand elasticities:

Price elasticity: $-0.088 \times \dfrac{100}{10.898} = -0.807$

Tuition elasticity: $0.138 \times \dfrac{14}{10.898} = 0.177$

Cross-price elasticity: $-0.076 \times \dfrac{110}{10.898} = -0.767$

The equation has an adjusted $R^2$ of 0.67. This means that 67 percent of the variation in the dependent variable can be explained by variations in the independent variable. Once again, only those familiar with this type of business can really evaluate the explanatory power of this estimated equation. However, 0.67 is a higher $R^2$ than is found in most empirical studies of consumer demand that use cross-sectional data.

To conduct the $t$-test, we first divide the standard errors (cited in parentheses) into their respective coefficients and compare these $t$-ratios with the appropriate values in Table B.4 in Appendix B. At the 0.05 level of significance, two-tail test, we see that the critical $t$-value for 25 degrees of freedom is 2.06. Using this critical level, we see that the variables $X_1$, indicating the price of pizza, and $X_3$, indicating the price of soft drinks, are statistically significant.

As for the policy implications of these regression findings, suppose you are an entrepreneur who is considering starting a chain of pizza parlors on college campuses across the country. The price inelasticity of pizza implies that you should try to use advertising and promotion instead of price reductions as a means of boosting sales. Moreover, the statistical significance of the coefficient of the price variable would give you a great deal of confidence that you should not try to reduce the price. Although the tuition coefficient did not prove to be statistically significant, the relatively low tuition elasticity of demand might lead you to conclude that the locations of your pizza parlors should not be confined to any particular type of institution of higher education. Based on the fairly high cross-price elasticity between soft drink prices and the demand for pizza, once the pizza parlors are established you might want to consider reducing the price of beverages as a way to boost demand for pizza.

### THE *F*-TEST

There is another test of statistical significance, called the *F*-test, that is commonly used in regression analysis. This test measures the statistical significance of the entire regression equation rather than of each individual coefficient (as the $t$-test is designed to do). Earlier, we stated that $R^2$ is the measure of the explanatory power of the regression model. In effect, the $F$-statistic is a test of the statistical significance of $R^2$. The null hypothesis of the $F$-test can be expressed as follows:

$$H_0 : b_1 = b_2 = \cdots = b_k = 0$$

where $k$ equals the number of independent variables in the regression equation.

If the null hypothesis is true, virtually no relationship exists between the dependent variable and the $k$ independent variables for the population, and whatever the value of $R^2$ (i.e., the proportion of the variation in $Y$ explained by $X$), it is most probably a chance occurrence in the sampling process.

The $F$-value can be defined as

$$F = \frac{\text{Explained variation}/k}{\text{Unexplained variation}/(n - k - 1)}$$

where the explained variation is $\sum (\hat{Y} - \overline{Y})^2$, the unexplained variation is $\sum (Y - \hat{Y})^2$, $n$ is the sample size, and $k$ is the number of independent variables. It can also be expressed in terms of the value of $R^2$:

$$F = \frac{R^2/k}{(1 - R^2)/(n - k - 1)} \tag{5.14}$$

The procedure for using the $F$-value in the $F$-test is similar to the use of the $t$-value in the $t$-test. A critical value for $F$ is established depending on the degree of statistical significance that the researcher wishes to set. Typically, the significance level is set at 0.05 or 0.01. The critical $F$-values corresponding to these acceptance levels are shown in Table B.3 in Appendix B. As can be seen, there are two "degrees of freedom" values that must be incorporated in the selection of the critical $F$-value. One value relates to the numerator of the equation for $F$, and the other relates to the denominator. Given this background information, we can now interpret the $F$-value for our multiple regression equation for pizza demand. With a sample size of 30 and four independent variables ($n = 30$ and $k = 4$), the $F$-table indicates that at the 0.05 level, the critical $F$-value for 4 and 25 degrees of freedom is 2.76. At the 0.01 level, the critical $F$-value is 4.18.

Because the estimated equation's $F$-value of 15.80 (reported in Equation (5.12)) exceeds both of these critical values, we can conclude that our entire regression model accounts for a statistically significant proportion of the variation in the demand for pizzas. In general, it is fairly easy for a regression model to pass the $F$-test. The null hypothesis, which states that there is no relationship between the dependent variable and *all* of the independent variables, is a rather stringent statement. As long as some of the independent variables in the regression equation truly help to explain the variance in the dependent variable, the $F$-test will more than likely indicate a statistically significant regression model. In fact, it can be seen in Equation (5.14) that for some given sample size and set of independent variables, the higher the $R^2$, the greater the $F$-value.

Another way to view the general tendency of a regression equation to pass the $F$-test is to recognize that regression models that *do not* pass the test must indeed be inferior. In any event, even if the $F$-statistic indicates the overall statistical significance of the regression model, there is still a need to subject each independent variable to individual testing. For this, we rely on the $t$-test.

# The Use of Regression Analysis to Forecast Demand

In addition to helping researchers understand more about the determinants of demand, regression analysis can be used simply as a tool for forecasting. In the next chapter, we will discuss this topic in much greater detail. For now, let us just state that once the regression coefficients have been estimated, arriving at a forecast value of the demand for a particular good or service is simply a matter of assigning values to the independent variables. For example, suppose the regression analysis of time series data resulted in the following estimate of the demand for pizza:

$$Q = 100 - 20P + 100I + 15AD + 10P_{hd}$$

where  $Q$ = Demand for pizza (in millions of slices per year)
       $P$ = Price of pizza (in cents)
       $I$ = Per-capita income (in thousands of dollars)
      $AD$ = Advertising expenditures (in millions of dollars)
    $P_{hd}$ = Price of hot dogs (in cents)

If we assume that $P = 100, I = 5, AD = 30$, and $P_{hd} = 125$, our forecast for the quantity of pizza demanded for the coming year will be 300 (million slices). However, when regression analysis is used for forecasting, the same care that was taken in assessing the statistical significance of the individual regression coefficients must be applied. This is because the forecast is based on a sample of data. To take into account that the forecast value of 300 is based on a sample and is therefore subject to a sampling error, we use a measure called the **standard error of the estimate (SEE).** This term is also included as a regular part of the computer printout of any software regression program. As a matter of fact, it can be shown that the standard error of the coefficient ($SE_{\hat{b}}$) is actually derived from the SEE of the regression equation.

According to statistical theory, we can expect that the true (but unknown) value of $Y$ will be within a range determined by the estimated value, plus or minus the product of the standard error of the estimate and the appropriate $t$-value. In notational form,

$$\hat{Y} \pm t_{n-k-1}\text{SEE}$$

For example, suppose the estimated regression equation for the pizza demand was generated from a sample size of 27 and had a SEE of 25. Given the previous values, we can say with 95 percent confidence that the actual demand for pizza is $300 \pm 2.074 (25)$, or a range of 248.15 to 351.85.[9] Caution should be exercised when developing the forecast range for the dependent variable of the estimated regression equation. Statistical theory shows that as the given values of the independent variables (e.g., price, income, price of related products) move further away from their mean values, the forecast range widens for any given level of confidence.

---

[9]According to the $t$-table, the critical $t$-value with 22 degrees of freedom (i.e., $n - k - 1$, or $27 - 5$) is 2.074. If a greater degree of confidence were desired, the range of the expected value of the demand for pizza would obviously widen. For example, at the 99 percent confidence level, the critical $t$-value with 22 degrees of freedom is 2.819.

# Additional Topics on the Specification of the Regression Model

## PROXY AND DUMMY VARIABLES

One of the most challenging aspects of regression analysis (or, for that matter, any type of statistical analysis) is obtaining sample data suitable for use in the analysis. For example, economic theory indicates that "tastes and preferences" is an important determinant of consumer demand. But how do we measure this factor? A researcher who cannot obtain direct information about tastes and preferences may have to use a proxy variable to represent this factor in the regression equation. Level of education and gender of consumers are possible proxy variables for tastes and preferences. Those with higher levels of formal schooling might have different tastes or preferences for a particular good or service. Women might have different tastes or preferences than men. Even differences in residential location might reflect differences in tastes and preferences. For example, the authors have observed that supermarkets in the northeast region of the United States carry a proportionally larger stock and variety of Italian foods than those in other parts of the country. On the other hand, the variety and quantity of Mexican food on supermarket shelves in the Midwest, the Southwest, and on the Pacific Coast are substantially greater than in the Northeast.

In certain instances, for variables such as location and gender to be used in regression analysis, they must be quantified. This can be done by creating a dummy or binary variable, which takes the value of 1 if the unit of observation falls into a particular category and 0 if it does not. For example, we can assign the value of one to a female consumer and zero to a male. In this manner, dummy variables can be created for any nonquantitative factor.

A useful way to consider a dummy variable in a regression equation is as a "shift" factor. For example, in our regression analysis of the demand for pizza by college students, the coefficient of the dummy location variable was estimated to be $-0.54$. Suppose we graphed the demand equation implied by the values provided in Equation (5.13). This is shown in Figure 5.16. The original demand curve indicates the demand by those students who attend schools outside of urban areas (i.e., $X_4 = 0$). To determine the demand by those students who attend school in urban areas, we simply assign the value of 1 to the $X_4$ variable. This gives us the second demand curve shown in Figure 5.16. In effect, the change in $X_4$ has caused the original curve to shift downward.

## NONLINEAR RELATIONSHIPS

The method of least squares finds the best linear relationship between the dependent and independent variables. However, in certain instances, economic theory, experience, or simple observation of the scatter plot may lead researchers to suspect that the relationship between the dependent and independent variables is nonlinear. For example, suppose data on income ($X$) and the demand for restaurant meals ($Q_D$) for a sample of households yields the scatter plot shown in Figure 5.17a. As you can see, the scatter implies a nonlinear relationship between income and the demand for restaurant meals. Such nonlinear representations are still suitable for estimation with the use of linear regression analysis. For example, we could specify a polynomial regression model in which the independent term, $X$, is raised to the second as well as to the first degree. Figure 5.17b illustrates this option. We could also specify our regression equation in terms of a

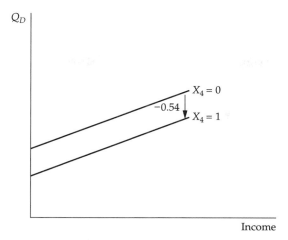

**FIGURE 5.16** Effect of the Dummy Variable

power function. Figure 5.17*c* illustrates this possibility. In either case, the idea is to use the method of least squares to estimate the coefficients of the equations. The usual tests and statistics (e.g., *t*-test, *F*-test, $R^2$) are still used in evaluating the regression results.

When using the power function, we first apply a logarithmic transformation to the original specification. For example, let the original equation be as follows:

$$Q_D = aX^b$$

where $Q_D$ = Demand for restaurant services (number of times a person eats in a restaurant per year)

$X$ = Annual income

Taking the log of both sides of the equation gives us the following logarithmic transformation:

$$\log Q_D = \log a + b \log X$$

To perform a regression analysis on this type of nonlinear data, we first find the logs of each of the values of $Y$ and $X$ in the sample data. We then regress $\log Y$ on $\log X$ using the method of least squares. One way in which the transformed regression equation can be evaluated is to compare its $R^2$ with that of a simple linear equation (i.e., $Q_D = a + bX$). If the $R^2$ of the transformed power equation is greater than that of the simple linear expression, it would appear that the nonlinear model offers a better explanation for the variance of $Q_D$.

The use of a *log-linear* equation in regression analysis is particularly appealing for economists because for relatively small changes in $X$, the estimated coefficient of the log of $X$ can indicate the *percentage change in Y relative to the percentage change in X*.[10] In other words, the coefficients of the transformed variables are in fact measures of the point elasticity of demand with respect to each variable. For example, if the estimated value of $b$ in the preceding equation were 1.2, then we could immediately interpret restaurant dining as a "superior" product because its income elasticity is greater than unity.

---

[10]For a discussion of the meaning of the coefficients in a log-linear regression equation, see the discussion of the basic mathematics of the Cobb-Douglas function in chapter 7.

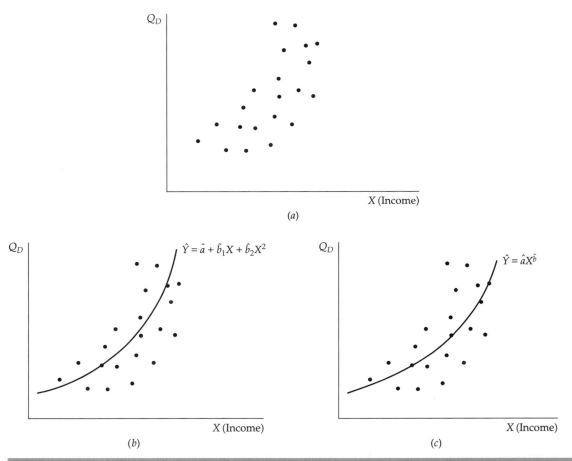

**FIGURE 5.17** Nonlinear Relationships

## Problems in the Use of Regression Analysis

A full discussion of the problems that may arise in regression is clearly beyond the scope of this chapter and this text. As mentioned at the outset of this chapter, entire textbooks and whole courses ranging from introductory to advanced are dedicated to the study of regression analysis. Nonetheless, we should cite and briefly explain some of these problems so that readers unfamiliar with this topic will gain an appreciation of the real challenges awaiting those who wish to apply regression analysis to business and economic research.

### THE IDENTIFICATION PROBLEM

The identification problem presents perhaps the greatest challenge to those using regression analysis to estimate the demand for a particular good or service. To explain

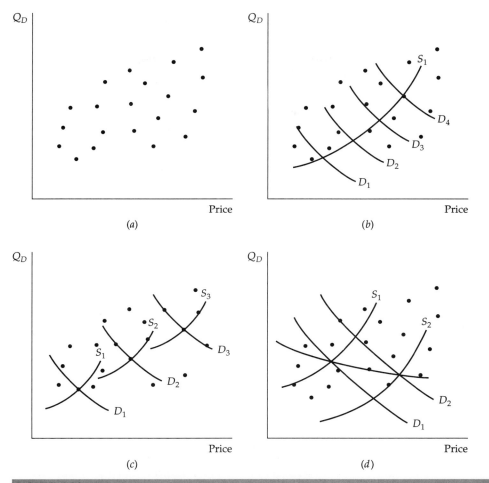

**FIGURE 5.18** The Identification Problem

this problem, let us return to our pizza example. Suppose we had time series data relating the per-capita consumption of pizza with the price of pizza over a 20-year period. The scatter plot of this information is shown in Figure 5.18a. Notice that the scatter tends to slope upward and that a least squares regression estimate would reflect this pattern of relationship. Does this mean that the consumers of pizza behave irrationally and demand more pizza at higher prices? Common sense would balk at such a conclusion, but then why the positive coefficient of the price variable in the demand equation? The alert reader will state that what we have identified as a demand equation is probably some sort of supply equation or perhaps, the result of the movement in *both* supply and demand for pizza over the past 20 years. As can be seen in Figure 5.18b, if the supply remained constant over the past 20 years while demand shifted upward (because of changes in such factors as income, number of buyers, and tastes and preferences over this time period), the regression equation would really be a reflection of the supply curve $S_1$. If the supply increased but demand increased more than the supply, then the regression estimate would really be a reflection of the intersection of the various $S$ and $D$ curves in Figure 5.18c. Figure 5.18d shows still another possibility. In this case, supply shifts more than demand, so that the estimated regression line is downward sloping and more like what we would expect of a demand curve. Nonetheless, this estimated demand curve is flatter than the true demand curves, which have gradually shifted to the right over the years. Thus, the regression estimate of the relationship between price and quantity demanded would be biased in the sense that it would indicate a much greater price elasticity than actually exists in the population of pizza consumers.

There are advanced estimation techniques, such as the methods of *two-stage least squares* and *indirect least squares,* that can help the researcher deal with samples in which the simultaneous shifting of demand and supply takes place. Essentially, these techniques involve the simultaneous consideration of the supply and demand equations with the use of a single regression equation. A discussion of these techniques lies outside the scope of this text. But the principal point to remember is that if the identification problem is not recognized and dealt with by the researcher, the method of ordinary least squares will result in biased estimates of the regression coefficients.

## MULTICOLLINEARITY

One of the key assumptions made in the construction of the multiple regression equation is that the independent variables are not related to each other in any systematic way. If this assumption is incorrect, then each of the estimated coefficients may give a distorted view of the impact of the change in each of the independent variables. For example, suppose a regression model states that the demand for luxury foreign-made automobiles depends on price, income, and education. The latter variable is included because education is a proxy for tastes and preferences, and those with higher levels of education are hypothesized to have a greater preference for luxury foreign cars. But, as you would expect, education and income are closely associated. If their values tend to move up and down together, the least squares method may arbitrarily assign a high value to the coefficient of one variable and a low coefficient value to the other. In effect, if two variables are closely associated, it becomes difficult to separate out the effect that each has on the dependent variable. The existence of such a condition in regression analysis is called *multicollinearity.*

If the regression results pass the $F$-test (the measure of the overall statistical significance of the regression equation) but fail the $t$-test for each of the individual regression coefficients, it is usually a sign that multicollinearity is present in the sample data. Multicollinearity can also be detected by examining the correlation coefficient between two variables suspected of being closely related.[11] As a rule of thumb, correlation coefficients of 0.7 or more provide a basis for researchers to suspect the existence of multicollinearity.

---

[11]The correlation coefficient is a measure of the degree of association between two variables. This measure, denoted $r$, ranges from a value of $-1$ (perfect negative correlation) to 1 (perfect positive correlation).

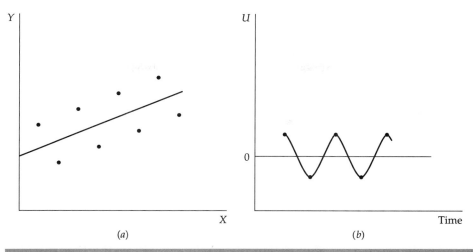

**FIGURE 5.19** Autocorrelation

If multicollinearity is a serious problem in the regression analysis, it will tend to introduce an upward bias to the standard errors of the coefficients. This will tend to reduce the *t*-values (which, you will recall, are computed using the standard errors of the coefficients). This makes it harder to reject the null hypothesis and, of course, to identify statistically significant independent variables in the regression model.

It should be pointed out, however, that if the researcher simply wishes to use the estimated regression coefficients as a basis for forecasting future values of the dependent variable, multicollinearity does not pose a serious problem. It is only when the researcher wishes to understand more about the underlying structure of the demand function (i.e., what are the key determinants of demand) that this particular statistical problem should be resolved. Most software packages automatically produce a correlation coefficient matrix for the entire set of independent variables used in the regression equation. A standard remedy for multicollinearity is to drop one of the variables that is closely associated with another variable in the regression equation.

## AUTOCORRELATION

Autocorrelation is a problem that is usually encountered when time series data are used. For this reason, it is often referred to as *serial correlation.* Let us use the case of simple regression, involving only the dependent variable $Y$ and one independent variable, $X$. Essentially, autocorrelation occurs when the $Y$ variable relates to the $X$ variable according to a certain pattern. For example, in Figure 5.19*a,* the scatter plot reveals that as $X$ increases (presumably over time), the $Y$ value deviates from the regression line in a very systematic way. In other words, the *residual term,* or the difference between the observed value of $Y$ and the estimated value of $Y$ given $X(\hat{Y})$ alternates between a positive and a negative value of approximately the same magnitude throughout the range of $X$ values. In fact, if we were to plot these residuals on a separate graph, they would have the pattern shown in Figure 5.19*b.*

One possible cause of autocorrelation is that there are effects on $Y$ not accounted for by the variables included in the regression equation. It might also be that the true relationship between $Y$ and the independent variable(s) is nonlinear. But regardless of the reason, if autocorrelation is present in the regression analysis, it creates a problem for the validity of the $t$-test. Simply stated, autocorrelation tends to increase the likelihood that the null hypothesis will be rejected. This is because autocorrelation gives a downward bias to the standard error of the estimated regression coefficient ($SE_{\hat{b}}$). Recalling that the $t$-value is defined as $(\hat{b} - b)/SE_{\hat{b}}$, we can see that a smaller $SE_{\hat{b}}$ would tend to increase the magnitude of the $t$-value, other factors held constant. Thus, in the presence of autocorrelation, researchers may well declare that certain independent variables have a statistically significant impact on the dependent variable when in fact they do not. From a policy standpoint, suppose that the estimated coefficient of the advertising variable in a regression model of demand passed the $t$-test when it really should not have. A firm might then be led to increase its advertising expenditures when in fact it should be looking at other ways to expand demand (e.g., through promotions, alternative channels of distribution, or price actions).

It may be difficult to identify autocorrelation simply by observing the pattern of the residuals of a regression equation. A standard test for identifying the presence of this problem is the *Durbin-Watson test*. The Durbin-Watson statistic (i.e., DW) is now routinely calculated in regression software packages and is presented automatically in the computer printout. As in the case of the $t$-test and the $F$-test, there is a Durbin-Watson table listing the critical values of this statistic for a given level of significance (usually the 0.05 level). We have included such a table in the appendix at the back of this text (see Table B.5). As a rule of thumb, if the DW statistic is around 2, there is in all probability no autocorrelation present in the data. Should the DW statistic indicate the presence of autocorrelation, there are certain things a researcher can do to correct the problem. These include transforming the data into a different order of magnitude or introducing leading or lagging data in the time series.

## THE SOLUTION

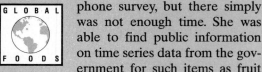

As it turned out, the task of generating a statistical model was not as simple as Jennifer Harrah had anticipated. The key problem was the lack of data. The product was brand new for Global Foods, so there was no historical information that the company could provide for use as time series data in the regression analysis. She could have generated cross-sectional data by conducting a tele-phone survey, but there simply was not enough time. She was able to find public information on time series data from the government for such items as fruit juices, soft drinks, and beer, but these were aggregated by product type, and no other information besides average price was available. The only data set she could find within the time allowed was part of a market research study

*(Continued)*

conducted in the 1950s by the *National Bottler's Gazette*. This study looked at the per-capita consumption of soft drinks by state, along with the average annual temperature of the state and its per capita income. These figures are shown in Table 5.3.[12] She conducted a regression analysis of these cross-sectional data using the following model:

$$Q = a + b_1 INC + b_2 TEMP$$

where $Q$ = Per-capita annual consumption of soft drinks
INC = Per-capita annual income
TEMP = Average annual temperature

The results of the computer analysis are shown in Table 5.4. Temperature has a sizable as well as a statistically significant impact on soft drink consumption. Every additional degree of average annual temperature results in an increase in per-capita soft drink consumption by 4.7 bottles. Using the "rule of 2," we can see that the *t*-value of 5.70 is clearly

significant. The estimated coefficient for the income variable is interesting. First, its negative value indicates that a soft drink is an "inferior" product. Higher levels of income result in lower per-capita consumption, and lower income implies higher consumption. However, the *t*-value of −1.2 is below the critical *t*-value. Thus, income cannot be considered a statistically significant determinant of soft drink consumption. The adjusted $R^2$ of 0.46 indicates that about one-half of the variation in soft drink consumption can be accounted for by the variation in per-capita income and average annual temperature. This is to be expected, considering the fact that cross-sectional data are used and that only two independent variables were incorporated into the equation. Nonetheless, the *F*-value of 21.37 indicates that the $R^2$ is statistically significant, because the critical value of *F* at the 0.05 level with 2 and 45 degrees of freedom is about 3.20.

Jennifer wanted to include price in her regression model. Unfortunately, no time series data were available for price. There were some cross-sectional data on the average prices in different regions of the country, but these data were not suitable for regression analysis, because the prices were basically the same for all regions. Regression analysis requires *variation* in the values of the independent variables. Otherwise, there is no scatter plot to which to fit the regression line.

---

[12]The authors debated whether to use artificially created data to demonstrate all of the topics presented in this chapter or to use real data, which would limit the application of regression analysis. The latter option was chosen because in actual business situations, the lack of good data is far more limiting than either one's knowledge of statistical analysis or the computing power available to "crunch" the numbers. The soft drink consumption figures from the study by the *National Bottler's Gazette* were originally presented in a market research textbook now out of print. Unfortunately, this text did not cite the date when the figures were obtained.

*(Continued)*

**TABLE 5.3  Soft Drink Consumption, Temperature, and Income by State**

| State | Consumption of Soft Drinks per Capita | Per Capita Income (Hundreds) | Mean Annual Temperature, °F |
|-------|---------------------------------------|------------------------------|------------------------------|
| Alabama | 200 | $13 | 66 |
| Arizona | 150 | 17 | 62 |
| Arkansas | 237 | 11 | 63 |
| California | 135 | 25 | 56 |
| Colorado | 121 | 19 | 52 |
| Connecticut | 118 | 27 | 50 |
| Delaware | 217 | 28 | 52 |
| Florida | 242 | 18 | 72 |
| Georgia | 295 | 14 | 64 |
| Idaho | 85 | 16 | 46 |
| Illinois | 114 | 24 | 52 |
| Indiana | 184 | 20 | 52 |
| Iowa | 104 | 16 | 50 |
| Kansas | 143 | 17 | 56 |
| Kentucky | 230 | 13 | 56 |
| Louisiana | 269 | 15 | 69 |
| Maine | 111 | 16 | 41 |
| Maryland | 217 | 21 | 54 |
| Massachusetts | 114 | 22 | 47 |
| Michigan | 108 | 21 | 47 |
| Minnesota | 108 | 18 | 41 |
| Mississippi | 248 | 10 | 65 |
| Missouri | 203 | 19 | 57 |
| Montana | 77 | 19 | 44 |
| Nebraska | 97 | 16 | 49 |
| Nevada | 166 | 24 | 48 |
| New Hampshire | 177 | 18 | 35 |
| New Jersey | 143 | 24 | 54 |
| New Mexico | 157 | 15 | 56 |
| New York | 111 | 25 | 48 |
| North Carolina | 330 | 13 | 59 |
| North Dakota | 63 | 14 | 39 |
| Ohio | 165 | 22 | 51 |
| Oklahoma | 184 | 16 | 82 |
| Oregon | 68 | 19 | 51 |
| Pennsylvania | 121 | 20 | 50 |
| Rhode Island | 138 | 20 | 50 |
| South Carolina | 237 | 12 | 65 |
| South Dakota | 95 | 13 | 45 |
| Tennessee | 236 | 13 | 60 |
| Texas | 222 | 17 | 69 |
| Utah | 100 | 16 | 50 |
| Vermont | 64 | 16 | 44 |
| Virginia | 270 | 16 | 58 |
| Washington | 77 | 20 | 49 |
| West Virginia | 144 | 15 | 55 |
| Wisconsin | 97 | 19 | 46 |
| Wyoming | 102 | 19 | 46 |

*(Continued)*

**TABLE 5.4  Excel Regression Analysis Output**

*Regression Statistics*

| | |
|---|---|
| Multiple R | 0.697953501 |
| R Square | 0.487139089 |
| Adjusted R Square | 0.464345271 |
| Standard Error | 49.71283142 |
| Observations | 48 |

*Anova*

| | df | SS | MS | F | Significance F |
|---|---|---|---|---|---|
| Regression | 2 | 105633.7976 | 52816.9 | 21.371544 | 2.98532E-07 |
| Residual | 45 | 111211.4524 | 2471.366 | | |
| Total | 47 | 216845.25 | | | |

| | Coefficients | Standard Error | t Stat | P-value | Lower 95% | Upper 95% |
|---|---|---|---|---|---|---|
| Intercept | −54.841134 | 63.45499732 | −0.864252 | 0.3920329 | −182.6460536 | 72.96379 |
| X Variable 1 | −2.20457538 | 1.825233618 | −1.207832 | 0.2334217 | −5.880784437 | 1.471634 |
| X Variable 2 | 4.719982058 | 0.828234444 | 5.698848 | 8.722E-07 | 3.05183233 | 6.388132 |

Variable 1 = income per capita
Variable 2 = average temperature

## Summary

This chapter has presented an introduction to regression analysis, the method most commonly utilized by economists for estimating the demand for goods and services. Actually, this chapter's material is only a small part of econometrics, which is the application of multivariate statistical analysis to economic theory. The primary importance of this chapter is as an aid in understanding how the techniques of regression analysis may be applied to businesses interested in finding out more about the quantitative aspects of the demand for their products. Readers should appreciate the challenge of applying regression analysis and other statistical techniques to business problems because of the difficulty of obtaining accurate and reliable data.

The process of applying regression analysis to the estimation of demand can be summarized in the following steps:

1. Specification of the regression model of demand
2. Collection of the relevant data
3. Estimation of the regression equation
4. Analysis and evaluation of the regression results (e.g., $t$-test, $F$-test, $R^2$), and adjustment or correction for any statistical problems (e.g., multicollinearity, autocorrelation, incorrect functional form)
5. Assessment of regression findings for use in making policy decisions

In a formal econometrics course, most of the emphasis is placed on steps 1, 3, and 4 (i.e., the more technical aspects of this type of statistical analysis). In business, the most important steps are 2 and 5. Powerful computers and sophisticated software packages are available to everyone today at such a reasonable cost that it has become elementary to apply regression analysis to the estimation of demand or any other aspect of business research. The real challenge is to obtain *good* data and to apply judiciously the results of the regression analysis to the managerial decision-making process. In these two areas of regression analysis, no textbook or course can take the place of actual hands-on experience.

## Important Concepts

**Alternative hypothesis:** In regression analysis, the hypothesis that stands in contrast to the null hypothesis. It generally states that the true (but unknown) population coefficient is some value other than zero. (p. 175)

**Coefficient of determination ($R^2$):** A measure indicating the percentage of the variation in the dependent variable accounted for by variations in some designated independent variable. Its value ranges from 0 to 1. Zero indicates that variations in the independent variable account for none of the variation in the dependent variable. One indicates that 100 percent of the variation in the dependent variable can be accounted for by the variations in the independent variable. In multiple regression analysis, this measure is referred to as the *multiple coefficient of determination.* (p. 159)

**Coefficients of the regression equation:** Also referred to as *parameters,* the values that indicate the quantitative impact on the dependent variable of a unit change in an independent variable. The main objective of regression analysis is to estimate the values of these coefficients from a sample of data. For this the method of ordinary least squares is often employed. (p. 164)

**Consumer survey:** The attempt to obtain data about demand directly by asking consumers about their purchasing habits through such means as face-to-face interviews, focus groups, telephone surveys, and mailed questionnaires. (p. 152)

**Cross-sectional data:** Data on a particular set of variables for a given point in time for a cross section of individual entities (e.g., persons, households, cities, states, countries). (p. 154)

**Degrees of freedom:** An adjustment factor that is required in conducting the *t*-test. This number is found by subtracting the number of independent variables plus 1 from the number of observations in the sample; that is, d.f. $= n - (k + 1) = n - k - 1$. (p. 176)

**F-test:** A test for the statistical significance of the $R^2$ value. If this test is passed, a researcher can be quite confident that all of the estimated coefficients of a regression model together are not zero for the population under study. (p. 159)

**Method of ordinary least squares (OLS):** In simple regression analysis, a method designed to fit a line through a scatter of points indicating values of a dependent variable and an independent variable in such a way that the sum of the squared deviations of the points from the line is minimized. (p. 164)

**Null hypothesis:** In regression analysis, the hypothesis used in testing for the statistical significance of the estimated regression coefficient. It states that the true (but unknown) regression coefficients for the population are zero. (p. 175)

**One-tail test:** This refers to the nature of the alternative hypothesis in the *t*-test. If the alternative hypothesis states that the population coefficient is positive, then the upper tail of the *t*-distribution is used. If the alternative hypothesis states that the population coefficient is negative, then the lower tail is used. In either case, only one tail is used. (p. 180)

**Regression analysis:** A statistical technique for finding the best relationship between a dependent variable and selected independent variables. If one independent variable is used, this technique is referred to as *simple regression.* If more than one independent variable is used, it is called *multiple regression.* (p. 153)

**Rule of 2:** A general rule of thumb employed by economists in conducting the *t*-test. Essentially, it states that any *t*-ratio of 2 or more indicates that the estimated coefficient is statistically significant at the 0.05 level. (p. 158)

**Standard error of the coefficient ($SE_b$):** A measure of the deviation of an estimated regression coefficient from the hypothesized value of the true (but unknown) population coefficient. In the *t*-test, the standard error of a particular estimated coefficient is divided into this coefficient, thereby indicating the *t*-value. (p. 158)

**Standard error of the estimate (SEE):** A measure of the deviation of the estimated value of the dependent variable, given the values of the independent variables. In forecasting, the standard error of the estimate is used to develop an interval that contains the true value of the dependent variable, subject to a designated degree of confidence. (p. 185)

***t*-table:** A numerical table indicating the different values of the *t*-ratio and the frequency of their occurrence in a *t*-distribution whose mean value is zero. (p. 176)

***t*-test:** A test for the statistical significance of the estimated regression coefficients. If a coefficient passes this test, then a researcher can be quite confident that the value of the true population coefficient is not zero. (p. 158)

**Time series data:** Data for a particular set of variables that track their values over a particular period of time at regular intervals (e.g., monthly, quarterly, annually). (p. 154)

**Two-tail test:** A *t*-test in which the alternative hypothesis states that the population coefficient may be either positive or negative (i.e., it is not zero); that is, either the upper or the lower tail of the *t*-distribution may be used. (p. 180)

## Questions

1. Explain the difference between time series data and cross-sectional data. Provide examples of each type of data.
2. Would there be any differences in the set of variables used in a regression model of the demand for consumer durable goods (e.g., automobiles, appliances, furniture) and a regression model of the demand for "fast-moving consumer goods" (e.g., food, beverages, personal care products)? Explain.
3. Explain the difference between a deterministic model and a probabilistic model of the relationship between a dependent variable and one or more independent variables.
4. Briefly explain the meaning of $R^2$. A time series analysis of demand tends to result in a higher $R^2$ than one using cross-sectional data. Why do you think this is the case?
5. Overheard at the water cooler: "My regression model of demand is better than the one that the consultant prepared for us because it has a higher $R^2$. Besides, my equation has three more independent variables and so is more complete than the consultant's." Comment on this statement. Would you agree with the speaker? Explain.
6. Summarize the steps involved in conducting the *t*-test. What is the basis for using the "rule of 2" as a convenient method of evaluating *t*-ratios?
7. Briefly explain the meaning of the *F*-test. Why do you think this test is considered to be more important in multiple regression analysis than it is in simple regression analysis?
8. What is *multicollinearity?* How can researchers detect this problem? What is the impact of this problem on the regression estimates? What steps can be taken to deal with this problem?
9. What is the identification problem? What effect will this problem have on the regression estimates of a demand function? Explain.

## Problems

1. In the first several years of the 1990s, the consumer electronics industry had high hopes for the success of a type of compact disc player that displays sophisticated audio and video programs on a television set. The initial price of this product, which would enable users to scan programs ranging from the complete works of William Shakespeare to a cookbook with more than 450 recipes with color photographs and voiceovers, was set at about $1,000.
   a. Suppose you were asked to conduct market research for this product. Is it possible to use regression analysis for a product such as this, which had never before been on the market? If you believe so, how would you have gone about conducting this research?

**b.** As data accumulated about this product's sales, suggest the types of variables that could have been included in a regression analysis of the demand for this new type of CD player.

**c.** What does the current popularity of multimedia personal computers (PCs with speakers and CD-ROM drives) tell you about the difficulties of using regression (or, for that matter, any other quantitative technique) to forecast a product's demand?

2. One of the most difficult tasks in regression analysis is to obtain the data suitable for quantitative studies of this kind. Suppose you are trying to estimate the demand for home furniture. Suggest the kinds of variables that could be used to represent the following factors, which are believed to affect the demand for any product. Be as specific as possible about how the variables are going to be measured. Do you anticipate any difficulty in securing such data? Explain.

| Determinants of Demand for Furniture | Suggested Variables to Use in Regression Analysis |
|---|---|
| Price | |
| Tastes and preferences | |
| Price of related products | |
| Income | |
| Cost or availability of credit | |
| Number of buyers | |
| Future expectations | |
| Other possible factors | |

3. You are the manager of a large automobile dealership who wants to learn more about the effectiveness of various discounts offered to customers over the past 14 months. Following are the average negotiated prices for each month and the quantities sold of a basic model (adjusted for various options) over this period of time.

**a.** Graph this information on a scatter plot. Estimate the demand equation. What do the regression results indicate about the desirability of discounting the price? Explain.

| Month | Price | Quantity |
|---|---|---|
| Jan. | 12,500 | 15 |
| Feb. | 12,200 | 17 |
| Mar. | 11,900 | 16 |
| Apr. | 12,000 | 18 |
| May | 11,800 | 20 |
| June | 12,500 | 18 |
| July | 11,700 | 22 |
| Aug. | 12,100 | 15 |
| Sept. | 11,400 | 22 |
| Oct. | 11,400 | 25 |
| Nov. | 11,200 | 24 |
| Dec. | 11,000 | 30 |
| Jan. | 10,800 | 25 |
| Feb. | 10,000 | 28 |

**b.** What other factors besides price might be included in this equation? Do you foresee any difficulty in obtaining these additional data or incorporating them in the regression analysis?

4. The maker of a leading brand of low-calorie microwavable food estimated the following demand equation for its product using data from 26 supermarkets around the country for the month of April:

$$Q = -5,200 - 42P + 20P_X + 5.2I + 0.20A + 0.25M$$

$$(2,002) \quad (17.5) \quad (6.2) \quad (2.5) \quad (0.09) \quad (0.21)$$

$$R^2 = 0.55 \qquad n = 26 \qquad F = 4.88$$

Assume the following values for the independent variables:

$Q$ = Quantity sold per month
$P$ (in cents) = Price of the product = 500
$P_X$ (in cents) = Price of leading competitor's product = 600
$I$ (in dollars) = Per capita income of the standard metropolitan statistical area (SMSA) in which the supermarket is located = 5,500
$A$ (in dollars) = Monthly advertising expenditure = 10,000
$M$ = Number of microwave ovens sold in the SMSA in which the supermarket is located = 5,000.

Using this information, answer the following questions:
a. Compute elasticities for each of the variables.
b. How concerned do you think this company would be about the impact of a recession on its sales? Explain.
c. Do you think that this firm should cut its price to increase its market share? Explain.
d. What proportion of the variation in sales is explained by the independent variables in the equations? How confident are you about this answer? Explain.
5. A manufacturer of computer workstations gathered average monthly sales figures from its 56 branch offices and dealerships across the country and estimated the following demand for its product:

$$Q = +15,000 - 2.80P + 150A + 0.3P_{pc} + 0.35P_m + 0.2P_c$$

$$(5,234) \quad (1.29) \quad (175) \quad (0.12) \quad (0.17) \quad (0.13)$$

$$R^2 = 0.68 \qquad \text{SEE} = 786 \qquad F = 21.25$$

The variables and their assumed values are

$Q$ = Quantity
$P$ = Price of basic model = 7,000
$A$ = Advertising expenditures (in thousands) = 52
$P_{pc}$ = Average price of a personal computer = 4000
$P_m$ = Average price of a minicomputer = 15,000
$P_c$ = Average price of a leading competitor's workstation = 8,000

a. Compute the elasticities for each of the variables. On this basis, discuss the relative impact that each variable has on the demand. What implications do these results have for the firm's marketing and pricing policies?
b. Conduct a *t*-test for the statistical significance of each variable. In each case, state whether a one-tail or two-tail test is required. What difference, if any, does it make to use a one-tail versus a two-tail test on the results? Discuss the results of the *t*-tests in light of the policy implications mentioned.
c. Suppose a manager evaluating these results suggests that interest rates and the performance of the computer (typically measured in millions of instructions per second, or MIPS) are important determinants of the demand for workstations and must therefore be included in the study. How would you respond to this suggestion? Elaborate.

6. Deck & Blacker is a maker of small kitchen appliances. Its economist estimates the following demand for toaster ovens using data gathered over 16 quarters from ten major retail distributors of its product. This type of sample, which involves the use of cross-sectional and times series data, is referred to as a *pooled sample*. On the basis of this pooled sample of 160 observations, the economist estimated the following equation:

$$Q = 40 - 1.1P + 1.5A + 0.32I + 0.5H + 0.1P_c$$

$$(2.5) \quad (0.9) \quad (0.6) \quad (0.12) \quad (0.17) \quad (0.75)$$

$$R^2 = 0.91 \qquad SEE = 2.8 \qquad F = 311.43$$

The variables and the values inserted into the equation for purposes of forecasting are as follows:

$Q$ = Quantity demanded, in thousands
$P$ = Price, in dollars = 55
$A$ = Advertising expenditures, in thousands = 20
$I$ = Average household income, in thousands = 31
$H$ = Total number of residential sales, in thousands = 10
$P_c$ = Price of leading competitor, in dollars = 50

a. Should this company try to market its toaster ovens in upscale gourmet shops? Explain.
b. How concerned should this company be about price discounts by its leading competitor? Explain.
c. How effective do you think advertising is for this company?
d. Should this company consider discounting its price in order to gain market share at the expense of its competitors? Explain.
e. Assuming the values of the variables are given, indicate the 95 percent confidence interval of the forecast demand for toaster ovens.

7. You are given the following demand for European luxury automobiles:

$$Q = 1,000P^{-0.93}P_a^{0.75}P_j^{1.2}I^{1.6}$$

where $P$ = Price of European luxury cars
$P_a$ = Price of American luxury cars
$P_j$ = Price of Japanese luxury cars
$I$ = Annual income of car buyers

Assume that each of the coefficients is statistically significant (i.e., that they passed the *t*-test). On the basis of the information given, answer the following questions:
a. Comment on the degree of substitutability between European and American luxury cars and between European and Japanese luxury cars. Explain some possible reasons for the results in the equation.
b. Comment on the coefficient for the income variable. Is this result what you would expect? Explain.
c. Comment on the coefficient of the European car price variable. Is that what you would expect? Explain.

# Take It to the Net

We invite you to visit the Keat/Young page on the Prentice Hall Web site at:

**http://www.prenhall.com/keat**

for additional resources.

# CHAPTER 6

# Forecasting

## THE SITUATION

Frank Robinson, recently brought into Global Foods, Inc., to build a forecasting department, finds his new position to be very challenging and quite interesting. However, he also knows that forecasting, even in the relatively stable soft drink industry, can be a thankless task. From various forecast requests on his desk, he pulls out the one for the company's lemon-lime soda, Citronade, a brand recently purchased from an older, established company. He has been asked to estimate sales for the next year, and the deadline for his report is nearing. He has annual sales data for the last 11 years, and he also has sales data by quarter. In an industry where sales show considerable increases during the summer months, a forecast that estimates  sales for the seasons of the year is very important.[1]

Frank first looks at the annual data, and he quickly computes year-to-year changes. These numbers are shown in Table 6.1. He notices that, although sales were up in each of the years, the percentage growth from year to year appears to have a declining trend. He will have to consider this phenomenon when he makes his forecast.

Quarterly data are shown in Table 6.2. As he looks over these numbers, Frank realizes that he has several busy days ahead of him.

---

[1]Sales forecasts for a "real" company are usually made on a monthly, not a quarterly, basis. But for the purposes of this text, quarterly data will be utilized. This is done to economize on the quantity of data used. The methods employed in the analysis of the data are identical whether quarterly or monthly figures are employed.

*(Continued)*

| TABLE 6.1 | Sales of Citronade (in Thousands of Cases) | | |
| --- | --- | --- | --- |
| Year | Annual Sales | Change | Percent Change |
| 1989 | 3,892 | | |
| 1990 | 4,203 | 311 | 8.0 |
| 1991 | 4,477 | 274 | 6.5 |
| 1992 | 4,810 | 333 | 7.4 |
| 1993 | 5,132 | 322 | 6.7 |
| 1994 | 5,407 | 275 | 5.4 |
| 1995 | 5,726 | 319 | 5.9 |
| 1996 | 6,023 | 297 | 5.2 |
| 1997 | 6,360 | 337 | 5.6 |
| 1998 | 6,641 | 281 | 4.4 |
| 1999 | 6,954 | 313 | 4.7 |

| TABLE 6.2 | Quarterly Sales of Citronade, 1989–1999 (in Thousands of Cases) | | | | |
| --- | --- | --- | --- | --- | --- |
| Year | 1st Qtr | 2nd Qtr | 3rd Qtr | 4th Qtr | Total |
| 1989 | 842 | 939 | 1,236 | 875 | 3,892 |
| 1990 | 907 | 1,017 | 1,331 | 948 | 4,203 |
| 1991 | 953 | 1,103 | 1,406 | 1,015 | 4,477 |
| 1992 | 1,047 | 1,180 | 1,505 | 1,078 | 4,810 |
| 1993 | 1,124 | 1,267 | 1,576 | 1,165 | 5,132 |
| 1994 | 1,167 | 1,340 | 1,670 | 1,230 | 5,407 |
| 1995 | 1,255 | 1,403 | 1,766 | 1,302 | 5,726 |
| 1996 | 1,311 | 1,495 | 1,837 | 1,380 | 6,023 |
| 1997 | 1,390 | 1,565 | 1,940 | 1,465 | 6,360 |
| 1998 | 1,455 | 1,649 | 2,026 | 1,511 | 6,641 |
| 1999 | 1,536 | 1,714 | 2,103 | 1,601 | 6,954 |

# Introduction

One of the authors remembers a poster he saw, many years ago, on the wall of the office of the director of market research of a large manufacturing corporation. It said: "Forecasting is very difficult, especially into the future." One could add: "Accurate forecasting is even more difficult." Certainly, there is a great deal of truth in this statement. But despite the difficulty of forecasting, and forecasting accurately, it is an integral part of our lives. Many of us eagerly watch television weather forecasts or pay heed to the predictions of a favorite stock market guru, knowing only too well how inaccurate they may be. In an even less formal sense we make forecasts when we buy a lottery ticket, bet on a horse, or make a decision whether to carry an umbrella when we leave our house.

In the worlds of business, government, or even nonprofit institutions, forecasting becomes even more important. In a world where organizations and their environments are continually becoming more complex and changes occur more rapidly, decision makers need help in weighing many factors and understanding constantly changing relationships to arrive at decisions whose results have ever-increasing impacts.[2] Utilizing existing resources and acquiring additional resources appropriately requires maximum information about the company's future.

All organizations conduct their activities in an uncertain environment, and probably the major role of forecasting is to reduce this uncertainty. But no forecast, however extensive and expensive, can remove it completely. Managers who use forecasts in their

---

[2]The introductory sections of this chapter draw heavily on one of the leading books in the area of forecasting, Steven C. Wheelwright and Spyros Makridakis, *Forecasting Methods for Management,* 5th ed., New York: John Wiley and Sons, 1989.

work "need to develop realistic expectations as to what forecasting can and cannot do."[3] "Forecasting is not a substitute for management judgment in decision making; it is simply an aid to that process."[4]

### OBJECTIVES, PLANS, FORECASTS

Before we discuss the things that are forecast and methods of forecasting, a brief digression is needed to define and distinguish some business terms.

A business firm operates in such a way as to achieve set objectives. Plans are constructed and implemented to achieve these objectives. Forecasts are used both in setting objectives and in creating plans. Obviously, forecasts are intimately connected with objective setting and planning, but the functions are not identical.

The setting of objectives by a corporation was discussed in chapter 2. Objectives (or goals) are usually stated in terms of revenue or profit growth, profitability or return on investment, and resource growth and deployment. In order that corporate management can set reasonable targets for its objectives, it must have available the relevant forecasts, both for the short and long terms. Thus, corporate management will consult with economists to obtain the best estimates of how the economy will behave over the relevant time period. In addition, management will be interested in the forecast of sales for the company's industry. These forecasts are then utilized in the process of objective setting for the corporation as a whole and for its component parts. Both short-term and long-term objectives will be established. When these objectives are communicated from corporate headquarters to the various profit centers, the process of planning begins.

Corporate planners in all areas—sales, human resources, facilities, manufacturing, finance—will utilize an array of forecasts in constructing the various portions of the plan. Actually, a forecast may show what will happen under certain conditions and assumptions. In such cases, a planner works with these forecasts but also designs actions that may counteract or revise the forecast. If, for example, a forecast shows an unfavorable trend in the sales of a particular product for the next year, the plan may recommend actions that will counteract this prediction. Then, given the new tactics or strategies incorporated into the plan, the original forecast may be superseded by a new, revised forecast, with altered conditions and assumptions.

# Subjects of Forecasts

Business utilizes forecasting to obtain information about many subjects. In the final analysis, firms are interested in future sales and profits—the bottom line. But to get there, a large number of forecasts may be necessary. In this section of the chapter, we will outline the various categories of forecasts—from the most macro forecasts down to individual series.

The broadest economic forecast series is the gross domestic product (GDP), which describes the total production of goods and services in a country. Actually, some measures are available for the world economy, but these are usually composites of country

---

[3]Ibid., p. 44.
[4]Ibid., p. 30.

forecasts. GDP forecasting is usually accomplished with highly complex econometric models that contain hundreds of variables and a huge number of calculations.

There are also forecasts of GDP components, for instance, consumption expenditure, producer durable equipment expenditure, or residential construction, to name just a few. Thus, a company producing heavy machinery would be interested in data on producer durable equipment and a forest products company in construction statistics. Again, such forecasts could be provided to the company by an outside organization specializing in such activities.

A step down from macro forecasting is the industry forecast. The future sales of the soft drink industry as a whole would be included here. Of course, a forecast could also relate to the automobile industry, the steel industry, or any other. In addition, concern may lie with the future sales of a particular product within an industry, such as club soda or compact automobiles.

Finally, the subject of interest may be the sales of a specific product of a specific firm, such as the diet cola of Global Foods' soft drink division.

The preceding discussion of the forecast hierarchy has concentrated on sales forecasts. But the future estimates for a given firm could be for costs and expenses (in total or for various categories), employment requirements, square feet of facilities utilized, or anything else of importance to a company.

Our major emphasis in this chapter will be with forecasting the sales of a particular product of our hypothetical soft drink manufacturer. The forecast of GDP and its constituent parts will be considered to be assumptions underlying the firm's specific product forecast.

### DEMAND ESTIMATING AND DEMAND FORECASTING

In the preceding chapter, regression analysis and demand estimation were discussed. There is a great deal of similarity between demand forecasting and demand estimating. Each serves to increase the information available to decision makers. The difference between the two lies largely in the ultimate purpose of the analysis.

The demand estimating technique will be used by a manager interested in probing the effect on the demand (or quantity demanded) of a change in one or more of the independent variables. Thus, a pricing manager may want to know the impact on the sales of the company's club soda as a result of a price change, of a competitor's price changes, or, for example, of a change in the company's advertising expenses.

On the other hand, forecasting puts less emphasis on explaining the specific causes of demand changes and more on obtaining information regarding future levels of sales activity, given the most likely assumptions about the independent variables. Such information is then used in the construction of the company's plan. Indeed, in some cases, to be discussed later in this chapter, forecasting is achieved without the introduction of any causal factors; future sales are predicted solely by projecting the past into the future.

## Prerequisites of a Good Forecast

Certain conditions should be met by any good forecast. Unfortunately, this is not always possible.

First, a particular forecast must be consistent with other parts of the business. If you forecast 10 percent growth in the shipments of your product for next year, you must make sure that your manufacturing facilities have sufficient capacity to produce this increased amount, and that the additions to the labor force necessary to produce and sell this increased amount are in the company's plan for next year.

Second, a good forecast should usually be based on adequate knowledge of the relevant past. There are, of course, exceptions to this rule. Sometimes past experience is of no help in predicting future demand. This is the case if conditions have undergone a radical change. Thus, after World War II, forecasts for automobile and appliance sales could not rely on sales data of recent years, since these products were not produced during the country's involvement in the war. Moreover, any sales patterns that held for the prewar years could not be applied, because in 1946, when automobiles again rolled off the production line, the average age of the existing automobile stock was considerably higher than was customary, people had old cars or none at all, returning servicemen and women were new additions to the car market, and many people had saved up large amounts of money during the war years and were ready to spend.

In other instances, there may be no past on which to fall back. This could be the case for a new product or a technological breakthrough. Under these circumstances, analysts' judgments must be injected into the forecasting process. In some cases, "forecasts based purely on the opinions of 'experts' are used to formulate the forecast or scenario for the future."[5]

Third, a forecast should take into consideration the economic and political environment. If significant changes in economic conditions or in political institutions are expected within the forecast period, these events must be accounted for, since they may have a substantial effect on the future of the business.[6]

One other prerequisite, a rather obvious one, must be added. A forecast must be timely. Sometimes accuracy may have to be sacrificed to achieve timeliness. It serves no purpose to deliver an extremely accurate forecast that is too late to be acted on. As obvious as this point may be, it cannot be stressed strongly enough. Forecasters are often tempted to polish and improve their forecasts. Not only can such embellishment add costs that may not be worth the improvement in accuracy, it may also delay the publication of the estimate. This is particularly important at turning points in the forecast series. If the forecast is published too late to issue a warning, its great accuracy will be worthless.

## Forecasting Techniques

There are many different forecasting methods. One of the challenges facing a forecaster is choosing the right technique. The appropriate method depends on the subject matter to be forecast and on the forecaster, but we can discuss some of the factors that enter into consideration.[7]

---

[5]John E. Hanke and Arthur G. Reitsch, *Business Forecasting,* 5th ed., Englewood Cliffs, NJ: Prentice Hall, 1995, p. 521. This is another text we recommend for students who are interested in exploring the subject of forecasting in more detail.

[6]Taking potential changes in political institutions into account is of importance to multinational corporations, which operate in a large number of foreign countries, probably including those whose political directions are quite unstable and whose governments may be subject to radical changes.

[7]This section relies heavily on Wheelwright and Makridakis, *Forecasting Methods,* pp. 30–31.

1. The item to be forecast. Is one trying to predict the continuance of a historical pattern, the continuance of a basic relationship, or a turning point?
2. The interaction of the situation with the characteristics of available forecasting methods. The manager must judge the relation between value and cost. If a less expensive method can be used to achieve the desired results, it certainly should be.
3. The amount of historical data available.
4. The time allowed to prepare the forecast. Selection of a specific method may depend on the urgency of the situation.

One other point about forecasting cost and accuracy should be added here. Generally, when the requirements for forecast accuracy are high, more sophisticated and more complex methods may be used. Such methods are, as a rule, more costly. Thus, a manager will authorize greater expenditures when relatively high accuracy is warranted. However, "Empirical studies have shown that simplicity in forecasting methods is not necessarily a negative characteristic or a detriment with regard to forecasting accuracy. Therefore, the authors would advise against discarding simple methods and moving too quickly to replace them with more complex ones."[8]

Forecasting techniques can be categorized in many ways. We will use the following six categories:

1. Expert opinion
2. Opinion polls and market research
3. Surveys of spending plans
4. Economic indicators
5. Projections
6. Econometric models

As we will see in the following pages, some of the methods can be classified as qualitative, others as quantitative. **Qualitative forecasting** is based on judgments of individuals or groups. The results of qualitative forecasts may be in numerical form but generally are not based on a series of historical data.

**Quantitative forecasting,** on the other hand, generally utilizes significant amounts of prior data as a basis for prediction. Quantitative techniques can be naive or causal (explanatory). **Naive methods** project past data into the future without explaining future trends. **Causal** or **explanatory forecasting** attempts to explain the functional relationships between the variable to be estimated (the dependent variable) and the variable or variables that account for the changes (the independent variables).

Although more sophisticated statistical tools have grown in availability and usage by managers, a recent survey indicates that judgmental (or qualitative) methods still predominate in many business organizations. This survey of both large and small manufacturing companies (ranging in sales from $5 million to over $10 billion) found that 54 percent of the firms surveyed used judgmental forecasts mostly, while 34 percent

---

[8]Ibid., p. 309. This quote deals with the merits of relatively simple time series methods versus more complex explanatory techniques. "Thus, the evidence suggests that explanatory models do not provide significantly more accurate forecasts than time series methods, even though the former are much more complex and expensive than the latter" (p. 297).

used both judgmental and quantitative methods. As could be expected, large firms utilized quantitative methods more frequently. Among the more common judgmental forecasting methods used were manager's opinion, jury of executive opinion, and sales force composite. The more frequently used quantitative methods were moving averages, exponential smoothing, and projections. These methods are discussed at length in the remainder of this chapter. The author of the survey found the dominance of judgmental forecasting to be "disheartening to forecasters" as formal approaches have been available for years, and quantitative forecasting has been shown to be more accurate and subject to fewer biases leading to bad forecasts.[9]

## EXPERT OPINION

Various types of techniques fit into the category of expert opinion. Only a limited number will be discussed here.

One of these methods is called the **jury of executive opinion.** As the name implies, forecasts are generated by a group of corporate executives, who may be sitting around a table discussing the particular subject to be forecast. The members of the panel are experts in the subject matter, (representing sales, finance, production, and so on). These panels can be interorganizational (i.e., from different corporations) or intraorganizational (i.e., within one corporation), depending on the breadth of the subject. This technique is used widely and is often quite successful. The major drawback of this approach is that a panel member with a forceful personality but not necessarily the greatest amount of knowledge and judgment may exercise a disproportionate amount of influence.

Another, similar technique involves the solicitation of views of individual salespeople in a company to forecast sales. This approach could have been utilized in the situation outlined at the beginning of the chapter. After all, sales representatives are expected to have a finger on the pulse of the market. The biases inherent in this type of predictive apparatus are, however, obvious. "Often sales people are either overly optimistic or overly pessimistic. At other times they are unaware of the broad economic patterns that may affect demand."[10] The latter problem can be overcome to some extent by informing the respondents of general economic forecasts.

Another popular method of qualitative forecasting, utilized predominantly in predicting technological trends and changes, is the **Delphi method.** This technique was developed at the Rand Corporation in the 1950s. Delphi uses a panel of experts; however, unlike the jury of executive opinion, the participants do not meet to discuss and agree on a forecast. The entire process is carried out by a sequential series of written questions and answers. The reason for separating the experts is to avoid the potential pitfall cited previously.

A relatively early Delphi study was that of Gordon and Helmer, which asked experts to forecast six subjects as far as 50 years into the future: scientific breakthroughs, population growth, automation, space progress, probability and prevention of war, and

---

[9]Nada R. Sanders, "The Status of Forecasting in Manufacturing Firms," *Production and Inventory Management Journal,* 38, 2, 1997, pp. 32–37.
[10]Wheelwright and Makridakis, *Forecasting Methods,* p. 242.

future weapons systems.[11] To arrive at predictions, the Delphi procedure begins by asking (e.g., by letter) the members selected to reply to a set of questions. In this study, the experts were asked to specify what advances in automation would occur over the next 50 years and to estimate the time period of occurrence. When answers were received, a list of the items was compiled and sent back to the panel for further consideration. Several iterations of this procedure were conducted until the range of choices was narrowed and specific time ranking was established. Finally, a consensus (or convergence of opinion) is obtained. But there is no need for unanimity of opinion; the forecast can include a range of opinions.

The Delphi method has been used to advantage in technological predictions and has been applied in business situations as well. A 1971 study sponsored by Corning Glass investigated trends in residential housing in the ensuing 15 years. Included were forecasts of housing supply and demand, costs, monetary aspects, among others.[12]

Still, Delphi suffers from many drawbacks: "insufficient reliability, oversensitivity of results to ambiguity of questions, different results when different experts are used, difficulty in assessing the degree of expertise, and the impossibility of predicting the unexpected."[13] Given the long-term nature of Delphi predictions, these criticisms do not appear to differ greatly from those leveled against forecasts in general.

## OPINION POLLS AND MARKET RESEARCH

You are probably familiar with opinion polling, since most of us have at one time or another been subjected to telephone calls or written questionnaires asking us to assess a product—or sometimes a political issue. Rather than soliciting experts, opinion polls survey a population whose activity may determine future trends. **Opinion polls** can be very useful because they may identify changes in trends, which, as we will see later in this chapter, may escape detection when quantitative (both naive and explanatory) methods are used.

Opinion polls are usually conducted on samples of the population. Choice of the sample is of utmost importance, since the use of an unrepresentative sample may give completely misleading results. Further, the questions must be stated simply and clearly in order that they can be easily interpreted by respondents. Often a question is repeated in a somewhat different form so that the replies can be cross-checked.

Market research is closely related to opinion polling. Thorough descriptions of this method can be found in marketing texts. Market research will indicate "not only why the consumer is or is not buying (or is or is not likely to buy), but also who the consumer is, how he or she is using the product, and what characteristics the consumer thinks are most important in the purchasing decision."[14] This information can then be used to estimate the market potential and possibly the market share.

---

[11]T. J. Gordon and O. Helmer, *Report on a Long-Range Forecasting Study,* Rand Corporation, P-2982, September 1964. (Described in Harold Sackman, *Delphi Critique,* Lexington, MA: Lexington Books, 1975, pp. 37–39, 104.)
[12]Selwyn Enzer, *Some Prospects for Residential Housing by 1985,* Institute for the Future, R-13, January 1971. (Cited in Sackman, *Delphi Critique,* p. 99.)
[13]Wheelwright and Makridakis, *Forecasting Methods,* p. 326.
[14]Ibid., p. 245.

## SURVEYS OF SPENDING PLANS

The use of **surveys of spending plans** is quite similar to opinion polling and market research, and the methods of data collection are also quite alike. But while opinion polling and market research usually deal with specific products and are often conducted by individual firms, the surveys discussed briefly here seek information about "macro-type" data relating to the economy.

1. *Consumer intentions.* Since consumer expenditure is the largest component of the gross domestic product, changes in consumer attitudes and their effect on subsequent spending are a crucial variable in the forecasts and plans made by businesses. Firms producing consumer products and services are, of course, affected directly. But companies producing durable equipment will also feel the effect of any changes in this important segment of the economy. Two well-known surveys are reviewed here.

   a. *Survey of Consumers, Survey Research Center, University of Michigan.* This is probably the best known among the consumer surveys conducted. Initiated in 1946, it is conducted monthly. It contains questions regarding personal finances, general business conditions, and buying conditions. The answers to these questions are summarized into an overall index of consumer sentiment and a large number of indexes covering replies to the more detailed questions. Subscribers to this service receive analyses of the most recent surveys as well as a booklet of tables and charts showing trends.

   b. *Consumer Confidence Survey, The Conference Board.* A questionnaire is mailed monthly to a nationwide sample of 5,000 households. Each month a different panel of households is selected. The resulting indexes are based on responses to questions regarding business conditions (current and six months hence), employment conditions (current and six months hence), and expectations regarding family income six months hence. The replies are then summarized monthly into three indexes: the Consumer Confidence Index, the Present Situation Index and the Expectations Index. This survey has been published since 1967.

2. *Inventories and sales expectations.* A monthly survey published by the National Association of Purchasing Agents is based on a large sample of purchasing executives.

3. *Capital expenditure surveys.* In the last two editions of this text we reported on surveys conducted by the U.S. Department of Commerce, the Conference Board, and McGraw-Hill *Business Week.* Unfortunately, detailed surveys of capital expenditures have been discontinued by all three organizations. The Department of Commerce still publishes some historical data on an annual basis.[15]

---

[15]The authors inquired with these organizations regarding the existence of the surveys. Our respondent at *Business Week* told us the following: "To my knowledge, there is no capital spending survey that outlines plans for the following year in a detailed way. As an economic analyst, I find that distressing, especially given the rising importance of the fast-growing high-tech sector in assessing the economic impact of business investment. I hope someone will pick up the ball at some point."

## ECONOMIC INDICATORS

The difficult task of predicting changes in the direction of activity has been discussed previously. Some of the qualitative techniques discussed in the preceding sections are aimed at identifying such turns. The barometric technique of **economic indicators** is specifically designed to alert business to changes in economic conditions.

The success of the indicator approach to forecasting depends on the ability to identify one or more historical economic series whose direction not only correlates with but precedes that of the series to be predicted. Such indicators are used widely in forecasting general economic activity. Any one indicator series may not be very reliable; however, a composite of leading indicators can be used to predict. Such a series should exhibit a slowing (and an actual decrease) before overall economic activity turns down, and it should start to rise while the economy is still experiencing low activity.

Forecasting on the basis of indicators has been practiced in an informal fashion for many years. It is said that Andrew Carnegie used to assess the future of steel demand by counting the number of chimneys emitting smoke in Pittsburgh. Much of the work of establishing economic indicators was done at the National Bureau of Economic Research, a private organization. Today, economic indicator data are published monthly by The Conference Board in *Business Cycle Indicators*. These monthly data are reported in the press and are widely followed.[16]

There are three major series: leading, coincident, and lagging indicators. As their names imply, the first tells us where we are going, the second where we are, and the third where we have been. Although the leading indicator series is probably the most important, the other two are also meaningful. The coincident indicators identify peaks and troughs, and the lagging series confirms upturns and downturns in economic activity.

Many individual series are tracked monthly in the *Business Cycle Indicators,* but only a limited number are used in the construction of the three major indexes. The leading indicator index contains 10 series, and the coincident and lagging indicators are made up of 4 and 7 components, respectively. All the series making up the indexes are listed in Table 6.3.

It is rather evident why some of the indicators qualify as leading. They represent not present expenditures, but commitments indicating that economic activity will take place in the future. Among these are manufacturers' new orders and building permits. Others are not quite as obvious. But one would expect employers to increase the hours of their work force as they increase production before committing themselves to new hiring. Stock market prices and money supply are usually thought to precede cycles.

Combining the individual series into overall indexes involves a number of statistical steps. First, each individual series is standardized to avoid undue influence of the more volatile components. Each series is then assigned a weight within the composite index. Then the leading and lagging indexes are adjusted to facilitate comparison with the coincident index. A trend adjustment is also made. The index has a base period of 1992 = 100.[17]

---

[16]The data can also be accessed on the World Wide Web at http://www.tcb-indicators.org

[17]An explanation of methods to compute, update, and standardize the indexes is available on the Web site cited in note 16.

| TABLE 6.3 Economic Indicators |
| --- |

*Leading indicators*
1. Average hours, manufacturing
2. Average weekly initial claims for unemployment insurance
3. Manufacturers' new orders, consumer goods, and materials
4. Vendor performance, slower deliveries diffusion index
5. Manufacturers' new orders, nondefense capital goods
6. Building permits, new private housing units
7. Stock prices, 500 common stocks
8. Money supply, M2
9. Interest rate spread, 10-year Treasury bonds minus federal funds
10. Index of consumer expectations

*Coincident indicators*
1. Employees on nonagricultural payrolls
2. Personal income less transfer payments
3. Industrial production
4. Manufacturing and trade sales

*Lagging indicators*
1. Average duration of unemployment
2. Inventories to sales ratio, manufacturing, and trade
3. Change in labor cost per unit of output, manufacturing
4. Average prime rate
5. Commercial and industrial loans
6. Consumer installment credit to personal income ratio
7. Change in consumer price index for services

How good a forecaster are the leading indicators? To answer this question, we must establish some criteria. First, how many months of change in the direction of the index are necessary before a turn in economic activity is expected? A general rule of thumb is that if, after a period of increases, the leading indicator index sustains three consecutive declines, a recession (or at least a slowing) will follow. On this basis, the leading indicators have predicted each recession since 1948.[18] Second, how much warning do the indicators give (i.e., by how many months do they lead) of the onset of a recession? Since 1948, the three-dip sequence has preceded the beginning of a recession by anywhere from 0 to 18 months.[19] Another way to evaluate the amount of lead time is to refer to *Business Cycle Indicators,* which shows the number of months between the turning point in the index and the change in the direction of general economic activity:

---

[18]George R. Green and Barry A. Beckman, "Business Cycle Indicators: Upcoming Revision of the Composite Indexes," *Survey of Current Business,* October 1993, pp. 44–51.
[19]Ibid.

| Cycle | Peak | Trough |
|-------|------|--------|
| 1960–61 | 10 | 3 |
| 1969–70 | 8 | 7 |
| 1973–75 | 9 | 2 |
| 1980–80 | 15 | 3 |
| 1981–82 | 3 | 8 |
| 1990–91 | 6 | 2 |

It is obvious that the lead times vary considerably. So we can sum up by observing that leading indicators do warn us about changes in the direction of economic activity, but they really do not forecast lead times reliably. If this were the only criticism that could be leveled against this barometer of the economy, we could probably cope with it quite easily. Unfortunately, there are other, probably more severe, drawbacks:

1. In some instances, the leading indicator index has forecast a recession when none ensued. For instance, the index declined for several months in 1966. Although a decline in the growth of the economy (a growth recession) followed, there was no "official" recession.[20]
2. A decline (or a rebound after a decline) in the index, even if it forecasts correctly, does not indicate the precise size of the decline (or rise) in economic activity.
3. The data are frequently subject to revision in the ensuing months. It is not uncommon for a particular month to show a drop in the index only to have the revisions change the direction of the index one or two months later. Thus, the final data may signal a different future from the one suggested by the originally published data.

The preceding criticisms of this forecasting method are certainly significant. But they indicate that this technique should be improved rather than discarded. The existing indicators are reevaluated periodically, and new ones are developed. As the structure of the economy changes, some of the indicators lose their relevance. The present index may be overly weighted toward manufacturing activities and neglects service industries, which make up a continuously increasing portion of our economy. The growing importance of international trade and capital flows suggests the inclusion in the index of a series reflecting these activities. In the meantime, the use of leading indicators has spread to a large number of foreign countries.

In short, despite its drawbacks, the index of leading indicators (and the other two indexes as well) is a useful tool for businesspeople and will continue to be closely watched. As always, reliance on this method must be tempered by the knowledge of its imperfections.

## PROJECTIONS

Earlier in this chapter, we discussed several qualitative methods of forecasting. We then moved to a discussion of economic indicators, a quantitative method. To continue the presentation of quantitative techniques, we now turn to **trend projections,**

---

[20]An "official" recession is pronounced by the National Bureau of Economic Research, which dates peaks and troughs.

which we previously identified as a naive form of forecasting. Several different methods will be discussed, but they all have a common denominator: past data are projected into the future without taking into consideration reasons for the change. It is simply assumed that past trends will continue. Three projection techniques will be examined here:

1. Compound growth rate
2. Visual time series projection
3. Time series projection using the least squares method

If annual data are to be forecast, any of these three methods can be used. However, more frequent data, such as monthly or quarterly, may be necessary. If there appear to be significant seasonal patterns in the data, a smoothing method must be applied. The moving-average method of smoothing will be discussed along with the least squares time series projection.

**MODULE 6A**

### Constant Compound Growth Rate

The constant **compound growth rate** technique is extremely simple and is widely used in business situations. When quick estimates of the future are needed, this method has some merit. And, as we will find out, it can be quite appropriate when the variable to be predicted increases at a constant percentage (as opposed to constant absolute changes). But care must be exercised not to apply this technique when it is not warranted.

The most rudimentary application of this method is to take the first and last years of past data, and to calculate the constant growth rate necessary to go from the amount in the first period to the amount in the last. This problem is solved in the same way as if we were to calculate how much a specific sum deposited in an interest-bearing account grows in a certain number of years at a constant rate of interest that is compounded annually. Suppose $1,000 is deposited at the beginning of the year and earns interest at the rate of 7 percent. How much will this deposit be worth at the end of the year? That is easy: $1,000 plus the 7 percent interest. The solution can be expressed in shorthand mathematical notation as follows:

$$E = B + Bi = B (1 + i)$$

where $E$ = Account balance at the end of the year
$B$ = Original deposit
$i$ = Rate of interest

Thus,

$$1,000(1.07) = 1,070$$

Now, if this year-end amount remains in the account for another year, the entire $1,070 will earn interest, of $74.90. Thus, the balance at the end of the second year will be $1,144.90. The second-year balance could have been obtained directly by compounding two years of interest on the original deposit, as follows:

$$1,000 \times 1.07 \times 1.07$$

or

$$1,000 \times (1.07)^2$$

If the deposit is left in the account for any number of years, the ending balance can be found with the following equation:

$$E = B(1 + i)^n$$

where $n$ represents the number of years. If $n$ is large, the calculation can become somewhat complex. Table B.1 in Appendix B to this book will make the computation much easier.[21] To find the amount to which a deposit of $1,000 will grow in 10 years at 7 percent interest, look up the factor in the table and multiply it by 1,000. The factor is 1.9672; therefore, the balance after ten years will be $1,967.20.

Frank Robinson can use the same table to make his projection for Citronade sales. The first period and the last period amounts are known, and the missing number is the growth rate, which, of course, has the same meaning as the interest rate in the preceding example. To solve for the growth rate, the previous formula is revised as follows:

$$(1 + i)^n = E/B$$

Applying this formula to the 1989 and 1999 sales of Citronade from Table 6.1,

$$6,954/3,892 = 1.7867$$

Since there are ten years intervening between the two sales periods, the growth rate can be found by entering the table at ten periods and moving to the right until a number close to 1.7867 is found. At 6 percent, the factor is 1.7908. Thus, the growth rate of Citronade over the last ten years is just under 6 percent.

Can, therefore, next year's sales be estimated at 7,371,000 cases, a 6 percent annual increase? Looking at the year-to-year increases in Table 6.1, Robinson noticed that the growth rate achieved in the early years (through 1993) has not been approached since. Whereas during the first four years of the available data, growth ranged between 6.5 and 8 percent, the second four years registered increases between 5 and 6 percent, and the rise in the last two years was less than 5 percent. Growth has been declining over the ten-year period.

This illustrates a major problem that is frequently encountered when the compound growth rate method of projection is employed. The only two numbers considered in determining the growth rate were the first and the last; any trends or fluctuations between the original and terminal dates are disregarded. Thus, when year-to-year percentage growth is not stable, any estimates based on this result can be misleading.

Figure 6.1 illustrates what may happen. The data plotted in the graph show a strong increase in each year except for the last value, which may have been caused by an exceptional occurrence such as a severe recession or a strike. If the compound growth rate approach is used, any forecast based only on the first and last observations may be quite misleading.

In summary, the compound growth rate (or CGR, as it is popularly known) method can often be useful, particularly when results are required quickly and a rough approximation is sufficient. But its drawbacks are significant and must always be considered.

---

[21]Of course, any number of hand-held calculators will make this computation even easier.

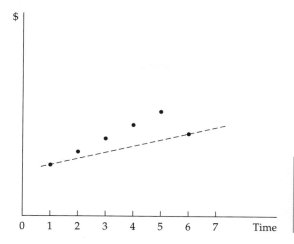

**FIGURE 6.1** An Example in Which the Constant Compound Growth Rate Approach Would Be Misleading

## Visual Time Series Projections

A series of numbers is often difficult to interpret. Plotting the observations on a sheet of graph paper (or entering paired data into a computer plotting program) can be very helpful since the shape of a complicated series is more easily discerned from a picture.

Frank Robinson did just that. He had two types of graph paper available to him. One was the familiar kind, with arithmetic scales on both axes, which he used to plot the annual data of Citronade sales, as shown in Figure 6.2. The observations appear to form a relatively straight line. As a matter of fact, one could easily draw a straight line just by

**FIGURE 6.2** Annual Sales of Citronade (1989–1999)

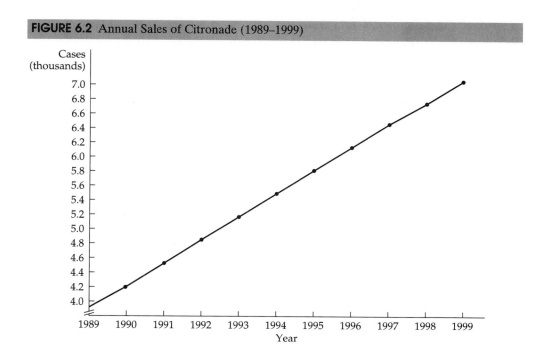

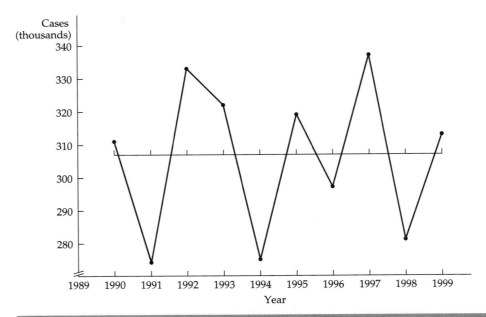

**FIGURE 6.3** Annual Increase in Citronade Sales (1989–1999)

putting a ruler through the observations, so that some points fall above and some below the line. Projecting the line to 2000 would give us a fairly good prediction—if the growth, in absolute number of cases, reflects past increases. The reason that a straight line is such a good fit is that the absolute annual increases in sales fluctuate around their mean of 306,000 cases without exhibiting any kind of trend (Figure 6.3).

There is another type of graph paper often used to observe trends—semilogarithmic. This graph has an arithmetic scale along the horizontal axis, but the vertical axis transforms numbers into a logarithmic format. Equal distances between numbers on the vertical scale represent a doubling. Thus, the distance between 1 and 2 is the same as that between 2 and 4, between 4 and 8, and so on.[22] In the semilogarithmic format, if observations that exhibit a constant growth rate are plotted, they will fall on a straight line.[23]

---

[22]Incidentally, the point of origin on the vertical axis is 1, not 0.

[23]A simple example will explain why a constant percentage growth rate shows up as a straight line on a logarithmic scale. Assume that the first period's quantity is 100 and that it grows by 20 percent each year. Then translate each number into a common logarithm, and calculate the differences for each series:

| Raw Data | Absolute Difference | Logarithm | Difference in Logarithms |
|---|---|---|---|
| 100 | | 2.0 | |
| 120 | 20 | 2.0792 | 0.0792 |
| 144 | 24 | 2.1584 | 0.0792 |
| 172.8 | 28.8 | 2.2375 | 0.0791 |
| 207.36 | 34.56 | 2.3167 | 0.0792 |

Although the absolute differences increase, the differences between logarithms remain constant. Thus, if the vertical scale of a graph is shown in terms of logarithms, constant percentage differences will plot as a straight line.

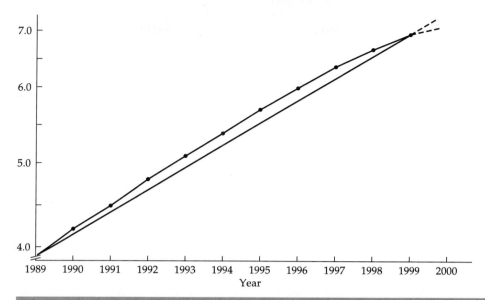

**FIGURE 6.4** Semilogarithmic Graph of Changes in Citronade Sales

The data for Citronade, as can be seen in Figure 6.4 where the annual observations are plotted, indicate growth at a decreasing rate. Thus, if Frank Robinson were to base his projections on this line, he would have to continue the curve on its decreasing slope.

Frank found that the compound growth rate for Citronade sales from 1989 to 1999 was 6 percent. A line representing an annual growth rate of 6 percent in Figure 6.4 is a straight line, since constant growth is assumed. But a projection of the straight line would result in a higher sales estimate for 2000 than if the decreasing year-to-year percentage of growth were taken into consideration.

Thus, a quick estimate of next year's sales can be made by just extending one of the lines that were drawn. If the average of the ten years of absolute growth—306,000—were used, 2000 sales would be 7,260,000 cases, a 4.4 percent increase from the 1999 total of 6,954,000 cases. This would correspond closely to the value produced by extending the line formed by the actual observations in Figure 6.4, which exhibits an increase at a decreasing rate. Using the compound growth rate of 6 percent—plotted as a straight line in Figure 6.4—would indicate sales of about 7,371,000 cases and would, as previously discussed, result in too high an estimate.

Although under some circumstances this type of forecast may be sufficiently accurate, most forecasters would feel that a more detailed estimate—particularly given the seasonal nature of soft drink demand—is essential. Thus, Frank will move on to perform a time series analysis using a least squares equation, and also to identify the seasonal pattern of Citronade sales.

## Time Series Analysis

In this section we will continue to explore the **time series** method of projection. However, instead of visual estimation, a more precise statistical technique will be employed: the method of least squares. This method was introduced in the last chapter and was used to estimate demand. Whereas demand estimation requires the use of one or more independent variables, and the interactive relationship between these variables is of great importance, in the context of time series analysis there is only one independent variable: time. Thus, this system of forecasting is "naive," because it does not explain the reason for the changes, it merely says that the series of numbers to be projected changes as a function of time.

Despite the mechanical nature of this type of forecast, time series analysis has much to recommend it:

1. It is easy to calculate. Presently, a large number of software packages on the market will compute the least squares trend line in various ways—linear, curvilinear, or exponential.
2. It does not require much judgment or analytical skill by the analyst. It merely assumes that the pattern of prior periods will repeat into the future.
3. Unlike visual projection, it describes the line that exhibits the best possible fit for past data. In addition, it provides the analyst with information regarding the statistical errors contained in the results and gives an indication of how statistically significant the results are.
4. Finally, except when an absolute turn in the series occurs, the projection based on this method of analysis is usually reasonably reliable in the short run.

The fact that time series analysis does not take into consideration causative factors does not mean that an analyst using this method should not consider additional information about changes in the underlying forces. Any analyst using this naive method of prediction should try to fine tune the conclusions based on information that could alter the results.[24]

When data are collected over a number of periods in the past, they usually exhibit four different characteristics:

1. *Trend.* This is the direction of movement of the data over a relatively long period of time, either upward or downward.
2. *Cyclical fluctuations.* These are deviations from the trend due to general economic conditions. For instance, if one were to observe data for the GDP over time, a long-run upward trend would be evident. Also evident in this series would be movement around that trend as the economy rises more quickly or less quickly (or actually declines).
3. *Seasonal fluctuations.* A pattern that repeats annually is characteristic of many products. Toy sales tend to rise briefly before Christmas. Fashions have spring and fall seasons. In the soft drink industry, the expectation is for higher sales during the warmer periods of the year (i.e., June through September). Thus, time series in which data are collected more frequently than annually (monthly, quarterly) can exhibit seasonal variations.
4. *Irregular.* Departures from the norm may be caused by special events, such as strikes or catastrophes. They occur randomly and do not repeat regularly, if at all,

---

[24]It is essential that all changes and alterations are well documented by the analyst so that a trail to her reasoning can be established.

and they certainly cannot be predicted. Actually, these random fluctuations do not have to be caused by any dramatic events. They may just represent "noise" in the series, since events never occur in a completely regular, stable manner.

Thus, time series data can be represented by the following mathematical expression:

$$Y_t = f(T_t, C_t, S_t, R_t)$$

where $Y_t$ = Actual value of the data in the time series at time $t$
$T_t$ = Trend component at $t$
$C_t$ = Cyclical component at $t$
$S_t$ = Seasonal component at $t$
$R_t$ = Random component at $t$

The specific form of this equation could be additive:

$$Y_t = T_t + C_t + S_t + R_t$$

Other forms could also exist. The specification most commonly used is the multiplicative form:

$$Y_t = (T_t)(C_t)(S_t)(R_t)$$

Thus, the changes in the actual values ($Y_t$) are determined by four factors. The task of the analyst is to "decompose" the time series of $Y$ into its four components.

We can now return to Frank Robinson's problem of forecasting Citronade sales not only for the entire year of 2000, but for each of the quarters. This entire procedure is summarized in Table 6.4.

**Seasonality**     The process of decomposition starts with identifying and removing the seasonal factor from our series of numbers in order to calculate the trend. We will use the method of **moving averages** to isolate seasonal fluctuations.

**Column 1:**   This column simply represents all the quarters of the 11 years, 1989 through 1999, numbered sequentially.

**Column 2:**   All the quarterly data, originally shown in Table 6.2, are listed here.

**Column 3:**   The first step in the deseasonalizing process is to calculate a quarterly average for the first year (i.e., the first four quarters). The result is 973.0, so this number is placed next to quarter 3 in this column. The next number is obtained by moving down one quarter: The first quarter is dropped, the fifth quarter is added, and the average of quarters 2, 3, 4, and 5 is calculated to be 989.3. This number is placed next to quarter 4. The same procedure is then followed for the rest of the quarters. Because of the averaging, the data for the first two quarters and the last quarter are lost.

The first moving average was placed next to the third quarter. It could also have been placed next to the second quarter. Actually, the average of four quarters belongs between the second and third quarters. This computation is made in column 4.

**Column 4:**   An average of two adjacent numbers in column 3 is calculated and placed at the third quarter. Because 973.0 in column 3 should have appeared between quarters 2 and 3, and 989.3 should have been between quarters 3

**TABLE 6.4  Citronade Quarterly Sales Analysis**

| (1)<br>Quarter | (2)<br>Actual | (3)<br>Moving<br>Average | (4)<br>Centered<br>Moving<br>Average | (5)<br>Ratio<br>Actual/<br>CMA[d] | (6)<br>Adjusted<br>Seasonal<br>Factors | (7)<br>Data<br>Deseason-<br>alized[b] | (8)<br>Trend | (9)<br>Cycle<br>and<br>Irregular[c] | (10)<br>Cycle |
|---|---|---|---|---|---|---|---|---|---|
| 1 | 842 | | | | 0.889 | 947.1 | 940.2 | 100.74 | |
| 2 | 939 | | | | 0.991 | 947.5 | 959.5 | 98.75 | 100.69 |
| 3 | 1,236 | 973.0 | 981.2 | 1.260 | 1.231 | 1,004.1 | 978.8 | 102.58 | 99.98 |
| 4 | 875 | 989.3 | 999.0 | 0.876 | 0.889 | 984.3 | 998.1 | 98.61 | 100.49 |
| 5 | 907 | 1,008.8 | 1,020.6 | 0.889 | 0.889 | 1,020.2 | 1,017.4 | 100.28 | 99.30 |
| 6 | 1,017 | 1,032.5 | 1,041.6 | 0.976 | 0.991 | 1,026.2 | 1,036.7 | 98.99 | 100.56 |
| 7 | 1,331 | 1,050.8 | 1,056.5 | 1.260 | 1.231 | 1,081.2 | 1,156.0 | 102.39 | 100.19 |
| 8 | 948 | 1,062.3 | 1,073.0 | 0.884 | 0.889 | 1,066.4 | 1,075.3 | 99.17 | 99.83 |
| 9 | 953 | 1,083.8 | 1,093.1 | 0.872 | 0.889 | 1,072.0 | 1,094.6 | 97.94 | 99.01 |
| 10 | 1,103 | 1,102.5 | 1,110.9 | 0.993 | 0.991 | 1,113.0 | 1,113.9 | 99.92 | 99.55 |
| 11 | 1,406 | 1,119.3 | 1,131.0 | 1.243 | 1.231 | 1,142.2 | 1,133.2 | 100.80 | 99.93 |
| 12 | 1,015 | 1,142.8 | 1,152.4 | 0.881 | 0.889 | 1,141.7 | 1,152.4 | 99.07 | 100.13 |
| 13 | 1,047 | 1,162.0 | 1,174.4 | 0.892 | 0.889 | 1,177.7 | 1,171.7 | 100.51 | 99.85 |
| 14 | 1,180 | 1,186.8 | 1,194.6 | 0.988 | 0.991 | 1,190.7 | 1,191.0 | 99.97 | 100.50 |
| 15 | 1,505 | 1,202.5 | 1,212.1 | 1.242 | 1.231 | 1,222.6 | 1,210.3 | 101.01 | 99.87 |
| 16 | 1,078 | 1,221.8 | 1,232.6 | 0.875 | 0.889 | 1,212.6 | 1,229.6 | 98.61 | 100.29 |
| 17 | 1,124 | 1,243.5 | 1,252.4 | 0.897 | 0.889 | 1,264.3 | 1,248.9 | 101.23 | 100.22 |
| 18 | 1,267 | 1,261.3 | 1,272.1 | 0.996 | 0.991 | 1,278.5 | 1,268.2 | 100.81 | 100.49 |
| 19 | 1,576 | 1,283.0 | 1,288.4 | 1.223 | 1.231 | 1,280.3 | 1,287.5 | 99.44 | 100.18 |
| 20 | 1,165 | 1,293.8 | 1,302.9 | 0.894 | 0.889 | 1,310.5 | 1,306.8 | 100.28 | 99.57 |
| 21 | 1,167 | 1,312.0 | 1,323.8 | 0.882 | 0.889 | 1,312.7 | 1,326.1 | 98.99 | 99.92 |
| 22 | 1,340 | 1,335.5 | 1,343.6 | 0.997 | 0.991 | 1,352.2 | 1,345.4 | 100.50 | 99.63 |
| 23 | 1,670 | 1,351.8 | 1,362.8 | 1.225 | 1.231 | 1,356.6 | 1,364.7 | 99.41 | 99.96 |
| 24 | 1,230 | 1,373.8 | 1,381.6 | 0.890 | 0.889 | 1,383.6 | 1,384.0 | 99.97 | 99.99 |
| 25 | 1,255 | 1,389.5 | 1,401.5 | 0.895 | 0.889 | 1,411.7 | 1,403.3 | 100.60 | 100.03 |
| 26 | 1,403 | 1,413.5 | 1,422.5 | 0.986 | 0.991 | 1,415.7 | 1,422.6 | 99.52 | 99.87 |
| 27 | 1,766 | 1,431.5 | 1,438.5 | 1.228 | 1.231 | 1,434.6 | 1,441.9 | 99.50 | 99.75 |
| 28 | 1,302 | 1,445.5 | 1,457.0 | 0.894 | 0.889 | 1,464.6 | 1,461.2 | 100.23 | 99.78 |
| 29 | 1,311 | 1,468.5 | 1,477.4 | 0.887 | 0.889 | 1,474.7 | 1,480.5 | 99.61 | 100.14 |
| 30 | 1,495 | 1,486.3 | 1,496.0 | 0.999 | 0.991 | 1,508.6 | 1,499.8 | 100.59 | 99.48 |
| 31 | 1,837 | 1,505.8 | 1,515.6 | 1.212 | 1.231 | 1,492.3 | 1,519.1 | 98.24 | 99.91 |
| 32 | 1,380 | 1,525.5 | 1,534.3 | 0.899 | 0.889 | 1,552.3 | 1,538.4 | 100.91 | 99.84 |
| 33 | 1,390 | 1,543.0 | 1,555.9 | 0.893 | 0.889 | 1,563.6 | 1,557.7 | 100.38 | 100.48 |
| 34 | 1,565 | 1,568.8 | 1,579.4 | 0.991 | 0.991 | 1,579.2 | 1,577.0 | 100.14 | 99.75 |
| 35 | 1,940 | 1,590.0 | 1,598.1 | 1.214 | 1.231 | 1,576.0 | 1,596.2 | 98.73 | 100.29 |
| 36 | 1,465 | 1,606.3 | 1,616.8 | 0.906 | 0.889 | 1,647.9 | 1,615.5 | 102.00 | 100.28 |
| 37 | 1,455 | 1,627.3 | 1,638.0 | 0.888 | 0.889 | 1,636.7 | 1,634.8 | 100.11 | 100.90 |
| 38 | 1,649 | 1,648.8 | 1,654.5 | 0.977 | 0.991 | 1,664.0 | 1,654.1 | 100.59 | 99.69 |
| 39 | 2,026 | 1,660.3 | 1,670.4 | 1.213 | 1.231 | 1,645.8 | 1,673.4 | 98.35 | 99.78 |
| 40 | 1,511 | 1,680.5 | 1,688.6 | 0.895 | 0.889 | 1,699.7 | 1,692.7 | 100.41 | 99.89 |
| 41 | 1,536 | 1,696.8 | 1,706.4 | 0.900 | 0.889 | 1,727.8 | 1,712.0 | 100.92 | 100.41 |
| 42 | 1,714 | 1,716.0 | 1,727.3 | 0.992 | 0.991 | 1,729.6 | 1,731.3 | 99.90 | 99.47 |
| 43 | 2,103 | 1,738.5 | | | 1.231 | 1,708.4 | 1,750.6 | 97.59 | 99.75 |
| 44 | 1,601 | | | | 0.889 | 1,800.9 | 1,769.9 | 101.75 | |

[a]Column 2 ÷ Column 4.
[b]Column 2 ÷ Column 6 × 100.
[c]Column 7 ÷ Column 8 × 100.

**TABLE 6.5   Averaging of Seasonal Factors**

| Year | First Quarter | Second Quarter | Third Quarter | Fourth Quarter | Total |
|------|------|------|------|------|------|
| 1989 |       |       | 1.260 | 0.876 |       |
| 1990 | 0.889 | 0.976 | 1.260 | 0.884 |       |
| 1991 | 0.872 | 0.993 | 1.243 | 0.881 |       |
| 1992 | 0.892 | 0.988 | 1.242 | 0.875 |       |
| 1993 | 0.897 | 0.996 | 1.223 | 0.894 |       |
| 1994 | 0.882 | 0.997 | 1.225 | 0.890 |       |
| 1995 | 0.895 | 0.986 | 1.228 | 0.894 |       |
| 1996 | 0.887 | 0.999 | 1.212 | 0.899 |       |
| 1997 | 0.893 | 0.991 | 1.214 | 0.906 |       |
| 1998 | 0.888 | 0.997 | 1.213 | 0.895 |       |
| 1999 | 0.900 | 0.992 |       |       |       |
| Average | 0.890 | 0.992 | 1.232 | 0.889 | 4.003 |
| Adjusted Average | 0.889 | 0.991 | 1.231 | 0.889 | 4.000 |

**Column 5:** and 4, the average of these two, 981.2, is correctly placed at quarter 3. All centered moving averages are placed in column 4. With this procedure, the next to the last number is now lost.

**Column 5:** We now obtain the seasonal factors. They are the ratios obtained by dividing the actual numbers in column 2 by the centered moving averages of column 4. Observing the numbers in column 5, it can be seen that every fourth quarter, starting with quarter 3 (i.e., quarters 3, 7, 11, and so on), has a factor greater than 1. These quarters represent the summer months (July to September), when soda consumption is at its peak. It can also be seen that data for the second calendar quarters (i.e., quarters 6, 10, 14, and so on) are rather close to 1, while the quarters representing fall and winter are generally below 0.9.

**Column 6:** To obtain a quarterly seasonal index, we must average the ratios obtained by quarter in column 5. This is done in Table 6.5. The quarterly patterns are quite obvious.[25]

The four averages should add to 4; they do not because of rounding. A minor adjustment must now be made. The results are then transferred to column 6 of Table 6.4.

**Column 7:** When the actual data of column 2 are divided by the seasonal factors of column 6, the deseasonalized series of numbers in column 7 is obtained. Both the actual and the deseasonalized data have been plotted in Figure 6.5. The latter series, as should be expected, is much smoother than the former.

---

[25]There appears to be a minor downward trend in the third-quarter data. This will be discussed later.

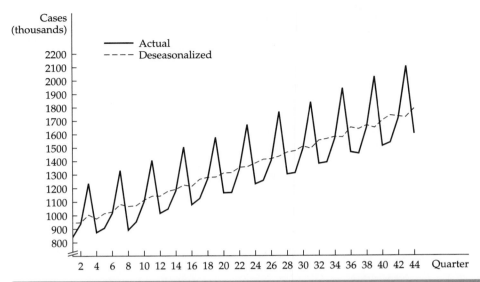

**FIGURE 6.5** Citronade Sales Deseasonalized

The first step of the decomposition procedure has now been completed:

$$(T \times C \times S \times R)/S = T \times C \times R$$

The new series has eliminated the seasonality. The next step is to calculate the trend.

**The Trend Line**     Computation of the trend utilizes the least squares method. The dependent variable is the deseasonalized series in column 7 of Table 6.4. The independent variable is time. Each quarter is numbered consecutively; although the initial number usually does not matter, it is easiest and most logical to start with 1. Thus, the consecutive numbers in column 1 of Table 6.4 represent the independent variable.

The form of the equation depends on the shape of the deseasonalized series. A casual observation of the deseasonalized series appears to indicate that a straight line would be most appropriate, but we actually tried three different possibilities:

Straight line: $Y = a + b(t)$

Exponential line:[26] $Y = ab^t$

Quadratic line:[27] $Y = a + b(t) + c(t)^2$

Although all three calculations gave acceptable results, the simplest—the straight line—gave the best statistical answers. Its coefficient of determination ($R^2$) was .996, and the *t*-statistic for the independent variable was 103.6—highly significant.

---

[26]This is the equation that would best fit a straight line on a semilogarithmic chart, representing constant percentage growth from period to period.
[27]This equation would fit a curve on a graph with arithmetic scales.

The exponential and quadratic equations also had very high $R^2$s, but their *t*-statistics were considerably lower (and the squared term in the latter was actually not statistically significant).

The straight-line trend equation was

$$Y = 920.90 + 19.2957t$$

**Column 8:** Using this equation, we arrive at the trend numbers in column 8.

**Column 9:** Then, by dividing the data in column 7 by those in column 8, we eliminate the trend from the deseasonalized series. In terms of the fraction used previously,

$$(T \times C \times R)/T = C \times R$$

Thus, only the cycle and random elements remain in column 9, which is in percentage form.

**Cycle and Random Elements**    At this point we could stop the analysis and do a forecast. The data in column 9 fluctuate rather irregularly within a range of about 5 percentage points. Part of this variation is due to random factors, which cannot be predicted and therefore should be ignored. However, there could be some longer business cycle wave in the data. To isolate the cycle, another smoothing operation can be performed with a moving average.

**Column 10:** The preferred length of the moving-average period cannot be determined except in each individual case. In our illustration we used three periods. If the moving average correctly eliminates the random variations remaining in column 9, then the swings that appear in column 10 should represent a cyclical index.

When the index rises above 100 percent, the indication is that economic activity is strong; the opposite holds for index numbers below 100 percent. The data in column 10 fluctuate very little—less than 2 percentage points. Therefore, no great adjustment is needed here. However, if the indication is that the economy is in a downturn, which may be expected to have some influence on soft drink sales, then a minor forecast adjustment can be made. Such an adjustment can be based on current general forecasts for the economy as a whole or on the latest published leading economic indicators.

### Forecasting with Smoothing Techniques

Before we leave the section on projections, one other naive method should be mentioned. This method involves using an average of past observations to predict the future. If the forecaster feels that the future is a reflection of some average of past results, one of two forecasting methods can be applied: simple moving average or exponential smoothing.

The smoothing techniques, either moving average or exponential smoothing, work best when there is no strong trend in the series, when there are infrequent changes in the direction of the series, and when fluctuations are random rather than seasonal or cyclical. Obviously, these are very limiting conditions and greatly circumscribe the usefulness of these methods. However, if a large number of forecasts are needed quickly and if the estimates involve only one period into the future, then one of these two techniques can be employed—as long as their drawbacks are well understood by the forecaster.

**TABLE 6.6  Moving Average Forecasting**

| Period | Actual | Three-Month Moving Average Forecast | Absolute Error | Squared Error | Four-Month Moving Average Forecast | Absolute Error | Squared Error | Five-Month Moving Average Forecast | Absolute Error | Squared Error |
|---|---|---|---|---|---|---|---|---|---|---|
| 1 | 1,100 | | | | | | | | | |
| 2 | 800 | | | | | | | | | |
| 3 | 1,000 | | | | | | | | | |
| 4 | 1050 | 967 | 83 | 6,944 | | | | | | |
| 5 | 1,500 | 950 | 550 | 302,500 | 988 | 513 | 262,656 | | | |
| 6 | 750 | 1,183 | 433 | 187,778 | 1,088 | 338 | 113,906 | 1,090 | 340 | 115,600 |
| 7 | 700 | 1,100 | 400 | 160,000 | 1,075 | 375 | 140,625 | 1,020 | 320 | 102,400 |
| 8 | 650 | 983 | 333 | 111,111 | 1,000 | 350 | 122,500 | 1,000 | 350 | 122,500 |
| 9 | 1,400 | 700 | 700 | 490,000 | 900 | 500 | 250,000 | 930 | 470 | 220,900 |
| 10 | 1,200 | 917 | 283 | 80,278 | 875 | 325 | 105,625 | 1,000 | 200 | 40,000 |
| 11 | 900 | 1,083 | 183 | 33,611 | 988 | 88 | 7,656 | 940 | 40 | 1,600 |
| 12 | 1,000 | 1,167 | 167 | 27,778 | 1,038 | 38 | 1,406 | 970 | 30 | 900 |
| 13 | | 1,033 | | | 1,125 | | | 1,030 | | |
| Total | | | 3,133 | 1,400,000 | | 2,525 | 1,004,375 | | 1,750 | 603,900 |
| Mean | | | 348 | 155,556 | | 316 | 125,547 | | 250 | 86,271 |

*Note:* Some of the squared errors appear to be incorrect; this is so because decimals have been omitted.

**Moving Average**     The average of actual past results is used to forecast one period ahead. The equation for this construction is simply

$$E_{t+1} = (X_t + X_{t-1} + \cdots + X_{t-N+1})/N$$

where $E_{t+1}$ = Forecast for the next period $(t + 1)$
$X_t, X_{t-1}$ = Actual values at their respective times
$N$ = Number of observations included in the average

The forecasts for Citronade, with their strong trend and seasonal patterns, would certainly not lend themselves well to this simple projection method. Instead, a hypothetical example will be used. Twelve observations are shown in the second column of Table 6.6.

The forecaster must decide how many observations to use in the moving average. The larger the number of observations in the average, the greater the smoothing effect. If the past data appear to contain significant randomness while the underlying pattern remains the same, then a larger number of observations is indicated. However, the analyst must remember that more historical data will be needed for the forecast if a large number of past data are to be included in the base. In Table 6.6 , three moving averages have been computed—three, four, and five months. The resulting estimates are shown in the forecast columns. For example, the forecast of 967 units in period 4 of the three-month moving average was obtained as follows:

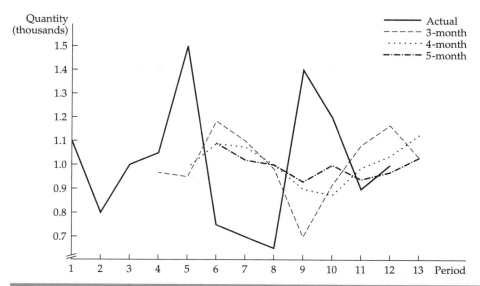

**FIGURE 6.6** Forecasting with Moving Averages

$$E_4 = (X_1 + X_2 + X_3)/N$$
$$= (1,100 + 800 + 1,000)/3$$
$$= 2,900/3 = 967$$

The three forecast columns diverge widely. These variations are shown graphically in Figure 6.6. As more observations are included in the moving average, the forecast line becomes smoother.

Which moving average should be used? One selection method is to calculate the mean error and the mean squared error of the differences between the actual data and the forecast.[28] The series with the smallest squared error would be preferred. In the example of Table 6.6, the five-month moving average minimizes the deviations.

**Exponential Smoothing**     The moving-average method awards equal importance to each of the observations included in the average, and gives no weight at all to observations preceding the oldest data included. However, the analyst may feel that the most recent observation is more relevant to the estimate of the next period than previous observations. In that case, it is more appropriate to employ the **exponential smoothing** method, which allows for the decreasing importance of information in the more distant past. This is accomplished by the mathematical technique of geometric progression.

---

[28]The formula for the mean squared error is

$$\frac{\sum_{n=1}^{N}(E_n - X_n)^2}{N}$$

Instead of the mean squared error, we could calculate the root mean squared error by taking the square root of the above equation.

**TABLE 6.7  Exponential Smoothing Forecasting**

| | | Smoothing Factor = 0.2 | | | Smoothing Factor = 0.4 | | | Smoothing Factor = 0.8 | | |
|---|---|---|---|---|---|---|---|---|---|---|
| Period | Actual | Forecast | Absolute Error | Squared Error | Forecast | Absolute Error | Squared Error | Forecast | Absolute Error | Squared Error |
| 1 | 1,100 | | | | | | | | | |
| 2 | 800 | 1,100 | 300 | 90,000 | 1,100 | 300 | 90,000 | 1,100 | 300 | 90,000 |
| 3 | 1,000 | 1,040 | 40 | 1,600 | 980 | 20 | 400 | 860 | 140 | 19,600 |
| 4 | 1,050 | 1,032 | 18 | 324 | 988 | 62 | 3,844 | 972 | 78 | 6,084 |
| 5 | 1,500 | 1,036 | 464 | 215,667 | 1,013 | 487 | 237,364 | 1,034 | 466 | 216,783 |
| 6 | 750 | 1,128 | 378 | 143,247 | 1,208 | 458 | 209,471 | 1,407 | 657 | 431,491 |
| 7 | 700 | 1,053 | 353 | 124,457 | 1,025 | 325 | 105,370 | 881 | 181 | 32,897 |
| 8 | 650 | 982 | 332 | 110,375 | 895 | 245 | 59,910 | 736 | 86 | 7,443 |
| 9 | 1,400 | 916 | 484 | 234,467 | 797 | 603 | 363,779 | 667 | 733 | 536,915 |
| 10 | 1,200 | 1,013 | 187 | 35,109 | 1,038 | 162 | 26,207 | 1,253 | 53 | 2,857 |
| 11 | 900 | 1,050 | 150 | 22,530 | 1,103 | 203 | 41,156 | 1,211 | 311 | 96,528 |
| 12 | 1,000 | 1,020 | 20 | 403 | 1,022 | 22 | 472 | 962 | 38 | 1,434 |
| 13 | | 1,016 | | | 1,013 | | | 992 | | |
| Total | | | 2,728 | 978,180 | | 2,886 | 1,137,973 | | 3,043 | 1,442,033 |
| Mean | | | 248 | 88,925 | | 262 | 103,452 | | 277 | 131,094 |

*Note:* Some of the squared errors appear to be incorrect; this is so because decimals have been omitted.

Older data are assigned increasingly smaller weights; the sum of the weights, if we approached an infinitely large number of observations, would equal 1. All of the complex formulations of the geometric series can be simplified into the following expression:

$$E_{t+1} = wX_t + (1 - w)E_t$$

where $w$ is the weight assigned to an actual observation at period $t$.

Thus, to make a forecast for one period into the future, all that is needed is the previous period's actual observation and the previous period's forecast. The analyst does not need the extensive historical data required for the moving-average method. The most crucial decision the analyst must make is the choice of the weighting factor. The larger the $w$ (i.e., the closer to 1), the greater will be the importance of the most recent observation. Therefore, when the series is rather volatile and when $w$ is large, the smoothing effect may be minimal. When $w$ is small, the smoothing effect will be considerably more pronounced. This result can be seen in Table 6.7 and Figure 6.7, where $w$s of 0.2, 0.4, and 0.8 have been used.[29] Which weights should be used? We can again calculate the mean squared error, as was done in Table 6.7. Using $w = 0.2$ minimizes the error, so this is the best weight for this set of data.

Both of these naive forecasting techniques have their advantages and disadvantages. The simplicity of the methods is certainly an advantage. However, their usefulness is limited to cases where there is an underlying stability (i.e., no trend) with period-

---

[29]Note that the forecast for period 2 in each case is the actual observation of period 1. Since there is no forecast for period 1, a forecast must be made up. Any number could have been used, but the actual observation is probably the most logical choice.

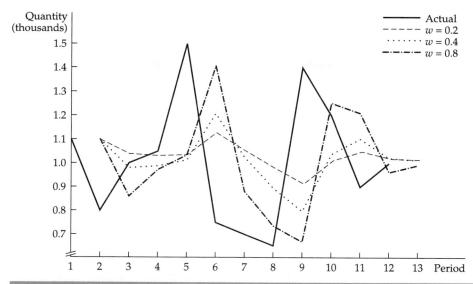

**FIGURE 6.7** Exponential Smoothing Forecasting

to-period random fluctuations. When a trend or a repeating pattern of fluctuations is present, the time series method with deseasonalization is a much better technique to use. In any case, the two methods just discussed should be employed only for extremely short-term estimates—preferably just one period into the future.

## ECONOMETRIC MODELS

Up to this point, all of the quantitative forecasting techniques discussed can be classified as naive. In this section of the chapter, our brief discussion will concentrate on models that are termed *causal* or *explanatory*. These **econometric models** were described in detail in chapter 5.

Regression analysis is an explanatory technique. Unlike the case of a naive projection, which relies on past patterns to predict the future, the analyst performing regression analysis must select those independent (or explanatory) variables that are influential in determining the dependent variable. Although simple projection models often give adequate results, the use of explanatory variables in the analysis can enhance the accuracy as well as the credibility of the estimates. Of course, no regression equation will explain the entire variation of the dependent variable, since, in most economic relationships, there are numerous explanatory variables with complex interrelationships. As already explained in chapter 5, the person performing the analysis will have to settle for the inclusion of a limited number of variables, an equation that approximates the functional relationships, and results that explain a significant portion of but not the entire variation in the dependent variable.

The regression methods previously described employ a single equation to make estimates. An analysis estimating the demand for soft drinks was described in the previous chapter. Here we will discuss a few studies of single-equation regression models of demand in which many of the variables are in the form of time series.

Among the many studies of automobile demand, the one written by Daniel Suits[30] is quite interesting. He combined the demand equations for new cars and used cars into one, as follows:

$$\Delta R = a_0 + a_1 \Delta Y + a_2 \Delta P/M + a_3 \Delta S + a_4 \Delta X$$

where $R$ = Retail sales, in millions of new cars
$Y$ = Real disposable income
$P$ = Real retail price of new cars
$M$ = Average credit terms (number of months of the average installment contract)
$S$ = Existing stock, in millions of cars
$X$ = Dummy variable

All of the variables are in terms of first differences; thus, the equation estimates year-to-year changes. The years 1942 through 1948 have been excluded from the time series because of the war years, when no automobiles were produced, and the immediate post-war period, when significant distortions existed in the automobile market.

The dummy variable $X$ takes into account the fact that not all the remaining years in the series can be treated equally. The years 1941, 1952, and 1953 were considered exceptional. The first two were assigned a value of $+1$, the third a value of $-1$, and all the other years a value of 0.

Having specified the equation, Suits calculated the coefficients (the *a*s) and tested the results by predicting 1958 new auto sales. "The demand equation predicts a level of sales of slightly less than 6.0 million. This compares favorably with a preliminary estimate of 6.1 million actual sales for the year and stands in sharp contrast with sales forecasts of 6.5 million and over, which were common in the industry at the start of the year."[31]

Another economist studied the demand for computers.[32] He specified the following equation in terms of logarithms:

$$\log(y_t/y_{t-1}) = a_0 - a_1 \log p_t - a_2 \log y_{t-1}$$

where $y_t$ = Stock of computers in year $t$
$y_{t-1}$ = Stock of computers in year $t-1$
$p$ = Real price of computers

The demand in this equation is measured as the percentage change in the stock of computers from one year to the next.

A last example will be given for coffee demand in the United States.[33] Coffee demand was estimated with the following equation:

$$Q = b_0 + b_1 P_0 + b_2 Y + b_3 P + \sum_{i=1}^{3} b_4 D_i + b_5 T$$

[30]Daniel B. Suits, "The Demand for New Automobiles in the United States, 1929–1956," *Review of Economics and Statistics,* August 1958, pp. 273–80.
[31]Ibid., p. 273.
[32]Gregory Chow, "Technological Change and the Demand for Computers," *American Economic Review,* December 1967, pp. 1117–30.
[33]Cliff J. Huang, John J. Siegfried, and Farangis Zardoshty, "The Demand for Coffee in the United States, 1963–1977," *Quarterly Review of Economics and Business,* 20, 2 (summer 1980), pp. 36–50.

where $Q$ = Per-capita (population over age 16) quantity of coffee
$P_0$ = Real retail price of coffee, per pound
$Y$ = Real per-capita disposable income
$P$ = Real retail price of tea, per quarter pound
$D_i$ = Binary (dummy) variable for quarters of the year
$T$ = Time trend

The authors found that coffee consumption is sensitive to its own price, that there had been a long-term decline in coffee consumption, and that significantly less coffee was consumed during the spring and summer months. The other coefficients did not turn out to be statistically significant. Thus, the consumption of coffee could be estimated from the time trend, from the quarterly changes, and from an assumption made regarding coffee prices.

In each of these studies, the numerical coefficients (the *a*s and the *b*s) were obtained by regression analysis. To forecast using these equations, it is necessary, of course, to make estimates of each of the independent variables for the period indicated.[34] Alternative forecasts can be created by assuming different values for each of the independent variables.

An important warning is in order regarding the use of regression equations for forecasting. All the parameters (coefficients) in a regression equation are estimated using past data (whether time series or cross-sectional analysis has been employed). The forecast based on such estimates will be valid only if the relationships between the dependent variable and the independent variables do not change from the past into the future. Literally, a regression equation is valid only within the limits of the data used in it. When we venture outside these limits (i.e., forecast with independent variables outside the range of the past), we are treading on dangerous ground. Still, forecasting with the least squares method is a much-used technique, often employed quite successfully. But its limitations must not be forgotten by the analyst.

Although many forecasting problems can be solved with the use of single-equation regression models, there are instances when one equation is not sufficient. In such cases, economists often turn to multiple-equation systems. Extremely large models used by economists to predict the GDP and its component parts are examples of such models, which may include hundreds of variables and equations.

A single-equation model can be used when the dependent variable can be estimated using independent variables that are determined by events not part of the equation. But what happens when the determining variables are determined by other variables within the model? Then a single equation is insufficient.

In a multiple-equation system, variables are referred to as *endogenous* and *exogenous*. Endogenous variables are comparable to the dependent variable of the single-equation model; they are determined by the model. However, they can also influence other endogenous variables, so they may appear as "independent" (i.e., on the right side of the equation) variables in one or more of the equations. Exogenous variables are from outside the system and are not determined within it; they are truly independent variables.

The following is an example of an extremely simple two-equation model of the private economy:

---

[34]In the case of lagged variables, actual data may be available. See, for instance, $y_{t-1}$, the stock of computers at the end of the previous year in the equation used in Chow, "Technological Change."

$$C = a_0 + a_1 Y$$

$$Y = C + I$$

where $C$ = Consumption
$Y$ = National income
$I$ = Investment

Here $C$ and $Y$ are endogenous variables. $I$ is assumed (rather unrealistically) to be exogenous, or determined by forces outside the system of equations.

Another simple multi-equation model represents the interrelationships of activities within a firm:

$$\text{Sales} = f(\text{GDP}, \text{Prices})$$

$$\text{Cost} = f(\text{Quantity of product}, \text{Factor prices})$$

$$\text{Expenses} = f(\text{Sales}, \text{Factor prices})$$

$$\text{Product price} = f(\text{Cost}, \text{Expenses}, \text{Profit})$$

$$\text{Profit} = \text{Sales} - \text{Cost} - \text{Expenses}$$

Here there are five endogenous variables. The exogenous variables are GDP, Quantity of product, and Factor prices. These equations are given in functional form only. The specific forms of the equations would, of course, have to be specified.

Such systems of equations would then be solved to obtain all of the coefficients. The statistical methods used to solve for all the numerical values are beyond the scope of this textbook.

## International Application: Forecasting Exchange Rates

In chapter 2, the additional challenges facing a multinational corporation were discussed. Such a corporation must forecast sales, expenses, and cash flows for its operations in different countries. The results from these transactions generated in the home country will depend on the exchange rate between the foreign and domestic currency. Often a company makes substantial investments in foreign operating facilities from which it expects to obtain cash flows. Thus, multinational corporations (MNCs) are vitally interested in forecasting exchange rates in both the short and long run.

A frequently used method to forecast exchange rates for relatively short periods into the future is through the forward rate. In order to understand this, two types of exchange rates must be defined:

1. Spot exchange rate—the price of one currency against another for transactions being completed immediately.
2. Forward exchange rate—the price of one currency against another for a transaction that will occur at some point in the future.

An extremely active exchange market exists, and financial officers can easily ascertain both spot and forward rates for the ten major currencies, which represent a predominant portion of all transactions. One view of the forward rate is that it represents the market's consensus on what the future spot rate should be. Thus, if today's spot rate is $1.494 for 1 British pound sterling, and the 90-day forward rate is $1.485, then one can argue that the market consensus is that the pound will decrease in value by $0.009 relative to the U.S. dollar 90 days hence.

Is the forward rate a good predictor of the spot exchange rate for major currencies? On the average, the forward rate will be equal to the future spot rate; in other words, negative and positive errors in the forecasts will be offset. It can, therefore, be said that the forward rate is an unbiased forecaster of the spot rate. It makes for a best-guess forecast. However, this does not make it an accurate forecast at any one time. Still, for the short run, it is probably as good an estimator as we have. In addition to its lack of accuracy, other shortcomings must be considered:

1. The present exchange rate system does not permit currencies to float freely. Governments interfere in the exchange rate markets when they consider it to be of benefit to their country's economy.
2. While forward rates can be established for relatively long periods into the future (in some cases, they can go out as far as ten years), by far the largest volume of forward contracts is for 180 days or less.
3. Reliable forward markets exist only for currencies of the leading industrial economies of the world.

Longer-term exchange rate forecasts often utilize econometric models. A major problem in constructing these multiple regression models is in finding appropriate reliable independent variables. In most cases, the independent variables are stated in terms of differentials between the domestic and foreign measures, such as:

1. Growth rates of GDP
2. Real interest rates
3. Nominal interest rates
4. Inflation rates
5. Balance of payments

A significant number of complex models are in use today. Here we will use a simple hypothetical model to illustrate the estimate of a relationship between the domestic currency and a foreign currency:

$$E_t = a + bI_t + cR_t + dG_t$$

where $E$ = Exchange rate of a foreign currency in terms of the domestic currency
$I$ = Domestic inflation rate minus foreign inflation rate
$R$ = Domestic nominal interest rate minus foreign nominal interest rate
$G$ = Domestic growth rate of GDP minus the growth rate of foreign GDP
$t$ = Time period
$a, b, c, d$ = Regression coefficients

Such forecasts have all the advantages and disadvantages usually found in the application of regression analysis to economic problems:

1. Which variables should be included?
2. What form should the regression equation adopt?
3. Are accurate measurements of independent variables available? Data may be inadequate for other than the major industrial countries.

**4.** In order to forecast exchange rates, it may be necessary to forecast the independent variables. And it is not surprising that it may be as difficult to forecast independent variables accurately as it is to forecast the exchange rates themselves.

By now the reader has probably concluded that forecasting exchange rates is not an easy task. But then, no forecasts are easy. The accuracy of exchange rate forecasts has been inconsistent at best. However, this should not deter business people from attempting to make such forecasts. Even if inaccurate, they enhance a manager's knowledge of her environment and provide a manager with insights into the economic variables that affect international decision making.

The discussion of this subject has been limited to its bare essentials. Students interested in studying this topic further can do so by reading one of several textbooks dealing with international financial management.[35]

## THE SOLUTION

Frank Robinson is now ready to make his forecast for 2000. He will do it in three steps:

**1.** He will project the trend for the four quarters of 2000.

**2.** He will apply the seasonal factors.

**3.** He may then make an adjustment for cyclical influences.

Since the trend equation is $Y = 920.9 + 19.2957(t)$, his trend forecasts will be as follows:

1st qtr: $920.9 - 19.2957 (45) = 1,789.2$
2nd qtr: $920.9 - 19.2957 (46) = 1,808.5$
3rd qtr: $920.9 - 19.2957 (47) = 1,827.8$
4th qtr: $920.9 - 19.2957 (48) = 1,847.1$

Next, each of these results must be multiplied by the seasonal factors:

1st qtr: $1,789.2 \times 0.889 = 1,590.6$
2nd qtr: $1,808.5 \times 0.991 = 1,792.2$
3rd qtr: $1,827.8 \times 1.231 = 2,250.0$
4th qtr: $1,847.1 \times 0.889 = 1,642.1$

Frank noticed, however, that the seasonal factors in Table 6.5 exhibit some trends over the 11 years. The third-quarter factor has been decreasing and the first- and fourth-quarter factors appear to be rising. To see the effect of these changes, Robinson decides to use the average of the last three observations for each quarter (and adjust to a total of 4, as was done previously). When he applies his new factors to the trend numbers, he obtains the following results:

1st qtr: $1,789.2 \times 0.894 = 1,599.5$
2nd qtr: $1,808.5 \times 0.993 = 1,795.8$
3rd qtr: $1,827.8 \times 1.213 = 2,217.1$
4th qtr: $1,847.1 \times 0.900 = 1,662.4$

He decides that this last computation is more valid. The last step in his procedure is to evaluate the effect of cycles and random factors. He decides that the cycle's influence on soft drink sales will be neutral in the coming year. Although an estimate of random factors cannot be made, Frank knows that the company has plans to implement a strong advertising campaign on behalf of Citronade during the second quarter

*(Continued)*

[35]For example, Dennis J. O'Connor and Alberto T. Bueso, *International Dimensions of Financial Management,* New York: Macmillan, 1990. The preceding discussion has drawn on material contained in this book.

of 2000. At this point, however, he does not have sufficient information regarding the effect of advertising on sales. He makes a note to mention that in his report as a possible plus and to try to make some quantitative estimates later.

An additional point deserves attention. We have assumed that the product whose sales Frank is forecasting has been in existence for at least 11 years. Had this been a new flavor, not previously produced, the forecast would have been much more difficult. If competing companies had been selling a similar product in the past, market information would be available in terms of very detailed statistics published by the beverage industry. Frank could then base his forecast on these data and assume some pattern of market penetration for the new brand. If, however, this is a completely new flavor not previously produced in the industry, it may be necessary to conduct market research to establish a base for a forecast. Another method would be to study the sales patterns of other soft drink products from point of introduction and to base the new product forecast on their histories.

## Summary

Forecasting is an important activity in many organizations. In business, forecasting is a necessity.

This chapter has summarized and discussed a number of forecasting techniques. Six categories of forecasts were included:

1.  *Expert opinion* is a qualitative technique of forecasting based on the judgment of knowledgeable people. Such forecasts can be developed by panels of experts. The Delphi method is another type of expert opinion forecast that is generally applicable in forecasting technological advances.
2.  *Opinion polls and market research* are conducted among survey populations, not experts, to establish future trends or consumer responses.
3.  *Surveys of spending plans* are concerned with such important economic data as capital expenditures and consumer sentiment. The forecasts are based on replies to questionnaires or interviews.
4.  *Economic indicators* are indexes of a number of economic series intended to forecast the short-run movements of the economy, including changes in direction.
5.  *Projections,* a quantitative method, employ historical data to project future trends. Usually, no causes for trends are identified. This chapter discussed compound growth rate projections as well as visual and least squares projection techniques.
6.  *Econometric models* are explanatory or causal models in which independent variables that influence the statistic to be forecast are identified. Both single- and multiple-equation models were discussed briefly.

The chapter also examined the decomposition of least squares projections into trends, seasonal and cyclical fluctuations, and irregular movements.

One other naive forecasting method was mentioned: forecasting with smoothing techniques. Smoothing techniques fall into two major categories, moving averages and exponential smoothing, and are useful when there are no pronounced trends in the data and when fluctuations from period to period are random.

## Important Concepts

**Causal (explanatory) forecasting:** A quantitative forecasting method that attempts to uncover functional relationships between independent variables and the dependent variable. (p. 206)

**Compound growth rate projection:** Forecasting by projecting the average growth rate of the past into the future. (p. 213)

**Delphi method:** A form of expert opinion forecasting that uses a series of written questions and answers to obtain a consensus forecast, most commonly employed in forecasting technological trends. (p. 207)

**Econometric forecasting model:** A quantitative, causal method that utilizes a number of independent variables to explain the dependent variable to be forecast. Econometric forecasting employs both single- and multiple-equation models. (p. 227)

**Economic indicators:** A barometric method of forecasting in which economic data are formed into indexes to reflect the state of the economy. Indexes of leading, coincident, and lagging indicators are used to forecast changes in economic activity. (p. 210)

**Exponential smoothing:** A smoothing method of forecasting that assigns greater importance to more recent data than to those in the more distant past. (p. 225)

**Jury of executive opinion:** A forecast generated by experts (e.g., corporate executives) in meetings. A similar method is to ask the opinion of sales representatives who are exposed to the market on a daily basis. (p. 207)

**Moving-average method:** A smoothing technique that compensates for seasonal fluctuations. (p. 219)

**Naive forecasting:** Quantitative forecasting that projects past data without explaining the reasons for future trends. (p. 206)

**Opinion polls:** A forecasting method in which sample populations are surveyed to determine consumption trends. (p. 208)

**Qualitative forecasting:** Forecasting based on the judgment of individuals or groups. Also called *judgmental forecasting.* (p. 206)

**Quantitative forecasting:** Forecasting that examines historical data as a basis for future trends. (p. 206)

**Surveys of spending plans:** Examination of economic trends such as capital expenditures, consumer sentiment, and inventory. (p. 209)

**Time series forecasting:** A method of forecasting from past data by using least squares statistical methods. A time series analysis usually examines trends, cyclical fluctuations, seasonal fluctuations, and irregular movements. (p. 217)

**Trend projection:** A form of naive forecasting that projects trends from past data. Trend projections usually employ compound growth rates, visual time series, or least squares time series methods. (p. 213)

## Questions

1. Discuss the basic differences among forecasting, planning, and objective setting.
2. Despite the many inaccuracies present in the making of forecasts, forecasting is a very important activity in a large business firm. Why?
3. "The best forecasting method is the one that gives the highest proportion of correct predictions." Comment.
4. Enumerate methods of qualitative and quantitative forecasting. What are the major differences between the two?
5. Discuss the benefits and drawbacks of the following methods of forecasting:
   a. Jury of executive opinion
   b. The Delphi method
   c. Opinion polls
   Each of these methods has its uses. What are they?

**6.** Here are the numbers for the leading economic indicators as published in 1990:

| | |
|---|---|
| January | 145.4 |
| February | 144.1 |
| March | 145.4 |
| April | 145.2 |
| May | 146.0 |
| June | 146.2 |
| July | 146.2 |
| August | 144.4 |
| September | 143.2 |
| October | 141.5 |
| November | 139.7 |
| December | 139.5 |

1982 = 100
*Source:* U.S. Department of Commerce, Bureau of Economic Analysis, *Survey of Current Business,* March 1991, p. C-1.

What conditions do you think they forecast for 1991?

**7. a.** Why are manufacturers' new orders, nondefense capital goods, an appropriate leading indicator?

**b.** Why is the index of industrial production an appropriate coincident indicator?

**c.** Why is the average prime rate charged by banks an appropriate lagging indicator?

**8.** Discuss some of the important criticisms of the forecasting ability of the leading economic indicators.

**9.** What is meant by "naive" forecasting methods? Describe some of the methods that fall within this category.

**10.** Manhattan was allegedly purchased from Native Americans in 1626 for $24. If the sellers had invested this sum at a 6 percent interest rate compounded semiannually, how much would it amount to today?

**11.** The compound growth rate is frequently used to forecast various quantities (sales, profits, and so on). Do you believe this is a good method? Should any cautions be exercised in making such projections?

**12.** Explain the meaning of *semilogarithmic scale.* When can it be used, and what are its advantages?

**13.** Describe projections that use either moving averages or exponential smoothing. Under what conditions can these techniques be used? Which of the two appears to be the more useful?

**14.** How do econometric models differ from "naive" projection methods? Is it always advisable to use the former in forecasting?

**15.** Which of the following forecasting methods are appropriate for predicting business cycles?
**a.** Trend projections
**b.** Leading economic indicators
**c.** Lagging economic indicators
**d.** Survey methods
Explain.

**16.** You have been asked to produce a forecast for your company's new product, bottled water. Discuss the kind of information you would look for in order to make this forecast.

**17.** Why do you think that a survey of planned capital expenditure would be of great importance? (At the time of this writing, several of these surveys have been discontinued.)

## Problems

**1.** If the sales of your company have grown from $500,000 five years ago to $1,050,150 this year, what is the compound growth rate? If you expect your sales to grow at a rate of 10 percent for the next five years, what should they be five years from now?

**2.** Based on past data, Mack's Pool Supply has constructed the following equation for the sales of its house brand of chlorine tablets:

$$Q = 1,000 + 100t$$

where $Q$ is quantity and $t$ is time (in years), with 1995 = 0.

**a.** What is the sales projection for 2000?

**b.** The tablet sales are seasonal, with the following quarterly indexes:

| | |
|---|---|
| Quarter 1 | 80% |
| Quarter 2 | 100% |
| Quarter 3 | 125% |
| Quarter 4 | 95% |

What is the quarterly sales projection for 2000?

**3.** The sales data over the last ten years for the Acme Hardware Store are as follows:

| | | | |
|---|---|---|---|
| 1990 | $230,000 | 1995 | $526,000 |
| 1991 | 276,000 | 1996 | 605,000 |
| 1992 | 328,000 | 1997 | 690,000 |
| 1993 | 388,000 | 1998 | 779,000 |
| 1994 | 453,000 | 1999 | 873,000 |

**a.** Calculate the compound growth rate for the period of 1990 to 1999.

**b.** Based on your answer to part *a*, forecast sales for both 2000 and 2001.

**c.** Now calculate the compound growth rate for the period of 1994 to 1999.

**d.** Based on your answer to part *c*, forecast sales for both 2000 and 2001.

**e.** What is the major reason for the differences in your answers to parts *b* and *d*? If you were to make your own projections, what would you forecast? (Drawing a graph will be very helpful.)

**4.** The sales data for the Tough Steel Hardware Company for the last 12 years are as follows:

| | | | |
|---|---|---|---|
| 1988 | $400,000 | 1994 | $617,000 |
| 1989 | 440,000 | 1995 | 654,000 |
| 1990 | 480,000 | 1996 | 700,000 |
| 1991 | 518,000 | 1997 | 756,000 |
| 1992 | 554,000 | 1998 | 824,000 |
| 1993 | 587,000 | 1999 | 906,000 |

**a.** What is the 1988–1999 compound growth rate?

**b.** Using the result obtained in part *a,* what is your 2000 projection?

**c.** If you were to make your own projection, what would you forecast? (Drawing a graph will be very helpful.)

**5.** The Miracle Corporation had the following sales during the past ten years (in thousands of dollars):

| | | | |
|---|---|---|---|
| 1990 | 200 | 1995 | 302 |
| 1991 | 215 | 1996 | 320 |
| 1992 | 237 | 1997 | 345 |
| 1993 | 260 | 1998 | 360 |
| 1994 | 278 | 1999 | 382 |

**a.** Calculate a trend line, and forecast sales for 2000. How confident are you of this forecast?

**b.** Use exponential smoothing with a smoothing factor $w = 0.7$. What is your 2000 forecast? How confident are you of this forecast?

**6.** You have the following data for the last 12 months' sales for the PRQ Corporation (in thousands of dollars):

| | | | |
|---|---|---|---|
| January | 500 | July | 610 |
| February | 520 | August | 620 |
| March | 520 | September | 580 |
| April | 510 | October | 550 |
| May | 530 | November | 510 |
| June | 580 | December | 480 |

**a.** Calculate a three-month centered moving average.

**b.** Use this moving average to forecast sales for January of next year.

**c.** If you were asked to forecast January and February sales for next year, would you be confident of your forecast using the preceding moving averages? Why or why not?

**7.** Office Enterprises (OE) produces a line of metal office file cabinets. The company's economist, having investigated a large number of past data, has established the following equation of demand for these cabinets:

$$Q = 10,000 + 60B - 100P + 50C$$

where $Q$ = Annual number of cabinets sold

$B$ = Index of nonresidential construction

$P$ = Average price per cabinet charged by OE

$C$ = Average price per cabinet charged by OE's closest competitor

It is expected that next year's nonresidential construction index will stand at 160, OE's average price will be $40, and the competitor's average price will be $35.

**a.** Forecast next year's sales.

**b.** What will be the effect if the competitor lowers its price to $32? If it raises its price to $36?

**c.** What will happen if OE reacts to the decrease mentioned in part *b* by lowering its price to $37?

**d.** If the index forecast was wrong, and it turns out to be only 140 next year, what will be the effect on OE's sales?

**8.** The gross domestic product of the United States, both in current and real dollars, from 1984 to 1995 was as follows:

|      | *Current* | *Real (1992 = 100)* |
|------|-----------|---------------------|
|      | *($ in billions)* |             |
| 1984 | 3,902 | 5,140 |
| 1985 | 4,181 | 5,324 |
| 1986 | 4,422 | 5,488 |
| 1987 | 4,692 | 5,650 |
| 1988 | 5,050 | 5,865 |
| 1989 | 5,439 | 6,062 |
| 1990 | 5,744 | 6,136 |
| 1991 | 5,917 | 6,079 |
| 1992 | 6,244 | 6,244 |
| 1993 | 6,558 | 6,390 |
| 1994 | 6,947 | 6,611 |
| 1995 | 7,270 | 6,762 |

**a.** Fit a linear (straight-line) trend to each of the data sets.
**b.** Now fit an exponential trend to these data.
**c.** Based on both the linear and exponential trend lines, what would have been your GDP (both current and real) forecast for the years 1996 and 1997?
**d.** Would any of these trend lines be good predictors of GDP? Why or why not?

**9.** An economist has estimated the sales trend line for the Sun Belt Toy Company as follows:

$$S_t = 43.6 + 0.8t$$

$S_t$ represents Sun Belt's monthly sales (in millions of dollars), and $t = 1$ in January 1995. The monthly seasonal indexes are as follows:

| January | 60 | April | 110 | July | 90 | October | 110 |
|---------|-----|-------|-----|------|-----|---------|-----|
| February | 70 | May | 110 | August | 80 | November | 140 |
| March | 85 | June | 100 | September | 95 | December | 150 |

Forecast monthly sales for the year 2000.

**10.** The U.S. population figures from 1978 to 1996 are as follows (in thousands):

| 1978 | 222,285 | 1985 | 238,466 | 1991 | 252,636 |
|------|---------|------|---------|------|---------|
| 1979 | 225,055 | 1986 | 240,651 | 1992 | 255,382 |
| 1980 | 227,726 | 1987 | 242,804 | 1993 | 258,089 |
| 1981 | 229,966 | 1988 | 245,021 | 1994 | 260,602 |
| 1982 | 232,188 | 1989 | 247,342 | 1995 | 263,039 |
| 1983 | 234,307 | 1990 | 249,949 | 1996 | 265,453 |
| 1984 | 236,348 |      |         |      |         |

**a.** Calculate the following:
   **(1)** A linear trend
   **(2)** An exponential trend
   **(3)** Compound growth rate
**b.** Forecast the 1997 and 1998 population figures from your calculations.
**c.** The actual population figure in 1997 was 267,901 (thousand) and in 1998 270,290 (thousand). Which of the three calculations gave you the best forecast?

**11.** You have sales for the Walgreen Company (in millions of dollars) and the Gross Domestic Product (in billions of dollars) for the years 1983 to 1997.

| | Walgreen Sales | | | | Gross Domestic Product | | |
|---|---|---|---|---|---|---|---|
| 1983 | 2,361 | 1990 | 6,048 | 1983 | 3,515 | 1990 | 5,744 |
| 1984 | 2,745 | 1991 | 6,733 | 1984 | 3,902 | 1991 | 5,917 |
| 1985 | 3,162 | 1992 | 7,474 | 1985 | 4,181 | 1992 | 6,244 |
| 1986 | 3,660 | 1993 | 8,295 | 1986 | 4,422 | 1993 | 6,558 |
| 1987 | 4,282 | 1994 | 9,235 | 1987 | 4,692 | 1994 | 6,947 |
| 1988 | 4,884 | 1995 | 10,395 | 1988 | 5,050 | 1995 | 7,270 |
| 1989 | 5,380 | 1996 | 11,778 | 1989 | 5,439 | 1996 | 7,662 |
| | | 1997 | 13,363 | | | 1997 | 8,111 |

**a.** Calculate the following:
   **(1)** A straight-line trend
   **(2)** An exponential trend
   **(3)** A regression with GDP as the independent variable
**b.** Walgreen's sales in 1998 were $15,307 (000,000), and the 1998 GDP was $8,509 (000,000,000). Which of the three calculations gives the best fit and the best estimate of Walgreen's sales in 1998?

---

## Take It to the Net

---

We invite you to visit the Keat/Young page on the Prentice Hall Web site at:

**http://www.prenhall.com/keat**

for additional resources.

---

## Appendix 6A

## Forecasting and the Computer[36]

Forecasting, in particular time series analysis, plays a fundamental role in the world of business and government. Among major topics covered in this chapter, classical decomposition and simple exponential smoothing are just two of the many procedures that forecasters have developed over the years. Simple exponential smoothing (sometimes called Brown's simple exponential smoothing[37]) is appropriate if there is no apparent trend to the data. If the data exhibit some pronounced linear or nonlinear trend, then Brown's method gives poor forecasts. Brown modified this procedure (traditionally called Brown's double exponential smoothing), but the method developed by Holt[38] is considered superior. Holt's method tries to find the equation of the line that fits the data, with more weight on recent observations and less weight on distant past observations. This method has two smoothing equations. The first finds an estimate for the intercept for the trend line, while the second estimates the slope of the trend line. Each equation has its own smoothing constant, and thus the forecaster must find the optimal values for each.

If the time series shows seasonal effects, the classical decomposition method discussed in the text can be used, but a more sophisticated method was developed by Winters.[39] This method is essentially a "superset" of Holt's method. There are three smoothing equations, each with its own smoothing constant. The first two find the intercept and slope of the linear trend line for the data, while the third finds estimates for the seasonal indices. If the data are quarterly, there would be four seasonal factors, monthly data have twelve seasonal factors, and so on. These seasonal indices are used as multiplicative factors in the forecast model. That is, the forecast found by the trend line is tempered by the seasonal index. Once again, the researcher is forced to find the optimal smoothing constants.

Other more sophisticated procedures exist, including the methods developed by Box and Jenkins.[40] This procedure also requires that certain statistical parameters be optimized, and the amount of work to do this becomes prohibitive if done by hand. Because of these issues, researchers can find many forecasting software programs on the market. Traditionally, if you wanted a "top-notch" forecasting program, you would buy a dedicated, standalone product. However, general statistical software packages have expanded and enhanced their forecasting modules, and some of these rival their standalone counterparts. The advantage of buying a general statistical software package is that the learning curve is small when you jump to the forecasting features. Because most forecasters perform statistical analysis also, the additional cost of the forecasting module could be lower than purchasing a dedicated forecasting program. However, if you

---

[36]This appendix was written by Jack Yurkiewicz, Professor of Management Science, Lubin School of Business, Pace University. The authors are very grateful for Professor Yurkiewicz's contribution.

[37]R. G. Brown, *Smoothing, Forecasting and Prediction of Discrete Time-Series,* Englewood Cliffs, NJ: Prentice Hall, 1962.

[38]C. C. Holt, "Forecasting Seasonal and Trends by Exponentially Weighted Moving Averages," Office of Naval Research, Memorandum 52, 1957.

[39]P. R. Winters, "Forecasting Sales by Exponentially Weighted Moving Averages," *Management Science,* 6 (1960), pp. 324–42.

[40]G. E. P. Box, G. M. Jenkins, and G. C. Reinsel, *Time Series Analysis, Forecasting and Control,* 3d ed., Englewood Cliffs, NJ: Prentice Hall, 1994.

want some of the more sophisticated forecasting methods (beyond exponential smoothing and Box-Jenkins procedures, such as spectral analysis or state-space models) then you must buy a dedicated forecasting program that offers these procedures.

Most of the forecasting software currently available offers "ease-of-use" and "ease-of-learning" attributes. You can usually import your data from a spreadsheet (some products make this importation easier than others) and the software will make a time plot automatically. The time plot is usually the first step in the forecasting process, for then the researcher, based on the appearance of the data, can choose an appropriate forecasting technique.

Some programs help the researcher in choosing the most appropriate procedure for the particular time series data. The extent of help offered allows us to categorize forecasting software into three groups. The first category can be called "automatic" software. In these products, the user enters or imports data and asks the program to "analyze" it. Considering various diagnostic tests, the software responds with a "recommended" method that should give the "best" forecasts. If the user concurs with the recommendation, the program will then proceed to find the optimal parameters for the proposed procedure, get the forecasts and corresponding statistics and make forecast plots. Users can manually override the recommended procedure and choose their preferred methodology. The software will then get the optimal parameters for the chosen model and the associated output.

Although it is always prudent to warn users to be leery of using these automatic programs as "black boxes," recently released software has made great strides in the accuracy of their recommendations.

The second software category can be called "semiautomatic." The software does not make a recommendation for the methodology best suited for the data. Users must choose the appropriate procedure from a list of procedures available. The program will then find the optimal parameters for the model chosen, make forecasts, and get the appropriate statistics and plots. The user of such software must obviously have a solid knowledge of forecasting and the various associated techniques. Most of the forecast software currently on the market falls into this category, and all of the general statistics programs with forecasting modules are also in this group.

The third software category can best be called "manual." Here the user must specify both the method and the parameters. The program will not find these parameters. Thus, the user must execute many "runs" for a time series, each time noting the corresponding output statistics. The session ends after many iterations, when the user either finds the "best" parameters or becomes tired, whichever comes first. There are few dedicated forecasting or general statistics programs that fall into this category, but because of their limited utility, purchasing them is not recommended.

To help researchers in deciding which software is most appropriate for their needs, *OR/MS Today,* from the Institute for Operations Research and Management Sciences, publishes a survey[41] every two years that describes the currently available forecast software. The survey gives the software's features (automatic, semiautomatic, or manual), methodology available, prices, and other issues. Other forecasting and statistical journals publish similar articles.

---

[41]J. Yurkiewicz, "Forecasting Software Survey: A Guide to a Fast Growing Discipline," *OR/MS Today,* December 1997, pp. 70–75.

# CHAPTER 7

# The Theory and Estimation of Production

## THE SITUATION

The meeting of Global Foods' top production managers must have been important because it was attended by CEO Bob Burns as well as by Jim Hartwell, vice president of manufacturing. Its purpose was to go over the plans for rolling out the company's new bottled water product, *Waterpure.* Christopher Lim, manager of the company's largest bottling plant, in St. Louis, Missouri, knew that this product was considered to be the hope of the sagging beverage division. He also suspected that there was going to be more than the usual plans for the bottling operation because of the additional presence of Nicole Goodman, senior VP of marketing.

The meeting began with a few opening remarks by the CEO about the phenomenal growth of the bottled water industry and how and why Global Foods hoped to get into this market. Chris noticed that all but a few of the 15 people at the meeting had their own bottle of water in front of them and thought that this more than any other statistic made the point. Then came the surprise. The opening presentation was given by the senior VP of marketing, not manufacturing.

Nicole Goodman began to make a compelling case for a radical change in the packaging of this product. "You all have seen how Coca-Cola has spent millions of dollars in advertising and packaging in order to focus on the shape of its original glass bottle and how Pepsi-Cola recently changed the look of its label and logo. But packaging can be considered even more important in the market for bottled water, because after all what are we selling?"

"What I propose is that we combine the tradition of Coca-Cola with the design innovation of Pepsi-Cola and a French company that makes another beverage called "Orangina" to create our own distinct packaging. We propose to sell our water in a green glass bottle

*(Continued)*

shaped like a bottle of champagne. To go along with this packaging, we intend to advertise our product as the "champagne of bottled water."

"How original," thought Chris. "I seem to recall that some time ago a beer company used a similar tag line in their advertising. But forget the advertising, doesn't she realize how expensive it is to use glass rather than plastic? There has to be a reason why both Coke and Pepsi don't use glass for most of their bottling, particularly here in the States."

As if in anticipation of Chris's negative thoughts, Nicole continued by saying, "I know some of you might be thinking that this champagne idea is not very original. But our market research indicates that people between

the ages of 15 and 35 are the key consumers of bottled water, and so most of our potential customers will be too young to remember that Miller beer commercial. We in marketing realize that it will be you in manufacturing that will actually implement our "creative" ideas. We know that this will present some interesting production challenges in terms of the set-up of the fill lines, the stacking of the cases for shipment and delivery, and so on. But I know you're up to the challenge. We want to begin a pilot program in one of our bottling plants. In consulting with both Bob and Jim, they both recommended strongly that we begin with our bottling plant in St. Louis. Chris, we want you to put together a plan for rolling out our new product in the next quarter."

## The Production Function

Christopher Lim's concerns are certainly justified. No matter how much revenue is generated by the marketing plan, if the cost of production cannot be contained, the company will not be able to earn an acceptable level of profit. In economics, the analysis of cost begins with the study of the production function. The **production function** is a statement of the relationship between a firm's scarce resources (i.e., its **inputs**) and the output that results from the use of these resources. Economic cost analysis can then be seen as the application of a monetary unit such as dollars to measure the value of this input usage in the production process. Therefore, both this chapter on production and the following chapter on cost really deal with the same general topic of economic cost analysis. Because of the length and complexity of this topic, we have divided its presentation into two separate chapters.

In mathematical terms, the production function can be expressed as:

$$Q = f(X_1, X_2 ....... X_k) \tag{7.1}$$

where $Q$ = Output
$X_1 ....... X_k$ = Inputs used in the production process

Note that we assume that this relationship between inputs and output exists for a specific period of time. In other words, $Q$ is *not* a measure of accumulated output over time. There are two other key assumptions that you should be aware of. First, we are assuming some given "state of the art" in the production technology. Any innovation in production (e.g., the use of robotics in manufacturing or a more efficient software package for financial analysis) would cause the relationship between given inputs and their output to change. Second, we are assuming that whatever input or input combinations are included in a particular function, the output resulting from their utilization is at the maximum level. With this in mind, we can offer a more complete definition of a production function:

> A production function defines the relationship between inputs and the maximum amount that can be produced within a given period of time with a given level of technology.

For Christopher's company, the $X$s could represent raw materials, such as carbonated water, sweeteners, and flavorings; labor, such as assembly line workers, support staff, and supervisory personnel; and fixed assets, such as plant and equipment.

For purposes of analysis, let us reduce the whole array of inputs in the production function to two, $X$ and $Y$. Restating Equation (7.1) gives us

$$Q = f(X,Y) \tag{7.2}$$

where $Q =$ Output
$\quad X =$ Labor
$\quad Y =$ Capital

Notice that although we have designated one variable as labor and the other as capital, we have elected to keep the all-purpose symbols $X$ and $Y$ as a reminder that any two inputs could have been selected to represent the array.

As stated earlier, in economic analysis the distinction between the short run and the long run is not related to any particular measurement of time (e.g., days, months, or years). Instead it refers to the extent to which a firm can vary the amounts of the inputs in its production process. Thus, a **short-run production function** shows the maximum quantity of a good or service that can be produced by a set of inputs, assuming that the amount of at least one of the inputs used remains unchanged. A **long-run production function** shows the maximum quantity of a good or service that can be produced by a set of inputs, assuming that the firm is free to vary the amount of *all* the inputs being used.

A hypothetical production function with two inputs is displayed in Table 7.1. The numbers in the matrix indicate the amount of output that would result from various combinations of $X$ and $Y$. For example, the use of 2 units of $X$ and 2 units of $Y$ yields 18 units of output. Adding one more unit of $X$ while holding constant the amount of $Y$ yields an additional 11 units of output ($Q = 29$). Increasing both $X$ and $Y$ by 1 unit yields 41 units of output. The additional 1 unit of $X$ with $Y$ unchanged is considered to be a "short-run" change. An increase in both inputs by 1 unit is a "long-run" change.

# A Short-Run Analysis of Total, Average, and Marginal Product

Before we go on to a more detailed analysis of the production function, certain key terms employed throughout this chapter should be clarified. First, economists use a number of alternative terms in reference to inputs and output:

| TABLE 7.1 Representative Production Table | | | | | | | | |
|---|---|---|---|---|---|---|---|---|
| **Units of Y Employed** | | | | *Output Quantity (Q)* | | | | |
| 8 | 37 | 60 | 83 | 96 | 107 | 117 | 127 | 128 |
| 7 | 42 | 64 | 78 | 90 | 101 | 110 | 119 | 120 |
| 6 | 37 | 52 | 64 | 73 | 82 | 90 | 97 | 104 |
| 5 | 31 | 47 | 58 | 67 | 75 | 82 | 89 | 95 |
| 4 | 24 | 39 | 52 | 60 | 67 | 73 | 79 | 85 |
| 3 | 17 | 29 | 41 | 52 | 58 | 64 | 69 | 73 |
| 2 | 8 | 18 | 29 | 39 | 47 | 52 | 56 | 52 |
| 1 | 4 | 8 | 14 | 20 | 27 | 24 | 21 | 17 |
| | 1 | 2 | 3 | 4 | 5 | 6 | 7 | 8 |
| | | | | *Units of X Employed* | | | | |

| **Inputs** | **Output** |
|---|---|
| Factors | Quantity ($Q$) |
| Factors of production | Total product (TP) |
| Resources | Product |

Second, in the short-run analysis of the production function, two other terms besides the quantity of output are important measures of the outcome. They are **marginal product (MP)** and **average product (AP).** If we assume $X$ to be the variable input, then

$$\text{Marginal product of } X \ = \ \text{MP}_X \ = \ \frac{\Delta Q}{\Delta X}, \text{holding } Y \text{ constant}$$

$$\text{Average product of } X \ = \ \text{AP}_X \ = \ \frac{Q}{X}, \text{holding } Y \text{ constant}$$

In other words, the marginal product can be defined as the change in output or **total product** resulting from a unit change in a variable input, and the average product can be defined as the total product (TP) per unit of input used.

The data in Table 7.2 shows a short-run production function. Here we see what happens to output when increasing amounts of input $X$ are added to a fixed amount of input $Y$ ($Y = 2$). Table 7.3 restates this information by focusing on the impact on TP, MP, and AP resulting from increases in $X$, while holding $Y$ constant at 2 units. The impact is also illustrated in the graphs in Figure 7.1. These tables and the figure indicate that the total product is 8 when 1 unit of $X$ is used, it increases to a maximum of 56 when 7 units of $X$ are used, and it decreases to 52 units when unit 8 of the $X$ input is added. Also notice in Table 7.3 that MP begins at 8 units, increases to a maximum of 11, and falls off to an ultimate value of $-4$. Average product also begins at 8, increases to a maximum of 9.67, and then drops to 6.5 units when 8 units of $X$ are combined with the fixed amount of $Y$. The pattern of these changes can be seen in Figure 7.1. The total product is plotted in Figure 7.1*a,* and the average and marginal products are plotted in Figure 7.1*b.*

We can observe that when $Q$, the quantity of the total product, reaches its maximum, MP $= 0$. We see also that initially (as more units of $X$ are added to the production

**TABLE 7.2** Short-Run Changes in Production Showing Factor Productivity

| Units of Y Employed | | | Output Quantity (Q) | | | | | |
|---|---|---|---|---|---|---|---|---|
| 8 | 37 | 60 | 83 | 96 | 107 | 117 | 127 | 128 |
| 7 | 42 | 64 | 78 | 90 | 101 | 110 | 119 | 120 |
| 6 | 37 | 52 | 64 | 73 | 82 | 90 | 97 | 104 |
| 5 | 31 | 47 | 58 | 67 | 75 | 82 | 89 | 95 |
| 4 | 24 | 39 | 52 | 60 | 67 | 73 | 79 | 85 |
| 3 | 17 | 29 | 41 | 52 | 58 | 64 | 69 | 73 |
| 2 | (8) | (18) | (29) | (39) | (47) | (52) | (56) | (52) |
| 1 | 4 | 8 | 14 | 20 | 27 | 24 | 21 | 17 |
| | 1 | 2 | 3 | 4 | 5 | 6 | 7 | 8 |

*Units of X Employed*

process), MP is greater than AP, and it then becomes less than AP. Furthermore, MP = AP at AP's highest point. Because we are dealing with incremental unit changes in the input, it is difficult to see these points in Table 7.3, but they can be seen clearly in Figure 7.1. In the next section we will have more to say about the pattern of change in *Q*, AP, and MP and, more important, the reasons for the pattern of change.

## THE LAW OF DIMINISHING RETURNS

The key to understanding the pattern of change in *Q*, AP, and MP is the phenomenon known as the **law of diminishing returns.** This law states:

As additional units of variable input are combined with a fixed input, at some point the additional output (i.e., marginal product) starts to diminish.

Diminishing returns are illustrated in both the numerical example in Table 7.3 and the graph of these same numbers in Figure 7.1. As you examine this information, think "change" as you see the word "marginal." Therefore, the "marginal product" of an in-

**TABLE 7.3** Short-Run Production Function: Q, MP, AP

| Variable Input (X) | Total Product (Q or TP) | Marginal Product (MP) | Average Product (AP) |
|---|---|---|---|
| 0 | 0 | | |
| 1 | 8 | 8 | 8 |
| 2 | 18 | 10 | 9 |
| 3 | 29 | 11 | 9.67 |
| 4 | 39 | 10 | 9.75 |
| 5 | 47 | 8 | 9.4 |
| 6 | 52 | 5 | 8.67 |
| 7 | 56 | 4 | 8 |
| 8 | 52 | −4 | 6.5 |

(*a*) Total product

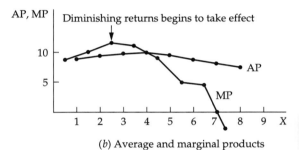

(*b*) Average and marginal products

**FIGURE 7.1** Short-Run Production with $Y = 2$

put such as labor is the change in output resulting from an additional unit of input. Notice in Table 7.3 that we have placed the marginal product *between* each interval of input and the resulting output. For example, the marginal product of the first unit of input, 8, is placed between 0 and 1 input or between 0 and 8 units of output. Continuing on, we see that marginal product reaches its maximum of 11 between the second and third units of input. It is precisely at this point, 2.5 units of input, that we can say the law of diminishing returns will begin to take effect.[1]

In situations in which it would not be possible to consider intervals of less than one unit, it is necessary to approximate the point at which diminishing returns occurs. Suppose you were a manager who could actually measure and track your employees' marginal product. The first person's MP would be 8, the second one would be 10 and the third person's would be 11. It would be only on the addition of the fourth person that you

[1]The idea that diminishing returns will occur at this point is based on an analysis using calculus, in which the first derivative of the total product function, marginal product, is set to zero. The amount of input that fulfills this condition, is then considered the exact point at which marginal product is maximized and the law of diminishing returns will begin to take effect. See Appendix B at the end of this chapter for a complete explanation of this approach.

would realize that the law of diminishing returns had occurred because this person's MP would be less than that of the previous worker. In summary we can say that, given the numbers in Table 7.3, the law of diminishing returns occurs in theory precisely at 2.5 units of input. In practice, a manager would have to add a fourth unit of labor in order to observe the law in action.

There are two key concerns of a practical nature that we advise readers to keep in mind when considering the impact of the law of diminishing returns in actual business situations. First, there is nothing in the law that states *when* diminishing returns will start to take effect. The law merely says that if additional units of a variable input are combined with a fixed input, *at some point,* the marginal product of the input will start to diminish. Therefore, it is reasonable to assume that a manager will only discover the point of diminishing returns by experience and trial and error. Hindsight will be more valuable than foresight. Second, when economists first stated this law, they made some very restrictive assumptions about the nature of the variable inputs being used. Essentially, they assumed that all inputs added to the production process were exactly the same in individual productivity. The only reason why a particular unit of input's marginal product would be higher or lower than the others used was because of the order in which it was added to the production process.

Let us examine more closely the possible reasons for the occurrence of diminishing returns. Essentially, these reasons have to do with the physical limitations of the fixed input and the variable inputs that are added to this fixed input. Suppose that we assume that the numbers in Table 7.3 represent a simple manufacturing situation where the variable input is labor and the fixed input is the factory and its machinery. Suppose that more labor is added to this fixed capital. Clearly when no workers are employed, TP or output is zero. The first worker produces 8 units. Thus, his marginal product (MP) is equal to 8 and his average product (AP) is also equal to 8. When 2 workers are used, their combined efforts yield a total product (TP) of 18. This implies that 2 people working together can produce more than the sum of their efforts working as separate individuals. (AP of one worker = 8 and AP of the two workers = 9.) Moreover, we see that the MP of the second worker is greater than that of the first (MP of second worker = 10, > MP of first worker = 8).

Because it is assumed in economic theory that each worker is equally productive, this must mean that the effect of teamwork and specialization enables additional workers to contribute more than those added previously to the production process, a phenomenon that we can refer to as "increasing returns." But as still more workers are added, there are fewer and fewer opportunities for increasing returns through specialization and teamwork and at some point additional workers result in diminishing returns. Eventually, there may be so many workers relative to the fixed capacity that they may start to interfere with each other's activities. In this case, the additional workers lead to negative marginal returns, causing the total product to decrease. We see this occurring in Table 7.3 when the eighth person is added to the production process. In this case, the old adage "too many cooks spoil the soup" seems to have been realized.

Economists who first thought about the law of diminishing returns relied primarily on deductive reasoning rather than empirical verification to explain the law's existence. It was critical for them to establish this law because it then helped to explain the "Three Stages of Production" and the phenomenon of increasing marginal cost (explained in detail in the next chapter). Furthermore, when this law was established in the nineteenth century, the primary examples used to illustrate its impact on production involved agriculture, with land being the fixed factor of production, and farmers being the variable factors. At some point, it was reasoned, with a fixed amount of land, additional farm workers would result in diminishing amounts of additional harvested output.

To illustrate this law with more contemporary examples, we offer an example based on an actual situation involving a soft drink bottling facility. In addition, we provide two examples related to information technology.

### The Sorting of Refillable Glass Bottles

In the early days of the soft drink industry, most drinks were packaged in returnable, refillable glass bottles. Now most drinks are packaged in plastic bottles or aluminum cans. But in some parts of the United States (particularly in Michigan) and in many parts of the rest of the world, returnable, refillable bottles are still used extensively.

There are three basic ways to sort and clean the returned bottles: (1) a totally automatic sorting system, (2) a totally manual sorting system, and (3) a hybrid system. The choice of system depends primarily on the anticipated volume of returned bottles. A typical manual sorting area is about 30 feet long and there is usually no room in a plant for expansion. Each sorter requires about 3 feet of space in which to work. A conveyor carrying the returned empties runs along a wall and sorters work from one side of this conveyor.

The standard productivity measure used in a plant is "cases sorted per person-hour." If only one person is sorting bottles, she will not be able to keep up with the flow. The bottles tend to back up, and the system has to stop while the sorter tries to catch up.[2] In an interview with a bottling plant manager, the authors learned that typically two sorters per flavor are used.[3] Thus, if five flavors need to be sorted, ten people work at the conveyor belt. These ten sorters take up the maximum length of the sorting area (30 feet) if the recommended amount of 3 feet per person is allocated. The plant manager explained that if more than 10 sorters are used, productivity tends to decrease because the workers start to get in each other's way. Although no quantitative detail was provided, we think that readers can well imagine that at this point, the law of diminishing returns would be starting to take effect, with each additional worker beyond ten sorting less returned bottles than the previously added worker.

*Fixed input:*   Machinery and working area square footage

*Variable input:*   People working as sorters

### Development of Applications Software

Suppose you are the manager of a team of software engineers that is developing a new program to help companies to make their computer systems compliant with the demands of the year 2000 (often referred to as the "Y2K" problem). Suppose your project management plan calls for writing approximately 500 lines of program code every day in order to reach the objective. You have a team of five programmers each writing about 100 lines of code a day. To speed things up (as January 1, 2000 rapidly approaches), you

---

[2]Readers can imagine that this is very much what might happen in stage I of the production process. (See next section for Stages of Production.)

[3]Interview with a former student of one of the authors, who used to work as a bottling plant manager for Pepsi-Cola.

decide to add more programmers to your team. You notice that the first additional person you add (the sixth member of the team) adds only 90 lines of code and the next person hired after that adds only 80 lines. Assuming that the two additional programmers are equally skilled and work well as team members with the established group, you conclude that the law of diminishing returns must be at work.

*Fixed input:*  the programming language and the hardware used to develop the applications program

*Variable input:*  software programmers

### Response Time on a Data Network

You are a manager of a data communications network that is responsible for issuing approval codes for a credit card operation. After a credit card is swiped, the data is sent from the merchant's bank to the bank that issued the cardholder the card via the data communications network. The approval code comes back to the merchant within an average of three seconds. The merchants complain that this is too long. Software programmers are put to work to make the adjustments in software that will reduce the average to two seconds. Ten programmers working 10 hours a week for two weeks reduce the response time down to two seconds. Merchants continue to complain and want the average reduced further to one second. As the network manager, you try again with another 10 programmers working the same amount of time as the previous addition of programmers. You find that the same additional time and effort does not yield the desired one-second reduction in response time. You conclude that the law of diminishing returns is at work.

*Fixed input:*  the technological infrastructure (i.e., the hardware and bandwidth of the transmission facilities of the physical network and the limits and capabilities of the software)

*Variable input:*  software programmers

In summary, all of these examples illustrate how diminishing returns can be caused by the physical limitations of fixed capital such as machinery and workspace, the technological limitations of computer hardware and software, and the personnel and management problems caused by increasing numbers of people working with a fixed capacity.

### THE THREE STAGES OF PRODUCTION IN THE SHORT RUN

The short-run production function can be divided into three distinct **stages of production.** To illustrate this phenomenon, let us return to the data in Table 7.3 and Figure 7.1. For your convenience, Figure 7.1 has been reproduced as Figure 7.2. As the figure indicates, stage I runs from zero to four units of the variable input $X$ (i.e., to the point at which average product reaches its maximum). Stage II begins from this point and proceeds to seven units of input $X$ (i.e., to the point at which total product is maximized). Stage III continues on from that point. According to economic theory, in the short run, "rational" firms should only be operating in stage II. It is clear why stage III is irrational: the firm would be using more of its variable input to produce less output! However, it may not be as apparent why stage I is also considered irrational. The reason is that if a firm were operating in stage I, it would be grossly underutilizing its fixed capacity. That

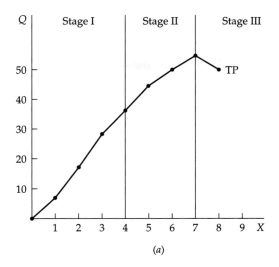

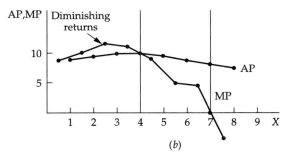

**FIGURE 7.2  The Three Stages of Production**

is, it would have so much fixed capacity relative to its usage of variable inputs that it could increase the output per unit of variable input (i.e., average product) simply by adding more variable inputs to this capacity. Figure 7.3*a* summarizes the three stages of production and the reasons that the rational firm operates in stage II of the short-run production function.

   If you are still not clear about the irrational nature of stage I, there is an alternative explanation. In Figure 7.3*b*, we have designated two levels of variable input usage: $X_1$ and $X_2$. Here we see that the average product is the same whether $X_1$ or $X_2$ units of the variable input are used. If output per variable input is the same regardless of which input level is used, the firm should employ $X_2$ because the total product will be higher.

**MODULE 7A**
**MODULE 7B**
**MODULE 7C**

### DERIVED DEMAND AND THE OPTIMAL LEVEL OF VARIABLE INPUT USAGE

Given that a firm's short-run production has only one "rational" stage of production (i.e., stage II), we must still determine the level of input usage within stage II that is best for the rational, profit-maximizing firm. To demonstrate how we determine the optimal level of input usage within stage II, we have created another numerical illustration, shown in Table 7.4. In this table we observe that stage II occurs from 60,000 to 80,000 units of total product. In terms of labor input, this stage II ranges

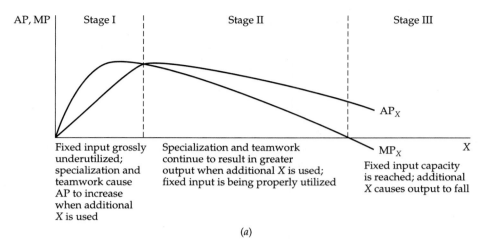

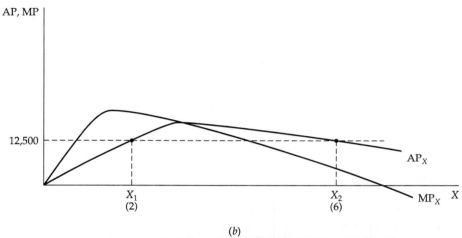

**FIGURE 7.3** Explanation of Production Stages

from four to eight units of input. But which level of output (or input) usage should we consider to be optimal? In answering this question, note that this table resembles the set up of a spreadsheet program, because MP is placed at the *same* level of output that results from an additional unit of input rather than *between* the two levels of output as shown in Table 7.3. In fact, we have provided you with an Excel exercise so that you can experiment with your own variations of the example shown in Table 7.4.

The answer to this question is based on a concept introduced in chapter 4, derived demand. Recall that the demand for inputs is derived from the demand for their output. In other words, it would do no good for the firm to decide how many units of variable input to use without knowing how many units of output it could sell, the price of the product, and the monetary costs of employing various amounts of the $X$ input.

**TABLE 7.4   Combining Marginal Revenue Product (MRP) with Marginal Labor Cost (MLC)**

| Labor Unit (X) | Total Product (Q or TP) | Average Product (AP) | Marginal Product (MP) | Total Revenue Product (TRP) | Marginal Revenue Product (MRP) | Total Labor Cost (TLC) | Marginal Labor Cost (MLC) | TRP − TLC | MRP − MLC |
|---|---|---|---|---|---|---|---|---|---|
| 0 | 0 | | 0 | 0 | | 0 | | 0 | 0 |
| 1 | 10,000 | 10,000 | 10,000 | 20,000 | 20,000 | 10,000 | 10,000 | 10,000 | 10,000 |
| 2 | 25,000 | 12,500 | 15,000 | 50,000 | 30,000 | 20,000 | 10,000 | 30,000 | 20,000 |
| 3 | 45,000 | 15,000 | 20,000 | 90,000 | 40,000 | 30,000 | 10,000 | 60,000 | 30,000 |
| 4 | 60,000 | 15,000 | 15,000 | 120,000 | 30,000 | 40,000 | 10,000 | 80,000 | 20,000 |
| 5 | 70,000 | 14,000 | 10,000 | 140,000 | 20,000 | 50,000 | 10,000 | 90,000 | 10,000 |
| 6 | 75,000 | 12,500 | 5,000 | 150,000 | 10,000 | 60,000 | 10,000 | 90,000 | 0 |
| 7 | 78,000 | 11,143 | 3,000 | 156,000 | 6,000 | 70,000 | 10,000 | 86,000 | −4,000 |
| 8 | 80,000 | 10,000 | 2,000 | 160,000 | 4,000 | 80,000 | 10,000 | 80,000 | −6,000 |

*Note:* $P$ = Product price = \$2
$W$ = Cost per unit of labor = \$10,000
MRP = MP $\times$ P
TLC = $X \times W$
MLC = $\Delta$TLC/$\Delta X$

To see exactly how this works, assume that a firm is operating in a perfectly competitive market for its input and its output. That is, it can sell as many units of the product as it wants as long as it does so at the going market price. Moreover, it can hire as many $X$ inputs as it desires as long as it pays these inputs the going market price (i.e., the competitive wage rate). Note that four new measures are added to Table 7.4:

*Total revenue product* (TRP): The market value of the firm's output, computed by multiplying the total product by the market price ($Q \times P$).
*Marginal revenue product* (MRP): The change in the firm's total revenue product resulting from a unit change in the number of inputs used ($\Delta$TRP/$\Delta X$). It can also be computed by multiplying the marginal product by the product price (MP $\times$ P).
*Total labor cost* (TLC): The total cost of using the variable input, labor, computed by multiplying the wage rate (which we assume to be some given and constant dollar amount) by the number of variable inputs employed (Wage rate $\times$ X).
*Marginal labor cost* (MLC): The change in total labor cost resulting from a unit change in the number of variable inputs used. Because the wage rate is assumed to be constant regardless of the number of inputs used, the MLC is the same as the wage rate.[4]

---

[4]This term is also referred to as *marginal resource cost* (MRC) and *marginal factor cost* (MFC). By assuming that the firm hires workers in a perfectly competitive labor market, we also assume that it can hire as many workers as it chooses at some going market wage rate determined by the supply and demand for this particular type of worker. This would not be the case if the firm were operating in an imperfectly competitive labor market. We will not consider the imperfectly competitive case in this text. Interested readers should consult any economics principles or intermediate microeconomics text for a full discussion on this type of labor market and its impact on the input decisions of the firm.

In deriving the figures for these measures in Table 7.4, we have assumed a product price of $2 and a wage rate of $10,000 per unit. Given these figures, you can see that a rational firm would want to hire 6 units of labor. Up to that point it pays for the firm to add more labor because the additional **marginal labor cost (MLC)** to the firm to do so is more than made up for by the additional **marginal revenue product (MRP)** brought in by the sale of the increased output. Beyond that point the firm would pay more in additional labor cost than it would receive in additional revenue.

Can you discern how the demand for the output is incorporated into this analysis, that is, how the demand for the input $X$ is actually derived from the demand for the output? Suppose the market demand increased and drove the market price up to $4. This would increase the market value of the labor input's efforts. In other words, the market value of each additional labor unit's contribution to the total product would double. This increase in the labor input's MRP would then justify the firm's use of a seventh unit of labor. Thus, an increase in the market demand for the output leads to an increase in the demand by the firm for labor input, all other factors held constant. The original figures from Table 7.4 as well as the case in which market price is assumed to increase to $4 are illustrated in Figure 7.4.

We can summarize this relationship between the demand for the output and the demand for the input in terms of the following optimal decision rule:

A profit-maximizing firm operating in perfectly competitive output and input markets will be using the optimal amount of an input at the point at which the monetary value of the input's marginal product is equal to the additional cost of using that input—in other words, when **MRP = MLC.**

**FIGURE 7.4** The Effect of Increased Market Price on the Demand for Labor

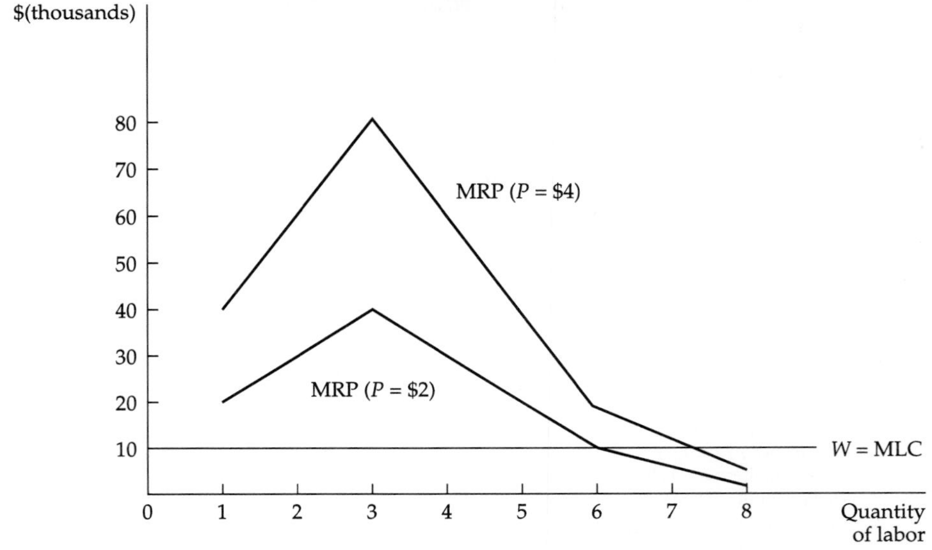

## THE CASE OF MULTIPLE INPUTS (ABRIDGED VERSION)

The purpose of this section is to present a relatively nonquantitative explanation of optimal input decisions involving two or more inputs. For a complete treatment of multiple inputs using numerical tables, graphs, and algebraic equations, please refer to Appendix 7A at the end of this chapter.

In the example illustrated in Table 7.4, we showed how a firm could use the concept of equalizing at the margin to determine the optimal usage level of a single variable input. This same equalizing concept applies to a situation in which two or more inputs are being considered. In the multiple input case, we must consider the relationship between the *ratio* of the marginal product of one input and its cost to the *ratio* of the marginal product of the other input (inputs) and its (their) cost. Expressed mathematically for "$k$" inputs:

$$\frac{MP_1}{W_1} = \frac{MP_2}{W_2} = \frac{M_k}{W_k}$$

Let us consider the case of a global manufacturing company that has manufacturing facilities in two different countries: a high-wage country and a low-wage country. We can analyze this problem by treating labor in the high wage country as one input and labor in the other country as another input. At first glance, it might seem obvious that a country seeking to minimize its costs and hence maximize its profits should try to manufacture as much as possible in the low-wage country. This would mean using mostly the low-wage labor input. But production theory suggests that the firm should not only look at input costs but also the marginal products of each input *relative* to their respective costs.

Suppose you are the production manager of a company that makes computer parts and peripherals in Malaysia and Costa Rica. At the current levels of production and input utilization in the two countries, you find that:

Marginal Product of labor in Malaysia ($MP_{Mal}$) = 18
Marginal Product of labor in Costa Rica ($MP_{CR}$) = 6
Wage rate in Malaysia ($W_{Mal}$) = \$6/hr.
Wage rate in Costa Rica ($W_{CR}$) = \$3/hr.

How much would you produce in each manufacturing facility? Because labor is cheaper in Costa Rica, you might be tempted to produce most of your output in that country. However, a closer look at the MP:wage ratios reveals the opposite conclusion. That is,

$$\frac{MP_{Mal}}{W_{Mal}} > \frac{MP_{CR}}{W_{CR}} \quad \text{or} \quad \frac{18}{\$6} > \frac{6}{\$3}$$

This means that at the margin, the last dollar spent on a unit of labor in Costa Rica would yield 2 units of output (6/\$3), while in Malaysia, the last dollar spent would result in three additional units of output (18/\$6). This inequality implies that the firm should begin to shift more of its production away from Costa Rica to Malaysia, until the two ratios are equalized. In theory, this optimal or equilibrium point would occur because as more labor is used in Malaysia, the law of diminishing returns would start to reduce the MP of labor in this country. With less labor being used in Costa Rica, the law of diminishing returns would work in reverse, causing the marginal product of labor in this country to rise. Of course, all this assumes a short-run condition whereby the complementary fixed inputs used along with labor remain constant.[5]

Once the implication of the basic model is understood, other factors can be brought in. If these factors outweigh the MP-input cost criteria, a company may well modify its decision. For example, despite Malaysia's higher MP/wage ratio, there may be political and economic risk factors to consider. (This was indeed the case when the Malaysian government imposed foreign exchange controls in 1998 by requiring foreign investors to keep their profits in Malaysia for at least one year before they could be repatriated.) On the other hand, Costa Rica is a fairly stable economy with leaders who do not seem to want to impose any such trade and finance restrictions. Its proximity to U.S. markets would also reduce transportation costs. Furthermore, it has a democratic government (with no standing army) and a highly skilled work force with strong English language skills.[6]

## The Long-Run Production Function

In the long run, a firm has time enough to change the amount of all of its inputs. Thus, there is really no difference between fixed and variable inputs. Table 7.5 uses the data first presented in Table 7.1 and illustrates what happens to total output as both inputs *X* and *Y* increase one unit at a time. The resulting increase in the total output as the two inputs increase is called **returns to scale.**

Looking more closely at Table 7.5, we see for example that if the firm uses 1 unit of *X* and 1 unit of *Y*, it will produce 4 units of output. If it doubles its inputs (i.e., 2 units of *X* and 2 units of *Y*), it will produce 18 units of output. Thus, a doubling of inputs has produced more than a fourfold increase in output. Proceeding further, we notice that an additional doubling of inputs (i.e., 4 units of *X* and 4 units of *Y*) results in more than a threefold increase in output, from 18 to 60. What we are observing in this table is *increasing returns to scale.*

According to economic theory, if an increase in a firm's inputs by some proportion results in an increase in output by a greater proportion, the firm experiences *increasing returns to scale.* If output increases by the same proportion as the inputs increase, the firm experiences *constant returns to scale.* A less than proportional increase in output is called *decreasing returns to scale.*

You might simply assume that firms generally experience constant returns to scale. For example, if a firm has a factory of a particular size, then doubling its size along with

---

[5]Over time, there might be another factor causing the two ratios to begin to equalize. If there are enough companies that see this inequality, their combined increase in demand for labor in Malaysia may start to drive up the wage rate in this country, while a decrease in demand for labor in Costa Rica may slow the rate in increase in wage rates or even cause them to fall. Thus equalizing at the margin could take place because of changes in the values of the denominators of the ratios as well as the value of their numerators.
[6]Although the numerical example above is entirely hypothetical, it seems that Costa Rica is actually an important factor in the international location decisions of some important global firms. In 1997, PC manufacturer AST shifted its call center operations to handle customer service inquiries originating in the United States from San Jose, California to San Jose, Costa Rica. About 500 jobs were involved. Also in that same year, Intel decided to locate a chip manufacturing facility in that country, passing over such countries as Malaysia and Ireland.

**TABLE 7.5   Returns to Scale**

| Units of Y Employed | Output Quantity | | | | | | | |
|---|---|---|---|---|---|---|---|---|
| 8 | 37 | 60 | 83 | 96 | 107 | 117 | 127 | (128) |
| 7 | 42 | 64 | 78 | 90 | 101 | 110 | (119) | 120 |
| 6 | 37 | 52 | 64 | 73 | 82 | (90) | 97 | 104 |
| 5 | 31 | 47 | 58 | 67 | (75) | 82 | 89 | 95 |
| 4 | 24 | 39 | 52 | (60) | 67 | 73 | 79 | 85 |
| 3 | 17 | 29 | (41) | 52 | 58 | 64 | 69 | 73 |
| 2 | 8 | (18) | 29 | 39 | 47 | 52 | 56 | 52 |
| 1 | (4) | 8 | 14 | 20 | 27 | 24 | 21 | 17 |
| | 1 | 2 | 3 | 4 | 5 | 6 | 7 | 8 |

*Units of X Employed*

a doubling of workers and machinery should lead to a doubling of output. Why should it result in a greater than proportional or, for that matter, a smaller than proportional increase? For one thing, a larger scale of production might enable a firm to divide up tasks into more specialized activities, thereby increasing labor productivity. Also, a larger scale of operation might enable a company to justify the purchase of more sophisticated (hence, more productive) machinery. These factors help to explain why a firm can experience increasing returns to scale. On the other hand, operating on a larger scale might create certain managerial inefficiencies (e.g., communications problems, bureaucratic red tape) and hence cause decreasing returns to scale. More will be said about the factors that can cause increasing or decreasing returns to scale in the next chapter, when we discuss the related concepts of economies and diseconomies of scale.

One way to measure returns to scale is to use a coefficient of output elasticity:

$$E_Q = \frac{\text{Percentage change in } Q}{\text{Percentage change in all inputs}}$$

Thus,

If $E > 1$, we have increasing returns to scale (IRTS).
If $E = 1$, we have constant returns to scale (CRTS).
If $E < 1$, we have decreasing returns to scale (DRTS).

Another way of looking at the concept of returns to scale is based on an equation that was first presented at the outset of this chapter:

$$Q = f(X, Y) \tag{7.3}$$

Recall in the original specification of this equation that it may include as many input variables as necessary to describe the production process (i.e., $i$ variables). For ease of discussion, we will limit this number to two: $X$ and $Y$. Now suppose that we increase the amount of each input by some proportion $k$. For example, if we increase the inputs by 10 percent, $k = 1.10$. If we double the inputs, $k = 2.0$. Of course, $Q$ is expected to increase by some proportion as a result of the increase in the inputs. Let $h$ represent the magnitude of this increase. Expressed in terms of Equation (7.3),

$$hQ = f(kX, kY) \tag{7.4}$$

Using this notation, we can summarize returns to scale in the following way:

If $h > k$, the firm experiences increasing returns to scale ($E_Q > 1$).
If $h = k$, the firm experiences constant returns to scale ($E_Q = 1$).
If $h < k$, the firm experiences decreasing returns to scale ($E_Q < 1$).

We will illustrate returns to scale with several numerical examples. Suppose we have the following production function:

$$Q_1 = 5X + 7Y$$

If we use 10 units of each input, the output will be

$$Q_1 = 5(10) + 7(10)$$
$$= 50 + 70 = 120 \text{ units}$$

Now let us increase each input by 25 percent (i.e., $k = 1.25$). This will give us

$$Q_2 = 5(12.5) + 7(12.5)$$
$$= 62.5 + 87.5 = 150$$

The 25 percent increase in $X$ and $Y$ has led to a proportional increase in output (i.e., 150 is 25 percent more than 120).

We can also illustrate the concept of returns to scale graphically. Figure 7.5 shows the three possible types of returns to scale. In each case, we assume that the inputs ($X$ and $Y$) are increased by the same proportion; thus, they are both included on the horizontal axis. Obviously, these graphs are idealized representations of returns to scale. In reality, we would not expect the changes in output relative to the changes in inputs to behave in such a smooth and orderly fashion.

**FIGURE 7.5** Graphic Representations of Returns to Scale

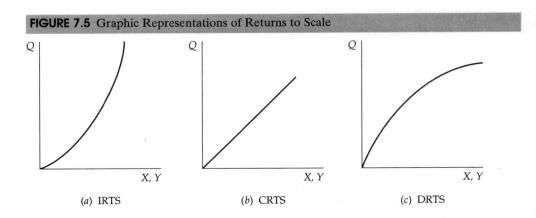

(a) IRTS  (b) CRTS  (c) DRTS

# The Estimation of Production Functions

Following our examination of demand theory, we turned to the subject of demand estimation. Now it is time to examine another of a managerial economist's important tasks, the estimation of production functions. This section will deal with three major topics. First, we will discuss the possible shapes of production functions. Second, we will discuss the Cobb-Douglas production function, a form which has been commonly used by economists since its introduction in the 1920s. Last, we will look at the data needed for estimation and some of the production function studies published by economists.

## THE VARIOUS FORMS OF A PRODUCTION FUNCTION

Earlier in this chapter, the short-run production function was introduced. As you remember, the short run is characterized by the existence of a fixed factor to which we add a variable factor. Thus, the simple function, containing just one variable factor and one fixed factor, can be written as follows:

$$Q = f(L)_K$$

where output $Q$ is determined by the quantity of the variable factor $L$ (labor) with the fixed factor $K$ (capital) given.[7]

The theoretical part of this chapter assumed that the production function starts with increasing marginal returns followed by decreasing marginal returns. In other words, all three stages of production are present. This situation is represented by a cubic function:

$$Q = a + bL + cL^2 - dL^3$$

where $a$ is the constant and $b$, $c$, and $d$ are coefficients. Figure 7.6a shows the total product line,[8] and Figure 7.6b shows the average and marginal product curves. All three stages of production are present.

It is possible, however, that the data employed in the estimate will exhibit diminishing marginal returns but no stage I. Such an estimate is represented by the quadratic function

$$Q = a + bL - cL^2$$

Figures 7.7a and 7.7b depict total and unit product curves respectively. Both of these graphs show diminishing marginal returns, but increasing marginal returns and thus stage I are absent.[9]

---

[7]In the prior discussion the letters $X$ and $Y$ designated inputs. This emphasized the production function's generality. Here we will use $L$ (for labor) and $K$ (for capital), since these are the letters that are frequently employed to indicate variable and fixed factors. In long-run analysis, of course, both $L$ and $K$ are variable.

[8]Total product curves should, in theory, be drawn from the origin, since it is most likely that no production would occur in the absence of any variable factor. However, when production functions are estimated using regression analysis, it is probable that the fitted line will have a positive or negative $y$-intercept. Thus, in the equations which follow we will include the intercept $a$. It should be noted that this $y$ value probably has no economic significance.

[9]If the intercept is present, average product is equal to $a/L + b - cL$. However, if the intercept is omitted, the average product will be a straight line, as shown in Figure 7.7b.

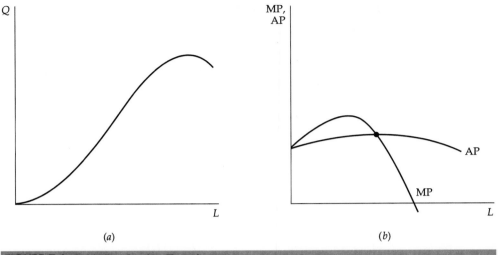

$Q$       (a)     $L$

MP, AP    (b)    AP   MP   $L$

**FIGURE 7.6** Cubic Production Function

In performing empirical research, it may be possible to identify a linear production function, $Q = a + bL$. This function exhibits no diminishing returns; the total product will be a straight line with slope $b$, and both the MP and AP lines will be horizontal and equal.[10] Of course, a straight-line production function may hold in some real situations,

**FIGURE 7.7** Quadratic Production Function

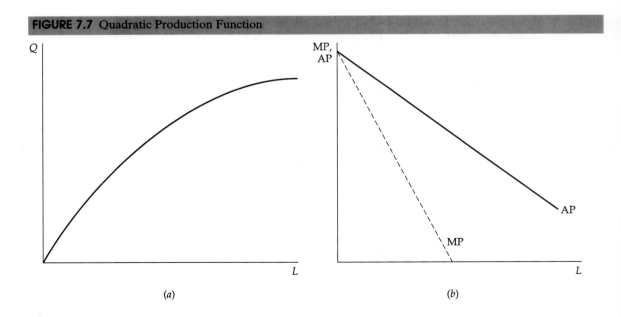

$Q$       (a)     $L$

MP, AP     AP    MP    (b)    $L$

---

[10]Again, if the intercept is present, the average product will show a decline. If, however, the intercept is omitted, the average product will be horizontal and equal to marginal product.

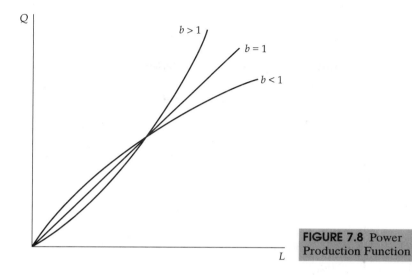

**FIGURE 7.8** Power Production Function

but given the existence of a fixed factor, constant marginal product should not be expected to prevail over a wide range of quantities produced.

Another form of the production function is the **power function,** which takes the following form:

$$Q = aL^b$$

The shape of this production function depends on the exponent $b$, as is shown in Figure 7.8.

A major advantage of the power function is that it can be transformed into a linear function when it is expressed in logarithmic terms, making it amenable to linear regression analysis:

$$\log Q = \log a + b \log L$$

The direction of marginal product depends on the size of the exponent $b$. If $b > 1$, marginal product is increasing; if $b = 1$, it is constant; and if $b < 1$, it is decreasing. It cannot, however, exhibit two directions for marginal product on the same function, as was possible with the cubic equation form. This function is used frequently in empirical work. One reason for its popularity is that it can be readily transformed into a function with two or more independent variables:

$$Q = aX_1^b \, X_2^c \,\ldots\ldots X_n^m$$

Using more than one independent variable in a production function is certainly more realistic than limiting the analysis to only one, and when it is assumed that all inputs are variable, we have then moved from short-run analysis to the long run. Indeed, this function can be employed in both analyses. In a simple two-variable model (e.g., labor and capital), the power function permits the estimation of marginal product (e.g., when labor changes and capital remains the same) and of returns to scale (when both variables change).

## THE COBB-DOUGLAS PRODUCTION FUNCTION

The **Cobb-Douglas production function** was introduced in 1928,[11] and it is still a common functional form in economic studies today. It has been used extensively to estimate both individual firm and aggregate production functions. It has undergone significant criticism but has endured. "It is now customary practice in economics to deny its validity and then to use it as an excellent approximation."[12] It was originally constructed for all of the manufacturing output ($Q$) in the United States for the years 1899 to 1922. The two inputs used by the authors were number of manual workers ($L$) and fixed capital ($K$). The formula for the production function, which was suggested by Cobb, was of the following form:

$$Q = aL^b K^{1-b}$$

What are the important properties of this function that have kept it popular for the last 70 years?

1. To make this equation useful, both inputs must exist for $Q$ to be a positive number. This makes sense, since total product is a result of combining two or more factors.[13]
2. The function can exhibit increasing, decreasing, or constant returns. Originally, Cobb and Douglas assumed that returns to scale are constant. The function was constructed in such a way that the exponents summed to $b + 1 - b = 1$. (A brief description of the mathematics of the Cobb-Douglas function can be found in Appendix 7B.) However, in later studies, they (as well as other researchers) relaxed this requirement and rewrote the equation as follows:

$$Q = aL^b K^c$$

Under this construction, if $b + c > 1$, returns to scale are increasing and if $b + c < 1$, returns are decreasing.[14] Constant returns exist when $b + c = 1$.
3. The function permits us to investigate the marginal product for any factor while holding all others constant. Thus it is also useful in the analysis of short-run production functions. In the two-factor model discussed here the marginal product of labor turns out to be $MP_L = bQ/L$, and the marginal product of capital is $MP_K = cQ/K$, (The mathematics of this result are shown in Appendix 7B.) Each of the two coefficients will usually be less than 1, and this will mean that they each exhibit diminishing marginal returns. Thus, production takes place in stage II, which is the relevant area of production.
4. The elasticity of production is an important concept as discussed previously. In the Cobb-Douglas function, the elasticities of the factors are equal to their exponents, in this case $b$ and $c$. Thus, the elasticities of labor and capital are constants.

---

[11]C. W. Cobb and P. H. Douglas, "A Theory of Production," *American Economic Review*, 8, 1 (March 1928, suppl.), pp. 139–65. Charles W. Cobb was a mathematician; Paul H. Douglas was an economist, and later a U.S. senator from Illinois.
[12]George J. Stigler, *The Theory of Price*, 4th ed., New York: Macmillan, 1987, p. 153.
[13]If an additive function (such as $Q = a + bL + cK$) were employed, output would still be positive even if one of the two inputs were zero.
[14]Of course, if the function contained more than two factors, the exponents would still have to equal more than one for increasing returns, less than one for decreasing, and one for constant.

5. Since a power function can be converted to a linear function by using logarithms, it can be estimated by linear regression analysis which makes for a relatively easy calculation with any software package.

6. Although we have limited our discussion to just two input variables ($L$ and $K$), Cobb-Douglas can accommodate any number of independent variables, as follows:

$$Q = aX_1{}^b X_2{}^c X_3{}^d \ldots\ldots X_n{}^m$$

7. A theoretical production function assumes that technology is constant. However, the data fitted by the researcher may span a period over which technology has progressed. One of the independent variables in the above equation could represent technological change (a time series) and thus adjust the function to take technology into consideration.

The Cobb-Douglas function has the following shortcomings:

1. The Cobb-Douglas cannot show the marginal product going through all three stages of production in one specification. (A cubic function would be necessary to achieve this.)

2. Similarly, it cannot show a firm or industry passing through increasing, constant, and decreasing returns to scale.

3. There are also important problems with specification of data to be utilized in empirical estimates. These problems will be discussed next.

## STATISTICAL ESTIMATION OF PRODUCTION FUNCTIONS

Let us turn now to a description of the data that would be utilized in empirical estimates of production functions. Later, we will also review some published studies. When the statistical estimate concerns a plant, or group of plants, the data will come from company records—accounting, employment, purchasing, manufacturing, and others.

If only one product is produced in a plant, $Q$ is specified in physical units (e.g., number, tons, gallons). However, if a plant produces a number of different products, and it is not possible to segregate properly the inputs and outputs of the products, estimation becomes considerably more difficult. In such a case, the investigator probably must settle for some measure of value, assigning weights to products depending on the value (in terms of cost or selling price) produced. There are some obvious problems with this procedure. First of all, over time the data will have to be deflated to account for price or cost changes. Second, the price or cost of a product may not be an exact reflection of the inputs combined in the total value. However, until better measurement methods are found, such valuing methods will have to suffice.

Measuring inputs also can vary in the level of difficulty. Inputs should be measured as "flow" rather than "stock" variables, and this is not always possible.[15]

Usually, the most important input is labor. Hours of labor input are probably the best measure for our purposes. Data for direct labor hours are ordinarily available from company records. If they are not, then number of direct workers is the next best choice. However, it must be remembered that number of workers is a stock variable and does

---

[15]Flows measure the usage of services consumed in producing a product, whereas stocks represent the amounts of factors present and available for productive use.

not necessarily represent the amount of labor expended in production. For materials, a physical measure is again best. In some cases, such data are readily available (weight of materials consumed, for instance). Of course, since we do not wish to proliferate the number of independent variables, choosing only the most important raw material may be indicated. Alternatively, a combination (by weight or value) may prove to be a viable option. Utilities (electricity, gas, etc.) may also be included; in this case, physical quantities should be fairly easily obtained.

The most difficult input variable is the all-important capital input. How can one measure the use of plant, machinery, and equipment in production? Since different components of plant and equipment are of varying durability and different input intensity, usage per period is very hard to establish. In some cases, periodic depreciation may be an indicator of capital use. However, depreciation as recorded in the company's books is often based on accounting convention or legal requirement. Further, the projected depreciation life of a piece of equipment tends to depend on tax rules, since the firm wishes to take advantage of the fastest write-off permitted for tax purposes. Some capital items, such as land, are not depreciated at all. Unless some rather consistent measurement of capital usage can be designed by the researcher (and this is certainly a formidable task), the common method of measuring capital by the use of a stock variable (e.g., fixed assets) is probably indicated. Obviously, this is not a perfect solution, since the price of these assets depends on when the assets were acquired. Thus, the asset figure must be adjusted by a price index. Should gross fixed assets (i.e., the original cost of all plant and equipment) be used, or net fixed assets (gross assets minus accumulated depreciation)? Again, this is a difficult question. There is no specific answer. The method used must be determined by the investigator as that which is most reasonable (and available) for each specific case.

If the production function estimate is to be accomplished using regression analysis, then we must choose between time series and cross-sectional analysis. The former would be preferable if data have been collected over a period of time in a given plant. However, it would be necessary to make adjustments for inflation if the variables are in monetary (rather than physical) terms. Also, a time variable (or a dummy variable) may have to be employed to account for changes in technology.

Cross-sectional analysis is favored when the data collected cover a number of plants in a given time period. But here again, problems may arise. The various plants may not employ the same level of technology. If the data are in monetary terms, an adjustment for differential price or wage levels at different geographical locations would be necessary.

While a theoretical production function assumes that output is produced at the most efficient input combinations, in reality such an ideal situation is certainly not assured whichever estimating method is used. Ultimately, there is no perfect way to measure and analyze the data. The researcher must choose the most appropriate method.

### A Numerical Example of a Cobb-Douglas Production Function

A cross-sectional sample of 20 soft drink bottling plants has been selected. The data are given for a specific month in 1998. Only two independent variables are used: (1) number of direct workers and (2) plant size. Plants range from 1 to 1.75, based on a size and capacity measure developed by engineers.

Production, the dependent variable, is stated in terms of gallons of product shipped during the period. Table 7.6 contains the data and the results of the analysis.

The Cobb-Douglas function of the form $Q = aL^bK^c$ was applied to the numbers. The regression output in the table shows the results.[16] The regression equation is as follows:

$$Q = 15.14L^{0.66}K^{0.32}$$

$R^2$ (the coefficient of determination) is quite high, showing that 98 percent of the deviations are explained. The two coefficients are significantly different from zero since they both pass the $t$-test.[17] The sum of the two coefficients is 0.985. Because this result is so close to 1, it can be assumed that the plants exhibit constant returns to scale. Each of the inputs indicates decreasing marginal returns.

### Two Studies of Individual Production Functions

In 1967, a study of the production function of the Pacific halibut industry was published. A Cobb-Douglas function appeared to give good results and showed that constant returns are probably the rule in this industry. A "good captain" variable was added—a confidential rating of the management abilities of the captains of the 32 boats in the sample. It was found that good captains made a difference.[18]

A more recent study included management in the production function equation. This study dealt with a sample of plants of a multinational consumer goods manufacturer. Time series and cross-sectional data were combined to obtain 127 observations over eight years (1975–1982). Management was measured as a performance ranking of each plant in terms of three criteria—output goal attainment, cost over- or underfulfillment, and quality level of output. The results showed that the management variable was statistically significant. Another feature of this study was the conclusion that increasing returns existed up to a certain plant size and that decreasing returns resulted at larger sizes.[19]

### AGGREGATE PRODUCTION FUNCTIONS

A large proportion of the studies performed using the Cobb-Douglas function did not deal with data for individual firms, but rather with aggregations of industries or even the economy as a whole. Although much of this work has proved to be quite fruitful in describing production functions, the interpretation of the results may not be quite as meaningful as for individual production functions. When data for the economy as a whole are used, the model must accommodate different technologies and different processes and thus does not represent a specific technological process of a given firm.

---

[16]The results were calculated using the Excel regression analysis program. The raw data were transformed into logarithms, and a straight-line regression in logarithms was computed. The constant of 1.18 is a logarithm, and 15.14 is its anti-log.

[17]Labor's $t$-test is significant at the 1 percent level, and capital's is significant at the 5 percent level.

[18]Salvatore Comitimi and David S. Huang, "A Study of Production and Factor Shares in the Halibut Fishing Industry," *Journal of Political Economy,* August 1967, pp. 366–72.

[19]Robert N. Mefford, "Introducing Management into the Production Function," *Review of Economics and Statistics,* February 1986, pp. 96–104.

**TABLE 7.6 Production Function: Soft Drink Bottling**

| Total Product | Labor | Capital |
|---|---|---|
| 97 | 15 | 1.00 |
| 98 | 17 | 1.00 |
| 104 | 20 | 1.00 |
| 120 | 22 | 1.00 |
| 136 | 22 | 1.25 |
| 129 | 25 | 1.25 |
| 145 | 30 | 1.25 |
| 170 | 32 | 1.25 |
| 181 | 35 | 1.25 |
| 166 | 30 | 1.50 |
| 175 | 35 | 1.50 |
| 190 | 38 | 1.50 |
| 212 | 42 | 1.50 |
| 220 | 44 | 1.50 |
| 207 | 45 | 1.50 |
| 228 | 44 | 1.75 |
| 226 | 47 | 1.75 |
| 240 | 52 | 1.75 |
| 270 | 55 | 1.75 |
| 280 | 58 | 1.75 |

*Summary Output*

*Regression Statistics*

| | |
|---|---|
| $R$ Square | 0.980965846 |
| Adjusted $R$ Square | 0.978726534 |
| Standard Error | 0.020818585 |
| Observations | 20 |

| | Coefficients | Standard Error | t Stat |
|---|---|---|---|
| Intercept | 1.1800154 | 0.096022924 | 12.288892 |
| X Variable 1 | 0.6643702 | 0.075371367 | 8.8146228 |
| X Variable 2 | 0.3214714 | 0.147006777 | 2.1867796 |

When the aggregation is done at the level of an industry rather than the overall economy, the assumption of similar technology is more appropriate, but even in such a case many dissimilarities may occur.

Gathering data for such aggregate functions can be difficult. For the economy as a whole, gross national or domestic product—in real terms—could be used to measure output. For specific industries, data from the Census of Manufactures or the production index published by the Federal Reserve Board can be employed. Data for investment and depreciation by industry are also available for the construction of appropriate indexes for the capital variable. The Bureau of Labor Statistics publishes a great deal of data on employment and work hours.

Cobb and Douglas performed their earliest study on U.S. manufacturing in the form of a time series regression for the years 1899–1922. Using the original version of their formula, they obtained the following result:

$$Q = 1.01L^{0.75}K^{0.25}$$

Other studies used the same technique with similar results.

In 1937, David Durand suggested that the equation should not necessarily limit the results to constant returns to scale.[20] After Durand's article, it was accepted that the exponents in the equation no longer had to equal 1. Douglas corrected the original study and found that the coefficient of labor was reduced to about two-thirds, whereas capital's exponent rose to about one-third. But the sum of the two exponents still summed to about 1, and thus constant returns to scale appeared to prevail.[21]

At about the same time, cross-sectional analysis, rather than time series, came into use, and most of the studies done since then have utilized this technique. The observations were now individual industries in a particular year. Many other studies were conducted on data from the United States, Australia, Canada, and New Zealand. In a majority of these investigations, the sum of the exponents turned out to be very close to 1.

In another study, the author performed a cross-sectional study of 18 industries using data from the Census of Manufacturers.[22] The observation units were individual states. Three independent variables were used:

1. Production worker hours
2. Nonproduction worker years
3. Gross book value of depreciable and depletable assets

The dependent variable, *Q,* was represented by the value added in each industry.

The results showed that the sums of the three exponents in the 18 industries ranged from about 0.95 to 1.11, indicating a span from decreasing to increasing returns. Tests of significance showed that in only 5 of the 18 industries was the sum of the coefficients significantly different from 1. Thus, again, in the majority of cases, constant returns to scale appeared to dominate.

# The Importance of Production Functions in Managerial Decision Making

As stated in the introductory section of this chapter, the production function is an important part of the economic analysis of the firm because it serves as the foundation for the analysis of cost. You will see this in the next chapter. But for managers, an understanding of the basic concepts discussed in this chapter also provides a solid conceptual

---

[20]David Durand, "Some Thoughts on Marginal Productivity with Special Reference to Professor Douglas," *Journal of Political Economy,* 45, 6 (December 1937) pp. 740–58.

[21]The history of the Cobb-Douglas function and the major studies were summarized by Douglas himself in his article, "The Cobb-Douglas Production Function Once Again: Its History, Its Testing, and Some New Empirical Values," *Journal of Political Economy,* 84, 5 (October 1976), pp. 903–15.

[22]John R. Moroney, "Cobb-Douglas Production Functions and Returns to Scale in U.S. Manufacturing," *Western Economic Journal,* 6, 1 (December 1967), pp. 39–51.

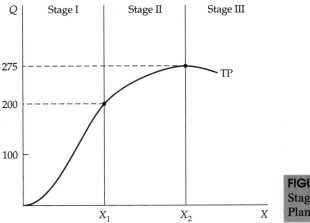

**FIGURE 7.9** Production Stages and Capacity Planning

framework for decisions involving the allocation of a firm's resources both in the short run and in the long run. Another key management principle illustrated in the economic theory of production is planning, discussed in the following subsection.

## CAREFUL PLANNING CAN HELP A FIRM TO USE ITS RESOURCES IN A RATIONAL MANNER

In our discussion of the short run, we stated that a firm is expected to have three stages of production. Stage I represents the underutilization of a firm's fixed inputs relative to its variable ones. Stage III represents an overutilization of its fixed inputs relative to its variable ones. Indeed, firms operating in this stage would find their total output *decreasing* as they increased their variable input. The only stage for a rational firm to be in is stage II. Assuming that this information is well known to managers, why would a firm find itself in stage I or III? The answer is, of course, that production levels do not depend on how much a company wants to produce, but on *how much its customers want to buy.*

Suppose we consider the short-run production function shown in Figure 7.9. As we can see, stage II applies to production levels between $Q_1 = 200$ and $Q_2 = 275$. If people want to buy less than 200 units or more than 275 units, for example, then in the short run the firm would be forced to operate in either stage I or stage III.

The information in Figure 7.9 implies that for a firm to avoid having to operate in either stage I or stage III, there must be careful planning regarding the amount of fixed inputs that will be used along with the variable ones. In business, this is often referred to as *capacity planning.* For example, if the firm anticipated that the demand for its product would be in the range of 200 to 275, then the capacity implied in Figure 7.9 is perfect for its needs. However, if a firm forecasts the demand to be greater than 275, it would have to consider increasing its capacity so that stage II would include the higher level of output. By the same token, if the firm forecasts a demand less than 200, it would have to consider decreasing its capacity. These alternative capacity levels are illustrated in Figure 7.10.

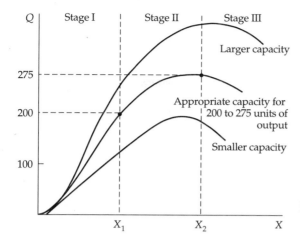

**FIGURE 7.10** Adjusting Capacity Based on Demand

Good capacity planning requires two basic elements: (1) accurate forecasts of demand and (2) effective communication between the production and marketing functions (particularly in large organizations, where these functions are often handled by separate work groups). The first element is rather obvious but, as you have seen in chapters 5 and 6, not very easy to achieve. The second element may not be so obvious, especially for those who have not had work experience in large organizations. It is not uncommon for manufacturing people to proceed merrily with their production plans on a purely technical basis (i.e., from a strictly engineering point of view) without fully incorporating the marketing plans of those whose main responsibility is to sell the products. It is also quite possible for marketing people to try to sell as many units of the product as possible (as marketing people are supposed to do) without consulting the production people as to whether the firm has the capacity to meet the increase in demand. A full discussion of these problems of management and organization is beyond the scope of this book. However, they are mentioned to underscore the importance for managers of understanding production theory.

## Call Centers: Applying the Production Function to a Service

Most production function examples involve manufacturing or agriculture. To illustrate how the concepts in this chapter can be used for a service activity, let us consider the example of a call center. A *call center* is a physical concentration of service representatives providing inbound or outbound communications with a company's customers. Perhaps you have seen pictures of call centers for QVC or LL Bean, in which hundreds of customer service representatives are situated in rows upon rows of cubicles in a large building that appears to be the size of a football field. The earliest call centers were run by the telephone companies themselves, particularly in cases where customer assistance was often required for domestic as well as international calling. As airline, hotel, and car rental businesses began to expand in the 1970s and 1980s, so too did their call center operations. During this time, there was also a tremendous expansion in the credit and charge card industry, and companies such as American Express and banks issuing MasterCard and Visa expanded their call center operations in order to communicate with their growing number of cardholders.

In the 1990s, the number and importance of call centers in the United States dramatically increased due to a combination of lower calling charges stemming from increasing competition among telecommunications companies, rapid growth and intense competition in the finance, retail, travel, and entertainment industries, and breakthroughs in the application of digital technology to voice, data, and video communications. Today, the call center has also become an integral part of multinational business activities.

For purposes of discussion, we will consider the production function of a call center handling inbound calls from customers inquiring about various aspects of their service.[23]

*Output:* The number of calls handled by customer representatives

In the service industry, the quality of a unit of service may be intrinsically tied to the length of time that it takes to "produce" the service (i.e., the amount of time a call representative spends with a customer). Nevertheless, we will handle this complexity by simply assuming that $Q$ is equal to an incoming call that lasts an average of 300 seconds.

*Input: Labor:* The call center representative

In the United States, there are a number of cities that have established themselves as attractive locations for call centers because they have large pools of qualified labor that are available at wage rates relatively lower than the major metropolitan areas. High on the list of these cities are Sioux Falls, South Dakota, Jacksonville and Tampa, Florida, St. Louis, Missouri, and Salt Lake City, Utah (primarily because of the large concentration of people with foreign language skills).

Sometime in the year 2000, industry experts believe that improvements in technology and reductions in costs will create the next generation of "Virtual Call Centers." Hardware and software for both information processing and distribution will enable customer service representatives to access information and provide customer support from any location to any customer at any time. To use industry jargon, the ability to provide call center support will be "channel and location–independent." This means that very shortly, if not already, companies will be able to draw on a global pool of labor to work as call representatives. (See also "International Applications: International Call Centers," following this section.)

*Input: Capital:* Hardware, software, and office facilities

Examples of types of operating systems used by call centers are Windows NT, OS/2, Novell Netware, Unix, DOS, Windows 95, and various systems provided by Unisys. These operating systems can be combined with dumb or 3270 terminals or PC workstations. There are a number of emerging technologies and applications software of importance to

---

[23]Interviews with representatives from MasterCard International and Bell Atlantic Corporation; "Top 10 Technologies: A New Millennium for the Card Industry," Faulkner and Gray, New York, 1998 pp. 1–5.

call center activities, such as Voice Response Unit (VRU) and Automatic Call Distribution (ACD), which automate the switching that route calls to customer service representatives.

Recently, a new technological concept has emerged known as the "Intelligent Center," which shifts the focus of call center activities from answering inbound queries to selling products on both inbound and outbound calls. Key technologies for the Intelligent Center include Computer-Telephony Integration (CTI) and middleware. Imagine you are a typical caller inquiring about the balance on your loan at your bank. Before a representative answers the phone, you are asked to key in your account number. When a representative answers, a window pops up on his or her terminal screen showing your complete financial history. Based on the assessment of your financial condition, the representative may then tell you about the possibility of consolidating all your loans into a home equity loan or of considering the purchase of supplementary life insurance. Many more Internet and Intranet applications will soon be combined with conventional call center operations. So, for example, it will someday be possible for you to type up your application for life insurance and then e-mail it to the bank while talking to its call center representative.

Given these inputs and output, the call center's short-run production function and the three stages of production might be expressed as follows:

$$Q = f(X, Y)$$

where $Q$ = number of 300-second calls

$X$ = variable input (this includes customer services representatives and the complementary hardware such as PCs, desks, and software if site licenses are sold on a per-user basis)

$Y$ = fixed input (this includes the call center building, hardware such as servers and telecommunications equipment, and software site licenses up to the designated maximum number of users)

Using this basic production function, it is possible to consider a number of applications of concepts. The following are offered as examples.

*Three Stages of Production:* Stage I could be a situation in which there is so much fixed capacity relative to number of variable inputs that many representatives sit around idle, waiting for calls to come in. Stage II could be a situation in which representatives are constantly occupied and callers are connected to representatives immediately after the call is answered or are kept waiting no more than a certain amount of time (e.g., three minutes). If callers are kept waiting for longer than three minutes, the call center manager might consider adding more call center representatives. Stage III could be a situation in which callers begin to experience a busy signal on a more frequent basis or call representatives may begin to experience a slower computer response or more frequent computer "down times." These are all technical manifestations of overloaded computer processing power or transmission capacity (i.e., insufficient bandwidth).

*Input Combinations:* There are a number of input combinations that could be considered in the operation of a call center. To begin with, there is the location trade-off in which the productivity of call center representatives in two or more locations might be considered relative to the cost of each representative (including wages, training costs,

costs associated with turnover rates, etc.). If a global search for the best location is involved, then the further consideration of language skills would have to be made.

Another trade-off involves capital and labor. The cost of upgrading the hardware and software used by each representative could be measured against the number of representatives utilized in the call center. For example, the installation of an automated call distribution system could result in the reduction in the number of representatives working at any time in the center.

*Returns to Scale:* One can well imagine that a call center would be amenable to increasing returns to scale. This is evidenced by the number of smaller companies who outsource their operations to companies that specialize in call center operations. These "third-party" vendors are able to provide call center services at a lower cost to the company mainly because their size enables them to take advantage of increasing returns to scale.

# International Application: International Call Centers

Technology and falling costs of telecommunications have made it economically feasible for call centers to be located almost anywhere in the world. As mentioned in an earlier section, a computer manufacturing company has relocated the entire help-desk operation for its American customers to San Jose, Costa Rica. MasterCard International has a call center in St. Louis, Missouri, that handles calls reporting lost or stolen cards from all over the world. Two additional examples reported in the popular press reinforce the global nature of call centers. An article in the *Financial Times* discusses how Salt Lake City has become an attractive site for global call centers.[24] This is because of the high concentration of people in the work force who speak a foreign language, having learned the language while serving their two years of missionary work for the Mormon Church in different parts of the world. But quite often, global call center representatives need to know more than just a foreign language. According to the article, the American representatives who handled the overflow of calls going to a center in the United Kingdom had to be trained in "pounds and pence, spelling differences and place names, not to mention the British sense of humor."

Another article in the *New York Times* discusses a small town in Sweden that is being saved by call centers.[25] Over the last several decades, it has been increasingly difficult for this town to keep its young people from leaving in search of gainful employment in urban centers such as Stockholm. But now that a sort of "cottage industry" of call centers has been established, there are opportunities for young people to earn a decent salary without having to move away. Perhaps the next call you make to an 800 number will be answered by someone in Florida or South Dakota . . . or perhaps Sweden or Ireland. On a personal note, one of the authors made a reservation from a town outside of London for a hotel owned by an American company. The representative who answered had a somewhat unusual accent. Upon inquiry, he said he was a Finnish national working in a call center in Dublin, Ireland.

---

[24]Alan Cane, "Telephone Contact with Customers Is Ripe for Outsourcing," *The Financial Times,* September 13, 1996.
[25]Warren Hoge, "Arvidsjaur Journal: Sweden's Frozen North Can Be Balmy for Business," *New York Times,* August 21, 1998.

## THE SOLUTION

To: Robert Burns, CEO,
   Nicole Goodman, SVP of
   Marketing, and
   Jim Hartwell, SVP of
   Manufacturing

From: Christopher Lim, Production
   Manager

Re: The Economic Feasibility of
   Packaging in Glass Bottles and
   Key Related Issues

Before beginning plans to bottle and distribute *Waterpure,* I feel that I must bring up certain production issues that I was not able to cover at our meeting last week. I have had considerable experience in glass packaging from my previous job as head of bottling for our Latin American beverage division. Glass is a more expensive material than either plastic or aluminum. With the latest slump in aluminum prices and technology developments in plastic, the price differential is widening even further. The reason why glass is so expensive is that it is much heavier and more fragile than these other materials. This causes higher production costs because (1) there are more back injuries to employees (thereby increasing our medical insurance premiums), (2) there is a need for special handling care (e.g., bottle carriers, protective cardboard), (3) breakage occurs, and (4) the greater weight increases the cost of fuel used in transportation.

We use a considerable amount of glass bottles in emerging market countries because the total cost differential between glass and aluminum or plastic is not as great in these countries. For example, because of lower labor costs in South America, we can better afford to use the more labor-intensive process of handling the heavy glass bottles. And the machinery to blow out the plastic pellets into 1- and 2-liter bottles is a lot more expensive in these countries than here in the United States. Furthermore, people in emerging market countries seem to like the idea of receiving their deposit back when returning glass bottles, however small the amount might seem to you to be.

However, a real issue that I think we should address even before devising a packaging, production, and distribution plan is the source of our bottled water. As you know, to be considered "spring water," bottled water must actually come from a spring. The industry has grown so rapidly over the past few years that companies are having a harder time finding good sources of spring water. I have heard of bottled water companies hiring geologists to look for water just as oil companies hire them to look for new sources of oil. Therefore, we should consider the cost of "manufacturing" the product itself—water—before even considering the cost of packaging. I eagerly await your response to the issues raised in this memo.

## Summary

The topics in this chapter represent the foundation for the economic analysis of supply. After all, people may be very willing to purchase a firm's product at a certain price, but will the firm be willing to supply the product at this price? The answer to this question begins with the relationship between the firm's inputs and the resulting output, that is, the firm's production function. In the short run, where at least one of the firm's inputs is fixed, we have learned that the firm is subject to the law of diminishing returns and the three stages of production. This means that as additional inputs are added to the fixed input, at some point the additional output (i.e., marginal product) resulting from the additional input will start to diminish. Once this level of production is exceeded, the output per unit of variable input (i.e., average product) will reach a maximum and then start to diminish. The point of maximum average product marks the end of stage I and the beginning of stage II, the stage in which the rational firm should be operating. The use of still more units of variable inputs will eventually cause the total output to decline (i.e., cause MP to assume negative values). By assigning monetary values to both the variable input and the output along with the use of marginal analysis, we were able to determine precisely where in stage II the firm should be operating. A similar analysis can be used to derive the conditions for the optimal use of more than one input. (See Appendix 7B.)

The long-run function, in which a firm is able to vary all of its inputs, was also considered in this chapter. When a firm is able to vary its entire scale of production, it may experience varying returns to scale. That is, the increase in output may be proportional, less than proportional, or greater than proportional to the increase in all of its inputs.

Most studies of production functions have used an exponential expression that results in a monotonically increasing output as inputs are added. This model was introduced by Cobb and Douglas in the 1920s. The original studies utilized the time series method of analysis, but researchers soon switched to cross-sectional regression, which they found more useful. The Cobb-Douglas function permits the investigation of both marginal product in short-run situations (with the presence of a fixed factor) and returns to scale in the long run. It is difficult to summarize the large number of studies conducted over the years, but the results generally indicate that constant returns to scale are the rule in manufacturing industries in the United States as well as in other countries.

In the next chapter, we present an analysis of a firm's cost function. We will then see how a solid background in the economic analysis of production will provide a better understanding of the cost structure of a firm, in both the short and the long runs.

## Important Concepts (Items with * are discussed in Appendix 7A or 7B)

**Average product (AP):** The total product divided by the number of units of a particular input employed by the firm. (p. 245)

**Cobb-Douglas production function:** A power function in which total quantity produced is the result of the product of inputs raised to some power (e.g., $Q = aL^b K^c$). (p. 262)

**Inputs:** The resources used in the production process. Examples in economic analysis generally involve the inputs *capital* (representing the fixed input) and *labor* (representing the variable input). Other terms used in reference to these resources are *factors* and *factors of production.* (p. 243)

* **Isocost:**   A line representing different combinations of two inputs that a firm can purchase with the same amount of money. In production analysis, the isocost indicates a firm's budget constraint. (p. 290)

* **Isoquant:**   A curve representing different combinations of two inputs that produce the same level of output. (p. 283)

**Law of diminishing returns:**   A law stating that as additional units of a variable input are added to a fixed input, at some point the additional output (i.e., the marginal product) will start to diminish. Because at least one input is required to be fixed for this law to take effect, this law is considered a short-run phenomenon. (p. 246)

**Long-run production function:**   The maximum quantity of a good or service that can be produced by a set of inputs, assuming that the firm is free to vary the amount of *all* inputs being used. (p. 244)

**Marginal labor cost (MLC):**   The additional cost to the firm of using an additional unit of labor. This is also referred to as *marginal factor cost* (MFC) or *marginal resource cost* (MRC). Labor is used in this term because it is the most commonly used variable input in the economic analysis of production. (p. 254)

**Marginal product (MP):**   The change in output resulting from a unit change in one of the firm's variable inputs. (p. 245)

* **Marginal rate of technical substitution (MRTS):**   Given two inputs $X$ and $Y$, the marginal rate of technical substitution of $X$ for $Y$ represents the reduction in $Y$ relative to the amount of $X$ that a firm must add to replace $Y$ to maintain the same amount of output. Mathematically speaking, it is represented by the slope of some given isoquant or $\Delta Y/\Delta X$ ($\delta y/\delta x$ for continuous isoquants). (p. 286)

**Marginal revenue product (MRP):**   The additional amount of revenue resulting from the use of an additional unit of a variable input. It can be calculated by taking an input's marginal product and multiplying it by the market price of the product. For example, given some input $i$, that $\text{MRP}_i = \text{MP}_i \times P$. (p. 254)

**MRP = MLC rule:**   A rule that guides a firm in its decision about how many units of a variable input it should use relative to its fixed input. The rule states that the firm should employ a particular input up to the point at which the revenue contribution of the additional input is equal to the cost incurred by the firm to employ this particular input. In the case of more than one input, this condition applies separately for every input used by the firm. (p. 254)

**Power function:**   A mathematical function of the form $Y = X^n$, where $n$ is a fixed number and $X$ takes positive values continuously. (p. 261)

**Production function:**   The maximum quantity of a good or service that can be produced by a set of inputs. Production functions are divided into two types: short run and long run. (p. 243)

**Returns to scale:**   The increase in output that results from an increase in all of a firm's inputs by some proportion. If the output increases by a *greater* proportion than the increase in inputs, the firm is experiencing increasing returns to scale. If the output increases by the *same* proportion as the inputs, the firm is experiencing constant returns to scale. Finally, if the output increases by a *smaller* proportion than the increase in inputs, the firm is experiencing decreasing returns to scale. (p. 256)

**Short-run production functions:**   The maximum quantity of a good or service that can be produced by a set of inputs, assuming that the amount of *at least one* of the inputs used remains unchanged as output varies. (p. 244)

**Stages of production:**   In a short-run production function, there are three stages of production. Stage I starts at zero and ends at the point where the firm has reached the maximum level of *average* product. Stage II continues from this point on to the point at which the firm has reached the maximum level of *total* product. Stage III continues from this point on. Economic theory suggests that the rational firm will try to produce in the short run in stage II. In stage I the firm would be underutilizing its fixed inputs, and in stage III it would be overutilizing its fixed inputs. (p. 250)

**Total product (TP):**   The firm's output for a given level of input usage, also referred to as *quantity,* or simply $Q$. (p. 245)

## Questions

1. Explain the difference between a short-run and long-run production function. Cite one example of this difference in a business situation.
2. Define the *law of diminishing returns.* Why is this law considered a short-run phenomenon?
3. What are the key points in a short-run production function that delineate the three stages of production? Explain the relationship between the law of diminishing returns and the three stages of production.
4. Explain why a firm's adherence to the MRP = MLC rule enables it to find the optimal number of units of a variable input to use in the short-run production process.
5. Define returns to scale. Why is this considered a long-run phenomenon?
6. According to the rule for optimal input usage, a firm should hire a person as long as her marginal revenue product is greater than her marginal cost to the company. It is well known that many companies have management training programs in which new trainees are paid relatively high starting salaries and are not expected to make substantial contributions to the company until after the program is over (programs may run between 6 to 18 months). In offering such training programs, is a company violating the optimality rule? Explain.
7. Explain the relationship between marginal product and average product. Why can we expect marginal product to equal average product at average product's maximum point?
8. Cite and discuss possible reasons a firm may actually find itself operating in stage I or stage III of the short-run production function.
9. Discuss the problems of measuring productivity in actual work situations. How might productivity be measured for each of the following industries?
   a. Education (e.g., elementary and secondary education, higher education—undergraduate and graduate)
   b. Government (e.g., the Social Security Office, the Internal Revenue Service)
   c. Manufacturing (e.g., soap and toothpaste, computers, heavy machinery)
   d. Finance and insurance (e.g., banks, insurance companies, brokerage houses)
10. For those of you with current or previous work experience, how is (was) productivity measured in your organization?
11. What are the two statistical methods most frequently used to estimate production functions? What are the advantages and disadvantages of each of these two methods?
12. Design a study of a production function for a steel mill and another one for a call center. Which variables would you use, and what statistical method would you select for each function? In general, compare and contrast the production function for a product and one for a service.

Refer to Appendix 7A and 7B to help you answer questions 13–16.
13. What are the properties of the Cobb-Douglas function $Q = aL^bK^{1-b}$. What conceptual change occurs when the equation is changed to $Q = aL^bK^c$?
14. In a power function $Q = aV^b$, how can you tell whether diminishing marginal returns are present?
15. When a Cobb-Douglas function with at least two inputs shows the existence of constant returns to scale, it implies that the marginal product of each input is diminishing. True or false? Explain.
16. Write a production function equation that expresses the existence of diminishing marginal returns. How will this equation differ from one that shows both increasing and decreasing marginal returns?

## Problems

1. Indicate whether each of the following statements is true or false. Explain why.
   **a.** When the law of diminishing returns takes effect, a firm's average product will start to decrease.
   **b.** Decreasing returns to scale occurs when a firm has to increase all of its inputs at an increasing rate in order to maintain a constant rate of increase in its output.
   **c.** A linear short-run production function implies that the law of diminishing returns does not take effect over the range of output being considered.
   **d.** Stage I of the production process ends at the point where the law of diminishing returns occurs.
2. The Oceanic Pacific fleet has just decided to use a pole-and-line method of fishing instead of gill netting to catch tuna. The latter method involves the use of miles of nets strung out across the ocean and therefore entraps other sea creatures besides tuna (e.g., porpoises and sea turtles). Concern for endangered species was one reason for this decision, but perhaps more important was the fact that the major tuna canneries in the United States will no longer accept tuna caught by gill netting.

   Oceanic Pacific decided to conduct a series of experiments to determine the amount of tuna that could be caught with different crew sizes. The results of these experiments follow.

| Number of Fishermen | Daily Tuna Catch (lb) |
|---|---|
| 0 | 0 |
| 1 | 50 |
| 2 | 110 |
| 3 | 300 |
| 4 | 450 |
| 5 | 590 |
| 6 | 665 |
| 7 | 700 |
| 8 | 725 |
| 9 | 710 |

   **a.** Determine the point at which diminishing returns occurs.
   **b.** Indicate the points that delineate the three stages of production.
   **c.** Suppose the market price of tuna is $3.50/pound. How many fishermen should the company use if the daily wage rate is $100?
   **d.** Suppose a glut in the market for tuna causes the price to fall to $2.75/pound. What effect would this have on the number of fishermen used per boat? Suppose the price rose to $5.00/pound. What effect would this have on its hiring decision?
   **e.** Suppose the firm realizes that to keep up with the demand for tuna caught by the more humane pole-and-line method of fishing, each of its boats must catch at least 1,000 pounds of fish per day. Given the preceding data, what should it consider doing? Explain.
3. A firm has the following short-run production function:

$$Q = 50L + 6L^2 - 0.5L^3$$

   where $Q$ = Quantity of output per week
   $L$ = Labor (number of workers)

**a.** When does the law of diminishing returns take effect?

**b.** Calculate the range of values for labor over which stages I, II, and III occur.

**c.** Assume each worker is paid $10 per hour and works a 40-hour week. How many workers should the firm hire if the price of the output is $10? Suppose the price of the output falls to $7.50. What do you think would be the short-run impact on the firm's production? The long-run impact?

**4.** The owner of a small car-rental service is trying to decide on the appropriate numbers of vehicles and mechanics to use in the business for the current level of operations. He recognizes that his choice represents a trade-off between the two resources. His past experience indicates that this trade-off is as follows **(see Appendix 7A for help in answering this question):**

| Vehicles | Mechanics |
|----------|-----------|
| 100 | 2.5 (includes one part-timer) |
| 70 | 5 |
| 50 | 10 |
| 40 | 15 |
| 35 | 25 |
| 32 | 35 |

**a.** Assume the annual (leasing) cost per vehicle is $6,000 and the annual salary per mechanic is $25,000. What combination of vehicles and mechanics should he employ?

**b.** Illustrate this problem with the use of an isoquant/isocost diagram. Indicate graphically the optimal combination of resources.

**5.** An American company that sells consumer electronics products has manufacturing facilities in Mexico, Taiwan, and Canada. The average hourly wage, output, and annual overhead cost for each site are as follows:

|  | *Mexico* | *Taiwan* | *Canada* |
|---|---|---|---|
| Hourly wage rate | $1.50 | $3.00 | $6.00 |
| Output per person | 10 | 18 | 20 |
| Fixed overhead cost | $150,000 | $90,000 | $110,000 |

**a.** Given these figures, is the firm currently allocating its production resources optimally? If not, what should it do? (Consider output per person as a proxy for marginal product.)

**b.** Suppose the firm wants to consolidate all of its manufacturing into one facility. Where should it locate? Explain.

**6.** The owner of a car wash is trying to decide on the number of people to employ based on the following short-run production function:

$$Q = 6L - 0.5L^2$$

where $Q$ = Number of car washes per hour
$L$ = Number of workers

**a.** Generate a schedule showing total product, average product, and marginal product. Plot this schedule on a graph.

   **b.** Suppose the price of a basic car wash (no undercoating, no wax treatment, etc.) in his area of business is $5. How many people should he hire if he pays each worker $6/hour?

   **c.** Suppose he considers hiring students on a part-time basis for $4/hour. Do you think he should hire more workers at this lower rate? Explain.

**7.** The Noble Widget Corporation produces just one product, widgets. The company's new economist has calculated a short-run production function as follows:

$$Q = 7V + 0.6V^2 - 0.1V^3$$

where $Q$ is the number of widgets produced per day and $V$ is the number of production workers working an eight-hour day.

   **a.** Develop a production schedule with $V$ equaling 1 to 10.

   **b.** Calculate average and marginal products.

   **c.** Draw a graph.

**8.** Suppose Noble's production function (see problem 7) is as follows:

$$Q = 7V - 0.5V^2$$

where $Q$ is the number of widgets produced per day and $V$ is the number of production workers working an eight-hour day.

   **a.** Develop a production schedule with $V$ equaling 1 to 10.

   **b.** Calculate average and marginal products.

   **c.** Draw a graph.

   **d.** Discuss the difference between the form of the production function in this problem and the form in problem 7. Discuss, among other things, the implications for the three stages of production.

**9.** The International Calculator Company of Hong Kong produces hand-held calculators in its plant. It tries to keep the number of workers in the plant constant, so that the only variable factor that can be measured is materials. Over the last seven monthly periods, the data for materials and quantity produced were the following:

| Materials | Quantity |
|-----------|----------|
| 70 | 450 |
| 60 | 430 |
| 80 | 460 |
| 95 | 490 |
| 77 | 465 |
| 100 | 550 |
| 85 | 490 |

   **a.** Calculate a Cobb-Douglas production function of the form $Q = aM^b$.

   **b.** Discuss the important properties of your results.

   **c.** What is the marginal product of materials?

**10.** The Brady Corporation has 11 plants located around the world. In a recent year, the data for each plant gave the number of labor hours (in thousands), capital (total net plant assets, in millions), and total quantity produced:

| Capital | Labor | Quantity |
|---------|-------|----------|
| 30 | 250 | 245 |
| 34 | 270 | 240 |
| 44 | 300 | 300 |
| 50 | 320 | 320 |
| 70 | 350 | 390 |
| 76 | 400 | 440 |
| 84 | 440 | 520 |
| 86 | 440 | 520 |
| 104 | 450 | 580 |
| 110 | 460 | 600 |
| 116 | 460 | 600 |

The plants all operate at a similar level of technology, so that a production function can be derived from the data.

**a.** Use a Cobb-Douglas production function to calculate a regression, and discuss the important characteristics of your results, such as the form of the equation, $R^2$, and the statistical significance of the coefficients.

**b.** Calculate the estimated production for each plant.

**c.** Does the result indicate constant, decreasing, or increasing returns to scale?

**d.** What are the elasticities of production of labor and of capital? What is the meaning of the elasticities?

**e.** Is the marginal product of labor decreasing?

Refer to Appendix 7A and 7B for help in answering problems 11–15.

**11.** Show what will happen to the following diagram as a result of the changes listed.

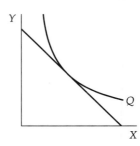

**a.** The firm's budget increases.

**b.** The price of $Y$ decreases.

**c.** The price of $X$ decreases.

**d.** $Y$ becomes more expensive, and $X$ becomes less expensive.

**e.** Technology makes the $Y$ input more productive.

**f.** Technology increases the productivity of both inputs by the same proportion.

**12.** Suppose you are given the following production function:

$$Q = 100K^{0.5}L^{0.5}$$

**a.** Use this function to generate the data for the following table:

| K | | | | | | | | | |
|---|---|---|---|---|---|---|---|---|---|
| 8 | | | | | | | | | |
| 7 | | | | | | | | | |
| 6 | | | | | | | | | |
| 5 | | | | | | | | | |
| 4 | | | | | | | | | |
| 3 | | | | | | | | | |
| 2 | | | | | | | | | |
| 1 | | | | | | | | | |
| 0 | 1 | 2 | 3 | 4 | 5 | 6 | 7 | 8 | L |

**b.** Identify as many isoquants as you can.

**c.** Comment on the returns to scale exhibited in this figure. (*Suggestion:* Start by assuming one unit of $L$ and one unit of $K$ are used. Then systematically increase both inputs by some given proportion.)

13. Following are different algebraic expressions of the production function. Decide whether each one has constant, increasing, or decreasing returns to scale.

   **a.** $Q = 75L^{0.25}K^{0.75}$
   **b.** $Q = 75A^{0.15}B^{0.40}C^{0.45}$
   **c.** $Q = 75L^{0.60}K^{0.70}$
   **d.** $Q = 100 + 50L + 50K$
   **e.** $Q = 50L + 50K + 50LK$
   **f.** $Q = 50L^2 + 50K^2$
   **g.** Based on the answers for the preceding equations, can you make any generalizations about the functional form of a production equation, the relative magnitudes of the coefficients, and the nature of the returns to scale? Explain.

14. Use the production matrix presented to answer the following questions.

| Y | | | | | | | | | |
|---|---|---|---|---|---|---|---|---|---|
| 8 | 31 | 67 | 101 | 133 | 161 | 184 | 202 | 213 | |
| 7 | 30 | 62 | 93 | 122 | 147 | 168 | 184 | 193 | |
| 6 | 27 | 54 | 82 | 108 | 130 | 149 | 168 | 163 | |
| 5 | 23 | 45 | 69 | 91 | 108 | 126 | 137 | 142 | |
| 4 | 17 | 34 | 54 | 72 | 89 | 101 | 108 | 111 | |
| 3 | 12 | 25 | 38 | 54 | 65 | 74 | 79 | 79 | |
| 2 | 6 | 14 | 24 | 33 | 44 | 54 | 47 | 43 | |
| 1 | 3 | 7 | 11 | 17 | 27 | 19 | 16 | 8 | |
| | 1 | 2 | 3 | 4 | 5 | 6 | 7 | 8 | X |

   **a.** Determine the returns to scale for this matrix. (Start with one unit of $X$ and one unit of $Y$.)
   **b.** Suppose the firm has a budget of $100 and that the price of $Y$ is $20 and the price of $X$ is $10. What is the optimal combination of inputs $X$ and $Y$ for this firm?
   **c.** Suppose the prices of $Y$ and $X$ are now $10 and $20, respectively. What effect will this have on the firm's optimal input combination?
   **d.** Illustrate the answers to the preceding questions with the use of an isoquant/isocost diagram.

**15.** The economist for the ABC Truck Manufacturing Corporation has calculated a production function for the manufacture of their medium-size trucks as follows:

$$Q = 1.3L^{0.75}K^{0.3}$$

where $Q$ is number of trucks produced per week, $L$ is number of labor hours per day, and $K$ is the daily usage of capital investment.

**a.** Does the equation exhibit increasing, constant, or decreasing returns to scale? Why?

**b.** How many trucks will be produced per week with the following amounts of labor and capital?

| Labor | Capital |
|-------|---------|
| 100 | 50 |
| 120 | 60 |
| 150 | 75 |
| 200 | 100 |
| 300 | 150 |

**c.** If capital and labor both are increased by 10 percent, what will be the percentage increase in quantity produced?

**d.** Assume that only labor increases by 10 percent. What will be the percentage increase in production? What does this result imply about marginal product?

**e.** Assume that only capital increases by 10 percent. What will be the percentage increase in production?

**f.** How would your answers change if the production function were $Q = 1.3L^{0.7}K^{0.3}$ instead? What are the implications of this production function?

# Take It to the Net

We invite you to visit the Keat/Young page on the Prentice Hall Web site at:

**http://www.prenhall.com/keat**

for additional resources.

## Appendix 7A

## The Multiple-Input Case

In this appendix, we examine in greater detail the more general case in which a firm seeks the optimal combination of inputs, rather than simply the optimal level of one particular input. For explanatory purposes, we will address the problem of determining the optimal combination of inputs using the two-input case. Mathematically, there is no problem in considering any number of inputs, but we will use two inputs for ease of graphical illustration. Nonetheless, it should be noted that the decision rule for determining the optimal combination of inputs is the same whether two inputs or more than two are used in the production process.

From the standpoint of economic theory, the two-input case can be considered either a short-run or a long-run analysis, depending on what assumption is made about the nature of the firm's inputs. If we assume that the firm has only two inputs (or, more realistically, that all of its inputs can be divided into two basic categories), then the two-input case must be considered a long-run analysis because, in effect, all of the firm's inputs are allowed to vary. However, if the firm is assumed to have other inputs that are being held constant while the two inputs are being evaluated, then the analysis must be considered short run. Readers should be able to discern from the context of our discussion which case applies for our examples.

To illustrate the two-input case, we will use the data in Table 7.1, reproduced as Table 7A.1. Suppose the firm produces 52 units of output ($Q = 52$). According to the table, the firm can employ the following combinations of inputs $Y$ and $X$ respectively: 6 and 2, 4 and 3, 3 and 4, 2 and 6, and 2 and 8. Together, they form the isoquant shown in Table 7A.1. An **isoquant** is a curve representing the various combinations of two inputs that produce the same amount of output. Notice that isoquants for $Q = 29$ and $Q = 73$ are also shown in Table 7A.1. The isoquant for $Q = 52$ is plotted in Figure 7A.1.

**TABLE 7A.1  Representative Production Table Illustrating Isoquants**

| Units of Y Employed | | | | Output Quantity (Q) | | | | |
|---|---|---|---|---|---|---|---|---|
| 8 | 37 | 60 | 83 | 96 | 107 | 117 | 127 | 128 |
| 7 | 42 | 64 | 78 | 90 | 101 | 110 | 119 | 120 |
| 6 | 37 | 52 | 64 | 73 | 82 | 90 | 97 | 104 |
| 5 | 31 | 47 | 58 | 67 | 75 | 82 | 89 | 95 |
| 4 | 24 | 39 | 52 | 60 | 67 | 73 | 79 | 85 |
| 3 | 17 | 29 | 41 | 52 | 58 | 64 | 69 | 73 |
| 2 | 8 | 18 | 29 | 39 | 47 | 52 | 56 | 52 |
| 1 | 4 | 8 | 14 | 20 | 27 | 24 | 21 | 17 |
| | 1 | 2 | 3 | 4 | 5 | 6 | 7 | 8 |
| | | | | *Units of X Employed* | | | | |

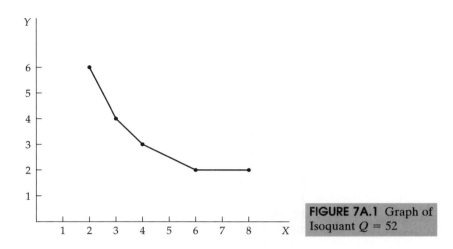

**FIGURE 7A.1** Graph of Isoquant $Q = 52$

A continuous production function, in which inputs are assumed to be perfectly divisible, is illustrated in Figure 7A.2. Here the isoquant appears as a smoothed out version of that depicted in Figure 7A.1. Notice that both the discrete and continuous isoquants are downward sloping and convex to the origin.

The latter characteristic means that the slope of the isoquant becomes less steep as one moves downward and to the right. These characteristics pertain to the degree to which the two inputs can be substituted for one another.

## Substituting Input Factors

The degree of substitutability of two inputs is a measure of the ease with which one input can be used in place of the other in producing a given amount of output. To explain this further, let us use the example of the making of soft drinks. Consider the ingredients listed on the label of a typical soft drink:

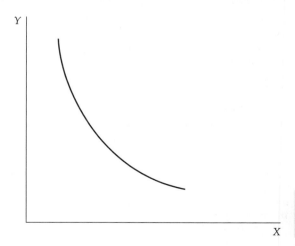

**FIGURE 7A.2** Isoquant for Continuous Production Function

| TABLE 7A.2 | Input Combinations for Isoquant $Q = 52$ | |
|---|---|---|
| **Combination** | **Y** | **X** |
| A | 6 | 2 |
| B | 4 | 3 |
| C | 3 | 4 |
| D | 2 | 6 |
| E | 2 | 8 |

back at the algebraic expression of MRTS ($X$ for $Y$), we see that it is the measure of the slope of the isoquant.

To see exactly how MRTS is measured along the isoquant, let us use the discrete case illustrated in Table 7A.1. The different input combinations that can be used to produce 52 units of output are summarized in Table 7A.2. The changes in $Y$ and $X$ as one moves from combination A to E are shown in Figure 7A.5. Moving from combination A to E, we measure the marginal rate of substitution of $X$ for $Y$ as follows:

| *Movement* | $MRTS\ (X\ for\ Y) = \dfrac{\Delta Y}{\Delta X}$ |
|---|---|
| A to B | $\dfrac{-2}{1}$ |
| B to C | $\dfrac{-1}{1}$ |
| C to D | $\dfrac{-1}{2}$ |
| D to E | $\dfrac{0}{2}$ |

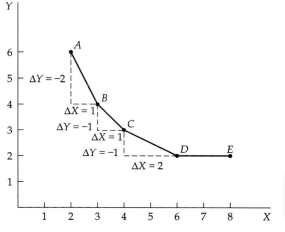

**FIGURE 7A.5**
Measuring MRTS along an Isoquant

Notice that because the isoquant is downward sloping, $\Delta Y/\Delta X$, or the MRTS, will always have a negative value. However, in discussing the economic significance of MRTS, it is easier to treat it as a positive value. Therefore, let us for the moment simply drop the negative sign. Thus, for example, the MRTS between A and B becomes: MRTS $= \frac{2}{1}$. Between B and C and between C and D, the MRTS values are 1 and $\frac{1}{2}$, respectively. Expressed as an absolute value, MRTS can be clearly seen to diminish as we move from combination A to combination E. Economists refer to this phenomenon as the *law of diminishing marginal rate of technical substitution.* As you might expect, this relates to the law of diminishing returns.

When we move from A to B, we substitute one unit of $X$ for two units of $Y$. In other words, the loss in output resulting from the use of two fewer units of $Y$ can be made up for by adding one unit of $X$. When we move from B to C, the loss in output resulting from the use of one fewer unit of $Y$ must be made up for by adding one unit of $X$. From C to D we see that the loss in output resulting from the use of one fewer unit of $Y$ must be made up for by adding two units of $X$. Finally, when we move from D to E, we find that rather than substituting $X$ for $Y$, we must add more units of $X$ to maintain the output level at 52.

Apparently, as we move from A to D, increasingly more $X$ must be added relative to the amount of $Y$ taken out of the production process to maintain the same amount of output. We started out by having to add only one unit of $X$ to replace two units of $Y$ and ended up having to add two units of $X$ to replace one unit of $Y$. In other words, as more $X$ is used relative to $Y$ in the production process, the productivity of $X$ diminishes relative to $Y$. This is a result of none other than the law of diminishing returns. Recall that this law states that as additional units of a variable factor are added to a fixed factor, at some point the additional output starts to diminish. If this holds true when one of the inputs is fixed, it must certainly hold when this same input is reduced.

To understand fully why increasingly more of input $X$ is needed to compensate for the loss of a given amount of input $Y$ to maintain the same output, we need to incorporate the concept of marginal product into our analysis. Looking back at Table 7.1 (reproduced as Table 7A.3 for your convenience), we observe that the movement from A to B actually involves two distinct steps. First, input $Y$ is reduced by 2 units (from 6 to 4), resulting in a reduction in output by 13 units (from 52 to 39). This is indicated by the downward-pointing arrow in Table 7A.3. Next input $X$ is added to the production process to compensate for the reduction in $Y$. As can be seen in the table, an additional unit of $X$ is required to restore the output to its original level of 52. This is indicated by the right-pointing arrow in the table.

Recall from an earlier discussion that the marginal product is defined as the change in output relative to the change in some given input. In this case, the movement from A to B in two separate steps reveals that the marginal product of input $Y$ is

$$\frac{\Delta Q}{\Delta X} = \frac{-13}{-2} = 6.5$$

The marginal product of input $X$ is

$$\frac{\Delta Q}{\Delta X} = \frac{13}{1} = 13$$

**TABLE 7A.3   Representative Production Table**

| Units of Y Employed | Output Quantity (Q) | | | | | | | |
|---|---|---|---|---|---|---|---|---|
| 8 | 37 | 60 | 83 | 96 | 107 | 117 | 127 | 128 |
| 7 | 42 | 64 | 78 | 90 | 101 | 110 | 119 | 120 |
| 6 | 37 | 52 | 64 | 73 | 82 | 90 | 97 | 104 |
| 5 | 31 | 47 | 58 | 67 | 75 | 82 | 89 | 95 |
| 4 | 24 | 39 | 52 | 60 | 67 | 73 | 79 | 85 |
| 3 | 17 | 29 | 41 | 52 | 58 | 64 | 69 | 73 |
| 2 | 8 | 18 | 29 | 39 | 47 | 52 | 56 | 52 |
| 1 | 4 | 8 | 14 | 20 | 27 | 24 | 21 | 17 |
| | 1 | 2 | 3 | 4 | 5 | 6 | 7 | 8 |

*Units of X Employed*

Proceeding next to combination C and then on to D using the same two-step process gives us the following ratios of the marginal products of $X$ and $Y$: between B and C, $MP_X/MP_Y = 1$; between C and D, $MP_X/MP_Y = 1/2$.

In reviewing the ratios of the marginal products of $X$ and $Y$ along the isoquant $Q = 52$, you probably have spotted a very important link between the MRTS, the slope of the isoquant, and these ratios. Indeed, they are all equal. More specifically,

$$\text{MRTS} = \frac{\Delta Y}{\Delta X} = \frac{MP_X}{MP_Y} \qquad (7A.1)$$

This equation is illustrated in Table 7A.4.

Because Equation (7A.1) will play an important part in a later section of this appendix, let us briefly explain its derivation. Consider once again the movement along an isoquant between two given points. As illustrated using specific numbers in the previous pages, this movement involves two distinct steps: the reduction in one input (e.g., input $Y$) and the increase in the other input (e.g., input $X$). The decrease in the output resulting from a decrease in input $Y$ can be stated as

$$-MP_Y \times \Delta Y$$

**TABLE 7A.4   $MP_X/MP_Y$ in Relation to MRTS ($X$ for $Y$)**

| Combination | Q | Y | $MP_X$ | X | $MP_Y$ | MRTS ($X$ for $Y$) | $MP_X/MP_Y$ |
|---|---|---|---|---|---|---|---|
| A | 52 | 6 | | 2 | | | |
| | | | 13 | | 6.5 | 2 | 2 |
| B | 52 | 4 | | 3 | | | |
| | | | 11 | | 11 | 1 | 1 |
| C | 52 | 3 | | 4 | | | |
| | | | 6.5 | | 13 | 1/2 | 1/2 |
| D | 52 | 2 | | 6 | | | |

The increase in output resulting from an increase in input $X$ can be stated as

$$\text{MP}_X \times \Delta X$$

Along the isoquant, the output level must be maintained at a constant level. Thus,

$$\frac{\text{MP}_Y}{\Delta Y} = \frac{\text{MP}_X}{\Delta X}$$

Rearranging the terms in this equation and remembering that MRTS = $\Delta Y / \Delta X$ gives us

$$\text{MRTS} = \frac{\Delta Y}{\Delta X} = \frac{\text{MP}_X}{\text{MP}_Y}$$

## The Optimal Combination of Multiple Inputs

Earlier we stated that the determination of the optimal combination of imperfectly sub-stitutable inputs depends on both their relative prices and on the degree to which they can be substituted for one another. In the previous section, you learned that the degree to which one input can be substituted for another is actually a reflection of the relation-ship between their marginal products. Therefore, the optimal combination of inputs de-pends on the relationship between the inputs' relative marginal products and their rel-ative prices. In the case of two inputs, we can state this relationship mathematically as

$$\frac{\text{MP}_X}{\text{MP}_Y} = \frac{P_X}{P_Y} \tag{7A.2}$$

To demonstrate this relationship we will use **isocost** curves and combine them with the isoquant curves developed in the previous section. First we will rearrange Equation (7A.2) in the following way:

$$\frac{\text{MP}_X}{P_X} = \frac{\text{MP}_Y}{P_Y} \tag{7A.3}$$

In other words, two inputs are combined in the best possible way when the marginal product of the last unit of one input in relation to its price is just equal to the marginal product of the last unit of the other input in relation to its price.

Let us now return to the more formal economic analysis of optimal input combi-nations by explaining the optimality rule with the use of isoquants and isocost curves. Suppose $P_X = \$100$ and $P_Y = \$200$. Suppose further that a firm has a budget of $1,000 to spend on inputs $X$ and $Y$. At these prices and this expenditure limit, any of the com-binations of $X$ and $Y$ in Table 7A.5 could be purchased.

Algebraically, the budget can be expressed as follows:

$$E = P_X \times X + P_y \times Y \tag{7A.4}$$

where $E$ = Total budget allotment for inputs $X$ and $Y$
$\quad P_X$ = Price of $X$
$\quad P_Y$ = Price of $Y$
$\quad\quad X$ = Quantity of input $X$
$\quad\quad Y$ = Quantity of input $Y$

| TABLE 7A.5 | Input Combinations for $1,000 Budget | |
| --- | --- | --- |
| Combination | X | Y |
| A | 0 | 5 |
| B | 2 | 4 |
| C | 4 | 3 |
| D | 6 | 2 |
| E | 8 | 1 |
| F | 10 | 0 |

In other words, the amount spent for $X$ and $Y$ is equal to the number of units of $X$ multiplied by its price plus the number of units of $Y$ multiplied by its price. In this case,

$$\$1,000 = \$100X + \$200Y \tag{7A.5}$$

Using this equation to plot the numbers in Table 7A.5, we obtain the isocost curve shown in Figure 7A.6.

Note that the isocost curve is linear because the prices of the inputs are constant. A few algebraic manipulations of Equation (7A.4) will indicate that the prices of the inputs in relation to each other (i.e., $P_X/P_Y$) are represented by the slope of the isocost line:

$$E = P_X \times X + P_Y \times Y \tag{7A.6}$$

$$P_Y \times Y = E - P_X \times X$$

$$Y = \frac{E}{P_Y} - \frac{P_X}{P_Y} \times X$$

Figure 7A.7 combines the isocost curve shown in Figure 7A.6 and the isoquant shown in Figure 7A.5. Note that the isocost line and the isoquant are tangent to each other between points (4,3) and (6,2). This means that between these two points the

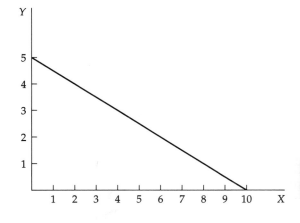

**FIGURE 7A.6**
Isocost Curve for Inputs $X$ and $Y$

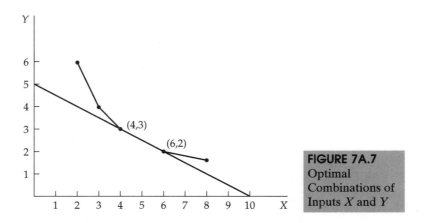

**FIGURE 7A.7**
Optimal
Combinations of
Inputs *X* and *Y*

slopes of the two curves are identical. Therefore, if the slope of the isocost line is $-P_X/P_Y$ and the slope of the isoquant is $-MP_X/MP_Y$, then between these two points

$$\frac{MP_X}{MP_Y} = \frac{P_X}{P_Y}$$

If we cancel the negative signs on both sides of the equation, we arrive at the optimality rule first stated in Equation (7A.2). Given a budget of $1,000 and the input combinations represented by the isoquant in Figure 7A.7, the firm would employ the optimal combination of inputs if it used either four units of *X* and three of *Y* or six units of *X* and two of *Y*.

We are not able to find a unique combination of inputs because we have used a discrete set of input combinations. Graphically, we can show quite easily how the use of a continuous production function enables us to find one optimal input combination. In Figure 7A.8, we have combined the isocost curve with a series of smoothed or continuous production isoquants. Point *B* represents the firm's optimal combination of inputs. Let us explain why.

To begin with, point *D* must be ruled out because at that point the firm would not be spending the full amount of its budget allotment. On the other hand, point *E* represents a combination beyond the limits set by the budget. This leaves points *A, B,* and *C,* each representing a combination that can be purchased with the budget allotment. Of these three points, point *B* represents the best combination because the firm would be producing the maximum amount given its budget limitation.

In terms of the marginal analysis developed previously, we can see that point *B* is the only one that fulfills the optimality condition expressed in Equations (7A.2) and (7A.3). That is, at point *B,* the slope of the isocost curve and the slope of the isoquant are identical. (Recall that the slope of a continuous isoquant is measured by the slope of the line tangent to the curve at a particular point.) Therefore, at point *B,* $MP_X/MP_Y = P_X/P_Y$.

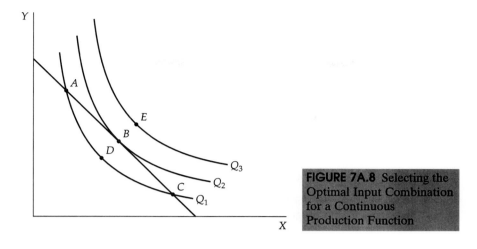

**FIGURE 7A.8** Selecting the Optimal Input Combination for a Continuous Production Function

## The Optimal Levels of Multiple Inputs

By following the optimality condition first presented in Equations (7A.2) and (7A.3), a firm ensures that it will be producing in the least costly way, regardless of the level of output. Therefore, Equation (7A.2) could be more specifically called the condition for cost minimization. But how much output should the firm be producing? The answer to the question, as was the case for a single input, depends on the demand for the product.

As you recall, the decision regarding the number of units of a single input to use was based on the condition $P_X = \text{MCL} = \text{MRP}_X$. That is, the firm should use the $X$ input up to the point at which its cost (i.e., $P_X$) just equals the market price of the additional input's efforts (i.e., $\text{MRP}_X$). By the same token, the decision rule for two or more inputs requires that the firm use each input up to the point

$$P_i = \text{MRP}_i \qquad\qquad \textbf{(7A.7)}$$

where $P_i$ = Price of input $i$
$\qquad \text{MRP}_i$ = Marginal revenue product of input $i$

If the firm is utilizing two inputs ($X$ and $Y$), its optimality condition is

$$P_X = \text{MRP}_X \text{ and } P_Y = \text{MRP}_Y \qquad\qquad \textbf{(7A.8)}$$

We can explain the rationale for the optimality condition with two or more inputs simply by saying that what applies in the case of one input must apply to more than one input. However, there is a more formal explanation in microeconomic theory using several terms and concepts that will not be presented in detail until chapter 9. Nonetheless, following is a brief version of this theoretical explanation.

According to economic theory, the firm that wishes to maximize its profit will always try to operate at the point where the extra revenue received from the sale of the last unit of output produced is just equal to the additional cost of producing this output. In other words, its optimal level of production is at the point where marginal revenue (MR) is equal to marginal cost (MC). In chapter 9, you will learn in much greater detail about the rationale and application of the MR = MC rule. For now, let us simply explain the justification for the rule governing the optimal use of more than one input.

Marginal cost, or MC, is the cost of producing an additional unit of output. Using the terms developed in previous examples in this chapter,

$$\text{MC} = \frac{P_i}{\text{MP}_i} \qquad (7\text{A}.9)$$

where $MC$ =   Marginal cost of production
$P_i$ =   Price of the input $i$ (i.e., the cost to the firm of using an additional unit of the input $i$)
$\text{MP}_i$ =   Marginal product of the input $i$

For example, suppose the input used is labor (measured in hourly units), and the price of labor is the wage rate given to the firm under perfectly competitive labor market conditions. Assume a wage rate of $10 per hour. Assume also that a particular hour of labor has a marginal product of 20 units of output. On a per-unit basis, these additional 20 units will cost the firm $0.50 (i.e., $10/20) to produce. In other words, at this point the marginal cost is $0.50.

Let us assume that the firm is operating at the profit-maximizing level of output—in other words, at the point where

$$\text{MR} = \text{MC} \qquad (7\text{A}.10)$$

Let us also assume that the firm employs two inputs, $X$ and $Y$. Substituting Equation (7A.9) into (7A.10) gives

$$\text{MR} = \frac{P_X}{\text{MP}_X} \text{ for the } X \text{ input} \qquad (7\text{A}.11)$$

$$\text{MR} = \frac{P_Y}{\text{MP}_Y} \text{ for the } Y \text{ input}$$

Rearranging terms gives us

$$P_X = \text{MR} \times \text{MP}_X \text{ and } P_Y = \text{MR} \times \text{MP}_Y \qquad (7\text{A}.12)$$

Since $\text{MR} \times \text{MP}_i = \text{MRP}_i$, the firm will be satisfying the optimality condition with that combination of $X$ and $Y$ at which

$$P_X = \text{MRP}_X \text{ and } P_Y = \text{MRP}_Y \qquad (7\text{A}.13)$$

In short, the optimal level of multiple inputs occurs when the additional revenue that each input accounts for is just equal to the additional cost to the firm of using each of the inputs. Another way to view this optimality condition is to remember that it is actually derived from the assumption that the firm is already producing at the profit-maximizing level of output (i.e., where MR = MC). This, in turn, implies that the firm is combining its inputs in an optimal fashion. If not, then it could not possibly be maximizing its profit.

Figure 7A.9 illustrates the difference between the cost-minimizing and the profit-maximizing combinations of inputs. You can see that any one of the points along the "expansion path" represents the cost-minimizing combination of inputs $X$ and $Y$. However, suppose that the MR = MC rule for profit maximization dictates that a firm pro-

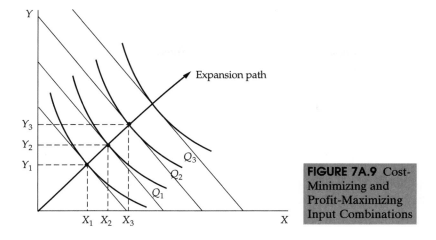

**FIGURE 7A.9** Cost-Minimizing and Profit-Maximizing Input Combinations

duce $Q_3$ units for sale in the competitive marketplace. As you can see, this implies that only one combination of inputs ($X_3$ and $Y_3$) should be used. All the other combinations of inputs will be cost-efficient but will not enable the firm to maximize its profits.

Incidentally, when returns to scale are measured, economists always assume that the firm is operating with the optimal combination of inputs. In Figure 7A.10, we view returns to scale "from above" rather than "from the side" as we did back in Figure 7.5. In this figure the different levels of output resulting from increases in input are found on a ray from the origin. (This ray is actually the locus of points indicating the optimal combination of inputs for different levels of budgetary constraint.) As implied by the hypothetical numbers assigned to the isoquants, the values of these isoquants in relation to the values of the optimal input combinations indicate whether the firm is experiencing increasing, constant, or decreasing returns to scale.

**FIGURE 7A.10** Optimal Input Combinations and Returns to Scale

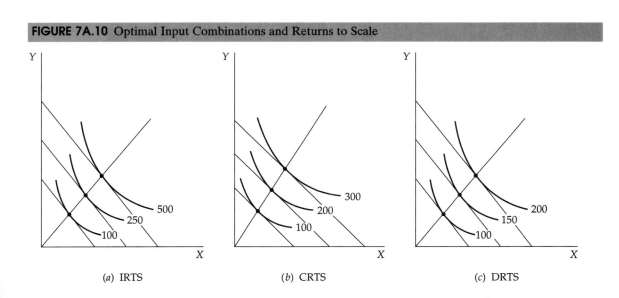

(*a*) IRTS

(*b*) CRTS

(*c*) DRTS

## Appendix 7B

## Expressing the Production Function with the Use of Calculus

In this chapter, we have relied primarily on tables and graphs to illustrate our analysis of the production function. This appendix shows you how calculus can be used in the analysis.

# A Brief Review of the Production Function

The production function expresses the relationship between the output and one or more inputs. The output is referred to either as *total product* (TP) or $Q$ (quantity). We began our analysis of the production function by presenting the relationship between different combinations of two inputs (i.e., labor and capital) and output in a numerical table (see Table 7B.1). As already explained, the production function takes the general form:

$$Q = f(L,K) \tag{7B.1}$$

where $Q$ = Quantity of output
$L$ = Labor (i.e., the variable input)
$K$ = Capital (i.e., the fixed input)

By stating this general functional form in more specific terms, we have an equation that can be used to generate a tabular model of the production function.

One popular form is the *Cobb-Douglas* production function. It can be stated as follows:

$$Q = AL^aK^b \tag{7B.2}$$

$Q$, $L$, and $K$ have the same definitions as in Equation (7B.1). The values for $A$, $a$, and $b$ determine the actual values in the production table. For example, suppose $A = 100$, $a = 0.5$, and $b = 0.5$. The production function would be

$$Q = 100L^{0.5}K^{0.5} \tag{7B.3}$$

This equation can be used to generate the numbers in Table 7B.1.

**Table 7B.1   Cobb-Douglas Production Function**

| $K$ | Output Quantity | | | | | | | |
|---|---|---|---|---|---|---|---|---|
| 8 | 282 | 400 | 488 | 564 | 628 | 688 | 744 | (800) |
| 7 | 264 | 373 | 456 | 528 | 588 | 644 | (700) | 744 |
| 6 | 244 | 345 | 422 | 488 | 544 | (600) | 644 | 688 |
| 5 | 223 | 315 | 385 | 446 | (500) | 544 | 588 | 628 |
| 4 | 200 | 282 | 346 | (400) | 446 | 488 | 528 | 564 |
| 3 | 173 | 244 | (300) | 346 | 385 | 422 | 456 | 488 |
| 2 | 141 | (200) | 244 | 282 | 315 | 345 | 373 | 400 |
| 1 | (100) | 141 | 173 | 200 | 223 | 244 | 264 | 282 |
| | 1 | 2 | 3 | 4 | 5 | 6 | 7 | 8 |

# Marginal Product: The First Derivative of the Total Product Function

As shown in the discussion of isoquants, the marginal product expressed in terms of calculus is the partial derivative of the total product function. We can use the Cobb-Douglas form of the production function shown in Equation (7B.3) to illustrate how the derivative is used to find this marginal product.

Suppose we want to find the marginal product of the fourth unit of labor added to the production process, assuming that we are currently using four units of capital. We simply take the partial derivative of the equation with respect to $L$, set $L = 4$ and $K = 4$, and find the resulting value of total product:

$$\frac{\delta Q}{\delta L} = 100(0.5)L^{-0.5}K^{0.5}$$

$$= 100(0.5)4^{-0.5}4^{0.5}$$

$$= 50$$

In Table 7B.1 we note that the marginal product of the fourth unit of labor assuming 4 units of capital is 54 (i.e., $400 - 346$). The two values differ because the use of calculus actually enables us to compute marginal product right at the point at which four units of labor are being used, rather than that amount of output resulting from the addition of the fourth unit.

# Converting the Cobb-Douglas Function into a Linear Form

**1.** The Cobb-Douglas function is nonlinear; it is an exponential function. However, it can be converted into a linear function in terms of logarithms:

$$Q = aL^bK^c$$

$$\log Q = \log a + b\log L + c\log K$$

**2.** The original form of the function was

$$Q = aL^bK^{1-b}$$

This model assumes constant returns to scale. In other words, if both labor and capital inputs are changed by a certain proportion $s$, $Q$ will also change by $s$:

$$Q = a(sL)^b(sK)^{1-b}$$

$$= a(s^bL^b)(s^{1-b}K^{1-b})$$

$$= (s^bs^{1-b})(aL^bK^{1-b})$$

$$= (s^{b+1-b})(Q)$$

$$= s^1Q$$

Thus, the new quantity, $Q$, will equal the old quantity times $s$—the proportion by which both $L$ and $K$ changed.

The later version of the function relaxed the requirement of constant returns since it permitted $b + c$ to be less than, equal to, or greater than 1. In this case, the results would be as follows:

$$Q' = a(sL)^b (sK)^c$$
$$= a (s^b L^b)(s^c K^c)$$
$$= a(s^{b+c})(L^b K^c)$$
$$= (s^{b+c})(Q)$$

If $b + c > 1$, then for an input change $s$, $Q$ will increase by more than $s$ (i.e., increasing returns). If $b + c < 1$, the increase in $Q$ will be less than $s$ (i.e., decreasing returns).

**3.** The marginal product of a factor is the partial derivative of quantity of output with respect to the factor:

$$MP_L = \delta Q/\delta L$$
$$= abL^{b-1}K^{1-b}$$
$$= abL^b L^{-1}K^{1-b}$$
$$= bL^{-1}Q$$
$$= bQ/L$$

Similarly, the marginal product of capital, $MP_K$, equals $cQ/K$ or $(1 - b) Q/K$.

**4.** The elasticity of production measures the sensitivity of total product to a change in an input in percentage terms:

$$E_Q = \frac{\text{Change in } Q\ (\%)}{\text{Change in input }(\%)}$$

or, in the case of labor,

$$\Delta Q/Q \div \Delta L/L = \Delta Q/Q \times L/\Delta L = \Delta Q/\Delta L \times L/Q = \Delta Q/\Delta L \div Q/L$$

$\Delta Q/\Delta L$ is, of course, the marginal product of labor; $Q/L$ is the average product of labor (with capital held constant). Thus, the elasticity of production is equal to the marginal product divided by the average product. It was shown that the marginal product of labor is $bQ/L$ and, as we have just pointed out, the average product of labor is $Q/L$. Dividing $MP_L$ by $AP_L$,

$$MP_L/AP_L = bQ/L \div Q/L = bQ/L \times L/Q = b$$

Thus, the elasticity of production for labor is $b$ (and for capital, it is $c$). These are the original constant exponents of the Cobb-Douglas function. For any percentage increase (or decrease) in the quantity of a factor, holding quantity of the other factor or factors the same, the increase (or decrease) in total product will be a constant percentage. And since the exponents are less than 1, the percent increase in total product is less than the increase in the quantity of the factor.

# The Optimal Combination of Two Inputs

In the main body of this chapter, we showed that if a firm is producing a level of output that maximizes its profit, then it must be using its inputs in such a way that the marginal revenue product of every input used is equal to its price (or cost). In other words, if a firm uses $k$ inputs, then

$$\text{MRP}_1 = \text{Cost of input 1}$$

$$\text{MRP}_2 = \text{Cost of input 2}$$

$$\vdots$$

$$\text{MRP}_k = \text{Cost of input } k$$

Earlier we showed why a rational firm would be using its inputs in the most cost-efficient manner if it combined them in such a way that the ratio of each input's marginal product relative to its price is equal for all inputs used:

$$\frac{\text{MP}_1}{P_1} = \frac{\text{MP}_2}{P_2} = \cdots = \frac{\text{MP}_k}{P_k}$$

In this section, we employ calculus to demonstrate mathematically why this is so.

We begin by stating the profit function in the following manner:

$$\pi = \text{TR} - \text{TC} \tag{7B.4}$$

where $\pi$ = Total profit
TR = Total revenue
TC = Total cost

By definition, total revenue is equal to price times quantity:

$$\text{TR} = P \times Q \tag{7B.5}$$

where $P$ = Price of the output
$Q$ = Quantity of output sold

Total cost is equal to the amounts of the inputs used multiplied by their respective prices. Let us assume that the firm is using two inputs, labor and capital, and that their prices are the wage rate and some rental cost of using the capital. Thus, we can say that

$$\text{TC} = wL + rK \tag{7B.6}$$

where $L$ = Labor
$K$ = Capital
$w$ = Wage rate of labor
$r$ = Rental cost of using capital

Substituting Equations (7B.6) and (7B.5) into Equation (7B.4) gives us

$$\pi = PQ - (wL + rK) \tag{7B.7}$$

As you know, the production function can be stated in general terms as

$$Q = f(L, K) \tag{7B.8}$$

Substituting this equation into Equation (7B.7) gives us

$$\pi = Pf(L, K) - wL - rK \tag{7B.9}$$

To find the level of input that will maximize the firm's profit, we can take the partial derivative of the profit function with respect to each of the inputs, $L$ and $K$, while holding the other one constant and set each equal to zero:

$$\frac{\delta\pi}{\delta L} = Pf_L - w = 0 \tag{7B.10}$$

$$\frac{\delta\pi}{\delta K} = Pf_K - r = 0 \tag{7B.11}$$

If we express Equations (7B.10) and (7B.11) in terms of the prices of the inputs, we obtain

$$w = Pf_L \tag{7B.12}$$

$$r = Pf_K \tag{7B.13}$$

Recall that the definition of the marginal product of a particular input is the change in output with respect to a change in that input. In other words

$$MP_L = f_L \tag{7B.14}$$

$$MP_K = f_K \tag{7B.15}$$

Recall further that the definition of the marginal revenue product (MRP) is the MP of a particular input multiplied by product price. Thus, Equations (7B.12) and (7B.13) are nothing more than a restatement of the conditions necessary for the optimal use of inputs discussed earlier in the main body of this chapter. That is,

$$Pf_L = MRP_L = w \tag{7B.16}$$

$$Pf_K = MRP_K = r \tag{7B.17}$$

Now that we have established the relationship, we can easily use the same equations and notations to show how the condition necessary for the most cost-efficient combination of inputs is derived. If we divide equation (7B.12) by Equation (7B.13), we obtain

$$\frac{w}{r} = \frac{Pf_L}{Pf_K}$$

The $P$s in the denominator and the numerator on the right-hand side cancel out, giving

$$\frac{w}{r} = \frac{f_L}{f_K}$$

Using the definitions of marginal product stated in Equations (7B.14) and (7B.15) and rearranging the terms gives the condition for the most efficient combination of input usage:

$$\frac{MP_L}{w} = \frac{MP_K}{r} \tag{7B.18}$$

# CHAPTER 8

# The Theory and Estimation of Cost

## THE SITUATION

To: Nicole Goodman, SVP of Marketing

From: Christopher Lim, Production Manager

Re: Sources of spring water

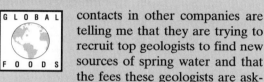

Thank you for considering fully my idea of using plastic instead of glass bottles for *Waterpure*. This memo is to express my concern for another manufacturing problem: the high cost of supplying the product itself. As you well know, for us to label and advertise *Waterpure* as spring water, it must actually *be* spring water. My concern is that the attempt by companies to meet the huge demand for bottled spring water is making it increasingly difficult to find new natural sources of this product. Some of my contacts in other companies are telling me that they are trying to recruit top geologists to find new sources of spring water and that the fees these geologists are asking for their exploration work are starting to make them look like free-agent baseball players.

My main concern is that the heavy, up-front cost of exploring for new sources may well increase our fixed costs of production to the point where it may not make good economic sense to get into this market. I do not like being seen as the perennial naysayer in this whole project, but I thought I had better bring to your attention this other key factor in the management of the cost of operations.

## The Importance of Cost in Managerial Decisions

As the old adage goes, "buy low and sell high." This chapter concerns the part about buying low. Cost has become particularly important in recent years as increasing competitive pressures, changing technology, and customer demand have made it harder for firms to achieve high profit margins by raising their prices. Recall in chapter 1 our discussion of how changing economics forced companies from a "cost-plus" stage to one where "cost management" became preeminent (see pp. 6-7). The most commonly used way to contain or to cut costs over the past decade has been to reduce the number of people on a company's payroll. *Restructuring, downsizing, rightsizing, redundancy,* and *force management* are all terms that have at one time or another been used in reference to this action. In addition, companies have resorted to outsourcing and the relocation of manufacturing facilities to lower-wage countries to reduce their costs.

In 1997 Sara Lee, a company that manufacturers a wide variety of consumer products, including frozen desserts, women's pantyhose, men's underwear, and pork sausages, adopted a cost-cutting strategy that became known in the popular press as "deverticalization." That is, the company began to sell off the basic components of its manufacturing processes, such as textile mills and slaughter houses. In fact, its CEO was quoted as saying that his "role model" was Nike, a company noted for outsourcing the making of its shoes to companies in low-wage Asian countries.[1]

Another common way in which companies have tried to cut costs to remain competitive is to merge, consolidate, and then reduce headcount. It is no surprise that megamergers making the news in recent years primarily involve companies that have been experiencing considerable changes in the economics of their business. Commercial financial services and banks (e.g., Citicorp and Travelers, Bank of America, and Nations Bank), pharmaceuticals (e.g., SmithKline and Beecham, Glaxo and Wellcome, Sandoz and Eli Lilly) and telecommunications (e.g., SBC and Pacific Telesis—soon to be joined by Ameritech, Bell Atlantic and Nynex—soon to be joined by GTE). As this chapter is being written, Exxon was proceeding with its plans to merge with Mobil, and BP, fresh from its merger with Amoco, announced that it intended to acquire Arco, another major oil producer. These mergers clearly will have profound effects on the competitive landscape of the oil industry. Nonetheless, an important reason for these mergers is the cost savings from the economies of scale.[2]

As explained earlier, the economic analysis of cost begins with the production function. We therefore begin the analysis of cost by showing the links between production and cost functions. But before doing so, we review briefly the particular way in which cost is defined and used in economic analysis.

## The Definition and Use of Cost in Economic Analysis

In a typical business organization, cost is generally considered the domain of the accounting department. Its presentation to the outside world (e.g., to bankers, bond holders, investors, and suppliers) is based on generally accepted rules of accounting (GAAP). For purposes of internal analysis and decision making, the definition of cost is based on the concept of relevancy. By definition, a cost is considered to be relevant if it is affected by a management decision. Any cost not affected by a decision is considered irrelevant. Both economists and managerial or cost accountants (as opposed to financial accountants) use the concept of **relevant cost** when analyzing business problems and recommending solutions. Following are some important ways to distinguish between relevant and irrelevant cost.

---

[1]Roger Lowenstein, "Instrinsic Value: Remember When Companies Made Things?" *The Wall Street Journal,* September 18, 1997.
[2]For a good overview of the "merger mania" of the late 1990s, see Richard Teitlebaum, "Mergers, Mergers Everywhere, But Do Shareholders Benefit?" *New York Times,* November 29, 1998.

## HISTORICAL VERSUS REPLACEMENT COST

Suppose a manufacturer of a video game system has an inventory of $750,000 worth of 16-bit chips left over from a discontinued system. Strong protectionist measures by Congress have created a shortage of these chips, driving their market value up to $1,000,000. Meanwhile, the firm decides to reenter the video game market. (This time, it will manufacture the product in Thailand and will begin production with the leftover inventory of chips.) How much will it cost the firm to use this inventory? Although the **historical cost** is $750,000, the replacement value is $1,000,000. According to the principle of relevant cost, the firm should use the latter figure in computing its cost of reentering the video game market.[3] Let us see why this is so.

If the firm were to decide not to proceed with the project but instead to sell its inventory of chips in the open market, it could receive the full market value of $1,000,000. Therefore, by using the chips, it is forgoing the opportunity to receive $1,000,000 for their sale. Moreover, if it decided to buy chips rather than use its inventory, it would have to pay $1,000,000 for the same quantity that it holds in inventory. The $1,000,000 is the relevant sum because it is the amount that has an impact on the alternatives being considered.

## OPPORTUNITY COST VERSUS OUT-OF-POCKET COST

Previous discussions pointed out that **opportunity cost** is one of the most important and useful concepts in economic analysis because it highlights the consequences of making choices under conditions of scarcity. We can now use this term in a more specific way to help explain the concept of relevant cost. Opportunity cost, as you recall, is the amount or subjective value that is forgone in choosing one activity over the next best alternative. This type of cost can be contrasted with "out-of-pocket cost." On occasion, economists refer to opportunity cost as *indirect cost* or *implicit cost,* and refer to out-of-pocket cost as *direct cost* or *explicit cost.*

In the case of the company with the inventory of computer chips, we can clearly see that the opportunity cost of using the inventory in its second attempt to penetrate the video game market involves the cost of not being able to resell the inventory for $1,000,000. Seen in this way, this sum is the firm's "relevant opportunity cost." The $750,000 is not relevant because it is not the opportunity cost of going ahead with the project. Incidentally, the firm's out-of-pocket cost of using chips would be the cost of buying additional chips for the production process. For example, if the firm decides that it needs $1,500,000 worth of chips (at current market prices) in the first year of the project's operation, we can infer that this figure consists of $1,000,000 in opportunity cost and $500,000 in additional out-of-pocket cost.

## SUNK VERSUS INCREMENTAL COST

Let us evaluate the cost to the firm of using its inventory of chips with a reversal in market conditions. Instead of the firm's inventory increasing in value, suppose something happens to cause its value to fall to $550,000. For example, the introduction of a 32-bit

---

[3]The recording of the cost of an asset for purposes of financial reporting is subject to generally accepted accounting principles (GAAP), which state that assets and liabilities should be recorded in financial statements at historical cost. Inventories may be reported at historical cost or current market value, whichever is lower. But regardless of the rule set for external reporting, economists and cost accountants (as opposed to financial accountants) recommend that a firm use current market value for internal management decisions.

video game system drastically reduces the demand for and price of the 16-bit system. Under these circumstances, how much will it cost the firm to use the inventory for which it originally paid $750,000? To answer this question, we employ the distinction that economists make between *incremental* and *sunk* costs. **Incremental cost** is the cost that varies with the range of options available in a decision. **Sunk cost** is the cost that does not vary in accordance with the decision alternatives. Our computer manufacturer has already paid $750,000 for the chips and can really do nothing about the fact that changes in market conditions have driven the value of the chips down to $550,000. If the firm decides to sell the inventory, it will receive at the most only $550,000. If it decides to go ahead with the project, the incremental cost (i.e., the part of its cost that is affected by the decision) of using the inventory of chips will be $550,000 and not $750,000. And, as you have probably already concluded, the $200,000 difference between these two sums must be considered a sunk cost to the firm. As it turns out, the $550,000 can also be considered the opportunity cost of using the chips instead of selling them. Therefore, in summary, the firm should consider $550,000 to be the relevant cost of using its inventory of chips, because it is an *incremental opportunity cost.*

A dramatic example of the use of incremental and opportunity costs to determine relevant cost is the case of a new technology suddenly rendering the entire inventory of chips obsolete. For example, the introduction of a 64-bit game system would virtually destroy the market for 16-bit games. In this event, no one would want to buy the chips at any price, and the value of this inventory would be reduced to zero. The entire $750,000 investment in inventory would be considered a sunk cost to the firm. Furthermore, since the resale value of the inventory is zero, the firm's use of the chips in its project would not incur an opportunity cost.[4] In economic terms, the chips would represent a "free resource" because there would be no amount forgone with their use in the project. Would the firm be tempted to use the chips simply because of this? Would you want to build a new video game system with obsolete chips? If people will not buy the product, there would indeed be a high opportunity cost in terms of forgone sales.

## The Relationship between Production and Cost

The economic analysis of cost is tightly bound to the economic analysis of production discussed in the previous chapter. As a matter of fact, one can say that the cost function used in economic analysis is simply the production function expressed in monetary rather than physical units. Furthermore, all the limiting assumptions used in specifying the short-run production function apply to the short-run cost function. The only additional assumption needed to determine the short-run economic cost function pertains to the prices of the inputs used in the production process. Here we assume that the firm acts as a "price taker" in the input market; that is, it can hire or use as many or as few inputs as it desires, as long as it pays the going market price for them.

Table 8.1 presents an example of the numerical relationship between production and cost in the short run. The cost of using the variable input is determined by multi-

---

[4]We will avoid using the term *indirect cost* in reference to opportunity cost because some readers may confuse it with another definition. In manufacturing, *indirect cost* usually refers to the cost of using labor not directly involved in the making of a product (e.g., finance, personnel, research and development, and other support or staff functions).

**TABLE 8.1  Relationship between Production and Cost, Short Run**

| Total Input (L) | Q | TVC (L × $500) | MC (ΔTVC/ΔQ) | Reference Point in Figure 8.1 |
|---|---|---|---|---|
| 0 | 0 | 0 | | |
| | | | 0.50 | |
| 1 | 1,000 | 500 | | A(A') |
| | | | 0.25 | |
| 2 | 3,000 | 1,000 | | B(B') |
| | | | 0.16 | |
| 3 | 6,000 | 1,500 | | C(C') |
| | | | 0.25 | |
| 4 | 8,000 | 2,000 | | D(D') |
| | | | 0.50 | |
| 5 | 9,000 | 2,500 | | E(E') |
| | | | 1.00 | |
| 6 | 9,500 | 3,000 | | F(F') |
| | | | 1.42 | |
| 7 | 9,850 | 3,500 | | G(G') |
| | | | 3.33 | |
| 8 | 10,000 | 4,000 | | H(H') |
| | | | −3.33 | |
| 9 | 9,850 | 4,500 | | |

plying the number of units by the unit price. In this case, each unit of labor is assumed to be the equivalent of a 40-hour work week. The weekly wage rate is $500. As indicated in the table, when the total product ($Q$) increases at an *increasing* rate, **total variable cost (TVC)** increases at a *decreasing* rate. When $Q$ increases at a *decreasing* rate, TVC increases at an *increasing* rate. Plotting these numbers on a graph makes it quite apparent that total variable cost is a "mirror image" of total product (Figure 8.1.)

In the previous chapter, the marginal product was defined as the change in total product divided by the change in the amount of the variable input used in the production process. Similarly, the rate of change in total variable cost is called **marginal cost.** Expressed in symbols,

**FIGURE 8.1** Short-Run Production and Cost

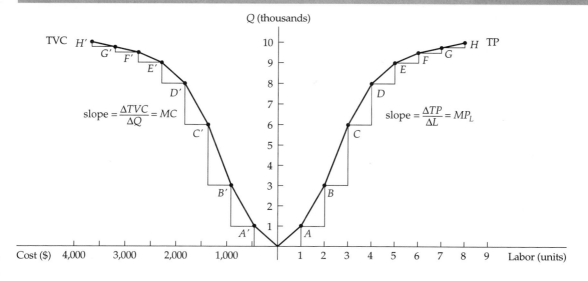

$$\text{MC} = \Delta\text{TVC}/\Delta Q \quad \text{or} \quad \text{MC} = \Delta\text{TC}/\Delta Q$$

Note that marginal cost is either the change in total variable cost or the change in total cost with respect to the change in output. This is because the **total fixed cost** component of **total cost** never changes as output increases. Using marginal cost and marginal product, we can restate the relationship shown in Figure 8.1 in this way: When the firm's marginal product is increasing, its marginal cost of production is decreasing; when its marginal product is decreasing (i.e., *when the law of diminishing returns takes effect*), its marginal cost is increasing.

The relationship between diminishing returns and increasing marginal cost can also be illustrated algebraically. First, assume that the variable input is labor ($L$), and its unit cost is some given wage rate ($W$). Now let us start by defining marginal cost as:

$$\text{MC} = \frac{\Delta\text{TVC}}{\Delta Q} \tag{8.1}$$

Since $\text{TVC} = L \times W$, we can say that

$$\Delta\text{TVC} = \Delta L \times W \tag{8.2}$$

Substituting Equation (8.2) into Equation (8.1) gives us

$$\text{MC} = \frac{\Delta L \times W}{\Delta Q} = \frac{\Delta L}{\Delta Q} \times W \tag{8.3}$$

Recalling the definition of MP, we know that $\text{MP}_L = \Delta Q/\Delta L$. Incorporating this observation into Equation (8.3) gives us

$$\text{MC} = \frac{1}{\text{MP}} \times W = \frac{W}{\text{MP}} \tag{8.4}$$

Clearly, Equation (8.4) tells us that, assuming a constant wage rate, MC will decrease when MP increases and will increase when MP decreases (i.e., when the law of diminishing returns takes effect).

In economic theory, the relationship between diminishing returns and marginal cost represents a key link between a firm's short-run production function and its short-run cost function because it is the law of diminishing returns that gives the short-run cost function its distinctive nonlinear form. Consequently, as will be seen in ensuing sections of this chapter, the firm's total cost, total variable cost, average cost, average variable cost, and marginal cost functions are all constructed in accordance with this nonlinearity.

## The Short-Run Cost Function

This section deals with the focal point of this chapter: the firm's short-run cost function. A numerical model of the behavior of the firm's short-run cost is shown in Table 8.2. Before commenting on each of the columns in the table, let us review all of the assumptions that economists make in specifying a model of this kind.

**1.** The firm employs two inputs, labor and capital.

**TABLE 8.2  Total and Per-Unit Short-Run Cost**

| Quantity (Q) | Total Fixed Cost (TFC) | Total Variable Cost (TVC) | Total Cost (TC) | Average Fixed Cost (AFC) | Average Variable Cost (AVC) | Average Total Cost (AC) | Marginal Cost (MC) |
|---|---|---|---|---|---|---|---|
| 0 | 100 | 0.00 | 100.00 | | | | |
| 1 | 100 | 55.70 | 155.70 | 100.00 | 55.70 | 155.70 | 55.70 |
| 2 | 100 | 105.60 | 205.60 | 50.00 | 52.80 | 102.80 | 49.90 |
| 3 | 100 | 153.90 | 253.90 | 33.33 | 51.30 | 84.63 | 48.30 |
| 4 | 100 | 204.80 | 304.80 | 25.00 | 51.20 | 76.20 | 50.90 |
| 5 | 100 | 262.50 | 362.50 | 20.00 | 52.50 | 72.50 | 57.70 |
| 6 | 100 | 331.20 | 431.20 | 16.67 | 55.20 | 71.87 | 68.70 |
| 7 | 100 | 415.10 | 515.10 | 14.29 | 59.30 | 73.59 | 83.90 |
| 8 | 100 | 518.40 | 618.40 | 12.50 | 64.80 | 77.30 | 103.30 |
| 9 | 100 | 645.30 | 745.30 | 11.11 | 71.70 | 82.81 | 126.90 |
| 10 | 100 | 800.00 | 900.00 | 10.00 | 80.00 | 90.00 | 154.70 |
| 11 | 100 | 986.70 | 1,086.70 | 9.09 | 89.70 | 98.79 | 186.70 |
| 12 | 100 | 1,209.60 | 1,309.60 | 8.33 | 100.80 | 109.13 | 222.90 |

2. The firm operates in a short-run production period. Labor is its variable input, and capital is its fixed input.
3. The firm uses the inputs to make a single product.
4. In producing the output, the firm operates at a given level of technology. (Recall that in our discussion of the short-run production function, we assumed that the firm uses state-of-the-art technology in the production process. The same holds when we talk about short-run cost.)
5. The firm operates at every level of output in the most efficient way.
6. The firm operates in perfectly competitive input markets and must therefore pay for its inputs at some given market rate. In other words, it is a price taker in the input markets.
7. The firm's underlying short-run production function is affected by the law of diminishing returns.

As we proceed in this chapter, you will see why these assumptions are crucial to the understanding of the short-run cost function.

The variables listed in Table 8.2 are defined as follows:

*Quantity* (Q): The amount of output that a firm can produce in the short run. (*Total product* is also used in reference to this amount.)
*Total fixed cost* (TFC): The total cost of using the fixed input $K$.
*Total variable cost* (TVC): The total cost of using the variable input $L$.
*Total cost* (TC): The total cost of using all of the firm's inputs (in this case, $L$ and $K$).
*Average fixed cost* (AFC): The average or per-unit cost of using the fixed input $K$.
*Average variable cost* (AVC): The average or per-unit cost of using the variable input $L$.
*Average total cost* (AC): The average or per-unit cost of using all of the firm's inputs.

*Marginal cost* (MC): The change in a firm's total cost (or, for that matter, its total variable cost) resulting from a unit change in output.

The important relationships among these various measures of cost can be summarized as follows:

$$TC = TFC + TVC$$

$$AC = AFC + AVC \ (or \ TC/Q)$$

$$MC = \Delta TC/\Delta Q \ (or \ \Delta TVC/\Delta Q)$$

$$AFC = TFC/Q$$

$$AVC = TVC/Q$$

In evaluating the schedule of numbers in Table 8.2, note that as a matter of convenience, we have considered unit changes in output over the range of production being considered. Since $\Delta Q$ will always be equal to 1, we can quickly figure the marginal cost as output increases. For example, the marginal cost of the second unit of output is simply the change in the firm's total cost (or total variable cost) between one unit and two units of production. In Table 8.2, we observe that this amount is $49.90.

As output increases from 0 to 12, observe what happens to the various measures of cost. Total fixed cost, as expected, remains constant at $100 over the range of output. Total variable cost increases at a decreasing rate, but when the fourth unit of output is produced, it starts to increase at an increasing rate. The same is true for total cost. When the numbers are plotted on a graph (see Figure 8.2*a*), the rate of change in total cost can be seen as the slope of the TC curve. The constancy of fixed cost is depicted by the horizontal line emanating from the corresponding point on the *Y*-axis.

**FIGURE 8.2** Total Cost, Total Variable Cost, Total Fixed Cost, Average Cost, Average Variable Cost, and Marginal Cost

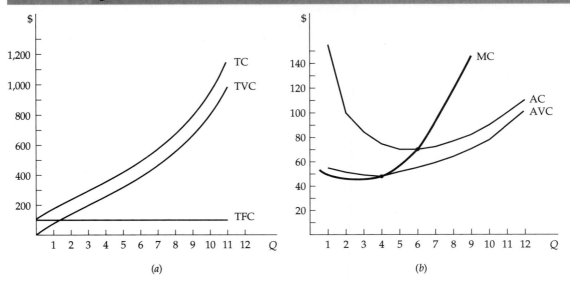

(*a*)                    (*b*)

As for the per-unit cost measures, we see that **average fixed cost (AFC)** declines steadily over the range of production. This is to be expected, because a constant sum of $100 is being divided by the larger amounts of output. **Average variable cost (AVC)** declines, reaches a minimum at four units of output, and then starts to increase. **Average total cost (ATC)** behaves in a similar fashion but reaches its minimum point at six units of output. Marginal cost declines and then starts to increase once the third unit of output is produced.

Notice in Table 8.2 that the values for marginal cost are placed between the output intervals, indicating that this measure of cost shows how total cost changes as a result of a unit change in quantity. For this same reason, marginal cost data are also plotted on a diagram between the output intervals. This particular way of showing marginal cost graphically can be seen in Figure 8.2, along with the average total cost and average variable cost curves.

Figure 8.2 shows a particular relationship between marginal cost and the two other per-unit cost measures that is not as evident in Table 8.2. Notice that when marginal cost is equal to average variable cost, the latter measure is at its minimum point. (This occurs at four units of output.) When marginal cost is equal to average cost, average cost is at its minimum point. (This occurs at six units of output.) Another way to describe these relationships is to state that as long as marginal cost is below average variable cost, average variable cost declines as output increases. However, when marginal cost exceeds average variable cost, average variable cost starts to increase. The same relationship holds between marginal cost and average total cost. The economic significance of these relationships will be explained in chapter 9. But for now, it is important at least to note these relationships among the different per-unit measures of cost. Summarizing these relationships in abbreviated form:

When MC < AVC, AVC is falling.
When MC > AVC, AVC is rising.
When MC = AVC, AVC is at its minimum point.

To summarize the relationship between marginal cost and average cost, simply substitute AC for AVC.

It is important to understand how the concept of relevant cost can be incorporated into the analysis of short-run cost. Suppose a firm is currently producing six units of output per period and is considering increasing this amount to seven. In deciding whether to produce the seventh unit of output, the relevant cost is the marginal cost. In other words, it is the *change* in total cost and not the total cost itself that must be considered. This is because whether the firm produces six or seven units of output per time period, it still must pay the same amount of fixed cost. By evaluating the change in total cost, the firm automatically excludes fixed cost from consideration.

## INCREASING COST EFFICIENCY IN THE SHORT RUN

As will be seen in chapters 9 through 12, the short-run cost function plays a central part in the economic analysis of production and pricing. For now, we can appreciate the value of this model by considering the ways in which a company might attempt to become more economically efficient. The assumptions listed when the model was specified provide a convenient guide.

To start with, the model assumes that the firm is already operating as efficiently as possible. If we assume that the firm is in fact operating as best it can with state-of-the-art technology, then the only possibility to reduce cost in the short run is for the inputs to decrease in price. If this were to happen, there would be a downward shift in the

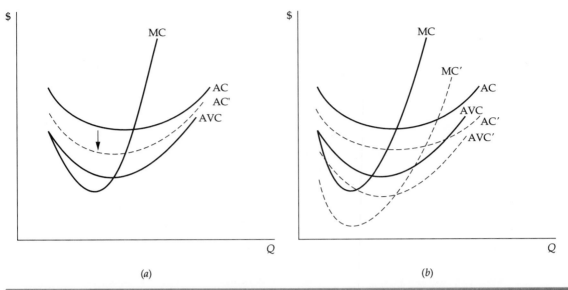

**FIGURE 8.3** Effects on Short-Run Cost Structure of Price Changes in Variable and Fixed Inputs

firm's short-run cost curves. This effect is shown in Figure 8.3*a* and *b*. Notice that a reduction in the firm's fixed cost (e.g., a reduction in rental payments) would simply cause the average cost line to shift downward, whereas a reduction in the firm's variable cost (e.g., a reduction in wage rates or raw materials costs) would cause all three cost lines—AC, AVC, and MC—to shift. MC actually shifts downward and to the right.

The purchase of capital equipment was not considered in the discussion because we assumed it to be our model's fixed input. Actually, the addition of capital equipment could be considered a short-run change *if we assume labor to be the fixed input.* For example, a workforce of a certain size might be given additional machinery with which to work. The point is that in the short-run analysis of cost, at least one of the inputs must be held constant.

**MODULE 9A**

### ALTERNATIVE SPECIFICATIONS OF THE TOTAL COST FUNCTION

In economic analysis, the most common form of the short-run cost function is the one that has been used thus far in this chapter. That is, the **total cost function** is specified as a cubic relationship between total cost and output. As output increases, total cost first increases at a decreasing rate, and then at some point it increases at an increasing rate. By now you should be well aware that this is due to the underlying relationship between the firm's variable input and the resulting output. Total cost increases at a decreasing rate because the firm is experiencing increasing returns to its variable input. When the law of diminishing returns takes effect, the firm begins to experience decreasing returns to its variable factor, thereby causing its total cost to begin increasing at an increasing rate.

In addition to this cubic form of the cost function, two other important functional relationships between total cost and output are considered in economic analysis. One is a quadratic relationship, and the other is a linear one. These relationships along with the

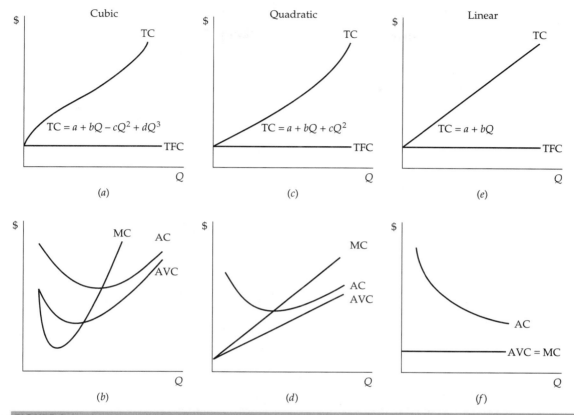

**FIGURE 8.4** Alternative Representations of Total, Average, and Marginal Costs

cubic cost function are shown in Figure 8.4. This figure also shows the general algebraic expressions for the three forms of total cost. These variations can be explained once again by the underlying relationship between the firm's variable input and the resulting output. In Figure 8.4c we can see that the quadratic total cost function increases at an increasing rate from the outset of production. This implies that the law of diminishing returns takes effect as soon as the firm starts to produce. On the other hand, the linear cost function, shown in Figure 8.4e, indicates that total cost increases at a constant rate. Think about this for a moment. What does this mean in terms of the underlying relationship between the firm's variable input and its output? It means that the firm is experiencing neither increasing nor diminishing returns as its variable input is added to its fixed input. Each additional unit of variable input adds the *same* amount of additional output (marginal product) throughout the short-run range of production. Therefore, the change in the total cost relative to the change in output (which, as you recall, is indicated by the slope of the total cost line) is the same throughout the range of output considered.

Rather than discuss the different specifications of the firm's short-run cost function in terms of total cost, it might be easier and more meaningful to discuss the alternative forms in terms of unit costs, both average and marginal. Thus, instead of referring to total cost "increasing at an increasing rate," we can simply say that the firm's marginal cost is increasing. An increase in total cost at a constant rate means a constant marginal cost. We can also use Figure 8.4 to illustrate this point.

In Figure 8.4*b,* we see the familiar set of short-run cost curves depicted earlier. As output increases, marginal cost falls, reaches a minimum, and then starts to increase (as the law of diminishing returns takes effect). As it increases, marginal cost intersects with average variable cost and average total cost at their respective minimum points, for reasons explained earlier. In Figure 8.4*d,* we see that marginal cost increases as soon as production begins, just as we noted when evaluating the slope of the total cost function. As in the case of Figure 8.4*b,* marginal cost intersects average variable cost and average cost at their minimum points.

In the case of the linear cost function, shown in Figure 8.4*f,* the horizontal marginal cost line denotes that marginal cost remains constant as output increases. But also witness that marginal cost is equal to average variable cost, unlike the cases in Figure 8.4*b* and *d.* To illustrate this relationship, consider the following numerical example. Suppose you are given the following cost function:

$$\text{TC} = 100 + 0.50\,Q \tag{8.5}$$

Assuming the intercept and slope coefficients represent dollar units, this function tells us that the firm's total fixed cost is \$100 and its marginal cost is \$0.50. That is, each additional unit of production adds \$0.50 to the firm's total cost. Omitting the fixed cost component of the equation gives us

$$\text{TVC} = 0.50\,Q \tag{8.6}$$

Recall by definition that AVC = TVC/*Q.* Dividing Equation (8.6) by *Q* gives an AVC of \$0.50, which is the same as the marginal cost.

The mathematics of this example may seem rather trivial. Nonetheless, it is important to elaborate on this relationship between average variable cost and marginal cost because these two measures of cost are often used interchangeably in the business world. For example, when cost accountants use the term *standard variable cost,* they are usually referring to *both* marginal cost and average variable cost. In so doing, they are assuming that the total cost function is linear, that the firm experiences neither increasing nor diminishing returns in the short run. The importance of these assumptions as well as the role of the linear total cost function in economic analysis will be discussed further in appendix 8B and chapter 11.

# The Long-Run Cost Function

### THE RELATIONSHIP BETWEEN LONG-RUN PRODUCTION AND LONG-RUN COST

In the long run, all inputs to a firm's production function may be changed. Because there are no fixed inputs, there are no fixed costs. Consequently, all costs of production are variable in the long run. In most work situations, managers of firms make decisions about production and cost that economic theory would consider short-run in nature. For example, they might have to decide how many labor hours are required for a par-

**TABLE 8.3   Long-Run Cost Function**

| Scale of Production (Capacity Level) | Total Product (Output/Mo) | Long-Run Total Cost (LRTC) | Long-Run Marginal Cost (LRMC) | Long-Run Average Cost (LRAC) |
|---|---|---|---|---|
| A | 10,000 | 50,000 | $5.00 | $5.00 |
| B | 20,000 | 90,000 | 4.00 | 4.50 |
| C | 30,000 | 120,000 | 3.00 | 4.00 |
| D | 40,000 | 150,000 | 3.00 | 3.75 |
| E | 50,000 | 200,000 | 5.00 | 4.00 |
| F | 60,000 | 260,000 | 6.00 | 4.33 |

ticular project or whether the existing work force requires more machinery to meet increased demand.[5] But from time to time, managers must make long-run production decisions. That is, they must consider possible changes in *all* of the firm's inputs and, hence, changes in all of the firm's cost of operation. Decisions of this kind are considered by economists to be part of a manager's planning horizon.

In explaining the nature of the long-run cost function, we begin with a schedule of numbers showing a firm's long-run cost function in relation to its long-run production function. Unlike the case of short-run cost presented in Table 8.2, the hypothetical numbers in Table 8.3 are based on the assumption that greater amounts of output are the result of increases in *all* of the firm's inputs. Consistent with this assumption, this table implies that the firm would incur no cost if it chose not to produce any output, because in the long run there is no fixed cost.

As output increases, observe that total cost increases, but not at a constant rate. As with the short-run function, the rate of change of the long-run total cost function is called the marginal cost (long-run marginal cost, to be more precise). In looking at the long-run marginal cost column in Table 8.3, we see that this measure at first decreases, then is constant, and finally increases over the range of the output. The numbers in Table 8.3 are plotted on a graph in Figure 8.5. The rate of change in the long-run total cost can be seen by observing the slope of this curve as well as by observing the behavior of the long-run marginal cost curve.

The reason for this particular behavior of the firm's long-run marginal cost (or the rate of change in its long-run total cost) pertains to returns to scale. As explained in the previous chapter, economists hypothesize that a firm's long-run production function may at first exhibit increasing returns, then constant returns, and finally decreasing returns to scale. This being the case, we would expect a firm's long-run cost to change in a reciprocal fashion.

When a firm experiences increasing returns to scale, an increase in all of its inputs by some proportion results in an increase in its output by some *greater* proportion. Assuming constant input prices over time, this means that if the firm's output increases by

---

[5]Recall that we stated earlier that the "short run" in economic theory requires only that at least one of the inputs in the production function be held constant. Thus, we can treat the addition of capital equipment as a short-run change if the amount of factory space or the amount of labor, for example, remains unchanged.

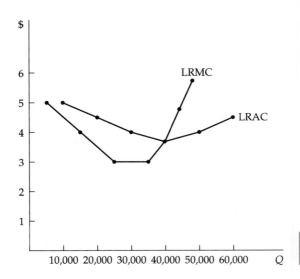

**FIGURE 8.5** Long-Run Average and Marginal Cost

some percentage, its total cost of production increases by some *lesser* percentage. The graphs in Figure 8.6 illustrate the reciprocal behavior of long-run cost and long-run production.

It is important to stress that although the long-run cost function appears to exhibit the same pattern of behavior as the short-run cost function, the reasons for their respective patterns are entirely unrelated. The short-run cost function is affected by increasing and diminishing returns, a phenomenon that is assumed to take effect when at least one of the inputs is held constant, and the long-run function is affected by increasing and decreasing returns to scale, a phenomenon assumed to take effect when all of the firm's inputs are allowed to vary. Figure 8.7 serves as a reminder of this distinction.

## ECONOMIES OF SCALE

One of the measures of cost in Table 8.3 has yet to be discussed: long-run average cost. This variable is the key indicator of a phenomenon called **economies of scale.** If a firm's long-run average cost declines as output increases, the firm is said to be experiencing economies of scale. If long-run average cost increases, economists consider this to be a sign of **diseconomies of scale.** There is no special term to describe the situation in which a firm's long-run average cost remains constant as output increases or decreases. We shall simply say that such a firm experiences neither economies nor diseconomies of scale. Figure 8.8 illustrates a typical U-shaped average cost curve reflecting the different types of scale economies that a firm might experience in the long run.

The primary reason for long-run scale economies is the underlying pattern of returns to scale in the firm's long-run production function. Further evaluation of Table 8.3 indicates that as long as marginal cost is falling, it is less than long-run average cost and in effect pulls the average down—a sure sign of economies of scale. However, once the firm starts to experience decreasing returns to scale, its long-run marginal cost begins

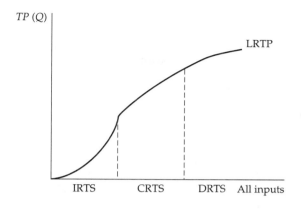

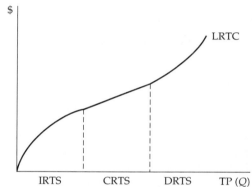

**FIGURE 8.6** Returns to Scale for Long-Run Total Cost and Long-Run Total Production

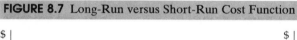

**FIGURE 8.7** Long-Run versus Short-Run Cost Function

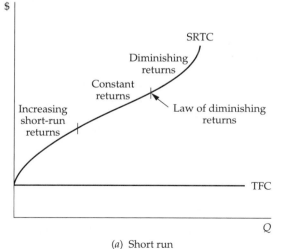

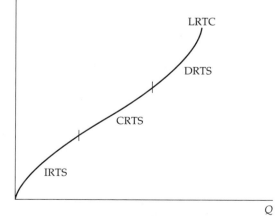

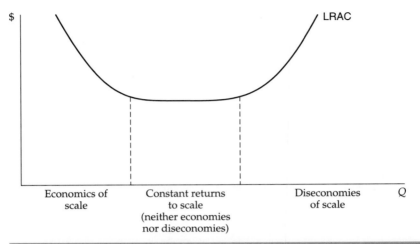

**FIGURE 8.8** Long-Run Average Cost

to rise. Eventually it becomes greater than long-run average cost, causing LRAC to rise and signifying diseconomies of scale.[6]

Scale economies and diseconomies may result from factors besides those relating to returns to scale. These other factors pertain primarily to the prices of the firm's inputs. For example, as the firm's scale of production increases, it may be able to exert some market power over its suppliers and thus receive volume discounts for bulk purchases of raw materials and component parts. Another example involves a firm's use of capital equipment with better *price-performance ratios.* As the firm increases its scale of production, it may be worthwhile to buy more cost-effective machinery whose price and capacity could not be justified at smaller scales of production. Only a few years ago, a typical illustration cited by economists of this type of scale economy was the computer. But with the advent of personal and midsize computers, there are now machines with prices and levels of computing power that are appropriate for firms of all sizes. Furthermore, with the tremendous advances in technology and software, the prices of the machines relative to their computing power (i.e., their price-performance ratios) do not differ much among the various sizes of computers.

We should briefly mention two other factors contributing to economies of scale. First, larger firms may be able to raise funds in capital markets at a lower cost than smaller ones. For instance, a large company may be able to secure short-term funds in the commercial paper market and long-term funds in the corporate bond market, whereas a small company may be able to secure borrowed funds only from a bank. Generally, the interest rates that firms must pay for funds in money and capital markets are

---

[6]You should recognize the relationship between LRMC and LRAC to be the same mathematically as the relationship between SRMC and SRAC. That is, regardless of whether a short- or a long-run time period is assumed, when the marginal is below the average, it brings the average down. When the marginal is above the average, it pulls the average up.

less than for bank loans with comparable maturities. Second, a large firm may be able to take advantage of economies resulting from the spreading out of promotional costs. If a firm expands its scale of production, it may not have to expand its advertising budget by the same proportion, if at all. The same can be said about research and development expenditures.

As far as diseconomies of scale are concerned, if the firm's scale of production becomes so large that it begins to affect substantially the total market demand for its inputs, it may start to increase the price of these inputs. A typical case is the expansion of a major employer in a local area with a relatively fixed supply of labor. If the firm's higher scale of production sufficiently increases its demand for labor, it could begin to drive up local wage rates.

Another factor not related to the long-run production function that could cause diseconomies of scale is a firm's transportation costs. As a firm increases the production capacity of a particular manufacturing facility, per-unit transportation cost tends to rise rather than to fall. This is largely because transportation costs involve more than just the delivery of goods from one point to another. In addition, there are handling expenses, insurance and security expenses, and inventory costs (as goods await shipment). Increases in these types of expenses help to increase the total transportation cost to the extent that average transportation cost increases as well. Furthermore, basic delivery expenses may rise at a faster rate than other kinds of cost if the firm has to ship the additional output to farther destinations. Economists hypothesize that eventually the increase in unit transportation cost will more than offset the fall in unit cost due to economies of scale. If this happens, then diseconomies of scale (i.e., rising average total cost) will result. Table 8.4 summarizes the key reasons for economies and diseconomies of scale. Factors that primarily relate to returns to scale are noted with an asterisk.

### TABLE 8.4  Factors Affecting Economies and Diseconomies of Scale

*Possible Reasons for Economies of Scale*

Specialization in the use of labor and capital*
Indivisible nature of many types of capital equipment*
Productive capacity of capital equipment rises faster than purchase price
Economies in maintaining inventory of replacement parts and maintenance personnel*
Discounts from bulk purchases
Lower cost of raising capital funds
Spreading of promotional and research and development costs
Management efficiencies (line and staff)*

*Possible Reasons for Diseconomies of Scale*

Disproportionate rise in transportation costs
Input market imperfections (e.g., wage rates driven up)
Management coordination and control problems*
Disproportionate rise in staff and indirect labor*

*Indicates reason related directly to economies or diseconomies of scale in the long-run production function.

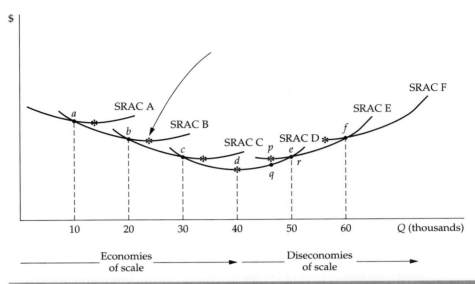

**FIGURE 8.9** Capacity Level and Short-Run Average Cost

## THE LONG-RUN AVERAGE COST CURVE AS THE ENVELOPE OF SHORT-RUN AVERAGE COST

Up to now, we have been discussing long-run average cost as part of the firm's planning horizon. That is, the firm is assumed to be free to choose any level of capacity that it wants, because in our theoretical long-run time period, all inputs may vary. However, once a firm commits itself to a certain level of capacity, it must consider at least one of the inputs fixed as it varies the rest. In terms of production cost, this means that once a capacity level is decided on, the firm must work with a short-run cost function. We can illustrate this by returning to the example in Table 8.3.

Suppose that the capacity levels shown in the table represent plants of increasing size. Figure 8.9 shows these capacity levels in relation to each plant's short-run average cost curve. The points labeled *a* through *f* represent the levels of output and average cost shown in Table 8.3. The dotted lines passing through the points indicate the short-run average cost curves that we imagine to exist once the firm has locked into one of the plant sizes represented by the labeled points.

As expected, short-run average cost (SRAC) curves for the larger plants are positioned to the right of the curves for smaller ones, indicating greater production capacity. For example, SRAC B is to the right of SRAC A because plant B is larger than plant A. But, as noted in Figure 8.9, plants with larger capacities are greatly influenced by economies and diseconomies of scale. Because of the impact of economies of scale, plant B's SRAC curve is positioned below as well as to the right of plant A's, so that the minimum point of B's SRAC curve is *lower* than that for A. The same can be said for plant C's minimum SRAC in relation to plant B's and for D's in relation to C's. However, because of the impact of diseconomies of scale, plant E's SRAC curve is positioned above and to the right of D's, and plant F's is above and to the right of E's. That is, the SRAC curves of plants larger than plant D have progressively higher minimum average cost points. For reference, the minimum SRAC points for all of the plants are marked in Figure 8.9 with asterisks.

Another important aspect of Figure 8.9 is that none of the labeled dots is at the lowest point of its respective short-run average cost curve *except for the dot representing plant D.* For example, the asterisk marking plant B's minimum short-run average cost depicts a level above the average cost that would be incurred by plant C in the short run for a comparable level of production (see arrow in Figure 8.9). A logical extension of this illustration is the observation that if a firm wants to produce between 20,000 and 30,000 units of output per month, it would be better off utilizing the manufacturing capacity provided by plant C than to try to increase the usage of the smaller plant B. To understand the full economic implication of this observation, it is necessary to take a slight detour in our discussion to explain the particular way in which economists represent plant capacity with the use of short-run average cost curves.

You will recall that the typical short-run average cost curve (based on a cubic total cost function) declines, reaches a minimum point, and then rises as the firm produces more with some fixed amount of input. By definition, economists consider the lowest point of the short-run average cost curve to represent the firm's maximum capacity. Although "maximum capacity" usually denotes the physical limit of production (i.e., a plant simply cannot produce any more output), Figure 8.9 shows that a firm is clearly capable of producing beyond the output level at which average cost is at its lowest point. Rather than try to figure out the reason for this particular use of the term, just remember that for economists, "maximum plant capacity" coincides with a level of output that costs a firm the least amount per unit to produce in the short run.[7]

Thus, Figure 8.9 shows that over certain ranges of output, a firm is better off operating a larger plant at less than maximum capacity than a smaller plant at maximum capacity. The average cost of production in the larger plant is lower than the lowest possible average of production in the smaller plant. What causes this to happen? Economies of scale, of course. Because of this phenomenon, we can expect that over certain ranges of output, the reduction in average cost resulting from the economies of using a larger plant will be greater than the reduction in average cost resulting from operating a smaller plant at its most efficient (the economic "maximum") level of capacity!

As a cautionary note, we should add that once diseconomies of scale take effect, it is better for a firm to operate a plant of a given size beyond its "maximum capacity" than to build a plant of a larger size. We leave it to you to work through a detailed explanation of this observation. Suffice it to say that the reasoning is very similar to the explanation regarding the impact of economies of scale. (If you need help, refer to Figure 8.9, points *p, q,* and *r.*)

Looking at Figure 8.9 from another perspective, we can see that the firm's long-run average cost curve is actually the envelope of the various short-run average cost curves. As such, the long-run curve outlines the lowest per-unit costs that the firm will incur over the range of output considered, given the possibility of using plant sizes A through

---

[7]Economists sometimes refer to this point as "minimum efficiency scale," or MES. This term is generally used in industrial organization textbooks.

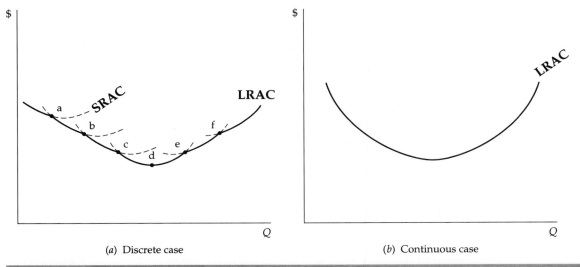

**FIGURE 8.10** Forming LRAC Curve from SRAC Curves

F. Figure 8.10*a* illustrates this point. As the number of choices of plant size approaches infinity, the envelope becomes a continuous version of the graph; this version is shown in Figure 8.10*b*. You should recognize it as the long-run average cost curve first shown in Figure 8.8.

### USING LONG-RUN AVERAGE COST AS A DECISION-MAKING TOOL: THE IMPORTANCE OF COORDINATING PRODUCTION PLANS WITH MARKET FORECASTS

In planning for its long-run capacity, which plant size should a firm choose? Using the schedule of numbers in Table 8.3, we can see that if a firm decides to build plant A, then the lowest per-unit cost of production it can expect is $5. But if it decides to build a plant with greater capacity—for instance, plant C—the potential for reducing per-unit cost is considerable because of economies of scale. Using plant C, the firm could produce its output for as little as $4 per unit. Indeed, this is where accurate forecasts of product demand are needed to help the firm plan for the best plant size. There would be no sense in investing in plant C, for example, if monthly demand is only 20,000. In this case, the smaller plant B would be more suitable. Actually, given the plant size options shown in Table 8.3 and Figure 8.9, we see that it is not necessary for a firm to forecast a specific amount of demand, but it should at least have a good idea of what the range of demand will be in the future. Table 8.5 presents a schedule showing the most appropriate plant size for different ranges of demand and production.

You should recognize that because diseconomies of scale take effect when plant E is used, plant D is appropriate for a wider range of production than the other plants. The penalty for selecting the inappropriate level of capacity is the incurrence of unnecessary cost, whether the actual demand turns out to be above or below the range used as

TABLE 8.5 Optimal Plant Size According to Expected Demand

| Units of Output Produced Based on Expected Demand | Appropriate Plant Size |
|---|---|
| 0 to 10,000 | A |
| 10,000 to 20,000 | B |
| 20,000 to 30,000 | C |
| 30,000 to 50,000 | D |
| 50,000 to 60,000 | E |
| 60,000 to 70,000 (not shown on graph) | F |

a basis for the firm's decision on long-run production capacity. In Figure 8.11, we can see that if the firm had decided to build plant B and the demand turned out to be 25,000, it would lose on a per-unit basis the amount depicted by the arrow. If demand were such that it required the firm to produce only 5,000 units per month, the firm would suffer a similar type of loss.

As a final comment on long-run cost, it is very easy to put the onus for picking the best level of long-run capacity on the market forecasters. After all, their estimates of future demand should be the main guide for the decision makers who plan production capacity. Nevertheless, the production people in a business could become carried away with considerations of production capacity and efficiency for their own sake (e.g., "let us build a plant of the size that will enable us to benefit substantially from economies of scale") and convince the management to overbuild the company's long-run capacity. Certainly, optimal long-run production decisions require a balanced contribution from both the engineers and the marketing people.

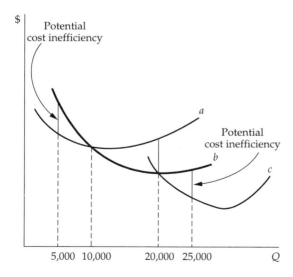

FIGURE 8.11 Unnecessary Costs Due to Inappropriate Plant Size

# The Learning Curve

The **learning curve** is a line showing the relationship between labor cost and additional units of output. Its downward slope indicates that this additional cost per unit declines as the level of output increases because workers improve with practice. The reduction in cost from this particular source of improvement is often referred to as the *learning curve effect*.

Specifically, a learning curve is measured in terms of the percentage decrease in additional labor cost each time output doubles. Table 8.6 presents data for an "80 percent" learning curve. Each time the output doubles, the cost of producing the next increment of output decreases to 80 percent of the previous level (i.e., declines by 20 percent). As you can see in this table, the first unit costs $100,000; the second unit costs 80 percent of this amount, or $80,000; the fourth unit costs 80 percent of this amount, or $64,000; and so on. Notice that the percentage reduction is actually with respect to labor hours. However, given some wage rate (in this case, $10/hour), the labor cost decreases by the same percentage. The data in Table 8.6 are plotted in Figure 8.12.

There is a mathematical formula for determining the pattern of reduction in labor cost based on a selected percentage decline. This formula is

$$Y_x = Kx^n$$

where  $Y_x$ = Units of factor (labor hours) or cost to produce $x$th unit
$K$ = Factor units or cost to produce $k$th (usually first) unit
$x$ = Product unit (the $x$th unit)
$n$ = log $S$/log 2
$S$ = Slope parameter

For an 80 percent learning curve, the number of direct labor hours required to produce the eighth unit of output is

### TABLE 8.6  Numerical Example of the Learning Curve

| Unit Number | Unit Labor Hours | Cumulative Labor Hours | Cumulative Average Labor Hours | Unit Labor Cost | Cumulative Average Labor Cost |
|---|---|---|---|---|---|
| 1 | 10,000 | 10,000.0 | 10,000 | $100,000 | $100,000 |
| 2 | 8,000 | 18,000.0 | 9,000 | 80,000 | 90,000 |
| 4 | 6,400 | 31,421.0 | 7,855.3 | 64,000 | 78,553 |
| 8 | 5,120 | 53,459.1 | 6,682.4 | 51,200 | 66,824 |
| 16 | 4,096 | 89,201.4 | 5,575.1 | 40,960 | 55,751 |
| 32 | 3,276.8 | 146,786.2 | 4,587.1 | 32,768 | 45,871 |
| 64 | 2,621.4 | 239,245.3 | 3,738.2 | 26,214 | 37,382 |
| 128 | 2,097.2 | 387,439.5 | 3,026.9 | 20,972 | 30,269 |
| 256 | 1,677.7 | 624,731.8 | 2,404.6 | 16,777 | 24,046 |

Wage rate = $10/hr.

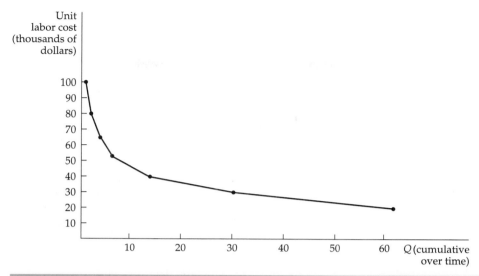

**FIGURE 8.12** An 80 Percent Learning Curve

$$S = .8$$

$$Y_8 = 100,000 \, (8)^{\log .8/\log 2}$$

$$= 100,000 \, (8)^{-.322}$$

$$= \frac{100,000}{8^{.322}}$$

$$= \frac{100,000}{1.9535} = 51,200$$

This answer conforms to Table 8.6 and Figure 8.12. You may want to try constructing other learning curves based on different percentages, or refer to learning curve tables in an engineering textbook.

Although the learning curve is expressed in terms of the marginal cost of production, the impact of improving with practice can also be seen in terms of the decline in average cost. Table 8.6 also shows the cumulative labor cost and the cumulative average labor cost of producing various levels of output. As can be seen, the average labor cost also decreases, although not as sharply as the marginal labor cost. In any case, the learning curve effect clearly has an impact on the short-run cost presented earlier. In particular, the learning curve effect causes the short-run average cost curve to shift downward. This is shown in Figure 8.13.

The Japanese have been frequently cited in academic studies and in the popular press for their use of the learning curve in driving down costs. This is most dramatically shown in their production of computer chips and consumer electronics. Their particular use of the learning curve involves accelerating production experience

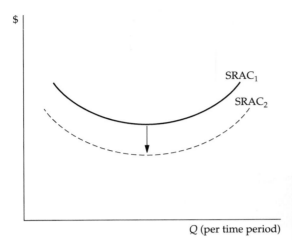

**FIGURE 8.13** Impact of Learning Curve Effect on Short-Run Average Cost per Time Period

through aggressive price-cutting measures. The price cuts enhance sales and give them production experience more rapidly. This in turn helps to drive down costs of production faster. The tactic of learning curve pricing is illustrated in Figure 8.14.

In concluding this section on the learning curve effect, we should note that this phenomenon was first observed in the production of aircraft more than 50 years ago. The reason cited for the learning curve effect was the repetition of tasks performed by workers actually manufacturing the product (e.g., direct labor). Later on, the experience gained from repetition by those indirectly related to the production process

**FIGURE 8.14** Pricing Based on Learning or Experience Curve

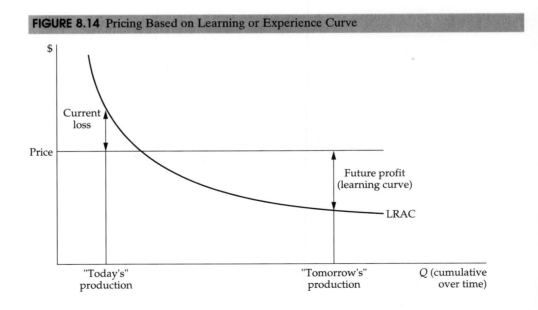

(e.g., engineers and researchers) was also included in this phenomenon. Thus, such factors as the development of new process and engineering methods, the substitution of lower-cost materials or processes, and product redesign were also considered as factors causing unit costs to decrease as production levels increased. The recognition of these additional factors prompted the use of the broader term **experience curve.** Today, *experience curve* and *learning curve* are generally used interchangeably. However, some business managers and consultants still prefer to make a distinction between the two terms.

# Economies of Scope

Before summarizing this chapter, we should introduce briefly a concept often used in business but that does not quite fit into the conventional economic theory of cost, namely, **economies of scope.** This term can be defined as

> the reduction of a firm's unit cost by producing two or more goods or services jointly rather than separately.

The effort by our hypothetical firm Global Foods, Inc., to increase its profits by expanding into the soft drink industry offers a good example of a company seeking to take advantage of economies of scope. The company already has the knowledge, experience, and skills to produce and distribute processed food items and hopes to use these attributes in the production and distribution of soft drinks.

In a sense, the concept of economies of scope is closely related to economies of scale. Engaging in more than one line of business may require a firm to have a certain minimum scale of operation. Another way to view this relationship between scale and scope is to consider that a company's expansion into different lines of business naturally increases its scale of operation.

Economies of scope is a very important concept in the production of services as well as goods. As an example, Fingerhut is a catalog company that specializes in selling products to lower-income households (i.e., below $29,200 per year). The company assumes a higher risk but charges higher prices for their products to compensate for this. In recent years, the increased marketing of credit cards by banks to the same lower-income households that are targeted by Fingerhut have hurt the company's sales. In retaliation, Fingerhut began offering credit cards to its catalog customers through a separate subsidiary, Metris. The key to this company's success is a list of 30 million names that Fingerhut accumulated over the years from its direct mail business. This list contains critical information not generally available through the credit bureaus that issuers of credit cards use, such as occupation, number of children, hobbies, home ownership, and spending and payment patterns. Most important, the list includes 11 million "no-pays" that are purged from every direct mail campaign or solicitation.[8] Thus, we have a good example of how economies of scope is achieved through the sharing of a database between two separate lines of business.

---

[8]Joseph B. Cahill, "Credit Companies Find Tough Rival at Bottom of Consumer Market," *The Wall Street Journal,* December 29, 1998.

# Examples of Ways Companies Have Cut Costs to Remain Competitive

The consideration of cost in business decisions often evokes mixed feelings among managers. This is because efforts to reduce costs may involve the downsizing of staff, the layoff of workers, reductions in discretionary expenses for such things as training and travel, or the elimination of executive perquisites such as corporate jets. In contrast, efforts to increase revenues involve growth and all of the activities that accompany it (such as new hires, better equipment, new offices, and increases in discretionary spending and perquisites). Yet, from an objective standpoint, it is clear that a dollar saved, given some level of output and revenue, adds as much to the bottom line as an additional dollar of revenue, given some level of output and cost. Following are some recent examples of firms that implemented various cost-cutting methods or procedures in order to remain competitive.

1.  *The Strategic Use of Cost: The Case of Southwest Airlines*[9]

    Southwest Airlines began in 1967 as a small operation aimed at improving air service between Houston, Dallas-Fort Worth, and San Antonio, Texas. Today it is a formidable competitor in the short-haul (500 miles or less) air transportation market. Indeed, there are now certain routes (for example, Burbank, California to Las Vegas, Nevada) that the major airlines such as American Airlines have withdrawn from since Southwest's entry into the market. Southwest Airlines has achieved this success by being the low-cost provider of short-haul service. Its everyday fares can be as low as one-third of the standard fares charged by the major airlines on short-haul routes.

    Among the key cost items that gives Southwest a cost advantage over American and the other major airlines is payroll (it employs nonunion personnel), food (no food is served on short-haul flights), and depreciation (Southwest's fleet is not as new as American's).

    It is more meaningful to look at Southwest's cost advantage not as a series of ad hoc cost-cutting measures, but as the consequence of its overall market strategy. When the founders of Southwest Airlines devised their strategy of providing low-priced air transportation in the short-haul market, it anticipated being able to keep costs down by virtue of the very strategy that they selected. By flying only on short-haul routes, Southwest needed only one type of aircraft (the Boeing 737). This meant less training costs for flying and maintenance as well as a lower inventory of replacement parts. Furthermore, short hauls require no in-flight meals. In addition, because it has positioned itself in the minds of its customers as a low-cost provider of air transportation, it can save more money by cutting out services or conveniences that customers generally expect from the major airlines. For example, Southwest does not take reservations, thereby saving money on staff and computer services. Whenever possible, it also uses secondary or alternative airports, thereby avoiding the higher landing fees charged by the major-hub airports.[10]

---

[9]For a good historical review of Southwest Airlines' start-up and operations, see Christopher H. Lovelock, "Southwest Airlines," Harvard Business School Case Study #575-060, 1975.

[10]Most of the material in this section was taken from Gene Walden and Edmund O. Lawler, *Marketing Masters: Secrets of America's Best Companies,* New York: HarperCollins, 1993, pp. 17–22.

Raw materials savings

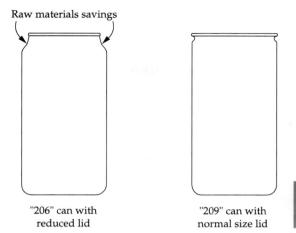

"206" can with
reduced lid

"209" can with
normal size lid

**FIGURE 8.15** Using Reduced-Lid Can to Achieve Raw Materials Savings

**2.** *Reduction in Cost of Materials*

Manufacturers are constantly seeking to cut costs by materials substitution or modification. In the beverage industry, one noticeable example of this is the reduction in the size of the lid of a 12-oz. aluminum can. Towards the end of the bottling process, each can on the conveyor belt passes a measuring device called a "fill height detector" that checks if there are at least 12 ounces of liquid in the container. Those with less are discarded. This measuring device shoots a gamma beam about one-quarter inch below the top of the can's lid. Because it is not necessary for the product to be filled to the very top of the can, the lid can be made slightly smaller by crimping the top portion of the can. The savings from the reduction in the aluminum content are considerable, given the millions of cans that are produced each year (Figure 8.15).

**3.** *Using Enterprise Resource Planning to Reduce Costs*

If you have management experience and a good working knowledge of the products of SAP, you can probably get a job in a consulting company or large corporation that offers a six-figure salary. SAP is the leading company that offers software products for "enterprise resource planning" or ERP. Other major companies offering these products are PeopleSoft, Baan, and QAD.

ERP is the industry term for software that enables companies to integrate their planning, scheduling, synchronization, and tracking of the entire chain of their production process. The use of ERP has helped companies to cut costs as well as increase revenues by getting the right products into the hands of their customers in the most timely and efficient way. SAP's Web site (http://www.sap.com) provides examples of how companies have saved money by using its products and services. For example, Larry Bergner, vice president of technology for the Earthgrains Company (owner and operator of 39 bakeries and dough plants in the United States, and 8 bakeries and one dough plant in Europe) said that the use of SAP's products "has allowed us to control our disbursements from one central location, giving us better management of our working capital. It's [also] enabled us to streamline our procurement cycle, with an immediate savings of millions of dollars per year."[11] No doubt similar savings also have been achieved by using other companies' ERP products and services.

**4.** *Reduction of Process Costs*

Cost savings stemming from the use of ERP has been getting most of the attention in the popular press and the literature on business studies. However, there are also more specific but equally important ways that appropriate software can help to cut costs. More companies are starting to require that their employees use software packages to file travel and expense reports electronically. Studies by American Express found that U.S. companies spent about $175 billion on travel and expenses in 1998 and that the use of electronic filing can cut the cost of processing expense reports from $36.46 per paper report to as low as $7.91.[12]

**5.** *Relocation to Lower-Wage Countries or Regions*

We have already noted how a number of American companies have decided to relocate to regions or countries where wages are lower to reduce the cost of production. American companies are not the only ones to take this cost-reducing measure. Japanese companies have been relocating to all parts of Southeast Asia. German companies have been moving to Central European countries such as Poland, where wages are less than one-tenth of the average rate in Germany. There are other examples, such as an Austrian company moving to Slovakia and a French company partnering with a German company to manufacture products in Hungary. Furthermore, manufacturing companies are not the only ones who can benefit from the move to lower-wage countries. A thriving software development industry has emerged in India, where American and European companies find that the average wage rate of an Indian programmer is about one-fourth of a comparable person in the United States.[13]

**6.** *Mergers, Consolidation, and Downsizing*

This particular approach to cost cutting has already been cited earlier in this chapter. A more detailed example is the case of SPX Corporation, a supplier of auto parts, technical systems, and industrial and electrical controls. In late 1998 it announced that it would close about 25 facilities and eliminate about 1,000 jobs as it restructures the operations of General Signal Corp, an industrial manufacturer that it had acquired in July of that year. The CEO of the company stated that "with the anticipated savings from these restructuring actions, which mitigate the current economic trends of our global markets, we remain confident in our 1999 earnings guidance of $4.85 per share, excluding special charges."[14]

---

[11]Retrieved February 12, 1999 from the World Wide Web:
http://www.sap.com/products/industry/consum/media/earthgr.htm
[12]"Software Is Easing Expense-Form Headaches" *The Wall Street Journal,* December 28, 1998.
[13]See Peter Gumbel, "Western Europe Finds That It's Pricing Itself Out of the Job Market," *The Wall Street Journal,* December 9, 1993; "Europe: The Push East," *Business Week,* November 2, 1994, pp. 48–49. Information about wage rates for Indian software programmers was acquired in an interview in November, 1998 with a representative from Tata, India's largest manufacturing, service, and information technology conglomerate.
[14]Emily R. Sendler, "SPX Plans to Trim Sites, Jobs in Restructuring," *The Wall Street Journal,* December 29, 1998.

**7.** *Layoffs and Plant Closings*

Sometimes, companies find it necessary to resort to simply laying off workers and closing down certain operations. As you will see in the next chapter, these companies find that certain plants may have reached the "shut-down" point. For example, in the same edition of *The Wall Street Journal* that contained the article on SPX, there was an article reporting that Cooper Industries, a Houston-based manufacturer of electrical tools and business products, planned to cut 3.5 percent of its workforce and to close more than a dozen manufacturing plants. Cooper has about 100 manufacturing plants around the world. Although it did not announce which plants would close, it did state that it would expand its Mexican facilities to manufacture certain products now made in the plants to be closed. Without knowing any further details, this seems to be a good illustration of item six of this list, regarding the relocation of companies to lower-wage countries.[15]

# International Application: Downsizing in Japan[16]

Although downsizing and restructuring have become practically a way of life for corporate America, the impression that most Americans have is that laying people off in Japan is simply not done. According to an article in *The Wall Street Journal,* the lifetime employment practices of large Japanese corporations may finally be changing because of the recession that has plagued the Japanese economy for most of the 1990s. In fact, in November 1998, the unemployment rate in Japan rose to 4.4 percent, matching that of the United States for the first time since Japan began keeping such statistics in 1953.

Ever since Japan's recovery after World War II, Japanese corporations prided themselves in catering not just to shareholders, but to a wider group of "stakeholders," including suppliers, borrowers, communities, and, of course, workers. As their economy worsened in the mid to late 1990s, Japanese corporations tried their best to hold on to their full-time male employees by assigning them to lower-level or "make-work" tasks. But while laying workers off is officially not done, many employers have begun to engage in de facto firings. For example, Hoya Corporation, a Tokyo optical glass maker, laid off about one-third of its work force through an early retirement program. Those who did not take the program would have faced pay cuts of 30 percent. One unnamed company supposedly ordered its older office workers to chop wood to persuade them to opt for retirement.

After the news about Japan's 4.4 percent unemployment rate was announced, Taichi Sakaiya, head of Japan's Economic Planing Agency, stated that American-style labor flexibility, "isn't necessarily desirable . . . it's inevitable."

---

[15]Anne Marie Borrego, "Cooper Industries to Cut Staff 3.5% and Close More Than a Dozen Plants," *The Wall Street Journal,* December 29, 1998.
[16]"Sign of Changed Times: Japan's Jobless Rate Rises to the U.S. Level," *The Wall Street Journal,* December 28, 1998.

## THE SOLUTION

To: Christopher Lim, Production Manager

From: Nicole Goodman, SVP of Marketing

Re: The Issue of an Adequate Supply of Spring Water

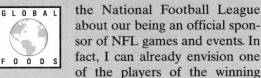

Thank you very much for your memo cautioning me on the ability of our company to find an adequate and continuing supply of spring water. In response to the issue you raised, I immediately arranged for a series of focus groups of consumers who drink bottled water. Surprisingly, our research found that people are interested in drinking *pure* water as much as they are in drinking *spring* water. The growing concern about the drinkability of tap water throughout the country is no doubt behind the increasing demand for bottled water.

I have consulted with Jim (Hartwell, SVP of manufacturing) and we believe that our solution is to bottle a water that has been subjected to "industrial strength filtering" (i.e., triple filtered), thereby enabling us to market the water as pure and even better than the water purified with home filtering devices. This purifying process, combined with elegant packaging in glasslike champagne bottles, our strong distribution system already in place for our food and carbonated soft drink products, and a strong advertising and promotion campaign, should help to establish Global Foods as a major player in the bottled water market within one year. In fact, our marketing plan calls for our gaining at least 10 percent of the total national market within the first year. We have already approached the National Football League about our being an official sponsor of NFL games and events. In fact, I can already envision one of the players of the winning Super Bowl team dousing the head coach with a bucket of *Waterpure*.

I realize that this filtered water approach will require us to make some investments in water treatment equipment. But I understand that we filter our water anyway (but not as much we would need to for our water product) before adding the flavorings and $CO_2$ to make our carbonated soft drinks. Thus, there would only be an incremental cost involved in raising the standard of purity of the water. I assure you that this marginal cost will be more than offset by the marginal revenue resulting from our sale of *Waterpure*.

As a final thought on this matter, I think it is interesting to note that when you raised the issue of the higher production costs associated with glass, we decided to go with plastic. This is an example of production and cost considerations outweighing a marketing idea. On the other hand, our decision to produce filtered water rather than spring water is an example of how the marketing objective of giving customers what they want (i.e., pure water, not necessarily natural spring water) led us to the more cost-effective method of production. I think it is great to see that marketing and production people can work so effectively together to improve the economics of the business. I look forward to working with you on this challenging new project that will help to keep the company's revenue engine humming.

## Summary

This chapter has been devoted to the analysis of the cost structure of the firm, both in the short run and the long run. In the short-run analysis, it is important to keep in mind that "behind the scenes," the law of diminishing returns causes the firm's marginal cost to increase, and that this increase in turn affects the pattern of behavior of the firm's average variable cost and average total cost. In the long-run analysis, it is important to recognize that certain factors may cause the firm's unit costs to decrease as its scale of operation increases. However, certain other factors may actually cause the unit cost to increase if the scale of operations becomes too large. In addition, other factors such as the learning curve effect and economies of scope must be taken into account in the long-run analysis of cost.

The material that has been covered in this chapter may seem rather mundane because of the great emphasis placed on defining the various cost terms used in economic analysis. However, your patience and thoroughness in reading this chapter will be rewarded when you read the next four chapters. There you will find that the material in this chapter, together with the analysis of demand presented in chapters 3 and 4, forms the core of the economic analysis of the firm. As you will learn, all the decisions involving the production and pricing of goods or services—and, in a much broader sense, the very desirability for a firm to be in a particular line of business—depend on the demand for the particular product, the cost at which the firm is able to provide this product, and the competitive structure of the market in which it is operating.

## Important Concepts (Items with * are discussed in Appendix 8B.)

**Average fixed cost (AFC):** The fixed cost per unit of output. (p. 309)

**Average total cost (AC or ATC):** The total cost per unit of output. (p. 309)

**Average variable cost (AVC):** The variable cost per unit of output. (p. 309)

**Diseconomies of scale:** The increase in the unit cost of production as the firm increases its capacity. Like economies of scale, this is considered to be a long-run phenomenon. Among the more important reasons a firm may experience rising unit costs as its scale of production increases are (1) management coordination and control problems and (2) a disproportionate increase in staff in relation to indirect labor. (p. 314)

**Economies of scale:** The reduction in the unit cost of production as the firm increases its capacity (i.e., increases all of its inputs). It is considered a long-run phenomenon. Among the reasons a firm experiences economies as its scale of production increases are (1) the ability to exact volume discounts from vendors, (2) the ability to utilize more fully specialization and division of labor, (3) the ability to justify the use of certain types of capital equipment or technology appropriate only for very large scales of production, and (4) management efficiencies resulting from an increased span of control at all levels of management. (p. 314)

**Economies of scope:** The reduction in cost resulting from the joint production of two or more goods or services. (p. 325)

***Engineering cost estimating:** A method of estimating long-run costs. Professionals familiar with production facilities calculate optimal combinations of inputs needed to produce given quantities of output. Monetary values are then assigned to obtain cost. (p. 352)

***Estimation of long-run cost functions:** Analysis that assumes that all factors, especially capital, are variable. Cross-sectional regression analysis is customarily employed in the estimation. (p. 346)

***Estimation of short-run cost functions:** An analysis in which certain factors are assumed to be fixed during the period analyzed. Time series regression analysis is customarily employed in the estimation. (p. 341)

**Experience curve:** The relationship between the unit cost of labor and all inputs associated with the production process (i.e., both direct labor, such as factory workers, and indirect labor, such as design engineers). (p. 325)

**Historical cost:** The cost incurred in a past activity (e.g., the purchase price of an asset or the cost of a project incurred up to the point at which a decision is to be made). (p. 303)

**Incremental cost:** The total cost associated with a particular decision (e.g., the cost of building an additional wing to an office building, the cost of going into the soft drink business). If incremental cost is considered on a per-unit basis, it becomes marginal cost. For example, incremental cost can be considered the change in total variable cost, whereas marginal cost can be considered the change in total variable cost divided by the change in output. (p. 304)

**Learning curve:** The relationship between the unit cost of labor and the total amount of output produced by labor that is directly associated with the production process (i.e., "direct labor"). Essentially, this concept is based on the principle that one improves with practice. The resulting productivity gains lead to a reduction in the direct labor cost of producing a unit of output. (p. 322)

**Marginal cost (MC):** The cost to a firm of producing an additional unit of an output. (p. 305)

**Opportunity cost:** The amount of subjective value forgone in choosing one activity over the next best alternative. (p. 303)

**Relevant costs:** Costs that are affected by a current decision alternative and that must therefore be taken into account in the decision. Variable costs and incremental costs are considered to be relevant costs. (p. 302)

**Sunk cost:** A cost incurred in the past that is not affected by a current decision. If a resource has no opportunity cost (i.e., it has no market value in an alternative use), it is considered to be sunk. A sunk cost is irrelevant to a current decision. (p. 304)

*** Survivorship technique:** A method for estimating long-run cost curves. The proportion of total industry output by firms of different sizes is observed over a period of time. That size segment of the industry that gains in proportion of industry output over time is deemed most efficient (lowest cost). (p. 353)

**Total cost (TC):** The total cost of production, including both total variable and total fixed costs. (p. 306)

**Total cost function:** Economic analysis considers three basic functional forms of total cost: cubic, quadratic, and linear. The microeconomic theory of the firm relies almost entirely on the cubic function, and break-even analysis generally uses the linear form. (p. 310)

**Total fixed cost (TFC):** A cost that remains constant as the level of output varies. In a short-run analysis, fixed cost is incurred even if the firm produces no output. (p. 306)

**Total variable cost (TVC):** The total cost associated with the level of output. This can also be considered the total cost to a firm of using its variable inputs. (p. 305)

## Questions

1. Define and compare the following types of cost:
   a. Sunk cost versus incremental cost
   b. Fixed cost versus variable cost
   c. Incremental cost versus marginal cost
   d. Opportunity cost versus out-of-pocket cost

2. Point out which costs in the preceding question are considered "relevant" and which are considered "irrelevant" to a business decision. Explain why.

3. Explain the relationship between a firm's short-run production function and its short-run cost function. Focus on the marginal product of an input and the marginal cost of production.

4. "If it were not for the law of diminishing returns, a firm's average cost and average variable cost would not increase in the short run." Do you agree with this statement? Explain.

5. Explain the distinction made in economic analysis between the short run and the long run.

6. Define *economies of scale.* How does this relate to returns to scale? Cite and briefly discuss the main determinants of economies of scale.

7. Define *diseconomies of scale.* Cite and briefly discuss the main determinants of this phenomenon.

8. Define *economies of scope.* Is this concept related to economies of scale? Explain.
9. Explain the relationship between the learning curve and a firm's cost function. Would economists consider the learning curve a short-run or a long-run phenomenon?
10. Define the *experience curve.* Compare its impact on a firm's cost function with that of the learning curve.
11. "Because of economies of scale, it is sometimes more cost effective for a firm to operate a large plant at less than maximum efficiency than a small plant at maximum efficiency." Do you agree with this statement? Explain.
12. When a company states its financial results in its annual report, it typically presents its income statement in the following way:

|   | Revenue |
|---|---|
| − | Cost of Goods Sold (including some depreciation) |
|   | Gross Profit |
| − | Selling, General and Administrative Expenses |
| − | Research and Development |
| − | Depreciation |
|   | Operating Profit |
| +/− | Net Interest (income and expense) |
|   | Net Profit before Income Taxes |
| − | Taxes |
|   | Net Profit after Income Taxes |

"Cost of goods sold" includes all costs directly associated with making a product or providing a service. In retail merchandising this cost is essentially the wholesale cost of goods sold.

Discuss the differences between cost of goods sold and the concept of relevant cost used in this chapter. Are there any situations in which selling, general and administrative expenses, or research and development expenses might be considered as part of a firm's relevant costs? Explain.

13. Overheard at the water cooler: "I think our company should take advantage of economies of scale by increasing our output, thereby spreading out our overhead costs." Would you agree with this statement (assuming this person is not your boss)? Explain.

Refer to Appendix 8B for help in answering questions 14 through 16.

14. Discuss the estimation of short-run cost functions. Which regression method is most frequently used, and what are some of the problems a researcher will encounter? What adjustment factors may have to be employed?
15. Discuss the estimation of long-run cost functions. Which regression method is most frequently used, and what are some of the problems a researcher will encounter? What adjustment factors may have to be employed?
16. Comment briefly on the following methods of cost estimation:
   **a.** Engineering costs
   **b.** Survivorship principle
   Discuss the strengths and shortcomings of these methods and the circumstances under which each can be applied.

## Problems

1. Based on your knowledge of the definition of the various measures of short-run cost, complete the table below.

| Q | TC | TFC | TVC | AC | AFC | AVC | MC |
|---|----|-----|-----|----|----|----|----|
| 0 | 120 | — | — | x | x | x | x |
| 1 | — | — | — | 265 | — | — | — |
| 2 | — | — | 264 | — | — | — | — |
| 3 | — | — | — | 161 | — | — | — |
| 4 | — | — | — | — | — | — | 85 |
| 5 | — | — | 525 | — | — | — | — |
| 6 | — | — | — | 120 | — | — | — |
| 7 | — | — | — | — | — | 97 | — |
| 8 | — | — | 768 | — | — | — | — |
| 9 | — | — | — | — | — | 97 | — |
| 10 | — | — | — | — | — | — | 127 |

2. Mr. Lee operates a green grocery in a building he owns in one of the outer boroughs of New York City. Recently, a large chemical firm offered him a position as a senior engineer designing plants for its Asian operations. (Mr. Lee has a master's degree in chemical engineering.) His salary plus benefits would be $95,000 per year. A recent annual financial statement of his store's operations indicates the following:

| | |
|---|---|
| Revenue | $625,000 |
| Cost of goods sold | 325,000 |
| Wages of workers | 75,000 |
| Taxes, insurance, maintenance, and depreciation on building | 30,000 |
| Interest on business loan (10%) | 5,000 |
| Other miscellaneous expenses | 15,000 |
| Profit before taxes | $175,000 |

If Mr. Lee decides to take the job, he knows that he can sell the store for $350,000 because of the goodwill built with a steady clientele of neighborhood customers and the excellent location of the building. He would still hold on to the building, however, and he knows he could earn a rent of $50,000 on this asset. If he did sell the business, assume that he would use some of the proceeds from the sale to pay off his business loan of $50,000. He could then invest the difference of $300,000 (i.e., $350,000 − $50,000) and expect to receive an annual return of 9 percent. Should Mr. Lee sell his business and go to work for the chemical company?

In answering this question, also consider the following information:

a. In his own business, Mr. Lee works between 16 and 18 hours a day, six days a week. He can expect to work between 10 and 12 hours a day, five days a week, in the chemical company.

b. Currently, Mr. Lee is assisted by his wife and his brother, both of whom receive no salary but share in the profits of the business.

c. Mr. Lee expects his salary and the profits of his business to increase at roughly the same rate over the next five years.

3. Joe enjoys fishing and goes out about 20 times per year. One day, his wife Sarah told him that fishing is simply too expensive a hobby. "I think that you should stop going fishing," she exclaimed. "I did a little calculation, and I figured that it costs us about $28.75 for every fish that you catch, because you usually catch about 20 fish per trip. Besides, I always end up having to clean them. We would be much better off buying ready-to-cook fish from the local fish market."

Comment on Sarah's remarks. Do you agree with her argument? Explain. (Following below are her cost estimates.)

| | |
|---|---:|
| Boat | $150 |
| (cost = $30,000, usable for 10 years, 20 outings per year) | |
| Boat fuel | 45 |
| Dock fees and insurance for the boat | 130 |
| (average per trip) | |
| Travel expenses to and from the lake | 25 |
| (100 miles @ $0.25 per mile: gas, oil, and tires, $0.18, and depreciation and insurance, $0.07) | |
| New fishing equipment purchases this year | 25 |
| (prorated over 20 trips) | |
| Annual fishing license | 35 |
| Bait and miscellaneous expenses | 50 |
| Food | 40 |
| Beverages | 35 |
| Traffic fine received on the way to the lake | 40 |
| Total cost per trip | $575 |

4. You are given the following cost functions:

$$TC = 100 + 60Q + 3Q^2 + 0.1Q^3$$
$$TC = 100 + 60Q + 3Q^2$$
$$TC = 100 + 60Q$$

a. Compute the average variable cost, average cost, and marginal cost for each function. Plot them on a graph.

b. In each case, indicate the point at which diminishing returns occur. Also indicate the point of maximum cost efficiency (i.e., the point of minimum average cost).

c. For each function, discuss the relationship between marginal cost and average variable cost and between marginal cost and average cost. Also discuss the relationship between average variable cost and average cost.

5. Decide whether the following statements are true or false and explain why.
   a. A decision maker must always use the historical cost of raw materials in making an economic decision.
   b. The marginal cost curve always intersects the average cost curve at the average cost's lowest point.
   c. The portion of the long-run cost curve that is horizontal indicates that the firm is experiencing neither economies nor diseconomies of scale.
   d. Marginal cost is relevant only in the short-run analysis of the firm.
   e. The rational firm will try to operate most efficiently by producing at the point where its average cost is minimized.
6. Indicate the effect that each of the following conditions will have on a firm's average variable cost curve and its average cost curve.
   a. The movement of a brokerage firm's administrative offices from New York City to New Jersey, where the average rental cost is lower
   b. The use of two shifts instead of three shifts in a manufacturing facility
   c. An agreement reached with the labor union in which wage increases are tied to productivity increases
   d. The elimination of sugar quotas (as it pertains to those firms that use a lot of sugar, such as bakeries and soft drink bottlers)
   e. Imposition of stricter environmental protection laws
7. You are given the following *long-run* cost function:

$$TC = 160Q - 20Q^2 + 1.2Q^3$$

   a. Calculate the long-run average cost and marginal cost. Plot these costs on a graph.
   b. Describe the nature of this function's scale economies. Over what range of output does economies of scale exist? Diseconomies of scale? Show this on the graph.

Refer to Appendix 8B for help in answering the following problems.

8. Over the last 50 years or so, many studies of cost curves have been published. The results of two of these are summarized here. In each case, interpret the equation and discuss the shapes of the total cost curve, the marginal cost curve, and the average cost curve.
   a. A study of a light plant over a six-month period resulted in the following regression equation:

$$Y = 16.68 + 0.125X + 0.00439X^2$$

   where $Y$ = Total fuel cost
   $X$ = Output

   b. An early study of the steel industry indicated the following results, based on annual data for 12 years.

$$Y = 182,100,000 + 55.73X$$

   where $Y$ = Total cost
   $X$ = Weighted output, in tons

   A time series analysis usually indicates a short-run cost study. Do you believe that a 12-year period is too long? Explain.
9. You have been presented with the following cost data and asked to fit a statistical cost function:

| Quantity | Total Cost |
|----------|-----------|
| 10 | 104.0 |
| 20 | 107.0 |
| 30 | 109.0 |
| 40 | 111.5 |
| 50 | 114.5 |
| 60 | 118.0 |
| 70 | 123.0 |
| 80 | 128.5 |
| 90 | 137.0 |
| 100 | 150.0 |

a. Plot the data on a graph, and draw a freehand curve that best fits the data.
b. Fit three possible statistical cost functions to the data. Use straight-line, quadratic, and cubic formulas. Do the results confirm the curve you drew in *a?*
c. Discuss the statistical results you obtained in *b.* Include in your discussion $R^2$, the coefficients, and the statistical significance of the coefficients.
d. If the data represent 10 months of production for one plant of a specific company, would you consider this to be a short-run analysis?
e. How would your answer to part *d* change if you were told that the data represent 10 different plants during a particular month of the year?

10. The economist for the Grand Corporation has estimated the company's cost function, using time series data, to be

$$TC = 50 + 16Q - 2Q^2 + 0.2Q^3$$

where TC = Total cost
    Q = Quantity produced per period

a. Plot this curve for quantities 1 to 10.
b. Calculate the average total cost, average variable cost, and marginal cost for these quantities, and plot them on another graph.
c. Discuss your results in terms of decreasing, constant, and increasing marginal costs. Does Grand's cost function illustrate all of these?

11. Discuss the following three cost functions:

$$TC = 20 + 4Q$$

$$TC = 20 + 2Q + 0.5Q^2$$

$$TC = 20 + 4Q - 0.1Q^2$$

a. Calculate all cost curves:
  • Total cost
  • Total fixed cost
  • Total variable cost
  • Average total cost
  • Average fixed cost
  • Average variable cost
  • Marginal cost

**b.** Plot these curves on graphs.

**c.** Compare the shapes of these curves and discuss their characteristics. (Particularly interesting should be the last cost function, whose shape is often found in engineering cost studies.)

12. The Central Publishing Company is about to publish its first textbook in managerial economics. It is now in the process of estimating costs. It expects to produce 10,000 copies during its first year. The following costs have been estimated to correspond to the expected copies.

|     |                             |          |
| --- | --------------------------- | -------- |
| a.  | Paper stock                 | $8,000   |
| b.  | Typesetting                 | $15,000  |
| c.  | Printing                    | $50,000  |
| d.  | Art (including graphs)      | $9,000   |
| e.  | Editing                     | $20,000  |
| f.  | Reviews                     | $3,000   |
| g.  | Promotion and advertising   | $12,000  |
| h.  | Binding                     | $22,000  |
| i.  | Shipping                    | $10,000  |

In addition to the preceding costs, it expects to pay the authors a 13 percent royalty and its salespeople a 3 percent commission. These percentages will be based on the publisher's price of $48 per textbook.

Some of the preceding costs are fixed and others are variable. The average variable costs are expected to be constant. While 10,000 copies is the projected volume, the book could sell anywhere between 0 and 20,000 copies.

Using the preceding data,

**a.** Write equations for total cost, average total cost, average variable cost, and marginal cost.

**b.** Draw the cost curves for quantities from 0 to 20,000 (in intervals of 2,000).

13. The Big Horn Corporation commissioned an economic consultant to estimate the company's cost function. The consultant collected a large amount of data for a number of years from the books of the corporation and came up with the following equation:

$$TC = 170 + 22Q + 1.5Q^2$$

where TC = Total cost (in thousands)

　　　　　$Q$ = Quantity produced per period

**a.** Plot this curve for quantities 1 through 15.

**b.** Calculate the average total cost, average variable cost, and marginal cost, and plot them on another graph.

**c.** Discuss your results in terms of decreasing, constant, and increasing marginal costs. Does Big Horn's cost function illustrate all of these?

# Take It to the Net

We invite you to visit the Keat/Young page on the Prentice Hall Web site at:

**http://www.prenhall.com/keat**

for additional resources.

## Appendix 8A

## A Mathematical Restatement of the Short-Run Cost Function

The general form of the short-run cost function is

$$TC = f(Q) \tag{8A.1}$$

where TC = Total cost
Q = Output

As stated in this chapter, three specific forms of this function are used in economic analysis: the cubic, the quadratic, and the linear. Microeconomic theory relies primarily on the cubic equation because it encompasses the possibility of increasing returns to a factor as well as diminishing returns. The quadratic form of the total cost function implies that only the law of diminishing returns affects the short-run relationship between a firm's output and its variable input. The linear form indicates that neither increasing nor diminishing returns to a factor take place in the short run as the firm uses additional units of its variable input. In this appendix, we use calculus to state the cubic equation, the one most frequently used in economic theory.

Consider the following equation (which, incidentally is the one used to generate the cost data in Table 8.2 and Figure 8.2):

$$TC = 100 + 60Q - 5Q^2 + 0.7Q^3 \tag{8A.2}$$

The total fixed-cost component of this equation is simply the constant term, 100. The balance of the right-hand side gives us total variable cost. The average and marginal costs can be derived from Equation (8A.2) using the definitions provided in the chapter, which are restated in the following equations:

$$\text{Average fixed cost (AFC)} = \frac{TFC}{Q} = \frac{100}{Q} \tag{8A.3}$$

$$\text{Average total cost (AC)} = \frac{TC}{Q} = \frac{100}{Q} + 60 - 5Q + 0.7Q^2 \tag{8A.4}$$

$$\text{Average varible cost (AVC)} = \frac{TVC}{Q} = 60 - 5Q + 0.7Q^2 \tag{8A.5}$$

$$\text{Marginal cost (MC)} = dTC/dQ = 60 - 10Q + 2.1Q^2 \tag{8A.6}$$

Notice that to find marginal cost, we simply took the first derivative of the total cost function stated in Equation (8A.2).

## Appendix 8B

## The Estimation of Cost

The literature of empirical economic inquiry deals heavily with estimation of cost curves. This work has its origins with Joel Dean, who wrote the first textbook on managerial economics, and conducted many of the studies, dating back to the 1930s.

As in the case of production functions, we are interested in estimating cost functions both in the short run and in the long run. The purposes of the estimation differ between the two functions. The short-run function helps to define short-run marginal costs and thus assists the manager in determining output and prices. In the long run, the decision that a firm faces involves building the most efficient size of plant. That determination will depend on the existence of scale economies and diseconomies.

Short-run cost functions (like short-run production functions) assume that at least one factor is fixed. Thus, cost is influenced by the quantity produced as changes occur in the variable factor. To estimate such a short-run function, we must find data in which quantity and costs change while certain factors change and others remain fixed. As in the section on production functions, we can make the simplifying assumption that in a two-input model, labor changes while capital remains fixed.

In investigating short-run cost functions using regression analysis, researchers have most frequently employed the time series technique with data for a specific plant or firm over time. It is important that when time series data are collected, the period over which observations are taken is limited to a relatively short span. A major reason is that the size of the plant or firm, as well as technology, should not change significantly during the time interval used in a short-run cost function. To conduct a meaningful analysis, there must be a sufficient number of observations, and there must be variations in production from observation period to observation period.[17] Thus, each observation period, where possible, should be limited to a month, and sometimes even a shorter period (a week or two weeks).

Long-run cost functions—the planning functions—allow for changes in all factors including plant size (or capital investment in general). Time series regression analysis could be used if changes in plant size occurred during the period studied. But such changes would probably occur in limited numbers at certain times, and would not provide a continuous series. For this reason, most studies of long-run cost functions have employed cross-sectional analysis. Observations are recorded in a specific time period (e.g., one year) for a number of different plants of different sizes with different amounts of inputs and outputs. We will discuss short-term and long-term analyses separately.

# The Estimation of Short-Run Cost Functions

### PROBLEMS AND ADJUSTMENTS
#### Economic versus Accounting Costs

Most empirical studies of cost functions have utilized accounting data that record the actual costs and expenses on a historical basis. However, decision-making data—

---

[17]Ideally, these changes in quantities produced should occur under relatively normal circumstances rather than due to some abnormal upheaval. Thus, production cuts because of plant damage or a strike, for instance, may not produce valid data.

economic data—should also include opportunity costs. No amount of adjustment will ever completely reconcile these concepts, but certain corrections can be made.

- Changes in prices of labor, materials, and other inputs must be adjusted so that current prices are used.[18]
- Costs that are not a function of output should be excluded. Because we are dealing with short-run cost functions, fixed costs should not have an influence on pricing or output decisions. Many analysts try to isolate only the direct costs of production, omitting fixed overhead expenses. But care must be taken to include all expenses that vary with output in the cost calculations.
- Closely allied to the previous point is the question of depreciation. Accountants usually record depreciation on a time-related basis. Depreciation is often not related to actual usage but follows accounting convention as adapted to tax rules. If "use" depreciation can be isolated from the accounting data, only that portion should be included in costs. But it must be kept in mind that recorded depreciation is based on the original cost of the equipment, whereas economic depreciation should be based on replacement value.

The problems that arise in the **estimation of short-run cost functions** because of differences between accounting and economic costs are the most difficult to solve. In most cases, some type of compromise is necessary. No definitive advice can be given here to prospective researchers. We can only point out the significant issues and suggest some possibly appropriate adjustments. What is done in the final analysis depends on the data available and the ability of the investigator to make the corrections.

### Rate Changes

In addition to inflationary changes in the prices of various inputs, costs can also change due to variations in tax rates, Social Security contributions, labor insurance costs (unemployment insurance or worker's compensation rates), and various benefit coverages that affect costs. Because most of these rate changes are not based on quantity produced, they should be excluded.

### Output Homogeneity

The problems encountered in cost estimation are similar to those discussed for the production function. The analysis is easiest when output is relatively homogeneous. If only one product is produced in the plant, the quantity produced (or shipped) can be handled in a rather uncomplicated manner. But if there are several products moving through the plant simultaneously, some weighting apparatus must be employed to obtain the quantity produced.[19]

---

[18]Since different inputs may incur different relative price changes, some factor substitution may result over time. It can only be hoped that such effects will not be significant, since they are extremely difficult, if not impossible, to remove.

[19]If a weighting scheme involving costs or direct inputs for each of the products is utilized, then, in a way, we are employing costs to determine output and then measuring costs as a function of this output. In other words, we are introducing a dependency into the relationship between costs and output, when we are really trying to determine the relationship between the two. This presents a serious problem. But again, as long as accounting and production records of a firm are employed, there is no easy way out of this dilemma.

## Timing of Costs

In many cases, costs and the service performed to create these costs do not occur at the same time. For instance, a machine that is in use continuously may be scheduled for maintenance periodically. In the airline industry, for example, major maintenance on engines is performed after a given number of flight hours. When such timing differences occur, care must be taken to spread the maintenance costs over the period of machine usage.

## Accounting Changes

When a time series analysis using accounting data is performed, it is very important that the researcher ascertain whether changes in accounting methods, such as depreciation methods and recording of development expenses, have occurred during the period included in the study. Such changes must be adjusted to reflect uniformity in the measurements over time.

Given all the warnings about the problems that can be encountered in empirical cost estimation, you may have been persuaded that no useful conclusions can be obtained from such studies. Actually, such difficulties have not turned away many economists. Starting with Dean in the 1930s and continuing until today, economic journals contain many articles investigating statistical cost functions. The studies have also been summarized in articles as well as books.

## THE SHAPES OF SHORT-RUN COST FUNCTIONS

Earlier in this chapter, three different specifications of cost functions were shown. Each represents a possible shape of the cost curves. The economist, after collecting and adjusting the data, will use one of these specifications to measure the relationship between cost and output. Other statistical functions could be employed (such as the Cobb-Douglas power function), but the three shapes are the ones most frequently encountered in statistical studies.

Figures 8.4*a* and *b* represent the normal theoretical function, which exhibits both decreasing and increasing marginal and average costs. The curves can be drawn in terms of total costs or unit costs. Figure 8.4*a* shows total cost.[20] The mathematical function that describes such a curve is a polynomial function of the third degree, that is, a cubic function:

$$TC = a + bQ - cQ^2 + dQ^3$$

where TC = Total cost
$Q$ = Total output

The negative sign preceding the quadratic term of the equation causes the total cost first to increase at a decreasing rate (decreasing marginal costs). Then the cubic term causes

---

[20]If only variable costs are estimated, this curve would be the variable cost curve. Theoretically, it should begin at the origin since there are no variable costs when production is zero. However, when the curves are statistically estimated, even if only variable costs are included, the line will most likely intercept the *Y*-axis at a point other than zero. From the investigator's viewpoint, this is not terribly important, since most of the observations included in the statistical estimate will not be anywhere near zero production. The intercept thus turns out to be meaningless.

it to increase at an increasing rate (increasing marginal costs). The average and marginal costs shown in Figure 8.4b can be expressed as follows:[21]

$$AC = a/Q + b - cQ + dQ^2$$
$$MC = b - 2cQ + 3dQ^2$$

If the data do not quite fit the cubic function, the quadratic function can be tested. The three equations in this case are as follows:

$$TC = a + bQ + cQ^2$$
$$AC = a/Q + b + cQ$$
$$MC = b + 2cQ$$

As can be seen in Figures 8.4c and d, the shapes of these functions differ substantially from the cubic function. The total cost curve consists of only that section that increases at an increasing rate. Thus, there are no decreasing marginal costs (increasing marginal product) in this construction. This can be seen in Figure 8.4d, where the MC curve is a straight line increasing at all points (i.e., not U-shaped).

A linear total cost function can also be fitted.[22] The three equations take the following form:

$$TC = a + bQ$$
$$AC = a/Q + b$$
$$MC = b$$

Figures 8.4e and f show the curves based on the linear form.[23] Note that the law of diminishing marginal returns has been eliminated. Each additional unit's cost is the constant, b. Thus, this specification of the cost curve exhibits strictly constant marginal costs. This type of analysis does not appeal intuitively to an economist, who knows that if units of a variable factor are continually added to a fixed factor (plant), somewhere at higher production levels unit costs must rise.

These three specifications can fit various types of cost data. But even when a really good set of data is available to the investigator, chances are that the range of observations will be rather limited and will tend to cluster around a midpoint. Very seldom will we have data corresponding to near-zero production, and very seldom will data be given for production equaling or exceeding theoretical capacity. Thus, the statistical results economists obtain may not reflect the behavior of costs at the two extremes of the curve. In the following discussion of some of the empirical work that has been performed in the past, we find that this is precisely the case.

---

[21]The average cost curve is obtained by dividing TC by $Q$. To obtain the marginal cost, some elementary calculus is needed. The marginal cost is the first derivative of the total cost function with respect to $Q$.

[22]In chapter 11, on break-even analysis, we use this function exclusively.

[23]The average total cost curve in this case declines continuously and approaches the marginal cost curve asymptotically. The reason for this, in the formula, is that the first term $a/Q$, decreases as $Q$ increases and the second term, $b$, is a constant. If we were dealing exclusively with variable costs, where the $a$ term does not exist (because costs are zero when production is zero), then $AVC = b$ and the marginal and average variable costs equal each other. This, of course, must be true, since if each additional (marginal) unit costs the same, then the average variable cost of each unit does not change and must equal the marginal cost.

## A SAMPLING OF SHORT-RUN COST STUDIES

There is a large number of cost studies from which we could choose for purposes of illustration. We have selected three studies covering different industries and different time periods. Although some of the estimating procedures have become somewhat more sophisticated over time, the studies all used time series regression analysis.

### The Hosiery Mill

One of several studies conducted by Joel Dean in the 1930s and 1940s focused on a mill of a large hosiery manufacturer.[24] Its equipment was highly mechanized and its labor skilled.

Data for 54 months from 1935 to 1939 were employed. During this period, the size of the plant did not change, and the equipment remained approximately the same. Production during these months varied from zero to near physical capacity. Direct labor, indirect labor, and overhead costs were included. These costs were adjusted by factor price indexes. Output was a weighted index of individual products, and the weights were based on relative labor costs. The result, using a linear regression form, was

$$TC = 2{,}935.59 + 1.998Q$$

where TC = Total cost
$Q$ = Output, in pairs of hosiery

The results were statistically significant, and the correlation coefficient was 0.973 (and, therefore, the coefficient of determination, $R^2$, was 0.947).

Quadratic and cubic equations were also calculated but did not show a good fit to the data. Thus Dean's analysis points to the existence of a straight-line total cost curve, a decreasing average total cost curve, and constant marginal costs.

### Road Passenger Transport

In the United Kingdom J. Johnston collected data from one of the larger transportation companies, with a fleet of some 1,300 vehicles, that operated some 45 million car miles per year.[25] The data were grouped into four-week periods over three years, 1949 to 1952. Production exhibited a marked seasonal pattern, so varying production amounts per period could be observed.

The costs included all the vehicle operations (wages, clothing, gasoline, oil, and tires), maintenance, depreciation (based on mileage), variable overhead, and a minor amount of fixed overhead. Output was measured in car miles during the period. The data were adjusted by individual price indexes where price changes had occurred.

Again, a straight-line total cost function provided the best fit:

$$TC = 0.65558 + 0.4433Q$$

where $Q$ represents car miles, in millions. The correlation coefficient was 0.95. So, as in Dean's study, the total cost curve was a straight line with constant marginal costs.

---

[24]Joel Dean, *Statistical Cost Functions of a Hosiery Mill,* Studies in Business Administration, 11, 4, Chicago: University of Chicago Press, 1941. This study and others have been reprinted in a volume of Dean's work, *Statistical Cost Estimation,* Bloomington: Indiana University Press, 1976.
[25]J. Johnston, *Statistical Cost Analysis,* New York: McGraw-Hill 1960, pp. 74–86.

## Plastic Containers

In a study conducted for 10 different products moving through a plant at the same time, 21 monthly observations were taken during the period of January 1966 to September 1967.[26] During this period plant capacity was fixed, and all input prices were also fixed by contract. Only direct costs of labor, machinery, and materials were included, so no allocation problems for overhead items had to be handled. The firm reported wide production fluctuations during the period, with several observations being somewhat above 90 percent of capacity level.

Time series regression analysis was calculated for each of the three functional forms. Again, the straight-line function exhibited the best fit for each of the 10 products. The squared and cubed terms were not statistically significant. Tests to investigate cost interrelationships among the products showed no influence.

The authors also tested for the firm's aggregate cost-output relationship. The total physical output was obtained by weighting each product by its base-period price. Again, the best results were given by a straight-line equation,

$$TC = 56{,}393 + 3.368Q$$

with the *t*-test significant at the 1 percent level and the $R^2$ a respectable 0.89.

## MARGINAL COST: U-SHAPED OR CONSTANT?

Each of the three studies just cited concluded that in the short run, the total cost curve is a linear function of production and that the marginal cost is constant. In addition to the hosiery mill, Dean also studied a furniture factory and a leather belt shop. Johnston conducted investigations into a food-processing firm and coal mining, among others. Studies of the steel industry, cement industry, and electric power were also done. Most of these came to conclusions similar to those of the three studies we described briefly. Actually, some of the researchers found decreasing marginal costs to be the rule.

Does that mean that economists should revise their thinking about U-shaped average and marginal cost curves? Although these findings should cause economists to pause and do some additional thinking, the results of these studies—even over the relatively long period of 50 or more years—can be reconciled with the traditional shapes of cost curves:

1. The data employed in most of the studies concentrated on output levels that were limited in range. Thus, even though in some cases production may have taken place at about 90 percent of capacity, it is quite possible that plants are built and equipped in such a way that unit costs are relatively constant over a fairly long range of outputs. The cost curves that economists draw, as we have seen in this chapter, show very distinct minimum points to show their importance to students of elementary economics. However, the bottom of the curve may represent a fairly wide interval, and unit costs may rise (quite sharply) only when physical capacity is reached. Figure 8B.1 shows an average cost curve (*A*) that most students have seen drawn on blackboards. But curve *B*, which still conforms to the economist's thinking about rising unit costs, may be the one that is more true to life. The minimum point of this curve is not as low as that on curve *A*, but there is a relatively

[26]Ronald S. Coot and David A. Walker, "Short-run Cost Functions of a Multi-product Firm," *Journal of Industrial Economics,* April 1970, pp. 118–28.

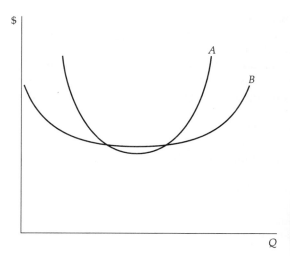

**FIGURE 8B.1** Theoretical versus Realistic Average Cost Curve

wide range of outputs on curve *B* where costs remain low—lower than for curve *A*. As production fluctuates from period to period, output is more likely to take place on the relatively constant unit cost segment on curve *B* than at curve *A*'s narrowly defined minimum.

2. Many economists explain straight-line cost curves by pointing out that although theory requires capital inputs to be fixed in the short run, they really are not. For instance, when production increases, a firm can easily set up an additional assembly line to keep the fixed/variable input ratio constant. Thus, since the fixed factor is utilized in a fixed proportion with the variable factor, increasing marginal cost will not necessarily occur.

3. Regression analysis is not a perfect tool. If most of the observations fall into an intermediate output range, there may just not be a sufficient number of observations at the extremes to convert a linear fit to a curvilinear one.

Thus, although economists would certainly feel more gratified if empirical work were to confirm their theories, the evidence of the studies is not so overwhelming that an immediate reevaluation of microeconomic theory is necessary. Further, real-life data seem to be consistent with the existence of upward-sloping marginal cost curves. We learned earlier that the upward-sloping short-run supply curve of a firm or industry is based on the existence of an upward-sloping marginal cost curve. The fact that rising demand for a product raises the price and causes an increase in quantity supplied in the short run is evidence of the existence of an upward-sloping supply curve that is theoretically explained by the existence of an upward-sloping marginal cost curve. Thus, despite some of the empirical findings, it appears that corporate managers act as if they were confronted by a marginal cost curve of the kind described by economic theory.

## The Estimation of Long-Run Cost Functions

The **estimation of long-run cost functions** presents some new challenges. As you will recall, in the economic long run, all costs are variable. That means that capital (plant and equipment), which is ordinarily held fixed in the short run, is now permitted to change.

As a matter of fact, it is precisely the goal of long-run cost analysis to trace unit costs for different sizes of plant and different amounts of equipment capacity. Our interest in long-run costs is to investigate the existence of returns to scale.

The question of costs in relation to size is important not only for planning decisions regarding plant or firm expansion. Firms must also consider costs when deciding on potential mergers. Will the synergy of the new units indicate a potential decrease in unit costs as a function of size?

When we speak of the long run, we may imagine that such research requires data for a given plant or firm over a considerable interval of time, so that changes in capacity can be observed. But even if such data are available, it is also important that technology is kept constant over this time period. Such a static situation would be extremely difficult to find.

Therefore, most long-run cost studies have employed cross-sectional regression analysis. This method has several advantages:

1. Observations are recorded for different plants (or firms) at a given point of time. Since different plants generally come in different sizes, the independent variable, quantity of output, can vary over relatively large ranges.
2. Since all observations are taken at a given point in time (e.g., one year), the technology is known and does not change. Under ideal circumstances, each plant will utilize that level of technology, within the known state of the art, that is most efficient for that specific plant. But this ideal is usually not reached, as is explained in the following discussion.
3. Adjusting the various costs for inflation or other price changes is not necessary under cross-sectional analysis. If annual observations are used for the sample of plants, an average figure for costs (e.g., per labor hour or ton of material) will be satisfactory. Only under conditions of very severe inflation—hyperinflation—would the averaging of annual costs become a significant problem, but any studies undertaken under such conditions would surely be of dubious quality in any case.

The use of the cross-sectional technique also creates some difficulties of which the researcher must be well aware. Just a few of these are the following:

1. Inflationary problems may be avoided by abandoning the time series method, but a new problem is introduced. Since the observations are taken from plants (or firms) in different geographical areas, we may encounter interregional cost differences in labor rates, utility bills, material costs, or transportation costs, for example. Adjustments to some common base must be made. But if relative prices of inputs differ, then the combination of inputs in a particular location may be a function of these relative differences. By adjusting prices to a specific benchmark, we may be obliterating the conscious choice made by management in a particular location based on relative prices of different inputs.
2. Although, as stated, the known state of the art for each firm is the same, it is not necessarily true that all plants are, at a given point of time, operating at the optimal level of technology. The assumption that each plant is operating most efficiently for its production level does not necessarily hold. This can be illustrated by drawing the familiar envelope curve. In Figure 8B.2 an envelope curve, *ABC,* is drawn. This long-run average cost curve represents all the optimal points of production. Point *B* is the minimum cost point, which represents the most efficient

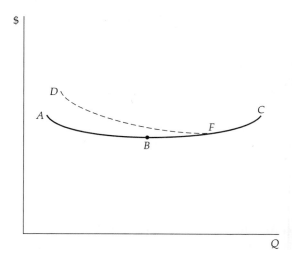

**FIGURE 8B.2** Optimal and Suboptimal Cost Curves

plant size. If, however, the plants in the sample do not operate at optimal points for any level of production, we may end up with observations along a curve such as *DF,* which will tend to be above the optimal curve, *ABC,* and which indicates not only a level but also a slope quite different from the optimal cost curve. There really is no way to correct for this potential error completely.

3. If accounting data are used to make the estimates, it is very important that the economist verify that there are no significant differences in the way costs are recorded on the firms' books of account. Although different depreciation procedures are the most important cause of discrepancies, varying inventory valuation methods and amortization of other expenses can lead to substantial distortions. The best possible adjustments must always be made.

4. Different companies may pay their factors differently. This is most important in the case of labor costs. Total labor costs can comprise varying fractions of wages and benefits (such as vacation time, holidays, and medical care). In some cases, employees may receive part of their income in stock, or stock may be sold to them at a discounted price. The estimator must be certain to include all relevant costs.

## A SAMPLING OF LONG-RUN COST STUDIES

As in the case of short-run costs, a large number of inquiries into the properties of long-run costs have been conducted over the last 50 years or so. A small number of these will be mentioned here to provide a flavor of method and results.

### Shoe Store Chain

In one of the early studies conducted by Joel Dean, the sample comprised 55 metropolitan area shoe stores owned by one firm.[27] "Such units possess the important ad-

---

[27]Joel Dean and R. Warren James, *The Long-Run Behavior of Costs in a Chain of Shoe Stores: A Statistical Analysis,* Studies in Business Administration, 12, 3, University of Chicago Press, 1942, reprinted in Dean, *Statistical Cost Estimation,* pp. 324–60.

vantage of being almost identical with respect to records, merchandise, layout, personnel and management methods."[28] Pairs of shoes were the output. Costs were mainly composed of selling expenses (including wages), handling expenses, and building expenses. Corporate allocations were omitted. The study was based on annual data for 1937 and 1938. Quadratic total cost curves gave the best fit for both years, indicating a U-shaped average cost curve and a rising marginal cost curve.

### Building Societies

In the United Kingdom, building societies are roughly equivalent to savings and loan associations in the United States. Johnston studied 217 such enterprises in the year 1953.[29] The companies were grouped into six size categories based on total annual revenue.

Johnston found that a U-shaped long-run cost curve existed for these enterprises. Cost in this study was measured as a ratio of management expenses to revenue. Middle-size societies were found to have the lowest ratio. However, when Johnston segregated the 217 observations into 149 societies with no branches and 68 with branches, somewhat different results appeared. Most of the firms in the former group were concentrated in the four lower size categories and most firms in the latter group were in the top four. When the nonbranch societies and the branch societies were analyzed separately, the former firms appeared to have a declining cost ratio whereas the companies with branches had a constant ratio. Thus, the appearance of a U-shaped average cost curve and, therefore, economies of scale at the low end and diseconomies of scale at the high end, were the result of two separate underlying patterns.

### Electric Utilities

The electric utility industry has been a frequent target of economists studying cost curves. Output is fairly easily defined (electricity produced), and the United States has a large number of independently owned utilities of many different sizes. Since these companies must regularly deal with state regulatory commissions in rate cases, they collect large volumes of data pertaining to costs and revenues. Utilities have also been observed to have constant productivity improvements and technological progress. The study summarized here was performed using 1971 data for 74 utilities.[30] Because the data are for 1971, this study rules out any effects of pollution control equipment on costs.

The major costs were best described by a quadratic function, which led to a U-shaped average cost curve. The cost coefficients were statistically highly significant. The authors identified the intervals for which economies of scale existed and the appropriate minimum cost point. They found that diseconomies of scale appeared beyond moderate firm size. Many earlier studies of utilities found economies of scale throughout the range of observations. This study, as well as another one for the year 1970[31] found the possibility of scale diseconomies in firms of larger size.

---

[28]Ibid., p. 325.
[29]Johnston, *Statistical Cost Analysis*, pp. 103–5.
[30]David A. Huettner and John H. Landon, "Electric Utilities: Scale Economies and Diseconomies," *Southern Economic Journal*, April 1978, pp. 883–912.
[31]L. R. Christensen and W. H. Greene, "Economies of Scale in U.S. Electric Power Generation," *Journal of Political Economy*, 84, 4 (August 1976), pp. 655–76.

### Financial Institutions

A more recent article reviewed some 13 studies that attempted to estimate economies of scale and economies of scope for credit unions, savings and loan associations, and commercial banks.[32] Economies of scale are defined as those associated with firm size, whereas economies of scope relate to the joint production of two or more products. "Economies of scale exist if per unit or average production costs decline as output rises. Economies of scope arise if two or more products can be jointly produced at a lower cost than is incurred in their independent production.[33] Each of the studies used a logarithmic function and employed similar measures of economies. The author summarized the results of these 13 studies as follows:

- Overall economies of scale appear to exist only at low levels of output, with diseconomies at larger output levels.
- There is no consistent evidence of global economies of scope.
- There is some evidence of cost complementarities (product-specific economies of scope).
- The results appear to exist generally across the three types of institutions studied as well as across different data sets and product and cost definitions.

### Bottling Plants

A few years ago, the authors received access to some confidential cost and production data for more than 30 bottling plants of a large company. The plant sizes and their production varied widely, and thus, the data for a specific time period lent themselves to a cross-sectional regression analysis. It was our aim to investigate the potential existence of an optimum plant size.

A straight-line total cost function obtained fairly good results. The $R^2$ equaled 0.62 (quite high for a cross-sectional analysis) and the slope coefficient was statistically significant. Surprisingly, when a cubic function was fitted, the results improved considerably. With the equation $TC = a + bQ + cQ^2 + dQ^3$, we obtained the following answers:

$$R^2 = 0.70 \qquad F\text{-statistic} = 24.87$$

|          | a     | b     | c      | d     |
|----------|-------|-------|--------|-------|
| Estimate | 0.078 | 0.891 | −0.096 | 0.004 |
| *t*-test |       | 3.653 | −2.240 | 1.910 |

The *t*-tests for coefficients *b* and *c* are significant, for *d,* slightly low. The *c* coefficient is negative, indicating that the total cost curve would first increase at a decreasing rate and then at an increasing rate—resulting in a U-shaped unit cost curve.

Another piece of data was available—the percentages of canned and bottled sodas. Because the cost of cans was lower than of bottles, we included the percent of canned soda production as another independent variable, with the following results:

$$R^2 = 0.83 \qquad F\text{-statistic} = 37.45$$

---

[32]Jeffrey A. Clark, "Economies of Scale and Scope at Depository Financial Institutions: A Review of the Literature," *Economic Review,* Federal Reserve Bank of Kansas City, September/October 1988, pp. 16–33.
[33]Ibid., p. 17.

|           | *a*      | *b*    | *c*      | *d*    | *e*      |
|-----------|----------|--------|----------|--------|----------|
| Estimate  | −0.177   | 1.316  | −0.146   | 0.006  | −1.575   |
| *t*-test  |          | 6.358  | −4.229   | 3.597  | −4.823   |

All *t*-tests are now significant and coefficient *e*, the percent of can production, has the correct (negative) sign, showing that production costs decrease as the proportion of cans increases.

Granted that we used only data for one period and that we did not refine these data, we still obtained some good results indicating a U-shaped average cost curve and an optimal plant size.

### Empirical Long-Run Cost Studies: Summary of Findings

Some of the studies just summarized show the possible existence of diseconomies of scale for larger firm and plant size. However, a majority of the empirically estimated functions suggest the existence of scale economies up to a point. As output increases to a substantial size, these economies rapidly disappear and are replaced by constant returns for long intervals of output. Most studies have not found the existence of declining average costs at very large quantities. And findings of diseconomies of scale for high rates of production are rather rare.

## TWO OTHER METHODS OF LONG-RUN COST ESTIMATING

The use of regression analysis in long-run (as well as short-run) cost estimating involves the use of accounting data. At the beginning of the discussion of cost estimating, we issued a warning that accounting magnitudes may not correspond to economic measures. However, all the analyses just reviewed employed accounting data and, through various adjustment procedures, attempted to make the numbers correspond more closely to the cost concepts meaningful to the economist. In addition, economists have tried to use methods that are not dependent on numbers drawn from companies' accounting records. Two techniques of analysis will be discussed briefly: the engineering cost method and the survivorship technique.

### Engineering Cost Estimates

Engineering costs are based on a thorough understanding of inputs and outputs and their relationships. Knowledgeable professionals will calculate the quantity of inputs needed to produce any quantity of outputs. These calculations are based on optimal assumptions (i.e., the largest output for a given combination of inputs). This is really a production function. From here it is a relatively easy step to apply monetary quantities to the inputs to arrive at costs.

The advantages of such a method are quite obvious. Technology is held constant. There are no problems of inflation. Problems of changing output mix are eliminated. As a matter of fact, such calculations are often made by corporations planning to introduce a new product. While the market research and product forecasting departments concentrate on preparing estimates of sales at different prices, cost estimators in a corporation (engineers and others) prepare estimates of costs for different levels of output. Then members of the pricing department take all the available data and calculate profitability at different prices and levels of output. It is through this process that product prices are obtained.

Although the **engineering cost estimating** technique avoids some of the pitfalls of regression analysis, it suffers from some problems of its own. First of all, the estimates represent what engineers and cost estimators believe cost should be, not necessarily what they actually will be. Since they are really forecasts, calculations may omit certain components that contribute to costs. Further, most of the time, only direct output costs are estimated. Other costs that may be directly associated with the product (such as some portion of overhead and direct selling expenses) are not included, or if they are, it is through some rather arbitrary allocation. Often such estimates are made on the basis of pilot plant operations and do not consider actual production, which may be attended by bottlenecks and other problems, causing costs to differ from those estimated.

Generally, engineering cost estimates will show declining unit costs up to a point and substantially flat unit costs at higher production quantities. The possible existence of diseconomies of scale is usually ignored.

It is quite possible for a study to combine engineering cost estimates for some segments of costs with utilization of accounting data for others. Such an analysis was performed some years ago, when a group of economists at the Transportation Center at Northwestern University published a forecast of aircraft prices.[34] One important step in arriving at the forecast was the calculation of aircraft operating costs. These were computed for a large number of different types of aircraft and utilized both actual data and engineering estimates. Crew salaries were calculated from a number of union contracts and compared with historical data to arrive at an average. Maintenance costs were calculated from a formula supplied by the Air Transport Association. Fuel consumption was obtained from engineering curves produced by aircraft manufacturers and airlines, and reconciled with some actual published data. Other costs (employee benefits, landing fees, liability and property damage insurance) were estimated in similar ways. The resulting curves reflected direct operating costs per aircraft mile for a series of different stage length categories ranging from 0–200 miles to 2,500 miles and over. The resulting cost curves generally exhibited a downward slope up to the limit of the stage length that each of the aircraft could fly nonstop.

### Survivorship Principle

A prominent American economist and Nobel Prize winner, George J. Stigler, developed an intriguing method for estimating long-run costs.[35] Stigler felt that the use of accounting data, with all their distortions and subsequent need for adjustments, made the validity of cost estimation based on such data questionable. His method was to observe an industry over time, categorize the firms in the industry by size (measured as a percent of total industry capacity or output), and then arrive at a conclusion regarding cost efficiency based on the relative growth or decline of these size categories. His results for the steel industry (using data for 1930, 1938, and 1951) showed that medium-size firms (defined as between 2.5 percent and 25 percent of industry capacity) appeared to have gained in share of total industry output over the 21-year period, from 35

---

[34]Stephen P. Sobotka, Paul G. Keat, Constance Schnabel, and Margaret Wiesenfelder, *Prices of Used Commercial Aircraft,* 1959–1965, Evanston, IL: Transportation Center at Northwestern University, 1959.
[35]George J. Stigler, "The Economies of Scale," *Journal of Law and Economics,* 1, 1 (October 1958), pp. 54–81.

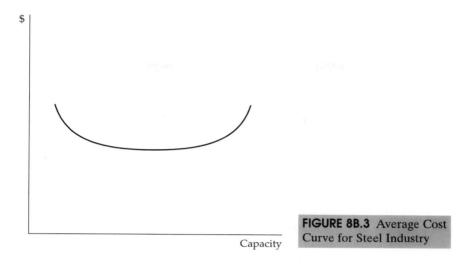

**FIGURE 8B.3** Average Cost Curve for Steel Industry

percent to 46 percent of total, whereas small firms (less than 2.5 percent of capacity) and large firms (actually just one firm, with over 25 percent of capacity) lost market share. Stigler concluded the existence of a U-shaped long-run average cost curve whose path first showed net economies of scale, then constant returns, and finally diseconomies of scale. Figure 8B.3 illustrates Stigler's conclusions.

Economists have continued to use the **survivorship technique** to investigate economies of scale. For example, a later study by R. P. Rogers examined economies of scale in steel manufacturing in the United States. The author measured the distribution of production in conventional steel mills in 1976 and 1987. He classified steel mills into four size categories by their annual capacity (1–1.49 million tons, 1.5–4.5 million tons, 4.5–7.5 million tons, and over 7.5 million tons). He then examined these four categories for the proportion of total capacity in the two years. He found that the 4.5–7.5 MT category increased its market share considerably. The results were consistent with a previous study by D. G. Tarr, who had used the engineering cost approach to estimate the minimum optimal size (MOS) of a steel mill. Tarr had found the MOS plant to be of 6 MT capacity, which is the midpoint of Rogers' findings.[36]

This survivorship principle is intuitively appealing due to its simplicity and avoidance of unreliable data. However, it also suffers some serious limitations. It is of no help in measuring costs for planning purposes. It merely tells us which company size appears to be more efficient; it says nothing about relative costs. Further, it implicitly assumes that the industry is highly competitive, so that survival and prosperity are solely a function of efficient use of resources and not of market power or the erection of barriers to entry. Changing technology and inflation over a long span can also cause distortions. As time passes, the structure of an industry can change in such a way that firms of certain size are favored over others.

---

[36]R. P. Rogers, "The Minimum Optimal Steel Plant and the Survivor Technique of Cost Estimation," *Atlantic Economic Journal,* 21 (September 1993), pp. 30–37; D. G. Tarr, "The Minimum Optimal Scale Steel Plant in the Mid-1970's," *FTC Working Paper, 3,* March 1997; D. G. Tarr, "The Minimum Optimal Scale Steel Plant," *Atlantic Economic Journal,* 12, 2 (1984), p. 122.

Moreover, although Stigler's analysis of the steel industry showed a U-shaped cost curve, he could not obtain similar results for the automobile industry, where the survivor cost curve showed declining and constant portions but there was no evidence of diseconomies of scale at high production quantities.

## Summary

Accounting data have generally been used to investigate short-run and long-run cost functions. These data present the researcher with a host of problems since the economic and accounting definitions of costs can differ substantially. Also, depending on how the data are collected, adjustments for price changes, geographical differentials, and other variations must be made.

Time series analysis has largely been used to estimate short-run costs, whereas the cross-sectional regression technique appears more suited for long-run cost estimation.

A large majority of these studies have concluded that marginal cost in the short run is relatively constant. In the long run economies of scale predominate at the low end of production, and at higher output, constant returns to scale appear to exist.

The upward-sloping—U-shaped—average and marginal cost curves postulated by economic theory tend to be the exception in empirical findings. Although such results should make economists pause and reexamine some of their theoretical conclusions, the studies have generally been conducted in such a way that the possibility of eventually rising marginal costs and diseconomies of scale cannot be discounted.

Some economists prefer not to use accounting data in their inquiries. Thus, two other methods of cost estimation were briefly described in the chapter. Engineering cost analysis is based on the expert knowledge of the relationship between inputs and outputs and standard costs. It avoids the use of accounting information and does not run into the problem of adjusting for changing technology and inflation. The survivorship method bases its findings on the change in the proportion of total industry output produced by firms of different size categories. It concludes that the more efficient firms will gain share of production at the expense of less efficient ones.

# CHAPTER 9

# Pricing and Output Decisions: Perfect Competition and Monopoly

For the job of product manager for the new beverage, *Waterpure,* Nicole Goodman, SVP of marketing, did not want a new MBA fresh out of the company's management training program. There was simply too much at stake to entrust the job to a rookie. She firmly believed that the job of bringing the new product to market should be given to a seasoned manager with a proven record of accomplishments. Finding a person with the necessary qualifications from within the company was not going to be easy, because all successful product managers were rapidly promoted to higher management positions. Nicole could have used a "headhunter" firm to find an outside person, but she pre-

ferred to give someone within the company a chance to make the project work.

"I've got just the person for you," the executive vice president exclaimed at lunch one day. "There is a real sharp manager over in market research. I think he was the one who did the background study on the soft drink market. It would be nice to give him a chance to put his ideas into practice."

The person recommended for this critical job was none other than Frank Robinson, the head of the forecasting department. (See chapter 6.) In his first meeting with Nicole after being hired, Frank was briefed on the job. "Because this new product is so important to the growth strategy of

*(Continued)*

our firm," Joan said, "and because of your experience and accomplishments, we decided that we wanted you rather than one of the outside people who were considered for the job.

"One of the first tasks you should pursue is an analysis of the optimal price of this beverage. Tell us what price we should charge to maximize our profit in this new venture. The CEO told us the other day that the Wall Street analysts were questioning our judgment in getting into such a crowded and highly competitive market. We need to prove as fast as possible that we made the right decision, so we want to maximize our profit in this venture in as short a time as possible.

"As always, the management committee has the final say on the price of the new beverage, just as for all our products and services. But don't get discouraged. As I know from the other products that I've managed, pricing is a very useful exercise because it forces one to bring together all the different elements of the business. The market research that you have already done on this product will provide you with a quantitative estimate of the demand as well as a general competitive analysis of the entire beverage industry. Our production people and cost accountants will give you the cost estimates. It will be up to you to put everything together to arrive at a suitable price for "Waterpure."

# Introduction

We are now completely ready to discuss management decisions concerning a firm's pricing and levels of output. In a broader sense, these two decisions are part of a larger exercise that business people often refer to as the *business case.*[1] In the process of deciding how much to produce and at what price, a manager is actually deciding whether it is worthwhile for the firm to supply this product.

Every pricing and output decision involves three key factors: cost, demand, and market structure. (These factors are also referred to in marketing textbooks as *the three Cs of pricing:* cost, customers, and competition.) We have already examined cost in chapter 8 and demand in chapters 3 and 4. In this chapter and the one to follow, we combine these two elements with the third, market structure, into a complete economic model of the pricing and output decision. In economic analysis, the nature of the competition that a firm faces is reflective of the market structure in which it competes. **Market structure** refers to the number and relative sizes of the buyers and sellers in a particular market. A "competitive" market structure implies that the number of buyers and sellers in a market is large enough that it is difficult if not impossible for any one buyer or seller to determine the market price.

---

[1]The term "business case" usually refers to the justification for allocating a firm's resources to a particular activity. Besides the consideration of the fundamental question, "Should we be in this business?" the business case usually includes the capital budgeting analysis that we discuss in chapters 13 and 14.

In a more formal way, economists divide market structure into four basic types: perfect competition, monopoly, monopolistic competition, and oligopoly. In this chapter, we will deal with a firm's pricing and output decisions in perfect competition and monopoly. We will cover the cases of monopolistic competition and oligopoly in the next chapter. Perfect competition and monopoly can be considered the two extreme market environments in which a firm competes. In perfect competition, there are so many sellers offering the same product that an individual firm has virtually no control over the price of its product. The interaction of supply and demand decides the price for all participants in this type of market. All an individual firm is able to do is to decide whether to compete in the market and how much output to produce.

In **monopoly,** there is only one seller and, consequently, the monopoly firm has a considerable amount of power to establish its price.

Monopolistic competition and oligopoly are somewhere in between the two extremes of perfect competition and monopoly in terms of a firm's power to establish the price. They are more typical of actual situations in which firms must compete. However, from a pedagogical standpoint, it is much easier to understand and appreciate the particulars of monopolistic competition and oligopoly if there is first a thorough understanding of the perfectly competitive and monopoly markets. Hence, the sequence of our presentation in this and the ensuing chapters. We begin our discussion of competition with a description of all four types of markets.

## MARKET STRUCTURE

Figure 9.1 formally outlines the ways in which economists divide up the different types of competition in the marketplace. The most important distinction is the degree to which firms in these markets exercise control over the price of their products. In the market labeled **perfect competition,** for example, it is virtually impossible for a firm to set the price of its product. There are so many firms in the market that buyers do not need to rely on any one firm to meet their demand. In other words, if a single firm decided to restrict its supply in order to extract a higher price, customers would simply turn to other sellers, who would gladly sell them the product at the going market price. So in effect, both buyers and sellers are **price takers.**

You might be thinking that a seller could exercise control over price by adding some sort of perceived value to the product. For instance, special packaging, added service, or simply "service with a smile" might make customers willing to pay more. But in a perfectly competitive market all products are standardized. That is, there is no way in which a firm can distinguish its products from those of all the other firms in the market.

How many times have you bought an item at a store only to find out the next day that you could have bought it for less at another store? Your first reaction might have been anger at the first store for charging you more. But a store can do this if there are people like you who do not have complete information about the selling prices of the item at various stores. As long as it is possible for you to check the prices at all stores, you really cannot blame the first store. This is why economists include the third characteristic of perfect competition cited in Figure 9.1. "Complete information" among consumers would make it impossible for this situation to occur. Buyers simply would know what everyone was selling the product for, and everyone would end up selling it for the same—or a very similar—price.

*Perfect Competition*
1. Large number of sellers and buyers
2. Standardized product
3. Complete information about market prices
4. Easy entry into and exit out of markets

*Monopoly*
1. One-firm industry
2. Unique product (no close substitutes)
3. Absolute control over supply within a price range
4. Entry into industry restricted by law or very difficult in practice

*Monopolistic Competition*
1. Large number of sellers acting independently
2. Product differentiation
3. Partial (and limited) control over product price
4. Easy entry into and exit from markets

*Oligopoly*
1. Relatively few sellers
2. Either standardized or differentiated products
3. Control over price closely circumscribed by the interdependence of the competing firms
4. Relatively difficult to enter

**FIGURE 9.1** The Four Basic Market Structures

The fourth characteristic of a perfectly competitive market is "easy entry and exit." This means that in a perfectly competitive market there are no legal or practical barriers to keep firms from entering or leaving the market. A patent is an example of a legal barrier to entry. Another is the monopoly rights granted by the government to a public utility. Import restrictions are also a form of market barrier to entry—in this case, against foreign sellers.

Examples of practical barriers to entry can be found in such markets as the American automobile manufacturing and breakfast food industries. High start-up capital requirements and strong brand identification by the general public have made it difficult for a firm to enter the American automobile industry—although foreign competition, particularly the Japanese, have certainly proved that it can be done. Strong brand identification and entrenched market distribution channels (e.g., supermarket shelf space garnered by food brokers) have made it difficult for any manufacturer of processed food to come into the breakfast foods market. In a perfectly competitive market, none of these barriers would exist.

Ease of exit from a market may at first seem a rather strange characteristic of a perfectly competitive market. After all, if a firm does not want to be in a particular business, is it not always free to leave? In certain regulated markets, firms are legally required to be in a market. For example, the concept of "universal service" still is an important part of the obligation of local telephone companies and power utilities. It requires these companies to provide service to everyone in the local market area, regardless of whether it is profitable for them to do so.[2] On rare occasions, the government may initiate efforts to keep a company from exiting the market. For example, in 1980, the federal government provided guaranteed bank loans to the Chrysler Corporation to ensure the automobile manufacturing capability of an American company. Chrysler eventually bounced back and in fact repaid its loans ahead of schedule. In 1998 it merged with the German company Daimler-Benz.

In the other three market types—monopoly, monopolistic competition, and oligopoly—sellers can exercise varying degrees of control over the prices of their products, otherwise referred to as **market power.** A closer look at the characteristics of these markets in Figure 9.1 will indicate why it is possible for these firms to enjoy what economists call "market power," or the power that a firm has to set its own price.

In the case of a *monopoly* market, there is only "one game in town." The single seller in the market has no competitor offering a close substitute for its product. Public utilities such as electric and water companies immediately come to mind. But the only jewelry store in a shopping center or a "last chance" gas station at the edge of the Nevada desert also enjoys a monopoly status.

*Monopolistic competition* (the subject of chapter 10) is a hybrid market. It is considered competitive because there are many sellers and because it is relatively easy to enter this market. But it is monopolistic because sellers try to differentiate their products as much as possible from those of their competitors. The best examples of this kind of market can be found in small businesses. Small retail stores (e.g., boutiques, luggage stores, shoe stores, stationery shops), restaurants, repair shops, laundries, and beauty parlors all compete in this type of market. One Chinese restaurant may attempt to differentiate itself by offering a cuisine from a relatively unknown region of China. A repair shop may try to distinguish itself from its competitors by opening seven days a week. If consumers perceive these differences to be important enough, these retail establishments may be able to charge a higher price than their competitors.

*Oligopoly* markets (also the subject of chapter 10) have relatively few sellers who are large in size (as measured by such indicators as market share, assets, and number of employees). A large part of the manufacturing sector in the United States is structured in this way. The makers of processed foods, appliances, computers, chemicals, cars, steel, personal care products, soft drinks, and airlines with national routes all compete in oligopolistic markets. These firms may either sell standardized products (e.g., aluminum, plastics, chemicals) or differentiated ones (e.g., cars, soap, breakfast cereals). Therefore, the key factor that gives rise to their market power is size.

# Pricing and Output Decisions in Perfect Competition

## THE BASIC BUSINESS DECISION

Imagine a firm that is considering entry into a market that is perfectly competitive. If it decides to compete in this market, it will have no control over the price of the product. Therefore, the firm's managers must make a business case for entering this market on the basis of the following questions:

---

[2]In late 1998, US West contested the obligation to provide telephone service to someone who lived high up on a mountain. The company petitioned its local public utilities commission to have the resident at least split the estimated cost of $70,000 to connect the house to the telephone network.

1. How much should we produce?
2. If we produce such an amount, how much profit will we earn?
3. If a loss rather than a profit is incurred, will it be worthwhile to continue in this market in the long run (in hopes that we will eventually earn a profit) or should we exit?

Perhaps even the output decision may seem superfluous. After all, is not the firm so small that it can sell as much as it wants without affecting the market price? Yes, but although the market price does not vary with an individual firm's level of output, the *unit cost* of production most certainly does. Think back to our discussion in chapter 8 about the cost of additional units of output. If we assume that marginal cost rises as output increases (thanks to the law of diminishing returns), then it seems reasonable to expect that eventually the extra cost per unit will exceed the selling price of the product. At this point, it no longer would make sense for a profit-maximizing firm to produce, because each additional unit sold would cost the firm more to produce than the price at which it could sell the product. Much more will be said about this shortly. But the point to emphasize here is that there is indeed a limit as to how much a perfectly competitive firm should produce in the short run. It is up to the firm to determine what this limit is.

Because the perfectly competitive firm must operate in a market in which it has no control over the selling price, there may be times when the price does not fully cover the unit cost of production (i.e., average cost). Thus, a firm must assess the extent of its losses in relation to the alternative of discontinuing production. In the long run, a firm that continues to incur losses must eventually leave the market. But in the short run, it may be economically justifiable to remain in the market, with the expectation of better times ahead. This is because in the short run, certain costs must be borne regardless of whether the firm operates. These fixed costs must be weighed against the losses incurred by remaining in business. It is reasonable to expect that a firm will remain in business if its losses are less than its fixed costs—at least in the short run.

## KEY ASSUMPTIONS OF THE PERFECTLY COMPETITIVE MARKET

As you are well aware, it is critical to know the assumptions made in the development of an economic model. Let us summarize the key assumptions made in analyzing the firm's output decision in perfect competition.

1. The firm operates in a perfectly competitive market and therefore is a price taker.
2. The firm makes the distinction between the short run and the long run.
3. The firm's objective is to maximize its profit in the short run. If it cannot earn a profit, then it seeks to minimize its loss. (See chapter 2 for a review of the goals of a firm.)
4. The firm includes its opportunity cost of operating in a particular market as part of its total cost of production.

All four assumptions have been discussed earlier, some in greater detail than others. But it might be useful to review certain aspects of these assumptions before proceeding to numerical and graphical examples.

For the economic analysis of a firm's output and pricing decisions to have a unique solution, the firm must establish a single, clear-cut objective. This objective is the maximization of profit in the short run. If the firm has other objectives, such as the maximization of revenue in the short run, the output that it would select would differ from the one based on this model. (See chapter 12, for a discussion of the Baumol revenue-maximization model.)

The consideration of opportunity cost in the cost structure of the firm is vital to this decision-making model. The firm must check whether the going market price enables it to earn a revenue that covers not only its out-of-pocket costs, but also the costs incurred by forgoing alternative activities. A brief numerical example should help to convey this point.

Suppose the manager of a "stop and shop" convenience store wants to own and operate a store of her own. She knows she will have to leave her job and use $50,000 of her savings (currently invested and yielding a 10 percent return). A statement of the projected cost of operating in the first year follows.

| | |
|---|---:|
| Cost of goods sold | $300,000 |
| General and administrative expenses | 150,000 |
| Total accounting cost | $450,000 |
| Forgone salary for being a store manager | 45,000 |
| Forgone returns from investments (100% return) | 5,000 |
| Total opportunity cost | $50,000 |
| Total economic cost (total accounting cost plus total opportunity cost) | $500,000 |

To keep this example as simple as possible, we did not include depreciation and taxes.

Suppose this budding entrepreneur forecasts revenue to be $500,000 in the first year of operation. From an accounting standpoint, her profit would be $50,000 ($500,000 − $450,000). But from an economic standpoint, her profit would be zero, since the revenue would just equal her total **economic cost.** Certainly, there would be nothing wrong with "breaking even" in the economic sense of the term, because this indicates that the firm's revenue is sufficient to cover both its out-of- pocket expense and its opportunity cost. Another way to view this situation is to note that when a firm "breaks even" in the economic sense, it is actually earning an accounting profit equal to its opportunity cost. In other words, if this entrepreneur's annual revenue is $500,000, she will earn an accounting profit that offsets the opportunity cost of going into business for herself. In economic terms, she would be earning a **normal profit.**

The reason for using the term "normal" can be seen in situations in which the entrepreneur's revenue is higher or lower than $500,000. Suppose her revenue is $550,000. In this case, she will earn a profit of $50,000 ($550,000 − $500,000). We refer to this sum as "above normal," "pure," or **economic profit** because it represents an amount in excess of the out-of-pocket cost plus the opportunity cost of running the business.

In the case where revenue is less than economic cost, clearly a loss is incurred. However, this **economic loss** might well coincide with a firm earning an accounting profit. For example, suppose our entrepreneur's revenue is $480,000. The economic loss would be $20,000 ($480,000 − $500,000), but the accounting profit would be $30,000 ($480,000 − $450,000). Table 9.1 summarizes the three scenarios discussed above.

With these assumptions in mind, we are now ready to discuss the decision-making process. Suppose that in determining whether to operate in a particular market at some

**TABLE 9.1   Normal Profit, Economic Profit, and Economic Loss**

|  | *Normal Profit* | *Economic Profit* | *Economic Loss* |
|---|---|---|---|
| Revenue | $500,000 | $550,000 | $480,000 |
| Accounting cost | 450,000 | 450,000 | 450,000 |
| Opportunity cost | 50,000 | 50,000 | 50,000 |
| Profit | 0 | $50,000 | ($20,000) |
|  | *Note:* Accounting profit for $50,000 equals the opportunity cost of $50,000. | Accounting profit of $100,000 exceeds the opportunity cost of $50,000. | Accounting profit of $30,000 is less than the opportunity cost of $50,000. |

level of output, the firm is faced with the short-run total cost structure presented in Table 9.2. (For convenience, the cost data are the same as those first presented in Table 8.2.)

Let us assume that the market price is $110. Given this price, the firm is free to produce as much as or as little as it desires. The demand, total revenue, marginal revenue, and average revenue schedules for this firm are shown in Table 9.3. Notice that because the price to the firm remains unchanged regardless of its output level, the total, marginal, and average revenue schedules do not resemble the schedules analyzed in chapter 4. As a price taker, the firm faces a demand curve that is "perfectly elastic." That is, customers are willing to buy as much as the firm is willing to sell *at the going market price*. This special type of demand curve can be seen in Figure 9.2. Moreover, the firm receives the same marginal revenue from the sale of each additional unit of product. This marginal revenue is simply the price of the product. Recall that the price is tantamount to average or per-unit revenue. Hence, a perfectly competitive firm's demand is

**TABLE 9.2   Total and Per-Unit Short-Run Cost**

| Quantity (Q) | Total Fixed Cost (TFC) | Total Variable Cost (TVC) | Total Cost (TC) | Average Fixed Cost (AFC) | Average Variable Cost (AVC) | Average Total Cost (AC) | Marginal Cost (MC) |
|---|---|---|---|---|---|---|---|
| 0 | 100 | 0.00 | 100.00 |  |  |  |  |
| 1 | 100 | 55.70 | 155.70 | 100.00 | 55.70 | 155.70 | 55.70 |
| 2 | 100 | 105.60 | 205.60 | 50.00 | 52.80 | 102.80 | 49.90 |
| 3 | 100 | 153.90 | 253.90 | 33.33 | 51.30 | 84.63 | 48.30 |
| 4 | 100 | 204.80 | 304.80 | 25.00 | 51.20 | 76.20 | 50.90 |
| 5 | 100 | 262.50 | 362.50 | 20.00 | 52.50 | 72.50 | 57.70 |
| 6 | 100 | 331.20 | 431.20 | 16.67 | 55.20 | 71.87 | 68.70 |
| 7 | 100 | 415.10 | 515.10 | 14.29 | 59.30 | 73.59 | 83.90 |
| 8 | 100 | 518.40 | 618.40 | 12.50 | 64.80 | 77.30 | 103.30 |
| 9 | 100 | 645.30 | 745.30 | 11.11 | 71.70 | 82.81 | 126.90 |
| 10 | 100 | 800.00 | 900.00 | 10.00 | 80.00 | 90.00 | 154.70 |
| 11 | 100 | 986.70 | 1086.70 | 9.09 | 89.70 | 98.79 | 186.70 |
| 12 | 100 | 1209.60 | 1309.60 | 8.33 | 100.80 | 109.13 | 222.90 |

| TABLE 9.3 | Revenue Schedules | | |
|---|---|---|---|
| Quantity | Price (AR) | TR | MR |
| 0 | 110 | 0 | |
| | | | 110 |
| 1 | 110 | 110 | |
| | | | 110 |
| 2 | 110 | 220 | |
| | | | 110 |
| 3 | 110 | 330 | |
| | | | 110 |
| 4 | 110 | 440 | |
| | | | 110 |
| 5 | 110 | 550 | |
| | | | 110 |
| 6 | 110 | 660 | |
| | | | 110 |
| 7 | 110 | 770 | |
| | | | 110 |
| 8 | 110 | 880 | |
| | | | 110 |
| 9 | 110 | 990 | |
| | | | 110 |
| 10 | 110 | 1,100 | |
| | | | 110 |
| 11 | 110 | 1,210 | |
| | | | 110 |
| 12 | 110 | 1,320 | |

also its marginal and its average revenue over the range of output being considered. Note in Figure 9.2 that the demand curve is also labeled "AR" and "MR."

Figure 9.3 compares the perfectly elastic demand curve with the typical downward-sloping linear demand curve used in chapter 4. It also shows the total revenue curves in relation to the two types of demand curves. As is the case with perfect elasticity, a downward-sloping demand curve is the same as the average revenue curve, because $P$ by definition is equal to AR. However, recall that a linear, downward-sloping demand curve is associated with a marginal revenue curve that is twice as steep. In addition, this type of demand results in a nonlinear total revenue curve that reaches a maximum at the point at which marginal revenue equals zero (see Figure 9.3$b$). In contrast, as shown in Figure 9.3$d$, there is no limit to the amount of total revenue that firms can garner in a perfectly competitive market. The more a firm produces, the more revenue it will

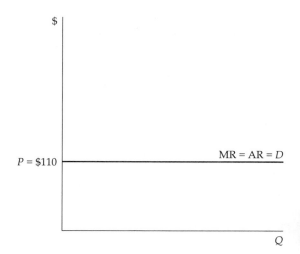

**FIGURE 9.2** Perfectly Elastic Demand Curve

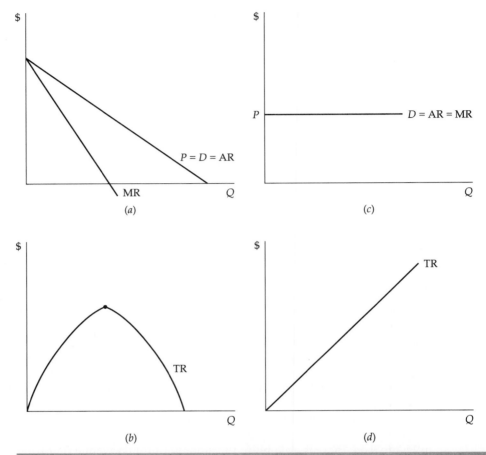

**FIGURE 9.3** Different Types of Demand Curves and Associated Total Revenue Curves

obtain. The limit to its output is based on revenue in relation to the firm's cost of production, that is, the profit earned at various levels of output.

Armed with its cost and revenue schedules, all that a firm needs to do is to combine the sets of information to find the level of output that maximizes its profit (or minimizes its loss).

**MODULE 9A**

### THE TOTAL REVENUE–TOTAL COST APPROACH TO SELECTING THE OPTIMAL OUTPUT LEVEL

The most logical approach to selecting the optimal level of output is to compare the total revenue with the total cost schedules and find that level of output that either maximizes the firm's profit or minimizes its loss. This is shown in Table 9.4 and Figure 9.4. As can be seen in the table and the figure, this output level is 8, at which the firm would be earning a maximum profit of $261.60. Graphically, this output level can be seen as the one that maximizes the distance between the total revenue curve and the total cost curve. By convention, this point has been labeled $Q^*$.

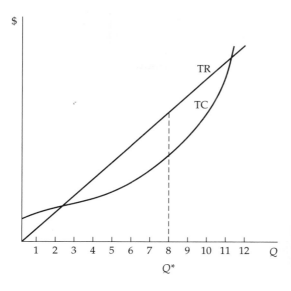

**FIGURE 9.4** Determining Optimal Output from Cost and Revenue Curves—Perfect Competition

## THE MARGINAL REVENUE–MARGINAL COST APPROACH
## TO FINDING THE OPTIMAL OUTPUT LEVEL

Marginal analysis is at the heart of the economic analysis of the firm. Once we explain how marginal analysis is used by the firm to determine its optimal level of output, we will rely primarily on this type of analysis throughout the rest of this chapter.

Table 9.5 presents the cost and revenue data on a per-unit basis. The marginal revenue and marginal cost columns contain the key numbers the firm must use to decide on

**TABLE 9.4  Cost and Revenue Schedules Used to Determine Optimal Level of Output**

| Quantity (Q) | Price (P) | Total Revenue (TR) | Total Fixed Cost (TFC) | Total Variable Cost (TVC) | Total Cost (TC) | Total Profit (π) |
|---|---|---|---|---|---|---|
| 0 | 110 | 0 | 100 | 0.00 | 100.00 | −100.00 |
| 1 | 110 | 110 | 100 | 55.70 | 155.70 | −45.70 |
| 2 | 110 | 220 | 100 | 105.60 | 205.60 | −14.40 |
| 3 | 110 | 330 | 100 | 153.90 | 253.90 | 76.10 |
| 4 | 110 | 440 | 100 | 204.80 | 304.80 | 135.20 |
| 5 | 110 | 550 | 100 | 262.50 | 362.50 | 187.50 |
| 6 | 110 | 660 | 100 | 331.20 | 431.20 | 228.80 |
| 7 | 110 | 770 | 100 | 415.10 | 515.10 | 254.90 |
| 8 | 110 | 880 | 100 | 518.40 | 618.40 | 261.60 |
| 9 | 110 | 990 | 100 | 645.30 | 745.30 | 244.70 |
| 10 | 110 | 1100 | 100 | 800.00 | 900.00 | 200.00 |
| 11 | 110 | 1210 | 100 | 986.70 | 1086.70 | 123.30 |
| 12 | 110 | 1320 | 100 | 1209.60 | 1309.60 | 10.40 |

**TABLE 9.5   Using Marginal Revenue (or Price) and Marginal Cost to Determine Optimal Output: *The Case of Economic Profit***

| Quantity (Q) | Marginal Revenue (MR = P = AR) | Average Fixed Cost (AFC) | Average Variable Cost (AVC) | Average Total Cost (AC) | Marginal Cost (MC) | Marginal Profit (Mπ) |
|---|---|---|---|---|---|---|
| 0 | 100 | | | | | |
| | | | | | 55.70 | 54.30 |
| 1 | 110 | 100.00 | 55.70 | 155.70 | | |
| | | | | | 49.90 | 60.10 |
| 2 | 110 | 50.00 | 52.80 | 102.80 | | |
| | | | | | 48.30 | 61.70 |
| 3 | 110 | 33.33 | 51.30 | 84.63 | | |
| | | | | | 50.90 | 59.10 |
| 4 | 110 | 25.00 | 51.20 | 76.20 | | |
| | | | | | 57.70 | 52.30 |
| 5 | 110 | 20.00 | 52.50 | 72.50 | | |
| | | | | | 68.70 | 41.30 |
| 6 | 110 | 16.67 | 55.20 | 71.87 | | |
| | | | | | 83.90 | 26.10 |
| 7 | 110 | 14.29 | 59.30 | 73.59 | | |
| | | | | | 103.30 | 6.70 |
| 8 | 110 | 12.50 | 64.80 | 77.30 | | |
| | | | | | 126.90 | −16.90 |
| 9 | 110 | 11.11 | 71.70 | 82.81 | | |
| | | | | | 154.70 | −44.70 |
| 10 | 110 | 10.00 | 80.00 | 90.00 | | |
| | | | | | 186.70 | −76.70 |
| 11 | 110 | 9.09 | 89.70 | 98.79 | | |
| | | | | | 222.90 | −112.90 |
| 12 | 110 | 8.33 | 100.80 | 109.13 | | |

its optimal level of output. Let us examine the marginal revenue and the marginal cost associated with additional units of output, starting with zero units. As you can see in Table 9.5, the first unit would result in additional revenue of $110 and cost the firm an additional $55.70 to make. The second unit would add another $110 to revenue and another $49.90 to the firm's total cost. Continuing in this manner, we observe that it would be worthwhile for the firm to produce more as long as the added benefit of each unit produced and sold (i.e., the marginal revenue) exceeds the added cost (i.e., the marginal cost). Because the marginal revenue is equal to the existing market price, it does not change as output increases. However, because of the law of diminishing returns, the firm's marginal cost begins to increase with the fourth unit of output. From that point on, each additional unit of output costs *increasingly more* to produce. Between zero and eight units of output, we observe that marginal revenue exceeds marginal cost. However, production of the ninth unit of output will cost the firm more than the revenue that it would add (MC = $126.90 and MR = $110). In Table 9.5, MR = MC actually occurs between eight and nine units of output, but we use eight as the approximate level of optimal output.

Using the relationship between marginal revenue and marginal cost to decide on the optimal level of output is referred to in economics as the **MR = MC rule.** The rule is stated as follows:

> A firm that wants to maximize its profit (or minimize its loss) should produce a level of output at which the additional revenue received from the last unit is equal to the additional cost of producing that unit. In short, MR = MC.

The MR = MC rule applies to any firm that wishes to maximize its profit, regardless of whether it has the power to set the price. However, in the particular case in which the firm has no power to set the price (i.e., it is a price taker), the MR = MC rule can be restated as the $P$ = **MC rule.** This is simply because when a firm is a price taker, its marginal revenue is in fact the going market price. (Refer to Figure 9.3 for an illustration of this.)

Table 9.5 shows that by following the MR = MC rule and producing eight units of output, the firm would earn a profit of $261.60 [8(AR − AC)], which is what we already learned by following the total revenue–total cost approach. Hence, the rule apparently works. Another way to think about MR and MC is in terms of marginal (i.e., additional) profit. If TR − TC is equal to total profit, then MR − MC must be equal to marginal profit. The last column in Table 9.5 indicates the amount of additional profit that would be earned by the firm in producing additional units of output. As you can see, this column is merely the difference between the MR column and the MC column. When MR is equal to MC, marginal profit must be zero. When marginal profit is equal to zero, it indicates that the firm can make no more *additional* profit and therefore should not produce at a higher level of output.

Of course, there is nothing to prevent the firm from producing more or less than eight units of output. As you can see in the last column of Table 9.4, it would still earn a profit if it produced at any of the output levels 2 to 12, but none of these amounts except 8 is the *maximum* that it could earn. Remember that we are now referring to *total revenue* and *total cost.* If the firm were to produce at the level where these two measures are equal, then clearly all it would be doing is earning a "normal" profit.

Although the optimal output level can be found just as easily by using the TR–TC approach, economists rely much more on the MR–MC approach in analyzing the firm's output decision. Essentially, this approach is an extension of the basic analytical technique of "marginal analysis" first introduced in the chapters on demand, production, and cost. Furthermore, the practical implications of this approach are similar to those discussed in these earlier chapters. Very often firms do not have the benefit of complete columns of numbers depicting cost and revenue. Instead, they must rely on actual cost and revenue data at a particular level of output and then conduct sensitivity analysis involving relatively small incremental changes around that level. As will be illustrated in the ensuing sections, "marginal analysis" is much better suited to this situation than "total analysis."

## The MR–MC Approach in Graphs

A graphical analysis using the MR–MC approach employs the data in Table 9.5 and is shown in Figure 9.5. Also shown is the firm's demand curve, a horizontal line intersecting the vertical axis at the level of the given market price of $110. Thus, the demand curve of this price-taking firm is "perfectly elastic." The optimal output level is clearly seen as the level at which the firm's MC line and its MR line (demand line) intersect. The amount of profit earned is represented by the shaded rectangle *ABCD*. Because these graphs will be utilized in this way throughout the rest of the chapter, it is crucial that you clearly understand their interpretation.

Points on each of the unit cost curves indicate the dollar value of the cost at different levels of output. Therefore, at output level $Q^*$, the average cost is represented by the distance between point $C$ and the horizontal axis (i.e., $CQ^*$). It follows that since total cost is average cost multiplied by the quantity of output, it is shown as the area of the rectangle determined by $OQ^*$ and $CQ^*$ (rectangle $ODCQ^*$). In the same manner, we can show that total revenue can be displayed as the rectangle determined by $OQ^*$ and $BQ^*$ (rectangle $OABQ^*$). Therefore, profit (i.e., the shaded rectangle $DABC$) can

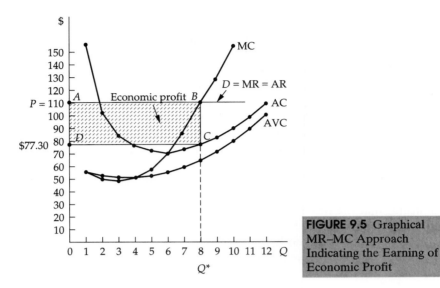

**FIGURE 9.5** Graphical MR–MC Approach Indicating the Earning of Economic Profit

be represented by the difference between the larger rectangle, depicting total revenue, and the smaller one, showing total cost.

## ECONOMIC PROFIT, NORMAL PROFIT, LOSS, AND SHUTDOWN

The preceding example assumed that the market price was high enough for the firm to earn an economic profit by following the MR = MC rule. But because the firm is just one of many price-taking sellers in this market, there is no reason to expect that market price will always be this beneficial for the firm. Given the vagaries of supply and demand, it is just as likely that a firm will be faced with prices that result in only normal profit—or worse, in operating losses. Tables 9.6 and 9.7 and Figure 9.6 demonstrate these possibilities. To focus on the marginal revenue–marginal cost approach, we include only the per-unit cost data in the tables and figure.

The situation depicted in Table 9.7 and Figure 9.6b indicates a loss for the firm. Does this mean that the firm should not be in this market? As you know, in the short run, the firm must bear certain fixed costs regardless of the level of its output. Using the data in Table 9.7, if the firm were to shut down its operations (i.e., if Q = 0), it would still have a fixed cost of $100. Given the market price of $58, we know that the best that a firm can do is to follow the MR = MC rule, produce five units of output, and lose $72.50. But if the firm were to shut down, it would lose $100 because this is the amount of fixed cost that it would incur, whether or not it operates in the short run. Therefore, with a market price of $58, *it would be better for a firm to operate at a loss than to cease its activities in this market.* This is illustrated in Figure 9.7a.

Another way to understand this rationale is to compare the firm's total revenue at the $58 price with its total variable cost, assuming a production level of five units. The total revenue is $290 ($P \times Q$), and the total variable cost is $262.50 ($Q \times$ AVC). Clearly, this revenue is sufficient to cover the firm's total variable cost. Moreover, the amount left over ($27.50) can be used to pay for a part of its fixed cost. Hence, we can also conclude that

**TABLE 9.6   Using Marginal Revenue (or Price) and Marginal Cost to Determine Optimal Output: The Case of Normal Profit**

| Quantity (Q) | Marginal Revenue (MR=P=AR) | Average Fixed Cost (AFC) | Average Variable Cost (AVC) | Average Total Cost (AC) | Marginal Cost (MC) | Marginal Profit (Mπ) | Total Profit Or Loss (Q[P−AC]) |
|---|---|---|---|---|---|---|---|
| 0 | 71.87 | | | | | | −100.00ᵃ |
| 1 | 71.87 | 100.00 | 55.70 | 155.70 | 55.70 | 16.17 | −83.83 |
| 2 | 71.87 | 50.00 | 52.80 | 102.80 | 49.90 | 21.97 | −61.86 |
| 3 | 71.87 | 33.33 | 51.30 | 84.63 | 48.30 | 23.57 | −38.28 |
| 4 | 71.87 | 25.00 | 51.20 | 76.20 | 50.90 | 20.97 | −17.32 |
| 5 | 71.87 | 20.00 | 52.50 | 72.50 | 57.70 | 14.17 | −3.15 |
| 6 | 71.87 | 16.67 | 55.20 | 71.87 | 68.70 | 3.17 | 0 |
| 7 | 71.87 | 14.29 | 59.30 | 73.59 | 83.90 | −12.03 | −12.04 |
| 8 | 71.87 | 12.50 | 64.80 | 77.30 | 103.30 | −31.43 | −43.44 |
| 9 | 71.87 | 11.11 | 71.70 | 82.81 | 126.90 | −55.03 | −98.46 |
| 10 | 71.87 | 10.00 | 80.00 | 90.00 | 154.70 | −82.83 | −181.30 |
| 11 | 71.87 | 9.09 | 89.70 | 98.79 | 186.70 | −114.83 | −296.12 |
| 12 | 71.87 | 8.33 | 100.80 | 109.13 | 222.90 | −151.03 | −447.12 |

ᵃ If $Q = 0$, firm still incurs a total fixed cost of $100 in the short run.

**TABLE 9.7   Using Marginal Revenue (or Price) and Marginal Cost to Determine Optimal Output: The Case of Economic Loss**

| Quantity (Q) | Marginal Revenue (MR = P = AR) | Average Fixed Cost (AFC) | Average Variable Cost (AVC) | Average Total Cost (AC) | Marginal Cost (MC) | Marginal Profit (Mπ) | Total Profit Or Loss (Q[P−AC]) |
|---|---|---|---|---|---|---|---|
| 0 | 58 | | | | | | −100.00 |
| 1 | 58 | 100.00 | 55.70 | 155.70 | 55.70 | 2.30 | −97.70 |
| 2 | 58 | 50.00 | 52.80 | 102.80 | 49.90 | 8.10 | −89.60 |
| 3 | 58 | 33.33 | 51.30 | 84.63 | 48.30 | 9.70 | −79.89 |
| 4 | 58 | 25.00 | 51.20 | 76.20 | 50.90 | 7.10 | −72.80 |
| 5 | 58 | 20.00 | 52.50 | 72.50 | 57.70 | 0.30 | −72.50 |
| 6 | 58 | 16.67 | 55.20 | 71.87 | 68.70 | −10.70 | −83.22 |
| 7 | 58 | 14.29 | 59.30 | 73.59 | 83.90 | −25.90 | −109.13 |
| 8 | 58 | 12.50 | 64.80 | 77.30 | 103.30 | −45.30 | −154.44 |
| 9 | 58 | 11.11 | 71.70 | 82.81 | 126.90 | −68.90 | −223.29 |
| 10 | 58 | 10.00 | 80.00 | 90.00 | 154.70 | −96.70 | −320.00 |
| 11 | 58 | 9.09 | 89.70 | 98.79 | 186.70 | −128.70 | −448.69 |
| 12 | 58 | 8.33 | 100.80 | 109.13 | 222.90 | −164.90 | −613.56 |

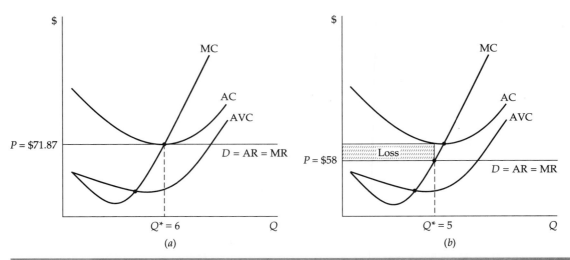

**FIGURE 9.6** (a) Normal Profit and (b) Economic Loss

as long as a firm's total revenue is greater than its total variable cost (or on a per-unit basis, as long as the market price exceeds average variable cost), it is better to operate than to shut down because at least part of its fixed cost will be defrayed. We refer to the amount by which total revenue exceeds total variable cost as the **contribution margin** (see Figure 9.7*a*). You should also recognize that the portion of fixed cost that is *not* covered by the contribution margin is in fact the amount of the firm's loss (i.e., $27.50 − $100 = −$72.50).

It is not always advisable to operate in the short run at a loss. Suppose the market price fell to $50. In this case, even if the firm followed the MR = MC rule, it would still incur a loss greater than it would have to bear by shutting down. This situation is not shown in a separate table but will be discussed in relation to the figures in Table 11.6. By literally following the MR = MC rule, the firm would be led to produce three units of output. But we can see that at this level, the total revenue of $150 ($50 × 3) would not even be enough to cover the firm's total variable cost of $153.90 ($51.30 × 3), resulting in a negative contribution margin of $3.90. Looking at this situation in terms of the firm's loss versus its fixed cost, we can see that its total loss of $103.90 is clearly greater than the fixed cost of $100 that it would incur if it decided to shut down its operations. (As you can see, the firm's loss is the combination of its fixed cost and negative contribution margin.) Thus, given the market price of $50, the firm would be better off by shutting down its operations. This is illustrated in Figure 9.7*b*.

Also shown in this figure is what economists refer to as the **shutdown point.** At this point, the market price is at a level in which a firm following the MR = MC rule would lose an amount just equal to its fixed cost of production. Expressed in another way, this price would result in a zero contribution margin. At the shutdown point, we assume that a firm would be indifferent about operating versus shutting down. However, it would certainly give strong consideration to ceasing to operate in the short run. As you can see, the shutdown point coincides with the point at which the firm's average variable cost is at its minimum.

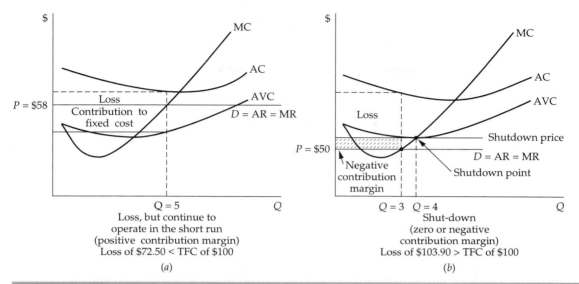

**FIGURE 9.7** Contribution Margin

## THE COMPETITIVE MARKET IN THE LONG RUN

Regardless of whether the market price in the short run results in economic profit, normal profit, or a loss for competing firms, economic theory states that in the **long run,** the market price will settle at the point where these firms earn a normal profit. This is because over a long period of time, prices that enable firms to earn above-normal profit would induce other firms to enter the market, and prices below the normal level would cause firms to leave the market. We just completed a discussion of the rationale for a firm's operating at a loss in the short run. However, in the long run, we assume that firms that are losing money would have to seriously consider leaving the market even if they have positive contribution margins. Recall that in the long run, firms have the time to vary their fixed factors of production. This means that they would have sufficient time to liquidate the fixed assets that account for their fixed costs.

We discussed the long-run adjustment process of entering and exiting firms in chapter 3. The entry of firms shifts the supply curve to the right, driving down market price. The exiting of firms shifts the supply curve to the left, placing upward pressure on market price. A firm's motivation to go into or get out of the market can now be examined in greater detail. There is only one price at which firms neither enter nor leave the market. This, of course, is the price that results in normal profits. The long-run process of entering and exiting firms is illustrated in Figure 9.8.

Figure 9.8*a* shows a hypothetical short-run situation in which the price (determined by supply and demand) is high enough to enable a typical firm competing in this market to earn economic profit. (Viewed in another way, given the market price, the firm's cost structure is low enough to enable it to earn economic profit.) Over time, new firms

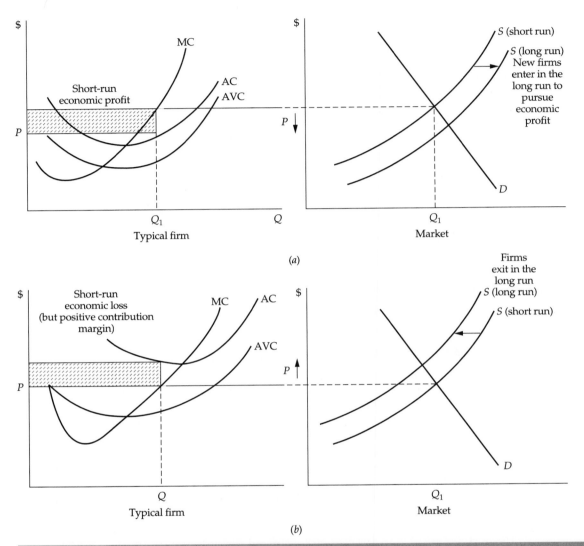

**FIGURE 9.8** Long-Run Effect of Firm's Entering and Exiting the Market

would enter the market, and the original firms would expand their fixed capacity in response to the incentive of economic profit. This would have the effect of increasing the market supply (shifting the supply curve to the right) and reducing the market price. At the point where firms earn only normal profit, this adjustment process would cease. Figure 9.8b shows the opposite case, in which a short-run loss incurred by firms in the market causes firms in the long run to leave the market. This causes price to rise toward the level in which the remaining firms would earn a normal profit.

The concept of a long-run "resting point" may seem a bit unrealistic. As much as we try to use real-world examples to support the theory of managerial economics, it is extremely difficult, if not impossible, to find examples of this principle in action. For one thing, in actual market situations, demand does not remain constant while supply adjusts toward the normal price. Tastes and preferences, the number of buyers, incomes, and prices of related goods are constantly changing. For another, the economic notion of the long run is a theoretical construct, not a period that can be measured in calendar time. If the market price has not reached the normal level, economists can say that the market is still adjusting toward long-run equilibrium. But herein lies the principal relevance of this concept to the real world of business. For business decision makers, the process of *adjustment* toward equilibrium is far more important than the equilibrium price itself.

An understanding of the conditions motivating market entry or exit over the long run should lead the firms to consider the following points:

1. The earlier the firm enters a market, the better its chances of earning above-normal profit (assuming a strong demand in this market).
2. As new firms enter the market, firms that want to survive and perhaps thrive must find ways to produce at the lowest possible cost, or at least at cost levels below those of their competitors.
3. Firms that find themselves unable to compete on the basis of cost might want to try competing on the basis of product differentiation instead.

## Pricing and Output Decisions in Monopoly Markets

**MODULE 9B
MODULE 9C**

A monopoly market consists of one firm. The firm *is* the market. Examples are gas and electric utilities and firms selling products under protection of U.S. patent laws. Prior to its breakup in 1984, AT&T was considered one of the largest monopolies in the world. The seven regional companies that were formed after divestiture still represent monopolies in many of the local calling areas within their respective regions. Most monopolies cited above are closely regulated by government or government-appointed agencies. (A notable exception is companies selling patented products.) Because this regulation severely constrains their ability to choose price and output levels, regulated monopolies are analyzed as a separate group of firms in chapter 15.

In the absence of regulatory constraints, the monopoly stands in counterpoint to the perfectly competitive firm. Firms in perfectly competitive markets have no power to set their prices; the monopoly firm has the power to establish any price that it wishes. If you were responsible for setting the price of a product that you alone were selling in the market, how much would you charge? The layperson's answer is usually "as much as I can" or "whatever the market will bear." On the surface, this answer seems reasonable enough. Unfortunately, it is too simplistic to be of much help to the monopolist. In 1948, when Polaroid first offered its camera, it could have charged any price that it wanted. The original price was $85 (which was a considerable sum at that time), but it could just as well have been $850 or $8,500. The market could have borne those prices because some people probably would have been willing to buy the camera at higher levels. The question is *how many* people would have bought the cameras and *when*. As it turned out, Polaroid offered five cameras for sale on the first day and sold them all in several hours. Who knows how long it would have taken them to sell the five units at $8,500?

The key point is that a monopoly firm's ability to set its price is limited by the demand curve for its product and, in particular, the price elasticity of demand for its product.

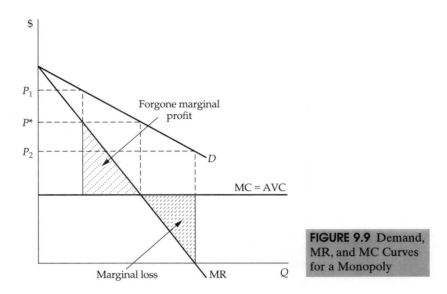

**FIGURE 9.9** Demand, MR, and MC Curves for a Monopoly

(Recall that according to the law of demand, people will buy more as price falls and vice versa.) The price elasticity of demand indicates how much more or less people are willing to buy in relation to price decreases or increases. If we assume that the firm's downward-sloping demand curve is linear, we know that as the price of the product falls, the marginal revenue from the sale of additional units falls, reaches zero, and then becomes negative. For purposes of illustration, let us also assume that the firm's marginal cost is constant in the short run. The linear, downward-sloping demand curve, the marginal revenue curve, and the constant marginal cost curve for such a firm are shown in Figure 9.9. Notice that if the firm charges too high a price (e.g., $P_1$), its marginal revenue will exceed its marginal cost; hence, it will be forgoing some amount of marginal profit (shown by the lighter shade). If the firm sets its price at too low a level, its marginal cost will exceed its marginal revenue, and the firm will experience a marginal loss (shown by the darker shade).

The ability of a monopoly to set its price is further limited by the possibility of rising marginal costs of production. If this is the case, then surely at some point the increasing cost of producing additional units of output will exceed the decreasing marginal revenue received from the sale of additional units. This begins at $Q'$, shown in Figure 9.10.

In conclusion, the firm that exercises a monopoly power over its price should not set its price at the highest possible level. Instead, it should set it at the *right* level. And what is this "right" level? It is the level that results in MR = MC.

To see how the MR = MC rule applies to the monopolist as well as to the perfect competitor, see Table 9.8. Note that the table presents only the cost data relevant to this example. For purposes of comparison, the same cost figures used in the previous section for the perfectly competitive firm have been selected.[3] But in

---

[3]By maintaining consistency in the cost data, we realize that we are sacrificing some realism because a monopoly would obviously produce more than a perfectly competitive firm. However, this shortcoming can be rectified by simply assuming that each unit of output is the equivalent of a larger number of units (e.g., $Q = 1 = 1,000$).

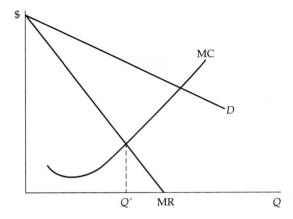

**FIGURE 9.10** Increasing Marginal Costs in Relation to Decreasing Marginal Revenue

this case, we assume that the firm is the "only game in town." Note that the price is not equal to the marginal revenue, because the firm is a price setter and not a price taker. Its demand schedule consists of columns 1 and 2, and the total revenue and marginal revenue schedules are those that normally accompany a downward-sloping demand curve.

Starting from the zero output level, let us consider the price, output, marginal revenue, marginal cost, and marginal profit as additional units of output are produced. You

**TABLE 9.8   Using Marginal Revenue and Marginal Cost to Determine Optimal Price and Output: The Case of Monopoly**

| Quantity (Q) | Price (P) | Total Revenue (TR) | Marginal Revenue (MR) | Average Total Cost (AC) | Total Cost (TC) | Marginal Cost (MC) | Total Profit (π) |
|---|---|---|---|---|---|---|---|
| 0 | 180 | 0 | | | 100.00 | | −100.00 |
| | | | 170 | | | 55.70 | |
| 1 | 170 | 170 | | 155.70 | 155.70 | | 14.30 |
| | | | 150 | | | 49.90 | |
| 2 | 160 | 320 | | 102.80 | 205.60 | | 114.40 |
| | | | 130 | | | 48.30 | |
| 3 | 150 | 450 | | 84.63 | 253.90 | | 196.10 |
| | | | 110 | | | 50.90 | |
| 4 | 140 | 560 | | 76.20 | 304.80 | | 255.20 |
| | | | 90 | | | 57.70 | |
| 5 | 130 | 650 | | 72.50 | 362.50 | | 287.50 |
| | | | 70 | | | 68.70 | |
| 6 | 120 | 720 | | 71.87 | 431.20 | | 288.80 |
| | | | 50 | | | 83.90 | |
| 7 | 110 | 770 | | 73.59 | 515.10 | | 254.90 |
| | | | 30 | | | 103.30 | |
| 8 | 100 | 800 | | 77.30 | 618.40 | | 181.60 |
| | | | 10 | | | 126.90 | |
| 9 | 90 | 810 | | 82.81 | 745.30 | | 64.70 |
| | | | −10 | | | 154.70 | |
| 10 | 80 | 800 | | 90.00 | 900.00 | | −100.00 |
| | | | −30 | | | 186.70 | |
| 11 | 70 | 770 | | 98.79 | 1086.70 | | −316.70 |
| | | | −50 | | | 222.90 | |
| 12 | 60 | 720 | | 109.13 | 1309.60 | | −589.60 |

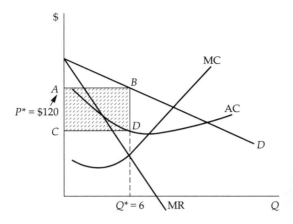

**FIGURE 9.11** Graphical Depiction of MR = MC Rule for a Monopoly

can see that as output increases, the marginal revenue associated with each unit exceeds the marginal cost up to six units. Beyond this level, the firm actually incurs a marginal loss. As the firm moves beyond this level, total profit is still positive, but it is not at its maximum. In other words, by following the MR = MC rule, a profit-maximizing firm would want to produce six units of output per time period. To do so, it would have to set a price of $120.

The way in which the MR = MC rule underlies the monopoly price can perhaps be more clearly seen in a graph. In Figure 9.11, we see that the firm would select *P*\* because, given the particular demand for the product, this is the price that would prompt customers to buy *Q*\*. And *Q*\* is the quantity that the firm would want to produce per time period because this is the amount at which the revenue received from the last unit produced is just equal to its cost (i.e., marginal revenue = marginal cost). With the same graphical references to total revenue and total cost as used in the analysis of perfect competition, we arrive at the measure of total profit as the shaded area *ABCD*.

In a perfectly competitive market, the short-run economic profit enjoyed by the monopoly firm in this example would be vulnerable in the long run to the entry of other firms wishing to earn similar amounts of profit. But because we assume it is a monopoly, this firm would not be subject to such threats in the long run. Nonetheless, the preceding illustration is not meant to give the impression that a monopoly automatically earns economic profit in either the short or the long run. Whether or not it does depends on the demand for its product. For example, a company may have a monopoly on a toy for children that is in great demand and consequently enables it to earn the kind of economic profit illustrated in Figure 9.11. But as the market demand is filled or as children begin to tire of the product, the demand could decline (e.g., the demand curve shifts to the left) to the extent that the firm earns only a normal profit or perhaps even incurs a loss.

Suppose a price-setting firm does not wish to maximize its short-run profit but instead wants to maximize its revenue. Let us explore this possibility using the data in

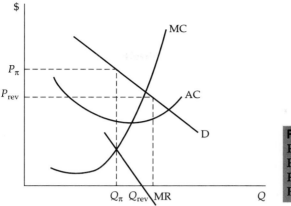

**FIGURE 9.12**
Relationship between the
Profit-Maximizing and
Revenue-Maximizing
Price and Quantity

Table 9.8. The price that maximizes the total revenue can be determined simply by observation. As you can see, by charging $90 for its product, the firm will receive the maximum total revenue of $810. You can also see that this revenue-maximizing price is lower than the one that maximizes the firm's total profit (i.e., $90 < $120). This relationship is illustrated in Figure 9.12. This dichotomy between **pricing for profit** and **pricing for revenue** will be discussed in greater detail in chapter 12.

## The Implications of Perfect Competition and Monopoly for Managerial Decision Making

After studying this chapter, it might appear to the reader that managers in a perfectly competitive or a monopoly market do not have much of a challenge in deciding on the price and output levels of their firm. In the case of perfect competition, the market price is determined for the managers by the forces of supply and demand. All that they have to do is to decide whether their cost structure will enable their firm to at least earn a normal amount of profit. In the case of monopoly, the fact that the firm has no competition enables its managers simply to follow the MR = MC rule to maximize its profit. We would agree with this view, particularly when the pricing and output challenges of these firms are compared with those in monopolistic competition and oligopoly. This will be evident when reading the next chapter. Nonetheless, as explained earlier, we have presented a detailed analysis of perfect competition and monopoly because those models serve as the basis from which pricing and output decisions in monopolistic competition and oligopoly can be better understood and appreciated. Besides this, we believe that the analysis of firms in perfect competition and monopoly offers lessons to managers that go beyond the routine application of the $P = MC$ or MR = MC rule.

The most important lesson that managers can learn by studying the perfectly competitive market is that it is extremely difficult to make money in a highly competitive market. Indeed, the only way for firms to survive in perfect competition is to be as cost efficient as possible because there is absolutely no way to control the price. Another lesson offered by the perfectly competitive model is that it might pay for a firm to move into a market before others start to enter. This might mean entering a market even before the demand is high enough to support an above-normal price. Spotting these market opportunities and taking the risk of going into these markets are key tasks of a good manager. Of course, the demand may never materialize or the long-run increase in supply might be so great that no one makes any money in this market. But that is all part of the risk that a manager must sometimes take. We will see more of the making of pricing and output decisions in highly competitive markets in the next chapter when we examine the case of monopolistic competition.

In monopoly markets not sanctioned by the government via regulations or patent laws, a monopoly presents a manager with somewhat of a paradox. What happens if the managers of a firm are so successful in beating the competition that the firm in fact becomes a monopoly, or at least one that exercises monopolistic power? Such was the case for IBM, which so dominated the mainframe computer market in the 1960s that in 1969 the Department of Justice instigated an antitrust suit against it to reduce its market power. The suit was eventually dropped in 1982. Such is the case in 1998 for Microsoft. This company, arguably one of the most successful companies in the history of the market economy, is being accused by the Department of Justice of violating the Sherman Anti-Trust Act, through its domination of the operating system for personal computers and its tie-in of its system with its Web browser product.

Our personal view on this matter is that a number of past examples indicate that changes in the economics of a business (i.e., customers, technology, and competition), eventually break down a dominating company's monopolistic power, no matter how invincible the company might seem (although some might argue that Microsoft will prove to be a major exception). Shortly after the Justice Department dropped the case against IBM, the company began to lose a considerable amount of business as personal computers, workstations, and client server networks became more important than the mainframe in many aspects of computing. Polaroid, the company which even today has a virtual monopoly on its instant developing camera, is no longer the company that it once was, thanks to the one-hour photo developing process, video cameras, and most importantly, digital cameras.

Perhaps one of the best examples of the vulnerability of a monopoly can be found in the pharmaceutical industry. Until the early 1990s, firms in this industry enjoyed among the highest profit margins and returns on equity of all the companies in the *Fortune* 500. However, a number of recent events have started to erode their profitability. To start with, companies that do not have the patent on a drug that treats a particular illness are coming up with what the industry calls "me-too" products. These are drugs that offer a therapy for the same illness but whose chemical compositions are different enough to come under different patents. Furthermore, patents are beginning to run out on a number of highly profitable drugs and generic drugs are entering the market at far lower prices. Finally, those who make the purchasing decisions are exerting much more market power than ever before. It used to be that the majority of purchasers were fee-based private physicians who wrote prescriptions regardless of price, partly because they knew that their patients would be reimbursed by third-party payers such as insurance companies. Now much more of the purchasing decisions are being made by cost-conscious health maintenance organizations, hospital associations, and networks of retail pharmacies.

The key lesson for managers to learn from the many examples of once-powerful monopolies or near-monopolies that have eventually been affected by changing economics is not to be complacent or arrogant and assume that their ability to earn economic profit can never be diminished. This is certainly the case for monopolistic competition and oligopoly, as you will see in the next chapter.

## International Application: Next Time You're in Tibet, Be Sure to Stop at the "Hard Yak Café"

In this chapter, you learned that if a firm is competing in a perfectly competitive market, its profits are subject to the vagaries of supply and demand. Imagine yourself as a yak herder in Tibet, where yak meat, along with "tsampa" (a mix of barley flour and rancid yak butter) and tea, is the staple food of the country. According to an article in the *New York Times,* "fierce competition has driven meat prices to the lowest in years."[4] One meat seller, in an interview with the *Times* reporter covering the story, described the situation succinctly enough: "Business is bad, too many sellers, not enough buyers."

Tibet experienced exceptionally bad weather in 1997–1998 (a rough winter followed by summer flooding) that would be expected to cause an increase in prices. However, what actually happened was that the bad weather led yak herders into thinking about the possibility of a repeat in the bad weather during the winter of 1998–1999. Assuming this to be the case, many herders decided to slaughter their yaks in the fall and take them to Lhasa, the capital of Tibet, where they had always gotten the highest prices. However, when they all arrived in the capital with their freshly killed product, the sudden increase in supply drove the price of yak meat to 75 cents a pound, about half the price of two years before.

There is nothing that the individual yak herder can do to offset the lower prices, because yak meat is a "standardized" product. However, we suspect that the price reduction may have at least helped those who buy the yak meat and sell it in restaurants. For example, the main restaurant in the Lhasa Hotel is called the "Hard Yak Café." No doubt the profit margin on their yak burgers has increased. But as you can well imagine from your knowledge of economic theory, the added profit should start to bring in more food establishments offering yak meat dishes. (Can the "Big Yak" be far behind?)

---

[4]This example is taken from "For the Bountiful Yak, the Road Ends Sadly Here," *The New York Times,* January 1, 1999.

## THE SOLUTION

Armed with all the available figures on the estimated cost and demand for *Waterpure*, Frank spent the next week trying to come up with an optimal price for the product. The weekly demand for the firm's bottled water product was estimated to be

$$Q_D = 2,000 - 1,000\,P \quad \textbf{(9.1)}$$

where $Q_D$ = Quantity of 12-ounce plastic bottles (in thousands)

$P$ = Price per container

Based on estimates provided by the bottling plant, Frank expressed the cost function as

$$TC = 150 + 0.25Q \quad \textbf{(9.2)}$$

where TC = Total cost per week (in thousands of dollars)

$Q$ = Output of 12-ounce plastic bottles (in thousands)

To find the optimal price on the basis of the MR = MC rule, Frank first found the total revenue and marginal revenue functions based on the data in Equation (9.1). Expressing this equation in terms of price,

$$P = 2 - 0.001Q \quad \textbf{(9.3)}$$

and substituting this into the equation for total revenue (i.e., TR = $P \times Q$), he found total revenue to be

$$TR = 2Q - 0.001Q^2 \quad \textbf{(9.4)}$$

To find marginal revenue, he took the first derivative of this equation and set it equal to the firm's marginal cost. (Based on Equation (9.2), he knew that the firm incurred a constant marginal cost of $0.25 per unit of the product.) He then solved for the quantity ($Q^*$) that satisfied the equality. Then he found the optimal price by substituting the value of this optimal quantity into Equation (9.3).

$$MR = \frac{dTR}{dQ} = 2 - 0.002Q \quad \textbf{(9.5)}$$

$$2 - 0.002Q = 0.25$$

$$Q^* = 875 \ (875,000 \text{ units per week})$$

$$P = 2 - 0.001\,(875)$$

$$P^* = 1.125 \quad \textbf{(9.6)}$$

$$= \$1.10 \text{ (rounding to the nearest 10 cents)}$$

Figure 9.13 shows Frank's solution on a per-unit basis.

Frank assumed that the main distributors of *Waterpure* would be small retail food establishments, which generally mark up the wholesale price of bottled water by about 100 percent. Therefore, Frank determined the wholesale price that Global Foods could charge the retail stores by simply taking 50 percent of the optimal price of $1.10. For every unit sold, the company would receive $0.55.

Frank then estimated the company's weekly profit from the production and sale of bottled water.

$$TR = \$0.55 \times 875$$

$$= 481.25, \text{ or } \$481,250$$

$$TC = 150 + 0.25\,(875)$$

$$= 368.75, \text{ or } \$368,750$$

$$\text{Total profit} = \$481,250 - \$368,750$$

$$= \$112,500$$

*(Continued)*

Although Frank realized that he had the optimal price for *Waterpure,* he also knew that there were already companies with established bottled water products in the market that were selling for about $1.25 a bottle. As the new entrant into the market, should Global Foods go along with the price established by the market leaders or should it try to sell it at a lower price? He was going to have to take this issue up with Nicole Goodman.

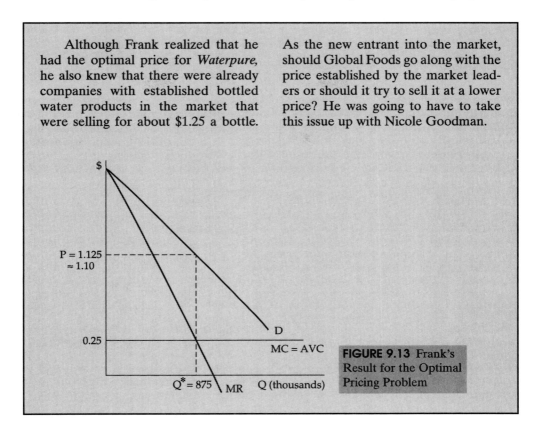

**FIGURE 9.13** Frank's Result for the Optimal Pricing Problem

## Summary

This chapter has presented a view of the pricing and output decisions facing firms in two extreme situations. In the case of perfect competition, the firm has virtually no power to set the price and is only able to decide to what extent (if at all) it wants to produce in this market, given the going market price. In the case of a monopoly, the firm *is* the entire market supply. This monopoly of supply gives the firm the power to set any price that it desires. In certain cases, this monopoly power is regulated by the government.

We demonstrated that firms wishing to maximize their short-run profit (or minimize their short-run loss) should establish their price and output levels according to the MR = MC rule. For those firms in perfectly competitive markets, MR is in fact equal to the price that has already been established for them by the forces of supply and demand. For these price-taking firms, the only task is to decide what output quantity results in the matching of the market price (i.e., marginal revenue) and the marginal cost of producing the last unit of its output. For the monopoly firm, following the MR = MC rule involves pricing the product at the level whereby the quantity that people purchase is the amount needed to bring MR in line with MC. We now turn to the cases between the two extremes of perfect competition and monopoly. For these "imperfect competitors," the MR = MC rule is an important part of their pricing decision. However, as we will show, the actions or reactions of their competitors also play a major role in the pricing of their products.

## Important Concepts

**Contribution margin:** The amount of revenue that a firm earns above its total variable cost. According to economic analysis, a firm experiencing a loss may continue operating in the short run if it has a positive contribution margin. A firm experiencing a negative contribution margin must shut down its operations because its revenue cannot even cover its variable costs of operations. (p. 370)

**Economic cost:** All cost incurred to attract resources into a company's employ. Such cost includes explicit cost usually recognized on accounting records as well as opportunity cost. (p. 361)

**Economic loss:** A situation that exists when a firm's revenues cannot cover its accounting cost as well as its opportunity cost of production. (p. 361)

**Economic profit:** Total revenue minus total economic cost. An amount of profit earned in a particular endeavor above the amount of profit that the firm could be earning in its next-best alternative activity. Also referred to as *abnormal profit* or *above-normal* profit. (p. 361)

**Long run (market analysis):** Firms are expected to enter a market in which sellers are earning economic profit. They are expected to leave a market in which sellers are incurring economic losses. (p. 371).

**Market power:** The power to establish the market price. (p. 359)

**Market structure:** The number and relative sizes of the buyers and sellers in a particular market. A "competitive" market structure implies that the number of buyers and sellers in a market is large enough that it is difficult, if not impossible, for any one buyer or seller to determine the market price. (p. 356)

**Monopoly:** A market in which there is only one seller for a particular good or service. There may be legal barriers to entry into this type of market (e.g., regulated utilities, patent protection). (p. 357)

**MR = MC rule:** A rule stating that if a firm desires to maximize its economic profit, it must produce an amount of output whereby the marginal revenue received at this particular level is equal to its marginal cost. This implies that those firms with market power must set a price that prompts buyers to purchase this particular level of output. (p. 366)

**Normal profit:** An amount of profit earned in a particular endeavor that is just equal to the profit that could be earned in a firm's next-best alternative activity. When a firm earns normal profit, its revenue is just enough to cover both its accounting cost and its opportunity cost. It can also be considered as the return to capital and management necessary to keep resources engaged in a particular activity. (p. 361)

**$P = MC$ rule:** A variation of the MR = MC rule for those firms operating in perfectly competitive markets. In such markets, firms are price takers. Thus, the price they must deal with (which has been determined by the forces of supply and demand) is in fact the same as a firm's marginal revenue. Firms using this rule must also be careful that the price is greater than average variable cost as well as equal to marginal cost (i.e., $AVC < P = MC$). If a firm cannot operate at the production level where this condition holds, it should shut down its operations. (p. 367)

**Perfect competition:** A market with four main characteristics: (1) a very large number of relatively small buyers and sellers, (2) a standardized product, (3) easy entry and exit, and (4) complete information by all market participants about the market price. Firms in this type of market have absolutely no control over the price and must compete on the basis of the market price established by the forces of supply and demand. (p. 357)

**Price takers:** Firms that operate in perfectly competitive markets. (p. 357)

**Pricing for profit:**   The method of pricing that follows the MR = MC rule. (p. 377)

**Pricing for revenue:**   The pricing of a product to maximize a firm's revenue. In this case, the firm would try to price its product to sell an amount of output whereby the revenue earned from the last unit sold would be equal to zero (i.e., MR = 0). Assuming that the firm faces a linear demand curve, the price it establishes to maximize revenue would be lower than the price that would maximize its profit. (p. 377)

**Shutdown point:**   The point at which the firm must consider ceasing its production activity because the short-run loss suffered by operating would be equal to the short-run loss suffered by not operating (i.e., the operating loss = total fixed cost). In a perfectly competitive situation, this point is found at the lowest point of a firm's average variable cost curve. If the market price falls to this point, the firm should consider shutting down its operations. Any price lower than this would dictate that the firm should cease its operations. (p. 370)

## Questions

1. What are the main characteristics of a perfectly competitive market that cause buyers and sellers to be price takers? Explain.

2. Explain the importance of free entry and exit in the perfectly competitive market. That is, if free entry and exit did not exist, what impact would this have on the allocation of resources and on the ability of firms to earn above-normal profits over time?

3. "The perfectly competitive model is not very useful for managers because very few markets in the U.S. economy are perfectly competitive." Do you agree with this statement? Explain. Regardless of whether you agree, what lessons can managers learn by studying perfectly competitive markets?

4. Explain why the demand curve facing a perfectly competitive firm is assumed to be perfectly elastic (i.e., horizontal at the going market price).

5. Explain why the demand curve facing a monopolist is less elastic than one facing a firm that operates in a monopolistically competitive market (all other factors held constant).

6. Use the model of perfect competition described in this chapter to explain, illustrate, or elaborate on the following statements.

   a. "Increasing competition from new firms entering the market is good because it means one is in a good business."

   b. "One important difference between an entrepreneur and a manager is that the former gets into a market before demand increases, while the latter gets into the market after the shift."

7. Explain the relationship between $P >$ AVC and a firm's contribution margin.

8. Why do economists consider zero economic profit to be "normal"?

9. "Economic profit" is a theoretical concept used to help explain the behavior of firms in competitive markets. Suggest ways in which this concept can actually be measured.

10. Explain why the $P =$ MC rule is the same as the MR = MC rule for perfectly competitive firms.

11. Explain why a price-setting firm will always set its revenue-maximizing price below the price that would maximize its profit.

12. Provide some examples of business cases that a typical firm must consider. If possible, use current examples reported in the business press.

13. How "perfectly" competitive do you think are the following markets: (1) stock market, (2) bond market, (3) foreign exchange market, (4) world sugar market, and (5) world oil market? Explain.

14. Explain how the concept of "economic profit" might help to explain the rationale for the government's granting of monopolies to those firms that protect their product with a patent.

## Problems

For certain questions, consult Appendix 9A.

1. Following is the graphical representation of a short-run situation faced by a perfectly competitive firm. Is this a good market for this firm to be in? Explain. What do you expect will happen in the long run? Explain.

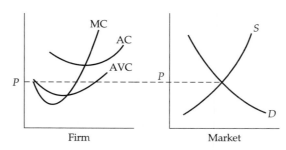

2. Indicate whether each of the following statements is true or false and explain why.
   a. A competitive firm that is incurring a loss should immediately cease operations.
   b. A pure monopoly does not have to worry about suffering losses because it has the power to set its prices at any level it desires.
   c. In the long run, firms operating in perfect competition and monopolistic competition will tend to earn normal profits.
   d. Assuming a linear demand curve, a firm that wishes to maximize its revenue will charge a lower price than a firm that wishes to maximize its profits.
   e. If $P > \text{AVC}$, a firm's total fixed cost will be greater than its loss.
   f. When a firm is able to set its price, its price will always be less than its MR.
   g. A monopoly will always earn economic profit because it is able to set any price that it wants to.

3. Kelson Electronics, a manufacturer of VCRs, estimates the following relation between its marginal cost of production and monthly output:

$$\text{MC} = \$150 + 0.005Q$$

   a. What does this function imply about the effect of the law of diminishing returns on Kelson's short-run cost function?
   b. Calculate the marginal cost of production at 1,500, 2,000, and 3,500 units of output.
   c. Assume Kelson operates as a price taker in a competitive market. What is this firm's profit-maximizing level of output if the market price is $175?
   d. Compute Kelson's short-run supply curve for its product.

4. A manufacturer of electronics products is considering entering the telephone equipment business. It estimates that if it were to begin making wireless telephones, its short-run cost function would be as follows:

| Q (Thousands) | AVC | AC | MC |
|---|---|---|---|
| 9 | 41.10 | 52.21 | 30.70 |
| 10 | 40.00 | 50.00 | 30.10 |
| 11 | 39.10 | 48.19 | 30.10 |
| 12 | 38.40 | 46.73 | 30.70 |
| 13 | 37.90 | 45.59 | 31.90 |
| 14 | 37.60 | 44.74 | 33.70 |
| 15 | 37.50 | 44.17 | 36.10 |
| 16 | 37.60 | 43.85 | 39.10 |
| 17 | 37.90 | 43.78 | 42.70 |
| 18 | 38.40 | 43.96 | 46.90 |
| 19 | 39.10 | 44.36 | 51.70 |
| 20 | 40.00 | 45.00 | 57.10 |

**a.** Plot the average cost, average variable cost, marginal cost, and price on a graph.
**b.** Suppose the average wholesale price of a wireless phone is currently $50. Do you think this company should enter the market? Explain. Indicate on the graph the amount of profit (or loss) earned by the firm at the optimal level of production.
**c.** Suppose the firm does enter the market and that over time increasing competition causes the price of telephones to fall to $35. What impact will this have on the firm's production levels and profit? Explain. What would you advise this firm to do?
**5.** This same manufacturer of electronics products has just developed a hand-held computer. Following is the cost schedule for producing these computers on a monthly basis. Also included is a schedule of prices and quantities that the firm believes it will be able to sell (based on previous market research).

| Q (Thousands) | Price | MR | AVC | AC | MC |
|---|---|---|---|---|---|
| 0 | 1,650 | | | | |
| 1 | 1,570 | 1,570 | 1,281 | 2,281 | 1,281 |
| 2 | 1,490 | 1,410 | 1,134 | 1,634 | 987 |
| 3 | 1,410 | 1,250 | 1,009 | 1,342.33 | 759 |
| 4 | 1,330 | 1,090 | 906 | 1,156 | 597 |
| 5 | 1,250 | 930 | 825 | 1,025 | 501 |
| 6 | 1,170 | 770 | 766 | 932.67 | 471 |
| 7 | 1,090 | 610 | 729 | 871.86 | 507 |
| 8 | 1,010 | 450 | 714 | 839 | 609 |
| 9 | 930 | 290 | 721 | 832.11 | 777 |
| 10 | 850 | 130 | 750 | 850 | 1,011 |

**a.** What price should the firm charge if it wants to maximize its profits in the short run?
**b.** What arguments can be made for charging a price *higher* than this price? If a higher price is indeed established, what amount would you recommend? Explain.
**c.** What arguments can be made for charging a *lower* price than the profit-maximizing level? If a lower price is indeed established, what amount would you recommend? Explain.

**6.** The manufacturer of high-quality flatbed scanners is trying to decide what price to set for its product. The costs of production and the demand for the product are assumed to be as follows:

$$TC = 500{,}000 + 0.85Q + 0.015Q^2$$

$$Q = 14{,}166 - 16.6P$$

**a.** Determine the short-run profit-maximizing price.

**b.** Plot this information on a graph showing AC, AVC, MC, P, and MR.

**7.** The demand and cost function for a company are estimated to be as follows:

$$P = 100 - 8Q$$

$$TC = 50 + 80Q - 10\,Q^2 + 0.6Q^3$$

**a.** What price should the company charge if it wishes to maximize its profit in the short run?

**b.** What price should it charge if it wishes to maximize its revenue in the short run?

**c.** Suppose the company lacks confidence in the accuracy of cost estimates expressed in a cubic equation and simply wants to use a linear approximation. Suggest a linear representation of this cubic equation. What difference would it make on the recommended profit-maximizing and revenue-maximizing prices?

**8.** Overheard at the water cooler: "The demand and cost estimates that were provided at the meeting are very useful [$Q = 90 - 6.5P$ and $TC = 150 + 3.5Q$]. Unfortunately, what we didn't realize at the time was that our fixed costs were underestimated by at least 30 percent. This means that we'll have to adjust upward our price by at least 30 percent to cover the added fixed cost. In any case, there is no way in the world that we can survive by charging less than \$9 for our product."

**a.** Comment on this statement. Do you agree with the speaker? Explain. Illustrate your answer with the use of a graph indicating the firm's short-run cost structure.

**b.** What price do you think this firm should charge if it wants to maximize its short-run profit?

**9.** Use the following equation to demonstrate why a firm producing at the output level where MR = MC will also be able to maximize its total profit (i.e., be at the point where marginal profit is equal to zero).

$$P = 170 - 5Q$$

$$TC = 40 + 50Q + 5Q^2$$

**10.** "In a perfectly competitive market, a firm has to be either *good* or *lucky*." Explain what is meant by this statement. Illustrate your answer with the use of the diagrams shown in Figures 9.5, 9.6, and 9.7.

---

## Take It to the Net

We invite you to visit the Keat/Young page on the Prentice Hall Web site at:

**http://www.prenhall.com/keat**

for additional resources.

## Appendix 9A

## The Use of Calculus in Pricing and Output Decisions

Thus far, we have discussed the firm's pricing and output decisions with the use of tabular and graphical examples. Using both the "total" approach and the "marginal" approach, we arrived at the MR = MC rule for determining the optimal level of output and price for those firms able to exercise market power. As a supplement, we now explain the MR = MC rule with the use of calculus.

To simplify our illustrations, we assume that the firm has a quadratic total cost function, rather than the cubic function used throughout the examples in the previous sections of this chapter.

# Perfect Competition

Suppose that you are the owner and operator of a perfectly competitive firm with the following total cost function:

$$TC = 2,000 + 10Q + 0.02Q^2 \tag{9A.1}$$

Suppose further that the current market price is \$25. By definition, $TR = P \times Q$, so your total revenue function can be stated as:

$$TR = 25Q \tag{9A.2}$$

Profit ($\pi$) is defined as $TR - TC$. Therefore, using Equations (9A.1) and (9A.2), your firm's profit function can be expressed as:

$$\pi = 25\,Q - (2,000 + 10Q + 0.02Q^2) \tag{9A.3}$$
$$= 25\,Q - 2,000 - 10Q - 0.02Q^2$$
$$= -2,000 + 15Q - 0.02Q^2$$

The optimal output level ($Q^*$) can be found at the point where your firm's marginal profit is equal to zero. In other words, additional units of output should be produced as long as your firm earns additional profit from their sale. Using calculus, the marginal profit can be expressed as the first derivative of the profit function:

$$\frac{d\pi}{dQ} = 15 - 0.04Q \tag{9A.4}$$

Setting Equation (9A.4) equal to zero and solving for the optimal level of output ($Q^*$),

$$15 - 0.04Q = 0 \tag{9A.5}$$
$$Q^* = 375$$

Returning to the total profit function presented in Equation (9A.3) and substituting $Q^*$ for $Q$ results in the following profit:

$$\pi = -2,000 + 15\,(375) - 0.02\,(375)^2 \tag{9A.6}$$
$$= \$812.50$$

We conclude that at the price of $25, the firm will earn maximum economic profit by producing 375 units of output per time period.

An alternative way of finding $P^*$ and $Q^*$ is to set the firm's marginal revenue function equal to its marginal cost function and then solve for $Q^*$. We already know that MR $= P$. The marginal cost function is the first derivative of the total cost function:

$$\text{MC} = \frac{d\text{TC}}{dQ} = 10 + 0.04Q \qquad \textbf{(9A.7)}$$

Setting MR equal to Equation (9A.7) and solving for $Q^*$ gives us

$$25 = 10 + 0.04Q \qquad \textbf{(9A.8)}$$
$$15 = 0.04Q$$
$$Q^* = 375$$

Comparison of Equations (9A.8) and (9A.5) provides a useful and concise explanation of the MR = MC rule. As you can see, using this rule is the mathematical equivalent of finding the level of output that maximizes the total profit function.

## Monopoly

As the manager of a product that only your company sells (e.g., a patent-protected product), suppose you are given the following information:

$$\text{TC} = 10{,}000 + 100Q + 0.02Q^2 \qquad \textbf{(9A.9)}$$
$$Q_D = 20{,}000 - 100P \qquad \textbf{(9A.10)}$$

You can use the same procedure employed in the case of perfect competition to find $Q^*$ and $P^*$.

First, determine your marginal revenue function. Because you are a price setter and not a price taker, you cannot assume that MR $= P$. Instead, you must derive the marginal revenue function from your firm's demand function, shown in Equation (9A.10). Because your objective is to find the level of output that will maximize your profit (i.e., $Q^*$), you must rearrange the terms in the equation so that price depends on the level of output:

$$P = 200 - 0.01Q \qquad \textbf{(9A.11)}$$

By definition, TR $= P \times Q$. So by substitution,

$$\text{TR} = (200 - 0.01Q)Q \qquad \textbf{(9A.12)}$$
$$= 200\,Q - 0.01Q^2$$

The marginal revenue function is the first derivative of the total revenue function:

$$\text{MR} = \frac{d\text{TR}}{dQ} = 200 - 0.02Q \qquad \textbf{(9A.13)}$$

From the example of perfect competition, we know that the first derivative of the total cost function is the marginal cost function:

$$\text{MC} = \frac{d\text{TC}}{dQ} = 100 + 0.04Q \qquad \textbf{(9A.14)}$$

Thus, the MR = MC rule is adhered to by setting Equation (9A.13) equal to Equation (9A.14) and solving for $Q^*$:

$$200 - 0.02Q = 100 + 0.04Q \qquad \textbf{(9A.15)}$$

$$0.06Q = 100$$

$$Q^* = 1{,}667 \text{ (rounded to the nearest whole number)}$$

To find $P^*$ we return to Equation (9A.11) and substitute $Q^*$ for $Q$.

$$P = 200 - 0.01\,(1.667) \qquad \textbf{(9A.16)}$$

$$P^* = \$183.33, \text{ or } \$183$$

At the rounded price of \$183, your firm can expect to sell 1,667 units of output per time period and earn an economic profit of \$73,333 (rounded to the nearest dollar). From the example on perfect competition, you should be aware of how the profit figure was determined.

• • •

As you can see from the preceding examples, the use of calculus offers a very concise way of explaining the output decision for price-taking firms in perfectly competitive markets and the pricing/output decision for monopoly firms. The same procedures could be applied for those firms in monopolistic competition and even for oligopolistic firms that have clear-cut roles as price leaders in their markets. However, tables and graphs similar to those used in previous sections of this chapter provide the same answers as the calculus method. Our intention is for this appendix to serve as a supplement rather than an advanced treatment of the pricing/output decision.

# CHAPTER 10

# Pricing and Output Decisions: Monopolistic Competition and Oligopoly

## THE SITUATION

In a meeting with Nicole Goodman, Frank Robinson explained the results of his price analysis. "My concern is that we know our optimal price, but do we really know how our competitors are going to react when we launch our product at this price point? Furthermore, I'm not sure the major players really consider us as a threat to their business, at least not yet. Therefore, can we assume that they will take us seriously?"

Nicole agreed, and suggested conducting further research. "One thing that we need is a complete list of prices of the major brands as well as the smaller brands," she began. "I was at a marketing conference in southern California last week and I noticed that the hotel that I stayed in had bottled water with the hotel name on the label in its minibar right next to one of the national brands."

"Leave it to California to come out with the trendiest products," Frank retorted.

"Not necessarily," said Nicole. "I heard that private labels are proliferating throughout the country. For example, there is even bottled water with the labels of cities and countries. And you might have heard that even McDonald's has its own bottled water that I understand is selling well in some markets. The other key information that we could use in making our

*(Continued)*

pricing decision is the perception of our product by potential consumers and their view of how much value our product provides them relative to our price. Perhaps it would be worthwhile

to hold a few focus groups to find this out."

"Good idea," said Frank. "I'll get on this right away and have a report for you in a couple of weeks."

# Introduction

In this chapter, we examine in detail the pricing and output decisions made by managers in two imperfectly competitive markets. More specifically, these two markets are called monopolistic competition and oligopoly. As stated earlier, in monopolistic competition and oligopoly, firms exercise various degrees of power to set the price, short of the power exercised by a monopoly. As in the case of perfect competition and pure monopoly, we assume that these imperfect competitors want to maximize their profit. This implies that they will want to produce an output level at which MR = MC. Therefore, they will set a price at which customers demand this particular level of output.

However, unlike the case of pure monopoly, monopolistic competitors and oligopolists have to consider the possible actions or reactions by competitors to the prices that they establish. Another way to look at this challenge is to recall our earlier comment that pricing involves three Cs: cost, customers, and competition. Because a perfect competitor has no control whatsoever over its price, it must only consider whether its cost is low enough to earn a profit at the going market price. A monopoly needs to be concerned with customers (in particular their demand elasticity) as well as cost. But as we will now explain, monopolistic competitors and oligopolists have to assess all three elements of cost, customers, and competition in their pricing decisions. We will first look at the pricing and output decision of a monopolistic competitor. We will then turn our attention to the oligopolist.

# Monopolistic Competition

Recall from our presentation on market structure in the previous chapter that **monopolistic competition** is a market in which there are many firms and relatively easy entry. These two characteristics are very similar to those of perfect competition. What enables firms to set their prices (i.e., to be monopolistic) is product differentiation. By somehow convincing their customers that what they are selling is not the same as the offerings of the other firms in the market, a monopolistic competitor is able to set its price at a level that is higher than the price established by the forces of supply and demand.

A good example of how product differentiation can turn a product sold in a perfectly competitive market into one in which a seller is able to exercise some degree of market power is the case of Tyson chicken. As in any other market for a commodity, poultry farmers face the uncertainty of price volatility that is characteristic of a perfectly competitive market. Don Tyson, founder of America's leading poultry company bearing his name, described this situation quite succinctly: "My daddy started raising chickens more than fifty years ago. The problem wasn't raising the chickens, it was trying to sell them at prices that seemed to vary every day or every hour."[1]

The solution for Tyson Foods to the problem of price volatility was "further processed value-enhanced poultry." This process of product differentiation began when Tyson realized that by selling Rock Cornish game hens by the hen and not by the pound, it could maintain its price point even when the price per pound was fluctuating. Once consumers got used to the idea that Tyson's hens were selling for a particular price, they continued to evaluate this price relative to their tastes and preferences, incomes, and the price of competing goods, regardless of what the price per pound happened to be.

In addition to changing the unit used in pricing its poultry, Tyson soon discovered that selling breaded chicken parts enabled it to set prices that were relatively immune to the fluctuating prices of fresh, unprocessed poultry. Then Tyson found that it could vary the seasoning in the breading to fit the particular tastes and preferences of any consumer. In so doing, it also recognized that it could prepare its chicken products to meet the special requirements of large customers such as fast-food and supermarket chains and institutions such as schools and hospitals. These large customers were interested in buying at the lowest possible price, but they were also interested in quality, consistency, and stability of supply. Therefore, Tyson could negotiate long-term price contracts with these large buyers, further protecting itself from the daily vagaries of the perfectly competitive market.

In economic analysis, we assume that the monopolistically competitive firm follows the MR = MC rule in order to maximize its profit (or minimize its loss). Therefore, as a matter of convenience, we employ the same graphical illustration for monopolistic competition that we used for the case of a monopoly market. This is shown in Figure 10.1*a*.

If the firm is in the situation depicted in Figure 10.1*a*, that is, if it is earning above-normal profit, then we can expect newcomers to be attracted to this market. The effect of this added competition on the monopolistic competitor can be seen in Figure 10.1*b*. Notice that the entry of new firms causes the original firm's demand curve to shift downward and to the left. If you are confused by this movement and the movement of the supply curve in the perfectly competitive market, remember that we are talking about this change from the point of view of the *individual firm*, not of the entire market. From an individual firm's perspective, the entry of additional firms in the market would decrease its market share by reducing the demand for its product. The leftward shift in the demand curve serves to illustrate this decline in market share. To be sure, this case assumes that the total market demand remains unchanged while the new firms are entering the market. If the total market demand were increasing while newcomers entered the market, the direction and extent of the shift in demand would be uncertain.

In the long run, economists hypothesize that the same situation would exist for monopolistic competition as for perfect competition: firms would be earning normal profit. If firms either earned above-normal profit or incurred losses, as shown in Figure 10.1*c*, then the entry or exit of firms, along with the adjustment of fixed capacity by existing

---

[1]This quote and the rest of the material on Tyson is taken from Gene Walden and Edmund Lawler, *Marketing Masters: Secrets of America's Best Companies,* New York: HarperBusiness, 1993, pp. 12–17.

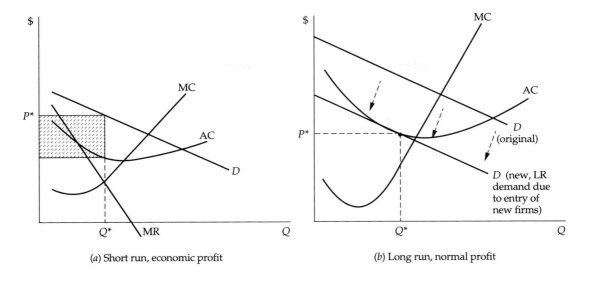

(a) Short run, economic profit

(b) Long run, normal profit

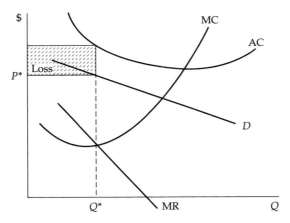

(c) Short or long run loss because demand is
below the level at which firm can set a
price to earn normal or economic profit.

**FIGURE 10.1** Monopolistic Competition

firms, would cause each individual firm's demand curve either to increase or decrease until firms in the market earned only normal profit. (See Figure 10.1b.)

Some of the best examples of monopolistic competition can be found among small businesses, particularly those in the retail trade or in services. Restaurants, grocery stores, dry cleaners, stationery stores, florists, hardware stores, pharmacies, and video rental stores are all markets in which entry is fairly easy and the number of sellers is relatively large. In these businesses, owner-managers may use location, "service with a smile," or a slightly different mix of product offerings to differentiate their business. For example, we have noticed that throughout the country, particularly in urban areas, sushi and Japanese food in general have begun to eclipse Chinese food in popularity. We believe that a growing concern about the fat content of food has contributed greatly to this shift in consumer preference. Several years ago, we began to notice an increasing number of Japanese restaurants in the New York City area that were opened and operated by ethnic Chinese. In addition, we began to notice a growing number of Chinese restaurants in New York City advertising the fact that they now had their own sushi bars.

The example of the Chinese restaurants serving sushi is a good illustration of one of the key characteristics of a monopolistically competitive market: ease of entry into the market. Although it is possible for sellers to differentiate their products, it is very easy for existing competitors to copy innovators or for new sellers to enter the market with their own version of an innovation. The next time you visit your local shopping area or mall, observe how easy it is for newcomers to begin selling a product or service that has been profitable for those already in the market. For example, when video rental stores first opened almost two decades ago, there were only one or two of them in shopping areas. Now there are many more and, in fact, a number of them have been forced to close as a result of the increasing number of competitors and other factors such, as pay-per-view television.

# Oligopoly

**Oligopoly** is a market dominated by a relatively small number of large firms. The products they sell may be either standardized or differentiated. Part of the control that oligopolists exercise over price and output stems from their ability to differentiate their products. But market power also stems mainly from the sheer size and dominance of the largest firms in this type of market.

The best examples of oligopoly in the U.S. economy are found in the manufacturing sector. Automobiles, appliances, mainframe computers, many types of processed foods (e.g., breakfast cereals and peanut butter), and beverages such as soft drinks and beer are all markets usually cited in introductory textbooks as examples of an oligopoly. Do not be misled by the number of brands in each of the markets. Although it is common knowledge that the U.S. automakers produce different makes and models, the general public is not as aware that the breakfast cereal industry consists essentially of four large food manufacturing concerns, notwithstanding the myriad of brand names and cereal types found on supermarket shelves. Examples of oligopolies that produce standardized products can be found in industries that produce raw materials such as steel, aluminum, copper, and various kinds of chemicals.

In 1994, there were over 4 million corporations and over 17 million partnerships and nonfarm sole proprietorships.[2] But only about 7,000 corporations had assets over $250 million, and two-thirds of these were in the finance, insurance, and real estate sector. Only 1,256 manufacturing corporations had assets over $250 million. Thus, we ask the question: "Just how concentrated is American industry?"

We will look at two measures that have been employed commonly to measure concentration. The first is the concentration ratio. A large amount of statistics on manufacturing corporations is published in the *Census of Manufactures*. For instance, in 1992

---

[2]*Statistical Abstract of the United States, 1997,* Table 834, p. 537.

**TABLE 10.1   Concentration Ratios in Manufacturing, 1992**

| SIC | Code and Industry | No. of Companies | Value of Shipments ($mil) | Percent of VS Accounted for by Largest 4 Cos. | 8 Cos. | HH Index |
|-----|-------------------|------------------|---------------------------|-----------------------------------------------|--------|----------|
| 3331 | Primary copper | 11 | 948 | 98 | 100 | 2,827 |
| 2111 | Cigarettes | 8 | 29,746 | 93 | (D) | (D) |
| 2082 | Malt beverages | 160 | 17,340 | 90 | 98 | (D) |
| 2043 | Cereal breakfast foods | 42 | 9,979 | 85 | 98 | 2,253 |
| 2771 | Greeting cards | 157 | 4,196 | 84 | 88 | 2,922 |
| 3221 | Glass containers | 16 | 4,860 | 84 | 93 | 2,162 |
| 3711 | Motor vehicles & bodies | 398 | 151,712 | 84 | 91 | 2,676 |
| 3861 | Photo equip. & supplies | 832 | 22,121 | 78 | 83 | 2,408 |
| 3571 | Electronic computers | 803 | 38,205 | 45 | 59 | 680 |
| 2911 | Petroleum refining | 131 | 136,579 | 30 | 49 | 414 |
| 2621 | Paper mills | 127 | 32,786 | 29 | 49 | 392 |
| 2834 | Pharmaceutical prepar. | 583 | 50,413 | 26 | 42 | 341 |
| 2731 | Book publishing | 2,504 | 16,753 | 23 | 38 | 251 |
| 2411 | Logging | 12,985 | 13,879 | 19 | 26 | 158 |
| 2421 | Sawmills | 5,302 | 21,065 | 14 | 20 | 78 |

D = Data omitted because of possible disclosure.

(the latest data available at this date), 41.4 percent of all manufacturing shipments was accounted for by the 200 largest companies,[3] representing a decrease in concentration from 1982, when it was 44.0 percent.

Generally, value of shipments is used by the U.S. Census Bureau to calculate these ratios. Companies are grouped by industry classification, and the data show the percentages of total shipments accounted for by the 4, 8, 20, and 50 largest companies. Table 10.1 summarizes some of the important statistics, specifically for companies with high and low concentration ratios. In particular, the percentage of the total value of shipments accounted for by the largest 4 and the largest 8 firms in an industry are shown.

Although these data are generally quite useful, they have several important limitations:

1. They are based on the similarity of the production process, but do not account for demand substitution (e.g., glass versus plastic containers).
2. Only U.S. production is included, imports are not accounted for.
3. Firms in some industries can easily modify their equipment to compete in other industries.
4. Some industries do not compete nationally. Thus, cement production shows a very low concentration ratio, but because of the high expense of transporting cement, companies operate locally, where their market share may be considerably higher.

---

[3]Most of the statistical information in this section was retrieved March 10, 1999 from the World Wide Web: www.census.gov/med/mancen/download/mc92cr.sum.

**5.** The statistics are not sensitive to differences within categories. For instance, each of the top four firms in an industry has 25 percent of the market, and the 4-firm ratio is 100. In another industry, the top firm has 94 percent of the market, and the next three have 2 percent each. Again, the ratio is 100, but surely the 94 percent firm has a considerably greater influence on pricing and behavior.

Another measure that considers the size distribution of firms in an industry is the Herfindahl-Hirschman index. The formula for this index is as follows:

$$HH = \sum_{i=1}^{n} S_i^2$$

where $n$ is the number of companies in the industry, and $S$ is the $i$th company's market share. The HH index is shown for the 15 industries in the last column of Table 10.1. The advantages of the HH index relative to concentration ratios are that

**1.** It uses the market share information about all the firms.
**2.** The squaring of individual market shares gives more weight to the larger firms.

The maximum HH index is 10,000—when there is just one firm in the industry. Using the prior example, the HH index will differentiate between an industry, where four firms equally share the total market (HH = 2,500), and an industry where the top firm has 94 percent and the other three 2 percent each (HH = 8,848). According to U.S. Department of Justice Merger Guidelines of 1982, "unconcentrated" markets are defined as those with an HH of less than 1,000. Table 10.2 shows selected markets dominated by a small number of companies and/or brands.

## Pricing in an Oligopolistic Market: Rivalry and Mutual Interdependence

Whether the sellers in an oligopolistic market compete against each other by differentiating their product, dominating market share, or both, the fact that there are relatively few sellers creates a situation where each is carefully watching the other as it sets its price. Economists refer to this pricing behavior as **mutual interdependence.** This means that each seller is setting its price while explicitly considering the reaction by its competitors to the price that it establishes.

In the 1930s, economist Paul Sweezy provided an early insight into the pricing dynamics of mutual interdependence among oligopoly firms by developing a **kinked demand** curve model.[4] The basic assumption of the Sweezy model is that a competitor (or competitors) will follow a price decrease but will not make a change in reaction to a price increase. Thus, the firm contemplating a price change may refrain from doing so for fear that quantities sold will be affected in such a way as to decrease profits.

If a firm lowers its price, this may have an immediate impact on the competition. This firm takes its action to increase sales by drawing customers away from the higher-priced competitors, but when competitors realize what is happening (i.e., their sales are

---

[4]Paul Sweezy, "Demand Under Conditions of Oligopoly," *Journal of Political Economy,* 47 (1939), pp. 568–73.

| TABLE 10.2   Selected Markets Dominated a Few Companies or Brands | |
| --- | --- |
| *Brand (Company)* | *Percentage of Market* |
| *Handheld Computers, 1996* | |
| Palm Computing (3 Com) | 62 |
| Hewlett-Packard | 16 |
| Others | 22 |
| *Leading Sports Drinks, 1997* | |
| Gatorade (Quaker Oats) | 79 |
| All Sport (PepsiCo) | 9 |
| Power Ade (Coca-Cola) | 9 |
| Others | 3 |
| *Ready-to-Drink Coffee Brands, 1997* | |
| Frappuccino | 64.1 |
| Nescafé | 10.8 |
| Others | 25.1 |
| *Salty Snack Makers, 1997* | |
| Frito-Lay | 54 |
| Borden (Wise) | 4 |
| Procter & Gamble | 4 |
| Others | 38 |
| *Powder Detergent Brands, 1997* | |
| Tide | 42.7 |
| Cheer | 9.7 |
| Gain | 8.5 |
| Surf | 7.3 |
| Arm & Hammer | 5.8 |
| Private Label | 2.8 |
| Other Brands | 23.2 |
| *DVD Disc Companies, 1997* | |
| Warner Home Video | 50.68 |
| Columbia | 16.72 |
| Disney | 7.73 |
| Universal Home Video | 7.14 |
| Others | 17.73 |

*Source: Market Share Reporter, 1999.*

declining), they will quickly follow the price cut to maintain their market share. If this firm undertakes the opposite action—a price increase—assuming incorrectly that competitors will follow suit, its sales will drop markedly if competitors fail to do so.

It is easy to demonstrate the "kink" in such a demand curve with the graph in Figure 10.2. Let us assume that the original price and quantity are found at point *A*. If the

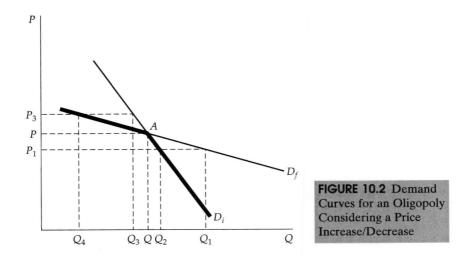

**FIGURE 10.2** Demand Curves for an Oligopoly Considering a Price Increase/Decrease

firm lowers its price, expecting that quantity demanded will move along the more elastic demand curve $D_f$ and this result materializes, then it will gain a relatively large quantity of additional sales for a relatively small decrease in price. If it lowers its price from $P$ to $P_1$, it will expect to increase its sales from $Q$ to $Q_1$. This is the relevant demand curve for the firm if other companies do not retaliate. Our firm would thus gain customers at the expense of competition. However, if competitors do react and match the price cut, our company will increase its sales only to $Q_2$, along demand curve $D_i$; this is the relevant demand curve when all companies in the industry decrease their price equally. There will be a relatively small increase in sales, since all prices in the industry are lower, but not nearly as much as the company expected when it reduced its price.

On the other hand, suppose our company decides to raise its price, anticipating that competitors will follow the increase. It thus expects to move along $D_i$ to $Q_3$ when it boosts its price to $P_3$. It would thus sustain some loss in sales while benefiting from a significantly higher price. However, suppose its competitors refuse to play along and keep their prices unchanged. The company's situation now becomes more precarious, since its quantity sold drops to $Q_4$: the demand curve for the firm alone is much more elastic than if all firms raise their prices in unison.

The prospect of being stung by such action will make the company much more loath to change its price from $P$. From that vantage point, it will appear to the company that the appropriate demand curve is $D_i$ if price is lowered and $D_f$ if the price is increased. The upper portion of $D_f$ and the lower portion of $D_i$ can be seen to form a kinked demand curve around point $A$; thus, the name of Sweezy's model. These relevant portions of the two demand curves are boldly outlined in Figure 10.2.

Now that we have developed a demand curve for this oligopolist, we can derive a marginal revenue curve as well. This marginal revenue curve will be discontinuous: there will be a gap at the point where the kink occurs. As we know, a company will maximize its profits at the point where marginal cost equals marginal revenue. The two marginal cost curves drawn in Figure 10.3 both imply the same price and quantity, at point $A$. Thus, a significant change in costs could occur for our firm, but it will not react by changing its price. Actually, the price may remain unchanged even if the demand curve

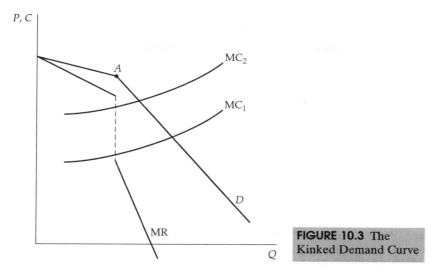

**FIGURE 10.3** The Kinked Demand Curve

moves to the right or left, as long as the kink remains at the same price level. Hence, it can be concluded that under the circumstances described, a kinked demand curve will result in price rigidities despite changes in demand and cost.

Over the years, the kinked demand curve has been challenged by other economists. In particular, Nobel Prize laureate George Stigler investigated several oligopolistic industries and found little empirical support for Sweezy's model. Stigler found that in these industries, price increases were followed as quickly as were price decreases.[5] Such findings, of course, contradict the existence of the kink. Further, the model does not explain how the price was originally set at the kink. Was it originally set where marginal revenue equaled marginal cost, or was it by some other means, such as tradition?

One commonly held view of how the price at point *A* is determined involves the concept of an industry **price leader.** This is the firm that dares to break out of the pack without fearing the consequences spelled out in the kinked demand model. If this firm decides to raise its price, it assumes all others will follow. If this firm decides to lower its price, it assumes the others may follow but will not go even lower, thereby triggering a price war that would hurt the entire industry.

In oligopolistic markets in the United States, the role of the price leader is usually assumed by the company with the largest share of the market. For example, General Motors is often the first to announce price increases for the next year's line of cars and trucks. IBM often sets the pace for the rest of the industry in large, mainframe computers. Different companies in the industry may take the leader role in setting prices for different products. Sometimes companies take turns in setting the price. In one instance, Coca-Cola may set the price of its product; in others Pepsi-Cola may take the lead. This rotation in the leadership position indicates that it is not always the largest company

---

[5]George J. Stigler, "The Kinky Oligopoly Demand Curve and Rigid Prices," *Journal of Political Economy,* October 1947, pp. 432–39. Similarly, see Julian J. Simon, "A Further Test of the Kinky Oligopoly Demand Curve," *American Economic Review,* December 1969, pp. 971–75.

that is the first to raise or lower the price. For example, in early 1999, after several years of strong demand, the major airlines decided to raise the price of their full-fare coach seats by about 2 percent. First to make this move was Delta Airlines. When this was first reported in the newspaper, industry analysts were wondering whether the other major airlines would follow. The next day, it was announced that they had.[6] Although Delta is not the leader based on market share (see chapter 15), it served as the industry leader in this particular case.

Price leaders are not always followed. Every so often, the popular press reports some price leader announcing a "rollback" in prices once it finds out that its competitors have refused to follow its lead in raising prices. Uncertainty also surrounds price cuts. The case of "Marlboro Friday" is a good example of this. On April 2, 1993, Philip Morris announced a reduction of 40 cents per pack in the price of its leading brand, Marlboro. When a company spokesperson was asked what Philip Morris expected to happen as a result of this cut, this person could only respond by saying it would have to wait and see.[7] We believe that Philip Morris was waiting for the reaction of its largest competitors, R.J. Reynolds-Nabisco and the American Tobacco Company. As it turned out, the competition's immediate response was to offer a $4 rebate via a mail-in coupon attached to each carton of their brands of cigarettes. With their power of hindsight, marketing analysts have severely criticized the economic wisdom of Philip Morris's drastic pricing action.

Worse than the uncertainty following a price cut is the outbreak of a price war. These wars have been observed with unsettling frequency in the airline industry. Also from time to time the "cola wars" break out between Coca-Cola and Pepsi-Cola in different regional markets in the United States.

As you can see, for oligopolistic firms price leadership is a critical accompaniment to mutual interdependence. Without leadership, there would be no orderly mechanism for these firms to set or change their prices—at least no legal way. Throughout this discussion of oligopoly pricing, it might have occurred to you that an easy solution to this quandary would be for all the firms to get together and set the price that they feel is in their best interest. This would be considered collusion and is illegal under existing U.S. laws of commerce.

One of the more celebrated cases of price fixing occurred in the 1950s involving the conviction of a number of executives in the electric industry. (See chapter 12 for details.) A more recent example occurred in early 1994, when the U.S. Department of Justice announced that it had gotten six U.S. airlines to settle a price fixing suit in which they were accused by the Justice Department of "using their jointly owned computerized ticket-information system to gain as much as $1.9 billion in fare increases through illegal price fixing from 1988 to 1992."[8]

The only kind of legal price fixing that is possible is in international markets. A group of sellers that operates internationally with a formal agreement to control price and output levels of its products is called a *cartel*. The OPEC cartel is probably the best known of these groups. We discuss cartels in greater detail in chapter 12.

---

[6]Laurence Zucherman, "Several Major U.S. Airlines Lift Fares Across the Board," *New York Times,* January 30, 1999.
[7]"Marlboro Friday, Still Smoking," *Advertising Age,* March 28, 1994, p. 62; "Don't Underestimate the Champ," *Forbes,* May 10, 1993.
[8]*International Herald Tribune,* March 18, 1994.

# Game Theory and the Pricing Behavior of Oligopolies

The economic concepts and tools of analysis that we have used throughout this text are all part of the microeconomic theory of the firm. The basic implication of this theory for managers is that the optimization of their firm's economic situation (i.e., profit maximization or loss minimization) requires that they base their output and pricing decisions on the MR = MC rule. Assuming that a manager has sufficient information to determine the firm's marginal cost and marginal revenue, this rule can be very useful in practical business situations. This is certainly the case in the perfectly competitive, monopoly, and monopolistically competitive markets.

But the one critical situation in which the MR = MC rule is seriously limited is in a market where pricing and output decisions are made by managers who anticipate or react to the pricing and output decisions of their competitors as they themselves try to determine the optimal level of price and output. The kinked demand model tries to explain why the prices in such markets tend to be very similar for each competitor, but it does not explain how and why this "administered price" is established in the first place.[9]

Over the past decade, managerial economics texts have sought to remedy this by introducing **game theory** into the analysis of pricing and output decisions in oligopoly markets. We believe game theory does add to the understanding of pricing and output decisions in oligopoly markets. We cannot do justice here to the coverage of this material because entire courses and textbooks are devoted to this subject. We can however, explain briefly the essence of this theory and provide a simple example of how the theory might be used to analyze an oligopolist's strategy, particularly in pricing.

Game theory is concerned with "how individuals make decisions when they are aware that their actions affect each other and when each individual takes this into account."[10] This definition should come as no surprise, given that game theory is utilized by economists especially to help them understand mutually interdependent behavior. There are many different types of games, each characterized by a unique set of assumptions concerning such conditions as the number of players, the stakes involved, whether there must be a winner and a loser, and whether the decisions taken are simultaneous or sequential. But regardless of the conditions, the essential idea in game theory is to apply the logic of mathematics to arrive at a "solution," or in economic terms, an "equilibrium."

For example, one of the most well-known and frequently cited game in economics textbooks is one called "Prisoners' Dilemma." This variation is considered to be a *two-person, non-zero-sum, noncooperative* game with a *dominant strategy.* In other words, both players may gain or lose, depending on the actions each chooses to take. In a *zero-sum* game, one player's gain is the other's loss and vice versa. The noncooperative feature of the game implies that opponents are not allowed to share information with each other. A dominant strategy means that there is one strategy that is best for a person, no matter what the other one does.

---

[9]In the early 1900s, the French economist Cournot developed a mathematical model to explain how a price is determined in a "duopoly" market in which there are just two competitors. However, the model did not take into account the possibility of actions and reactions between the two competing firms.
[10]H. Scott Bierman and Luis Fernandez, *Game Theory with Economic Applications,* Addison-Wesley, 1998, p. 4.

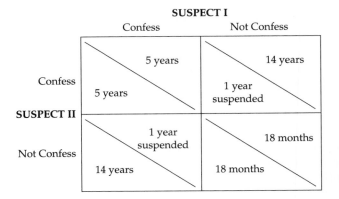

**FIGURE 10.4**
Prisoners' Dilemma:
Payoff Matrix

The particulars of prisoners' dilemma are essentially as follows.[11] Two individuals commit a serious crime together and are apprehended by the police. They know that there is insufficient evidence to convict them of the crime. At worst, they risk being charged and convicted of the less serious offense of loitering near the scene of the crime, which involves a lesser prison sentence. The police interrogate them separately. During this procedure, the suspects are not allowed to communicate with each other. If one suspect confesses, then he will get a minimum sentence (that could be suspended) for cooperating with the authorities, while the other will receive the maximum sentence. If both talk, then each will receive a moderate sentence somewhere between the minimum and the maximum. Given these conditions, what should each suspect do? Game theory provides an answer.

All solutions in game theory involve what economists call an equilibrium condition. In Prisoners' Dilemma, equilibrium means that each suspect must feel that he or she is in the best possible situation, *no matter what the other person is thinking of doing.*[12] Let us use a numerical illustration to show what the equilibrium situation would look like for each suspect.

Let us assume that the options for each prisoner and the consequences of selecting each option can be represented in the payoff matrix seen in Figure 10.4. For each suspect, the options are to confess or remain silent. If they both confess, the matrix indicates that they would each receive 5-year sentences. If one confesses and the other remains silent, then the "stool pigeon"[13] would get a 1-year suspended sentence, while his tight-lipped partner would receive a 14-year prison term. If they both remained silent, then they would both receive an 18-month sentence. Game theorists believe that ultimately both suspects would decide to confess. This is because if one decides not to confess, there is always the strong possibility that the other will in fact confess, thereby leaving the first with the worst possible pay-off, a 14-year sentence. The prospects of this

---

[11]There are numerous versions of the prisoners' dilemma story. This one is based on Andrew Schotter, *Microeconomics: A Modern Approach,* Addison-Wesley, 1998, chapter 7, and on J. R. McGuigan, R. C. Moyer, and F. H. Harris, *Managerial Economics,* South-Western College Publishing, 1999, pp. 539–45.
[12]Economists often refer to this situation as "Nash equilibrium," after the U.S. economist John Nash, who first proposed this in 1951 and who received a Nobel Prize in economics for his work in game theory.
[13]We recognize that there are more current terms for this type of person but we are hoping that we have some readers who on occasion watch a James Cagney movie on television.

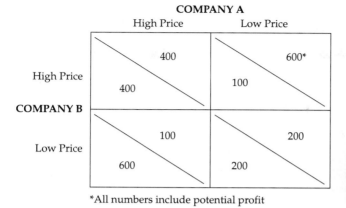

**FIGURE 10.5** Oligopoly Pricing Using the Prisoners' Dilemma: Payoff Matrix Model

*All numbers include potential profit

possibility would prompt her to confess. Assuming each suspects' reasoning to be the same, both would end up confessing. In the formal language of game theory, the situation in which both suspects confess is called a "dominant strategy equilibrium."

At this point readers might be wondering what is the relation of alleged criminals to oligopolistic pricing. Instead of alleged criminals, suppose we use two companies competing in a market for a product in which price is a key consideration in the purchasing decisions of consumers. In place of "confess" or "not confess" we can use the options "high price" and "low price." In place of prison sentences, we can use profit.

Figure 10.5 shows two companies, A and B, and the expected profit that each hopes to gain by charging a high or low price relative to the price charged by the other. It is easy to see that real two-company combination such as Coca-Cola and PepsiCola, IBM and Compaq, or Miller and Budweiser could be used as the A and B companies. As a test of your understanding of the Prisoners' Dilemma, what would be the dominant strategy equilibrium in this version of the game?

If your answer is that both companies would charge the low price, you would be absolutely right. Although the high price would be better for each company independently of the other, the point of this game is that each would always be thinking of the possibility of the other setting a low price (i.e., the equivalent of confessing). Therefore, as a sort of "second-best solution," each would chose the more secure situation of the low price, thereby dispensing with the fear of the other gaining an advantage by setting a lower price.

Is game theory interesting? It certainly can be fascinating and as we said earlier, interested students can take courses devoted entirely to this subject. Does game theory provide insights into oligopolistic behavior? To be sure, even the most elementary of games such as Prisoners' Dilemma offers greater insight than early models of oligopoly pricing behavior such as the kinked demand model. Can game theory be applied to actual business situations? Can it help managers to make actual strategic decisions? Here is where it becomes somewhat controversial.

Recently game theory has proven to be quite helpful for certain wireless companies that were bidding for the rights to use certain radio frequency ranges for digital wireless telecommunications services. However, for many business professors and practitioners, game theory continues to be a more theoretical than practical tool of analysis. For example, the authors of a relatively recent article on corporate strategy state that

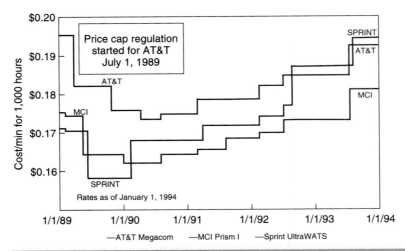

**FIGURE 10.6** Long-Distance Telephone Service Pricing, 1989–1994.

*Source: Business Communications Review,* p. 17.

many examples of competitive interaction are too rich and full of possible moves and countermoves to be modeled by game theory, which requires very precise and somewhat simplified characterizations of strategy.[14]

An author of a textbook on strategy has this to say about the subject:

> Game theory's preoccupation with equilibrium has resulted in its prediction of an enormous range of outcomes from a variety of highly stylized situations involving few exogenous variables and highly restrictive assumptions. The result is a mathematically sophisticated body of theory that in terms of application to strategic management suffers from unrealistic assumptions, lack of generality, and an analysis of dynamic situations through a sequence of static equilibriums.[15]

We tend to agree with the above criticisms and offer an illustration of the market for long-distance telephone service as an example of game theory's limitations. When AT&T's telephone monopoly in the United States was broken up in 1983, it was widely believed that competition would drive down the prices of long-distance telephone services. And during the second half of the 1980s, this was indeed the case. However, as shown in Figure 10.6, in the first half of the 1990s, prices actually began to edge back up. The fact that the prices of the big three long-distance companies all tended to fall and rise together does seem to indicate the existence of mutual interdependence. But could Prisoners' Dilemma have been used to predict the case of high (or higher) prices? This

---

[14]M. J. Chen and G. Miller, "Competitive, Attack, Retaliation, and Performance," *Strategic Management Journal,* 15, 5 (February 1994), p. 98.
[15]Robert M. Grant, *Contemporary Strategy Analysis: Concepts, Techniques, Applications,* 2nd ed., Cambridge, MA: Blackwell, 1995, p. 13.

is doubtful because, to begin with, the solution for this game involves both parties setting low prices.

Besides being unable to predict price changes, particularly price increases, game theory—despite the many variations of games—is limited if the rules of the game change, or if competitors decide simply to "play" another game. For example, regardless of a price increase or decrease in long-distance telephone services, it is evident to anyone that telephone rates are extremely complex. Consider a price plan offered by AT&T in the mid 1990s, called Uniplan. Following is a brief description of the pricing structure of this plan.

> Uniplan includes a volume discount, based on monthly usage, plus additional discounts applied to the remainder that are based on the total revenue and term commitment. For example, the Uniplan outgoing service uses AT&T's Megacom Plus rates, which average 24 cents per minute for domestic calls originating via switched access, and 18 cents per minute for dedicated access. Incoming calls are billed at about 26 cents per minute for switched access (i.e., Ready Linetype 800 services) and about 21 cents per minute for calls delivered via dedicated T1.
>
> Once combined monthly usage at these rates reaches $1,000, a discount ranging between 10 and 17 percent (for $15,000) is applied. Remaining outgoing costs can be further reduced anywhere from 5 to 15 percent, and remaining incoming costs by 9 to 15 percent. These additional discounts are available only if a customer commits to spending from $1,000 to $50,000 a month for a term of 12 to 36 months.[16]

Then at some point in the late 1990s, Sprint decided to change the rules of the game by offering something that customers were eager to have: pricing simplicity. Sprint's "Ten cents a minute" campaign, regardless of its restrictions related to day of week and time of day, clearly signalled a new way of competing. Then a company called U.S. Telecom began offering its "10-10-321" discount calls, known in the industry as a "dial-around" service. This had such an effect on the market share of the big three long-distance carriers, that one of them, MCI (now MCI-WorldCom) bought U.S. Telecom and expanded the dial-around service even further. AT&T, fearful of customers finding out that they could get the same long-distance phone services at a discount by using a 10-10-XXX prefix, refused to get into this market. Finally, in mid-1998, it was forced to initiate its own dial-around service under the label "Lucky Dog." Those wishing to use essentially the same AT&T service at a lower price can call 10-10-345.

## Industrial Organization and Strategy

In an effort to expand the application of the analysis of oligopoly markets to management decision making, a number of managerial economics texts have begun to discuss strategic issues, particularly those based on the works of the strategist/economist Michael Porter. We begin this discussion by first presenting a general introduction to industrial organization, the field of study from which some of professor Porter's key ideas derive.

---

[16]"Voice Networks Pricing Update," *Business Communications Review,* February 1994, p. 15.

Industrial organization shares some similarity with managerial economics. Both investigate the application of microeconomics to business affairs. But while managerial economics applies theory to questions of managerial decision making, industrial organization studies ways that firms and markets are organized and how this organization affects the economy from the view point of social welfare (i.e., maximizing the well-being of consumers and producers).

To discuss the question of oligopolistic behavior, we first looked at the composition of U.S. industry to ascertain the existence of an oligopolistic market structure. We now discuss the effect oligopolistic industries have on economic activity.

## TWO MODELS OF INDUSTRIAL CONCENTRATION

Looking over the entire range of industry concentration data published by the U.S. Census Bureau, we find that "unconcentrated" industries outnumber "concentrated" industries by a wide margin. But the real important question to ask regarding industry concentration is whether and how it influences the performance of industries with few dominant firms (i.e., industries that appear to be oligopolistic). Two approaches to the study of industrial organization have dominated the discussion. The first, the **structure-conduct-performance (S-C-P) paradigm,** has been predominant since the 1940s until its critics, proponents of the price theory approach, began to challenge it in the 1970s. As so often is the case, the two explanations of industrial behavior were advanced by two of the leading schools of economic thought in the United States, Harvard University and the University of Chicago, respectively. A brief coverage of the two analytical methods follows.[17]

### The Structure-Conduct-Performance (S-C-P) Paradigm

The causality in this theory runs only in one direction. Industry performance is caused by industry's conduct, which in turn is determined by the industry's structure. We start with structure that is shaped by the demand and supply conditions prevalent in the industry. For instance, if an industry's product demand tends to be inelastic, then market prices would be higher than if demand were more elastic. Growth patterns and substitutability would also affect structure. On the supply side, technology is an important factor. The existence of economies of scale will determine the number of firms, which can operate profitably in the industry.

These basic conditions thus determine industry structure: the number of firms in an industry, conditions of entry, and product differentiation. The structure of the industry then directly influences the way the industry operates—its conduct. Conduct entails primarily pricing strategies and other activities such as advertising, product development, legal tactics, and choice of product, as well as the potential for collusion among companies and mergers, which may further endanger the competitive nature of the industry. "The essence of the structuralist approach is a presumption that industries having fewer (and larger) firms will tend to engage in conduct inconsistent with the norms of perfect competition."[18]

---

[17]The following discussion is based on two texts on industrial organization: Dennis W. Carlton and Jeffrey M. Perloff, *Modern Industrial Organization,* 2d ed., New York: HarperCollins, 1994; and William E. Shugart II, *The Organization of Industry,* Homewood, IL: Irwin, 1990.

[18]Shugart, *The Organization of Industry,* p. 9.

The next step in the S-C-P model is to link conduct to performance. As mentioned, the usual normative standard adopted by economists is the maximization of society's welfare. An industry market with great concentration will fall far short of reaching such a goal. Its performance will be marked by both productive and allocative inefficiencies. Prices will be above marginal costs, the choice and quality of products will not be ideal, technological progress may be slowed down, and ultimately profits will be higher than under competitive circumstances. This high level of profitability arises from the industry's pricing policy and not because of any cost advantages.

We have now connected the three parts of the S-C-P model. A necessary corollary of the results of this approach is that high industry concentration becomes a reason for government intervention proceeding against possible mergers and even trying to deconcentrate industries.

## The "New" Theory of Industrial Organization

A competing view of industrial organization is offered by a theory stating that there is no necessary connection between industry structure and performance that uniquely leads to maximum social welfare. It argues that the study of industry organization should utilize and apply microeconomic price theory. Thus, for instance, higher profit levels in more concentrated industries may be caused by economic efficiencies rather than pricing strategies. In other words, a small number of efficient firms can survive better than a larger number of firms that cannot take advantage of economies of scale. In fact, certain industries may not be able to support many firms on an acceptable profit level. Another argument involves the potential for collusion in concentrated industries. George Stigler concluded that while industry concentration makes collusion more likely, collusive agreements (cartels) are inherently unstable because they are expensive to enforce and because participants have incentives to cheat.[19]

A large number of studies examining the links between industry concentration and profits have been produced. The results, particularly in the earlier studies, appear to point to direct correlation between concentration and profit levels. However, the evidence is at best rather weak. Many later studies cast doubt on the earlier results, showing that what appeared to be a link between concentration and profits was actually due to other industry characteristics and often disappeared over the long run. For instance, one researcher found that cost reductions were significantly greater in increasingly concentrated industries, and even though price reductions to consumers were less than cost savings realized, consumers benefited from considerable price advantages.[20]

Another, more recent, addition to the above discussion and the notion that industry profits are not necessarily a function of industry structure is Baumol's theory of "contestable markets."[21] The idea is that performance by firms is ultimately influenced, not

---

[19]G. J. Stigler, "A Theory of Oligopoly," *Journal of Political Economy,* 72 (February 1964), pp. 44–61. Another argument made by the S-C-P approach is the monopolistic implications caused by tie-in sales. This point is discussed in chapter 12.
[20]S. Peltzman, "The Gains and Losses from Industrial Concentration," *Journal of Law and Economics,* 20 (October 1977), pp. 229–63.
[21]W. J. Baumol, "Contestable Markets: An Uprising in the Theory of Industry Structure," *American Economic Review,* 72 (March 1982), pp. 1–15.

by the presence of competition, but by the threat of potential competition. Contestability comes in several forms. An extreme case is perfect contestability, which implies that entry by new firms is free and exit is costless. In such cases, existing firms will not be able to sell their product at prices exceeding marginal costs. Of course, in industries where entry and exit are difficult and costly, such competitive threat would not be present. Still, if outsiders have access to the industry's technology and if assets are nonspecialized so that their costs can be recouped upon exit, such a competitive threat is powerful.

The debate between the advocates of the S-C-P paradigm and the price theory approach has now continued for many years and neither side has gained clear dominance. Market structure is still very important, particularly from a public policy point of view. But other factors must also be considered in deciding what are the important influences affecting social welfare.

## STRATEGY AND THE IDEAS OF MICHAEL PORTER

In the late 1970s, Michael Porter, an economics professor from the Harvard Business School, began publishing articles on strategy that would have a profound impact on the study of this subject. As with all innovative ideas, his work has been subject to counterarguments and criticism over the years.[22] Nevertheless, many of the terms and concepts that he introduced have become a part of the everyday vocabulary of the business strategist. In our discussion of strategy, we have chosen to limit coverage to his ideas about strategy because they are most directly related to the study of the economics of the firm and industry economics.

Porter did not dwell on theoretical issues about the links between industry structure, business conduct, and performance and whether a concentrated industry structure leads to a misallocation of a country's resources. Instead, he used the concepts of the S-C-P approach to industry economics as the basis for understanding the strategic challenges facing the managers of firms as they seek to maximize their firm's profit. His **"Five Forces" model,** shown in Figure 10.7, illustrates the various factors that affect the ability of any firm in the industry to earn a profit.

If buyers as well as suppliers do not exert much market power and there is little threat from either new competitors or the use of substitute products, firms in the industry are likely to earn relatively high returns on their investment. An extreme example of this is the market for operating systems software for personal computers . . . as long as you think of Microsoft as *the* company in this industry. It is easy to see the influence of the microeconomic theory of the firm on Porter's ideas when you compare the five forces with the characteristics of the different market types shown earlier in Figure 9.1. For example, "Entry Barriers" is related to "free entry and exit." If it is easier to enter, firms in the industry are less able to exercise market power and hence are less likely to have a relatively high return on investment.

After establishing a model for analyzing the overall profitability of an industry, Porter proceeded to discuss what kind of strategy would enable a specific firm in the industry to earn a return higher than the industry average. This above-average return

---

[22]For a good review of Porter's ideas on strategy together with the developments in the entire field of study over the past 30 years, see Henry Mintzberg, Bruce Ahlstrand, and Joseph Lampel, *Strategy Safari: A Guided Tour Through the Wilds of Strategic Management,* New York, The Free Press, 1998.

# The Porter Competitive Framework

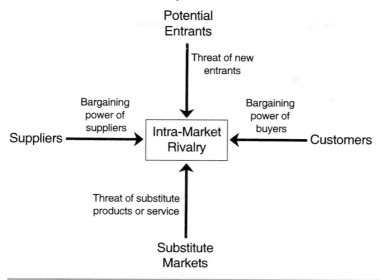

**FIGURE 10.7** The Porter Competitive Framework

*Source:* Adapted from Michael Porter, *Competitive Strategy,* New York: The Free Press, 1980, p. 4.

can be considered akin to "economic" or "above-normal" profit. Porter offers two generic strategies for earning an above-average return on investment. The first is the "differentiation" approach, the second is "cost leadership" approach. There is actually a third approach, in which a firm could exercise either differentiation or cost leadership for a particular market segment rather than for the entire market of potential buyers.

We also can see the influence of the microeconomic theory of the firm in this aspect of Porter's ideas on strategy. The cost leadership approach appears to be based on perfect competition, while the differentiation approach can be seen as related to the case of a monopoly or monopolistically competitive market. Recall that in the perfectly competitive market, all firms are price takers. The only way in which a particular firm in this market can earn an economic profit is to keep its cost structure low enough so that when $P = MC$, there is still a positive difference between $P$ and AC. In our view, this is where Porter came up with the idea of the cost leadership approach.

In the case of monopoly or monopolistic competition, product differentiation results in a downward sloping demand and an MR curve that lies below this demand line. Following the MR = MC rule enables a firm to set a price on the demand line that is higher than its AC, assuming of course that the demand curve itself is high enough to allow this to happen. The extreme case of this was shown in the example of pure monopoly. Not only is the product different, it is unique. In the case of monopolistic competition, the above-normal profit enjoyed by the differentiating firm may be reduced as the entry of firms in the long run shift a firm's demand curve to the left. But Porter would say that those firms that have a solid differentiation strategy would not be affected by the new entrants as much as those who allow their products to be "commoditized."

# International Application: Expanding Beyond One's Borders

Companies most likely to expand beyond their borders are oligopolies. An oligopolistic company generally has more resources to invest in a global expansion. Moreover, as the domestic market matures and limits the ability of large dominating firms to grow organically, these firms have more of an impetus to expand outside of their own country. This phenomenon is amply supported by the history of the global expansion of American-based multinationals, particularly those in the manufacturing sector (e.g., IBM and Hewlett-Packard, General Motors and Ford, Compaq and Dell, Colgate Palmolive and Procter & Gamble).

In the 1990s, certain large retail companies have tried to repeat the successes of their manufacturing counterparts, but with limited results. For example, Wal-Mart's early efforts in Brazil and Argentina were stymied by their lack of knowledge of local shopping patterns and tastes. Their efforts to expand in England were met with resistance from local communities afraid of what might happen to smaller shops on the high streets of their towns. But Wal-Mart has continued its global efforts, as evidenced by the company's purchase in 1998 of a large German retail chain.[23]

The decade of the 1990s witnessed the emergence of the megastore in the retail book industry, with Barnes and Noble and Borders leading the way in "land-based" stores, while Amazon.com came from nowhere to establish itself first in cyberspace. Barnes and Noble quickly followed suit on the Internet.[24] Thus on a national level, retail book selling has clearly become an oligopolistic market, being dominated by the three giant book retailers.

Borders has not been as aggressive as Barnes and Noble in following Amazon.com into the business of on-line selling, preferring instead to try their luck with traditional brick and mortar expansion into other countries. Obviously, their first efforts must focus on English-speaking countries and so they have targeted England, Australia, and Singapore first. Interestingly enough, this global expansion was greatly helped by changes in government and industry regulation. In 1995, an industry agreement in the U.K. that barred retailers from selling books at discount prices was dropped. In Singapore, liberal copyright laws allow Borders to ship in most of its book inventory from the United States without having to incur the added cost of setting up a local distribution network.

Local bookstores are not necessarily going to roll over and let the Americans take over, at least not in the U.K. W.H. Smith is already established throughout the U.K. as a dominant retailer of books and magazines. In early 1998, two other of Britain's leading retail booksellers, Waterstone's and Dillons, merged to form HMV Media Group. It will open a megastore on London's Oxford Street that is larger than the one recently opened by Borders only a few doors away.

---

[23]On a visit to Prague in 1994, one of the authors, Philip Young, was surprised to see a Kmart in the middle of the city. It was clearly positioned as a full-price, full-service retail store and looked much more like an anchor store in an upscale mall such as Macy's or Dillard's than a typical store in the suburbs of the United States. On a visit to Prague in 1999, the other author, Paul Keat, noticed that Kmart was replaced by Tesco, a British-owned supermarket.

[24]All the information on retail book selling was taken from "2 Peoples Separated by Ocean, Not by Borders," *The New York Times,* January 1, 1999.

**THE SOLUTION**

A few weeks later Frank again met with Nicole. He recommended selling *Waterpure* for $1.00 instead of the $1.10 suggested by the MR = MC analysis. His focus-group studies showed that people paid more attention to a 25-cent than a 15-cent difference. The average price of the major national brands was $1.25.

"I believe the 25-cent difference will be really noticeable to the consumer," Frank explained. "After all, we're new entrants into the market and we can use this lower price to attract customers away from the competition. At least they'll be more inclined to give our product a try. But we're not going to sell this product as a private label or discount product. According to your marketing plan, Nicole, we're going to be putting a lot of money into advertising to build brand awareness among consumers."

"That's just it, Frank, we are in fact going to be positioning *Waterpure* as a premium product, as good as any other national brand, if not better," Nicole responded. "If we're going to position our product in this way, we have got to use our price in support of this. If we set the price at $1.00 and then decide to raise it to $1.25 after it gains customer acceptance, they may not go along with this increase. We have to use promotion and advertising more than price to build our brand in the marketplace. Why don't we just match the competition's $1.25?"

"It makes sense to me," Frank answered. "The one thing we don't want to do is to trigger a price war. If any of our competitors with established brands decides to match or even beat our lower price, then the whole industry might suffer. As it now stands, I guess we're all doing very well if we can get people to pay more than a dollar for a bottle of water."

"Hey, now I've really got you thinking like a marketing person, Frank. Remember, demand is based on the customer's *perception* of value and not the intrinsic value of the product. If we can use advertising to support the price of $1.25, that's going to be the key to our success. Besides, you're right about a price war—I don't even want to think about starting a price war with the likes of Nestlé, Pepsi, and Coke."[1]

---

[1]Pepsi's main product is Aquafina, a tap water that is purified with triple filtration and a process known as "reverse osmosis." Nestlé's leading bottled brands are Perrier, Deer Park, Poland Spring, and Calistoga. Coca-Cola is developing its own bottled water brand and also is a major distributor of branded bottle water.

## Summary

The pricing and output decisions in imperfectly competitive markets are the most challenging because managers must consider all three of the key elements of pricing: cost, customers, and competition. Economic theory provides a useful rule for finding the price and output level that will enable a firm to maximize its profit or minimize its loss in the short run. This rule requires a firm to set a price that will result in a level of demand at which the marginal revenue earned for selling the last unit produced just equals its marginal cost of product. If this MR = MC rule enables a monopolistically competitive firm to earn an economic profit, then new entrants into the market will enter and all firms in the market will on the average be able to earn only normal profit.

Oligopolistic firms must contend with the possible pricing actions and reactions of their competitors. This type of mutual interdependence in pricing makes it extremely difficult to determine the precise optimal price for a firm. In certain instances, pricing in an oligopolistic market is set by a price leader. This possibility and others will be explored in the next chapter.

## Important Concepts

**Five Forces model:** Model developed by Michael Porter that shows the key factors that affect the ability of a firm to earn an economic profit: potential entrants, bargaining power of suppliers, bargaining power of buyers, threat of substitute products or services, and intramarket rivalry. Also referred to as the Porter Competitive Framework. (p. 408)

**Game theory:** A formal mathematical approach to the study of how individuals make decisions when they are aware that their actions affect each other and when each individual takes this into account. (p. 401)

**Kinked demand:** A theoretical construction that attempts to explain price rigidities in oligopolistic markets. (p. 396)

**Monopolistic competition:** A market distinguished from perfect competition in that each seller attempts to differentiate its product from those of its competitors (e.g., in terms of location, efficiency of service, advertising, or promotion). Good examples of this type of market can be found in small businesses, particularly those in the retail trade. (p. 391)

**Mutual interdependence:** A situation in which each firm in the market sets a price based on its costs, price elasticity, *and* anticipated reaction of its competitors. This type of pricing situation prevails in oligopolistic markets. (p. 396)

**Oligopoly:** A market in which there is a small number of relatively large sellers. Pricing in this type of market is characterized by mutual interdependence among the sellers. Products may either be standardized or differentiated. (p. 394)

**Price leader:** One company in an oligopolistic industry establishes the price, and the other companies follow. Two types of price leadership, barometric and dominant, are discussed in chapter 12. (p. 399)

**Structure-Conduct-Performance (S-C-P) paradigm:** An approach to studying industrial economics that states that an industry's structure determines an industry's conduct, which in turn affects the industry's performance. The key factors that shape industry structure are the number of firms in the industry, the conditions of entry and exit, and product differentiation. (p. 406)

## Questions

1. Explain the key difference between perfect competition and monopolistic competition.
2. Assume that firms in the short run are earning above-normal profits. Explain what will happen to these profits in the long run for the following markets.
   a. Pure monopoly
   b. Oligopoly
   c. Monopolistic competition
   d. Perfect competition
3. In certain industries, firms buy their most important inputs in markets that are close to perfectly competitive and sell their output in imperfectly competitive markets. Cite as many examples as you can of these types of businesses. Explain why the profits of such firms tend to increase when there is an excess supply of the inputs they use in their production process.

4. "In the short run, firms that seek to maximize their market share will tend to charge a lower price for their products than firms that seek to maximize their profit." Do you agree with this statement? Explain.

5. Explain why it is sometimes difficult to apply the MR = MC rule in actual business situations.

6. Define *mutual interdependence.*

7. Why do oligopolists often rely on a price leader to raise the market price of a product?

8. How does one determine whether a market is oligopolistic? Is it important for managers to recognize the existence of oligopolistic competitors in the markets in which their companies operate? Explain.

9. In the following list is a number of well-known companies and the products that they sell. Which of the four types of markets (perfect competition, monopoly, monopolistic competition, and oligopoly) *best* characterizes the markets in which they compete? Explain why.
   a. McDonald's—hamburgers
   b. Exxon—gasoline
   c. Dell—personal computers
   d. Heinz—ketchup
   e. Procter & Gamble—disposable diapers
   f. Kodak—photographic film
   g. Starbucks—gourmet coffee
   h. Domino's—pizza
   i. Intel—computer chip for the PC

10. This chapter discussed how a game called Prisoners' Dilemma could be used to show how two competing firms might establish their prices. What other variables besides price might be considered in this particular type of analysis? What are some limitations to using this analysis in actual business situations?

11. Briefly explain the Structure-Conduct-Performance approach to the study of industrial economics.

12. Compare and contrast Porter's Five Forces model with the four basic types of markets first described in chapter 9 in the section, "Market Structure."

## Problems

1. A group of five students has decided to form a company to publish a guide to eating establishments located in the vicinity of all major college and university campuses in the state. In planning for an initial publication of 6,000 copies, they estimated the cost of producing this book to be as follows:

| | |
|---|---|
| Paper | $12,000 |
| Research | 2,000 |
| Graphics | 5,000 |
| Reproduction services | 8,000 |
| Miscellaneous | 5,000 |
| Personal computer | 2,000 |
| Desktop publishing software | 500 |
| Overhead | 5,500 |
| Binding | 3,000 |
| Shipping | 2,000 |

By engaging in this business, the students realized that they would have to give up their summer jobs. Each student made an average of $4,000 per summer. However, they felt that they could keep expenses down by doing much of the research for the book by themselves with no immediate compensation.

They decided to set the retail price of the book at $12.50 per copy. Allowing for the 20 percent discount that retail stores in their state generally required, the students anticipated a per-unit revenue of about $10.00. The director of the campus bookstore advised them that their retail price was far too high, and that a price of about $8.75 would be more reasonable for a publication of this kind.

One of the students, who was a math and statistics major, asked the bookstore manager to provide her with historical data on sales and prices of similar books. From these data, she estimated the demand for books of this kind to be

$$Q = 18,500 - 1,000P$$

where $Q$ = Number of books sold per year
  $P$ = Retail price of the books

**a.** Construct a numerical table for the retail demand curve, and plot the numbers on a graph. Calculate the elasticity of demand for the interval between $12.50 and $8.00.

**b.** Do you think the students should follow the store manager's advice and price their book at $8.75? Explain. If you do not agree with this price, what would be the optimal price of the book? Explain.

**c.** Assuming that the students decide to charge the optimal price, do you think that they should proceed with this venture? Explain.

**d.** Assuming that the student's demand equation is accurate, offer some possible reasons why the bookstore manager would want to sell the book at the lower price of $8.75.

2. Use the same data presented in problem 1 to answer the following questions:

**a.** Explain the impact on the optimal price of designating the "miscellaneous" cost item as fixed versus variable. (Hint: Do the pricing analysis assuming miscellaneous is a fixed cost and compare it to an analysis that assumes it is a variable cost.)

**b.** Under what circumstances do you think the average variable cost would *increase* (as is generally expected in the economic analysis of cost)? Do you think the law of diminishing returns would play a role in increasing AVC? Explain.

**c.** Under what circumstances do you think the average variable cost would *decrease?* Explain.

3. A firm in an oligopolistic industry has identified two sets of demand curves. If the firm is the only one that changes prices (i.e., other firms do not follow), its demand curve takes the form $Q = 82 - 8P$. If, however, it is expected that competitors will follow the price actions of the firm, then the demand curve is of the form $Q = 44 - 3P$.

**a.** Develop demand schedules for each alternative and draw them on a graph.

**b.** Calculate marginal revenue curves for each.

**c.** If the present price and quantity position for the firm is located at the intersection of the two demand curves, and competitors follow any price decrease but do not follow a price increase, show the demand curve relevant to the firm.

**d.** Draw the appropriate marginal revenue curve.

**e.** Show the range over which a marginal cost curve could rise or fall without affecting the price the firm charges.

4. Indicate whether each of the following statements is true or false and explain why.

**a.** A competitive firm that is incurring a loss should immediately cease operations.

**b.** A pure monopoly does not have to worry about suffering losses because it has the power to set its prices at any level it desires.

   **c.** In the long run, firms operating in perfect competition and monopolistic competition will tend to earn normal profits.

   **d.** Assuming a linear demand curve, a firm that wishes to maximize its revenue will charge a lower price than a firm that wishes to maximize its profits.

   **e.** In an oligopoly, the firm that has the largest market share will also be the price leader.

   **f.** The demand curve facing a firm in a monopolistically competitive market is more elastic than one facing a pure monopoly.

**5.** A phenomenon in the retail merchandising of food and clothing in the United States and the United Kingdom is the growing popularity of private-label (also called store-brand) products. These products are priced at a lower level than the premium national brands. Use the concepts of price elasticity and relevant cost to explain the profitability of these products from the point of view of

   **a.** the retail stores that sell these private-label products.

   **b.** the manufacturers of these private-label products.

   If you were the manager of a national premium brand, what would you do to fight the growing competition of private labels?

**6.** Suppose three firms face the same total market demand for their product. This demand is

| P | Q |
|-----|--------|
| $80 | 20,000 |
| 70 | 25,000 |
| 60 | 30,000 |
| 50 | 35,000 |

   Suppose further that all three firms are selling their product for $60 and each has about one-third of the total market. One of the firms, in an attempt to gain market share at the expense of the others, drops its price to $50. The other two quickly follow suit.

   **a.** What impact would this move have on the profits of all three firms? Explain your reasoning.

   **b.** Would these firms have been better off in terms of profit if they all had raised the price to $70? Explain.

**7.** A firm has the following short-run demand and cost schedule for a particular product:

$$Q = 200 - 5P$$

$$TC = 400 + 4Q$$

   **a.** At what price should this firm sell its product?

   **b.** If this is a monopolistically competitive firm, what do you think would start to happen in the long run? Explain.

   **c.** Suppose in the long run, the demand shifted to $Q = 100 - 5P$. What should the firm do? Explain.

**8.** Suppose there are three firms with the same *individual* demand function. This function is $Q = 1,000 - 40P$. Suppose that each firm has a different cost function. These functions are:

$$\text{Firm 1: } 4,000 + 5Q$$

$$\text{Firm 2: } 3,000 + 5Q$$

$$\text{Firm 3: } 3,000 + 7Q$$

   **a.** What price should each firm charge if it wants to maximize its profit (or minimize its loss)?
   **b.** Explain why the answer to the preceding question indicates that two of the firms should charge the same price and the third should charge a higher price.
   **c.** Which firms will be most vulnerable to a price war? Explain.
 9. You and a competing firm are the only sellers of a new product. You are engaged in an intense battle for initial market share. You both realize that the one who captures most of the market share will be the one who spends the most on advertising and promotion. You are the marketing manager and you have up to $1 million for advertising and promotion for all your products. You have to decide how much of your budget you should allocate to the marketing of the new product. Construct a payoff matrix similar to the one shown in Figure 10.5.
   Note: Make whatever assumptions that you need about your opponent's spending on advertising and marketing.
10. Professor Michael Porter's generic strategy options for competing are the differentiation approach and the cost leadership approach. The first involves competing by having a better product and the second by having a lower cost than one's competitors. Relate this strategy to the monopolistically competitive model presented in this chapter. In particular, use the diagram in Figure 10.1 to explain the rationale for Porter's generic strategies.

## Take It to the Net

We invite you to visit the Keat/Young page on the Prentice Hall Web site at:

**http://www.prenhall.com/keat**

for additional resources.

# 11

# Break-Even Analysis (Volume-Cost-Profit)

October and November of each year are extremely busy months for the department of financial planning at Global Foods, Inc. It  is during this period that the financial plan for the next two years is prepared. As is customary in business, greater emphasis is always placed on the first of the two years. Planning data are collected from all departments— covering projected sales, costs, and expenses. After checking as much as possible to ensure reasonability and accuracy, the department consolidates the numbers to obtain a planned income and expense statement. The plans are prepared along profit center lines, usually by specific flavors of the products.

Suzanne Prescott is the senior analyst responsible for the company's new bottled water product, *Waterpure*. She and her assistant have worked on this project for two weeks and have completed the profit plan, which she will present to the manager of the

financial planning department. The first page of the long and detailed presentation shows the summary income statement for the *Waterpure* profit center for the year 2000 (Table 11.1).

Suzanne has kept her manager, Dorothy Simon, informed regarding the progress of the plan. As is quite common during a corporate planning cycle, their final discussion has been delayed several times due to late data, changed numbers, and missed schedules. Thus, Suzanne and Dorothy are meeting just one day before the results are to be presented to the company's controller. Dorothy agrees with the method with which the plan has been put together and with the results Suzanne has presented. But she expects that the controller will require additional information. She asks Suzanne whether she has performed a sensitivity analysis calculating profit results if sales were to be 10 percent lower or 10 percent higher than planned. She is

*(Continued)*

also interested in the level of sales at which profit would be zero to establish the "worst case." Suzanne admits that this analysis is incomplete due to lack of time. Since the presentation must be ready the next day, there is not enough time to rework the complete plan to obtain the alternative results. Suzanne will therefore have to devise a method by which she can obtain some good estimates for the "what-if" cases, estimates sufficiently reliable to show the controller. She remembers that in graduate school, she learned a method called break-even or volume-cost-profit analysis. Fortunately, she happens to have a few old textbooks in her office.

**TABLE 11.1   Income Statement for Waterpure Profit Center**

|  | *Plan for 2000 ($000)* |
|---|---|
| Sales | $5,000 |
| Cost of sales: | |
|    Materials | 800 |
|    Labor | 1,000 |
|    Overhead | 950 |
|       Total cost of sales | 2,750 |
| Gross profit | 2,250 |
| Selling and administrative expenses | 1,150 |
| Research and development expenses | 300 |
| Total expenses | 1,450 |
| Net earnings before taxes | $800 |

## Introduction

The analysis to be described in this chapter is derived from price/output decision making in the short run, which was discussed in the previous two chapters.

The graph illustrating the firm's decision-making mechanism with some form of imperfect competition[1] in the short run is presented in Figure 11.1a. The variable cost at first exhibits increasing marginal product (or decreasing marginal costs), but as quantity rises, decreasing marginal returns begin. Profit is achieved at quantities between $Q_1$ and $Q_2$, and there is a unique maximum profit point at $Q_m$, where the vertical distance between TR and TC is the largest.[2]

The TC curve in Figure 11.1b is the same as in Figure 11.1a, but the TR curve is a straight line. This represents the case of perfect competition under which the firm is able to sell any number of units it produces at a given price. As in the imperfectly competitive case, profit is present between quantities $Q_1$ and $Q_2$ and is maximized at $Q_m$.

---

[1] Either monopoly or monopolistic competition.
[2] This is, of course, the point at which marginal cost and marginal revenue are equal.

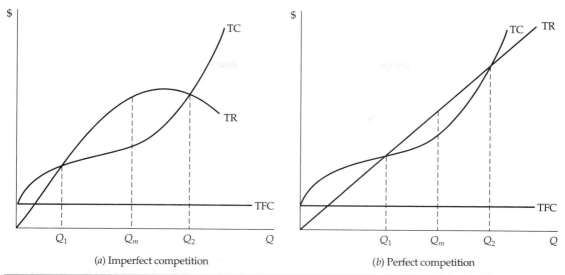

(a) Imperfect competition          (b) Perfect competition

**FIGURE 11.1**  Total Revenue and Cost Functions

Both of these cases should be quite familiar. In this chapter, we will simplify these two situations even further in the discussion of what is commonly referred to as **break-even analysis** or *volume-cost-profit* analysis.

The concept of fixed costs will be retained, as will the straight-line total revenue curve. The change arises in the treatment of variable costs, which in both the competitive and monopoly cases assumed the presence of first decreasing and then increasing marginal cost. For the present analysis, constant marginal cost will be assumed. Consequently, the variable cost curve (again added to the fixed-cost line) will be a straight line, since if marginal cost is constant, so is average variable cost. This construction is presented in Figure 11.2.

Thus, break-even analysis can be seen as a simplification of the usual short-run analysis in economics:

1. It assumes that in the short run there is a distinction between variable and fixed costs.
2. It assumes linearity (i.e., straight-line curves) throughout the entire analysis.
3. It implicitly assumes the presence of perfect competition since the price is considered to be the same regardless of quantity. (This procedure is followed, however, more for convenience than for theoretical reasons and can be changed.)[3]
4. The straight-line cost curve implies that marginal product is neither increasing nor decreasing, and that the entire range of the graph exhibits constant average variable and marginal costs. However, as with the straight-line total revenue curve, the

---

[3]It also must be understood that the horizontal (quantity) axis on graphs used in economics tends to measure very large quantity intervals. To claim that exact relationships hold over these long intervals is rather unrealistic. It is done for convenience and ease of exposition. But a firm will generally not consider such wide-ranging alternatives. It is much more likely that a company, given a particular level of production, will try to analyze some limited deviations from that level to, say, 5–10 percent higher or 5–10 percent lower. In such a limited interval, it is quite possible that a significant price change may not be necessary. Thus, even if the particular firm is not in a perfectly competitive market, a straight-line total revenue curve (i.e., no price change) in the relevant range may be close to reality.

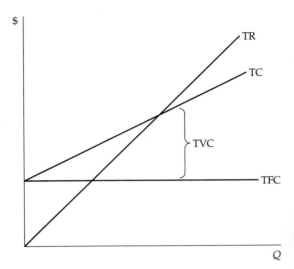

**FIGURE 11.2** Total Revenue and Cost Curves (Constant Average Variable Cost)

presence of constant returns for the entire range is not essential (see footnote 3). With the relevant range of decision making limited to some reasonable interval on the horizontal (quantity) axis, it is quite conceivable that the variable cost per unit will not change significantly. So, the ultimate presence of diminishing marginal returns is not denied in this analysis. Even if some change were to occur, it may not be large enough to affect the final results seriously. Figure 11.3 illustrates this point. The vertical distance between the two lines in the delineated interval is not great, nor is the difference in slope. Thus, the marginal costs specified by the two curves will not exhibit extreme differences.

Furthermore, as mentioned in the discussion of empirical cost estimates, the existence of constant unit variable costs in industry over a considerable range of quantities is a distinct possibility.

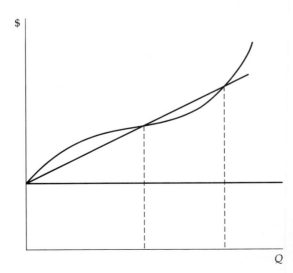

**FIGURE 11.3** The Implicit Assumption of Constant Returns

There are, however, some important differences between customary economic analysis and the break-even method that should not be overlooked.

1. The short-run economic chart shows two points where economic profits are zero, and maximum profit is identified somewhere between these two points. In break-even analysis, there is only one no-profit (break-even) point. As quantities rise beyond this point, profit increases continuously until, presumably, capacity is reached, and no additional quantities of product can be achieved.[4] At this point, costs become infinitely high, and the total cost line would thus cross the total revenue line.

2. There is also a major difference between the objectives of the two analyses. In chapters 9 and 10, interest focused on the question of resource allocation—the effect of a price change or a cost change on the quantity produced. In break-even analysis, the question is, What impact does a change in quantity have on variable costs and profit?

3. The third difference lies in the use of the cost concept. Economic costs, as previously discussed, are based on replacement costs and include imputed costs and normal profit. Break-even analysis, as practiced in business, usually relies on accounting costs (often standard costs as used in cost accounting), which include explicit costs only and represent historical data. However, in this case, careful treatment of data could convert accounting data into economic cost data. For instance, as will be shown later, a "required" minimum profit, which can represent the normal profit, can be included in the calculation.

## The Break-Even Point

**MODULE 11A**
**MODULE 11B**

The first of the calculations we will examine identifies the quantity at which the company will just break even—no profit, no loss. But this is not the point where company executives wish the firm to be. The break-even point merely sets the stage to investigate the relationship between quantity of the product, the cost to produce this quantity, and the profit—hence the name *volume-cost-profit* analysis.

The same abbreviations used in previous chapters will be utilized here:

| | |
|---|---|
| $P$ = Price | TC = Total cost |
| TVC = **Total variable cost** | $Q$ = Quantity produced |
| AVC = Average variable cost | TR = Total revenue |
| TFC = **Total fixed cost** | $\pi$ = Profit |

The very simple equation for profit is:

$$\begin{aligned} \pi \; &= \; TR - TC \\ &= \; TR - TVC - TFC \\ &= \; (P \times Q) - (AVC \times Q) - TFC \\ &= \; Q(P - AVC) - TFC \end{aligned}$$

---

[4]Because break-even analysis deals with the short run only, capacity does not change.

To obtain the **break-even point,** total revenue is set equal to total cost:

$$TR = TVC + TFC$$

$$(P \times Q) = (AVC \times Q) + TFC$$

$$(P \times Q) - (AVC \times Q) = TFC$$

$$Q(P - AVC) = TFC$$

Thus, the break-even quantity is

$$Q = TFC/(P - AVC)$$

For example, if $P = \$5$, $AVC = \$3$, and $TFC = \$20,000$,

$$Q = 20,000/(5 - 3) = 20,000/2 = 10,000$$

This result can be checked as follows:

| | |
|---|---|
| Total revenue (10,000 × $5) | $50,000 |
| Total variable cost (10,000 × $3) | 30,000 |
| Total fixed cost | 20,000 |
| Total cost | 50,000 |
| Profit | $ 0 |

If the quantity produced is larger than 10,000 units, a profit will result. If quantity drops below 10,000, the company will incur a loss. Table 11.2 illustrates the revenue, costs and profits resulting from changes in quantity, and Figure 11.4 graphs the results.[5]

What happens to the break-even point when one or more of the variables change? An increase in the average variable cost will increase the slope of the total cost curve, and increase the break- even point (a decrease will cause the opposite). Figure 11.5a illustrates an increase in the average variable cost to $3.33, and a resulting increase in the break-even point to 12,000 units. A change in the unit price will change the slope of the total revenue curve; a price increase (decrease) will decrease (increase) the break-even point. Figure 11.5b demonstrates a 10 percent price increase to $5.50, which causes the break-even point to drop to 8,000 units.

An increase (decrease) in fixed costs will cause a parallel shift up (down) in the costs curves and an increase (decrease) in the break-even point. If fixed cost were to increase to $25,000 (with price and average variable cost remaining at $5 and $3, respectively), the break-even point would rise to 12,500. Students can easily calculate and graph this or any other result.

## Break-Even Revenue

**MODULE 11C**

Under certain circumstances, the product price and the unit variable costs may not be available. This will happen—frequently—when more than one product is produced in a plant. Since each of the different products being manufactured side by side has a dif-

---

[5]The table and graph were generated with a Microsoft Excel program.

### TABLE 11.2   Break-Even Analysis

*Variables*

| | |
|---|---|
| Price per unit | 5.00 |
| Variable cost per unit | 3.00 |
| Total fixed cost | 20000 |

*Results*

| | |
|---|---|
| Break-even quantity | 10000 |
| Break-even revenue | 50000 |

| Units | Fixed Cost | Variable Cost | Total Cost | Revenue | Profit |
|-------|-----------|---------------|-----------|---------|--------|
| 0 | 20000 | 0 | 20000 | 0 | −20000 |
| 5000 | 20000 | 15000 | 35000 | 25000 | −10000 |
| 1000 | 20000 | 30000 | 50000 | 50000 | 0 |
| 15000 | 20000 | 45000 | 65000 | 75000 | 10000 |
| 20000 | 20000 | 60000 | 80000 | 100000 | 20000 |
| 25000 | 20000 | 75000 | 95000 | 125000 | 30000 |
| 30000 | 20000 | 90000 | 110000 | 150000 | 40000 |
| 35000 | 20000 | 105000 | 125000 | 175000 | 50000 |
| 40000 | 20000 | 120000 | 140000 | 200000 | 60000 |

### FIGURE 11.4 Break-Even Analysis

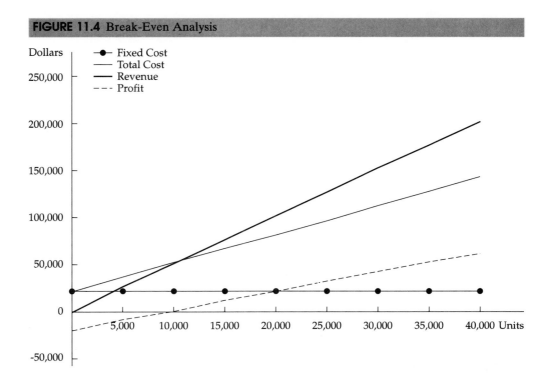

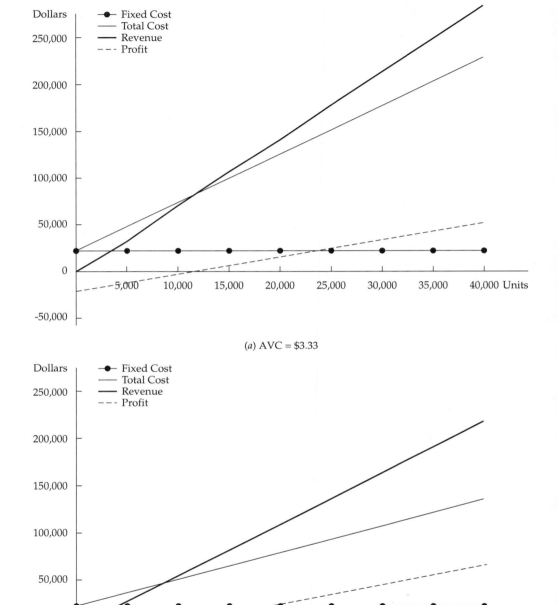

(*a*) AVC = $3.33

(*b*) P = $5.00

**FIGURE 11.5** Effect of Variable Change on Break-Even Analysis

ferent price and a different unit variable cost, it is difficult to utilize the formula of the previous section to establish the break-even point of the plant.

A weighted price and unit cost can be calculated for the products if the various products are produced in constant proportions. If we assume that variable costs are a constant percentage of total revenue, then we can calculate **break-even revenue** directly. Again we are assuming that the relationship between average variable cost and price for each product remains the same and the quantities of the various products are produced in constant proportions. Such an assumption does not appear to be unrealistic for relatively small changes in total revenue.

Starting with the equation that shows revenue at break-even,

$$TR = TVC + TFC$$

we now convert TVC into a constant fraction of total revenue.

If $a$ = TVC/TR, then TVC = $a \times$ TR, where $a$ is a constant less than 1. The break-even total revenue then becomes

$$TR = TFC/(1 - a)$$

For example, if TFC = 20,000 and $a$ = 0.6, then break-even TR equals 50,000, which is the same result as obtained previously, since if $P$ = 5, and AVC = 3, $a$ = 0.6 expresses the same relationship.

# Required Profit

If the only objective of this analysis were to find the point at which a plant or a company breaks even, not much would be accomplished. For a company to prosper, it must earn profits, not just break even. If a firm has a particular dollar profit objective per period, a small adjustment of the break-even equation will provide the appropriate output measure. A specific, fixed dollar amount of **required profit** can be handled as an addition to fixed cost; it also does not change as a function of quantity.

Continuing the illustration that has been used throughout this chapter, if the owners of the firm require a $10,000 profit, the equation is altered as follows:

$$Q_\pi = (TFC + \text{Profit requirement})/(P - AVC)$$
$$= (20,000 + 10,000)/(5 - 3)$$
$$= 30,000/2 = 15,000$$

where $Q_\pi$ stands for break-even with profit requirement.

If a specific profit per unit of product is required, this unit profit must be added to the average variable cost. For instance, suppose the company's objective is 40 cents profit per unit. Then AVC is changed to $3.40, and

$$Q_\pi = 20,000/1.60 = 12,500$$

Earlier in this chapter it was stated that the calculation of cost in volume-cost-profit analysis usually involves the use of accounting data. However, the "required profit" concept can easily be interpreted to represent the implied or opportunity costs that economists find crucial to the analysis of the firm. Thus, the profit measure, whether total or per unit, can be the normal profit, which is the minimum amount necessary to cause the owner to continue operating this business.

# Degree of Operating Leverage

**MODULE 11D**

Since volume-cost-profit analysis is concerned with the effect of a change in quantity of product on the profits of a firm, we must develop a method to quantify this effect. Such a method, called **degree of operating leverage (DOL)** is, in fact, a type of elasticity formula. The calculation result is a coefficient that measures the effect a percentage change in quantity has on the percentage change in profit.

$$\text{DOL} = \frac{\%\Delta\pi}{\%\Delta Q}$$

The percent change in profit can be written as follows:

$$\%\Delta\pi = \frac{\Delta\pi}{\pi} = \frac{\Delta Q(P - \text{AVC})}{Q(P - \text{AVC}) - \text{TFC}}$$

The percent change in quantity equals $\Delta Q/Q$. Putting these two expressions together:

$$\frac{\Delta Q(P - \text{AVC})}{Q(P - \text{AVC}) - \text{TFC}} \div \frac{\Delta Q}{Q} = \frac{\Delta Q(P - \text{AVC})}{Q(P - \text{AVC}) - \text{TFC}} \times \frac{Q}{\Delta Q} = \frac{Q(P - \text{AVC})}{Q(P - \text{AVC}) - \text{TFC}}$$

Thus,

$$\text{DOL} = \frac{Q(P - \text{AVC})}{Q(P - \text{AVC}) - \text{TFC}}$$

To better explain the meaning of DOL, let us use the example of the preceding section. At a production of 15,000 units, profit was $10,000. DOL can now be measured at the 15,000 quantity:

$$\text{DOL} = \frac{15{,}000\,(5 - 3)}{15{,}000\,(5 - 3)\ - 20{,}000} = \frac{30{,}000}{10{,}000} = 3$$

DOL = 3 means that, at $Q = 15{,}000$, a 1 percent change in quantity will result in a 3 percent change in profit (and a 10 percent change in $Q$ will lead to a 30 percent change in profit. Also, a 15 percent change will bring about a 45 percent change, etc.). The DOL effect can be seen in terms of an income statement at quantities of 13,500 and 16,500 (a 10 percent decrease and a 10 percent increase):

|                     | $Q = 13{,}500$ | $Q = 15{,}000$ | $Q = 16{,}500$ |
| ------------------- | --------- | --------- | --------- |
| Total revenue       | $67,500   | $75,000   | $82,500   |
| Total fixed cost    | 20,000    | 20,000    | 20,000    |
| Total variable cost | 40,500    | 45,000    | 49,500    |
| Total cost          | 60,500    | 65,000    | 69,500    |
| Profit              | $7,000    | $10,000   | $13,000   |

At a quantity of 13,500, profit is $7,000, or 30 percent less than at a quantity of 15,000 units. Conversely, at a quantity of 16,500 units, the profit is $13,000, or 30 percent larger.[6]

The importance of the degree of operating leverage is that it reveals to management the effect on profits of a small change in quantity. This construction will hold only, of course, as long as all variables remain the same (i.e., price, average variable cost, and total fixed cost).

The relative sizes of fixed and variable costs influence the level of the DOL coefficient. A plant with high fixed costs and low variable costs will have a higher DOL than a plant with lower fixed costs and higher variable costs. The former plant will also have a higher break-even point. The significance of this relationship is that a firm with high fixed costs—a capital-intensive firm—will usually achieve break-even at a higher quantity, but since it has a higher DOL, its profits will grow at a relatively high rate when production rises above break-even. Its profits will also decline more quickly during downturns in economic activity, and the firm will become unprofitable at a relatively high point of production (since its break-even quantity will be high). On the other hand, a plant with lower fixed costs and higher variable costs—a labor-intensive plant, perhaps somewhat obsolete—will break even at lower quantities, and its profits will tend to rise or fall less quickly when quantity produced moves up or down.

Thus, the break-even quantity and the DOL can have a very significant influence on a firm deciding whether or not to convert from an old—labor-intensive—manufacturing facility to a more modern, automated (i.e., capital-intensive) plant. For example, using the income statement presented at the beginning of this chapter, let us assume that the average variable costs per unit are $2.75 and total fixed costs are $1,450.[7] The break-even point for a $5 price is easily calculated as 644 units (rounded to the nearest integer).

Now suppose that additional, more up-to-date machinery were installed in the plant, increasing annual fixed costs to $2,000 and driving average variable costs down to $2.25. The break-even point for the modernized plant will have increased to 727 units. Why, then, should the company invest in the new machinery? Since the newly equipped plant enjoys a higher degree of operating leverage, its profits will rise more quickly with increases in production. At some quantity, the modernized plant and the old one will achieve equal profits. In this case, the point of equality is 1,100 units, at which both plants will show a profit of $1,025.[8]

At the production level of 1,100 units, the DOL values for the old and modernized plants are 2.41 and 2.95, respectively. Thus, if more than 1,100 units are to be produced annually in the future, the profit from the modernized plant will be greater. If, however,

---

[6]The degree of operating leverage can be calculated at any point in the profit or loss area. However, it cannot be calculated at the break-even quantity, since a percentage change in profit from zero does not make sense. (The denominator of the DOL formula is zero at break-even quantity.)

[7]All dollar and unit numbers (except price and variable cost per unit) are in thousands.

[8]This point is calculated as follows:

$$Q(P - AVC_a) - TFC_a = Q(P - AVC_b) - TFC_b$$

where the subscripts $a$ and $b$ denote the old plant and the modernized plant, respectively.

$$Q(2.25) - 1,450 = Q(2.75) - 2,000$$
$$0.5Q = 550$$
$$Q = 1,100$$

The profit for a quantity of 1,100 units is $1,025 for each plant.

| TABLE 11.3 Break-even and DOL Data for Old versus Modernized Plants | | |
|---|---|---|
| | *Old Plant* | *New Plant* |
| Price per unit | 5.00 | 5.00 |
| Variable cost per unit | 2.75 | 2.25 |
| Total fixed cost | 1,450 | 2,000 |
| Break-even quantity | 644 | 727 |
| Break-even revenue | 3,222 | 3,636 |
| *Equal Profit* | | |
| Quantity | 1,100 | 1,100 |
| Profit | 1,025 | 1,025 |
| Degree of operating leverage at equal-profit quantity | 2.41 | 2.95 |

the quantity is expected to remain at 1,000 units per year as in the company's plan, modernization would not be advisable at this time. The data for the present example are shown in Table 11.3.[9]

## The Uses and Limitations of Volume-Cost-Profit Analysis

Volume-cost-profit analysis is a very useful tool under certain circumstances, but its limitations must be understood. When a corporation prepares its financial plan for the next year or even the next two years, it usually engages in what is referred to as "bottom-up" planning, a process that is not only time consuming but extremely detailed. Many parts of the corporate organization contribute data on sales forecasts, prices, manufacturing costs, administrative and marketing expenses, and other measures. Data may be generated from every department in the corporation. Consolidating these data and making various changes in them before bringing a final plan up to top management for approval is a mammoth undertaking. A corporation would not use volume-cost-profit analysis for this type of planning.

The main use of this analysis lies in calculating alternative cases in a restricted period of time. It can also be used to make small, relatively quick corrections. In addition, during early stages of the plan, when detailed data are not yet available, estimates using variable and fixed costs can be used to establish some rough benchmarks for the eventual detailed plan.

However, despite its usefulness, break-even analysis has some important limitations, some of which have already been mentioned.

**1.** It assumes the existence of linear relationships, constant prices, and constant average variable costs. However, the use of linear construction, although limiting,

---

[9]This table was produced using a simple Excel program. Three variables ($P$, AVC, TFC) must be entered for each of the plants.

serves the intended purpose for this analysis. When the effects of relatively small changes in quantity are measured, linear revenues and variable costs are certainly good approximations of reality.

2. It is assumed that costs (and expenses) are either variable or fixed. Such an assumption is not completely realistic, but again, within a limited range of quantities it can be accepted. The existence of fixed costs limits this analysis to the short run. Changes in capacity are ordinarily not considered.

3. For break-even analysis to be used, only a single product must be produced in a plant or, if there are several products, their mix must remain constant.

4. The analysis does not result in identification of an optimal point; it focuses on evaluating the effect of changes in quantity on cost and profits.

A good indication of the usefulness and versatility of break-even analysis is the large number of hits that can be obtained when surfing the Internet. In addition to a considerable number of college course offerings including this subject and offers of software programs, here are a few examples of what we found:

1. Break-evens in cattle production and other farming operations
2. Break-evens in retail fuel pricing
3. Break-even analysis in hotel management
4. Break-evens in transportation (analysis of railroad routes and airline load factors)
5. A discussion by the Saskatchewan Office of Economic and Co-operative Development on the use of break-even analysis by management
6. Break-even projections for an Internet Kiosk

## An Application: The Restaurant Industry

The following is an illustration of the application of break-even analysis to the restaurant industry. While the numbers that follow are hypothetical, they are based on a survey conducted in conjunction with the National Restaurant Association. The study compared a full-menu restaurant with a fast-food restaurant. Costs and expenses were classified into fixed and variable. It is interesting to note that a large percentage of payroll costs was considered fixed (for skeleton staff necessary to run a restaurant).

|  | *Full-Menu Restaurant* | *Fast-Food Restaurant* |
|---|---|---|
| Revenue | $950,500 | $622,100 |
| Fixed cost | 445,700 | 260,700 |
| Variable cost | 459,500 | 280,900 |
| Profit | $45,300 | $80,500 |

From the preceding numbers, several inferences result:

1. The fast-food restaurant has a higher profit margin than the full-menu restaurant, 12.9 percent against 4.8 percent.
2. The break-even points are at revenues of $862,800 and $475,300, respectively.

**3.** The degree of operating leverage for the full-menu restaurant is 10.8 against the fast-food restaurant's 4.2 at the revenue levels given previously.[10] An increase in the full-menu restaurant's revenue would increase its profits at a much faster rate than a similar revenue increase in the fast-food restaurant's revenue.

Thus, the study concludes that volume-cost-profit analysis "can help you understand your establishment's cost structure, and help improve your decision making by quantifying the effect of specific policy decisions on the bottom line."[11]

---

[10]The formula for the degree of operating leverage is TR $(1 - a)$/[TR $(1 - a)$ − TFC], where $a$ is the fraction TVC/TR.

[11]Carol Greenberg, "Analyzing Restaurant Performance," *The Cornell H.R.A. Quarterly,* May 1986, pp. 9–11.

---

## THE SOLUTION

To calculate results for *Waterpure* sales of 10 percent more and 10 percent less, Suzanne Prescott needs to make estimates of price per unit, average variable cost, and total fixed cost. She had the production figure and price per case of $5. Breaking up the cost and expense numbers into fixed and variable components was a much more difficult task. Working with her assistant, she arrived at the following estimated breakdown:

| Cost of sales ($000) | |
| --- | --- |
| Variable materials and labor | $1,800 |
| Variable overhead | 500 |
| Fixed overhead | 450 |
| Expenses ($000) | |
| Variable selling and administrative | 450 |
| Fixed selling and administrative | 700 |
| Fixed research and development | 300 |

Thus, total fixed costs were found to be $1,450, and total variable cost $2,750 or $2.75 per unit.

She calculated the break-even point as follows:

$$\frac{1,450}{5 - 2.75} = 644$$

For the +10 percent and −10 percent she used the DOL equation:

$$\frac{1,000\,(5 - 2.75)}{1,000\,(5 - 2.75) - 1,450} = \frac{2,250}{800}$$

$$= 2.8125$$

For every 1 percent change in quantity, profit will change by 2.8125 percent. Thus, if quantity changes by 100 units (i.e., 10 percent), profit will change by 28.125 percent, from its $800 level down to $575 or up to $1,025.

Suzanne proceeded to prepare the presentation chart showing the planned figures, the two 10 percent variations, and the worst case. Table 11.4 illustrates the results. She is now ready for the next day's meeting with the controller.

*(Continued)*

**TABLE 11.4   Alternative Plans for Year 2000 ($000)**

|  | Best Estimate | +10% | −10% | Worst Case |
|---|---|---|---|---|
| Quantity | 1,000 | 1,100 | 900 | 644 |
| Sales | $5,000 | $5,500 | $4,500 | $3,222 |
| Cost of Sales |  |  |  |  |
| Variable mat. & labor | 1,800 | 1,980 | 1,620 | 1,160 |
| Variable overhead | 500 | 550 | 450 | 322 |
| Fixed overhead | 450 | 450 | 450 | 450 |
| Total cost of sales | 2,750 | 2,980 | 2,520 | 1,932 |
| Gross Profit | 2,250 | 2,520 | 1,980 | 1,290 |
| Expenses |  |  |  |  |
| Variable selling & admin. | 450 | 495 | 405 | 290 |
| Fixed selling & admin. | 700 | 700 | 700 | 700 |
| Fixed research & devel. | 300 | 300 | 300 | 300 |
| Total expenses | 1,450 | 1,495 | 1,405 | 1,290 |
| Net earnings before taxes | $800 | $1,025 | $575 | $(0) |

## Summary

Break-even (volume-cost-profit) analysis is a simplification of the economic analysis of the firm. It involves several limiting assumptions, such as constant prices and constant average variable costs. Since fixed costs are an essential component of this technique, it is strictly a short-run tool. Yet, despite these simplifications—and possibly because of them—break-even analysis is a very useful aid to an economic or financial analyst. It is, however, necessary to be aware of the method's limitations.

Several specific tools were discussed. The first was the break-even formula itself stated in terms of quantities of production units. If a single product cannot be identified, then a break-even formula for total revenue can be used.

Since the firm's objective is certainly not to break even but to achieve profitability, an equation was developed to identify the required quantity of production, given a lump-sum profit requirement or a profit-per-unit requirement.

To measure the effect of change in quantity on profits, the concept of degree of operating leverage was introduced. This elasticity-like formula measures the relation between a percentage change in quantity sold and a percentage change in profit. This equation was also shown to be useful in comparing two plants employing differing technologies (and therefore having different relationships between fixed and variable costs) or in making decisions on modernizing a plant.

The usefulness of break-even analysis in evaluating alternatives and in making quick corrections was discussed. The limitations in the application of this technique were also pointed out.

## Important Concepts

**Break-even analysis:**   Also called *volume-cost-profit analysis,* a simplification of the economic analysis of the firm that measures the effect of a change in quantity of a product on the profits of the firm. (p. 419)

**Break-even point:**   The level of output at which the firm realizes no profit and no loss. (p. 422)

**Break-even revenue:**   The amount of revenue at which the firm realizes no profit and no loss. (p. 425)

**Degree of operating leverage (DOL):**   An elasticity-like formula that measures the percentage change in profit resulting from a percentage change in quantity produced or revenue. (p. 426)

**Required profit:**   Profit that can represent the opportunity cost or the normal profit and that can be incorporated in the break-even formula. A fixed dollar amount of required profit can be handled as an addition to fixed cost; a specific profit per unit of product can be added to the average variable cost. (p. 425)

**Total fixed cost (TFC):**   A cost that remains constant as the level of output varies. In a short-run analysis, fixed cost is incurred even if the firm produces no output. Also referred to simply as *fixed cost.* (p. 421)

**Total variable cost (TVC):**   The total cost associated with the level of output. This can also be considered the total cost to a firm of using its variable inputs. Also referred to simply as *variable cost.* (p. 421)

## Questions

1. Although volume-cost-profit analysis uses graphs similar to those used by economists, the analysis differs in content. Discuss these differences.
2. Does the volume-cost-profit method analyze short-run or long-run situations? Why?
3. What is the difference between fixed costs and constant costs?
4. How realistic is the assumption of constant variable unit costs in volume-cost-profit analysis? Does it detract a great deal from the value of this analysis? Explain briefly.
5. What is the effect on break-even quantity of
   **a.** A decrease in unit price?
   **b.** A decrease in average variable cost?
   **c.** A decrease in fixed cost?
   Assume some numbers and illustrate the effect by drawing graphs showing the break-even point.
6. Business risk is usually defined in terms of variations of return (or profit) to a firm due to changes in activity resulting from changes in general economic activity. Can the degree of operating leverage therefore be described as a measure of business risk? Why?
7. Would you expect a company whose production is rather stable from period to period and growing slowly from year to year to have relatively high fixed costs?
8. How would you account for required profit in the break-even formula when
   **a.** Profit is set as a requirement for a time period (e.g., a year)?
   **b.** Profit is set as a specific monetary amount per unit?
9. Can the degree of operating leverage be measured at the break-even quantity point? Why or why not?
10. Is volume-cost-profit analysis a good planning tool? Discuss briefly.
11. What are some useful applications of volume-cost-profit analysis?

## Problems

1. The Automotive Supply Company has a small plant that produces speedometers exclusively. Its annual fixed costs are $30,000, and its variable costs are $10 per unit. It can sell a speedometer for $25.

**a.** How many speedometers must the company sell to break even?
**b.** What is the break-even revenue?
**c.** The company sold 3,000 units last year. What was its profit?
**d.** Next year's fixed costs are expected to rise to $37,500. What will be the break-even quantity?
**e.** If the company will sell the number of units obtained in part *d* and wants to maintain the same profit as last year, what will its new price have to be?

2. Writers' Pleasure, Inc. produces gold-plated pen and pencil sets. Its plant has a fixed annual cost of $50,000, and the variable unit cost is $20. It expects to sell 5,000 sets next year.

**a.** In order to just break even, how much will the company have to charge for each set?
**b.** Based on its plant investment, the company requires an annual profit of $30,000. How much will it have to charge per set to obtain this profit? (Quantity sold will still be 5,000 sets.)
**c.** If the company wants to earn a markup of 50 percent on its variable costs, how many sets will it have to sell at the price obtained in part *b*?

3. Bikes-for-Two, Inc., produces tandem bicycles. Its costs have been analyzed as follows:

| | |
|---|---|
| *Variable Cost* | |
| Materials | $30/unit |
| Manufacturing labor | 3 hours/unit ($8/hour) |
| Assembly labor | 1 hour/unit ($8/hour) |
| Packing materials | $3/unit |
| Packing labor | 20 minutes/unit ($6/hour) |
| Shipping cost | $10/unit |
| | |
| *Fixed Costs* | |
| Overhead labor | $50,000/year |
| Utilities | $5,000/year |
| Plant operation | $65,000/year |
| | |
| *Selling Price* | $100/unit |

**a.** Calculate the break-even quantity.
**b.** Calculate the break-even revenue.
**c.** Develop a chart to show profits at quantities of 2,000, 4,000, 6,000, 8,000, and 10,000.

4. Music Makers Company, a wholesale distributor, is considering discontinuance of its line of tapes due to stiff competition from CDs and other new, technologically advanced recordings. The variable cost of its tapes last year was about 40 percent of its tape revenue, and the allocated fixed cost equaled $100,000 per year. Last year's sales were $250,000, but it is expected that in the future, annual revenue will drop by 20 percent and variable costs will rise to 50 percent of revenue (because of price reductions). Will tapes still be profitable for the company?

5. The ABC Company sells widgets at $9 each; variable unit cost is $6, and fixed cost is $60,000 per year.

**a.** What is the break-even quantity point?
**b.** How many units must the company sell per year to achieve a profit of $15,000?
**c.** What will be the degree of operating leverage at the quantity sold in part *a*? In part *b*?
**d.** What will be the degree of operating leverage if 30,000 units are sold per year?

6. Two companies, Perfect Lawn Co. and Ideal Grass Co., are competing in the manufacture and sale of lawn mowers. Perfect has a somewhat older plant and requires a variable cost of $150 per lawn mower; its fixed costs are $200,000 per year. Ideal's plant is more automated and thus has lower unit variable costs of $100; its fixed cost is $400,000. Since the two companies are close competitors, they both sell their product at $250 per unit.

   **a.** What is the break-even quantity for each?

   **b.** At which quantity would the two companies have equal profits?

   **c.** At the quantity obtained in part *b,* what is each company's degree of operating leverage?

   **d.** If sales of each company were to reach 4,500 units per year, which company would be more profitable? Why?

**7.** Elgar Toaster Co. is contemplating a modernization of its antiquated plant. It now sells its toasters for $20 each; the variable cost per unit is $8, and fixed costs are $840,000 per year.

   **a.** Calculate the break-even quantity.

   **b.** If the proposed modernization is carried out, the new plant would have fixed costs of $1,200,000 per year, but its variable costs would decrease to $5 per unit.

      **(1)** What will be the break-even point now?

      **(2)** If the company wanted to break even at the same quantity as with the old plant, what price would it have to charge for a toaster?

   **c.** If the new plant is built, the company would want to decrease its price to $19 to improve its competitive position.

      **(1)** At which quantity would profits of the old and the new plants be equal (assuming the price of a toaster is $20 for the old plant but $19 for the new)? How much would the profit be at this quantity?

      **(2)** Calculate the degree of operating leverage for each plant at the quantity obtained in part (1).

      **(3)** If sales are projected to reach 150,000 units per year in the near future, would you recommend construction of the new plant? Why or why not? (Assume that both plants have the capacity to produce this quantity.)

**8.** The Saline Company produces and sells rock salt. Its annual fixed cost was $10,000. During the past year, the company sold 8,000 bags of its product. It estimates that at this level of sales its degree of operating leverage is 1.5.

   **a.** How much was Saline's profit last year?

   **b.** At which level of production would the company just break even?

**9.** The Amazing Book Co. sells a selection of paperbacks at an average price of $9. Its fixed costs are $400,000 per year and the unit variable cost of each paperback is $4 on average.

   **a.** Calculate the company's break-even quantity.

   **b.** The company's sales target for the year is 100,000 units. What will be its profit?

   **c.** At the beginning of the year the unit variable cost rises to $5. If the company wants to achieve the same profit as obtained in item b, how many books will it have to sell?

   **d.** At the beginning of the year, the company installs new billing equipment. Its fixed costs rise to $450,000. If the company wants to remain on target to sell 100,000 units and preserve the profit obtained in item b, what price will it have to charge per book?

   **e.** An early review of competitive price forces the company to drop its average price to $8. If it still targets its sales at 100,000 units and will settle for a profit of $50,000, what is the maximum unit variable cost it can afford? (TFC = $400,000)

   **f.** If the average price during the year is $8, the unit variable cost remains at $4, how many books must the company sell to achieve the profit obtained in item b? (TFC = $400,000)

## Take It to the Net

We invite you to visit the Keat/Young page on the Prentice Hall Web site at:

**http://www.prenhall.com/keat**

for additional resources.

# CHAPTER 12

# Special Pricing Practices

## THE SITUATION

One of the most difficult challenges in the food and beverage industries is the establishment of effective channels of distribution. 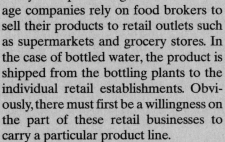 Many food-processing and beverage companies rely on food brokers to sell their products to retail outlets such as supermarkets and grocery stores. In the case of bottled water, the product is shipped from the bottling plants to the individual retail establishments. Obviously, there must first be a willingness on the part of these retail businesses to carry a particular product line.

The task of establishing the relationship between Global Foods, Inc. and the retail stores was given to Rebecca James, assistant vice president of marketing of the beverage division. Since the product, *Waterpure,* was so new, she found considerable resistance among the major supermarket chains to carrying Global's line of bottled water. Thus far, she had been able to sell relatively small volumes to smaller grocery stores, convenience stores, delicatessens, and sandwich shops. Then

she learned that a large catering company that provided food service in major airports all across the country wanted to carry an additional line of bottled water. This firm had put out a request for bids to all the major beverage companies and also to Global Foods. After all, Global had an established reputation in the food business.

Rebecca was eager to land this major account. But she also realized that her bid would have to be considerably lower than that offered to her present customers. However, this lower price would be more than made up by the potential volume of sales, as well as by the creation of a base from which to further penetrate the market for bottled water. But she was not quite sure how to decide on the price she should recommend. She decided to consult with Philip Olds, an executive in the company's foods service division. Philip had considerable experience in preparing bids on large customer contracts.

# Introduction

In chapters 9 and 10 we discussed output and pricing decisions under different market arrangements. We will now continue this discussion and apply our knowledge to pricing decisions made in specific situations. We will also be confronted by some complications: whereas we have previously assumed that a firm produces only one product, we will now have to allow for the pricing of several products simultaneously. The situations we will encounter in this chapter usually occur under imperfectly competitive conditions.

# Cartel Arrangements

Competition is a very tough taskmaster. To survive in competition in the long run, a company must operate at its most efficient (minimum) cost point, and it will earn no more than a normal return. Thus, there is always an incentive for a company to try to become more powerful than its competitors—in the extreme, to become a monopolist. In an oligopolistic type of industry, where there are several powerful firms, it would probably be impossible for one firm to eliminate all the others. So, in order to reap the benefits of a monopoly (i.e., higher profits, stable market shares and prices, and the general creation of a more certain and less competitive environment), it may be advisable for companies in the industry to act together as if they were a monopoly. In other words, they all agree to cooperate with one another; they form a **cartel.** Cartel arrangements may be tacit, but in most cases some sort of formal agreement is reached. The motives for cartelization have been recognized for many years. Indeed, an early recognition can be found in a passage in Adam Smith's famous book: "People of the same trade seldom meet together, even for merriment and diversion, but the conversation ends in a conspiracy against the public, or in some contrivance to raise prices."[1]

Cartels were made illegal in the United States with the passage of the Sherman Anti-Trust Act of 1890. Thus, most "official" cartels are found in countries other than the United States. Probably the most famous cartel in existence today is the Organization of Petroleum Exporting Countries (OPEC). But there are others, such as the IATA (International Air Transport Association), to which U.S. airlines can belong. Collusive agreements have existed in the United States as well. One of the most famous cases of price and market share fixing was in the electrical industry and involved General Electric, Westinghouse, and other large corporations. The case was tried and concluded in 1961 and resulted in prison sentences for several executives and large fines. This case, and a more recent one, that of the Archer-Daniels-Midland Company, will be described briefly following a discussion of the characteristics and effects of cartels.

Cartels may not flourish in all oligopolistic markets. Following are some of the conditions that influence the formation of cartels.

---

[1]Adam Smith, *An Inquiry into the Nature and Causes of the Wealth of Nations,* New York: Modern Library, 1937, p. 128.

1. The existence of a small number of large firms facilitates the policing of a collusive agreement.
2. Geographical proximity of the firms is favorable.
3. Homogeneity of the product makes it impossible for cartel participants to cheat on one another by emphasizing product differences.
4. The role of general business conditions presents somewhat contradictory arguments. Cartels are often established during depressed industry conditions, when companies attempt to forestall what they consider to be ruinous price cutting. However, it also appears that cartels disintegrate as demand for the product falls, and each member thinks it can do better outside the cartel. The cartel may then reestablish itself during the recovery period. Thus, cartels can form or fall apart during either phase of the business cycle.[2]
5. Entry into the industry must be difficult. The case of OPEC is a good example. It is impossible for countries that do not possess the basic resource to begin petroleum production and compete for monopoly profits.
6. If cost conditions for the cartel members are similar and profitability thus will not differ greatly among members, cartels will be easier to maintain. Product homogeneity, mentioned earlier, will contribute to cost uniformity.

The ideal cartel will be powerful enough to establish monopoly prices and earn maximum monopoly profits for all the members combined. This situation is illustrated in Figure 12.1. For simplicity, assume that there are only two firms in this oligopolistic industry. The total industry demand curve is shown in Figure 12.1c. The marginal revenue curve is constructed for this demand curve in the usual manner. Each of the two competitors (illustrated in Figures 12.1a and b) has its respective average total cost and marginal cost curves, which can differ.

The two individual marginal cost curves are then added horizontally, and the result is plotted on the industry graph ($MC_T$). Industry output will take place where $MC_T$ equals the industry marginal revenue, and the price charged will be found by drawing a vertical line to the demand curve (point A). This is, of course, the classic monopoly situation, and monopoly profits will be maximized at this point.

The next step is to establish how much each of the two companies will sell at this price. In order that the entire industry output be sold, each company will sell that output corresponding to the point at which a horizontal line drawn from the $MC_T = MR_T$ intersection on the industry graph crosses the marginal cost curve of each of the two firms. It can be seen that each of the two firms will produce different quantities and achieve different profits depending on the level of the average total cost curve at the point of production. Generally, the lower-cost company will be the more profitable one (profits for the two companies are shown by the hatched areas in Figure 12.1). This result, although maximizing combined profits, may also be one of the reasons for the subversion of cartels. A very efficient company with low average costs, and most likely with

---

[2]A very cogent description of this phenomenon can be found in George J. Stigler, *The Theory of Price,* New York: Macmillan, 1949, pp. 274–75. Stigler also puts forward the idea that, regardless of the level of business activity, government action in support of such collusion is an important factor in a cartel's success. An important example is the U.S. National Recovery Act (NRA) of the 1930s, later declared unconstitutional by the Supreme Court.

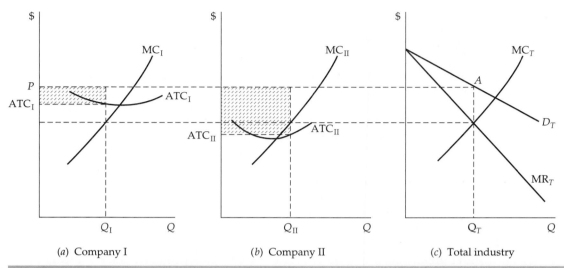

**FIGURE 12.1** The Ideal Cartel

excess capacity under cartel conditions, may find it profitable to cheat by offering its product at a lower price and capturing a larger share of the total business.

Such a cartel may be unstable. Unless strictly enforced, cartels will have a tendency to break down. Secret price cuts may be extremely profitable because (if the product is undifferentiated) the demand curve for an individual firm in a cartel will be quite elastic. Cartel subversion often occurs during slumps in demand, as individual members will be looking to increase their share to avoid significant quantity decreases.

It must also be remembered that collusion is costly. First, there is the cost of forming the cartel. Second, there is a cost of monitoring the actions of the cartel members and of enforcing the rules to minimize cheating. There is also the potential cost of punishment by authorities. Thus, in the end, cartelization may not necessarily be profitable. In short, the additional revenues obtained by cartel members due to collusion must exceed the costs just described. We can, therefore, state that while profit maximization is the incentive that leads to collusion, it may also be the cause of a cartel's breakdown.

Cartels often have agreements specifying the market share of each participant. Such allotments may be based on history, or they can be arranged to give each member a certain geographical area. Collusion can also exist in much more informal ways. Thus, physicians within a geographical area coincidentally charge similar fees for their services. Trade associations are often suspected of collecting and conveying information that will lead to the fixing of prices.

## TWO CASES OF PRICE FIXING BY CARTELS

A classic case of price fixing and market sharing ended in February 1961 in a Philadelphia court, when 7 executives of General Electric, Westinghouse, and other companies were sent to prison and fined; 23 others were given suspended sentences and fined; and 29 companies were fined a total of approximately $2 million. Starting shortly after World War II, this conspiracy involved a number of heavy electrical equipment products, such as switching gear, circuit breakers, transformers, and turbine engines. The companies involved pleaded guilty and "no contest" to the federal indictments.

The story of these collusive practices reads like a mystery story.[3] There were meetings in hotel rooms during conventions of the National Electric Manufacturers Association. There were hotel meetings at various locations in which the participants did not register under their company affiliations and recorded trips to other locations in their expense accounts. There were code numbers given to each company. There were telephone calls at the participants' homes and even a conspiratorial round of golf.

A recent case is that of the Archer-Daniels-Midland Company (ADM), a large agricultural business with annual revenues of approximately $14 billion. In October 1996, ADM pled guilty to price fixing of two of its products, lysine, a feed supplement, and citric acid, a food additive. Four Asian firms were implicated in the lysine conspiracy, and four European companies were involved in the citric acid case. The price fixing and division of markets was arranged in a series of secret meetings in many locations, including Mexico City, Paris, Tokyo, and Atlanta. ADM was fined a total of $100 million, and in addition paid approximately $90 million to settle customer and stockholder suits.

Two years later, in September 1998, three ADM executives were convicted of participating in the case. One of them was the former vice chairman, Michael Andreas, son of ADM's chief executive officer and his likely successor. He was sentenced to two years in prison and assessed a $350,000 fine.[4]

## Price Leadership

When collusive arrangements are not easily achieved, another type of pricing practice may occur under oligopolistic market conditions. This is the practice of **price leadership,** in which there is no formal or tacit agreement among the oligopolists to keep prices at the same level or change them by the same amount. However, when a price movement is initiated by one of the firms, others will follow. Examples of such practices abound. You may have observed that at two or more gasoline stations at the same intersection, prices for each grade of gasoline are either identical or almost the same most of the time. Another example is automobile companies, which in recent years have come up with rebate programs. Surely you have seen advertisements offering "$1,000 cash or 3.9 percent financing." One company is usually the first to announce such a program; the others follow in short order. Another case is IBM. For many years, in the 1950s and 1960s, IBM was considered to be the price leader in the computer industry. In fact, IBM's prices were considered to form an "umbrella" for industry pricing. It was said that IBM would establish a price, and since it was the most powerful and preferred manufacturer and thus could command a higher price (an umbrella over the others), its competitors would tend to set their prices at some slightly lower level for similar equipment.

---

[3]The description of this case has been obtained from two articles in *Fortune* (April 1961, pp. 132–37 ff, and May 1961, pp. 161–64 ff), and from *The Wall Street Journal,* January 10 and 12, 1962.
[4]N. Millman, "$100 Million Fine in ADM Guilty Plea," *Chicago Tribune,* October 16, 1996; G. Burns, "Three ADM Execs Found Guilty," *Chicago Tribune,* September 17, 1998; S. Kilman, "Jury Convicts Ex-Executives in ADM Case," *The Wall Street Journal,* September 18, 1998; S. Kilman, "Ex-Officials of ADM Given 2 Years in Jail," *The Wall Street Journal,* July 12, 1999.

We have just described two major variants of the price leadership phenomenon: barometric and dominant price leadership.

## BAROMETRIC PRICE LEADERSHIP

There may not be a firm that dominates all the others and sets the price each time. One firm in the industry—and it does not always have to be the same one—will initiate a price change in response to economic conditions, and the other firms may or may not follow the leader. If the **barometric price leader** has misjudged the economic forces, the other companies may not change their prices or may effect changes of a different, possibly lesser, magnitude. If the firm has correctly gauged the sentiment of the industry, all of the firms will settle in comfortably at the new price level. But if this does not happen, the price leader may have to retract the price change, or a series of iterations may be set in motion until a new price level, agreeable to all, is reached. Such a pattern of price changes has been observed in many industries, including automobiles, steel, and paper.

In recent years, the airline industry has furnished several examples of price leadership that was not followed. A recent, almost bizarre, example occurred in August 1998. First, Delta Air Lines and American Airlines raised leisure fares by 4 percent. When Northwest Airlines refused to match the increase, it was rescinded. A few days later, Northwest raised its fares and was matched by the others. Two days later Northwest rescinded the increase, and within a day other airlines followed. Then Northwest raised some of its fares again, only to pull some of them back, and actually decreased leisure fares in some of its markets. Other airlines then realigned their fares with those of Northwest.[5]

## DOMINANT PRICE LEADERSHIP

When an industry contains one company distinguished by its size and economic power relative to other firms, the **dominant price leadership** model emerges. The dominant company may well be the most efficient (i.e., lowest-cost) firm. It could, under certain circumstances, force its smaller competitors out of business by undercutting their prices, or it could buy them out on favorable terms. But such action could lead to an investigation and eventual suit by the U.S. Department of Justice under the Sherman Anti-Trust Act. To avoid such difficulties, the dominant company may actually act as a monopolist, setting its price at the point where it will maximize its profits, and it will permit the smaller companies to continue to exist and sell as much as they wish at the price set by the leader. The theoretical explanation of the dominant price leadership model is quite straightforward and is presented in all microeconomics textbooks. We will follow its development in Figure 12.2.

The demand curve for the entire industry is $D_T$. The marginal cost curve of the dominant firm is $MC_D$, and the sum of all the marginal cost curves of the follower firms is represented by $MC_R$. The demand curve for the leader, $D_D$, is derived by subtracting at each point the marginal cost curve of the followers from the total demand curve, $D_T$. The reason is that if the small firms supply the product along their combined marginal cost curve, $MC_R$, then the dominant firm will be left with product demand shown along

---

[5]This sequence of fare changes was reported in several issues of *The Wall Street Journal* between August 11, 1998 and the end of August.

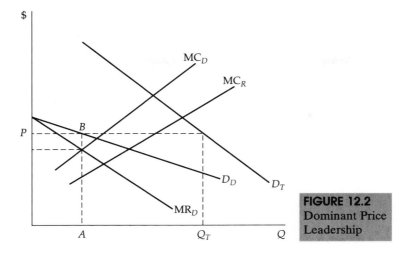

**FIGURE 12.2**
Dominant Price Leadership

$D_D.$ When the leader's marginal revenue curve, $MR_D$, is drawn in the usual manner, the leader can establish its profit-maximizing quantity at point *A,* and price at point *B.* This price is then accepted by the smaller firms in the industry, which will supply the rest of the market at this price. The followers are thus actually faced by a horizontal demand curve at price *P.*

Such an arrangement is satisfactory to the dominant firm. It maximizes profits and at the same time permits the small firms to exist, thus possibly avoiding legal action. On the other hand, the followers will be able to assure themselves of a piece of the market without inviting the possibility of a price war, which they would most likely lose.

As in the case of cartels, dominant price leadership arrangements tend to break down. As markets grow, new firms enter the industry and decrease the interdependence among the firms. Technological changes may bring changes in pricing, and in the long run the leadership of the dominant firm is likely to erode.

## Revenue Maximization

**MODULE 12A**

Another model of oligopolistic behavior was developed some years ago by the American economist William Baumol.[6] Ignoring interdependence, the **Baumol model** suggests that a firm's primary objective, rather than profit maximization, can be the maximization of revenue, subject to satisfying a specific level of profits. He gives several reasons for this objective, among them (1) a firm will be more competitive when it achieves large size (in terms of revenue) and (2) management remuneration may be more closely related to revenue than to profits.

This situation is depicted in Figure 12.3. The figure shows three solid curves. The total revenue curve is the usual one for a firm in imperfect competition, with revenue increasing at a decreasing rate because the firm is faced by a downward-sloping demand

[6]William J. Baumol, *Economic Theory and Operations Analysis,* 3rd ed., Englewood Cliffs, NJ: Prentice-Hall International Editions, 1972, chapter 13.

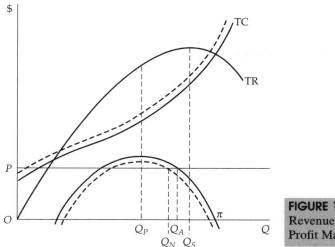

**FIGURE 12.3**
Revenue versus
Profit Maximization

curve.[7] The total cost curve also is no surprise; it indicates first decreasing and then, at higher production levels, increasing marginal cost. The third line represents profits. It is simply the vertical difference between the revenue and cost lines.

If the firm were a profit maximizer (the traditional economic objective), production would take place at point $Q_P$, where the profit line hits its peak. On the other hand, should the firm be a pure revenue maximizer, equilibrium would occur at output $Q_S$, where the total revenue curve reaches its peak. This point, as we learned earlier, occurs where demand elasticity is unity (i.e., marginal revenue equals zero).

However, revenue maximization is subject to the constraint that an acceptable profit level exists. This profit will tend to be at a lower level than the maximum achievable. Assuming that this acceptable level is at OP, output will settle at $Q_A$. This will achieve the highest possible revenue while satisfying the profit requirement. Thus, total revenue will be higher than would have been attained under conditions of profit maximization, but lower than if pure revenue maximization (without a minimum profit constraint) had been pursued.

An interesting implication of this model is the effect of a change in fixed costs. Recall that under conditions of profit maximization in the short run, a change in fixed costs will have no effect on price or quantity, since neither marginal revenue nor marginal cost is impacted, and thus the maximizing requirement of MR = MC will remain the same. However, in the Baumol model, a rise in fixed costs will raise the cost curve and decrease the profit line. Both new lines will be parallel to the old ones. The two broken lines in Figure 12.3 represent this shift. As can be seen, the existence of the profit constraint will cause output to decrease to $Q_N$. At this lower output, price will be higher.

Baumol's model is an interesting attempt to present an alternative to the traditional maximization hypothesis. Since his model has not been extensively tested, it is difficult to assess its validity. There have been some empirical studies investigating the relationship be-

---

[7]Thus, each quantity represents a different price.

tween executive pay and revenue (as opposed to profits), but no definitive verdict has been obtained. Some of the studies found a more solid relationship between executive pay and revenue, and others appeared to favor a relationship with profits. Still others arrived at ambiguous answers. One important question remains: Are corporate owners (stockholders) more concerned—and thus determine the market value of a corporation—with revenue or profitability? In the long run, the most likely answer is the latter. Thus, it is doubtful that Baumol's model, although possibly applicable to some corporate behavior in the short run, will ever replace the traditional profit-maximizing objective.

# Price Discrimination

Up to this point, we have assumed that a firm will sell identical products at the same price in all markets. (When the term *identical* is used in this context, it implies that the costs of producing and delivering the product are the same.) But such is not always the case. When a company sells identical products in two or more markets, it may charge different prices in the markets. Such a practice is usually referred to as **price discrimination.** The word *discrimination* here is not used in a normative sense; there is no judgment being made about whether this practice is good or bad. (The term *differential pricing* could be used instead, but the former term has become part of the everyday language of the economist.)

Price discrimination means one of the following:

1. Products with identical costs are sold in different markets at different prices.
2. The ratio of price to marginal cost differs for similar products.

The practice of price discrimination is not an isolated event. It occurs in many familiar situations. Later in this section we will cite a number of common examples. Here we will mention just two, to illustrate each general instance just listed. In the first case, price discrimination exists when an adult and a child are charged different prices for tickets (of the same quality and at the same time) at a movie theater. The latter can be illustrated by the selling of cosmetic items, identical except for names on the labels and the quality of packaging, for vastly different prices at department or specialty stores on the one hand and drug and discount stores on the other. The existence of price discrimination is caused by differing demand conditions, not by differences in cost.

Such discriminating price differentials cannot exist under all circumstances. In fact, two conditions are necessary for such a market arrangement:

1. The two or more markets in which the product is sold must be capable of being separated. Specifically, this includes the requirement that there can be no transfer or resale of the product (or service) from one market to the other. That is, there is no leakage among the markets. Only if the markets are sealed off from one another (by natural or contrived means) will the buyers in the various markets be unable to trade the products among these markets. And only in such a case will the seller be able to charge different prices without the price differential being nullified through competition. If the seller incurs costs in creating separate markets, these costs must be less than the additional revenue obtained from discrimination.
2. The demand curves in the segmented markets must have different elasticities at given prices. Without this condition, price discrimination would be futile.

The reason that companies attempt to engage in price discrimination is that it can enhance profits. From the viewpoint of the consumers of the product, those in the lower-price market may benefit compared to situations where a uniform price is charged. However, consumers in the higher-price market are at a disadvantage.

Economists normally identify three degrees of discrimination. First-degree discrimination is the most profitable for the seller, but it can be enforced only infrequently. Third-degree discrimination, which is not as profitable, is the most commonly observed, and we single it out for brief discussion in the next subsection.

1. First-degree discrimination exists when the seller can identify where each buyer lies on the demand curve and can charge each buyer the price he is willing to pay. Thus, the demand curve actually becomes the marginal revenue curve as faced by the seller. Of course, for the seller—a monopolist[8]—to achieve this advantageous position, it must have considerable information on where each of the buyers can be found on the demand curve, admittedly a herculean amount of market knowledge rarely attained. It is probably almost impossible to find such a pure case in real life, but let us attempt an example. A consumer purchasing a new automobile will generally bargain with the salesperson until they finally agree on a price. If the automobile dealer were clever enough to figure out the highest price that each individual was willing to pay, she could then conclude a deal with each customer at the maximum price (but only if no other dealer offered a lower price). Thus, each price the dealer obtains is on the buyers' demand curve. In reality, automobile dealers (and we must surely be thankful for this) are usually not endowed with such omniscience. We could stretch this example to apply to certain personal services such as medical or legal, where different customers (i.e., patients and clients) could be charged different fees based, for example, on their incomes.

2. Second-degree discrimination, although encountered somewhat more frequently than first degree, also is not commonplace in real life. It involves differential prices charged by blocks of services. An example is the way some public utilities price. They will charge the highest unit price (e.g., per kilowatt of electricity) for small quantities (at the top of the demand curve) and lower prices as the rate of consumption per period increases.[9] Thus, again, only if the monopolist seller has a great deal of information about the demand curve will it be able to roughly "skim" the curve and exact higher revenues from its customer set. To be able to engage in second-degree discrimination, a firm must be able to meter the services consumed by the buyers.[10]

3. Third-degree discrimination is by far the most frequently encountered. In this case, the monopolist segregates the customers into different markets and charges different prices in each. Such market segmentation can be based on geography, age, sex, product use, or income, for example.

---

[8]The assumption is usually made that a discriminating seller is a monopolist. But price discrimination also commonly exists in markets where competition is not perfect, not just in pure monopoly markets.
[9]The price differential here is not related to pricing at peak versus off-peak periods. Such pricing may be related to the cost of producing the service and therefore does not represent discrimination.
[10]Price discrimination can also be achieved by using a "two-part tariff," that is, charging a lump-sum fee and then charging for usage. Thus, buyers with greater demand will pay more. Examples of such charges would be a base fee charged by water and telephone companies.

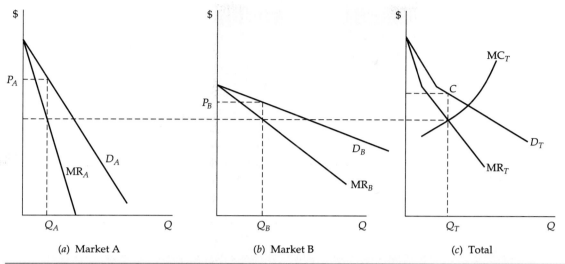

(a)  Market A          (b)  Market B          (c)  Total

**FIGURE 12.4** Third-Degree Price Discrimination

## THIRD-DEGREE DISCRIMINATION

If the firm can segment markets successfully, it can increase its profits above what they would be if a single price were charged. We will show the pricing results with graphs, and subsequently we will show a numerical example comparing the profitability of differential pricing versus uniform pricing as well as a mathematical solution. As shown in Figure 12.4, the company operates in two markets, A and B. In Figure 12.4a and b, it can be seen that A's demand curve is less elastic than B's. Figure 12.4c shows the horizontal summation of both demand and marginal revenue curves to represent the company's total market.

Because we assume that the products sold in the two markets are homogeneous, we can draw a marginal cost curve for the firm as a whole, as shown in Figure 12.4c. Output will take place at the point where MR = MC. Had a uniform price been charged, it would have been at point *C* on the aggregate demand curve. However, the firm can increase its profit by differentiating prices between the two markets. By drawing a horizontal line from the MR = MC intersection across the graphs for the two separate markets, we can allocate total production to the two markets. For each market, this will be the point where the horizontal line intersects the marginal revenue curve. Marginal revenue is thus the same for both markets. The price charged in each market can be found by drawing a vertical line at the corresponding quantity to the demand curve. Price will be considerably higher in market A, whose demand elasticity is lower.

A numerical example will illustrate third-degree discrimination.[11] Section A of Table 12.1 presents the demand schedule for two markets as well as the combined schedule for the entire market. Assume that fixed costs are $12,000 per period, and

---

[11]We have chosen to show a numerical example of price discrimination rather than a mathematical proof. The latter would have been more precise. However, the simpler numerical illustration should be more useful. A brief outline of a mathematical solution is presented in the next subsection.

## TABLE 12.1  Numerical Example of Third-Degree Discrimination

### A. Demand Schedules

| Price | Market A Quantity | Market B Quantity | Total Quantity |
|---|---|---|---|
| 36 | 0 | 0 | 0 |
| 30 | 475 | 25 | 500 |
| 24 | 900 | 100 | 1,000 |
| 18 | 1,100 | 400 | 1,500 |
| 12 | 1,300 | 700 | 2,000 |
| 6 | 1,450 | 1,050 | 2,500 |
| 0 | 1,500 | 1,500 | 3,000 |

### B. Total Market

| Price | Quantity | Total Revenue | Marginal Revenue | Fixed Cost | Aver. Var. and Marginal Costs | Total Cost | Profit |
|---|---|---|---|---|---|---|---|
| 36 | 0 | | | 12,000 | | 12,000 | −12,000 |
| 30 | 500 | 15,000 | 30 | 12,000 | 3 | 13,500 | 1,500 |
| 24 | 1,000 | 24,000 | 18 | 12,000 | 3 | 15,000 | 9,000 |
| 18 | 1,500 | 27,000 | 6 | 12,000 | 3 | 16,500 | 10,500 |
| 12 | 2,000 | 24,000 | −6 | 12,000 | 3 | 18,000 | 6,000 |
| 6 | 2,500 | 15,000 | −18 | 12,000 | 3 | 19,500 | −4,500 |
| 0 | 3,000 | 0 | −30 | 12,000 | 3 | 21,000 | −21,000 |

### C. Market A

| Price | Quantity | Total Revenue | Marginal Revenue | Fixed Cost | Aver. Var. and Marginal Costs | Total Cost | Profit |
|---|---|---|---|---|---|---|---|
| 36 | 0 | | | 6,000 | | 6,000 | −6,000 |
| 30 | 475 | 14,250 | 30 | 6,000 | 3 | 7,425 | 6,825 |
| 24 | 900 | 21,600 | 17 | 6,000 | 3 | 8,700 | 12,900 |
| 18 | 1,100 | 19,800 | −9 | 6,000 | 3 | 9,300 | 10,500 |
| 12 | 1,300 | 15,600 | −21 | 6,000 | 3 | 9,900 | 5,700 |
| 6 | 1,450 | 8,700 | −46 | 6,000 | 3 | 10,350 | −1,650 |
| 0 | 1,500 | 0 | −174 | 6,000 | 3 | 10,500 | −10,500 |

### D. Market B

| Price | Quantity | Total Revenue | Marginal Revenue | Fixed Cost | Aver. Var. and Marginal Costs | Total Cost | Profit |
|---|---|---|---|---|---|---|---|
| 36 | 0 | | | 6,000 | | 6,000 | −6,000 |
| 30 | 25 | 750 | 30 | 6,000 | 3 | 6,075 | −5,325 |
| 24 | 100 | 2,400 | 22 | 6,000 | 3 | 6,300 | −3,900 |
| 18 | 400 | 7,200 | 16 | 6,000 | 3 | 7,200 | 0 |
| 12 | 700 | 8,400 | 4 | 6,000 | 3 | 8,100 | 300 |
| 6 | 1,050 | 6,300 | −6 | 6,000 | 3 | 9,150 | −2,850 |
| 0 | 1,500 | 0 | −14 | 6,000 | 3 | 10,500 | −10,500 |

**TABLE 12.2  Profits from First-Degree Discrimination**

| Price | Quantity | | Revenue |
|-------|----------|--|---------|
| $30 | 500 | | $15,000 |
| 24 | 500 | | 12,000 |
| 18 | 500 | | 9,000 |
| 12 | 500 | | 6,000 |
| 6 | 500 | | 3,000 |
| Total revenue | | | $45,000 |
| Fixed cost | | $12,000 | |
| Variable cost (2,500 × $3) | | 7,500 | |
| Total cost | | | 19,500 |
| Profit | | | $25,500 |

that the average variable cost is constant (and consequently so is marginal cost) at $3 per unit.

If the company were to sell at a uniform price in both markets, it would maximize its profits at a price of $18. At that point, its profit would be $10,500. This can be seen in section B of Table 12.1. But if our company can separate the two markets, it can increase its total profit, as shown in sections C and D of the table. If it charges $24 per unit in market A and $12 per unit in market B, its profits will be $12,900 and $300, respectively. Thus, it will be able to increase its profit by $2,700.[12]

Had the company been able to carry out first-degree discrimination and sold to all potential customers at the prices they were willing to pay (with the exception of the last 500 units, which would not have been produced), its profits would have risen to $25,500, as shown in Table 12.2.

## A Mathematical Solution for Third-Degree Discrimination

We will discuss briefly a simple method to solve for prices and quantities in the presence of third-degree discrimination.

1. Assume that there are two markets, A and B, and the demand curves are straight lines, that is,

$$Q_A = a_A - b_A P_A \text{ and } Q_B = a_B - b_B P_B$$

---

[12]We have arbitrarily divided the fixed costs equally between the two markets. But this has no effect on the total profits of the company or on the levels of sales in the two markets that will lead to profit maximization. Indeed, we could have omitted the fixed costs altogether, and there would have been no impact, except that the profits would have been $12,000 higher in both cases. Also, it should be noted that the quantity sold in this case is somewhat higher than in the one-price case. This is an inaccuracy caused by using discrete numbers in our demand schedule. Had this case been solved mathematically, using calculus, this inaccuracy would not have arisen.

2. Reverse these equations so that $P$ is the dependent variable:

$$P_A = \frac{a_A}{b_A} - \frac{Q_A}{b_A} \text{ and } P_B = \frac{a_B}{b_B} - \frac{Q_B}{b_B}$$

3. Now calculate total revenue by multiplying by $Q$:

$$\text{TR}_A = \frac{a_A Q_A}{b_A} - \frac{Q_A^2}{b_A} \text{ and } \text{TR}_B = \frac{a_B Q_B}{b_B} - \frac{Q_B^2}{b_B}$$

4. Calculate the first derivative of total revenue to obtain marginal revenue:

$$\text{MR}_A = \frac{a_A}{b_A} - \frac{2Q_A}{b_A} \text{ and } \text{MR}_B = \frac{a_B}{b_B} - \frac{2Q_B}{b_B}$$

5. Now set the marginal revenue equal to the company's marginal cost, which we will assume to be a constant:

$$\text{MR}_A = \text{MC} \text{ and } \text{MR}_B = \text{MC}$$

6. Substituting for $\text{MR}_A$ and $\text{MR}_B$ and solving the two equations gives the quantity sold in each market.
7. From here it is easy to find the contribution profit for the two markets and for the combination of the two. Remember that because MC is a constant, average variable cost is constant also, so that total variable cost can be calculated simply by multiplying AVC ($= \text{MC}$) by the quantity. Fixed cost, if any, can then be subtracted.
8. If we wish to find out what the price would be if a uniform price were charged, we first add the two demand functions found in step 1. We then reverse the resulting equation in terms of price, as in step 2, and obtain marginal revenue. Marginal revenue is then equated to MC, and the price, quantity, and contribution profit are obtained in the same manner as in steps 3 to 7. The quantity sold will be the same as if discrimination existed, but the profit will be lower.

## EXAMPLES OF PRICE DISCRIMINATION

Price discrimination is an extremely common practice encountered in all types of situations. A number of rather common examples follow:

1. In the past, physicians often set their fees in accordance with patient income. In a way, it could be argued that such a fee arrangement was quite equitable: Those who can afford to pay higher prices will do so. However, as stated before, we are not concerned here with the normative aspects of differential pricing. The result of such a practice will still be an increase in the physician's income.

   Presently, medical price discrimination exists in a somewhat different guise. Physicians frequently charge a patient who has health insurance more for the same services than they charge a patient who does not. The difference cannot be explained by the cost incurred by the physician in filing insurance documents. However, the two conditions necessary for differential pricing exist. The elasticities in the two markets (uninsured and insured) are certainly different, and the markets are sealed from each other (either the patient has insurance or does not have it).

2. Very often, products going into the export market will be priced lower than those sold domestically. A major reason for the differential is that international competition is stronger than that faced by the firm in its (frequently sheltered) domestic markets. Thus, demand curves in international markets are more elastic. Japanese electronics and French wines are just two examples of such discrimination.

3. Many pubs and bars have "ladies' hours," and in the past, major league baseball parks had ladies' days on Wednesdays. In both cases, the price for women is lower than that charged their male counterparts.

4. Theaters, cinemas, and sports events often charge lower prices for children occupying equal accommodations as adults. The same arrangement is frequently offered to senior citizens.

5. Public transportation systems commonly offer reduced fares to senior citizens.

6. State universities charge higher tuition fees to out-of-state students, although there is no cost differential to the university between in-state and out-of-state students.

7. Public utilities (electric, gas, telephone) customarily charge higher rates to business customers than to residential customers.

8. University bookstores offer 10 to 15 percent discounts to faculty while charging full prices to students.

9. Individuals can order publications from publishers at lower prices than those charged to libraries and other institutions. Most professional journals are priced in this way.

10. Advancing technology is creating new avenues for practicing price discrimination, as shown in the following two examples:
    a. Last-minute airline ticket buyers can make special deals through the Web site "priceline.com."
    b. New software permits Web-based merchants to identify individual visitors to their Web sites, and to study their shopping behavior. Price-sensitive customers may be offered lower prices. This new approach is a variation on catalog retailers' policies of sending catalogs with different prices to different zip codes.[13]

We leave it to you to think of additional examples.[14] In all of these instances, different prices are charged at the same time. A senior citizen and a person 40 years of age traveling in the subway together will pay different fares. Differential utility charges to business and residential customers are in effect at the same time during the day.

However, there are also price differences that depend on when products or services are consumed:

---

[13]S. Woolley, "I got it cheaper than you," *Forbes,* November 2, 1998, pp. 82–84.
[14]Fare differentials in the airline industry are often mentioned as a prime example of price discrimination. A ticket bought well in advance, whose price is not refundable and which includes a weekend, is usually considerably cheaper than one that does not possess these characteristics. Vacation (elastic demand) and business (inelastic demand) travel are usually differentiated in this manner, and thus it may not be unusual for two travelers to sit next to one another on a plane and be paying vastly different fares. However, there are also differences in cost and risk to the airline between these two different fares, so that the two tickets are really not the same. If the fare differentials occur due to disparities in cost and risk, then this is not an example of price discrimination.

1. Theaters charge different ticket prices for matinees and evening performances.
2. Theaters charge higher ticket prices on weekends than on weekdays.
3. Daytime telephone rates are higher than nighttime rates.
4. Hotels catering mostly to business travelers charge lower room rates during weekends.

Are these also examples of price discrimination? Many economics texts subscribe to this notion. (Of course, where a firm's costs differ at different times, no price discrimination would be claimed.) However, if these are types of discrimination they do not really belong with the original examples given. After all, movements of a demand curve over time will change the prices of many products without the presence of price discrimination. What appears to be the case here is that weekend theater ticket demand, for example, is considerably higher than demand on a Tuesday or a Wednesday, while the supply curve is essentially vertical. And prices change as demand changes. Whether this qualifies as price discrimination is questionable.

## PRICING IN THE HOTEL INDUSTRY: EXAMPLE OF PRICE DISCRIMINATION

Differential room rates have existed in the hotel industry for a long time. However, we will not discuss in this section, for instance, the lower weekend rates that are standard at business hotels or the higher rates charged during the busy season by resort hotels. These intertemporal differences appear to be based on different levels of demand. Here we will be concerned with different rates charged to different customers at the same time (e.g., same day). In the following discussion we must remember an important fact attending the operation of a hotel: A large proportion of the cost of running a hotel is fixed. The variable cost of renting an empty room is relatively small. "To paraphrase one general manager, 'If I've got a warm body with money standing in front of me and cold sheets upstairs, I want to make a deal. As long as the customer is willing to pay more than my variable cost to clean that room, I'm going to make money.' "[15] Each additional rented room represents incremental revenue.

This situation leads to different types of price discrimination practices in the hotel industry.

Often a hotel will have several different rates, and the actual rate charged to a particular guest will depend on the bargaining skill of the customer and the knowledge of the innkeeper in estimating the highest price the potential patron is willing to pay. Thus, the revenue of the hotel may be found along the demand curve (if the manager is really proficient at estimating the customer's willingness to pay), and the result may approach first-degree discrimination. Figure 12.5 illustrates this situation with potential scenarios for three different prices.

However, the more typical way of discriminating is to segment the market. The simplest method is to separate leisure travelers from business travelers. The demand of the former is certainly more price elastic, since the room price is an important part of the total vacation expense. At the same time, vacation travelers may be willing to make an advance commitment, may stay for a longer time period, and are more flexible in their

---

[15]Richard D. Hanks, Robert G. Cross, and R. Paul Noland, "Discounting in the Hotel Industry: A New Approach," *The Cornell H.R.A. Quarterly,* February 1992, pp. 15–23. The discussion in this section is based largely on this article. The quote and all that follow also come from this article.

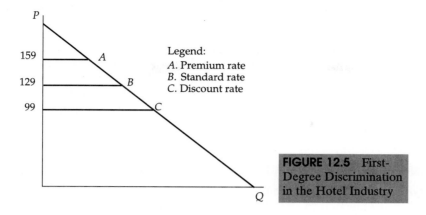

**FIGURE 12.5** First-Degree Discrimination in the Hotel Industry

Legend:
*A*. Premium rate
*B*. Standard rate
*C*. Discount rate

arrangements. The business travelers' demand is less price elastic; they are much more inflexible in making their arrangements (they must be in a certain place at a certain time); their commitments often cannot be made far in advance; perhaps most important is that they are in most cases not willing to stay over the weekend, when rates are often lowest. Figure 12.6 shows the two demand curves with possible prices.

"As customers have become more sophisticated in manipulating the current pricing system, hotels will eventually be forced to modify their pricing structure." A new approach is being introduced, which will "fence" customers into different rate categories tailored to specific needs so that higher-rate patrons will not be able to "trade down." Among the various methods to segment the customer sets will be the following:

1. Advance reservations and advance purchase
2. Rates differentiated depending on how many days in advance the reservations are made
3. Refundability
4. Flexibility to make changes in arrangements
5. Required time of stay

**FIGURE 12.6** Third-Degree Discrimination in the Hotel Industry

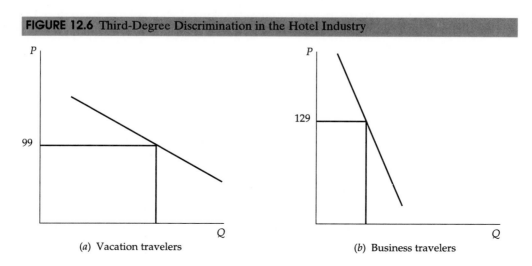

(*a*) Vacation travelers

(*b*) Business travelers

Hotels will be able to combine and alter these requirements ("fences") depending on the level of demand at any specific time. With these procedures, hotels will be able to penetrate their markets more deeply. However, such a multifaceted program also has its problems. First of all, to carry out this program effectively, hotels must have sophisticated computer-directed reservation systems and must be able to make rapid adjustments to ensure that they do not sell too many rooms at unnecessarily discounted rates. The administration of such a system may require additional staffing and additional costs, and management must be sure that the additional revenue derived from this system more than compensates for this cost.

## TYING ARRANGEMENTS: A POSSIBLE EXTENSION OF PRICE DISCRIMINATION

A *tying arrangement* (frequently referred to as a *tie-in sale*) exists when a buyer of one product is obligated to also buy a related (usually complementary) product from the same supplier. U.S. antitrust laws take a very dim view of tying arrangements, and a large number of court cases have declared this practice to be illegal. The reasoning behind this is that a firm will use its existing market power in the first (tying) product to suppress previously existing competition in the second (tied) product. The firm will thus extend its monopoly power.

Typically a tying arrangement will involve a major, often durable product and a low-value item that is usually complementary to the former.[16]

The legal argument claiming that tying arrangements cause an extension of monopoly appears flawed. If a company already has market power in the tying product it can maximize its monopoly profit. To tie another product to it may actually dilute its power, in that customers who buy the two complementary products are mainly interested in the total cost of the two products combined. Thus, if a tie-in sale arrangement causes the price of the tied product to increase, it may have to be made up by a decrease in the price of the tying product.

An alternative economic explanation of a tying arrangement is that it is a type of third-degree discrimination. A company may charge identical prices for the tying good. However, purchasers of the tying product may have different levels of demand for its usage. This quantity of demand can be "metered" by the tied product; purchasers who use the product with greater intensity will use a larger quantity of the tied product. Thus, the seller may charge a relatively reasonable price for the major product and collect monopoly profits on the lower-valued complementary product.

One of the more prominent cases in the history of this litigation was the U.S. government suit against IBM.[17] IBM rented its equipment on a monthly basis. All customers paid the same monthly rental whether they used the machine eight hours a day or two hours per week. Those customers who used the equipment with greater intensity had to use a larger number of punch cards. Thus, IBM really had a relatively inexpensive way to separate its customers into those who used the rented machines more intensively and those who used them only sporadically. And it could practice this

---

[16]To illustrate, some of the court cases involving tying arrangements have included riveting machines and rivets, computers and punch cards, camera film and film processing, condominiums and building management services.

[17]*International Business Machines Corporation v. United States,* 298 U.S. 392 (1936).

discrimination even while charging the same unit price for punch cards to all customers. "It is generally agreed that if the tying and tied goods are complementary in demand, then profit maximization under the price discrimination hypothesis will lead the seller to lower the price of the tying good (below the level that would prevail if the good were sold separately) and sell the tied good at a price above its marginal production cost."[18]

While price discrimination is a plausible explanation of tying arrangements, other arguments have been advanced:

1. *Quality control.* Firms have argued that tying arrangements are necessary to ensure the integrity of their product so they do not get blamed if an inferior tied good is used.
2. *Efficiencies in distribution.* A total lower cost can be attained if there are savings to the company in delivering both products.
3. *Evasion of price controls.* If there is a ceiling price on one of the two products, then selling the second product at a higher price will circumvent price control.

## SOCIAL WELFARE IMPLICATIONS OF PRICE DISCRIMINATION

As mentioned previously, U.S. antitrust laws look unfavorably at the practice of price discrimination, which is said to lead to a lessening of competition.

Under monopoly conditions an industry produces a smaller amount of product at a higher price than under competitive conditions. However, as we have seen, under price discrimination of the first and second degree, a company may produce a larger quantity than a single-price monopoly. Given the conditions of first-degree discrimination, the firm will charge prices along the demand curve all the way to the point where demand equals marginal cost. This, of course, results in a larger quantity than produced by a single-price monopoly. A similar situation would hold for second-degree discrimination. Thus, when price discrimination exists, total production may equal that which would exist under competitive circumstances.

In the case of third-degree discrimination, the situation is more ambiguous. As we have seen, as long as the demand curve for the monopolist is a straight downward-sloping line, the quantity produced will be the same under a single-price and a price-discrimination situation. However, under certain circumstances, production under discriminatory pricing may increase. This situation may occur if the demand curve is not a straight line, or if a one-price policy would not be profitable enough for a company to produce the product at all.

In the case of third-degree discrimination, customers in the market with lower price elasticity will pay higher prices, while those in an elastic demand market will pay lower prices than under conditions of a one-price monopoly. The implications here are uncertain, since it is very difficult to weigh the benefits bestowed on the latter compared to the costs imposed on the former as to their effect on total economic welfare. However, there is no question that the sellers in the discrimination case will benefit from the higher prices charged at least in a part of the market, thereby increasing their profits.

---

[18]Meyer L. Burstein, "The Economics of Tie-In Sales," *Review of Economics and Statistics,* 42 (February 1960), p. 69. Much of the preceding discussion is based on William F. Shughart II, *The Organization of Industry,* Homewood, IL: Irwin, 1990, pp. 307–14.

# Nonmarginal Pricing

Throughout this text we appear to have assumed that all businesspeople calculate demand and cost schedules, obtain marginal revenue and marginal cost curves, equate marginal revenue with marginal cost, and thus determine their profit-maximizing selling price and production quantity. But how many business owners or managers actually know how to make these calculations? And even if they have the knowledge, how many have the time and, even more important, sufficient information to make such calculations?

In fact, it is often claimed (as discussed in chapter 2) that businesses are really not profit maximizers, that they have other objectives. It has been said that management will seek only satisfactory levels of profit for the owners. The term *satisficing* has been used in this context.[19] Other corporate goals may also be important, such as the achievement of a desired market share, a target profit margin (i.e., percent of profits to revenue), or a target rate of return on assets (profit divided by assets) or on equity (profit divided by stockholder equity).

It also appears that one of the most popular pricing methods, believed to be pervasive throughout industry is the cost-plus or full-cost method, which at first glance seems not to employ the marginal pricing principle at all. It is this subject that we will discuss next.

### COST-PLUS PRICING

A researcher questioning a sample of businesspeople on their pricing methods, would probably be told by a majority that they simply calculate the variable cost of the product, add to it an allocation for fixed costs, and then add a profit percentage or markup on top of these total costs to arrive at **cost-plus price.**[20] Thus, for instance, if the direct (variable) cost of a product is $8, its allocated overhead is $6, and the desired markup is 25 percent, the price of the product will be $17.50 (8 + 6 + 0.25 × 14).[21]

Such a calculation appears to be extremely simple, and the whole method is often described as naive.[22] But this apparent simplicity hides some fairly difficult calculations and assumptions:

1. How are average variable costs calculated?
2. How are fixed costs allocated? And why are fixed costs included in the price calculation? Economic theory tells us that fixed costs do not affect price.[23]

---

[19]See Herbert Simon, "Theories of Decision Making in Economics and Behavioral Science," *American Economic Review,* 49 (June 1959), pp. 253–83. This condition usually prevails in large corporations, where professional managers may not act in conformance with the wishes of stockholders. In the textbooks on corporate finance, considerable attention is accorded this subject, which has been named "agency theory." It is based on a famous article by Michael C. Jensen and William H. Meckling, "Theory of the Firm: Managerial Behavior, Agency Costs, and Ownership Structure," *Journal of Financial Economics,* October 1976, pp. 305–60.

[20]One of the original studies was R. L. Hall and C. J. Hitch, "Price Theory and Business Behavior," *Oxford Economic Papers,* 2 (May 1939), pp. 12–45.

[21]Markup is ordinarily calculated as a percentage of cost. Profit margin is commonly computed as a percentage of price. Thus, a 25 percentage markup is equivalent to a 20 percent profit margin.

[22]It is said that restaurants usually mark up the food cost four times to arrive at the price of a menu item—a very simple calculation indeed.

[23]Only in the Baumol revenue maximization model does fixed cost enter into price determination.

**3.** How is the size of the markup determined? Usually, it is said that the markup should guarantee the seller a "fair profit," or some target profit margin or target rate of return. If this is the case, are demand conditions taken into consideration at all?

We will discuss these problems, and as we go through this analysis we may find that cost-plus pricing and marginal pricing have a lot in common.

In cost-plus pricing, costs, both variable and fixed overheads, are usually calculated at some standard or normal quantity, as is done by accountants. These are historical costs and do not appear to include an opportunity cost. But economic theory tells us that unit costs tend to vary with quantity, and the expected quantities may not correspond to those that result.[24] Also, as mentioned, fixed costs should not be used in the determination of prices.

However, if we take these criticisms in turn, the shortcomings of cost-plus pricing may not be as serious as they appear. There is no real reason why accounting costs cannot include some measure of opportunity cost. And even if it is not incorporated, a normal profit (another name for opportunity cost) certainly could easily be included in the markup. Now, it is often said that cost-plus pricing is a long-term concept. If that is the case, then, according to economic theory, all costs are variable; a cost allocation is then an estimate of the additional variable costs in the long run. Further, although economists like to draw nice U-shaped cost curves, it is quite possible that in the longer run the bottom portion of the average cost curve is quite shallow (saucer-shaped) and that over some production range it may appear to be almost horizontal.[25] In that case, as long as a firm is producing in the range at which standard costs are calculated, the problem of costs varying with quantity is obviated. Also, if the curve is relatively horizontal, marginal cost will be identical or almost identical to the average cost in that interval, and pricing on basis of average cost will thus be substantially similar to marginal cost pricing. In addition, economic theory tells us that, under perfect competition, in the long run all but normal profits will disappear. The markup, then, must certainly represent normal profit. It is more likely, however, that competition in the real world is not quite perfect, and the firm will therefore be faced by a downward-sloping demand curve.

This brings us to the question of the demand curve. If a markup is applied to obtain a "fair" profit, the implication is that demand conditions are not taken into consideration. But that would indicate almost complete inflexibility regarding the size of the markup. However, it has been observed in innumerable cases that markup percentages

---

[24]The accountant's cost for a normal quantity can be shown as one point on the economist's average cost curve:

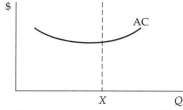

Point $X$ is the "normal" quantity at which costs would be calculated. But other quantities would be produced at different costs.

[25]This situation is consistent with constant returns to scale.

differ among different product lines of the same firm. The fact that a company accepts a lower markup for some products than others indicates that demand conditions and the competitive environment are included in the pricing decision making. As will be shown, the markup percentage tends to vary inversely with demand elasticity. This makes obvious sense: when a firm is faced by very strong competition, the demand curve facing it will tend to be nearly or completely horizontal: under those circumstances, the firm will not be able to afford a very large markup.

One other important point must be made. Not only will different markups be applied for different product lines of a given firm, but the markup will probably change on a given product from time to time. Such changes could be caused by changing demand or changing cost conditions. When this occurs, a firm will adjust its markup and, thus, its price to meet the new circumstances. Its purpose for such action is most probably to increase or protect its profits. And as long as a firm changes its prices to "do better," (i.e., increase its profit or minimize its loss), it is acting as if it has knowledge of its demand and cost curves: that is, it is acting consistently with marginal pricing.

It is certainly true that businesspeople do not have sufficient knowledge to estimate marginal revenue and marginal cost curves with any degree of accuracy. Thus, cost-plus pricing can be a substitute for marginal pricing in the absence of sufficient knowledge. But given the proclivity for firms to adjust their markups in response to demand and cost conditions in such a way as to improve profitability, profit maximization and cost-plus pricing can be quite compatible.

### An Arithmetic Reconciliation of Cost-Plus and Marginal Pricing

It can be shown mathematically that under certain circumstances, cost-plus pricing can be consistent with profit maximization (i.e., MR = MC).

Most microeconomics textbooks show the mathematical relationship among price, marginal revenue, and demand elasticity as follows.[26]

$$MR = P\left(1 + \frac{1}{E_p}\right)$$

As profit is maximized when MR = MC, we can rewrite the equation as

$$MC = P\left(1 + \frac{1}{E_p}\right)$$

Further, under certain conditions, marginal cost will equal average cost. Thus, our equation becomes

---

[26]The equation is derived in the following way: Total revenue (TR) equals price times quantity ($P \times Q$). To obtain marginal revenue, total revenue must be differentiated with respect to quantity:

$$MR = \frac{d\,TR}{dQ} = \frac{d(P \times Q)}{dQ} = P \times \frac{dQ}{dQ} + Q \times \frac{dP}{dQ} = P \times 1 + Q \times \frac{dP}{dQ} = P\left(1 + \frac{Q}{P} \times \frac{dP}{dQ}\right)$$

Note that the product inside the parentheses is the reciprocal of elasticity; hence,

$$MR = P\left(1 + \frac{1}{E_p}\right)$$

Remember that demand elasticity has a negative sign.

$$AC = P\left(1 + \frac{1}{E_p}\right)$$

and can then be rewritten as

$$AC = P\left(\frac{E_p + 1}{E_p}\right)$$

To show how price is based on average cost, we can rearrange the equation as

$$P = AC\left(\frac{E_p}{E_p + 1}\right)$$

Under conditions of cost-plus pricing,

$$P = AC\,(1 + M)$$

where *M* stands for the markup percentage. If the two previous equations are comparable, then

$$(1 + M) = \frac{E_p}{E_p + 1}$$

It can be shown that there is an inverse relationship between markup and demand elasticity. For example, if $E_p = -2$, then $(1 + M) = -2/-1 = 2$ and *M* is therefore 100 percent. If, however, $E_p = -5$, then $(1 + M) = -5/-4 = 1.25$, and markup is only 25 percent. This result is quite reasonable; it indicates that the less elastic the demand curve, the larger the markup will be.

Thus, under the not infrequent conditions where the average cost curve is constant in the relevant range of production, cost-plus pricing may give results identical to those that would be obtained if managers were pursuing profit maximization.

## INCREMENTAL PRICING AND COSTING ANALYSIS

We have just discussed the cost-plus method of pricing; it is considered to be a very popular pricing method. We explained that cost-plus pricing and marginal pricing can generally be reconciled. But there are difficulties with implementing marginal pricing in the real world. To do a good job of marginal pricing, a manager would have to have good estimates of the shape of demand and cost curves. Since it may be quite costly and certainly very difficult to estimate marginal quantities, businesses will often use incremental analysis to achieve the objective of profit maximization.

In a way, marginal and incremental analyses are very similar. But while *marginal* implies that we must estimate the revenue and costs created by one additional unit or the additional revenue obtained from one extra dollar of expenses, incremental analysis deals with changes in total revenue and total costs resulting from a particular decision to change prices, introduce a new product, discontinue an existing product, improve a product, or acquire additional machinery or plant. We have already discussed the question of incremental costs in chapter 8.

The important lesson to learn here is that only those revenues and costs that will change due to the decision should be considered. Thus, it is a mistake to include sunk costs in calculating the outcome. Furthermore, if costs such as fixed overhead are already being incurred and will not change (even though accountants may reallocate these costs), they are irrelevant to the decision. On the other hand, if a decision results in a change in revenues or costs of another product (possibly a complementary or substitute good), such an effect must be included in the analysis.

Obviously, this is an important subject to which we are devoting only a small amount of space here. However, incremental analysis is at the heart of the study of long-term investments. This is a subject discussed at greater length in chapter 13.

## Multiproduct Pricing

In economics much of the analysis makes use of simplifying assumptions. For example, we know that very few products in our economy are produced under conditions of perfect competition. Nevertheless, a large portion of our text—and all other economics texts—is devoted to its discussion. There are good reasons for this practice. First, perfect competition is the simplest of the economic models and is thus a good starting point for the discussion of more complex systems. Second, many markets, although not perfectly competitive (i.e., firms are faced by downward-sloping demand curves), can be analyzed as such because their behavior resembles perfect competition closely enough. Any predictions based on this analysis will be sufficiently accurate to obviate the need for more complex models.[27]

Another simplification frequently made in economic theory is assuming that a firm or a plant produces a single product. Up to this point, we have done so in this text. Actually, we first assumed that single products were sold in single markets, and later extended our analysis to operations in more than one market (price discrimination). Now we will provide a brief treatment of **multiproduct pricing,** cases in which a plant or a firm produces two or more products, which are, of course, the norm rather than the exception.

The various products produced by a firm can be independent of one another. This means that neither the demand for nor the cost of one product is affected by the demand for or cost of another product. In such a case, each product will be produced, as usual, at the level where its marginal revenue equals its marginal cost. The analysis can then proceed as if only one good were produced.

In most cases, however, there is some relationship among products produced by one firm. The relationships can exist either on the demand side or the cost side—or both. We can distinguish (at least) four different interrelationships:

1. Products are complements in terms of demand. One company may produce both personal computers and software, or a fast-food restaurant may sell both hamburgers and soft drinks.
2. Products are substitutes in terms of demand: A company may produce different models of a personal computer, or a soft drink company may bottle both cola and lemon-lime soda.

---

[27]It is the accuracy of the prediction provided by a model that is important to scientists, not the reasonability or realism of the assumptions. This point has been successfully argued by Milton Friedman in "The Methodology of Positive Economics," contained in his *Essays in Positive Economics,* Chicago: University of Chicago Press, 1953, pp. 3–43.

3. Products are joined in production. The extreme case of joint production occurs when two products are produced in fixed (or almost fixed) proportions, such as cattle production, which involves one skin and one carcass per steer.
4. Products compete for resources. If a company making different products that compete for the available resources produces more of one product, it will have to do so at the expense of producing less of other products. The production of different models of the same computer is an example.

Let us now discuss each of these cases.

## PRODUCTS COMPLEMENTARY IN DEMAND

When two products are complementary, an increase in the quantity sold of one will bring about an increase in the quantity sold of the other. This may be due to an increase in the demand for product A or a price decrease of product A (bringing about an increase in the quantity demanded). Products may be so closely related that they are bought in fixed proportions. An example is kitchen knives, each of which must be made of one wooden handle and one metal blade. Other complementary products are a personal computer and a keyboard, and still another example is an automobile body and a set of four wheels. Somewhat less fixed in proportion but still closely related products are razors and razor blades, tennis rackets and tennis balls, and computers and software. There are also more remotely related products where the demand for one can easily have a beneficial effect on the demand for the other. For instance, a popular textbook in economics published by a particular company may enhance the sales of a finance textbook by the same publisher.

The important point is that the demand for a product is affected not only by its price, by income, and by tastes, for example, but also very strongly by the prices of related commodities. This subject was discussed in chapter 3, where we defined the determinants of the demand curve in general. Here we will concentrate on the effects of complementary commodities on the revenues of one firm. Thus, if products A and B are complementary, a change in revenue from A will entail a change in the revenue from B. In both cases, profit maximization will occur at the familiar point where the marginal revenue of each product equals its marginal costs. Since each of the demand equations will include the prices of both products, the pricing problem will require the solution of simultaneous equations.

If managers had nice, neat demand and cost functions available for each of these products, they could arrive at the combined profit maximization positions using relatively simple mathematical formulas.[28] However, since in real life the decision maker would most likely not have sufficient data on hand, the maximization process would proceed along a trial-and-error course, where markups (and thus prices) for the products would be adjusted until the optimal combination is reached. Actually, the process

---

[28]For a two-product situation, a manager could calculate the marginal revenue for each of the interrelated products. Because

$$Q_A = f(P_A, P_B) \text{ and } Q_B = f(P_B, P_A)$$

then

$$MR_A = \frac{d\,TR_A}{dQ_A} + \frac{d\,TR_B}{dQ_A} \text{ and } MR_B = \frac{d\,TR_B}{dQ_B} + \frac{d\,TR_A}{dQ_B}$$

Each of the marginal revenues would be equated to their respective marginal costs simultaneously:

$$MR_A = MC_A \text{ and } MR_B = MC_B$$

would be even more complex in reality, as it is not only the complementary relationship between the firm's two products that has an important influence on the firm's revenue (and profit); competitors' products that are substitutes for our firm's products must also be considered in the process of price setting.

There is another instance in which a company must consider these interrelationships. It is not necessary that a firm produce two related products simultaneously. It may just produce one and be in the process of deciding whether to embark on the production of a complementary product. In calculating the profitability of such expansion, the company must include the increase in sales of and profit earned on the earlier product. If it omitted this positive effect, it would be understating the benefits of the new product. It may decide against the product's introduction when in fact the total profits of the company would increase if the new product were brought to market. As an example, suppose a successful producer of television sets is considering whether or not to introduce a new line of VCRs. In calculating the potential profitability of producing VCRs, the producer must include the possibility of enhanced sales (and profits) from its television line.

## PRODUCTS SUBSTITUTABLE IN DEMAND

A brief treatment of substitutability and pricing will suffice, as this case is extremely similar to that of complements. For substitutes, the effect to be considered is the decrease (increase) in revenue and profits of a second product if quantities bought of the first product rise (fall), either because of changes in demand or changes in price. Examples of such cases abound. Two different sizes of personal computers certainly are substitutes for one another. The different automobile models produced by one manufacturer (sedans versus convertibles, Honda Preludes versus Accords, Chevrolets versus Pontiacs, etc.) are relatively close substitutes, so it is necessary to price them jointly. Another example is Global Foods' soft drink division, which produces cola-type and non-cola-type sodas simultaneously.

Just as in the case of complementary products, substitution can occur when a new product is introduced. Thus, a computer manufacturer developing a new generation of computers must consider the impact that the introduction will have on similar but less advanced products now being marketed.

The analysis of these cases is basically the same as for complementary commodities. The marginal revenue of one product will be a function of the quantities sold of both commodities, and the prices of the two will be found by solving simultaneous equations. However, in this case, the sales of one product will have a negative impact on the sales of the other.

## JOINT PRODUCTS WITH FIXED PROPORTIONS

Certain products will be produced together from one set of inputs. In some instances, the two products will be produced in fixed proportions to one another. Although precisely fixed proportions may not occur often in the real world, relative fixity is commonly encountered, particularly in the short run. The example given earlier involved the products of a beef carcass and a hide (only one of each can be obtained from one steer). Other examples are soybean meal and soybean oil, and coconut milk and coconut meat. In many cases, there is a principal product and one or more byproducts.

Assume that products A and B are produced jointly in fixed proportions. Only one cost curve can be constructed in this case. However, the demand curves for the two

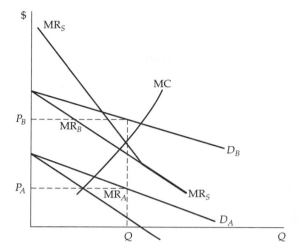

**FIGURE 12.7** Price Determination for Joint Products Made in Fixed Proportions

products are independent (e.g., the demand for coconut meat is not related to the demand for its milk). Thus, the two demand curves and their respective marginal revenue curves can be added vertically to obtain a total demand curve and a total marginal revenue curve. Observe, however, that when one of the separate marginal revenue curves goes negative, it becomes irrelevant to the solution of the problem, because no business would produce at a point where marginal revenue is negative. To the right of this point, the total marginal revenue curve will be coincident with the marginal revenue of the product that is still in the positive range. Production will take place (using our usual maximization rule) where total marginal revenue equals marginal cost. The prices of the two separate products can be found at the quantity indicated on their respective demand curves. Figure 12.7 shows the results. $D_A$, $D_B$, $MR_A$, and $MR_B$ are the demand and marginal revenue curves for the two products, and $MR_S$ represents the vertical summation of the two individual marginal revenue curves. (The summed demand curve is actually irrelevant to the solution of the problem and need not be shown.) As can be seen, $MR_S$ becomes identical with $MR_B$ to the right of the point where $MR_A$ becomes negative.

The curve MC represents the marginal cost of the joint product. Production will take place where marginal cost is equal to $MR_S$, which is at quantity $Q$ on the graph. The prices charged for the two products will be found on their respective demand curves at $P_A$ and $P_B$. An interesting aspect of this type of construction is that if the optimal production quantity were to the right (i.e., at higher quantities) of the point where one of the marginal revenue curves (in our case, that for product A) becomes negative, it would become profitable for the company to produce this total amount but not to sell quantities of product A beyond the point where its marginal revenue becomes zero. The company should discard the excess product A.

Another important point is the effect of the change in the demand for one of the two jointly produced products. If the demand for product B rises and the price of B thus increases, there will be a decrease in the price of A (as it will be produced at a lower point on its demand curve).

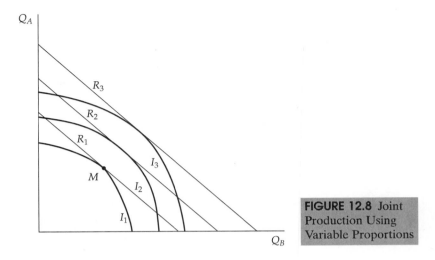

**FIGURE 12.8** Joint Production Using Variable Proportions

## JOINT PRODUCTS IN VARIABLE PROPORTIONS

When we relax the limitation of fixed proportions, we have the usual case of joint production. Indeed, when two products are produced from similar resources in variable proportions (i.e., if we produce more of one product we must produce less of the other) the situation is not dissimilar to the general case of production of different products with limited resources. We are essentially describing the "guns or butter" situation. Under short-run conditions, there is a given amount of resources with which the two products can be produced.

Figure 12.8 illustrates this situation. Curve $I_1$ is an isocost curve; the total cost of production is the same at each point. An essential requisite is that the curve be concave to the origin: as more of one product is produced, progressively larger quantities of the other must be given up. The isocost curve shows the alternative quantities of product A and B that can be produced. If the prices of the two products are constant regardless of quantity (i.e., we are implicitly operating under conditions of perfect competition), then a straight-line isorevenue curve can be drawn. At each point on $R_1$ in Figure 12.8, identical revenue is obtained. To optimize, the company will produce at the point of tangency between the isorevenue and isocost curves (point $M$ in the figure). This represents the highest revenue that the company can attain for a given total cost. If revenue at this point is greater than cost, economic profit will result.

The company could also move from one isocost curve to another (e.g., from $I_1$ to $I_2$ to $I_3$), and consequently from one isorevenue curve to another, representing the use of additional variable resources. Production would take place at the tangency point that results in the largest difference between total revenue and total cost. This point signifies the maximum economic profit the company can achieve. In the long run, these isocost curves would include changes in all resources, including those (such as plant and equipment) that are fixed in the short run. Under conditions of perfect competition, the optimal tangency would occur where total revenue just equals total cost, with no economic profit. At all other points, economic losses would be sustained.

We have limited our discussion to a simple model, utilizing only two products and assuming perfect competition. Much more complex models could be developed, involving more than two products, noncompetitive conditions, and demand interrelationships, for example. The results would be more difficult to obtain, and relatively complicated mathematical models would have to be introduced, but the principles of economic maximization would still apply. Whenever a company takes action in introducing a new product, producing more of one at the expense of another or eliminating a certain commodity from its product line, and when such action is taken to improve its short-run or long-run profitability, the company is guided by the basic principle of equating marginal cost with marginal revenue.

# Transfer Pricing

In today's complex industrial world, many companies have subdivided their operations into several groups or divisions. As a product moves from its early stages to the point where it is ready to be sold to consumers, it is passed from one operating division of the company to another. In the automobile industry, for example, various auto parts may be produced in different plants and then assembled into the finished product in yet another plant. Computer and peripheral equipment components may be produced in one plant and assembled into different products at other plants. Then, to sell the products, the marketing arm of the company may have to assemble the various individual machines into complete systems.

To continue this analysis, it is necessary to address the notion of *profit center,* a frequently used term that refers to a situation prevalent in large corporations. The management of each division is charged with a profit objective. Thus, each stage of production must measure its costs and then establish a price at which it will "transfer" its product to the next stage. However, if each intermediate profit center were to set its price to maximize its own profit, the price of the final product may not maximize the profit of the company as a whole, which is the appropriate objective. The price set by the division transferring the intermediate product becomes the cost of the division receiving this product. If that price is set too high, this may start a chain reaction resulting in the final product price being higher than the price which would maximize the company's profit. The **transfer pricing** mechanism must be geared toward maximizing total company profit; therefore, the final pricing policy may be dictated centrally from the top of the corporation.

Such processes can be extremely complicated, particularly if there are more than two steps in the transfer process. Further, the intermediate products may be only for internal usage. On the other hand, the producing division may also be selling its product in an external market, and the receiving division may be free to purchase the intermediate product from a competitor, if that would improve the company's profit situation. Let us discuss each of these cases in turn. To simplify matters, we will assume the existence of just two divisions, one that manufactures components (division C), and another that assembles them into the final product and sells it (division A).

## NO EXTERNAL MARKETS

If there is no possibility for division A to buy components from a competing firm and no possibility for division C to sell components to other companies, then the two divisions must deal with equal quantities; division C will produce exactly the number of components that will be utilized by division A for assembly and sales. The company will be faced by a demand curve for the final product and two marginal cost curves. The two MC curves, one for each division, will be summed vertically to obtain total marginal cost, and the company will maximize its total profit by equating the total marginal cost with marginal revenue. Production will take place at that intersection, and the price for the final product will be the corresponding price on the demand curve.

## EXTERNAL MARKETS

It may be possible for division C to sell its (intermediate) product in a competitive market and for division A to purchase division C's product (an identical product) in a competitive market. In that case, the pricing of the product will proceed as follows:

1. Division C will produce at the point where its marginal cost equals the market price. (Because we are assuming the existence of a competitive market, the demand curve is horizontal, resulting in a uniform price regardless of quantity.)
2. The cost of the intermediate product to division A is the market price. This will be added to division A's marginal cost curve to obtain the total marginal cost for the final product.
3. Production will take place at the quantity where the total marginal cost equals the marginal revenue for the final product.
4. If the final product quantity is less than the quantity of the intermediate product produced by C, then C will sell the surplus in the competitive external market. If the output of C is less than A wishes to buy, A will turn to the external market for the additional units of the intermediate product it needs to maximize company profit.

Of course, should division C for some reason attempt to price the intermediate product in excess of the market price, then A would buy all of the intermediate product in the external market.

## MULTINATIONAL TRANSFER PRICING

While transfer pricing presents a domestic company with many problems, the matter becomes even more complex when a multinational corporation is involved, where an internal transfer involves movement across borders. This additional complication arises from the fact that a transfer price may be manipulated in such a way as to transfer funds among countries or to affect a company's income tax liability. A company operating in countries A and B would certainly wish to increase its profit in country A, whose income tax rates are lower, at the expense of profit in high-tax country B. To do this, if the company ships components from its manufacturing facility in A to its assembly plant in

B, it would charge very high transfer prices, thus increasing its profitability in A and decreasing its profits in B.[29]

The United States as well as other countries have taken action to prevent such tax evasion by multinational companies. Section 482 of the U.S. Internal Revenue Code gives the IRS the authority to "shift around income and expense figures to arrive at what the government considers a more equitable result."[30] In such cases, the burden of proof is on the taxpayer to prove that the IRS has been incorrect in reallocating income.

The IRS requires that transfer pricing is done on an "arm's length" relationship. The best evidence of such relationship is that prices resemble those that would be established between two independent companies.

Transfer price proceedings have been a prominent activity of the IRS, and it was reported that in 1997 more than $4 billion of transfer pricing cases were being handled by the U.S. Tax Court.[31]

In 1994, Japanese tax authorities charged Coca-Cola Japan with a penalty tax of 15 billion yen (approximately $100 million), claiming that brand and royalty payments for three years (to March 1992) transferred by Coca-Cola to its U.S. parent were too high by $36 billion yen.[32]

A case involving a tax dispute over about $140 million occurred in Houston, Texas, in 1997. The case concerned a Mexican manufacturer of transformers, cable wire, and other products, Conductores de Monterrey, and a Houston distributor, Eletex, Inc. In the years 1988 to 1993, the latter incurred such large losses that it reported no taxable income. The question here was whether the two companies were really independent, or whether Eletex was a representative of Conductores.[33]

## Other Pricing Practices

**Price skimming** occurs when a firm is the first to introduce a product. It may have a virtual monopoly, and often will be able to charge high prices and obtain substantial profits before competition enters.

In **penetration pricing** a company sets a relatively low price in order to obtain market share.

---

[29]The relationship can be shown by the following simple equation:

$$\Delta T = Q \times \Delta P \times t_E - Q \times \Delta P \times t_M$$

where $\Delta T$ = the change in the total tax bill
$Q$ = the quantity of products shipped by E (exporter) to M (importer)
$\Delta P$ = the change in price of the product
$t_E$ and $t_M$ = the tax rates in the exporting and importing countries, respectively

If $t_E > t_M$, transfer price should be lowered, and if $t_E < t_M$, transfer price should be raised. How much prices can be changed to minimize total tax payments depends, of course, on the level of the transfer price that would be tolerated by the higher tax government. The equation would become more complex if we had included import duties.

[30]C. Carroll, "IRS Targets Local Company in 'Transfer Pricing' Case," *Houston Business Journal,* February 3, 1997.

[31]*Ibid.*

[32]E. Terazono, "Coca-Cola Faces Tokyo Penalty Tax," *Financial Times,* March 28, 1994.

[33]Carroll, "IRS Targets Local Company."

With **prestige pricing,** demand for a product may be higher at a higher price because of the prestige that ownership bestows on the buyer.

**Psychological pricing** takes advantage of the fact that the demand for a particular product may be quite inelastic over a certain range but will become rather elastic at one specific higher or lower price. Such a demand curve has the appearance of a step function.

Complete explanations of these pricing practices can be found in many marketing textbooks.

# International Application

### THE DECLINE OF EUROPEAN CARTELS

European governments have in the past tolerated and supported monopolies, and while pricing cartels have been illegal, they have flourished. But this situation is currently changing. Where monopolies existed, markets are now opening up.

For instance, in early 1998, when new rules permitted competition with Deutsche Telekom, TelePassport, a small company that discounts telephone services, signed up over 19,000 customers in 20 days. Deutsche Telekom then proceeded to cut its prices to fight this competition. Indeed, it was reported that, by the middle of 1999, prices of domestic long-distance calls had decreased by up to 85 percent. New telephone companies had obtained 35 percent of the long-distance and overseas call markets.

Airline monopolies have also been breaking up. Three small start-up companies have now captured 22 percent of the German market, and in Italy, several new small companies have decreased Alitalia's market share from 90 to 75 percent.

Although changes in the energy sector have been slow, and markets are opening only in 1999, some large consumers had already been able to secure lower electrical rates before that date. Enron Corporation, a Houston, Texas, company has entered the European market and is selling electricity. Progress may be slow, but freer markets are on the increase in Europe. "Once the ball starts rolling, competitive pressures will make things move very quickly," stated Mark E. Frevert, CEO of Enron's European unit.[34]

### THE EUROPEAN CARTON-BOARD CARTEL

A recent case involving 19 carton-board producers in ten European countries actually resembles the electrical manufacturers' case discussed previously.

In July 1994, the European Commission imposed record fines of $159 million on the 19 producers. The cartel involved a market-sharing agreement and orchestrated 6–10 percent price increases each six months during the period from 1987 to 1990. Monthly "social" meetings were arranged at luxury hotels (most frequently in Zurich). "The cartel's members then compared the state of their order books to judge when best to introduce a price increase. Sometimes the big producers agreed on temporary plant

---

[34]This section is based on T. Peterson, "The Cartels Are Finally Crumbling," *Business Week,* February 2, 1998, p. 52; R. Atkins, "German Phone Call Prices Cut," *Financial Times,* July 9, 1999.

stoppages to keep production under control."[35] Fake minutes were drawn up to disguise the business that was transacted.

The European Commission acted after complaints by the industry's customers about the continual price increases during a period of sharp economic downturn. In 1991, officials of the commission staged simultaneous raids on the producers and found private notes documenting the dates and amounts of price increases. One of the companies decided to admit to the conspiracy and aided the probe, which resulted in heavy fines.

---

### THE SOLUTION

Rebecca James went to see Philip Olds of the food division to solicit his advice on the bid she intended to make for the bottled water supply contract with the large airport catering company.

"One thing is certain," he said. "You have to bid at a price considerably lower than the price at which you sell to small retail stores. These stores have a leeway in how much they can charge their customers, since they are really selling convenience. A small variance in price is not going to change their sales significantly, so they will not stop buying from us as long as our price is not out of line.

"However, your potential new customer intends to give a contract to only one additional supplier, and 10 cents per case will make a large difference when hundreds of thousands of cases are involved. Thus, you will have to shave your markup as much as possible. It may turn out that you will make precious little profit, if any, on this contract."

Philip was telling Rebecca that the demand price elasticity of the large caterer was quite different from that of the small retailers. As a result,

Global Foods could sell to these two markets at different prices.

Rebecca is thus confronted with a case of price discrimination. The demand elasticities in the two markets are probably quite different; thus, higher prices can be charged in the market displaying lower elasticity. And the separation of the two markets (i.e., no cross-selling) represents the second important condition for the existence of price discrimination. Another important consideration for Rebecca is that the price to be charged must enable the company to gain a foothold in this large market (penetration or entry pricing).

Back in her office, Rebecca begins to work on determining the price. She assumes that the average cost per case of *Waterpure* for the two customers is the same. Although this is certainly not quite accurate (the large shipments the company will make to the new customer if the bid is won will probably create some cost savings), the unit cost differences probably will not be significant, so her analysis will lose little if she assumes equality.

She estimates the company's usual markup to be about 50 percent. After

*(Continued)*

---

[35]This discussion and quotation are based on Emma Tucker, "Price-fixing Cartel Given Record Fine by Brussels," *Financial Times,* July 14, 1994, and Emma Tucker, "Rise and Fall of a House of Cards," *Financial Times,* July 15, 1994.

some additional consideration, and a review of some data for the industry that she obtained, she feels that a 20 percent markup would put the company in a good competitive position.

Before making this recommendation to her boss, she will consult with the finance and accounting departments to determine what, if any, profit would be realized on this transaction. She will, of course, include this analysis with her recommendation. It is quite possible that at this low price profit will be extremely marginal, and she will then have to argue that obtaining a foothold in this market will have beneficial long-run consequences.

The decision that she has made has some rather important implica-

tions for the estimate of demand elasticities for the two classes of customers. The lower the demand elasticity, the higher will be the markup that a company can obtain. Following the equation developed previously,

$$(1 + M) = \frac{E_P}{E_P + 1}$$

(where demand elasticity is a negative number), an elasticity of 3 conforms to a markup of 50 percent, whereas an elasticity of 6 corresponds to a 20 percent markup. Of course, these numbers are approximations, but such an estimate could be of great help to Rebecca in her attempt to set the proper price.

## Summary

This chapter has built on the foundation laid in chapters 9 and 10 by applying the principles of pricing and output to specific pricing situations, most under conditions of imperfect competition. Briefly, we learned the following:

1. Cartels are formed to avoid the uncertainties of a possible reaction by one competitor to price and production actions by another. The firms in the industry agree on unified pricing and production actions to maximize profits. However, as history shows, such arrangements are not always stable.
2. Price leadership exists when one company establishes a price and others follow. Two types of price leadership were discussed: barometric and dominant.
3. Baumol's model describes the actions of a company whose objective is to maximize revenue (rather than profits) subject to a minimum profit constraint.
4. Price discrimination (or differential pricing) exists when a product is sold in different markets at different prices. Third-degree price discrimination is the most common. By charging different prices in separate markets that have demand curves with different price elasticities, a firm can increase its profits over what they would be if a uniform price were charged.
5. Cost-plus pricing appears to be a very common method. However, such pricing does not necessarily imply that marginal principles and demand curve effects are not taken into consideration.
6. Multiproduct pricing was examined, because most firms and plants produce more than one product at the same time. Multiple products produced by one firm can be complements or substitutes, both on the demand side and the supply side. Four

possible cases were discussed, and it was shown how application of the marginal principle brings about profit maximization.

7. Several other pricing practices were summarized. One was transfer pricing, which is used to determine the price of a product that progresses through several stages of production within a firm.

## Important Concepts

**Barometric price leadership:** In an oligopolistic industry, a situation in which one firm, perceiving that demand and supply conditions warrant it, announces a price change, expecting that other firms will follow. (p. 440)

**Baumol model:** A model hypothesizing that firms seek to maximize their revenue subject to some minimum profit requirement (i.e., the profit constraint). (p. 441)

**Cartel:** A collusive arrangement in oligopolistic markets. Producers agree on unified pricing and production actions to maximize profits and to eliminate the rigors of competition. (p. 436)

**Cost-plus pricing:** Also called *full-cost pricing,* a practice in which prices are calculated by adding a markup to total cost. (p. 454)

**Dominant price leadership:** In an oligopolistic industry, a firm, usually the largest in the industry, sets a price at which it will maximize its profits, allowing other firms to sell as much as they wish at that price. (p. 440)

**Multiproduct pricing:** Pricing that reflects the interrelationship among multiple products of a firm that are substitutes or complements. (p. 458)

**Penetration pricing:** A company charges a lower price than indicated by economic analysis in order to gain a foothold in the market. (p. 465)

**Prestige pricing:** A perception that charging a higher price will increase quantity sold because of the prestige obtained by the buyer. (p. 466)

**Price discrimination:** A situation in which an identical product is sold in different markets at different prices. (p. 443)

**Price leadership:** One company in an oligopolistic industry establishes the price, and the other companies follow. Two types of price leadership are common: barometric and dominant. (p. 439)

**Price skimming:** The practice of charging a higher price than indicated by economic analysis when a company introduces a new product and competition is weak. (p. 465)

**Psychological pricing:** The practice of charging, for example, $9.95 rather than $10 for a product in the belief that such pricing will create the illusion of significantly lower price to the consumer. (p. 466)

**Transfer pricing:** A method to correctly price a product as it is transferred from one stage of production to the next. (p. 463)

## Questions

1. "If a company sets its prices on the basis of a cost-plus calculation, it cannot possibly suffer a loss on its products." True or false? Comment.
2. Price discrimination is often defended on the basis of equity. What is meant by this statement? Comment on its validity.
3. Which products in each pair would tend to have higher markups in a supermarket?
   **a.** Cigarettes versus tomatoes
   **b.** Potatoes versus orange juice
4. Many years ago, a neighborhood lunch counter charged 15 cents for a cup of coffee and 15 cents for a buttered hard roll. One day, a customer ordered the two items and was told that the total price was 35 cents. When the customer asked which of the two items had been raised by 5 cents, the owner's condescending reply was, "Which do you think?" In your opinion, which of the two items was affected and why?
5. Differentiate *barometric* price leadership and *dominant* price leadership.
6. Is there a similarity between cartel pricing and monopoly pricing?

7. What conditions are favorable to the formation and maintenance of a cartel?
8. Can government be a potent force in the establishment and maintenance of monopolistic conditions? Name and describe such occurrences.
9. Describe the properties of the Baumol revenue maximization model. Do you consider this to be a good alternative to the profit maximization model?
10. Telephone companies charge different rates for calls during the day, in the evening, and at night or weekends. Do you consider this to be price discrimination?
11. Is cost-plus pricing necessarily inconsistent with marginal pricing?
12. Airline ticket prices may differ with respect to when the ticket is bought, how long a passenger remains on the trip (e.g., over a weekend) and other variables. Are these differences a case of price discrimination?
13. Does cost-plus pricing necessarily ignore the demand curve?
14. Define and describe (giving examples):
    a. Transfer pricing
    b. Psychological pricing
    c. Price skimming
    d. Penetration pricing
15. Under what circumstances would a discriminating monopolist produce a more socially optimal quantity than a nondiscriminating monopolist? Is there any situation under which a discriminating monopolist could produce the quantity that would be produced under competition?
16. Why should a government be concerned with the pricing of products that a company transfers to an affiliate in another country?

## Problems

1. There are only two firms in the widget industry. The total demand for widgets is $Q = 30 - 2P$. The two firms have identical cost functions, $TC = 3 + 10Q$. The two firms agree to collude and act as though the industry were a monopoly. At what price and quantity will this cartel maximize its profit?
2. An amusement park, whose customer set is made up of two markets, adults and children, has developed demand schedules as follows:

| Price ($) | Quantity Adults | Children |
|---|---|---|
| 5 | 15 | 20 |
| 6 | 14 | 18 |
| 7 | 13 | 16 |
| 8 | 12 | 14 |
| 9 | 11 | 12 |
| 10 | 10 | 10 |
| 11 | 9 | 8 |
| 12 | 8 | 6 |
| 13 | 7 | 4 |
| 14 | 6 | 2 |

The marginal operating cost of each unit of quantity is $5. (*Hint:* Since marginal cost is a constant, so is average variable cost. Ignore fixed cost.) The owners of the amusement park wish to maximize profits.

**a.** Calculate the price, quantity, and profit if
 **(1)** The amusement park charges a different price in each market.
 **(2)** The amusement park charges the same price in the two markets combined.
 **(3)** Explain the difference in the profit realized under the two situations.
**b.** (Mathematical solution) The demand schedules presented in problem 2 can be expressed in equation form as follows (where subscript $A$ refers to the adult market, subscript $C$ to the market for children, and subscript $T$ to the two markets combined):

$$Q_A = 20 - 1P_A$$
$$Q_C = 30 - 2P_C$$
$$Q_T = 50 - 3P_T$$

Solve these equations for the maximum profit that the amusement park will attain when it charges different prices in the two markets and when it charges a single price for the combined market.
**3.** The Bramwell Corporation has estimated its demand function and total cost function to be as follows:

$$Q = 25 - 0.05P$$
$$TC = 700 + 200Q$$

Answer the following questions either by developing demand and cost schedules (*hint:* use quantities from 1 to 14) or by solving the equations.
**a.** What will be the price and quantity if Bramwell wants to
 **(1)** Maximize profits?
 **(2)** Maximize revenue?
 **(3)** Maximize revenue but require the profit to be a minimum of $300?
**b.** Now assume that the cost function is $TC = 780 + 200Q$ while the demand function remains the same. What will the price and quantity be if Bramwell wants to
 **(1)** Maximize profits?
 **(2)** Maximize revenue?
 **(3)** Maximize revenue but require the profit to be a minimum of $300?
**c.** Why are the answers the same in $a(1)$ and $b(1)$ but different in $a(3)$ and $b(3)$?
**4.** The Great Southern Paper Company has the following marginal cost schedule for producing pulp:

| Quantity (tons) | Marginal Cost |
| --- | --- |
| 1 | $18 |
| 2 | 20 |
| 3 | 25 |
| 4 | 33 |
| 5 | 43 |

Pulp can be bought in the open market for $25 per ton. The marginal cost of converting pulp into paper is $MC = 5 + 5Q$, and the demand for paper is $P = 135 - 15Q$. Calculate the marginal cost of paper if the company produces its own pulp. What is the profit-maximizing quantity? Should the company purchase pulp from the outside or produce it inhouse?
**5.** The purchase price of Fancy Shoes, sold by Bradbury Footwear Stores, is $30 per pair. The company's economist has estimated the point price elasticity to be $-1.8$. What price should the company charge if it wants to maximize its profits?

6. An airplane manufacturer has annual fixed costs of $50 million. Its variable costs are expected to be $2 million per plane. If the manufacturer wants to earn a 10 percent rate of return on its investment of $400 million and expects to produce 100 aircraft this year, what will its markup on total cost have to be? If it expects to produce 150 aircraft, what will its markup have to be?

7. Schultz's Orchard grows only two types of fruit—apples and peaches—and over the years it has been able to chart two production levels and the resulting total cost. The figures are shown in the following table, where quantity produced is given in bushels.

| Apples | Peaches | Apples | Peaches |
|---|---|---|---|
| 900 | 0 | 1,400 | 0 |
| 800 | 200 | 1,200 | 300 |
| 600 | 400 | 900 | 600 |
| 400 | 500 | 700 | 700 |
| 250 | 550 | 300 | 850 |
| 0 | 600 | 0 | 900 |
| Total cost: $15,000 | | Total cost: $25,000 | |

This year it is expected that the price of apples will be $30 per bushel and that of peaches will be $45 per bushel.

What is the best production level at each cost? How much is the profit at each level?

8. The Prestige Office Equipment Company produces and sells different types of office furniture. One of the important items it sells is a high-quality desk. During the past year, Prestige sold 5,000 of these at a price of $500 each. The contribution profit for this line of furniture last year was $700,000.

A consultant suggests that Prestige decrease the price of each desk by $30. In his opinion, another 500 desks could then be sold, and the total profit would be maintained. A trade publication that employs an economist has estimated price elasticity of office furniture (including desks) to be about −1.8.

Assume that the variable unit cost per desk in the coming year will remain the same. Evaluate the consultant's proposal. Be sure to include in your answer the price elasticity assumed by the consultant, as well as the published elasticity estimate.

9. How can a multinational company with locations in two countries benefit from varying its transfer prices when income tax rates in the two countries differ? Design a simple numerical example to show how a company could decrease its income tax burden by changing its transfer price between countries A and B.

10. The royalties received by an author for writing a college text are frequently set a rate of about 15 percent of the publisher's book price. This may create a conflict between the goals of a profit-maximizing publisher and those of a royalty-maximizing author. As a student consumer (assuming that you have to pay for your textbooks), whose goal would be more beneficial to you? Why? Demonstrate this situation graphically (assume a downward-sloping demand curve).

## Take It to the Net

We invite you to visit the Keat/Young page on the Prentice Hall Web site at:

**http://www.prenhall.com/keat**

for additional resources.

# CHAPTER 13

# Capital Budgeting

## THE SITUATION

George Kline is the manager of Global Foods' capital planning department. He is responsible for analyzing projects that require extensive expenditures and whose payoffs occur over a significantly long period of time—capital budgeting projects. When the analysis is completed, George and his staff of five make presentations up the company hierarchy—to the treasurer (George's boss) and the vice president of finance. If the proposal is large enough, it may finally have to be approved by the Corporate Management Committee (a group composed of top executives).

George has in front of him two new project proposals that require extensive analysis by his staff. The first is the proposed expansion of company activities into a new geographical region. Global is investigating the possibility of entering a new region where its soft drink and bottled water products have not been marketed previously. Potential annual sales for this area have been estimated at 100,000,000 cases. A 4 percent annual increase in total consumption is forecast. The mar-

ket research people have estimated that, given an extensive advertising campaign, the first year's market share could reach 1 percent, and it may grow to some 5 percent four years later.

For the company to compete in this new area, it must establish a plant. An unused, somewhat obsolete bottling plant is available in the area for $5 million. The total costs of rebuilding and renovating the plant and purchasing and installing the new equipment are expected to amount to $2 million. During the first year, the company will incur expenses of recruiting a new workforce. Just before production starts in year two, there will be an extensive advertising and promotion campaign. These expenses are estimated at $750,000.

If Global Foods actually achieves a 1 percent share of the market, it will sell 1 million cases. Each case sells for $5. Production costs will be $2.50 per case. General and administrative expenses will be $650,000 during the first year. Of this amount, $500,000 is fixed; the remainder is a function of quantity.

*(Continued)*

473

Distribution and selling expenses will be 60 cents per case. Advertising expenses will be 5 percent of sales.

The cost of rebuilding and renovating the plant will be depreciated over 31 1/2 years. The remainder, $1 million (for new machinery, etc.), will be depreciated over seven years using the modified accelerated cost recovery system (MACRS). The purchase cost of the plant is to be allocated as follows: 10 percent for land, 50 percent for building, and 40 percent for equipment. The same methods of depreciation will be used. (Land is not depreciable.)

Global also expects that it will have to increase the size of its working capital by $750,000, to cover the additional inventory, accounts receivable, and cash for transactions.

The analysis will span seven years, including the first year of expenditures and six years of operations. This is a relatively conservative assumption—if the company cannot make a viable business of this plant over a seven-year time period, it would consider the operation too risky to undertake. Two other important pieces of information needed to complete the analysis are the following:

The company's marginal income tax rate (federal, state, and local) is 40 percent.

The cost of capital for this project will be 15 percent.

The second project George must consider is replacing an old depalletizing machine, which, although still in good working condition, is relatively slow and expensive to operate. A new machine will increase revenue and decrease operating and maintenance expenses. The total annual benefit from this will amount to $18,000.

A new machine will cost $100,000 and is conservatively expected to last ten years. The old machine has a present book value of $10,000. If properly maintained, it can be made to last another ten years. At that point it will have no market value. If sold today (there is a market for used depalletizers), it would have a cash value of $12,000.

The remaining depreciation life of the old machine is two years; it is being depreciated on a straight-line basis. The new machine will be depreciated over seven years, also using the straight-line method.

The company's income tax rate is 40 percent. The required rate of return (cost of capital), as this project is less risky than the expansion project, is 12 percent.

# Introduction

In chapter 2, we discussed the question of profit maximization as an objective of the firm. In all the chapters that followed we explicitly assumed that firms were actively pursuing this objective. We dealt with a firm's action during a specified period of time, such as a year, a month, or a day.[1] For example, a demand curve and revenues flowing to the firm were defined in terms of quantities per year; costs were stated in term of quantities pro-

---

[1]The only exception was the discussion of the learning curve, which was defined over a given production run, regardless of the time involved.

duced for the same period. Even when we discussed long-term relationships, such as the long-run cost curve (the envelope curve), where each point on the horizontal (quantity) axis represented a plant of a different size, we did not concentrate on how the firm changed from a smaller to a larger plant. It was merely accepted that at each point on the horizontal axis, different quantities were produced by plants of different capacities.

To increase production over time, a firm must invest in new capacity. Even for a firm to maintain level capacity, it must replace worn-out equipment and plant. Such action also involves investment of resources.

A company's decision to commit funds to obtain revenues not only in the current period, but also in future periods, has not yet been analyzed. A brief reference regarding the consideration of expenditures to obtain payoffs over a considerable period of time in the future was made in chapter 2, in the section on maximizing the wealth of stockholders. We are now prepared to discuss decisions leading to this maximization criterion.

The subject of capital budgeting is generally taught in courses in finance. Large portions of basic and more advanced courses are devoted to this topic, and in some schools the finance curriculum includes a one-semester course in capital budgeting. However, the principles of capital budgeting also are properly a part of microeconomic theory extended to multiperiod problems. The application of incremental and marginal analysis will be encountered in this chapter just as in all the previous ones. Thus, it is not only desirable to include a chapter on this subject, but it is essential to make this book a complete treatment of managerial economics.

## The Capital Budgeting Decision

**Capital budgeting** describes decisions where expenditures and receipts for a particular undertaking will continue over a period of time. These decisions usually involve outflows of funds (expenditures) in the early periods (sometimes just one expenditure will be made at the beginning of a project, as for the purchase of a new machine), and the inflows (revenues) start somewhat later and (it is hoped) continue for a significant number of periods.[2]

The following figure is a simple illustration of the components to be considered in making capital budgeting decisions. The figure shows one outflow at the beginning of the project and five inflows in subsequent periods. This model could represent the purchase of a new machine that will last five years and provide new revenues (or savings, if it decreases the cost of production) during that time. We could have shown an example with outflows occurring during, say, the first three years. Such outflows could represent a company's decision to build a new plant and equip it with new machines. Such a large investment could easily occur over a period of three years, and revenues would not start until the fourth year or even later.[3]

---

[2]Note that the term *flows,* meaning inflows or outflows, is being used in this chapter. In capital budgeting decisions, the quantities considered are the actual expenditures and receipts of cash, not quantities adjusted by accounting conventions, such as accruals. Cash flows are quite objective—either cash goes out or it comes in—and there are no allowances made for when revenues and expenses are recognized in the company's books of account.

[3]The replacement problem and the expansion proposal of the "Situation" are examples of these two types of projects.

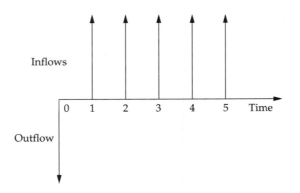

## TYPES OF CAPITAL BUDGETING DECISIONS

Now that we have described the general characteristics of a capital budgeting decision, we can list types of projects that fit this category.

*Expansion of facilities.* Growing demand for a company's products leads to consideration of a new or additional plant. Planning for other new facilities, such as sales offices or warehouses, would also be included here. George Kline's first project is an expansion proposal.

*New or improved products.* Additional investment may be necessary to bring a new or changed product to the market.

*Replacement.* Replacement decisions can be of at least two types: (1) replacement of worn-out plant and equipment or (2) replacement with more efficient machines of equipment that is still operating but is obsolete. George's second proposal falls in this group.

*Lease or buy.* A company may need to decide whether to make a sizable investment in buying a piece of equipment or to pay rental for a considerable time period.

*Make or buy.* A company may be faced with deciding whether to make a significant investment to produce components for its product or whether to forgo such investment and contract for the components with a vendor.

*Other.* The preceding list is certainly not complete, since a capital budgeting problem exists whenever initial cash outflows and subsequent cash inflows are involved. For instance, an advertising campaign or an employee training program would lend itself to the same method of analysis.

*Safety or environmental protection equipment.* Such investments may be mandated by law and therefore are not necessarily governed by economic decision making. However, if there are alternate solutions, capital budgeting analysis may be helpful in identifying the most cost-efficient alternative.

# Time Value of Money

If a capital budgeting problem simply involved the subtraction of outflows from inflows, the mechanics of obtaining a solution would be extremely easy. However, because the various flows occur at disparate times in the future, we must adjust these numbers to make them equivalent. Differences in the values of the flows are based on the **time value of money.**

All this term really means is that a dollar today is worth more than a dollar tomorrow. For example, if you were offered a choice between a gift of $100 today and the same amount one year from now (the receipt of both amounts being certain), you would most likely select the first alternative. If you were to take the $100 today and put it in a bank paying 5 percent interest, you would have $105 a year from now; thus, the $100 today would be equivalent to $105 a year later. As long as you have an opportunity to earn a positive return on your funds over the one-year period, a dollar today and a dollar a year from now are not equivalent. Some people would conclude that this phenomenon is due to the presence of inflation, that is, a decrease in the value of the purchasing power of money over time. But inflation is not a necessary condition. Certainly, during a period of rising prices, nominal interest rates will be higher than during times of price stability. However, even when inflation is absent, funds that are saved and invested will earn interest for their owner.

Thus, to put cash flows originating at different times on an equal basis, we must apply an interest rate to each of the flows so that they are expressed in terms of the same point in time. In capital budgeting calculations, cash flows are usually brought back from various points in the future to the beginning of the project—time zero. It is then said that all cash flows are discounted to the present to obtain a present value. This is a useful convention, although we could discount or compound the flows to any date.

Those of you who have had previous exposure to the mechanics of compounding and discounting will be able to move immediately into the discussion of the solution of capital budgeting problems that follows. However, those of you who are unfamiliar with the calculations or whose memory on this subject is somewhat hazy will benefit from reading Appendix 13A at the end of this chapter.

## Methods of Capital Project Evaluation

Various methods are used to make capital budgeting decisions, that is, to evaluate the worth of investment projects. Two methods that have been used for many years will be mentioned only briefly. They are the payback method and the accounting rate of return method. Although they are still often used in the business world, they have generally been judged to be inadequate.

The **payback** method calculates the time period (years) necessary to recover the original investment. The **accounting rate of return** is the percentage resulting from dividing average annual profits by average investment.[4] Among the many drawbacks of these methods is the fact that neither applies the criterion of the time value of money in its computations.[5] Readers who are not familiar with these two measures and are interested in learning about them will find more lengthy descriptions in any basic corporate finance textbook.

The two methods that do discount cash flows to a present value are **net present value (NPV)** and **internal rate of return (IRR).**[6] Both of these techniques satisfy the

---

[4]Note that the accounting rate of return uses profits, rather than cash flows, in its calculation.
[5]Another version of payback, the discounted payback method, utilizes time value of money calculations. But it does not consider cash flows received after the payback period has been reached.
[6]A third calculation method using discounted cash flows is called the *profitability index* or *index of present value.* This is a derivative of the other two methods and will not be discussed in this text. You should refer to any of the leading textbooks in managerial finance.

two major criteria required for the correct evaluation of capital projects: use of cash flows and use of the time value of money.

## NET PRESENT VALUE

The net present value (NPV) of a project is calculated by discounting all flows to the present and subtracting the present value of all outflows from the present value of all inflows. In simple mathematical terms,

$$\text{NPV} = \sum_{t=1}^{n} \frac{R_t}{(1 + k)^t} - \sum_{t=0}^{n} \frac{O_t}{(1 + k)^t}$$

where $t$ = Time period (e.g., year)
$n$ = Last period of project
$R_t$ = Cash inflow in period $t$
$O_t$ = Cash outflow in period $t$
$k$ = Discount rate (cost of capital)

Some of these terms must be explained further. Inflows are shown from period 1 to period $n$; however, inflows may not occur in all periods. Should the project under consideration be the construction of a plant, the time elapsed before the first shipment of product, and thus the first inflow, may not occur until period 3, for example. Remember that in George Kline's expansion project, inflows will not begin until the second period.

Outflows are shown starting in period 0 (i.e., at the very beginning of the project). Indeed, the only outflow may occur in period 0 if the proposal being evaluated is the purchase of a machine that will begin to produce cash inflows upon installation. The depalletizing machine is a case in point. On the other hand, the expansion proposal considered by Kline will have outflows in periods 0 and 1.

Thus, the two terms have been generalized to allow for inflows and outflows throughout the life of the project, even though flows of one kind or the other may not occur in all periods.

The **discount rate,** $k$, is the interest rate used to evaluate the project. This rate represents the cost of the funds employed (the opportunity cost of capital) and is often called the **cost of capital.** It can also be referred to as the *hurdle rate,* the *cut-off rate,* or the *minimum required rate of return.*[7]

To illustrate the net present value method, we will use a simple numerical example. A proposed capital budgeting project requires one initial investment of $100 today. Its expected life is 5 years, and the annual cash inflows will be $25, $35, $40, $40, and $30 in years 1 through 5, respectively. The cost of capital at which the cash flows will be discounted is 14 percent. The relevant amounts are as follows:

---

[7]The term *cost of capital* often applies to the overall average cost of funds for a corporation. This cost may differ from the rate used for a specific division of the company or for a particular capital budgeting proposal. One of the major reasons for the difference is risk (both business and financial risk). Thus, the corporation's cost of capital represents an average for the whole entity, but specific areas of the business may be more or less risky than the average and thus require higher or lower discount rates. Thus, the discount rate may differ from area to area or project to project within the same company.

| | | |
|---|---|---|
| *Inflows* | | |
| Year 1 | 25 × 0.8772 | $ 21.93 |
| 2 | 35 × 0.7695 | 26.93 |
| 3 | 40 × 0.6750 | 27.00 |
| 4 | 40 × 0.5921 | 23.68 |
| 5 | 30 × 0.5194 | 15.58 |
| | | $115.12 |
| | | |
| *Outflow, year 0* | | 100.00 |
| Net present value | | $ 15.12 |

All the estimated cash inflows have been brought back (discounted) to the present at the 14 percent cost of capital and then added. (The factors by which each of the cash flows is multiplied have been obtained from Table B.1c in Appendix B at the end of this text.) The total present value of cash outflows is deducted. In this case, there is only one outflow occurring at period 0 (now); thus, no discounting is necessary. The net present value equals $15.12. Should this proposal be accepted?

The answer is yes. The net present value for this program is positive. Stated somewhat differently, if we add all the cash inflows discounted at the cost of capital and deduct the cash outflow, we still have something left over. We expect to earn more than the cost of capital (i.e., the cost of financing this project). The proposal earns what the suppliers of capital require plus an additional amount.

We have arrived at the NPV rule for evaluating capital budgeting programs. If the NPV is positive, the project is financially acceptable. If NPV is negative, rejection is indicated. If NPV is exactly zero, this proposal is just earning the cost of capital; we are on the borderline. However, since the return just equals the required rate of return, the project appears to be acceptable.[8]

## INTERNAL RATE OF RETURN

Internal rate of return (IRR) is the second of the two methods we will discuss that discounts cash flows. However, rather than looking for an absolute amount of present-value dollars, as in the NPV analysis, we solve for the interest rate that equates the present value of inflows and outflows:

$$\sum_{t=1}^{n} \frac{R_t}{(1 + r)^t} = \sum_{t=0}^{n} \frac{O_t}{(1 + r)^t}$$

or

$$\sum_{t=1}^{n} \frac{R_t}{(1 + r)^t} - \sum_{t=0}^{n} \frac{O_t}{(1 + r)^t} = 0$$

[8]This case is similar to one encountered previously, in chapter 9. Production takes place at the point where marginal cost equals marginal revenue. If discrete quantities are involved, the cost of the "last" unit produced is the same as the revenue received from it; it earns no economic but only normal profit. In capital budgeting, the situation is really the same: the "last" proposal that would be accepted is the one that just earns the rate required by the suppliers of capital.

The *r* term in the equations is the internal rate of return—the unknown variable for which we solve. Actually, the IRR solution is only a special case of the NPV technique; the internal rate of return of a project is the discount rate that causes NPV to equal zero (which occurs when the project is just earning its cost of capital).

The calculation of the IRR can be easily accomplished with a hand-held business calculator or a computer (using, for instance, an Excel function), and this is what most people do. However, for our purposes, we will use the tables in Appendix B at the back of the text. In this case, the calculation may become rather cumbersome. Unless all cash inflows are uniform and there is only one outflow (in which case we can simply employ the annuity formula), it is necessary to find the answer by trial and error. One must first choose an applicable interest rate—and this may be no more than an educated guess—and then iterate until the correct answer is obtained.

Turn to the example used before. We found in the NPV analysis that, with a 14 percent cost of capital, net present value is positive ($15.12), so the internal rate of return must be greater than 14 percent. We will first try 18 percent (again using the factors in Table B.1*c*):

| Inflows | | |
|---|---|---|
| Year 1 | 25 × 0.8475 | $ 21.19 |
| 2 | 35 × 0.7182 | 25.14 |
| 3 | 40 × 0.6086 | 24.34 |
| 4 | 40 × 0.5158 | 20.63 |
| 5 | 30 × 0.4371 | 13.11 |
| | | $104.41 |
| | | |
| Outflow, year 0 | | 100.00 |
| Net present value | | $ 4.41 |

As the result is still positive, we will choose a higher discount rate, 20 percent:

| Inflows | | |
|---|---|---|
| Year 1 | 25 × 0.8333 | $ 20.83 |
| 2 | 35 × 0.6944 | 24.30 |
| 3 | 40 × 0.5787 | 23.15 |
| 4 | 40 × 0.4823 | 19.29 |
| 5 | 30 × 0.4019 | 12.06 |
| | | $ 99.63 |
| | | |
| Outflow, year 0 | | 100.00 |
| Net present value | | $ −0.37 |

NPV is now negative; 20 percent is too high. Thus, the result lies somewhere between 18 percent and 20 percent. It is readily seen that the IRR is much closer to 20 percent than to 18 percent, because $−0.37 is much nearer to 0 than is $4.41. A more precise answer can be obtained using linear interpolation; this would result in an internal rate of return of about 19.8 percent.

The accept/reject criterion for the internal rate of return is based on a comparison of the IRR with the cost of capital of the project. Although the cost of capital is not used in the calculation of the IRR, it is still an all-important component of decision making. If the internal rate of return is larger than the cost of capital—the required rate of return—of the proposal, it signals acceptance. If IRR < $k$, the proposed project should be rejected. If IRR = $k$, although it could be said that decision makers would be indifferent on whether to undertake the project, an argument can be made that the project is earning its cost of capital and therefore should be accepted at the margin.

**MODULE 13A**

## NPV VERSUS IRR

Two methods have just been described that conform to the criteria specified for a valid capital budgeting decision. Is one preferred over the other, or are the two equally valid?

In a large majority of cases, either NPV or IRR can be used with confidence. These two tests of investment worth give consistent accept/reject indicators. In other words, when

$$NPV > 0, IRR > k$$

$$NPV = 0, IRR = k$$

$$NPV < 0, IRR < k$$

Thus, either of the two measures gives the correct answer. In some cases, however, problems may arise.

When **independent projects** are being analyzed, both IRR and NPV criteria give consistent results. "Independent" implies that if a company is considering several projects at the same time, they can all be implemented simultaneously as long as they pass the NPV or IRR tests, and as long as funds are not limited. The adoption of one independent project will have no effect on the cash flows of another. For example, the two proposals on George Kline's desk are independent. Global Foods can expand into a new territory and replace the depalletizing machine at the same time. The acceptance of one proposal does not preclude executing the other.

However, proposals may be **mutually exclusive.** This occurs when two solutions for a particular proposal are offered, only one of which can be accepted. Suppose Global decides to acquire a new depalletizer. At this point, sales representatives from two manufacturers of these machines descend upon the company, and each offers a new version. But the company needs only one depalletizer. If both NPV and IRR are calculated, inconsistent recommendations can result. NPV analysis may suggest purchase of machine A, but IRR indicates machine B. Such disparate signals can occur if one or both of the following conditions are present:

1. The initial costs of the two proposals differ.
2. The shapes of the subsequent cash inflow streams differ; for instance, one alternative may have large early inflows with the other exhibiting increasing inflows over time.

The reason for the differences between IRR and NPV results is the implicit reinvestment assumption. In the NPV calculation, as inflows occur, they are automatically assumed to be reinvested at the cost of capital (the project's $k$). The IRR solution assumes reinvestment at the internal rate of return (the project's $r$).

Conflicting accept/reject signals may not occur frequently in capital project analysis, but they do occur and they may cause the analyst some anxious moments.

**TABLE 13.1 Two Mutually Exclusive Projects that Differ in Size**

| Project | t = 0 | t = 1 | t = 2 | t = 3 | t = 4 | t = 5 |
|---------|-------|-------|-------|-------|-------|-------|
| A | (1,500) | 580 | 580 | 580 | 580 | 0 |
| B | (1,000) | 400 | 400 | 400 | 400 | 0 |
| Cost of capital | | | 15.0% | | | |

| | *Internal Rate of Return* | *Net Present Value* |
|---|---|---|
| Project A | 20.1% | 156 |
| Project B | 21.9% | 142 |

| *Delta Project* | | | | | | |
|---|---|---|---|---|---|---|
| (A − B) | (500) | 180 | 180 | 180 | 180 | 0 |
| Internal rate or return | 16.4% | | | Net Present Value | | 14 |

*Project Evaluation at Several Discount Rates*

| | 0.00% | 5.00% | 10.00% | 15.00% | 20.00% | 25.00% |
|---|-------|-------|--------|--------|--------|--------|
| Project A | 820 | 557 | 339 | 156 | 1 | (130) |
| Project B | 600 | 418 | 268 | 142 | 35 | (55) |

## An Example

As mentioned previously, conflicting results can be caused by a difference in project size. Table 13.1 shows such a case. Two mutually exclusive projects are presented. Project A involves an original outlay of $1,500; its cash inflows are $580 per year for four years. Project B (which is a substitute for A) is somewhat less expensive—only $1,000—but the four cash inflows are also smaller, at $400 each. Each project has a four-year life and no salvage value. Proceeding in the normal way, we find that the IRR of project B is higher than that of project A—21.9 percent against 20.1 percent. If we were to go no further, basing our choice on a comparison of IRRs, project B would be selected. But if we perform an NPV calculation (at the company's cost of capital of 15 percent), project A tops B's NPV by $14 (i.e., $156 against $142). The IRR tells us to adopt project B, but if we want to maximize net present value, we should implement project A.

To resolve this dilemma, we calculate the NPV and IRR for an "incremental" (or *delta*) project. That is, we take the differences between the two project cash flows and create a delta project. If we undertake A rather than B, we must incur an additional original cash outflow (at $t = 0$) of $500 and receive in turn additional cash inflows of $180 for each of the next four years. Such a project, evaluated separately, would have an NPV of $14 and an IRR of 16.4 percent. This means that the additional outlay of $500 provides an incremental positive NPV ($14) and an internal rate of return (16.4 percent) that exceeds the 15 percent cost of capital. Thus, both criteria indicate that the additional investment of $500 is worthwhile. It follows that the NPV rule, which suggested project A, was the correct indicator, and that project A should be chosen over project B.

Figure 13.1 illustrates the relationship between the two projects. At the bottom of Table 13.1, the two projects have been evaluated at six different discount rates, and their respective NPVs have been plotted on the graph. When the discount rate is 0, the NPV

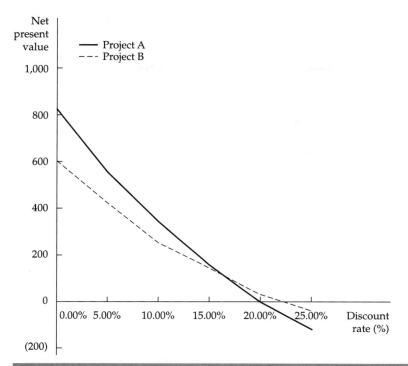

**FIGURE 13.1**  Net Present Value Profiles for Projects of Different Size

is merely the sum of all the cash flows (for project A, $-1{,}500 + 580 + 580 + 580 + 580$ = 820). This is shown on the vertical axis. On the horizontal axis, the projects' NPVs become 0 at their respective IRRs (20.1 percent for A and 21.9 percent for B). The two projects' NPVs cross at $111, at a discount rate of 16.4 percent, which is the IRR of the incremental project. To the left of this intersection, project A's NPV exceeds that of project B's, which creates a conflict, since project B's IRR (21.9 percent) is always higher than project A's (20.1 percent). Had the cost of capital been higher than 16.4 percent, project B would have been preferred under both methods, since it also would now have the higher NPV.

The second instance when the two measures give conflicting rankings occurs when the shapes of the cash inflow streams differ significantly. Although the initial outlays for both mutually exclusive projects are the same, one of the projects has a cash flow pattern that starts slowly and builds up, whereas the other has cash inflows that are initially large but decline over time. Table 13.2 shows the data for projects A and B; both start with a $5,000 investment. The results in this case are similar to those previously shown. Project A's NPV is considerably higher than B's, but the IRR's are again reversed. The interpretation of Table 13.2 and Figure 13.2 is the same as in the case of the two projects with differing sizes of investment. Project A is preferable at a cost of capital of 10 percent.

Another problem that may occur concerns the case of nonconventional cash flows. Conventional cash flows occur when cash outflows are followed by a series of cash inflows for the remainder of the project's life. In other words, over time, there is only one

**TABLE 13.2 Two Mutually Exclusive Projects with Different Cash Inflow Streams**

| *Project* | *t = 0* | *t = 1* | *t = 2* | *t = 3* | *t = 4* | *t = 5* |
|---|---|---|---|---|---|---|
| A | (5,000) | 500 | 2,500 | 5,000 | 0 | 0 |
| B | (5,000) | 3,500 | 2,800 | 500 | 0 | 0 |
| Cost of capital | | | 10.0% | | | |

| | *Internal Rate of Return* | *Net Present Value* |
|---|---|---|
| Project A | 20.4% | 1,277 |
| Project B | 22.4% | 872 |

| *Delta Project* (A − B) | *t = 0* | *t = 1* | *t = 2* | *t = 3* | *t = 4* | *t = 5* |
|---|---|---|---|---|---|---|
| | 0 | (3,000) | (300) | 4,500 | 0 | 0 |

| Internal rate of return | 17.6% | Net Present Value | 406 |
|---|---|---|---|

*Project Evaluation at Several Discount Rates*

| | *0.00%* | *5.00%* | *10.00%* | *15.00%* | *20.00%* | *25.00%* |
|---|---|---|---|---|---|---|
| Project A | 3,000 | 2,063 | 1,277 | 613 | 46 | (440) |
| Project B | 1,800 | 1,305 | 872 | 489 | 150 | (152) |

change from negative flows (outflows) to positive (inflows). But suppose there are two or more changes. If a project starts with a cash outflow followed by a series of cash inflows, and then ends up with a cash outflow (i.e., two changes in sign), two different rates of return will result. Such an answer is obviously not satisfactory. If NPV analysis is used, a single answer will be obtained.

Writers of financial and economic literature almost unanimously recommend NPV as the theoretically more correct measure. A full explanation of the reasons for this choice would be quite long. For the purpose of our limited exposition of this subject, let us mention just briefly two arguments:

1. The financial objective of the firm is the maximization of stockholder wealth, and the NPV method is more applicable to this end. Projects with the largest NPVs will add up to the highest present value for the business.
2. The NPV reinvestment assumption, at *k,* appears to be more realistic in most cases than reinvestment at *r* of a particular project.[9]

---

[9]There is a method that has gained favor and that corrects some of the problems encountered with the internal rate of return. It is called the *modified internal rate of return* (MIRR) and is calculated by discounting, at the cost of capital, all cash outflows to year zero and compounding all inflows to the end of the project. The discount rate that equates the sum of the ending values to the sum of the beginning values is the MIRR. Using this method reinvests the cash flows at the cost of capital. Also, the possibility of obtaining more than one solution (nonconventional cash flows) is eliminated. However, accept/reject signal conflicts with NPV can still occur. For a longer explanation, see Eugene F. Brigham, Louis C. Gapenski, and Michael C. Ehrhardt, *Financial Management: Theory and Practice,* 9th ed., Fort Worth, TX: Dryden, 1999, pp. 440–41.

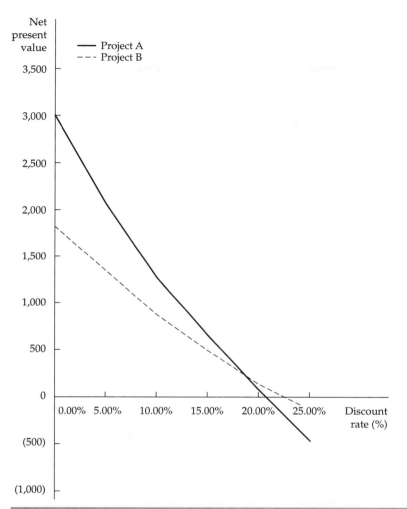

**FIGURE 13.2** Net Present Value Profiles for Projects with Different Cash Inflow Streams

Although NPV is recommended by theorists and textbook writers, in actual business practice, IRR is the more frequently used.[10] Why? Businesspeople—especially nonfinancial managers—are much more comfortable making their judgments by looking at percentages. The NPV number, a dollar figure, is not readily recognizable. (Incidentally, the second most popular technique cited in the Gitman and Forrester article in note 10 was the accounting rate of return, also expressed as a percentage. NPV came in third but was also frequently mentioned as the second choice.) Only in the case of mutually exclusive projects may IRR fail to give the correct signal. However, in many

---

[10]Harold Bierman, Jr., "Capital Budgeting in 1992: A Survey," *Financial Management,* Autumn 1993, p. 24; Lawrence J. Gitman and John R. Forrester, Jr., "A Survey of Capital Budgeting Techniques Used by Major U.S. Firms," *Financial Management,* Fall 1977, pp. 66–71.

evaluations—probably a majority—even where mutual exclusivity exists, the IRR and NPV methods will lead to consistent answers.

The fact that large corporations use one or the other of the evaluation methods incorporating the time value of money is important. Such was not the case 30 years ago. Only in the recent past have the more "scientific" ways of project assessment assumed prominence.

## Cash Flows

**MODULE 13B**
**MODULE 13C**

Up to this point the discussion has concentrated on the methods and mechanics of the capital budgeting process. Cash flows were assumed and put into the appropriate formulas for processing. The term *cash flow* has been used in abundance but has not been explained thoroughly.

When confronted with a capital budgeting proposal, the analyst's most difficult task is to enter the best estimates of cash flows into the analysis. Since all of the inflows and outflows are in the future, their amounts and timing are uncertain. Some of them can be assessed with relative certainty. For instance, if a replacement proposal is being considered, the cost of the new machine has probably been established. But as the analyst tries to assess future annual benefits and costs, the amount of uncertainty increases.

In most cases, capital budgeting analysts do not generate the inputs for the model. They obtain the estimates from other parts of the organization, such as market research, marketing, manufacturing, engineering, or service. There will be market forecasts, price estimates, and cost and expense forecasts. These data have to be examined for potential bias. Market forecasts may be too high, since the people who prepare them are interested parties. Costs often are underestimated. In general, estimated cash flows tend to be optimistic and must be adjusted to make them more realistic.[11]

The person organizing the data must understand the following points:

1. All revenues and costs must be stated in terms of cash flows.
2. All cash flows should be incremental. Only those flows that will change if the proposal is accepted should be recorded. For example, ongoing overhead costs, part of which may be allocated to the project under consideration, should be ignored.
3. Sunk costs do not count. Costs incurred prior to the time the project is being evaluated and that cannot be recouped if the project is implemented should be omitted from consideration.
4. Any effect on other parts of the operation must be taken into account. If the introduction of a new diet soda will have an adverse impact on sales of current soft drinks, this amount must be subtracted from the cash flows planned for the new product. On the other hand, impact may be positive. For example, if the company also sells alcoholic beverages, the introduction of a "light" tonic could enhance sales of the company's gin. These are, of course, examples of the familiar cases of

---

[11]Stephen W. Pruitt and Lawrence J. Gitman, "Capital Budgeting Forecast Biases: Evidence from the *Fortune* 500," *Financial Management,* Spring 1987, pp. 46–51.

substitutes and complements. Some idea of the size of cross-elasticities of demand is needed to estimate these impacts. Cost impacts must also be considered.

5. Generally, in capital budgeting analysis, interest paid on debt is not considered. Since interest is included in the discount rate, showing it as a cash outflow would amount to double-counting.

## TYPES OF CASH FLOWS

Cash flows come in many varieties. Some of the most common and important types are discussed next.

### Initial Cash Outflows

Cash flows occur at the inception of the project. If a new machine is installed, this represents a one-time outflow. But initial outflows can also be spread over a period of time, as mentioned previously.

### Operating Cash Flows

When a new project goes on line, it begins to generate cash inflows (revenues). Of course, it also generates cash outflows (costs and expenses), which must be subtracted from the inflows. In the early years of operations, outflows can exceed inflows; thus, the annual net outflow can continue even after the initial investment stage.

So far this exposition is relatively simple. But one of the expenses that accountants record in the income statement of a company is depreciation (and amortization). Obviously, this is not a cash flow; it is a bookkeeping entry to show that the value of the plant and equipment is declining. The actual cash flow occurred when the plant was built and the machinery purchased, and it was recorded as such in the capital investment analysis. If we were living in that ideal society with no income tax, we would simply ignore depreciation in calculating cash flows.

But because income taxes are a fact of life, they must be considered in the treatment of depreciation. The after-tax profit reflects the deduction of depreciation. But since depreciation did not result in a cash outflow, it has to be added back to the after-tax profit to obtain net cash flow.

An example will illustrate this procedure. If cash sales during a period are $100, cash costs and expenses are $50, depreciation of buildings and equipment is $20, and the income tax rate is 40 percent, then net cash flow for the period will be $38:

| | |
|---|---:|
| Sales | $100 |
| Costs and expenses | 50 |
| Depreciation | 20 |
|    Total costs and expenses | $ 70 |
| Net profit before tax | 30 |
| Income tax | 12 |
| Net profit after tax | $ 18 |
| Depreciation | 20 |
| Net cash flow | $ 38 |

For each of the periods (years), operating cash flows have to be calculated and the results discounted to the present.

### Additional Working Capital

In the case of an expansion proposal, in addition to new plant and equipment, increased working capital may be required. Inventories may be larger, accounts receivable may grow, and more cash may be needed to finance the transactions engendered by the growth in operations. Investing in working capital is a cash outflow that is similar in nature to an investment in brick and iron. We must account for it. However, there may not be a periodic write-down (i.e., depreciation) for such investments in the plan. When the proposed project comes to the end of its life, inventories will be used up, accounts receivable will be collected, and the additional cash will no longer be needed. So the same amount that was expended at the beginning of the program may be returned at the end—with one big difference: The cash outflow occurs at or near the beginning of the operations, whereas the inflow of the same amount occurs at the end and must be discounted to the present.

The ending amount of working capital may actually be less than the original investment since some accounts receivable may turn out to be uncollectible and some inventory may become obsolete. The actual loss on this decrease in working capital can be deducted from the cash flows for a tax benefit.

### Salvage or Resale Values

At the end of the project's life, a machine that has been completely depreciated (i.e., has an accounting book value of zero) may turn out to have a residual resale value or some scrap value. If cash can be obtained for it, a cash inflow will result.

But care must be exercised in including this cash flow. If the market value is greater than the book value, a profit will result, with inevitable tax consequences. Thus, if a fully depreciated piece of equipment is expected to bring in $5,000 in resale value at the end of the project life, and if the tax rate is 40 percent, then the actual cash flow will be only $3,000, since $2,000 must be paid in taxes. The formula for computing the cash flow in such a case is

$$SV - (SV - BV)\, T$$

where $SV$ = Salvage or resale value
  $BV$ = Book value
   $T$ = Tax rate

### Noncash Investment

Sometimes a new project involves an investment that does not require a cash flow. For instance, suppose an old, fully depreciated machine is standing on the factory floor. This machine is not needed for present production requirements. But then a new expansion proposal is accepted, allowing this old machine to be utilized. Does it represent a cash outflow? Yes, if the machine has a salvage value; no, if it has no market value at all. Thus, as in all cases of capital budgeting decisions, the alternatives have to be considered.

# Cost of Capital

In each of the capital budgeting decisions described, a certain cost of capital was assumed. Its derivation has not been explained. Much space is usually devoted to this subject in finance textbooks—an entire chapter or more. Such an exposition is beyond the scope of this text. However, a brief explanation of this important concept is essential.

To invest in capital projects, a company must obtain financing. Financing, of course, comes from different sources. There is debt, either short-term or long-term. Then there is equity. A company may retain earnings, which then become part of its equity, or it can issue new shares. Each type of financing must be paid for; each has its cost. It is these costs that establish a company's cost of capital. When all of the costs have been identified, they are combined to arrive at an average cost of capital for a given debt/equity mix.[12]

## DEBT

The cost of debt is the easier to explain. It is simply the interest rate that must be paid on the debt. But since interest expense is tax deductible, the actual cost of the debt to the company is the after-tax cost. The expression for the cost of debt is

$$\text{Interest rate} \times (1 - \text{Tax rate})$$

Which interest rate should be used? If a company already has debt outstanding, it pays a certain rate. But the rate being paid on past debt is not relevant. What is important to the company in measuring its cost of capital is the interest it would have to pay if it were to borrow today. Thus, the present rate being charged in the market for the kind of debt the company would issue (e.g., life to maturity, risk category) determines the company's cost of debt.

**MODULE 13D**

## EQUITY

The cost of equity is more difficult to obtain. A large body of literature exists on this subject, and there are different methods to arrive at this cost. Two of these will be described here.

### The Dividend Growth Model

The cost of equity is determined by the population of stockholders. Because the stockholders expect to receive dividends ($D$) plus a selling price ($P_n$) for the shares in the future, the price they are willing to pay for the stock today ($P_0$) is determined by discounting the future cash flows to the present at the rate of return ($k_e$) the stockholders require to buy the stock:

$$P_0 = \sum_{t=1}^{n} \frac{D_t}{(1 + k_e)^t} + \frac{P_n}{(1 + k_e)^t}$$

---

[12]Admittedly, there are other financial instruments with which a company obtains funds, such as preferred stocks or convertible bonds. However, this short description will limit itself to debt and common equity.

The stockholders will sell the shares at time $n$ to new stockholders, who again may hold the stock for a limited period before selling it to other stockholders, and so on. Since the buying and selling of the stock merely represent an exchange and thus cancel out, the net cash flow from this stock is the dividend, which will continue over an infinite period of time if it is assumed that the corporation will live in perpetuity. The equation showing an infinite stream of dividends can be written as

$$P_0 = \sum_{t=1}^{\infty} \frac{D_t}{(1 + k_e)^t}$$

The dividend does not have to be the same in each period. An assumption, referred to as the **dividend growth model,** is often made that the dividend will grow at a constant rate $(g)$ forever. The equation then converts to[13]

$$P_0 = \frac{D_0(1 + g)}{(1 + k_e)} + \frac{D_0(1 + g)^2}{(1 + k_e)^2} + \cdots + \frac{D_0(1 + g)^n}{(1 + k_e)^n}$$

which can be simplified to

$$P_0 = \frac{D_1}{k_e - g}$$

Because it is the cost of capital that we seek, the equation can be written in terms of $k_e$ as

$$k_e = \frac{D_1}{P_0} + g$$

Thus, this construction states that the cost of equity capital $(k_e)$ equals the dividend in year 1 divided by today's stock price—the dividend yield—plus the expected growth rate in the dividend. This formula is often referred to as the Gordon model, so named for Myron J. Gordon, an economist who has done a great amount of work in this area and who is credited with a major role in developing this model.[14]

The dividend growth model just presented is generally applicable when a company reinvests the earnings that have not been paid out as dividends. If a company issues new stock in the financial markets, it incurs an additional cost. The proceeds from the sale of the stock will be less than the current market price, $P_0$. The cost of underwriting the issue must be taken into consideration. If these costs, often referred to as *flotation costs, f,* are expressed as a percentage of $P_0$, the Gordon model converts to

$$k_0 = \frac{D_1}{P_0 (1 - f)} + g$$

---

[13]$D_0$ represents the most recent dividend paid, and thus $D_0(1 + g) = D_1$; $D_1$ is the dividend expected to be paid during the next period.
[14]See, for instance, Myron J. Gordon, *The Investment, Financing, and Valuation of the Corporation,* Homewood, IL: Irwin, 1962.

Obviously, the cost of external equity capital will be higher for newly issued stock than for retained earnings.[15]

While the Gordon model formula appears rather simple, it requires a forecast of growth. Forecasts, as we have found out, are always tenuous. Thus, the calculation of the cost of capital can be only as good as the estimates entered into it.

## The Capital Asset Pricing Model (CAPM)

The **capital asset pricing model** had its birth in the 1960s.[16] It is based on the principle that there is a relationship between risk and return. The more risky the investment, the higher will be the required return. Only a brief description of this model will be given here.

An important conclusion of this model is that the required rate of return[17] on a stock is a function of the volatility (market risk) of its returns relative to the return on a total stock market portfolio. This volatility is referred to as *beta* and is calculated by regression analysis. The variability of the individual stock's return is the dependent variable, and the variability of the market return is the independent variable. The higher the volatility of the individual stock's return compared to the market return, the higher the beta. A beta of 1.0 signifies that the stock's return is as volatile as the market's. If the beta is greater than 1.0, the stock's return is more variable and, therefore, the stock is more risky; the reverse situation holds when beta is less than 1.0.

One other item is included in this model, the riskless interest rate. The riskless rate is usually represented by interest paid on U.S. Treasury securities. The beta coefficient is used to arrive at the risk premium of the individual stock relative to the difference between the average return for the market portfolio and the riskless rate.

The required rate of return on an individual stock is calculated as follows:

$$k_j = R_f + \beta(k_m - R_f)$$

where $k_j$ = Required rate of return on stock $j$
$R_f$ = Risk-free rate
$k_m$ = Rate of return on the market portfolio

---

[15]The assumption of constant growth may not always be realistic. For a variable growth rate, the growth rate must be estimated for each period and the entire equation solved for $k_e$. For example, in the case of a company that expects rapid growth at first, then a slowdown, and finally some "normal" constant growth, the equation becomes somewhat complicated:

$$P_0 = \sum_{t=1}^{n} \frac{D_t}{(1 + k_e)^t} + \frac{D_{n+1}}{k_e - g}\left[\frac{1}{1 + k_e}\right]^n$$

where $n$ = Number of years of nonconstant growth
$g$ = Expected annual growth rate during the constant growth period
$D_t$ = Dividend expected in each year $t$ of the nonconstant growth period
$D_{n+1}$ = Dividend in first period of constant growth

For additional information on this construction, see any finance textbook, for instance, Brigham, Gapenski, and Ehrhardt, *Financial Management,* pp. 339–42. This method of calculation will be employed later in this chapter, in the section, "The Value of a Corporation."

[16]See, for instance, William F. Sharpe, "Capital Asset Prices: A Theory of Market Equilibrium under Conditions of Risk," *Journal of Finance,* 19 (September 1964), pp. 425–42.

[17]The rate of return for a period is defined as

$$\frac{\text{Dividend} \pm \text{change in stock price}}{\text{Stock price at the beginning of the period}}$$

This model has experienced immense popularity—and also criticism. Although it provides a logical explanation of maximizing behavior under conditions of risk, it suffers, as does the Gordon model, from difficulties of obtaining the relevant data. Probably one of the most serious objections is that the model tries to predict the present and future costs of equity capital with past data. It assumes, therefore, that the past relationship between stock return and market return will continue into the future. This, of course, is a shortcoming of all forecasts made using regression analysis.

Another criticism of CAPM lies in the fact that betas are not always stable. They vary depending on the time period used in making the analysis, and they are affected by the specific statistical method used. Thus, again, the cost-of-capital estimate is only as good as the data used in the computation and the method used. It is obvious that there is much work yet to be done to improve the estimates of the equity cost of capital.

**MODULE 13E**

### THE WEIGHTED COST OF CAPITAL

Despite the fact that the measurements of the components of capital costs are not entirely satisfactory, they are the best available at the present, and they are used in obtaining an overall cost of capital of the firm. This is achieved by weighting the various costs by the relative proportion of each component's value in the total capital structure.

A question arises at this point. Should the weights be based on book values (i.e., the numbers on the balance sheet) or market values? The answer is market values, since they reflect the actual values of the various components today, and the prices the securities would command if new financing is needed.

If debt makes up 20 percent and equity 80 percent of a company's financial structure, and their respective costs are 6 percent and 14 percent, the weighted cost of capital is

$$0.2\ (0.06) + 0.8\ (0.14) = 0.012 + 0.112 = 0.124 = 12.4 \text{ percent}$$

Since the cost of debt capital is usually lower than that of equity, this formula would indicate that a company can decrease its cost of capital (and thus increase the value of the firm) by increasing the ratio of debt to equity. This is misleading, however. As the proportion of debt increases (i.e., as leverage rises), the financial community will view the company as more risky. Consequently, the cost of both components, debt as well as equity, will rise, causing the weighted average to rise also. There is probably some point where the combination of components is optimal, and where the weighted cost of capital of a particular firm is at a minimum.

## The Capital Budgeting Model

In the arena of corporate decision making, capital budgeting is an application of the marginal revenue–marginal cost principle. Figure 13.3 illustrates this principle.

Assume that a company is faced with a menu of seven independent capital budgeting proposals. The capital planning department has analyzed each of them and has calculated the internal rate of return, which is the evaluation technique the company uses. In Figure 13.3, the projects have been ranked by IRR from highest to lowest. Each proposal is represented by a bar; its height represents the IRR, and the width indicates the size of the investment. If a line were drawn connecting the tops of the bars and then smoothed, it would resemble a marginal revenue curve. In this case, it would be a curve representing the internal rate of return on successive doses of investment—a marginal investment opportunity curve.

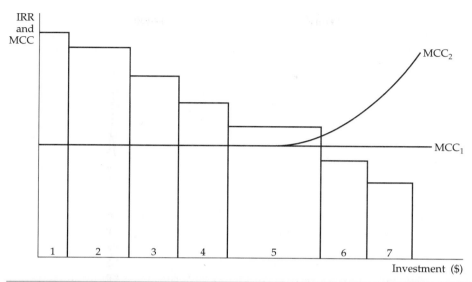

**FIGURE 13.3** The Capital Budgeting Decision

The marginal cost curve is based on the cost of capital. In Figure 13.3, two possible constructions of the cost of capital curve are shown. The first, a horizontal line ($MCC_1$), implies that a company can obtain the funds it needs at a set cost.

In the more likely case, as a company requires additional funds (i.e., moves from left to right on the graph), it will be forced to pay higher costs. We have already said that obtaining new equity carries a higher cost of capital than retained earnings. If a company has large requirements for investment funds, and after using up its retained earnings it must look to the outside equity market for additional financing, the marginal cost of capital will rise at that point. If the company's debt–equity ratio is considered optimal, the company will increase its debt proportionally to maintain it. As the company increases its borrowing, it will most likely be required to pay increasing interest rates for additional amounts of debt capital.

Thus, as the costs of both debt and equity rise, the marginal weighted cost of capital will show an increase as the corporation increases its demand for capital funds. Hence, it is considerably more realistic to draw the weighted marginal cost of capital as a rising curve ($MCC_2$), particularly after the capital budget of a certain size is reached.

The company will reach the optimal investment budget at the point where the marginal investment opportunity curve and marginal cost of capital curve intersect. This is, of course, the principle that was applied in the one-period case. In the example shown in Figure 13.3, the conclusion is that projects 1 through 5 should be accepted, and those with lower IRRs (projects 6 and 7) should be rejected.

The illustration shown here is a great simplification. A menu of projects will not usually be put on the table at one time. Projects typically arrive at the capital planning department at various times, and the proposals have to be evaluated one at a time. However, this simplification should be sufficient to show that capital budgeting is indeed an application of the marginal principle.

There is one other important point that must be made. We have just concluded that in order to arrive at an optimal capital budget, a company will accept all projects with positive NPV's (an exception, capital rationing, is discussed in the next section). However, if a firm operates in a competitive market, then in the long run, all NPV's will be reduced to zero. This is consistent with our discussion of competition in chapter 9, where we concluded that in a long-run equilibrium firms will earn only their normal profit. Of course, in reality, continuous changes in demand and supply conditions may prevent a static long-run equilibrium from ever being reached. Nevertheless, competitive forces will require companies to continue to innovate to maintain their market advantage or to attempt to create noncompetitive (monopolistic) conditions to produce economic profits—and positive NPV's—in the long run.

## Capital Rationing

The marginal rule indicates that the company should invest in every project whose IRR exceeds the marginal cost of capital or whose net present value is positive. However, some corporations impose an absolute limit on capital spending during a particular interval, and not all projects that pass the IRR or NPV test will be accepted. This situation, referred to as **capital rationing** occurs when management may not be willing to obtain external financing. There are various reasons for such a practice. For instance, there may be a reluctance to incur increasing levels of debt. Alternatively, management may not wish to add to equity in fear of diluting control. Thus, under capital rationing conditions, a company may have to reject otherwise acceptable projects to remain within its expenditure limit.

Assume that a corporation has evaluated five independent capital projects, with the results shown in Table 13.3. Each of the projects has a positive net present value and therefore should be undertaken under the usual rule. To embark on these five projects, the company would have to incur cash outflows of $250 and would obtain a net present value of $120.

However, the management of this firm has decreed that only $100 will be spent on capital projects at this time. Obviously, the company will not be able to maximize its net present value at $120. Which projects should it select? To create the most value it can under the circumstances, it will choose the combination of projects that will give the highest net present value within the spending constraint. This leads to the selection of projects A, C, and D. These three projects together will require an outlay of just $100 and will have a combined net present value of $60. No other combination of projects within the $100 spending constraint will achieve a net present value as high as $60.

Although the imposition of capital rationing does not appear to be rational maximizing behavior, it nevertheless occurs quite frequently. The final judgment on capital rationing is that it does not permit a company to achieve its maximum value.

| TABLE 13.3 | Investment Choices under Capital Rationing | |
| --- | --- | --- |
| Project | Original Investment | Net Present Value |
| A | $50 | $25 |
| B | 70 | 30 |
| C | 20 | 25 |
| D | 30 | 10 |
| E | 80 | 30 |

# The Value of a Corporation

We have just learned how to calculate the present value of a project given cash inflows and outflows over a period of time, and discounting these to the present using a discount rate, the cost of capital.

A similar method of computation can be employed to value a corporation as a whole. Of course, if the corporation's stock trades on a stock exchange and its debt is composed of publicly owned bonds, its market value can easily be established from published data. However, assume that you are one of the founders of a relatively small private corporation. You and the other owners are now planning to carry out an "initial public offering" (usually referred to as an IPO). How would you go about estimating what your company is worth?[18] To come up with some kind of a reasonable value figure, you will have to estimate your cash inflows and outflows several years into the future. To do a complete valuation job, it would be necessary to project your income statements and balance sheets. We will try to condense our procedure here by selecting the essential data we will need to make our computation without constructing complete financial statements.

To accomplish our objective we must start with the concept of **free cash flow.**[19] Free cash flow consists of funds that would be available to investors from operating cash flows after we subtract investments in working capital and fixed assets needed to operate and grow the company. These terms are defined as follows:

1. Operating cash flow = $EBIT \times (1-T)$ + Depreciation

    where $EBIT$ = Earnings before interest and tax (also frequently called operating profit)

    $T$ = Tax rate

2. New investment in operating working capital represents the annual increases in certain parts of current assets. In general, this would include increases in cash, accounts receivable, and inventories minus increases in accounts payable and accrued expenses.
3. Increases in fixed assets are increases in land, property, and equipment before subtracting depreciation (i.e., the gross increases in fixed assets).

Let us construct a simple example to illustrate the valuation method. Assume that in 1999, the following were the relevant numbers (in $000):

| | |
|---|---:|
| EBIT | $60 |
| Depreciation | 20 |
| Operating working capital | 80 |
| Gross fixed assets | 120 |

---

[18]The reader should notice that in calculating the value of this company we will use the nonconstant growth model, discussed in note 15 of this chapter.
[19]Free cash flow was mentioned briefly in chapter 2. Free cash flow is essentially the same as dividends, which were used to calculate the value of the common stock in that chapter. The following discussion has benefited from Brigham, Gapenski, and Ehrhardt, *Financial Management,* chapter 9.

Your company expects to have rather rapid growth during the next three years because of a new product you are bringing to the market. You expect, however, that after three years your competition will have caught up with you. Because you are not certain what new products you will introduce then, you make the conservative judgment that your company's free cash flow will increase at 6 percent per year for the foreseeable future. To calculate the free cash flow for the years 2000, 2001, and 2002, you have estimated the following:

|  | 2000 | 2001 | 2002 |
|---|---|---|---|
| EBIT | $90 | $110 | $125 |
| Depreciation | 30 | 35 | 40 |
| Operating working capital | 110 | 135 | 155 |
| Gross fixed assets | 160 | 190 | 220 |

EBIT and depreciation give us the two components of free cash flow. To calculate the other two, we must compute the year-to-year changes to obtain the cash outflow arising from an increase in those investments. Thus,

|  | 2000 | 2001 | 2002 |
|---|---|---|---|
| Operating working capital | $30 | $25 | $20 |
| Gross fixed assets | 40 | 30 | 30 |

We expect the income tax rate to be 40 percent in each of the years. Now we are ready to calculate the free cash flows for the three years:[20]

|  | 2000 | 2001 | 2002 |
|---|---|---|---|
| EBIT $\times (1 - T)$ | $54 | $66 | $75 |
| + Depreciation | 30 | 35 | 40 |
| − Increase in operating working capital | 30 | 25 | 20 |
| − Increase in gross fixed assets | 40 | 30 | 30 |
| Free cash flow | $14 | $46 | $65 |

The next step is to calculate the present value of the free cash flows. At this point we must establish the discount rate—the cost of capital. We estimate it to be 12 percent. Therefore, the present value of the above three cash flows at the end of 1999 will be the following (again using data from Appendix Table B.1*c*):

| Year 2000 | 14 × .8929 | 12.5 |
|---|---|---|
| 2001 | 46 × .7972 | 36.7 |
| 2002 | 65 × .7118 | 46.3 |
| Total |  | $95.5 |

[20]It is quite common for a new, small, and growing company to have negative free cash flows in its early years. Even though its EBIT is positive, it will have substantial cash outflows as it builds up its working capital and fixed asset base. To simplify matters, we have assumed positive free cash flows in each year.

Now we must account for the cash flows after the first three high-growth years. We had assumed previously that we would expect the normal long-term growth rate in free cash flow to be 6 percent. We can use the constant growth formula (Gordon model) to give us the answer. If free cash flow grows by 6 percent in 2003, then it will amount to $65 \times 1.06 = \$68.9$. As the cost of capital is 12 percent and the growth rate is 6 percent, our calculation will proceed as follows:

$$68.9/(0.12 - 0.06) = 68.9/(0.06) = 1148.3$$

The answer is the present value of all future cash flows at the beginning of year 2003 (or the end of 2002). To bring this amount back to the end of 1999, we must discount the amount for three years, or $1148.3 \times .7118 = 817.4$. The last step is to add the present value of the first three years to the present value of the growing perpetuity: $95.5 + 817.4 = 912.9$.

We have thus estimated the total value of your business to be $912,900. But as one of the owners of the business, you are interested in how much you could receive for your stock. We must now deduct any bank debt and long-term debt that you have on your balance sheet. Suppose that you had borrowed $300,000. Then the estimate of your stock value is $612,900. Let us assume that you and the other present owners wish to retain 20 percent of the stock ownership of the firm. This means you could expect to obtain $490,320 from your IPO.

Some cautions are in order. The result that we calculated is extremely sensitive to all the estimates we had made for cash flows, tax rates, and discount rates. The final results could differ substantially from our calculations. It would most likely be useful to do one or more additional calculations, using more optimistic and pessimistic assumptions, to help establish a range of potential outcomes.[21]

You would perform a similar calculation, if instead of an IPO, you were to consider a buyout offer by a large established firm in your industry. You would then be interested in determining the price at which you would be willing to sell your company. Again it would be useful to make several calculations to arrive at a desirable selling price. Further, if the acquiring firm should be able to achieve some synergies from taking over your firm, then the value of your company could be higher. That firm certainly made calculations similar to yours, and because of the synergies, they may have arrived at a higher figure. Thus, after you have bargained with the large firm, you may end up with a larger amount. And if you were lucky enough to have two large firms competing to acquire you, you may indeed strike a good bargain.

# International Application: Capital Budgeting in a Multinational Corporation

The capital budgeting process, as we have seen, is often quite complicated. Investment proposals are analyzed carefully, and then approvals must be obtained by management to implement these projects, particularly when the potential expenditures are large.

While this is true when proposals are confined to the company's domestic operations, the process becomes even more complex when a multinational corporation considers an investment in one of its foreign subsidiaries. Corporations invest in foreign countries for

---

[21]Sensitivity analysis calculations are discussed in detail in chapter 14.

many reasons. A corporation may be able to take advantage of lower production costs. The higher sales will permit a corporation to spread fixed costs (e.g., research and development). Because a company may be excluded from exporting its product due to various import restrictions, it protects its foreign markets if it can produce abroad. These and many other reasons have caused U.S. corporations to go international. Of course, making foreign investments may also carry considerable risk, which we will discuss in our next chapter. Here we consider only the complications that are inherent in making investments across national borders.

Since it is the domestic parent company that pays dividends to the stockholders, the parent will expect that at least some part of the foreign subsidiary's cash flow will be repatriated to the domestic company. However, in some cases, the foreign country may not permit a free flow of cash abroad. If this blockage is temporary, and the subsidiary has an opportunity to make an investment in its own country, then the effect may not be great or may even be advantageous. However, if it is more or less permanent, then this will decrease the cash flows to the parent. In some cases, taxes are imposed by the subsidiary's country when it remits dividends to its parent.

Income tax rates probably differ in the two countries. The foreign subsidiary pays a tax on its income. Usually this tax will be credited against the taxes the parent must pay on the income and dividends generated by the subsidiary. If the parent's tax is higher than the subsidiary's, the parent will have to pay this additional tax to its tax authority, thus decreasing the net cash flow it receives.

Various other cash flows can be obtained by the parent from its subsidiary. Frequently, there are licensing fees that must be remitted. Second, the parent may export certain components that the subsidiary will incorporate in its final product. These charges must be paid for; the transfer price of these components probably includes a profit to the parent, which must be accounted for in its income tax reports.

The differences in inflation rates and changes in currency exchange rates also may have a significant effect on the cash flows between the two organizations.

All of these events will most likely cause the cash flows from a project to the parent to be different from those received by its subsidiary. Thus, when the present values of the project are calculated both from the point of view of the parent and the subsidiary, substantial differences may occur. It may not be at all extraordinary for the net present value of a project to be positive to the subsidiary and negative to the parent.

Which of the two results should prevail? Theoretically, the parent's cash flows and net present value should determine the decision whether to invest. After all, it is the parent's cash flow that is used to pay shareholder dividends, and the net present value generated by the parent is instrumental in creating shareholder value. Thus, while it is important to analyze projects at the subsidiary's level, the parent's result should determine the final decision.[22]

---

[22]This section has benefited greatly from materials contained in David K. Eiteman, Arthur I. Stonehill, and Michael H. Moffett, *Multinational Business Finance,* 8th ed., Reading, MA: Addison-Wesley, 1998, pp. 585–87; and Dennis J. O'Connor and Alberto T. Bueso, *International Dimensions of Financial Management,* New York: Macmillan, 1990, pp. 431–42.

**MODULE 13F**

## PROJECT 1: EXPANSION PROPOSAL

George Kline is now ready to put some numbers together. He ascertains that the market forecast of 100 million cases pertains to Global's first year of production, and the 4 percent assumed growth rate will apply thereafter. Since the market research people expect, rather optimistically, that market share will grow to 5 percent after four years, George sets market share at 2, 3, and 4 percent respectively, for the interim years. He calculates the seven-year MACRS depreciation for the equipment using the midyear convention as required by the 1986 tax law. (Generally, under this law, only one-half of the first year's depreciation can be taken in the first year and one-half at the end. Thus, if a piece of equipment is depreciated on a seven-year basis, it will actually be depreciated over eight years. The depreciation percentages used in this example are 14 percent, 25 percent, 17 percent, 13 percent, 10 percent, 9 percent, 9 percent, and 3 percent.) Depreciation will start in year 2; thus, the equipment will not be fully depreciated at the end of six years; nor will the buildings. George assumes that the remaining book values will represent the market value at the end of year 7 and will be shown as cash inflows at that point. He also decides that of the original $750,000 cash outflow for working capital, 80 percent will be recovered as cash at the end of year 7 (some accounts receivable will not be collectible, and some inventory will be obsolete). The 20 percent loss will be tax deductible.

George now prepares his worksheet, shown in Table 13.4. The column labeled "Constant" contains the parameters established originally. (These constant parameters can be changed if different assumptions are to be used. A change in one of these will alter the entire line. This technique will be used in chapter 14 when we examine how any change in the assumptions will affect the results.) Most of the numbers in this table are self-explanatory, but a few comments should help. The start-up expense of $750 is tax deductible; thus, the cash outflow is $450. The cost of the plant is $3.5 million (50 percent of the purchase price plus $1 million for renovation). The cost of equipment is $3 million (40 percent of the original purchase price plus $1 million for new machinery). Land ($500,000) is assumed not to appreciate.

When the cash flows are obtained and discounted at the 15 percent required rate of return, the resulting NPV is a positive $3,553,000. The internal rate of return is 24.2 percent—considerably above the required rate.

George can therefore recommend the acceptance of this expansion project. However, since all of the cash flows are estimates into the future, there is probably considerable uncertainty about their accuracy. We will revisit this project in chapter 14 and will show how risk and uncertainty can be accommodated in our analysis.

## PROJECT 2: DEPALLETIZER REPLACEMENT

The original cash outflow at time 0 is $100,000. But if the investment in the
*(Continued)*

**TABLE 13.4** Expansion Project ($000)

| | Constant | Year 0 | Year 1 | Year 2 | Year 3 | Year 4 | Year 5 | Year 6 | Year 7 |
|---|---|---|---|---|---|---|---|---|---|
| Total market | 4.0% | | | 100,000 | 104,000 | 108,160 | 112,486 | 116,986 | 121,665 |
| Market share (%) | | | | 1.0 | 2.0 | 3.0 | 4.0 | 5.0 | 5.0 |
| Company sales (qty) | | | | 1,000 | 2,080 | 3,245 | 4,499 | 5,849 | 6,083 |
| Expenditures | | (5,000) | (2,000) | | | | | | |
| Working capital | | | (750) | | | | | | |
| Start-up expense | (750) | | (450) | | | | | | |
| Sales | 5.00 | | | 5,000 | 10,400 | 16,224 | 22,497 | 29,246 | 30,416 |
| Product cost | 2.50 | | | 2,500 | 5,200 | 8,112 | 11,249 | 14,623 | 15,208 |
| Distribution cost | 0.60 | | | 600 | 1,248 | 1,947 | 2,700 | 3,510 | 3,650 |
| G&A expense (fixed) | 500 | | | 500 | 500 | 500 | 500 | 500 | 500 |
| G&A expense (variable) | 3.0% | | | 150 | 312 | 487 | 675 | 877 | 912 |
| Advertising expense | 5.0% | | | 250 | 520 | 811 | 1,125 | 1,462 | 1,521 |
| Depreciation (plant) | 3,500 | | | 111 | 111 | 111 | 111 | 111 | 111 |
| Depreciation (equipment) | 3,000 | | | 420 | 750 | 510 | 390 | 300 | 270 |
| Total cost & expenses | | | | 4,531 | 8,641 | 12,478 | 16,749 | 21,384 | 22,173 |
| Net earnings before taxes | | | | 469 | 1,759 | 3,746 | 5,748 | 7,863 | 8,244 |
| Income tax | 40% | | | 188 | 704 | 1,498 | 2,299 | 3,145 | 3,298 |
| Net earnings after taxes | | | | 281 | 1,055 | 2,248 | 3,449 | 4,718 | 4,946 |
| Add: depreciation | | | | 531 | 861 | 621 | 501 | 411 | 381 |
| Operating cash flow | | | | 812 | 1,916 | 2,869 | 3,950 | 5,129 | 5,327 |
| Remaining values | | | | | | | | | |
| Land | | | | | | | | | 500 |
| Plant | | | | | | | | | 2,833 |
| Equipment | | | | | | | | | 360 |
| Working capital | 80.0% | | | | | | | | 660 |
| Total cash flow | | (5,000) | (3,200) | 812 | 1,916 | 2,869 | 3,950 | 5,129 | 9,681 |
| Net present value | 15.0% | | | | | | | | 3,553 |
| Internal rate or return | | | | | | | | | 24.2% |

new machine is made, the old one will be sold for $12,000. Since its book value is only $10,000, there would be profit from the disposal of used equipment of $2,000. The tax rate being 40 percent, the company would have to pay income tax of $800 on this profit; so the cash inflow from the sale of the old depalletizer would be $11,200.

The annual increase in operating cash flows would be $18,000. The new machine would be depreciated over seven years straight-line. The annual depreciation would, there-fore, be $14,286. The annual operating cash flow statement would be as follows:

| | |
|---|---|
| Revenue less cost | $18,000 |
| Depreciation | 14,286 |
| Net profit before taxes | $ 3,714 |
| Income tax | 1,486 |
| Net profit after taxes | $ 2,228 |
| Depreciation | 14,286 |
| Net cash flow | $16,514 |

*(Continued)*

| | |
|---|---:|
| Original investment at $t = 0$ | $ -100,000 |
| Cash proceeds from old machines at $t = 0$ | 11,200 |
| Annual cash flow from operations, years 1–7, | |
| at PV of annuity factor, 7 years at 12%: | |
| 16,514 × 4.5638 | 75,363 |
| Annual operating cash flows, years 8–10: | |
| Year 8    10,800 × 0.4039 | 4,362 |
| Year 9    10,800 × 0.3606 | 3,894 |
| Year 10   10,800 × 0.3220 | 3,478 |
| Depreciation of old machines forgone: | |
| 5,000 × 0.4 × 1.6091 | −3,380 |
| Net present value | $ −5,083 |

These cash flows would occur during the first seven years of operations. In years 8–10, there would be no depreciation tax shield. Thus, the annual operating cash flows would be:

| | |
|---|---:|
| Revenue less cost | $18,000 |
| Income tax | 7,200 |
| Net cash flow | $10,800 |

One additional piece of information must be included. If Global Foods had kept the old machine, it would be depreciated in years 1 and 2 at $5,000 annually. Since the tax rate is 40 percent, Global would save $2,000 each year in taxes—a cash inflow. If the old machine is sold, this depreciation tax shield will no longer be available. Consequently, the cash flows would be decreased by the present value of the two after-tax depreciation deductions.

Now the proposal can be put together: The IRR calculation would have given us 10.5 percent.

The result is a negative net present value (and an IRR less than the cost of capital). Acquisition of the new depalletizer is not indicated at this time. This is the recommendation the capital planning department will make. However, the decision could be reconsidered if any of the cash flow estimates should change.

## Summary

In this chapter we expanded the economic concept of profit maximization to multi-period projects.

Capital budgeting involves the evaluation of projects in which initial expenditures provide streams of cash inflows over a significant period of time. The process of evaluating capital proposals includes the following:

1. Estimating all incremental cash flows resulting from the project
2. Discounting all flows to the present
3. Determining whether a proposal should be accepted

Two methods were recommended for evaluating capital budgeting proposals—net present value and internal rate of return. These two criteria were compared as to their validity. It was found that, from a theoretical viewpoint, net present value is the more valid. However, there is much to recommend the use of IRR, and business, in fact, favors this technique. In most cases, both methods lead to the same answer.

The concept of the cost of capital was then developed, and methods of arriving at a weighted cost of capital were discussed.

Finally, using the economist's marginal revenue–marginal cost approach, it was shown that, to maximize its total value, a firm should accept any project whose IRR exceeds the marginal cost of capital.

## Important Concepts

**Accounting rate of return:** Also known as the *return on investment* (ROI) or *return on assets* (ROA), a method for evaluating capital projects. It is obtained by dividing the average annual profit by the average investment. (p. 477)

**Capital asset pricing model (CAPM):** A financial model specifying relationships between risk and return. An important part of the CAPM is the development of beta, which measures the market risk of a security and is a necessary ingredient in determining a stock's required rate of return. (p. 491)

**Capital budgeting:** An area of business decision making that concerns undertakings whose receipts and expenses continue over a significant period of time. (p. 475)

**Capital rationing:** The practice of restricting capital expenditure to a certain amount, possibly resulting in the rejection of projects that have a positive net present value and should be accepted to maximize the company's value. (p. 494)

**Cost of capital:** Also often referred to as the required rate of return, the hurdle rate, or the cutoff rate, the rate of return a company must earn on its assets to justify the using and acquiring of funds. (p. 478)

**Discount rate:** The rate at which cash flows are discounted. It is the required rate of return or cost of capital. (p. 478)

**Dividend growth model:** A method to arrive at the value of a security. Given the price of the security, it calculates the company's cost of equity as the dividend divided by the current stock price plus the growth rate in dividends (assumed to be constant). It is an alternative

method to CAPM in calculating the equity cost of capital. (p. 490)

**Free cash flow:** Funds that are available for distribution to investors. It includes operating cash flow after taxes minus (plus) increases (decreases) in operating working capital and fixed assets investment. (p. 495)

**Independent projects:** A situation in which the acceptance of one capital project does not preclude the acceptance of another project. (See *mutually exclusive projects.*) (p. 481)

**Internal rate of return (IRR):** One method of evaluating capital projects by discounting cash flows. The IRR is the interest rate that equates the present value of inflows with the present value of outflows, or, in other words, causes the net present value of the project to equal zero. (p. 477)

**Mutually exclusive projects:** A situation in which the acceptance of one project precludes the acceptance of another. (p. 481)

**Net present value (NPV):** A method of evaluating capital projects in which all cash flows are discounted at the cost of capital to the present and the present value of all outflows is subtracted from the present value of all inflows. (p. 477)

**Payback:** A method of evaluating capital projects in which the original investment is divided by the annual cash flow. It tells management how many years it will take for a project's cash inflows to repay the original investment. (p. 477)

**Time value of money:** Very basically, this means that a dollar today is worth more than a dollar tomorrow, because today's dollar will earn interest and increase in value. (p. 476)

## Questions

1. What is the objective of capital budgeting?
2. Name five types of decisions that utilize the capital budgeting method.
3. Define the *time value of money.*
4. How is net present value calculated? What is the decision rule for net present value?
5. How is the internal rate of return calculated? What is the decision rule for IRR?
6. The relationship between net present value and the internal rate of return is such that the IRR of a project is equal to the firm's cost of capital when the NPV of the project is $0. True or false? Explain.
7. Under which circumstances can the NPV and IRR calculations lead to conflicting results? What is the major reason for the difference? Which of the two methods is preferable? Why?
8. What are the major types of cash flows to be included in a capital budgeting analysis? Describe each.
9. Why is depreciation important in the analysis of a capital budgeting proposal?
10. Should a reallocation of fixed costs from other projects to the project being analyzed be included in the project's cash flows, if there is no net increase in cash outflow to the company? Why or why not?
11. You are analyzing a potential capital investment project involving a new product. As you are compiling all the relevant data for your analysis, you are informed of an expenditure that occurred during the prior year. The marketing research department of your company conducted an assessment of the demand for this new product. The cost of this research was $100,000 and was part of the company's expenses during the previous year. Is this relevant to your present analysis? Why or why not?
12. How is the company's optimal capital budget determined? Does the decision-making process in this case resemble the procedure used in determining the price and quantity of output? How?
13. How is the weighted cost of capital determined?
14. Discuss the two methods by which the costs of equity can be determined.
15. Define *beta.* How is it used to compute the required rate of return on a company's stock (the equity cost of capital)? An investment publication recently estimated the beta of Dominion Resources (a large electric utility company) to be .7, while the beta of Compaq (a computer manufacturer) was 1.55. Why is there such a large difference between the betas of the two companies? Which would you expect to have the higher required rate of return on its common stock?
16. Why is capital rationing not considered to be rational maximizing behavior?

## Problems

1. Jay Wechsler agrees to purchase a car from a local dealer, the Con Car Co. The purchase price is $15,000. Jay has the cash to pay the entire amount and wants to do so. Con's sales manager uses the following argument to convince him to finance the car: "All we require is a down payment of $3,000. Then you can borrow the $12,000 from our finance company at 12 percent. You will make monthly payments of $266.93 for five years (60 months), a total of $16,015.80. If you do that, you get to keep your $12,000. Now suppose you keep this money in a money market account that pays you 8 percent compounded quarterly. In five years the $12,000 will grow to $17,831.40. That means that you will be better off by $1,815.60 than if you pay the $12,000 in cash."

    Assume that all the numbers are correct. Does the offer sound too good to be true? Why? (This is an argument often used by automobile dealers. One of the authors encountered it not too long ago.)
2. Your firm has an opportunity to make an investment of $50,000. Its cost of capital is 12 percent. It expects after-tax cash flows (including the tax shield from depreciation) for the next five years to be as follows:

| Year 1 | $10,000 |
|--------|---------|
| Year 2 | 20,000 |
| Year 3 | 30,000 |
| Year 4 | 20,000 |
| Year 5 | 5,000 |

   **a.** Calculate the net present value.

   **b.** Calculate the internal rate of return (to the nearest percent).

   **c.** Would you accept this project?

**3.** You own a large collection of fine wines. You now decide that the time has come to consider liquidating this valuable asset. However, you predict that the value of your collection will rise in the next few years. The following are your estimates:

| Year | Today | 1 | 2 | 3 | 4 | 5 | 6 |
|------|-------|---|---|---|---|---|---|
| Value ($000) | 70 | 88 | 104 | 119 | 132 | 142 | 150 |

If you assume your cost of capital to be 10 percent, when should you sell your collection to maximize your NPV?

**4.** The Glendale Construction Company is considering the purchase of a new crane. Its cost would be $500,000. If it were to make the purchase, the company would sell its old crane, which still has a book value of $100,000 and which it could probably sell in the second-hand market for $70,000. If the tax rate is 40 percent, what would be the actual cash investment in the new crane?

**5.** As capital investment analyst for the Parkhurst Printing Corporation, you have been asked to evaluate the advisability of purchasing a new printing press to accommodate projected increases in demand. This new machine is expected to last five years, and you will be calculating the cash flows of the project for that period.

   The purchase price of the press is expected to be $140,000; in addition, it will cost $10,000 to install it. The press will be depreciated on a straight-line basis over five years to a zero salvage value. However, it is expected to have a market value of $10,000 at the end of five years.

   The press is expected to generate the following cash revenues and cash costs and expenses:

| | Year 1 | Year 2 | Year 3 | Year 4 | Year 5 |
|---|--------|--------|--------|--------|--------|
| Cash revenue | $50,000 | $80,000 | $80,000 | $80,000 | $40,000 |
| Cash cost and expense | 25,000 | 40,000 | 40,000 | 40,000 | 20,000 |

   Because of increased production, additional working capital of $15,000 will be needed at $t = 0$ (today) and will be returned at the end of the project (five years from now). The income tax rate is 40 percent, and the company's cost of capital is 12 percent. Calculate the net present value. Should the press be purchased?

**6.** The Gillmore Corporation is analyzing a new investment project. Cash flows for all the project years are being calculated. The following items, all pertaining to year 5, are directly associated with this project:

| | |
|---|---:|
| Sales | $800,000 |
| Manufacturing costs (including $40,000 of depreciation) | 380,000 |
| Selling expenses (including $20,000 of depreciation) | 170,000 |
| Research & development expenses | 50,000 |
| Fixed expenses reallocated from other products | 15,000 |
| Purchase of equipment | 30,000 |
| Sales of old equipment | 10,000 |
| Increase in working capital | 35,000 |
| Income taxes paid (on profits from this project) | 45,000 |

Calculate the cash flow in year 5 to be used in the computation of the present value of this investment.

7. The Colgate Distributing Company has the choice of furnishing its sales representatives with a car or paying a mileage allowance for the use of the representatives' own cars. If the company furnishes the car, it will pay all expenses connected with it, including gasoline for business mileage. The estimates are as follows:

Cost of car: $15,000
Estimated life: Four years
Depreciation method: Straight-line over four years (assuming no salvage value)
Expected sales value of car at end of four years: $2,500
Estimated annual operating costs:

| | |
|---|---:|
| Gasoline | $900 |
| License and insurance | 600 |
| Garaging | 300 |
| Maintenance | |
| Year 1 | 250 |
| Year 2 | 350 |
| Year 3 | 450 |
| Year 4 | 600 |

If the sales representatives use their own cars, the company will reimburse them at 35 cents per mile; the company estimates that each representative will drive 18,000 miles per year for business purposes. The company's cost of capital is 10 percent, and its income tax rate is 40 percent.

Should the company buy cars for its sales representatives or pay them a mileage allowance? Use the NPV method in your calculation.

8. The Manchester Tool Company is considering the replacement of an existing machine by a more efficient machine. The new machine costs $1,200,000 and requires installation costs of $150,000.

The present machine is four years old. It originally cost $800,000 and is being depreciated straight-line over ten years to a zero salvage value. Its market value today is $400,000. It can be used for the next six years; at that time, its market value will be zero.

The new machine has an expected life of six years and will be depreciated on a straight-line method over five years to a salvage value of zero. However, it is expected to have a market value of $200,000 at the end of six years.

The new machine will reduce operating costs by $250,000 per year. The company's income tax rate is 40 percent, and its cost of capital is 9 percent. Would you recommend that the old machine be replaced?

9. A company's common stock is currently selling at $40 per share. Its most recent dividend was $1.60, and the financial community expects that its dividend will grow at 10 percent per year in the foreseeable future. What is the company's equity cost of retained earnings? If the company sells new common stock to finance new projects and must pay $2 per share in flotation costs, what is the cost of equity?

10. Harvey Corporation's stock price today is $40. The most recent annual dividend it paid was $2. You estimate that the company's equity cost is 10 percent. If you expect the company's dividends to increase at a constant rate, what do you expect the growth rate to be?

11. A company has 1,000,000 shares of common stock outstanding, and the current market price is $50 per share. The company has also issued 20,000 bonds ($1,000 maturity value each), which are presently selling in the market at $980 each. The bonds are selling at a yield of 11 percent; the company expects to pay a dividend of $3 per share in the coming year, and the dividend is expected to grow at 8 percent per year. The company is in the 40 percent tax bracket. What is the weighted cost of capital?

12. A company has a beta of 1.3. The risk-free interest rate today is 8 percent, and the return on a market portfolio of stocks is 14 percent. (Therefore, the market risk premium is 6 percent, the difference between the market return and the risk-free return.)
    a. What is the required return (equity cost) on the company's stock?
    b. If the risk-free rate rises to 9 percent, what will be the required rate of return on the company's stock?
    c. If the beta of this company were 0.8, what would be its required rate of return?

13. Two mutually exclusive alternatives, projects C and D, have the following investments and cash flows:

|  | *Project C* | *Project D* |
|---|---|---|
| Investment at period $t = 0$ | $40,000 | $40,000 |
| Cash inflow at $t = 1$ | 10,000 | 20,500 |
| Cash inflow at $t = 2$ | 10,000 | 20,500 |
| Cash inflow at $t = 3$ | 47,000 | 20,500 |

    a. Calculate the net present value and internal rate of return of each project. The company's cost of capital is 12 percent.
    b. Which of the two projects would you accept? Explain.
    c. Sketch the two projects' NPV profiles.

14. The Berkshire Resort Hotel has planned several improvement projects. However, it has decided to restrict its capital expenditures to $340,000 during the next year. The following are the projects it has on its drawing board:

| | *Original Investment* | *Net Present Value* |
|---|---|---|
| Additional tennis court | $ 20,000 | $ 5,500 |
| Kitchen renovation | 50,000 | 14,000 |
| New children's playground | 60,000 | 12,500 |
| New bungalows | 100,000 | 22,500 |
| New golf clubhouse | 120,000 | 32,500 |
| Olympic-size swimming pool | 140,000 | 45,000 |
| New theater arena | 150,000 | 40,000 |

Which projects should it undertake?

## Take It to the Net

We invite you to visit the Keat/Young page on the Prentice Hall Web site at:

**http://www.prenhall.com/keat**

for additional resources.

## Appendix 13A

## Calculations for Time Value of Money

In this appendix, a brief explanation of the computation of the time value of money is given for readers not familiar with this subject. Modern technology has made these calculations very easy. Many computer programs have built-in time-value functions, and a large assortment of hand-held calculators will solve these problems using special keys. However, some people who use these methods do not understand the rationale for the answers and merely accept the results.

At the other extreme, the calculations could be made using exponentials and/or logarithms. Such a procedure may provide a thorough learning experience, but it is tedious and time consuming. Compound interest tables have been developed to provide a relatively easy tool for solving time-value problems. They will be found in Appendix B at the end of this book. Here we will walk through four types of calculations, each representing one of the four tables.

## The Future Value of a Single Sum

**MODULE 13AA**

If you deposit $1,000 in a savings account that pays 7 percent interest annually, and you do not withdraw this interest, the original amount will keep growing. (In real life, bank interest is usually compounded more frequently than once a year, but annual compounding will be assumed here. In other words, the 7 percent will be credited to the account once a year, at the end of the year.) One year later, $70 of interest will be added to the account, making the total balance $1,070. In mathematical terms, this occurrence can be written as follows: If $i$ equals the annual interest rate, then the amount of interest paid in one year equals $A$ times $i$, where $A$ is the original amount deposited. Thus, $B$, the ending balance in the account, will be

$$B = A + (A \times i) \qquad \text{or} \qquad B = A(1 + i)$$

In the present case, this will compute as

$$B = 1{,}000\,(1 + 0.07) = 1{,}000\,(1.07) = 1{,}070$$

Now, if \$1,070 is left in the account for another year, interest will be paid on the \$1,070:

$$B = 1{,}070\,(1.07) = 1{,}144.90$$

We could also find the answer in the following way:

$$B = 1{,}000 \times 1.07 \times 1.07 = 1{,}144.90$$

This expression simplifies to $1{,}000\,(1.07)^2$. Thus, in general terms,

$$FV = PV(1 + i)^n$$

where FV = Future value

PV = Present value

$i$ = Rate of interest

$n$ = Number of periods over which compounding takes place

Table B.1*a* in Appendix B at the end of this book presents the $(1 + i)^n$ factors for a large number of periods and interest rates. Thus, if you wish to find out how much your original \$1,000 will grow in eight years, you can look it up by moving down the leftmost (period) column to 8 and then moving to the right until you hit the 7 percent column. You will obtain an answer of 1.7182. Substituting into the general formula,

$$FV = 1{,}000\,(1.7182)$$

$$= 1{,}718.20$$

This table can also be used if you know the beginning and ending amounts and want to find the rate of interest it took to go from the first to the last amount. The formula for future value can be easily transformed to solve for the interest rate. If we refer to the number that appears in the table as "factor," then

$$FV = PV\,(\text{Factor})$$

$$\text{Factor} = FV/PV$$

Assume that you are saving for a particular purpose. You put aside \$1,000 today and want to have \$2,000 five years from now:

$$\text{Factor} = \frac{2{,}000}{1{,}000}$$

$$= 2$$

To find the answer, enter the table at five periods and move to the right until the number nearest to 2 is reached. This happens at 15 percent, where the $(1 + i)^n$ factor equals 2.0114. Thus, you would have to earn approximately 15 percent interest to double your amount in five years.[23]

---

[23]If more exact results are needed, linear interpolation should be used. We will not explain interpolation here. An explanation can be found in any basic mathematics text.

This type of calculation is employed frequently to obtain compound growth rates, a very popular concept in business.

# The Future Value of an Annuity

**MODULE 13AB**

In the previous section we dealt with the compounding of a single sum. But suppose that a uniform amount is set aside each period (e.g., each year), and we want to know how much will be in the account after several years.

For example, suppose five annual deposits of $500 each will be made to an account paying 7 percent annually, starting a year from now. What will be the amount at the end of five years? A simple diagram will illustrate:

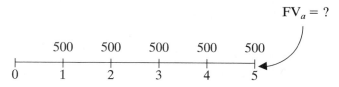

The first $500 will collect interest for four years, the second for three years, and so on. This problem could be solved by making all the separate calculations and adding the items:

$$FV_a = A (1 + i)^{n - 1} + A (1 + i)^{n-2} + \cdots + A (1 + i)^0$$

where $FV_a$ = Future value of the annuity
$A$ = Annuity

This expression simplifies to

$$\frac{(1 + i)^n - 1}{i}$$

Again, a table has been constructed to ease the effort involved in this calculation. Table B.1*b* in Appendix B shows the *sum of an annuity*. For the question posed here the answer is:

$$FV_a = A \text{ (Factor)}$$
$$= 500 \ (5.7507)$$
$$= 2,875.35$$

where "factor" is found in Table B.1*b*.

The preceding calculation solves for the future value of the annuity. But suppose we have a problem stated in the following form:

To finance the college education of a just-born child, the parents expect they will need $200,000 18 years from now. They believe that they can earn 7 percent on their savings. How much should they put aside each year? The future-value formula can be transposed to solve for the annuity, *A*:

$$A = FV_a/\text{Factor}$$
$$= 200,000/33.999$$
$$= 5,883$$

The parents will have to deposit $5,883 per year to have $200,000 in 18 years.

Table B.1*b* presents factors for ordinary annuities, which means that the first payment is made at the end of the first period and the last payment occurs on the final date. But suppose the payments are to start right now, and the last payment will occur at the beginning of the last period. Such a series of payments is usually referred to as an *annuity due,* and the diagram for such an arrangement, using data from the first example of this section, is:

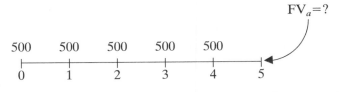

Table B.1*b* can still be applied, with one small change. The ordinary annuity factor in Table B.1*b* must be multiplied by $(1 + i)$. With interest again at 7 percent, the "annuity due" factor becomes 5.7507 times 1.07, or 6.1532. Thus, the result is

$$FV_a = 500 \ (6.1532)$$
$$= 3,077$$

Note that the amount accumulated at the end of five years is considerably larger than in the first example. The reason? Each of the contributions has an extra year to compound.

## Present Value of a Single Sum

**MODULE 13AA**

Suppose you are to receive a sum of $500 three years from now. You would like to receive the money today, and you would be willing to accept less, as an amount deposited today with interest would grow to a larger sum in three years. The question can be stated as follows: How much money accepted today would be equivalent to $500 three years from now? That depends, of course, on the rate of interest you earn on your money. As with our previous example, let us use a 7 percent interest rate.

Remember from our discussion of compounding a single sum that $FV = PV \ (1 + i)^n$. We are now attempting to solve the opposite problem: we know the future value and wish to find the present value. Therefore,

$$PV = \frac{FV}{(1 + i)^n}$$

Because

$$\frac{1}{(1 + i)^n} = (1 + i)^{-n}$$

this simple equation can be written as

$$PV = FV \ (1 + i)^{-n}$$

The number can be found in Table B.1*c*. We look up the three-year factor at 7 percent and find it to be 0.8163. Thus,

$$PV = 500\,(0.8163)$$

$$= 408$$

Incidentally, the present-value factors (Table B.1$c$) are reciprocals of the future-value factors (Table B.1$a$). Thus, if you have only one of these tables available, you can still do both future- and present-value calculations. For the preceding case, if only Table B.1$a$ were available, the solution would be as follows:

$$FV = PV\,(1 + i)^n$$

$$PV = \frac{FV}{(1 + i)^n}$$

$$= \frac{500}{1.225}$$

$$= 408$$

## Present Value of an Annuity

**MODULE 13AB**

Suppose that instead of receiving just one amount in the future, you expect to receive a series of uniform payments annually for four years starting a year from now (an ordinary annuity), or, as an alternative, you can receive a lump sum today. The single amount that would be equivalent to the annuity again depends on the interest rate you can earn. Assume that you are to receive four annual payments of $2,000. This is illustrated as follows:

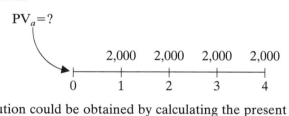

The solution could be obtained by calculating the present value of each payment using Table B.1$c$ and totaling the results. The first $2,000 would be discounted one year, the second two years, and so on. Using Table B.1$d$, however, avoids this time-consuming method. The factors contained in this table already include the discounting and summation of all the individual numbers. Thus, if the interest rate to be used is 8 percent, then

$$PV_a = A\,(\text{Factor})$$

$$= 2,000\,(3.3121)$$

$$= 6,624$$

where "factor" is found in Table B.1$d$. You would be indifferent between receiving a sum of $6,624 today and a series of four annual payments of $2,000.

The preceding calculations apply to an ordinary annuity. If the first payment is to be received today, a relatively simple adjustment must be made to the factors of Table B.1$d$.

A very relevant example of the present value of an annuity due is the case of a state lottery. You certainly have seen a banner headline such as "John P. Oliver Wins $5 Million in the Lottery." True, Mr. Oliver will receive $5 million (before he pays his taxes), but not all at one time. State lotteries frequently pay the winners in 20 equal installments; the first payment is received today and the other 19 are received annually starting one year from today. To convert the calculation to an annuity due, the ordinary annuity factor in Table B.1$d$ must be multiplied by $(1 + i)$. For 20 payments of $250,000 each, using an 8 percent interest rate, the 20-year factor is 9.8181 which, when multiplied by 1.08, becomes 10.6035. The calculation is as follows:

$$PV_a = A\ (10.6035)$$
$$= 250,000\ (10.6035)$$
$$= 2,650,875$$

Obviously, this amount is much less than the $5 million that was announced as Mr. Oliver's winning ticket. Still, more than $2.5 million dollars is not that bad.

There is one more exercise that should be examined in this section. Suppose we know the present value of the annuity and the interest rate, but the annuity payment is unknown. Assume that you wish to borrow $20,000 to be paid back over five years in equal installments at an interest rate of 9 percent. What will your annual payments be? The factors in Table B.1$d$ are again applicable, but we must reverse the formula:

$$PV_a = A\ (Factor)$$
$$A = \frac{PV_a}{Factor}$$
$$= \frac{20,000}{3.8897}$$
$$= 5,142$$

## More Frequent Compounding

All of the preceding examples were in terms of years—annual compounding. But compounding may occur more frequently. Banks advertise that they compound interest on savings accounts quarterly, monthly, or even daily. The more frequent the compounding, the greater the effect of the time value of money.

In the first section of this appendix, compounding of a single sum was discussed. The formula was

$$FV = PV\ (1 + i)^n$$

If compounding occurs more often than $n$—for instance, $m$ times $n$—then the compounding formula is revised as follows:

$$FV = PV\ (1 + i/m)^{mn}$$

Suppose a deposit of $10,000 pays an annual interest rate of 8 percent compounded semiannually, and the time elapsed is five years. The equation would be:

$$FV = 10,000 \, (1 + 0.08/2)^{5 \times 2}$$
$$= 10,000 \, (1.04)^{10}$$
$$= 10,000 \, (1.4802)$$
$$= 14,802$$

If compounding had been annual, the resulting amount would have been lower: 10,000 (1.4693) = 14,693.

On the other hand, with quarterly compounding:

$$FV = 10,000 \, (1.02)^{20}$$
$$= 10,000 \, (1.4859)$$
$$= 14,859$$

The more frequent the compounding, the larger will be the future value.

## Bond Values and Perpetuities

**MODULE 13AC**

One more application of present-value calculations will be discussed here. A corporate or government bond pays periodic interest and then repays the face value on the maturity date. Interest payments are generally fixed for the life of the bond and are expressed as a percentage of the face value. Whether market interest rates rise or fall during the life of the bond, the periodic interest paid will not change. However, the price of the bond will change so that the yield corresponds to the interest rate paid in the market for bonds of a similar risk class and length of life.[24]

As an example, we will take a bond with a face and maturity value of $1,000 (the usual amount in which bonds are denominated). It will mature in 20 years (it was originally a 30-year bond, issued ten years ago), and the stated interest rate is 8 percent. Thus, the annual interest payment is $80.[25]

Interest rates have risen recently, and today bonds with 20-year maturities yield 10 percent. But because the interest payment of $80 per year on the bond cannot be changed, the market value of the bond (the price someone would be willing to pay for it today) will have to decline. This situation is quite obvious. If bonds are now yielding 10 percent, a potential buyer of a $1,000 bond would require $100 of annual interest. The bond in our example pays $80 per year, with a final payment of $1,000 at maturity. To obtain its value when the current market yield is 10 percent, we compute the present value of a 20-year annuity of $80 at a 10 percent discount rate and add to it the present value of the maturity value, $1,000, also discounted to the present at 10 percent:

$$P_0 = 80 \, (8.5136) + 1,000 \, (0.1486)$$
$$= 681 + 149 = 830$$

---

[24]The riskier, or less safe, a bond, the higher will be the interest that the market will require. The longer the length of life of the bond, the higher will be the required interest, under normal circumstances.
[25]Bond interest is usually paid semiannually, but for this example, annual payments are assumed.

At $P_0 = 830$, representing the market price of the bond today, and a yield of 10 percent to maturity, this bond is equivalent to a bond selling today for $1,000 that pays $100 annually and will mature 20 years hence at $1,000.

Had interest rates dropped to 6 percent, the bond of our example, still paying $80 a year, would rise in price above its maturity value:

$$P_0 = 80\,(11.4699) + 1,000\,(0.3118)$$

$$= 918 + 312 = 1,230$$

Perpetual bonds do not exist in the United States. However, they have been issued elsewhere, for example, in the United Kingdom. Such bonds never mature, but they promise to pay a stated interest amount forever. If

$$P_0 = \text{Price of the bond today}$$

$$I = \text{Annual interest paid}$$

$$i = \text{Market interest rate}$$

then

$$i = \frac{I}{P_0}$$

and

$$P_0 = \frac{I}{i}$$

If the bond pays $80 a year and the market rate is 8 percent, the price of the bond today will be its face value of $1,000. However, should the market rate of interest for bonds of this type rise to 10 percent, the bond paying $80 per year will be worth

$$P_0 = \frac{80}{0.1} = 800$$

A bond selling for $800 and paying $80 a year yields precisely 10 percent in perpetuity.

Fluctuations in bond prices will be greater for any change in the market interest rate, the longer the period to maturity. The price of a bond that matures one year hence will not decrease much when market interest rates rise. On the other hand, the price of a perpetuity will fluctuate very significantly with changes in market interest yields.

# CHAPTER 14

# Risk and Uncertainty

**THE SITUATION**

When George Kline completed his analysis of the expansion proposal, he concluded that the company's plan for extending its activities into a new geographical region was desirable.[1] He had calculated a net present value that was positive and, consistently, an internal rate of return that exceeded the required rate of return (cost of capital).

He discussed his findings with his immediate manager, the company's treasurer. The treasurer agreed that the estimates used were the best available, and that even if some of them turned out to be overly optimistic, the project would still be acceptable. However, he indicated management's awareness that expanding into new,

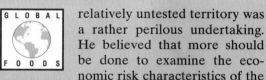

relatively untested territory was a rather perilous undertaking. He believed that more should be done to examine the economic risk characteristics of the project. Therefore, he asked George to perform additional risk analyses. George informed him that there are various techniques available, some of which involve statistical concepts. The treasurer suggested that George keep his analysis on a relatively simple level, but that it should be extensive enough that the vice president of finance and others who will be present when the proposal is presented can be comfortable with this important decision.

_____
[1]See "Solution" in chapter 13.

## Introduction

This chapter would be unnecessary if we were living in a world of perfect knowledge, where all future events could be determined with complete certainty.

Throughout this text, all quantities have been treated as if they were certain. Demand curves showed specific quantities that would be sold at specific prices. Cost curves showed definite dollar amounts of costs for specific quantities. In the preceding

**515**

chapter, on capital budgeting, the various estimates of cash flows for projects were treated as if they were known with certainty. In the real world, of course, most future events are not known with any degree of certainty. Managers must make decisions daily, relying on estimates they believe are reasonably reliable but by no means certain. Dealing with uncertainty and recognizing that future results may differ from well-constructed plans is a reality in the business world.

Although risk or uncertainty was not explicitly considered in the calculation of cash flows in the preceding chapter, there were several references to risk. For example, the replacement project was evaluated at a lower discount rate than the expansion project because the latter was considered to be more risky. Risk and uncertainty also played an important role in chapter 6, on forecasting. In this chapter, the meaning of the words *risk* and *uncertainty* will be explained, and the various methods of incorporating these concepts into economic analysis will be explored.

## Risk Versus Uncertainty

In economic or financial theory, the two terms **risk** and **uncertainty** have somewhat different meanings, even though they are often used interchangeably.[2] Although no future events are known with certainty, some events can be assigned probabilities, and others cannot. Where future events can be defined and probabilities assigned, we have a case of risk. Thus, for instance, a company's sales manager estimates that next year's sales of diet cola have a 25 percent probability to be 5 million cases, a 50 percent probability to be 6 million, and a 25 percent probability to be 7 million. If there is no way to assign any probabilities to future random events, we are addressing pure uncertainty. Even though this distinction is theoretically important, many writers omit it as a matter of convenience. We will follow this practice.

How are probabilities obtained? There are at least two ways. In the terminology of economist Frank Knight, probabilities can be classified as *a priori* or *statistical.*[3] The former can be obtained by repetition. Thus, if a true two-sided coin is flipped an infinite number of times, tails will come up on half the tosses and heads on the other half. When two dice are thrown, there are 36 possible combinations of numbers. Because there are six ways to obtain a 7, we can say that a 7 should appear on average once every six throws, if the two dice were thrown an infinite number of times. Instead of throwing the coin or dice an infinite number of times, we can specify the frequency based on general mathematical principles.

In everyday business, a priori probabilities cannot be specified. To assign probabilities to various outcomes, businesspeople must rely on statistical probabilities. These may be obtained empirically, based on past events. For instance, if a particular event has occurred once every ten times in the past, a 10 percent probability would be assigned to

---

[2]An early discussion of this distinction can be found in Frank H. Knight's *Risk, Uncertainty and Profit* (Boston: Houghton Mifflin, 1921, reprinted as no. 16 in a series of reprints by the London School of Economics and Political Science). Knight made the distinction as follows: "The essential fact is that 'risk' means in some cases a quantity susceptible of measurement, while at other times it is something distinctly not of this character . . . It will appear that a 'measurable' uncertainty, or 'risk' proper, as we shall use the term, is so far different from an unmeasurable one that it is not in effect an uncertainty at all" (pp. 19–20).
[3]Ibid., pp. 224–25. The names *objective* and *subjective* probabilities, respectively, can also be used.

it. If probabilities of future events are assigned based on the past, then we are assuming that the future is a mirror of the past (which in itself could be construed to be an a priori judgment). Alternatively, probabilities obtained from past events can be adjusted to reflect changed expectations for the future.

## Sources of Business Risk

Before discussing how risk should be treated in economic analysis, it is important that we first explain the reasons a businessperson faces an uncertain future. What are some of the sources of business risk?

First, there are general economic conditions. Firms face rising and declining phases of business cycles. Some success can be attained in forecasting economic fluctuations, but the timing of changes and the volatility of economic activity are never known with certainty. Moreover, the effects of movements in general economic activity on a specific firm or a specific product are not known ahead of time. Thus, a firm does not have the ability to completely prepare for these changes.

In addition to uncertainty with respect to the economy as a whole, there are fluctuations in specific industries, which are at least as uncertain and may not always coincide with those of the overall economy.

Further, the actions of a company's competition are certainly not known perfectly. Closely related to competitive actions are changes in technology. If a competitor effectively introduces an improved product, sales of a particular company or even an industry may suffer. For instance, the introduction of e-mail has cut into the fax machine business and one-hour film development has hurt Polaroid's business. On the other hand, a firm's own technological breakthrough may bring about considerably increased sales.

The vagaries of consumer demand create another source of risk for the businessperson. Successful products of one year or one season may become the discarded, unwanted items of the next. It is easy to find examples of such products. "Tickle-Me-Elmo" dolls—hot items for a year—met their demise. The fashion industry is notorious for changes in styles and skirt lengths from one year to another. The great boom in bowling in the 1960s disappeared some years later and caused serious dislocations for the leading companies in the industry.

Not all sources of uncertainty stem from the demand side. In the process of decision making, a company must also consider costs and expenses. When estimates of future expenditures are made, the company cannot be sure what the prices of its factors of production will be (unless they are stipulated in contracts into which a company has entered). Thus, the prices of materials, such as sugar, corn starch, and flavorings, can change, and so can the costs of electricity and other services. Labor costs and the cost of benefits are also subject to change unless union contracts are in existence.

It is easy to see that almost any future business event is attended by uncertainty. Both revenues and costs per period as well as the length of life of a product are uncertain. Obviously, this greatly complicates the jobs of managers.

However, it appears that in the future, companies may be able to considerably decrease risk in their operations. In a recent development, insurance companies have entered the field to protect companies from experiencing shortfalls in their financial results that result from events not within management control. Early in 1999, the Reliance Group introduced a product called Enterprise Earnings Protection Insurance.

Other insurance companies are also selling similar policies. Thus, for instance, British Aerospace PLC purchased a policy "that guarantees its aircraft-leasing business will generate $3.7 billion in revenue over the next 15 years."[4] The Toro Company, a manufacturer of snow blowers, has contracted for a policy that insures refunds that the company offered its customers based on amounts of snowfall. What falls within the definition of "management control" may not be quite clear. Reliance's new policy, for instance, does not cover accounting changes and employee strikes. It is probably too early to tell how successful these new products will be, but certainly the expansion of insurance into this area contains considerable risk for insurance companies.

## The Measures of Risk

When outcomes are uncertain, two measures that take risk into consideration are used.

First, not just one outcome but a number of outcomes is possible. Each potential result will have a **probability** attached to it. In making estimates of a future cash inflow, for example, the analyst must decide on the probability of each possible result and construct a probability distribution.

A **probability distribution** describes, in percentage terms, the chances of all possible occurrences. When all the probabilities of the possible events are added up, they must total 1, because all possibilities together must equal certainty. Thus, we may assign probabilities to various possible cash flows as shown in Table 14.1.

The interpretation of Table 14.1 is as follows: We estimate that possible cash flows from a project during the coming year will be $3,000, $4,000, $5,000, $6,000 or $7,000. Which of the five possible flows actually occurs will depend, for instance, on general economic conditions, the conditions in the industry, and the action of the competition. If all factors are favorable to the project, the cash flow will be $7,000; if unfavorable conditions prevail, the cash flow will be only $3,000. One of the other outcomes will emerge if some factors work to our benefit and others are unfavorable. Table 14.1 can also be translated into a bar chart, shown in Figure 14.1.

The assigned probabilities indicate that there is only a 10 percent chance that all the unfavorable predictions will materialize. Similarly, there is only one chance in ten (i.e.,

| TABLE 14.1 Probability Distribution for Cash Inflows | |
|---|---|
| *Cash Inflow* | *Probability* |
| 3,000 | 0.1 |
| 4,000 | 0.2 |
| 5,000 | 0.4 |
| 6,000 | 0.2 |
| 7,000 | 0.1 |

---

[4]D. Brady, "Is Your Bottom Line Covered?" *Business Week,* February 8, 1999, p. 86 (the full article is on pp. 85–86). All data in this paragraph are from this same source.

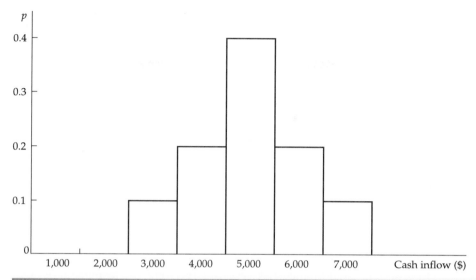

**FIGURE 14.1** Bar Graph of Data from Table 14.1

10 percent) that all of the favorable conditions will prevail. It is much more likely that some favorable and some unfavorable influences will ensue. Therefore, the probabilities for the intermediate cash flows are the highest.

Once we have established a probability distribution, we are ready to calculate the two measures used in decision making under conditions of risk.

**MODULE 14A**

### EXPECTED VALUE

From the numbers given in Table 14.1 we calculate a single value, the **expected value** of possible outcomes. The expected value is simply the average of all possible outcomes weighted by their respective probabilities.

$$\overline{R} = (3{,}000 \times 0.1) + (4{,}000 \times 0.2) + (5{,}000 \times 0.4) + (6{,}000 \times 0.2) + (7{,}000 \times 0.1)$$

$$= 300 + 800 + 2{,}000 + 1{,}200 + 700$$

$$= 5{,}000$$

where $\overline{R}$ represents the expected value. The generalized expression for expected value is as follows:

$$\overline{R} = \sum_{i=1}^{n} R_i p_i$$

where $\overline{R}$ = Expected value
$R_i$ = Value in case $i$
$p_i$ = Probability in case $i$
$n$ = Number of possible outcomes

| TABLE 14.2 | Calculation of Standard Deviation for Table 14.1 | | | |
|:---:|:---:|:---:|:---:|:---:|
| $R_i$ | $p_i$ | $(R_i - \overline{R})$ | $(R_i - \overline{R})^2$ | $(R_i - \overline{R})^2 p_i$ |
| 3,000 | 0.1 | −2,000 | 4,000,000 | 400,000 |
| 4,000 | 0.2 | −1,000 | 1,000,000 | 200,000 |
| 5,000 | 0.4 | 0 | 0 | 0 |
| 6,000 | 0.2 | 1,000 | 1,000,000 | 200,000 |
| 7,000 | 0.1 | 2,000 | 2,000,000 | 400,000 |
| | | | | 1,200,000 |

$$\sigma = \sqrt{1,200,000} = 1,095$$

Now that the weighted average—the expected value—has been obtained, we can determine the second measure, the one that specifies the extent of the risk.

## THE STANDARD DEVIATION

In economics and finance, risk is considered to be the dispersion of possible outcomes around the expected value. The greater the potential differences from the average, the greater the risk. Thus, to measure risk, we must find some yardstick that reflects the variation of possible outcomes from this average. A concept prominent in elementary statistics is used for this purpose—the standard deviation.[5]

The **standard deviation** is the square root of the weighted average of the squared deviations of all possible outcomes from the expected value:

$$\sigma = \sqrt{\sum_{i=1}^{n}(R_i - \overline{R})^2 p_i}$$

where $\sigma$ is the standard deviation. For the example in Table 14.1, the standard deviation is calculated in Table 14.2.

What is the meaning of a standard deviation of 1,095? First of all, since our probability distribution is symmetric, there is a 50 percent chance that the outcome will be larger than the expected value and a 50 percent chance that it will be less. The chance of a particular outcome occurring depends on how many standard deviations it is removed from the mean. Based on statistical theory describing the normal curve (which will be discussed more fully later), about 34 percent of all possible occurrences will be within one standard deviation of the mean, on each side of the mean, 47.7 percent within two standard deviations, and 49.9 percent within three standard deviations. Thus, given the expected value of 5,000 and standard deviation of 1,095, we conclude the following: There is 34 percent probability that the cash flow will fall between 5,000 and 5,000 − 1,095, or 3,905. In other words, there is a 16 percent probability that our cash flow will be 3,905 or lower. Further, because two standard deviations are equal to 2,190,

---

[5]If you wish to review the concept of standard deviation more thoroughly, any college statistics textbook can be consulted. See, for instance, Mark L. Berenson and David M. Levine, *Basic Business Statistics: Concepts and Applications,* 7th ed., Upper Saddle River, NJ: Prentice Hall, 1999.

**TABLE 14.3    Data for Project 2**

| $R_i$ | $p_i$ | $(R_i - \overline{R})$ | $(R_i - \overline{R})^2$ | $(R_i - \overline{R})^2 p_i$ |
|-------|-------|------------------------|---------------------------|------------------------------|
| 2,000 | 0.10 | −3,000 | 9,000,000 | 900,000 |
| 3,500 | 0.25 | −1,500 | 2,250,000 | 562,500 |
| 5,000 | 0.30 | 0 | 0 | 0 |
| 6,500 | 0.25 | 1,500 | 2,250,000 | 562,500 |
| 8,000 | 0.10 | 3,000 | 9,000,000 | 900,000 |
| | | | | 2,925,000 |

$$\overline{R} = 5,000$$

$$\sigma = \sqrt{2,925,000} = 1,710$$

there is a 2.3 percent probability (50 percent − 47.7 percent) that the cash flow will be 2,810 or lower. And it is almost certain that the cash flow will not fall below 1,715 (5,000 minus three standard deviations, or 3,285). The same reasoning leads us to conclude that chances are almost nil that the cash flow will exceed 8,285. There is a 16 percent probability that it will exceed 6,095, and so on.

The combination of the expected value and the standard deviation aids in making a decision between two projects. Suppose that we have to choose between project 1 (shown in Tables 14.1 and 14.2) and another, called project 2. Data for project 2 are shown in Table 14.3 and Figure 14.2 is the bar chart for this project.

**FIGURE 14.2** Bar Graph of Data from Table 14.3

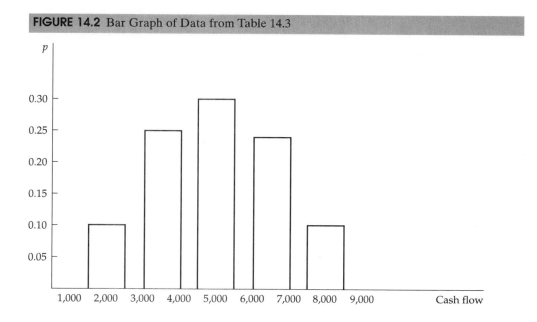

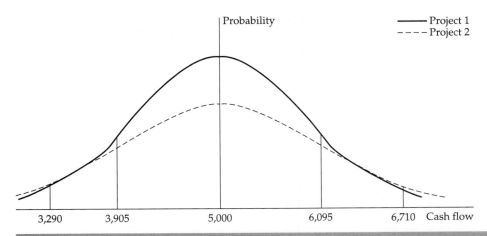

**FIGURE 14.3** Continuous Distributions for Projects 1 and 2

Since the expected values of the two proposals are identical, the decision will be made on the basis of the standard deviation. Project 2, with the greater standard deviation (1,710), is the riskier of the two. Generally, businesspeople are averse to risk; therefore, project 1, which has the lower risk, would usually be accepted.

## DISCRETE VERSUS CONTINUOUS DISTRIBUTIONS AND THE NORMAL CURVE

The frequency distributions that have been discussed so far are known as discrete.[6] The potential outcomes have been limited to just five numbers for each of the two projects. However, it is quite likely that other outcomes could occur—for instance, 4,679 or 6,227. If all possible outcomes are considered, we have a continuous distribution. The possible outcomes on a continuous distribution are often described by a bell-shaped curve, referred to as a *normal curve.* It is only on this type of curve that the properties of the standard deviation previously explained apply strictly. The two normal curves, shown in Figure 14.3, peak at the center, at the expected value, and are symmetrical on either side. Actually, the curves approach but do not reach zero at either end of the X-axis. Curves of this kind are called *asymptotic.*

With projects 1 and 2 drawn as continuous standard normal probability functions, project 1 exhibits a tighter curve, whereas project 2's curve is spread out over a much larger horizontal distance. Since project 1's standard deviation is 1,095, 34 percent of the area under its curve is between 5,000 and 3,905 (and also between 5,000 and 6,095). For project 2, whose standard deviation is 1,710, 34 percent of the area under the curve can be found between 5,000 and 3,290 (and also between 5,000 and 6,710).

The probabilities for any other range of numbers can be easily obtained from a table of values of the areas under the standard normal distribution function (see Table

---

[6]They are also symmetrical, which means that the observations to the left and to the right of the mean have the same probabilities and the same deviations from the mean.

B.2 in Appendix B at the end of this text). If, in assessing project 1, we wish to find the probability that the cash flow will be between, for example, 3,200 and 5,000, we can apply the following formula:

$$Z = \frac{X - \overline{R}}{\sigma}$$

where $Z$ = Number of standard deviations from the mean
$X$ = Variable in which we are interested

Thus,

$$Z = \frac{3,2000 - 5,000}{1,095} = \frac{-1,800}{1,095} = -1.64$$

The quantity 3,200 is 1.64 standard deviations below the mean. Looking up 1.64 in Table B.2, we find the value to be 0.4495. Thus, the probability that the cash flow will be between 3,200 and 5,000 is 45 percent. Since the left half of the normal curve represents 50 percent of all probabilities, we can also state that the chance of the cash flow being below 3,200 is 5.0 percent.

## THE COEFFICIENT OF VARIATION

When the expected values of two projects are equal, or at least close to one another, the standard deviation is a proper measure of risk. But since the standard deviation is an absolute measure, it may not serve our purposes if the two projects being compared have divergent expected values. For example, compare the two following hypothetical projects:

|  | *Expected Value* | *Standard Deviation* |
|---|---|---|
| Project A | 100 | 30 |
| Project B | 50 | 20 |

Project A has both the larger expected value and the larger standard deviation.

Since the expected values of the two projects are so dissimilar, an absolute measure of risk may not give an adequate answer. In such cases, another concept is introduced, the **coefficient of variation,** which measures risk relative to expected value. The simple formula for the coefficient of variation is

$$CV = \sigma/\overline{R}$$

For the two projects,

$$CV_A = 30/100 = 0.30$$

$$CV_B = 20/50 = 0.40$$

The coefficient of variation is greater for project B. Thus, despite the fact that project A's standard deviation is higher in absolute terms, its relative risk is lower. Since project A's expected value is greater and relative risk is smaller, project A is preferable.

The coefficient of variation will provide a satisfactory solution in most cases. However, when it does not, the businessperson will have to make a choice based on the perception of whether the risk is worth the potential return.[7]

## Capital Budgeting under Conditions of Risk

So far the discussion of expected value and risk has been limited to the results of one period only. However, the assessment of risk is even more important when plans span a term of several years. So we now turn to the question of how to deal with a capital investment proposal in which an initial outlay of funds promises to return cash flows over some period into the future. In chapter 13 the analysis of capital projects was discussed, but risk was not considered explicitly.

The first task is to calculate the net present value of the expected values obtained in each year, or the expected net present value. For a three-year project with one initial investment, we can use the following equation:

$$\overline{NPV} = \frac{\overline{R}_1}{1 + r_f} + \frac{\overline{R}_2}{(1 + r_f)^2} + \frac{\overline{R}_3}{(1 + r_f)^3} - O_0$$

or, in more general terms,

$$\overline{NPV} = \sum_{t=1}^{n} \frac{\overline{R}_t}{(1 + r_f)^t} - O_0$$

where $\overline{NPV}$ = Expected net present value
$\overline{R}_t$ = Expected values of the annual cash inflows
$O_0$ = Initial investment
$r_f$ = Risk-free interest rate

It should be noted that the expected cash flows are discounted at the riskless interest rate. Since risk is considered separately (in calculating the standard deviation), discounting at a rate that includes a risk premium could result in double-counting risk.[8]

---

[7]The economic theory of the marginal utility of money can also provide a way to incorporate risk in decision making. Although such an approach is quite elegant, it is somewhat doubtful that it can be utilized in most practical situations. To apply this approach, one would have to know the utility function of the decision maker, or of the stockholders the decision maker represents. This appears to be a rather monumental task. However, in the final analysis, it is the decision maker's perception of risk that determines the shape of the utility function. Thus, the decision is a subjective one. For a more detailed explanation of utility, see for example, Haim Levy and Marshall Sarnat, *Capital Investment and Financial Decisions,* 5th ed., Hertfordshire, England: Prentice Hall International, 1994, p. 221 ff. This exposition is based on the famous work of John Von Neumann and Oskar Morgenstern, *Theory of Games and Economic Behavior,* 2nd ed., Princeton, NJ: Princeton University Press, 1953.

[8]Actually, the use of the proper discount rate is subject to some controversy. In discounting at the risk-free rate, we have followed the method recommended in several books, Levy and Sarnat, *Capital Investment,* pp. 243–44; and James C. Van Horne, *Financial Management and Policy,* 10th ed., Upper Saddle River, NJ: Prentice Hall, 1995, pp. 179–81. However, other authors suggest that the company's (or the specific unit's or project's) risk-adjusted discount rate is more appropriate. See, for example, Lawrence J. Gitman, Michael D. Joehnk, and George E. Pinches, *Managerial Finance,* New York: Harper & Row, 1985, pp. 582–83; and Eugene F. Brigham and Louis C. Gapenski, *Intermediate Financial Management,* 5th ed., Fort Worth, TX: Dryden, 1996, p. 291. Using the lower, risk-free rate will increase the project's net present value and make it more acceptable.

**TABLE 14.4 Capital Budgeting Under Risk**

EXPECTED VALUE

| Year 0 | Year 1 | | Year 2 | |
|--------|--------|--------|--------|--------|
| | $p$ | $R$ | $p$ | $R$ |
| $-500$ | .2 | 300 | .25 | 400 |
| | .6 | 500 | .50 | 500 |
| | .2 | 700 | .25 | 600 |
| $\overline{R}$ | | 500 | | 500 |

$$r = 0.05$$
$$\overline{NPV} = 500/1.05 + 500/1.05^2 - 500$$
$$= 476 + 454 - 500 = 430$$

STANDARD DEVIATION

| | Year 1 | | | | Year 2 | | |
|---|---|---|---|---|---|---|---|
| $p$ | $(R - \overline{R})$ | $(R - \overline{R})^2$ | $(R - \overline{R})^2 p$ | $p$ | $(R - \overline{R})$ | $(R - \overline{R})^2$ | $(R - \overline{R})^2 p$ |
| .2 | $-200$ | 40,000 | 8,000 | .25 | $-100$ | 10,000 | 2,500 |
| .6 | 0 | 0 | 0 | .50 | 0 | 0 | 0 |
| .2 | $+200$ | 40,000 | 8,000 | .25 | $+100$ | 10,000 | 2,500 |
| | | | 16,000 | | | | 5,000 |

$$\sigma = \sqrt{16,000/1.05^2 + 5,000/1.05^4}$$
$$= \sqrt{14,512 + 4,114} = \sqrt{18,626} = 136$$

The standard deviation of the present value is

$$\sigma = \sqrt{\sum_{t=1}^{n} \frac{\sigma_t^2}{(1 + r_f)^{2t}}}$$

where $\sigma$ = Standard deviation of NPV

$\sigma_t$ = Standard deviation of each year's cash flow

Note that the exponent in the denominator of the expression is *2t*. Thus, the first year's $\sigma$ will be discounted at $(1 + r_f)^2$, the second at $(1 + r_f)^4$, and so on.

A simple numerical example will conclude this section. Table 14.4 shows that for a two-year project with a cash flow distribution and probabilities as specified, and with an initial investment of $500, the expected net present value is $430, and the standard deviation is 136. From these results we can conclude that chances are almost zero that NPV will be less than 22 (430 minus three standard deviations of 136) or more than 838 (430 plus three standard deviations of 136).

The preceding calculations are generally valid when the cash flows over the years are independent, that is, if in the case depicted in Table 14.4, the results in year 2 are not influenced by those of year 1.

# Two Other Methods for Incorporating Risk

Two other techniques of accounting for risk are commonly used. Both of these make the risk adjustment within the present-value calculation (without the use of the standard deviation), so that the final result is just one number: the net present value adjusted for risk. The two methods are

1. The **risk-adjusted discount rate (RADR),** in which the risk adjustment is made in the denominator of the present-value calculation
2. The **certainty equivalent,** in which the numerator of the present-value calculation is adjusted for risk

### THE RISK-ADJUSTED DISCOUNT RATE (RADR)

RADR is probably the most practical risk adjustment method and is the one most frequently used in business. In fact, we employed this technique in chapter 13 in the discussion of the cost of capital. The discount rate at which capital project flows are discounted to the present comprises two components, the riskless (or risk-free) rate, $r_f$, and the risk premium, RP:

$$k = r_f + \text{RP}$$

The risk-free rate is, in the ideal sense, the pure time value of money. Since such a rate is very difficult—if not impossible—to establish, it is usually represented by yields on short-term U.S. Treasury securities.[9] The risk premium represents a judgment as to the additional return necessary to compensate for additional risk.

For example, assume that the risk-free rate is 6 percent, but that a corporation uses a cost of capital of 10 percent for projects thought to carry average risk. The risk premium is 4 percent. However, that does not mean that each part of the company should always use the 10 percent discount rate. A company may be composed of divisions with different levels of risk. Suppose a company is made up of two divisions of similar size: the Sure division (for instance, a supermarket) and the Risk division (a high-tech operation). If these had been separate companies, their risk-adjusted discount rates would have been 8 and 12 percent respectively. These discount rates should be used rather than the average 10 percent for the company as a whole. If the average were to be used, the company's resources may be misallocated. For instance, a Sure division project with an IRR of 9.5 percent would have been rejected, while a Risk division project with an IRR of 11 percent would have been accepted. If the correct adjusted discount rates had been used, the Sure division project would have been accepted (its IRR is higher than its discount rate, and NPV is positive), while the Risk division project would have been rejected. Additionally, different projects within a division should often be evaluated at different discount rates. Suppose the Risk division is analyzing two projects, the development of a new product and the replacement of some inefficient equipment. Obviously, the former should be discounted at a higher rate than the latter because of the different levels of risk.

---

[9]Of course, even the shortest of U.S. Treasuries, the three-month bill, includes an inflation factor in its yield.

A recent study shows that about 70 percent of a sample of companies drawn from the *Fortune* 1,000 either individually measure project risk or group projects into risk classes.[10]

Of course, it must be recognized that developing risk-adjusted discount rates involves a large amount of judgment. But even if such adjustments are necessarily judgmental, they are very important. Companies with staffs capable of such refinements have developed some methods for differentiating discount rates.[11]

## CERTAINTY EQUIVALENTS

In calculating the risk-adjusted discount rate, the inclusion of risk in the calculation of present value is accomplished by altering the discount rate or the cost of capital, that is, the denominator of the discounting equation.[12] Another technique for including risk in the calculation of present values is to work through the numerator of the cash flow fraction; that is, the cash flow itself is adjusted to account for risk. Basically, this is accomplished by applying a factor to the cash flow to convert a risky flow into a riskless one. Since, as was said before, businesspeople tend to be risk-averse, they are expected to prefer a smaller cash flow that is certain (risk-free) over one that is attended by risky conditions. To accomplish this, the risky cash flow must be reduced by some amount, or multiplied by a number smaller than 1. We will refer to this adjustor as the *certainty equivalent factor.*

However, assigning a size to the certainty equivalent factor is fraught with at least as many problems as estimating the risk premium. But when all is said and done, the size of the certainty equivalent factor depends on the decision maker's attitude toward risk. Thus, if she decides that a specific risky cash flow (or the expected value of the risky cash flow) of $500 is equivalent to a risk-free cash flow of $450, the certainty equivalent factor, $a_t$, equals 0.9:

$$0.9 \times 500 = 450$$

So, for each risky cash flow, $R_t$, a certainty equivalent factor is assigned. If risk increases as a function of time, the certainty equivalent factors will decrease as we move into the future. For instance, a project could have the following cash flows and certainty equivalent factors:

| Period | $R_t$ | $a_t$ | $a_t R_t$ |
|--------|-------|-------|-----------|
| 1 | 100 | 0.95 | 95 |
| 2 | 200 | 0.90 | 180 |
| 3 | 200 | 0.85 | 170 |
| 4 | 100 | 0.80 | 80 |

[10]Lawrence J. Gitman and Vincent A. Mercurio, "Cost of Capital Techniques Used by Major U.S. Firms: Survey and Analysis of Fortune's 1000," *Financial Management,* winter 1982, pp. 21–29.
[11]See, for instance, Benton E. Gup and Samuel W. Norwood, III, "Divisional Cost of Capital: A Practical Approach," *Financial Management,* spring 1982, pp. 20–24. See also Grenville S. Andrews and Colin Firer "Why Different Divisions Require Different Hurdle Rates," *Long Range Planning,* 20, 5, 1987, pp. 62–68.
[12]In other words, the discounted cash flows can be expressed as follows:

$$PV = \sum_{t=1}^{n} \frac{\overline{R}_t}{(1 + r_t + RP)^t}$$

The risk is included in the formula by increasing the denominator for higher levels of RP.

The risk-free cash flows, $a_t R_t$, are obviously smaller than the risky flows, $R_t$, as would be expected for a risk-averse investor. These risk-free cash flows are then discounted at the risk-free interest rate to obtain the present value of the cash flows.

### RADR VERSUS CERTAINTY EQUIVALENTS

Two methods of accounting for risk without specifically calculating a standard deviation have just been presented. Which of the two is preferable? The certainty equivalent technique appears to be more sophisticated and is often recommended by people in academia. Businesspeople prefer RADR, which is by far the more frequently used technique. The reason for this preference is fairly obvious. It is considerably easier to make a rough estimate of the cost of capital than to specifically calculate each cash flow's certainty equivalent factor. However, it can be shown that the two methods arrive at identical results if the calculations and adjustments are made in a consistent manner.

The present value of a risky cash flow discounted at the risk-adjusted discount rate can be written as follows:

$$\frac{R_t}{(1 + k)^t}$$

On the other hand, the present value of a risk-adjusted cash flow discounted at the risk-free rate is:

$$\frac{a_t R_t}{(1 + r_f)^t}$$

If the two discounted cash flows are to be equal, then:

$$\frac{R_t}{(1 + k)^t} = \frac{a_t R_t}{(1 + r_f)^t}$$

$$a_t = \frac{(1 + r_f)^t}{(1 + k)^t}$$

Thus, the certainty equivalent factor is equal to $(1 + r_f)$ divided by $(1 + k)$, each term raised to the appropriate power. It must be noted that, in this solution, $a_t$ decreases over time while $k$ remains constant. This implies that given a constant $k$, risk increases over time. If this is the case, then using a constant $k$ is appropriate. However, there may be other cases in which risk does not grow with time. Therefore, an analyst should be aware that using a constant RADR may penalize longer-term projects that in fact do not exhibit higher risks.

# Sensitivity Analysis

**MODULE 14B**

**Sensitivity analysis** is a very pragmatic way to estimate project risk. It involves identifying the key variables that affect the results (the NPV of a project or its internal rate of return), and then changing each variable (and sometimes a combination of variables) to ascertain the size of the impact.

To explain and illustrate the concept of sensitivity analysis, we will utilize the data that were presented in Table 13.4 of the previous chapter. However, we will simplify the

| TABLE 14.5 Expansion Project: Sensitivity Analysis Worksheet ($000) | | | | | | | | | |
|---|---|---|---|---|---|---|---|---|---|
| | *Constant* | *Year 0* | *Year 1* | *Year 2* | *Year 3* | *Year 4* | *Year 5* | *Year 6* | *Year 7* |
| Total market | 4.0% | | | 100,000 | 104,000 | 108,160 | 112,486 | 116,986 | 121,665 |
| Market share (%) | | | | 1.0 | 2.0 | 3.0 | 4.0 | 5.0 | 5.0 |
| Company sales (qty) | | | | 1,000 | 2,080 | 3,245 | 4,499 | 5,849 | 6,083 |
| Expenditures | | (5,000) | (2,000) | | | | | | |
| Working capital | | | (750) | | | | | | |
| Start-up expense | (750) | | (450) | | | | | | |
| Sales | 5.00 | | | 5,000 | 10,400 | 16,224 | 22,497 | 29,246 | 30,416 |
| Prod. & distrib. cost | 3.10 | | | 3,100 | 6,448 | 10,059 | 13,948 | 18,133 | 18,858 |
| Variable expenses | 8.0% | | | 400 | 832 | 1,298 | 1,800 | 2,340 | 2,433 |
| Fixed costs | | | | 1,031 | 1,361 | 1,121 | 1,001 | 911 | 881 |
| Total cost & expenses | | | | 4,531 | 8,641 | 12,478 | 16,749 | 21,384 | 22,172 |
| Net earnings before taxes | | | | 469 | 1,759 | 3,746 | 5,748 | 7,863 | 8,244 |
| Income tax | 40% | | | 188 | 704 | 1,498 | 2,299 | 3,145 | 3,298 |
| Net earnings after taxes | | | | 281 | 1,055 | 2,248 | 3,449 | 4,718 | 4,946 |
| Add: depreciation | | | | 531 | 861 | 621 | 501 | 411 | 381 |
| Operating cash flow | | | | 812 | 1,916 | 2,869 | 3,950 | 5,129 | 5,327 |
| Remaining values | | | | | | | | | |
| Land | | | | | | | | | 500 |
| Plant | | | | | | | | | 2,833 |
| Equipment | | | | | | | | | 360 |
| Working capital | 80.0% | | | | | | | | 660 |
| Total cash flow | | (5,000) | (3,200) | 812 | 1,916 | 2,869 | 3,950 | 5,129 | 9,680 |
| Net present value | 15.0% | | | | | | | | 3,552 |
| Internal rate of return | | | | | | | | | 24.2% |

worksheet by combining product and distribution costs, which are a function of the number of cases shipped; by combining expenses, which are a percentage of dollar revenue; and by combining all the fixed costs. This is shown in Table 14.5.

We must now decide which of the lines in the projected cash flow statement will have the greatest impact on results. The following four items are probably key factors:[13]

1. Number of cases sold
2. Sales price
3. Product and distribution costs
4. Variable expenses

---

[13]We could have included a fifth variable, terminal values. We leave this calculation to the reader. Would variations in terminal values have an important effect on your final results?

**Table 14.6 Results of Sensitivity Analysis: Expansion Project (NPV in $000)**

| Change (%) | Sales | Sales Price | Cost | Variable Expenses |
|:---:|:---:|:---:|:---:|:---:|
| +40 | 7,524 | 15,731 | −4,655 | 2,493 |
| +30 | 6,531 | 12,687 | −2,603 | 2,758 |
| +20 | 5,538 | 9,642 | −552 | 3,023 |
| +10 | 4,545 | 6,597 | 1,500 | 3,287 |
| 0 | 3,552 | 3,552 | 3,552 | 3,552 |
| −10 | 2,559 | 507 | 5,604 | 3,817 |
| −20 | 1,567 | −2,537 | 7,656 | 4,082 |
| −30 | 574 | −5,582 | 9,708 | 4,347 |
| −40 | −419 | −8,627 | 11,760 | 4,611 |

Because the amount of capital expenditures is fairly certain, fixed costs will not be used as a test variable.

Next, a decision must be made on the range of the changes in the variables. The changes will be tested at 10 percent intervals between −40 percent and +40 percent. Admittedly, these are very wide ranges, and the extremes would represent very serious deviations from the best estimates. However, using such wide ranges is quite useful in pointing out by how much the forecasters would have had to miss their estimates to convert a positive NPV into a negative one. Furthermore, should a particular percentage point in between appear to be important for the analysis, it could easily be computed and added to the table of numbers. The results are summarized in Table 14.6.

Of the four variables selected for closer scrutiny, sales price appears to have the most serious impact. NPV turns negative if the price per case drops by a little over 10 percent. Of course, this will occur only if production and distribution costs do not decrease concurrently. But there is no reason that they should, unless the price decrease follows a cost decrease. Prices could decline for other reasons, such as intense competition.

Because a large amount of variable costs and expenses can be saved if sales quantities do not come up to the best estimate, a drop in sales of about 35 percent below estimated levels would have to occur before NPV would become negative. On the other hand, an increase of between 10 and 20 percent in production and distribution costs would make the NPV unacceptable. An error in the estimate of the relationship of variable expenses to revenue would not have a significant impact on net present value.

One other analysis should also be performed: the effect of an error in the assumed discount rate. Fifteen percent was the risk-adjusted rate that was employed. Since the internal rate of return on the project was 24.2 percent, it would take an increase of more than 9 percentage points to reverse the recommendation. That appears to be too large a margin to occur within any reasonable assumptions.

Sensitivity analysis is commonly used in business. Its outcomes can be displayed in a simple and straightforward manner. It permits analysts (and their managers) to evaluate each of the important variables and to examine the trade-offs among them. It can easily utilize a spreadsheet program to generate alternative results quickly.

# Simulation

Although the sensitivity analysis technique is popular with business, it does not make use of probability distributions. There is one method that does: simulation. In **simulation analysis,** each of the key variables is assigned a probability distribution. Thus, for instance, the sales variable of our previous example could be given the following distribution:

| Deviation From Estimate Value (%) | Probability | Cumulative Probability |
|:---:|:---:|:---:|
| −30 | 0.1 | 0.1 |
| −15 | 0.2 | 0.3 |
| 0 | 0.4 | 0.7 |
| +15 | 0.2 | 0.9 |
| +30 | 0.1 | 1.0 |

The column of cumulative probabilities indicates that there is a 10 percent chance that sales will be 30 percent lower than the base case. Furthermore, the probability is 30 percent that sales will be at least 15 percent below the base case, 70 percent that sales will not exceed the base estimate, and so on. Similar distributions would be estimated for the other important variables.

The device of random numbers is used to "simulate" a possible outcome. Suppose a random number generator with numbers from 1 to 100 is utilized. For this case, we can assign numbers from 1 to 10 to represent the −30 percent case. Any number between 11 and 30 (which has a 20 percent chance of being drawn) would stand for a −15 percent sales situation. All numbers between 31 and 70 would represent 0 percent deviation (the base case estimate) and so on.

We will also assign probability distributions to the other three variables considered to have significant impacts on net present value. The next step is to generate a random number for each of these four key variables, obtain the appropriate values, and calculate an NPV figure. This process will then be repeated a large number of times, each time generating another NPV figure. The NPVs thus generated will form a probability distribution and also enable the analyst to calculate a standard deviation as well as a $z$-statistic.[14]

To show how each NPV can be obtained, we will calculate one iteration with the distributions shown in Table 14.7. Suppose the random numbers generated turn out to be 24, 37, 69, and 29, respectively. These numbers are associated with sales 15 percent below expectations, sales price and costs at expected values (i.e., 0 percent deviation), and variable expenses 5 percent below the best estimates. They result in a net present value of 2,175 and an internal rate of return of 20.9 percent. If we repeat this operation

---

[14]The simulation procedure discussed here is based on a technique introduced by David B. Hertz in "Risk Analysis in Capital Investment," *Harvard Business Review,* January–February 1964, pp. 95–106, and "Investment Policies that Pay Off," *Harvard Business Review,* January–February 1968, pp. 96–108.

| TABLE 14.7 Simulation Analysis | | | | | |
|---|---|---|---|---|---|
| Sales: | | | | | |
| Deviation from expected value (%) | −30 | −15 | 0 | +15 | +30 |
| Probability | 0.1 | 0.2 | 0.4 | 0.2 | 0.1 |
| Cumulative probability | 0.1 | 0.3 | 0.7 | 0.9 | 1.0 |
| Sales price: | | | | | |
| Deviation from expected value (%) | −20 | −10 | 0 | +10 | +20 |
| Probability | 0.1 | 0.25 | 0.3 | 0.25 | 0.1 |
| Cumulative probability | 0.1 | 0.35 | 0.65 | 0.90 | 1.0 |
| Production and distribution costs: | | | | | |
| Deviation from expected value (%) | −10 | −5 | 0 | +5 | +10 |
| Probability | 0.1 | 0.15 | 0.5 | 0.15 | 0.1 |
| Cumulative probability | 0.1 | 0.25 | 0.75 | 0.9 | 1.0 |
| Variable expenses: | | | | | |
| Deviation from expected value (%) | −10 | −5 | 0 | +5 | +10 |
| Probability | 0.1 | 0.2 | 0.4 | 0.2 | 0.1 |
| Cumulative probability | 0.1 | 0.3 | 0.7 | 0.9 | 1.0 |

a large number of times—say one thousand—we will obtain a frequency distribution of NPVs. Such a procedure appears to be very time consuming and cumbersome. However, thanks to the existence of computers, a large number of iterations can be obtained quickly and effortlessly.

Simulation can be a good tool for decision making. However, the illustration used here is severely simplified and may not be sufficient for the solution of complex business problems. In obtaining the preceding solution, we made at least two assumptions that may have omitted some important relationships among the variables. First, we assumed that the deviations obtained with the use of random numbers remain the same in each year for which estimated cash flows were calculated. This need not be the case. A set of different random number calculations for each year may have been more appropriate. With the use of a computer, such calculations could have been taken care of quite efficiently.

Even more important, it has been assumed here that the four variables are statistically independent. It is much more likely that the various factors are interrelated. For example, a shortfall in market demand may have a negative effect on the price of each case of soft drinks. An unexpected increase in sales may have an effect on costs: in the short run, cost per unit may rise as plant employees work overtime at increased wages. If such interdependencies actually exist, they must be included in the simulation model. Such a model would, of course, be considerably more complex. A large number of estimates relating to these relationships would have to be made. And even though such a model would present the manager with a significant amount of useful information, the final decision, as in all cases, would still have to be based on the decision maker's judgment. In other words, no amount of data and information will substitute for mature business thinking.

# Decision Trees

One other method for making decisions under conditions of risk is the **decision tree.** This technique is especially suitable when decisions have to be made sequentially, for instance, if a decision two years hence depends on the outcome of an action undertaken today. Such decision making can be extremely complex, and the use of a tree diagram facilitates the process because it illustrates the sequence in which decisions must be made. It also compares the values (e.g., net present values) of the various actions that can be undertaken.

The best way to explain the technique is to use a relatively uncomplicated example. To manufacture a new product, a company must decide whether to buy a larger, more expensive, and more productive machine or a smaller, less expensive, and less productive one. If the demand for this new product turns out to be at the high end of the forecast, the purchase of the larger machine may turn out to be profitable; the smaller machine does not possess sufficient capacity to produce large quantities efficiently, and its purchase would require an additional machine to be purchased to satisfy the high demand. On the other hand, should the optimistic forecast turn out to be wrong, then the larger machine, if it were the one originally acquired, would not be used to capacity. The smaller machine, in this case, would be able to produce the quantities needed efficiently and profitably.

Such a scenario could be played out over several years, but we will assume that the life of this project, as well as of the machines, is just two years. The market and cash flow forecasts have been put together, and the decision tree analysis can begin. To simplify our task here, and also to save steps involving familiar calculations, we will assume that all flows occurring in the future (i.e., years 1 and 2) have already been converted to present values.

Table 14.8 shows all the probabilities and forecasts, and Figure 14.4 illustrates the decision tree with the resulting calculations. The first step in the analysis is to set up all the "branches" of the decision tree. As we move from left to right on the diagram, we are faced with decision points (e.g., acquire the large machine versus the small machine) and with chance events (e.g., the probabilities are 50/50 that the demand will be high/low). On the diagram, decision points are designated with squares and chance events with circles. When the entire tree is completed, the procedure is to move back from right to left, calculate the value of each branch, and where appropriate combine or eliminate branches.

Starting in the upper right, if the large machine is acquired and year 1 demand is high, there is a 75 percent probability that the second-year (present-value) cash flow will be $500 and a 25 percent probability that it will be $100. The expected value is, therefore, $400. If the first-year demand is high, cash flow will be $150 in year 1, so the present value of the cash flow of years 1 and 2 combined will be $550. If first-year demand is low, the expected value of the second set of branches will be $−37.50 (0.25 × 300 + 0.75 × −150). The cash flow in year 1 when demand is low is $−50, so the present value of the two cash flows combined will be $−87.50. As the probabilities are 50/50 that first-year demand will be high/low, the present value of cash flows, if the large machine is purchased, is $231.25 (0.5 × 550 + 0.5 × −87.50). Now the original investment of $250 must be deducted, and the result is an NPV of $−18.75.

If the small machine is acquired, a decision must be made at the end of year 1 if demand in that year is high: Should a second machine be purchased? If first-year demand

| TABLE 14.8 Decision Tree Inputs | | |
|---|---|---|
| DEMAND FORECASTS | | |
| Year 1: | High 50% | Low 50% |
| Year 2: | | |
| If year 1 is high: | High 75% | Low 25% |
| If year 1 is low: | High 25% | Low 75% |
| COST OF MACHINE | | |
| Large $250 | Small $150 | |
| CASH FLOWS (PRESENT VALUES) | | |
| If large machine is acquired: | | |
| Year 1: | | |
| If demand is high: | $150 | |
| If demand is low: | $−50 | |
| Year 2: | | |
| If year 1 demand is high: | | |
| If demand is high: | $500 | |
| If demand is low: | $100 | |
| If year 1 demand is low: | | |
| If demand is high: | $300 | |
| If demand is low: | $−150 | |
| If small machine is acquired: | | |
| Year 1: | | |
| If demand is high: | $100 | |
| If demand is low: | $30 | |
| Year 2: | | |
| If year 1 demand is high and second machine is acquired: | | |
| If demand is high: | $400 | |
| If demand is low: | $80 | |
| If year 1 demand is high and second machine is not acquired: | | |
| If demand is high: | $250 | |
| If demand is low: | $120 | |
| If year 1 demand is low: | | |
| If demand is high: | $150 | |
| If demand is low: | $0 | |

is high and the second machine is acquired, then the present value of the year 2 cash flow is $320 (0.75 × 400 + 0.25 × 80). If the second machine is not acquired, the cash flow is $217.50 (0.75 × 250 + 0.25 × 120). Since it would cost $150 to obtain the second small machine, the NPV of the former result is only $170 compared to $217.50. Therefore, the decision at this point would be not to expand productive capacity. We put an X over the "additional machine" branch in the tree to signify that we will ignore this branch as we continue our evaluation. So, if first-year demand is high with a cash flow of $100, the present value of the upper branch will be $217.50 + $100, or $317.50.

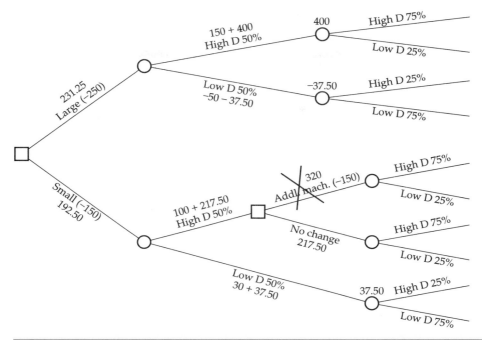

**FIGURE 14.4** Decision Tree Analysis

One more branch needs to be addressed. If the small machine is selected and demand is low in the first year, then the second-year expected value of the cash flow will be $37.50 (0.25 × 150 + 0.75 × 0). Adding the first-year cash flow to this branch, we obtain $67.50 ($37.50 + $30). To complete the calculation of the net present value for the small-machine alternative, each of the two present values must be multiplied by 0.5, since this is the probability that the first year's demand will be high/low: 0.5 × 317.50 + 0.5 × 67.50 equals $192.50. Subtracting the cost of the smaller machine, $150, we find that the net present value is $42.50. The final step is to compare the expected net present values of the two alternatives. The expected NPV if the large machine is acquired is $−18.75; if the smaller machine is selected, it is $42.50. Thus, it is obvious that the smaller machine is the better choice. Indeed, the large machine would have been unacceptable in any case, as its net present value is negative.

The preceding solution is not quite complete, as the decision is being made on the basis of expected net present value alone. There has been no calculation of standard deviations, so we have, in effect, ignored the differences in risk between the large- and small-machine alternatives. As mentioned in note 7 of this chapter, risk can also be measured by the use of utility analysis. Each of the outcomes could have been assigned an expected utility, and instead of maximizing net present value, as we did in this example, the objective would have been to maximize utility.

# Real Options in Capital Budgeting

The subject of decision trees, just discussed, points to a possible event we have not discussed previously: a capital budgeting decision does not have to be set in concrete at the beginning of the project.

Up to now, in analyzing capital budgeting decisions, we made estimates of costs, cash flows, life of the project, and probabilities of outcomes, and then proceeded to calculate the net present value or the internal rate of return. But we did not consider that there might be an opportunity for making changes in some aspects of the project while it is in progress or to make adjustments even before the project is started. The ability to make changes is commonly referred to as **real options** that are imbedded in the capital project.[15]

These real options may increase the value of a project above that resulting from a straightforward discounted cash flow calculation. The value of the option is the difference between the project's value with and without the option. We can represent this result with the following simple equation:

$$\text{Value of the project} = \text{NPV} + \text{option value}$$

Indeed, if such an option is taken into consideration, it may result in the acceptance of a project that was considered unacceptable without the option. (In other words, it can convert a project with a negative NPV to one with a positive NPV.)[16]

There are various forms of real options:

1. *Option to vary output.* Some projects can be structured to permit operations to expand if demand rises above expectations (this is usually called a *growth option*), or to contract operations if demand falters. It may even allow for a temporary shutdown of production.

2. *Option to vary inputs—flexibility.* A plant may include the possibility of operating with different types of fuel. While the original cost of the plant may be higher, switching from a more expensive fuel to a less expensive one may make the project more favorable. Another potential flexibility is that of taking advantage of different technologies depending on input costs.

3. *Option to abandon.* If, after the project has been started, results turn sour, it is possible that abandoning the project will improve its payoff. If the project can be sold for a price higher than the present value of its expected cash flows, or if its facilities can be utilized more favorably in another part of the company, then abandoning the project will enhance its value.

4. *Option to postpone.* An oil company may profit by postponing the extraction of oil from its field, if the current prices are low but are expected to rise in the future. A company may postpone the introduction of a new product pending completion of market research to better evaluate the product's potential.

---

[15]Real options have a similarity to financial options, which are an important subject in managerial finance. An option gives the holder the right, but not the obligation, to take an action in the future.

[16]For a more detailed introduction to real options, consult the following articles: A. K. Dixit and R. S. Pindyck, "The Options Approach to Capital Investment," *Harvard Business Review,* May–June 1995, pp. 105–115; and N. Kulatilaka and A. J. Marcus, "Project Valuation Under Uncertainty; When Does DCF Fail?" *Journal of Applied Corporate Finance,* 5, 3 (fall 1992), pp. 92–100. A leading book in this field is Lenos Trigeorgis, *Real Options,* Cambridge, MA: MIT Press, 1997. For a recent article on this subject, see P. Coy, "Exploiting Uncertainty," *Business Week,* June 7, 1999, pp. 118–124.

In both of these cases there is, of course, a cost involved in the postponement, whether it is the cost of delaying cash inflows or of incurring the expense of market research. However, the benefits of the postponement may exceed these costs, and thus create a positive value for the postponement option.

Another reason for postponement may be the expectation of decreases in interest rates. Lower interest rates would decrease the project's required rate of return and thus increase its present value. It must be remembered, however, that by postponing action, the company may lose the "first-mover" advantage.

5. *Option to introduce future products.* A company may be willing to launch a product with a negative NPV, if doing so gives it an option to gain an advantage when later versions of the product are introduced.

## AN ABANDONMENT OPTION

We will conclude this brief introduction to real options with a simple example. We will see that by including the option to abandon the project, we will convert a project with a negative NPV to a positive one.

The data for this project are as follows (all dollar amounts are in thousands):

1. The life of the project is 2 years.
2. The original cash outflow is $8,000.
3. The potential cash inflows in year 1 are $3,000 or $6,000, each with a probability of 50 percent.
4. If the first year's cash inflow is $3,000, the second year's cash inflows will be either $2,000 or $4,000, each with a probability of 50 percent.
5. If the first year's cash inflow is $6,000, the second year's cash inflows will be $5,000 or $7,000, each with a probability of 50 percent.
6. The project can be abandoned at the end of year one. The expected abandonment value is $3,500.
7. The project's discount rate is 10 percent.

The calculations are shown in Table 14.9. The upper third of the table shows the NPV calculation if abandonment is not included. The cash flows and their present value at period 0 are shown. Then the probabilities are calculated. Each of the four potential outcomes has a probability of 25 percent. The present value of the cash flows is $7,810, and the expected NPV is a negative $190. Thus, the project would be rejected.

In the second third of the table we show the present value at the end of period 1 of the year 2 cash inflows. We can see that if the first year's cash inflow was $3,000, and the second year's were either $2,000 or $4,000, the PV of these two cash flows at the end of year 1 is $2,727, less than the abandonment value. The expected $PV_1$ of the two higher cash flows is $5,455, well above the abandonment value.

In the last section of the table, we substitute the abandonment value of $3,500 into the calculation, and compute the expected $PV_0$. The expected $PV_0$ is now $8,161, which gives us a positive NPV of $161. With the abandonment option included, this has now become an acceptable project. The value of the option to abandon is $351.

We did not calculate the standard deviation for this problem. However, had we done so, it would have been lower when the option was considered than when we calculated a straight NPV without the option. Thus, inclusion of the option did not only increase the NPV of the project, but it also decreased its riskiness.

**TABLE 14.9  An Abandonment Option**

EXPECTED NET PRESENT VALUE CALCULATION

| Period 1 | | Period 2 | | Total | | | | Expected |
| CF | $PV_0$ | CF | $PV_0$ | $PV_0$ | $P_1$ | $P_2$ | $P_1 \times P_2$ | $PV_0$ |
|---|---|---|---|---|---|---|---|---|
| | | 2000 | 1653 | 4380 | | 0.5 | 0.25 | 1095 |
| 3000 | 2727 | | | | 0.5 | | | |
| | | 4000 | 3306 | 6033 | | 0.5 | 0.25 | 1508 |
| | | 5000 | 4132 | 9587 | | 0.5 | 0.25 | 2397 |
| 6000 | 5455 | | | | 0.5 | | | |
| | | 7000 | 5785 | 11240 | | 0.5 | 0.25 | 2810 |

|  |  |
|---|---|
| Total expected present value | 7810 |
| Initial investment | 8000 |
| Expected net present value | −190 |

PRESENT VALUE OF PERIOD 2 CASH FLOWS AT END OF PERIOD 1

| Period 2 CF | $PV_1$ | $P_2$ | Expected $PV_1$ |
|---|---|---|---|
| 2000 | 1818 | 0.5 | 909 |
| 4000 | 3636 | 0.5 | 1818 |
| | | | 2727 |
| 5000 | 4545 | 0.5 | 2273 |
| 7000 | 6364 | 0.5 | 3182 |
| | | | 5455 |

NET PRESENT VALUE WITH ABANDONMENT

| Period 1 CF | PV at 0 | $P_1 \times P_2$ | Expected $PV_0$ |
|---|---|---|---|
| 3000 | 5909* | 0.5 | 2955 |
| | 9587 | 0.25 | 2397 |
| 6000 | | | |
| | 11240 | 0.25 | 2810 |

|  |  |
|---|---|
| Total expected present value | 8161 |
| Initial investment | 8000 |
| Expected net present value | 161 |

*(3000 + 3500)/1.1 = 5909

# International Application: Risk in Capital Budgeting

In this chapter we have discussed methods to account for risk in the capital budgeting analysis of a corporation. When a corporation operates across national boundaries and is analyzing a long-term investment to be made in, for example, one of its foreign subsidiaries, it must take into consideration at least two additional sources of risk: exchange rate risk and political risk. We will discuss briefly both of these and then cite several real-life recent examples of political risk.

An increase in risk due to multinational operations can be accounted for either through decreasing cash flows (the certainty equivalents discussed previously) or through increasing the discount rate (see discussion of the risk-adjusted discount rate in this chapter). While both methods should ideally give the same final answer, the adjustment of cash flows is sometimes favored.

## EXCHANGE RATE RISK

A company is exposed to three types of exchange rate risk:

1. Operating (or economic): This measures the change in the present value of cash flows resulting from *unexpected* changes in exchange rates.
2. Transaction: This exposure occurs due to changes in exchange rates affecting existing outstanding obligations.
3. Accounting (or translation): This occurs due to the necessity of translating a subsidiary's financial statements denominated in a foreign currency into the parent's currency in the preparation of a consolidated statement. Changes in exchange rates can affect the consolidated equity.

In the context of capital budgeting, the first of the three, operating exposure, is by far the most important. It must be noted that exposure results only from unanticipated changes in the exchange rate. Expected changes should have been included in the analysis of the capital budgeting proposal. While a company can try to manage its transaction exposure by using various types of hedges, this cannot be accomplished in the case of operating exposure. A major reason for this is that hedging, which is limited to a few currencies, is usually done for relatively short periods, while capital budgeting projects often tend to extend over a considerable number of years into the future. The firm can best attempt to protect against this exposure by diversifying its operations over many countries, as well as diversifying its fundraising activities over a number of capital markets.

## POLITICAL RISK

*Political risk* can be defined as an action by a foreign government that is detrimental to the firm. Four types of such action can be enumerated:

1. *Regulation:* Such an action can include changes in taxes, labor law rules, minimum wages, and price controls. It should be noted that such regulation can affect local companies in the foreign country as well.
2. *Discrimination:* Potential actions include restrictions on the repatriation of dividends, special labor conditions, tariff and nontariff barriers, and also imposition of administrative rules (red tape) that will make operations prohibitively expensive. Such actions are probably the most frequent.
3. *Expropriation:* A government takes over foreign property, usually with the intention of operating the business itself. Expropriation can be done with fair compensation and with inadequate or no compensation. Of course, the question of what is "fair" is an extremely difficult one to answer.

**4.** *Wars and disorders:* These can lead to destruction of a firm's property.

It is important for a company to attempt to forecast political risk using the best information and advice that it can obtain. There is also the potential of insuring through the U.S. government–owned Overseas Private Investment Corporation (OPIC). This insurance can be obtained in dealing with developing countries and covers inconvertibility, expropriation, war, and political violence. Furthermore, a company can also reduce political risk by negotiating agreements with the government of the foreign country. There are also operating and financial strategies a company can adopt to decrease political risk. This brief discussion of financial risk cannot go into the details of such strategies; thorough descriptions can be obtained from books dealing with multinational corporate finance.[17]

### Examples of Political Risk

**1.** In Nigeria, violent confrontations between troops and protesters in the oil-rich region of the Niger Delta have caused serious disruption in oil production. Royal Dutch/Shell and Chevron production of about 200,000 barrels of oil per day is shut down as a result of this activity.
**2.** The arrest of the former President of Chile, Augusto Pinochet, in the United Kingdom has hurt the U.K.'s trade with Chile. It was reported that two contracts worth $20 million were lost by U.K. military manufacturers, and "some U.K. defense companies have reported a slowing down of activity with Chile . . ."
**3.** Turkey declared a boycott of Italian defense companies in retaliation for the latter's refusal to extradite Abdullah Ocalan, a Kurdish guerilla leader.
**4.** In February 1994, the government of Malaysia stopped awarding contracts to British companies. The reason was an allegation in the British press that Malaysian politicians were paid bribes, even linking the Malaysian prime minister to these transgressions. This ban was lifted six months later. While its effect appeared not to be too heavy, British companies lost some big contracts connected with the construction of a new airport in Kuala Lumpur.[18]

## CONTAINING INTERNATIONAL RISK

Operating internationally entails some additional risk, but a company can manage these exposures (and possibly benefit) by diversifying its operations and finances.

Suppose that due to a temporary disequilibrium, costs of production among different countries diverge. The company may be able to shift its production and sources of

---

[17]Two of the books on this subject, which have been mentioned before, are David K. Eiteman, Arthur L. Stonehill, and Michael H. Moffett, *Multinational Business Finance,* 8th ed., Reading, MA: Addison-Wesley, 1998, chapters 7, 16, and 17; and Dennis J. O'Connor and Alberto T. Bueso, *International Dimensions of Financial Management,* New York: Macmillan, 1990, chapters 6 and 11. Materials in these two texts have been utilized in this narrative.
[18]R. Corzine and W. Wallis, "Risk of More Disruption for Oil Companies," *Financial Times,* February 2, 1999 and W. Wallis, "Ethnic Fighting Flares in Nigerian Oil Delta," *Financial Times,* June 2, 1999; A. Parker, "Pinochet Arrest 'Hits Contracts,' " *Financial Times,* January 13, 1999; J. Blitz, "Turks to Boycott Italian Groups," *Financial Times,* November 23, 1998. The reports regarding Malaysia appeared in several issues of the *Financial Times,* February 25, 26–27, 28, March 1, 3, 8, and September 8, 1994.

materials and components from one country to another. Or, if product prices and profitability shift among countries, so can a company's marketing efforts. If temporary deviations occur in interest or exchange rates, a company may find it possible to decrease its cost of capital by moving its financing sources. Finally, a diversification strategy may avoid some of the dangers of political risk.[19]

## THE SOLUTION

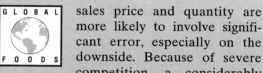

George Kline is now preparing to perform the risk analysis on the expansion project as requested by the treasurer. Although he is quite familiar with the various risk-adjustment techniques, he heeds the treasurer's suggestion to stay away from statistical refinements. He decides to use sensitivity analysis for his presentation. (As we used the expansion project data in explaining sensitivity analysis, we will now continue with the same data.)

George gives some thought to how to simplify Table 14.6 and show a combination of changes. He decides that he will present three summary estimates: worst case, base case, and best case. The base case will, of course, be the original analysis (developed in chapter 13). The worst case will show all variables on the unfavorable side, and the best case will be the opposite. He tries out several combinations. He believes that certain variables are more likely to contain larger errors than others. For instance, he postulates that production and distribution costs, with which the company has experience in other geographic areas, is a fairly good estimate. However, as this new market is not well known,

sales price and quantity are more likely to involve significant error, especially on the downside. Because of severe competition, a considerably higher sales price should not be expected. Also, because the company is attempting to penetrate a new market, the chances of falling short of the base estimate appear to be greater than those of surpassing it. He finally settles on the ranges shown in Table 14.10, which also include the resulting net present values and internal rates of return.

The worst case turns out to have a very negative NPV and an internal rate of return close to zero. To prepare for the presentation, George calculates several cases for which NPV is near zero and the internal rate of return is about 15 percent, which, of course, is the required rate. He is thus able to show the magnitude of the errors that would cause the company to be indifferent to this proposal. Three combinations that provide such results are shown in Table 14.11. Many other calculations could have been made, but at this point George feels that he has a good handle on the presentation.

*(Continued)*

---

[19]A more complete discussion of this subject can be found in Eiteman, Stonehill, and Moffett, *Multinational Business Finance,* pp. 244–47.

**TABLE 14.10 Three Possible Scenarios**

|  | Worst Case | Base Case | Best Case |
|---|---|---|---|
| Percentage differences: |  |  |  |
| Sales | −20 | 0 | +20 |
| Sales price | −15 | 0 | +5 |
| Prod. & distr. costs | +10 | 0 | −10 |
| Variable expenses | +10 | 0 | −10 |
| Net present value ($000) | −3,909 | 3,552 | 10,161 |
| Internal rate of return | 1.6% | 24.2% | 37.7% |

**TABLE 14.11 Additional Scenarios**

|  | Case 1 | Case 2 | Case 3 |
|---|---|---|---|
| Percentage differences: |  |  |  |
| Sales | −10 | −5 | −7 |
| Sales price | −6 | −7 | −5 |
| Prod. & distr. costs | +5 | +7 | +7 |
| Variable expenses | 0 | +5 | +4.5 |
| Net present value ($000) | −8 | −2 | 0 |
| Internal rate of return | 15.0% | 15.0% | 15.0% |

When the time for the presentation to top management arrived, George, accompanied by the treasurer, brought all of his charts to the conference room. George proceeded with his discussion, summarizing the forecasts and estimates and arriving at the recommended solution. He reviewed with management his sensitivity analysis, and the treasurer completed the presentation by recommending that the company go ahead and begin production in the new region.

George felt that his presentation went well, and the treasurer commended him for a good job. But a few days later, the treasurer called George into his office and told him that management had, at least for the time being, decided not to go ahead with expansion. He explained that management felt that this was not the right time to expand, given the economy's some-what cloudy future. Also, they considered the strength of their competition and decided that this was not the time to make the investment. Sensing George's disappointment, the treasurer assured him that he did an excellent job with the data he had. Actually, he said, the vice president of finance had told him to commend George for his substantial effort. "But that's the way things go in a large corporation," he continued. "You see, decisions are not always made on the basis of figures, however thoroughly they were developed. You must remember that in business, once the data have been put together, there is still the judgment factor that must be applied by management. After all, that's what top management gets paid for. I am sure that in the future, this or a similar project will be considered again."

## Summary

In this chapter the emphasis has been on incorporating risk into the capital budgeting process. The most common measure of risk in economic and financial literature is the standard deviation, which measures the dispersion around the mean of a distribution of possible outcomes. The coefficient of variation, which puts the standard deviation on a relative basis, helps in comparing projects with unequal expected net present values. The $z$-statistic is used to ascertain probabilities of an outcome being below a certain amount, above a certain amount, or within a range of amounts.

The calculation of the expected net present value and standard deviation for multi-period projects under conditions of statistical independence was also discussed.

In real business situations, these calculations are often not employed because of their complexity. Instead, the discount rate is frequently adjusted to incorporate risk; the risk-adjusted discount rate (RADR) is a technique that is dominant in business. Another method of accounting for risk, the certainty equivalent, can give results identical to those obtained using the RADR; however, because of its greater theoretical complexity and the difficulty of defining certainty equivalents, this method is not very popular in business.

Additional techniques were discussed. One whose use is quite widespread—sensitivity analysis—was used in solving the situation presented at the beginning of the chapter. Although it doesn't consider the probabilities of occurrence, this method calculates answers to a series of what-if questions. It pinpoints the specific variables (on either the revenue or the cost side) that will have large and small impacts on the results.

Other techniques also were presented. Simulation analysis requires specification of each risky input to arrive at an expected value and standard deviation. Calculations are relatively simple when independence among the variables is assumed, but can become extremely complex when interrelationships among the variables are taken into account. The decision tree method lends itself to sequential decision making. However, specifying sequences and the effects of one decision on another is extremely difficult. A brief and elementary introduction to real options explained how flexibility can be introduced into the capital budgeting process.

Although many techniques of accounting for risk were discussed in this chapter, it is obvious that none of these methods is completely satisfactory. However, the important lesson of this chapter is that risk is everpresent in business, and anyone engaging in business planning must be aware of the dangers of risky outcomes and be able to cope with the uncertainty of future events. Thus, the awareness of a risky situation may be more important than familiarity with any of the specific methods illustrated in this chapter.

## Important Concepts

**Certainty equivalent:** A certain (risk-free) cash flow that would be acceptable as opposed to the expected value of a risky cash flow. (p. 526)

**Coefficient of variation:** A measure of risk relative to expected value that is used to compare standard deviations of projects with unequal expected values. (p. 523)

**Decision tree:** A method used with sequential decision making in which a diagram points out graphically the order in which decisions must be made and compares the value of the various actions that can be undertaken. (p. 533)

**Expected value:** An average of all possible outcomes weighted by their respective probabilities. (p. 519)

**Probability:** An expression of the chance that a particular event will occur. (p. 518)

**Probability distribution:** A distribution indicating the chances of all possible occurrences. (p. 518)

**Real option:** An opportunity to make adjustments in a capital budgeting project in response to changing circumstances potentially resulting in improved results. (p. 536)

**Risk:** Refers to a situation in which possible future events can be defined and probabilities assigned. (p. 516)

**Risk-adjusted discount rate (RADR):** A value equal to the riskless (risk-free) interest rate plus a risk premium. The risk-free rate ideally is the pure time value of money, and the risk premium represents a judgment as to the additional return necessary to compensate for additional risk. (p. 526)

**Sensitivity analysis:** A method for estimating project risk that involves identifying the key variables that affect results and then changing each variable to measure the impact. (p. 528)

**Simulation analysis:** A method that assigns a probability distribution to each of the key variables and uses random numbers to simulate a set of possible outcomes to arrive at an expected value and dispersion. (p. 531)

**Standard deviation:** The degree of dispersion of possible outcomes around the mean outcome or expected value. It is the square root of the weighted average of the squared deviations of all possible outcomes from the expected value. (p. 520)

**Uncertainty:** Refers to situations in which there is no viable method of assigning probabilities to future random events. (p. 516)

## Questions

1. Distinguish *risk* and *uncertainty*. Distinguish *a priori* and *statistical* probabilities.
2. Enumerate causes of business risk.
3. The following are the probabilities and outcomes for an event:

| Probability | Outcome |
|---|---|
| 0.25 | 3,000 |
| 0.50 | 4,000 |
| 0.25 | 5,000 |

   Does the table represent a discrete or a continuous distribution? Distinguish the two.
4. You are comparing two potential mutually exclusive investment projects. You have calculated the expected NPV of project A to be $3,758 and that of project B to be $3,114. Can you be certain that you should recommend to your management to implement project A?
5. If two projects have different expected values, can the standard deviations be used to determine differences in risk?
6. Would a risk-averse person prefer a project whose distribution of potential outcomes can be drawn as a continuous normal curve with a very high peak and a steep decline around the peak?
7. Of what use is the table of values of areas under the standard normal distribution in determining the risk level of a project?
8. Define *coefficient of variation*.
9. "All our projects are discounted at the same interest rate," says the treasurer of a large company. Would you dispute the advisability of such a procedure?
10. Why do companies use the RADR method much more frequently than the certainty equivalent method? Can the two methods arrive at the same result?

11. Is a person who regularly goes to horse races (and places bets) and has insured his house against fire acting inconsistently?
12. Describe and give examples of
    **a.** Sensitivity analysis
    **b.** Simulation analysis
13. Explain the use of the decision tree in risk analysis. Is this a useful method? Is it the appropriate method for all types of analyses?
14. Why does the use of "real options" improve capital investment analysis? Under which circumstances would you recommend using real options?

## Problems

1. The Quality Office Furniture Company has compiled the year's revenue expectations and their probabilities:

| Sales ($000) | Probabilities |
|:---:|:---:|
| 240 | 0.05 |
| 280 | 0.10 |
| 320 | 0.70 |
| 360 | 0.10 |
| 400 | 0.05 |

Calculate
**a.** The expected revenue
**b.** The standard deviation
**c.** The coefficient of variation
2. If the probabilities in problem 1 had been 0.15, 0.2, 0.3, 0.2, and 0.15, recalculate the expected revenue, standard deviation, and coefficient of variation. Which of the two projections (in problem 1 and this problem) represents a riskier situation? Explain. Draw a bar graph for each situation.
3. The Learned Book Company has a choice of publishing one of two books on the subject of Greek mythology. It expects the sales period for each to be extremely short, and it estimates profit probabilities as follows:

| Book A | | Book B | |
|:---:|:---:|:---:|:---:|
| *Probability* | *Profit* | *Probability* | *Profit* |
| 0.2 | $2,000 | 0.1 | $1,500 |
| 0.3 | 2,300 | 0.4 | 1,700 |
| 0.3 | 2,600 | 0.4 | 1,900 |
| 0.2 | 2,900 | 0.1 | 2,100 |

Calculate the expected profit, standard deviation, and coefficient of variation for each of the books. If you were asked which of the two to publish, what would be your advice?

**4.** Suppose you can make an investment with the following possible rates of return:

| Probability | Rate of Return |
|:---:|:---:|
| 0.2 | −10% |
| 0.6 | 10% |
| 0.2 | 30% |

On the other hand, you can invest in a U.S. Treasury bill that earns a certain 7 percent. Evaluate the alternatives.

**5.** The Cactus Corporation is considering a two-year project, project A, involving an initial investment of $600 and the following cash inflows and probabilities:

| Year 1 | | Year 2 | |
|:---:|:---:|:---:|:---:|
| Probability | Cash Flow | Probability | Cash Flow |
| 0.1 | $700 | 0.2 | $600 |
| 0.4 | 600 | 0.3 | 500 |
| 0.4 | 500 | 0.3 | 400 |
| 0.1 | 400 | 0.2 | 300 |

**a.** Calculate the project's expected NPV and standard deviation, assuming the discount rate to be 8 percent.

**b.** The company is also considering another two-year project, project B, which has an expected NPV of $320 and a standard deviation of $125. Projects A and B are mutually exclusive. Which of the two projects would you prefer? Explain.

**6.** The Grand Design Corporation uses the certainty equivalent approach in making capital budgeting decisions. You are given the following data, for a particular project:

| Year | Cash Flow | Certainty Equivalent Factor |
|:---:|:---:|:---:|
| 0 | $−20,000 | 1.00 |
| 1 | 5,000 | 0.90 |
| 2 | 5,000 | 0.90 |
| 3 | 5,000 | 0.90 |
| 4 | 15,000 | 0.70 |

The risk-free discount rate is 4 percent, and the risk-adjusted discount rate is 12 percent. Calculate the net present value. Would you accept this project?

**7.** You have just been employed in the finance department of the Mahler Transportation Corporation. The first task you have been assigned is to recommend a method for evaluating risky projects. You have studied both the risk-adjusted discount rate (RADR) method and the certainty equivalent method, and you have been asked to evaluate the following project using both methods.

A four-year project involves an original cash outflow of $30,000; there will be (after-tax) cash inflows of $10,000 in each of the first three years and an inflow of $20,000 in the fourth year. You estimate that the risk-free interest rate is 8 percent and the project's risk premium is 4 percent.
  **a.** Calculate the net present value using RADR.
  **b.** Now calculate net present value using the certainty equivalent method, and show that the two methods give identical answers.

**8.** Project A has an expected net present value of $500 and a standard deviation of $125. Project B has a standard deviation of $100 and an expected net present value of $300. Which of the two projects would you select? Explain why.

**9.** Global Industries has calculated the return on assets (ROA) for one of its projects using the simulation method. By simulating the operations 1,000 times, they obtained an ROA of 16.7 percent and a standard deviation of 6.2. The results of the simulation conform quite closely to a normal curve.
  **a.** Draw a probability distribution using the given data.
  **b.** The company's objective is to achieve an ROA of 12 percent. What is the probability that the project will achieve at least that level?
  **c.** What is the probability of ROA being nonnegative?

**10.** The Great Pine Forest Corporation is analyzing an expansion project with the following information:

Initial investment:   $120,000
Depreciation life: five years—straight-line
Project life: five years
Additional working capital at $t = 0$   $20,000
Working capital returned at $t = 5$   $20,000
Expected salvage value at $t = 5$   $15,000
Tax rate: 34 percent
Cost of capital: 12 percent

|  | *Year 1* | *Year 2* | *Year 3* | *Year 4* | *Year 5* |
|---|---|---|---|---|---|
| Revenue | $50,000 | $80,000 | $80,000 | $80,000 | $40,000 |
| Cash costs | 30,000 | 30,000 | 25,000 | 25,000 | 25,000 |

  **a.** Calculate the present value of this project.
  **b.** Now conduct a sensitivity analysis as follows:
    **(1)** Assume the best case to have revenue 10 percent higher than just stated, costs 5 percent lower than given, and salvage value twice the amount given.
    **(2)** Assume the worst case to have revenue 10 percent lower than given, costs 5 percent higher than given, and salvage value to be 0.
  Show the results for the best case, the most likely case, and the worst case.

**11.** The Prime Time Printing Company is analyzing a two-year project, which would necessitate the purchase of a printing press. The demand for the product will depend on the expected state of the economy. The company's economist forecasts a 30 percent probability that the economy will be expanding strongly, a 50 percent probability that expansion will be normal, and a 20 percent probability of a weak expansion. These probabilities will hold for the next two years. The company has a choice of purchasing a large press for $50,000 or a smaller one for $40,000. The present value of potential cash flows (in $000) in year 1, given the state of the economy and the size of the equipment, is as follows:

| Year 1 | Large | Small |
|--------|-------|-------|
| 0.3 | 100 | 60 |
| 0.5 | 40 | 40 |
| 0.2 | −20 | 20 |

If year 1 has a strong expansion, then the probabilities and PV of cash flows (in $000) in year 2 will be the following:

| Year 2 | Large | Small |
|--------|-------|-------|
| 0.3 | 180 | 100 |
| 0.5 | 90 | 60 |
| 0.2 | 60 | 40 |

If year 1 has a normal expansion, then the probabilities and PV of cash flows (in $000) in year 2 will be the following:

| Year 2 | Large | Small |
|--------|-------|-------|
| 0.3 | 80 | 70 |
| 0.5 | 40 | 40 |
| 0.2 | 20 | 30 |

If year 1's expansion is weak, then year 2's PV of cash flows (in $000) will be:

| Year 2 | Large | Small |
|--------|-------|-------|
| 0.3 | 50 | 50 |
| 0.5 | 30 | 30 |
| 0.2 | −30 | 10 |

Calculate the expected NPV, the standard deviation, and the coefficient of variation for each alternative, and recommend which alternative should be selected.

12. The Bentley Manufacturing Company has an opportunity to purchase a patent for the manufacture of a new product for $200,000. It has three possible choices:
   **a.** It does not purchase the patent.
   **b.** It purchases the patent at the above price.
   **c.** It spends $50,000 on additional research to learn more about the feasibility and potential of this product, before deciding whether to purchase the patent.
   You have the task of making a recommendation. You have expended considerable effort in familiarizing yourself with this product and you have consulted with technical and market experts at your company. You have made the following estimates.

**a.** There is a 60 percent probability that the additional research will show this product to have a good market potential.

**b.** If the research results are favorable, the chances are 80 percent that the product will net the company $1,000,000; there is a probability of 20 percent that the income from it will be only $150,000.

**c.** If the research results are not favorable, there is a 90 percent probability that income will be $100,000 and 10 percent that it will be $800,000.

**d.** If, however, the company purchases the patent without any more research, your estimates are as follows:

| | |
|---|---|
| 30% probability | $1,000,000 |
| 40% probability | 500,000 |
| 30% probability | 150,000 |

Assume that all above numbers are in terms of present values. Using a decision tree, make your recommendation.

13. It has been your secret wish to own and operate an amusement park when you can afford to make the investment. That time has now arrived. There is a large empty lot at the outskirts of Phoenix, Arizona, owned by the city. The city is willing to lease one-half of this lot for 5 years with an option to lease both it and the other half for the next 5 years. In return for charging you a reasonable rent, the city will take ownership of your equipment at the end of the 5 or 10 years.

You have estimated your original investment to be $250,000. You expect your net cash flows (after lease payments, all other expenses and taxes) to be $55,000 for each of the first five years. If you exercise your option to continue with both parts of the property at the end of year 5, you will need to invest another $150,000 (for additional equipment and a miniature golf course). Because your cash flow estimates are now far into the future, you estimate a 50 percent probability that your annual cash flows will remain the same ($55,000) and a 50 percent probability that they will rise to $100,000 per year for the second five years. Your cost of capital is 12 percent.

**a.** Is the first five-year project acceptable?

**b.** What is the value of the total project if you exercise your option? What is the value of your option?

---

## Take It to the Net

We invite you to visit the Keat/Young page on the Prentice Hall Web site at:

**http://www.prenhall.com/keat**

for additional resources.

# CHAPTER 15

# Government and Industry: Challenges and Opportunities for Today's Manager

## THE SITUATION

Bill Adams, the chief information officer (CIO) of Global Foods, Inc., was faced with a serious challenge. Over the years, under his leadership, the company had built 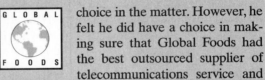 up a substantial private voice and data network. However, in a meeting he just attended with Bob Burns and the other company executives, he learned that Bob was going to launch a major outsourcing initiative to help the company focus on its *core competencies.* "Bill, we're not a telecom company," Bob told him at the meeting. "We're a food and beverage company. You must start to figure out a good way to let other people handle the communications." Bill knew that consultants the company had hired to help develop a business process reengineering program were the ones who had convinced Bob of the need to outsource noncore activities. Although it meant the eventual dismantling of his department, Bill knew that he had no choice in the matter. However, he felt he did have a choice in making sure that Global Foods had the best outsourced supplier of telecommunications service and so he set out to try to find the right one.

When Bill's staff put out the RFP (request for proposal), Bill was surprised at the number and diversity of the responses. He thought there would just be the usual cast of characters such as AT&T, MCI WorldCom, and Sprint. But in addition, his local telecommunications company, one of the "Regional Bell Operating Companies," put in a bid, along with a dozen or so smaller companies that had formed consortiums with big consulting companies such as EDS and Andersen Consulting. "The competitive landscape in telecommunications has really changed since the breakup of AT&T in 1984," Bill thought. "I guess this should help our company get a good deal. But we'll see."

# Introduction

The primary objective of this chapter is to discuss the impact of government policies on managerial decision making. When the government is involved in the market economy, it generally controls the behavior of buyers and sellers through a process of "indirect command." That is, rather than ordering buyers and sellers to allocate resources in a particular way, the government uses market incentives or disincentives. This "visible hand" of the government can take such forms as price controls, rules and regulations, taxes, and subsidies. In using the incentive of profit or the disincentive of loss, the government does not change the basic system of rewards and punishments used in the market. Instead, it simply alters the reward structure of a laissez-faire market so that resources are allocated more in accordance with government policy than with the actions of individual buyers and sellers.

In the following section, we will elaborate on the different roles that government plays in the market economy and the justification for such roles. We will then describe what it is like to do business with the U.S. government, which after all is one of the largest buyers of goods and services in the world. (This section is entirely new to this edition. It was written by Sylvia Von Bostel, a member of the staff of Booz-Allen & Hamilton, one of the world's top consulting companies. Its client list includes a number of agencies and departments of the federal government.)

# The Rationale for Government Involvement in a Market Economy

There are five major functions the government can perform in a market economy such as that of the United States. First, it provides a legal and social framework within which market participants buy and sell the goods and services produced by the economy's scarce resources. For example, the Food and Drug Administration (FDA) seeks to ensure that food and pharmaceutical companies sell products that meet certain standards of safety and quality.

Second, the government strives to maintain competition in markets for goods and services by trying to ensure that no one seller dominates the market in an unfair manner. Third, the government may decide to play a role in the redistribution of income and wealth. It can do so through the tax system (particularly through income taxes), and also through various types of government subsidies and grants for special-interest groups. For example, one of the major subsidies for middle- and upper-income in the United States is the ability to deduct interest payments on residential mortgages.

The fourth market-related function of government is the reallocation of resources. According to economic theory, a misallocation of resources results whenever a market has certain externalities or spillovers. That is, some of the benefits or costs associated with the production or consumption of a particular product accrue to parties other than the buyers or sellers of a product.

The fifth major function of government in a market economy is the stabilization of the aggregate economy. The market economy is prone to periodic upswings and downswings in economic activity. As you have probably already studied in a course in macroeconomics, governments can employ monetary and fiscal policy to deal with the problems of unemployment and inflation, which usually occur at different stages of the cycle.

One government function that does not quite fit into any of the five main categories is the regulation of natural monopolies. The economic definition of a **natural monopoly** is an industry in which a single firm can serve customers more efficiently than many smaller competing firms because of the predominance of economies of scale. Examples of natural monopolies are electricity and gas utilities and telephone services. However, over the past decade or so, there has been a movement by governments throughout the world to reduce the government ownership or regulation of these natural monopolies. Let us elaborate a bit further on two of the five main functions of government: providing a competitive framework for market participants and the reallocation of resources in the presence of market externalities.

## PROVIDING A LEGAL FRAMEWORK FOR COMPETITION: THE ANTITRUST LAWS

A thorough interpretation of antitrust laws would carry us beyond the scope of this book.[1] We here provide a brief review of the subject. The beginning of antitrust legislation in the United States dates back to the late nineteenth century in response to the formation of large corporations and the so-called "merger-to-monopoly" wave. While under common law various anticompetitive actions (e.g., price fixing) were not enforceable, stronger positive legal action appeared necessary. The first law to be passed was the Sherman Anti-Trust Act, followed by several others.

### The Sherman Anti-Trust Act (1890)

The two important sections of this law were the following:

Section 1: ... every contract, combination in the form of trust or otherwise, or conspiracy, in restraint of trade or commerce among the several states, or with foreign nations, is declared to be illegal ...

Section 2: ... every person who shall monopolize or attempt to monopolize any part of the trade or commerce among the several states, or with foreign nations, shall be deemed guilty of a felony ...

Section 1 outlawed explicit cartels. Section 2, which appeared to outlaw monopoly, was interpreted by the courts as a prohibition of "bad acts" and not monopoly per se.

### The Clayton Act (1914)

The Clayton Act was intended to strengthen and widen the application of antitrust enforcement, and specifically enumerated four forbidden practices:

Section 2: prohibits price discrimination that would "substantially lessen competition ..." It exempted price differentiation due to differences in quality, quantity, and costs of selling and transportation.

Section 3: Prohibits the use of tying or exclusive contracts that would lessen competition.

Section 7: Prohibits the acquisition of other companies through purchase of stock if this lessens competition.

Section 8: Restricts interlocking directorates.

The Clayton Act also provided for the recovery of treble damages by the injured party.

---

[1]A large number of texts on industrial organization treat this topic thoroughly. An example is Dennis W. Carlton and Jeffrey M. Perloff, *Modern Industrial Organization,* 2nd ed., New York: HarperCollins, 1994, chapter 20.

## The Federal Trade Commission Act (1914)

This law set up a new agency, the Federal Trade Commission (FTC), to investigate violations, enforce antitrust laws, and determine what actions constitute "unfair method of competition," which the law declared unlawful. The Wheeler-Lea Act (1938) extended FTC's authority to the protection of consumers.

## Subsequent Acts

The Robinson-Patman Act (1936) strengthened the price-discrimination provisions of the Clayton Act to include not only the lessening of competition, but also injury to or prevention of competition "with any person who either grants or knowingly receives the benefits of such discrimination, or with customers of either of them." This act was the result of political pressure by small independent grocery stores to make it difficult for large grocery chains to buy and sell at lower prices.

The Celler-Kefauver Act (1950) corrected some omissions of the Clayton Act. Specifically, it applied the law to mergers accomplished through asset acquisition (the Clayton Act applied only to acquisition of stock).

The Hart-Scott-Rodino Act (1976) imposed a premerger notification requirement on large firms (where the acquiring firm has at least $100 million in assets and $10 million in annual sales).

## Some Closing Remarks on Antitrust Laws

Over time, the interpretation and enforcement of antitrust laws has varied a great deal. Before leaving this subject, we will briefly discuss the two main schools of thought regarding the purpose of the antitrust law and comment on perhaps one of the most publicized antitrust cases in recent years: the United States Government versus the Microsoft Corporation.

One school of thought suggests that the main purpose of antitrust laws is economic efficiency. The laws act against practices that restrict output and raise prices. But not all mergers and agreements will create economic inefficiencies; instead they may lead to greater efficiency and lowering of costs. Thus, courts should interpret such actions case by case. The final goal of policy should be to enhance consumer welfare.

The opposing school of thought argues that the purpose of antitrust laws is actually to limit the power of large firms, and to protect smaller independent firms regardless of the effects on efficiency. This seemed to be particularly evident in the case of the Robinson-Patman Act, which was explicitly aimed at the protection of small grocery businesses. Obviously, this is an extremely complex issue that has not been solved in all these years, and probably will not for many years to come.

One high profile antitrust case that is occurring as the third edition of this text is being completed is the U.S. government's case against the Microsoft Corporation. In a nutshell, the U.S. government has charged that Microsoft has used its monopolistic powers to compete unfairly against the Netscape Communications Corporation in the Web browser market. (Microsoft also was accused of unfair practices against other companies; however, we will confine ourselves here to the government's case regarding Netscape.) By bundling its own product, Internet Explorer, with its Windows operating system, the government charges that the company gained an illegal competitive advantage against Netscape's Navigator. The thrust of the government's arguments rests on two points: (1) Microsoft indeed has monopolistic powers that violate current antitrust laws, and (2) Microsoft used these powers to unfairly restrict Netscape's ability to compete.

Readers can well expect that top economists were among the cast of expert witnesses called in to testify on behalf of either side. In a dramatic display of "You've got your expert and I've got mine," the government called in prominent economist Franklin M. Fisher of the Massachusetts Institute of Technology, and Microsoft countered with Richard L. Schmalensee, also of M.I.T. By coincidence (or perhaps not), Professor Fisher was Professor Schmalensee's Ph.D. thesis advisor.

Professor Fisher challenged the fairness of Microsoft's decision to imbed its browser into its Windows operating system, which has more than a 90 percent share of the market. Professor Schmalensee countered by saying that this is like saying that "consumers will be made better off if they are deprived, by court order, of Web-browsing functionality that Microsoft wishes to provide at zero marginal cost and that consumers are free to ignore or replace."[2] Professor Fisher argued, saying that the threat is not merely that Microsoft will wrest the browser market away from the current leader, Netscape Communications, but worse, that Microsoft might well use browser domination to eliminate competition in operating systems. He further charged that Microsoft's decision to give away its browser constituted an extreme form of "predatory pricing," designed to drive a competitor out of business. The arguments go much further, but these brief remarks should help to give readers an idea of just how difficult it is to actually prove a violation of antitrust laws, particularly when both lawyers and economists are involved. If the verdict goes against Microsoft, this case will probably go on for years until it reaches the Supreme Court.[3]

## DEALING WITH MARKET EXTERNALITIES: ANOTHER KEY FUNCTION OF GOVERNMENT IN THE MARKET ECONOMY

In the microeconomic theory of the firm, on which much of managerial economics is based, it can be shown that under conditions of perfect competition, an economy's scarce resources will be most efficiently allocated and social welfare will be maximized. This situation prevails when all costs are fully accounted for in the price of the product. However, there are frequent cases when not all costs are included in the price or when not all costs are compensated. Such situations give rise to externalities and result in market failure.

A **benefit externality** is one where not all costs are compensated. In other words, certain benefits accrue to third parties. For instance, a beautiful private garden will benefit people who walk by but this will not compensate the owner. Benefit externalities (sometimes called positive externalities) also arise in the case of information (several people can read the same newspaper) or from innovations that benefit many people. Because producers of these products cannot appropriate all the revenue, too little may be produced.

---

[2]"Trial's War of Economists Pits Student Against Teacher," *New York Times,* January 25, 1999.
[3]Readers should have no trouble finding material in the popular press about this case. However, two good sources that appeared around the time of the preparation of this edition are "As Microsoft Struggles with Antitrust Case, Tactical Errors Emerge," *The Wall Street Journal,* February 18, 1999, and "For Microsoft, Humbled May Not Mean Defeated," *New York Times,* February 28, 1999.

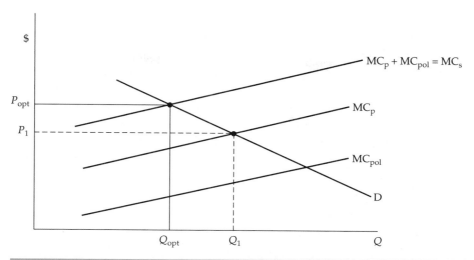

**FIGURE 15.1** Impact of the Marginal Cost of Pollution on Price

But **cost externalities** are the ones with which economists are mostly concerned. These are the cases where a producer does not pay all the costs generated by the product. The most popular example of cost externalities (also called negative externalities) in economic literature is pollution. A factory will produce both the product and pollution. But if it does not have to pay for the cost of the pollution it has created, the product will be priced based only on the "private" production costs. Thus, the product's price will be lower than if it had been fully costed, and too much of the product will be produced. This can be shown on a simple graph for a competitive industry, shown in Figure 15.1.

The marginal cost curve of the product is shown as $MC_p$. The price of the product will be $P_1$ and the quantity produced will be $Q_1$. The cost of pollution is not considered in this result. The marginal cost of pollution is shown as $MC_{pol}$.

The total cost of the product to the economy, the "social cost," is the vertical summation of $MC_p$ and $MC_{pol}$, or $MC_s$. If this cost had been included in the pricing of the product, then equilibrium would have been at $P_{opt}$ and $Q_{opt}$. Obviously, there will always be some pollution. If pollution were to be completely eliminated, then this industry would have to shut down and produce nothing. But this would not be an ideal situation, as there is demand for the product. The **socially optimal price** will occur at $P_{opt}$, where the price of the product is equal to marginal social cost. Note that at this point less pollution will be produced (and less of the product also) than under strictly competitive conditions where only $MC_p$ was priced into the product.

How can the optimal equilibrium be attained? The usual prescription is for government to act in one of two ways.[4] The first would be to restrict production to $Q_{opt}$. The other method is taxation. Ideally this tax would be equal to the $MC_{pol}$ curve. If such

---

[4]The entire subject of externalities and government intervention was first treated fully by a famous English economist, A. C. Pigou. See *The Economics of Welfare,* 4th ed., London: Macmillan, 1932.

a tax were levied, then "externalities would be internalized." A third, rather new way, under the 1990 Clean Air Act, is for the government to set maximum pollution levels, and then sell licenses to companies to give them the right to pollute.

### The Coase Theorem: An Alternative Treatment of Externalities

In 1960, Ronald Coase advanced the idea that government intervention to eliminate the effect of externalities is not necessary if property rights are correctly and clearly defined.[5] This is often referred to as the **Coase theorem.** Who has the right to pollute and who has the right to keep pollution low? If it were originally decided who owns the property in question, then bargaining between the two parties would result in an optimal solution, without government intervention, at the level that would have been brought about with a correct taxation policy.

Various examples of such a situation can be given. Let us assume a stream, on which we find a chemical plant and a fishing establishment. If the property rights to this stream go to the chemical plant, the fishing company will have to pay the plant to reduce the dumping of its waste into the stream. It will pay just up to the point where the marginal benefit to the fishermen (from harvesting more and healthier fish) will be just equal to the cost incurred by the chemical plant (in dumping its waste at a less convenient and more expensive location, or actually decreasing its production). On the other hand, if the fishing company has the property rights, the plant will have to pay the fishermen to permit the plant to dump waste. In both cases, the final result will be the same, and will take place at the optimal point that would have been achieved if a correct tax policy (i.e., taxes equal to the marginal cost of polluting) had been imposed.

Other examples of this kind abound. Coase, in his famous article, described the case of farmers growing grain in unfenced fields until a cattle rancher, whose cattle tend to damage the farmers' crops, arrives in the area. In addition, in his article, Coase cited a number of legal cases spanning back to the nineteenth century where the assignment of property rights was crucial in the decision.

While the Coase theorem poses very interesting questions regarding the need for government interference, it is important to look at its limitations. For instance, while optimal production levels are reached whichever party is assigned property rights, income distribution will be affected. In our example, if the chemical plant was awarded property rights, it will gain at the expense of the fishing industry. Thus, normative issues are not addressed by Coase.

But there are additional limitations. First, if transaction costs—i.e., the cost of obtaining an agreement between the two parties—are high, then bargaining may not be an ideal solution. Second, if one company engages in unfair bargaining, no reasonable agreement may be reached. And third, neither side may have complete information regarding the costs and benefits of arriving at the optimal solution.[6]

[5]Ronald Coase, "The Problem of Social Cost," *Journal of Law and Economics,* 3 (October 1960), pp. 1–44. This is a very long and complex article. For an excellent brief summary, see George J. Stigler, *The Theory of Price,* 4th ed., New York: Macmillan, 1987.
[6]A. M. Polinsky, "Controlling Externalities and Protecting Entitlements: Property Right, Liability Rule, and Tax-Subsidy Approaches," *Journal of Legal Studies,* 8, 1979, pp. 1–48.

# Doing Business with the U.S. Government[7]

Nowhere else do government policies and procedures have greater impact than on market segments where the government *is* the buyer. Such a market is sometimes described as a **monopsony,** or a market in which the product or service of a number of sellers is sought by only one buyer. In this section, we will focus on the U.S. government because of its size, reach, and impact on the U.S. economy. Conversely, we also will illustrate that a market economy can have a great impact on how the U.S. government acts as a buyer. The challenges of doing business with local and state governments are similar, although there may be specific differences in policies and procedures from those followed by the federal government.

The U.S. government is arguably the single biggest client in the world. In fiscal year 1998, federal receipts totaled $1.722 trillion, or 20.5 percent of gross domestic product. Total outlays were $1.653 trillion or 19.7 percent of gross domestic product.[8] Each year, the federal executive branch purchases about *$200 billion* in goods and services.[9] According to the Federal Procurement Data Center, part of the U.S. General Services Administration, every 20 seconds of each working day the U.S. government awards a contract with an average value of $465,000.[10] In such a market, government policies fundamentally shape the ways in which businesses behave.

## THE GOVERNMENT MARKET

Doing business with the federal government is highly complicated. Entire industries have emerged to explain how to be successful in this marketplace. Some companies choose not to do business with the government due to special accounting and reporting requirements, potential liabilities, profit limitations, and other statutory and regulatory controls. On the other hand, many companies have learned how to operate and prosper in this environment.

For the purposes of this discussion, we will approach this subject with three basic questions of *what? when?* and *how?* First, businesses look at *what* they believe the government will buy. This determines the way in which businesses define their product or service offerings. Related to this question is that of *when* the government plans to buy. This is a critically important factor and has an impact on whether short- or long-term investments are required. Third, businesses carefully monitor changes in federal acquisition policies that govern *how* the government will buy. This affects the way in which they develop their bidding strategies. Let us take a closer look.

### What the Government Buys

*What* the U.S. government buys is influenced by government strategic plans, budget and program input from federal departments and agencies, priorities set by the President, the availability of appropriated funds, congressionally mandated requirements,

---

[7]This section was written by Sylvia Von Bostel, on the staff of Booz-Allen & Hamilton.
[8]"The Budget System and Concepts," *Budget of the United States Government, Fiscal Year 2000,* Washington, DC: U.S. Government Printing Office, 1999.
[9]Retrieved February 3, 1999 from Federal Procurement Data System, General Services Administration World Wide Web site: fpds.gsa.gov
[10]"FPDS . . . the Competitor's Edge," retrieved February 3, 1999 from the World Wide Web: fpds.gsa.gov/fpds/compete

whether the federal budget is in surplus or deficit, and lots of politics. Businesses monitor this ever-changing environment, their government clients, and the entire federal budget process carefully. While perhaps 80 to 90 percent of the President's budget request is usually enacted, individual programs or projects can be eliminated, cut back, restricted, or limited in other ways. Sometimes Congress adds funding that was not requested. Any of these actions can have a significant impact on a business that has or is seeking a contract with the government.

The federal government's fiscal year begins on October 1, ends on September 30, and is named by the year in which it ends. Fiscal year 1999, for example, began on October 1, 1998, and ended on September 30, 1999. Each January the President announces priority initiatives and proposed funding in the President's State of the Union Address. The formal budget process begins with release of the *Budget of the United States Government* to Congress, which the President is required to submit to Congress by the first Monday in February.[11]

In reality, federal departments and agencies begin building their budgets two years in advance and, in addition to the fiscal year in question, look at "out years," or five to six years into the future. The White House, bipartisan commissions, independent panels, interagency councils, inspectors general, the General Accounting Office (the investigative arm of Congress), congressional committees, and federal departments and agencies themselves conduct many reviews that influence budget requests. The Office of Management and Budget (OMB) provides detailed instructions to federal departments and agencies about how to put their budgets together in *OMB Circular A-11,* "Preparation and Submission of Budget Estimates," a document that is updated annually to reflect changes in law. OMB collects the budget requests, "scrubs" the numbers, and puts together the President's budget.

Ultimately, it is the U.S. Congress that authorizes and appropriates the funds that can be obligated and expended for the purchase of goods and services. Once the President's budget is submitted to Congress, the annual appropriations process begins in earnest. There are 13 appropriations bills. In some years they are enacted separately. In others, due to lack of time or breakdowns in negotiations between the White House and Congress on major programs or policy issues, some or all appropriation bills are bundled in a large catchall piece of legislation. Appropriation bills or some stopgap legislation, referred to as "continuing resolutions," must be enacted by October 1 or parts or all of the federal government may be forced to "shut down."

## When the Government Buys

*When* the government plans to purchase goods or services is a critical factor in many ways. Learning about a major procurement when the government publishes a request for proposal usually means it is too late to be a player. Competitors who have been tracking the procurement, devising a strategy, and negotiating with teaming partners will have an advantage. For companies that develop and build prototypes and manufacture high-cost items requiring substantial long-term investment, serious delays can threaten their very survival and even lead to merger or acquisition. Unanticipated can-

---

[11]"Citizen's Guide to the Federal Budget," *Budget of the United States Government, Fiscal Year 2000.*

cellations due to budget cutbacks or major government shutdowns can result in layoffs, plant closings, and cash flow problems. One need only look at the consolidations that have been occurring in the defense and aerospace industries since the end of the Cold War to see the impact of changes of federal government budgets on private industry. (See the reference on p. 562 to Lockheed's efforts to enter the market for computer services.)

### How the Government Buys

*How* the government purchases goods and services has a major impact on bidding strategies. Government acquisition is controlled by two basic laws, the *Armed Services Procurement Act,* applicable to the Army, Navy, Air Force, Coast Guard, and NASA, and the *Federal Property and Administrative Services Act,* applicable to the General Services Administration and all other agencies. The Federal Acquisition Regulation System codifies and publishes uniform policies and procedures for acquisition by all federal agencies. It consists of the Federal Acquisition Regulation (FAR), which is the primary governmentwide document, and agency acquisition regulations that supplement the FAR. The Office of Federal Procurement Policy, part of the Office of Management and Budget, provides overall direction.[12]

Companies doing business with the government must comply with requirements and controls that do not exist in commercial transactions. These include competition requirements, profit restrictions, audits, bid protest rules, accounting system requirements, prohibitions against gratuities and certain hiring practices, and socioeconomic programs. The Federal Acquisition Regulation is divided into 53 parts. Part 15 deals exclusively with negotiated contracts. Parts 19–26 of the Federal Acquisition Regulation are dedicated to socioeconomic programs, for example, small business programs, the application of labor laws to government acquisitions, environment, conservation, occupational safety, and drug-free workplace, protection of privacy and freedom of information, foreign acquisition, the Indian incentive program, and historically black colleges and universities and minority institutions. Part 30 sets forth cost accounting standards and part 31 deals with contract cost principles and procedures. Part 52 is a long list of solicitation provisions and contract clauses, and includes a matrix listing of FAR provisions and clauses applicable to each principal contract type, for example, fixed-price supply or cost reimbursement research and development. Part 53 provides examples of standard forms, optional forms, and agency-specific forms.[13]

### THE GOVERNMENT AND THE MARKET ECONOMY

As stated, the market economy has a great impact on how the U.S. government acts as a buyer as well. During the 1980s it became apparent that the annual federal deficit and total national debt were reaching unacceptable levels, the Cold War was ending, and the nation was entering a new Information Age. Laws were enacted to enforce budget discipline and the federal government sought ways in which to become more efficient and

---

[12]"Authority·Policy·Laws·Regulations·Selling to the Federal Government," *Government Contracts Reporter,* Commerce Clearing House, Inc., June 14, 1989.
[13]*Federal Acquisition Regulation* as of January 1, 1998, Commerce Clearing House, Inc., 1998.

cost effective. It did this by adapting for its use successful business practices in the private sector such as total quality management, business process reengineering, downsizing, rightsizing, mergers, streamlining acquisitions, and shedding excess infrastructure. From the height of the defense buildup in the mid 1980s until around 1998, the Department of Defense reduced force structure by 35 to 40 percent.[14] Four Base Realignment and Closure (BRAC) Commissions between 1988 and 1995 proposed the closure or realignment of 152 major installations and 235 smaller installations.[15] While not all actions have occurred, approximately $14 to 15 billion in savings were achieved by 1998.[16]

In the 1990s, the federal government accelerated steps to further streamline its acquisition processes, adopt commercial practices, get away from detailed government specifications, buy commercial off-the-shelf items whenever possible, and emphasize performance-based or results-based management. Table 15.1 highlights some of the laws enacted during the 1990s.

One of the major impacts of these acquisition reforms of the 1990s was the increased use of the *Federal Supply Schedules* as a preferred way of doing business. Under the Federal Supply Schedules administered by the General Services Administration (GSA), companies apply to provide certain types of commercial items and services and are placed on a list of approved vendors, together with their price lists, which are posted on GSA's Web pages. Qualified vendors are able to market their products and capabilities to federal agencies. Federal agencies are able to find vendors on the list and use streamlined acquisition procedures to meet their requirements. Commercial items and services and off-the-shelf commercial items are also exempt from significant statutory and regulatory requirements, both at the contract and subcontract levels.

Around 1995, under the auspices of the National Performance Review, another phenomenon, sometimes referred to as *entrepreneurial government,* emerged. This brought the adaptation of commercial practices to a new level by actively sanctioning government "franchising," employee stock ownership programs (ESOPs) made up of former government employees, public–public competition, and public–private competition. The *Government Management Reform Act/Federal Financial Management Act of 1994,* cited in Table 15.1, established a franchise fund pilot program in six executive agencies. The fund is used to provide common administrative support services to the designated agency, but can also be used to provide services to other agencies on a competitive basis. As of July 1997, the Environmental Protection Agency, the departments of Commerce, Health and Human Services, Interior, Treasury, and Veterans Affairs were participating in the franchise fund program. Data centers at these six agencies gave up their operating budgets but recover their expenses by charging their own agencies and other government entities for the work they do.[17] US Investigations Services,

---

[14]William S. Cohen, Secretary of Defense, "The Secretary's Message," *Report of the Quadrennial Defense Review,* May 1997.
[15]William S. Cohen, Secretary of Defense, *Annual Report to the President and Congress,* 1998, p. 176.
[16]William S. Cohen, Secretary of Defense, Testimony before the House Armed Services Committee, "Hearing on the President's Fiscal Year 2000 Budget," February 2, 1999.
[17]"Battle Lines Drawn on FAA Contract," *Washington Technology,* July 10, 1997, page 1.

TABLE 15.1   Selected Laws Adopting Commercial Practices

| Year | Public Law | Key Provisions |
|------|-----------|----------------|
| 1990 | Chief Financial Officers Act | • Required the establishment of agency chief financial officers and designated a governmentwide CFO |
| 1993 | Government Performance and Results Act | • Established strategic planning and performance measurement requirements for federal agencies |
| 1994 | Government Management Reform Act, which contained the Federal Financial Management Act | • Required agencies and the government as a whole to produce annual audited financial statements<br>• Mandated direct deposit electronic funds transfers for all federal wage, salary, and retirement payments |
| 1994 | Federal Acquisition Streamlining Act | • Expanded the types of commercial items and services that the government could purchase using streamlined procedures<br>• Simplified payments for small purchases by increasing the use of governmentwide credit cards |
| 1996 | Federal Acquisition Reform Act | • Expanded the definition of commercial items and services and exempted them from the requirement for certified cost or pricing data and the federal government's cost accounting standards |
| 1996 | Information Technology Management Reform Act | • Required capital planning and investment control for information technology<br>• Called for the designation of a chief information officer at each executive agency |

*Sources: Chief Financial Officers Act of 1990,* Public Law 101–576, November 15, 1990; *Government Performance and Reform Act of 1993 (GPRA),* PL 103–62, August 3, 1993; *Government Management Reform Act of 1994 (GMRA),* PL 103–356, October 13, 1994; *Federal Acquisition Streamlining Act of 1994 (FASA),* PL 103–355, October 13, 1994; *Federal Acquisition Reform Act of 1996 (FARA),* PL 104–106, February 10, 1996; *Information Technology Management Reform Act of 1996 (ITMRA),* PL 104–106, February 10, 1996.

Inc. (USIS) is an ESOP formed in July 1996 by former federal civil servants in the Office of Federal Investigations, part of the Office of Personnel Management. USIS is the first employee-owned enterprise that involved a former federal agency, and has become the largest private investigations company in North America.[18]

In May 1997, the Federal Aviation Administration (FAA) awarded its Integrated Computing Environment-Mainframe and Networking (ICE-MAN) contract, worth up to $250 million over eight years, to the U.S. Department of Agriculture (USDA)

[18]"Live Long and Prosper," edited with permission from an article appearing in *Government Executive,* website of Foundation for Enterprise Development, http://www.fed.org/leading_companies/nov97/harper.html

computer center in Kansas City, Missouri. Under that contract, USDA operates the FAA's computer systems for payroll, personnel, and flight safety. Competitors included major corporations such as IBM, Unisys, Computer Sciences, and Lockheed Martin and at least one government agency, the Defense Information Systems Agency.[19]

Federal policy regarding the performance of commercial activities is set forth in *OMB Circular A-76,* first promulgated by the Bureau of the Budget in 1955 and reissued and revised many times since then, most recently in 1996. Circular A-76 states that in the process of governing, the government should not compete with its citizens and shall rely on commercially available sources to provide commercial products and services. When commercial performance of a government commercial activity is appropriate, A-76 requires that the cost of private sector versus government performance be compared to determine who will do the work. It also states that certain functions are so intimately related to the public interest as to mandate performance only by federal employees.[20]

In 1998, the *Federal Activities Inventory Reform Act* (FAIR) required federal agencies to review, inventory, and publicly list those functions that are not inherently governmental and that could therefore be performed by commercial entities. At the same time, FAIR statutorily sanctioned competition between federal agencies and the private sector. To address longstanding concerns in the private sector that government bids in public–private competitions do not fully reflect all costs, FAIR also required the Office of Management and Budget to issue guidance on conducting such competitions. To ensure realistic and fair cost comparisons, FAIR further directed federal agencies to ensure that all costs, including the costs of quality assurance, technical monitoring of the performance of a function, liability insurance, employee retirement and disability benefits, and all other overhead costs, be considered.[21]

These changes over the past 20 years are altering client relationships and redefining what it means to do business with the federal government. Much more business is being conducted using the *Federal Supply Schedules.* More A-76 competitions are being held to determine whether commercial activities should be performed by the government or by commercial entities. There have been major reforms to reduce bid protests and long procurement cycles. The potential value of large federal information technology contracts more frequently reaches or exceeds $100 million. The federal government has created "franchises" and ESOPs. Government agencies are competing against each other to perform administrative services, and companies find themselves bidding against their government clients to provide computer services. In the words of Aldous Huxley, this government market is a "brave new world," one that will certainly bring fascinating challenges in the new millennium.

---

[19]"FAA, $150M Iceman Cometh to USDA," *Federal Computer Week,* May 12, 1997, p. 1; "When the Government Hires the Government, FAA Awards Big Systems Contract to USDA, but to Private Contractors, It Doesn't Compute," *The Washington Post,* May 22, 1997; "Battle Lines Drawn on FAA Contract," *Washington Technology,* July 10, 1997, p. 1.

[20]*OMB Circular A-76,* March 1996.

[21]*Federal Activities Inventory Reform Act (FAIR),* Public Law 105–270, October 19, 1998.

# Government Deregulation, Mergers, and Acquisitions

For various historic, political, and economic reasons, certain major industries in the United States were subject to considerable government regulation. Telecommunications, electric and gas utilities, airlines, and commercial banks are perhaps the best examples. Beginning in the late 1970s and continuing on through the 1990s, the U.S. government in effect eliminated most if not all regulatory control that it had exercised over firms in these industries. Regardless of the original reasons for their regulation, the Government has assumed that by deregulating these industries, consumers will be better served by lower prices, better service, or more rapid introduction of technology that would ostensibly stem from a more competitive environment.

However, in recent years, the deregulation has apparently resulted in such a fiercely competitive environment that a number of companies in these industries have sought to merge or acquire other companies in order to survive and grow. This is somewhat ironic because one of the great concerns of antitrust policy in the United States has been the level of merger activity. As companies merge, is there a danger that their greater size makes them monopolistic and a threat to free competition? If so, then the very actions of the government to make certain industries more competitive may require it to assert its role as the arbiter of what constitutes "competition."

In commercial banking, the mergers (the combination of two firms or the acquisition of one firm by another) that have grabbed most of the headlines have been among the leading financial institutions. Citicorp merged with Traveler's Insurance to form Citigroup. Chemical Bank and Chase Manhattan, merged to become the Chase Bank. Bank of America merged with Nations Bank, BankOne merged with First Chicago, and Wells Fargo merged with Norwest.

In the market for local telecommunications service, the seven Regional Bell Operating Companies that were formed by the breakup of AT&T have become five, and may soon be reduced to four. Pacific Telesis merged with SBC under the name SBC and NYNEX merged with Bell Atlantic, retaining the name Bell Atlantic. As this edition is being prepared, SBC has sought the government's approval to acquire Ameritech, while Bell Atlantic has requested permission to merge with GTE, an independent telecommunications company that was never a part of the old Bell system. In the long distance market, WorldCom acquired MCI (pre-empting an effort by British Telecom to buy MCI) to form MCI WorldCom.

Airline companies in the United States have not been as active in mergers and acquisitions as their counterparts in the other two major deregulated industries, choosing instead to develop alliances in such areas as flight scheduling and terminal connections with international carriers (e.g., American Airlines with British Air, United Airlines with Lufthansa, and Delta Airlines with Air France). However, in early 1999, pilots of American Airlines staged a major "sick-out," causing widespread disruptions in service and resulting in hundreds of millions in lost revenue for the company. The cause of the pilot's work stoppage was their fear that American Airline's recent purchase of a small regional company, Reno Air, would eventually affect their compensation packages. At about the same time, the newspapers reported a possible purchase by United Airlines of America West, one of the smaller national carriers that had not been very profitable, despite an upturn in profits in the whole industry throughout the second half of the decade.

The recent increase in mergers in the deregulated industries is nothing new. The U.S. economy has passed through a number of merger waves since the end of the nineteenth century. During the 1980s and early 1990s, many mergers were motivated by low valuations of the target firms, which had been underperforming. In addition to mergers, this period also saw a large number of leveraged buyouts (LBO's), where public companies were taken private by groups of investors, using large amounts of debt to finance the transaction.[22] In the middle and late 1990s, mergers have been motivated primarily by the necessity to obtain greater efficiencies—economies of scale or scope—to be able to compete in a global economy. This impetus for merging with or acquiring companies is relevant for any industry where the intensity of competition has increased. As we have just pointed out, deregulated industries are perhaps the most dramatic example of situations where there is a sharp increase in competition, but certain other industries that have never been regulated also have undergone significant upheaval. In the automobile industry, mergers and acquisitions making the news include the merger of Daimler-Benz with Chrysler, the Ford Motor Company's purchase of Jaguar and of Volvo's motor vehicle division, and BMW's purchase of Rover. After several years of owning Rover, BMW continues to lose money from this operation and its CEO is being severely criticized for this purchase. BMW's current bad experience with Rover shows that not all mergers and acquisitions result in immediate economic gains (later in this section we summarize studies that have tracked the economic consequences of mergers and acquisitions).

There are many reasons behind merger activity. The basic motivation for mergers is to increase the value of the combined firms compared to their separate valuations. This simple idea is usually expressed with the following equation:

$$V_{A+B} > (V_A + V_B)$$

where $V$ stands for total market value, and A and B are the two companies involved in the merger.

Among the incentives to merge, some result in increased economic efficiency, but others do not. A partial list of incentives follows:

1. *Synergies in production.* If synergies exist, then the value of the combined companies should exceed the value of the two separately. Among the synergistic results we would find the following:
   a. *Revenue enhancements.* For example, a better distribution system for products when two companies combine may increase sales.
   b. *Operating economies.* These results would include economies of scale and/or scope. Economies could also be achieved through improved research and development (because of complementarities in technical skills resident in the two companies) or "management meshing," where the skills of the management of the companies complement each other. For instance, one company

---

[22]The ultimate goal was, of course, to streamline these companies, make them more efficient (possibly by disposing of some parts of the company), and eventually bring them back as publicly owned companies.

has strong marketing management while the other's managers have technical superiority.

   **c.** *Financial economies.* The combined company may be able to lower its cost of capital.

2. *Improved management.* In some cases, the acquired firm may lack good management skills, while the acquiring firm has a relative abundance of skilled managers. The merger will create an opportunity for improving the overall management level of the new company by eliminating poor managers.

3. *Tax consequences.* While a merger may not result in increased economic efficiency, it may reduce the tax bill of the two combined companies. If a company has been incurring losses, it will not be paying taxes. It will carry tax losses forward, and may reduce its tax liabilities in the future when it becomes profitable. By merging with a profitable company, it will be able to save taxes immediately, and increase the combined companies' cash flow even in the absence of any synergies.

   Taxes will also be decreased for a company with much cash and no great investment opportunities. If this company were to pay a large dividend, then its stockholders would pay taxes immediately; or if the company were to buy back its stock, stockholders could be liable for capital gains taxes. By using its cash to acquire another company, it will avoid creating tax liabilities.

4. *Managerial power.* Mergers may occur when the acquiring company's managers are seeking to increase their span of authority. While the acquisition of another company may expand the power of managers, it will, in many cases, not result in enhanced efficiency.

5. *Diversification.* During the 1960s, diversification was the ostensible motivation for a large number of mergers. Mergers among companies in unrelated fields of activity predominated. It was said that diversification could decrease the variability of sales and earnings and thus be of benefit to stockholders, even if no synergistic effects were present. This is a flawed argument. There is no reason why stockholders cannot achieve their own diversification by investing in both companies. This would be accomplished much more cheaply, since it would avoid the significant costs that would be incurred in completing the merger.

6. *Market power.* The combination of two or more powerful firms could lead to a decrease of competition in the industry. The result could be lower production, higher prices, and a negative effect on the efficient functioning of the economy. It is with these potential effects that U.S. antitrust laws are concerned.

A large number of studies have investigated the effects of mergers on stockholders and the economy. We summarize their results as follows:

1. There is general agreement that stockholders of the target companies are the big winners, gaining between 20 and 30 percent when their company is acquired. On the other hand, the stockholders of the acquiring firms gain very little, as their stock prices, on average, remain constant. Overall, there appears to be an increase in the value of the combined companies.

2. The evidence regarding increased profitability of merged firms is rather mixed.

3. Merger activity does not appear to have increased the level of industry concentration.

4. There appears to be no decrease in research and development activity of merged firms, contrary to the opinion of some commentators.

## International Application: Regulators Around the World Try to Hold Back the "Red Team's" Global Expansion[23]

Throughout this text, we have been talking about a fictional company, Global Foods, that is trying to compete in the soft drink market primarily against the "Red Team" and the "Blue Team." Although we had no particular company in mind when we created this firm, one possible candidate for the real Global Foods is Cadbury Schweppes, a British company that sells a variety of confections and soft drinks. A decision it made in early 1999 to sell all of its non-U.S. business to the Coca-Cola Company provides us with a very good example of the international dimension of the relationship between government and industry.

At one time, Cadbury Schweppes' strategy was to become the world's leading seller of non-cola soft drinks. Some of its well-known trademarked brands include Dr. Pepper, Seven-Up, Canada Dry, and Schweppes ginger ale. However, it apparently decided that the resources needed to be a global bottler and marketer of soft drinks are beyond what it had prepared to allocate and thus decided to focus its soft drink business solely in the United States. This is understandable, because the annual per-capita consumption of soft drinks in the United States of 500 12-oz. can equivalents is decidedly greater than any other country in the world (the next highest is the United Kingdom with about 100 cans per capita).

The Coca-Cola Company has 50 percent of the world market share of soft drinks, followed by PepsiCo, Inc. with slightly over 20 percent. Cadbury Schweppes is a distant third with 7.4 percent. The rest of the market is made up of a number of smaller firms. Coca-Cola ended up as the company that successfully bid for Cadbury's non-U.S. soft drink business, with a price of $1.85 billion. If this acquisition is made, then clearly Coca-Cola would become even more dominant in the world soft drink market. But as of this writing regulators in a number of key countries around the world are apparently worried about precisely this fact.

After the deal was announced, regulators in Australia, Belgium, and Germany raised objections and those in Spain and Mexico began to scrutinize it very closely. While this was happening, Coca-Cola's plans to buy Orangina from Pernod Ricard of France for about $800 million was blocked by the French authorities.[24] The specific market share figures in these countries help to explain their regulators' concern. For example, in Australia, Coca-Cola has about 63 percent market share, PepsiCo has 14 percent, and Cadbury Schweppes has about 14.7 percent. Coke's purchase of the Cadbury brands would give it almost 80 percent of the soft drink business in this country.

---

[23]This section is based on "Unquenchable Thirst," *Financial Times,* April 30, 1999.
[24]Recall the mentioning of this product in chapter 7.

---

**THE SOLUTION**

Bill's office was inundated with proposals. The four that made the "short list" were from AT&T, EDS, SBC, and Bell Atlantic. AT&T's proposal made the final cut because it had recently bought IBM's data network and because they were the most experienced in the telecommunications outsourcing business. EDS is known primarily for its data-processing expertise, but its recent acquisition of some of MCI WorldCom's data communications services gave it an advantage as a leading integrator of computer and telecommunications services.

SBC and Bell Atlantic were the two regional bell operating companies that had the most data communications capability. Eager to enter the major leagues, they both came in with lower bids than either AT&T or EDS. However, what surprised Bill the most was how fast the regional bells had progressed in offering data com-

G L O B A L
F O O D S

munications service. For example, in early 1999, SBC had acquired a significant equity stake in Williams, a private company that had developed a nationwide fiber optic cable data network. Bell Atlantic stated that it could provide the latest technology in the area known as "virtual private networks." These were services that used the public network and defined the capacity and features for a client based on software rather than on hardware configurations, called in the industry *bandwidth on demand*. "Regardless of which company we choose," Bill thought to himself, "it is a win for us. Deregulating the telecommunications industry has given us, the customer, more choices, the latest technology, and lower prices. After reviewing these proposals, I realize that outsourcing noncore activities can be financially as well as strategically justified."

---

## Summary

We have illustrated specifically how various business decisions can be influenced by government involvement in the market economy. As we discussed in chapter 1, the primary advantage of the market process over the command and traditional processes is the efficient manner in which market participants allocate a country's scarce resources. Throughout this text, we have tried to show how managers, equipped with an understanding of the major factors of the market process (supply, demand, production, cost, and competition) and various quantitative tools of analysis are able to make optimal decisions to help their firms maximize economic profit.

However, managers often must take government involvement into account in the making of an optimal decision. This is particularly true when managers operate on a global basis and must deal with the laws and regulations of different governments. Coca-Cola's intended purchase of Cadbury Schweppes non-U.S. soft drink business provided a good case in point. To be sure, government laws and regulations can reduce a firm's profits. But at the same time, as we have shown, the government itself is a major customer and so businesses can in fact profit by being suppliers to the government's demand for various goods and services. Today's manager must be equally versed in matters of government as well as private industry.

## Important Concepts

**Benefit externalities:** Benefits that accrue to individuals other than those who have paid for a particular good or service, also referred to as *positive benefits, spillover benefits, third-party benefits,* and *social benefits.* The demand for products with external benefits tends to be understated in the market. (p. 554)

**Coase Theorem:** The idea, developed by Ronald Coase, that government intervention to eliminate the effect of externalities is not necessary if property rights are correctly and clearly defined. (p. 556)

**Cost externalities:** Costs incurred by individuals other than those who produce a particular good or service, also referred to as *negative costs, spillover costs,* and *social costs.* The supply of goods whose production involves cost externalities tends to be overstated in the market. A good example of cost externalities is environmental pollution. (p. 555)

**Monopsony:** A market in which there is only one buyer. The government procurement office is often cited as a good example of a monopsony. (p. 557)

**Natural monopoly:** An industry in which a single large firm can serve customers more efficiently than many smaller ones because of economies of scale. (p. 551)

**Socially optimal price:** The price of a good or service that is equal to its marginal cost of production. (p. 555)

## Questions

1. What is the rationale for government involvement in the market economy? (Cite the five points presented at the outset of this chapter.)
2. Define *benefit* and *cost externalities.* Explain why situations involving benefit externalities tend to result in an underallocation of society's scarce resources, and why situations involving cost externalities tend to result in an overallocation of society's scarce resources.
3. What is the role of government in dealing with benefit externalities? With cost externalities?
4. Suppose a chemical company was fined for violating certain antipollution laws. As the spokesperson for the Environmental Protection Agency, how would you explain the economic reasons for these actions to angry customers of this company who were forced to pay more for the chemicals as a result of this government action?
5. "The reason the government has to step in and 'internalize' benefit and cost externalities is because people are basically selfish." Do you agree with this statement? Explain.
6. Briefly discuss the Coase theorem. What does this theory imply about the role of government in dealing with market externalities?
7. Based on the information presented in this chapter and on your own reading, do you think Microsoft is operating as an illegal monopoly? Explain.
8. In 1998, American Express announced that it was not going to bid for a renewal of its contract with the federal government to provide its purchasing card for government employees. The

government replaced it with Visa and MasterCard purchasing cards. Why do you think American Express decided not to continue this particular business with the federal government? Briefly elaborate.

9. Discuss the economic justification for a merger. In particular, how might these reasons apply to companies now merging in the following industries: oil, automobiles, telecommunications, electric power, commercial banks?

## Take It to the Net

We invite you to visit the Keat/Young page on the Prentice Hall Web site at:

**http://www.prenhall.com/keat**

for additional resources.

# 16

# Managerial Economics in Action: The Case of the Semiconductor Industry

Throughout this text, we have presented examples of ways that economic concepts can be applied to business situations faced by many different companies in a variety of industries, including our hypothetical company, Global Foods Inc., which competes in the beverage industry. In this concluding chapter, we focus on one industry and on one actual company in this industry. We selected the semiconductor industry because it is an excellent example of a market that is constantly buffeted by the economic forces of supply and demand. We selected Standard Microsystems because its recent experiences clearly reveal how challenging it is for a company to compete in such a market.

We start by presenting in its entirety an analysis of the semiconductor industry conducted by researchers at Standard & Poor's. Readers may also wish to refer to reports on this industry by other sources such as Value Line or the research provided by analysts in stock brokerage firms. Following the industry study, we examine some of the key economic challenges that have been faced by Standard Microsystems. We conclude this chapter with a letter written by the CEO of this company to its shareholders and employees at about the time that this text was being revised. At the beginning of this text, we introduced readers to Bob Burns, a fictional CEO, who had to deal with a number of economic problems and challenges. At the close of this text, readers have the chance to review a letter from a real CEO describing the economic challenges faced by his company. We can think of no better way to dramatize the importance for managers of understanding economic concepts and tools of analysis.

## Industry Analysis

Following is an analysis by Standard & Poor's of the semiconductor market, reprinted in its entirety. Passages related directly to the economic concepts and tools of analysis presented in this text are in boldface type. Each highlighted passage is followed by brief comments and a citation of chapter and pages to which the reader may want to return for additional review.

# Chip Market Meltdown[1]

Several factors have converged to create a severe slump that has gripped nearly every sector of the global semiconductor industry. **Among the factors playing prominent roles in the downturn are the global economic slowdown, chronic industry overcapacity, weak pricing, and the emergence of the sub-$1000 personal computer (PC).**

***Comment:*** *Chronic industry overcapacity can be represented by a rightward shift in the supply curve; emergence of the sub-$1000 PC by the leftward shift in the demand curve (decrease in the price of a substitute product causes a decrease in the good in question). Weak pricing can be shown by the downward pressures on price caused by the surplus resulting from the greater supply and lower demand (Figure 16.1).*

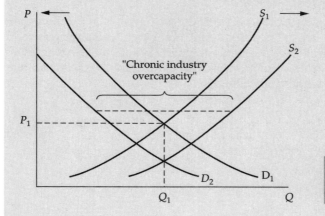

**FIGURE 16.1** Market for Chips Used in PCs Selling for More than $1,000

*Reference: nonprice determinants of demand and supply, ch. 3 (pp. 71–72, 75)*

Most recent data published by the Semiconductor Industry Association (SIA) reveal continued contraction in the chip market, providing little hope for a near term bounce-back. In July 1998, worldwide semiconductor sales were down 17% from the year earlier period, representing the worst monthly comparison thus far in 1998. The Japanese market, down more than 30% that month was the hardest hit. While nearly two-thirds of Japan's decline was attributed to the sharp depreciation of the yen versus the dollar (because sales are denominated in dollars), weak end market demand and persistent pricing pressures remained evident. Europe, off just 3.9% in July, was the strongest geographic region.

----

[1]*Industry Surveys: Semiconductors,* Standard & Poor's, October 29, 1998, pp. 1–4.

## WORSE THAN PRIOR DOWNTURNS

Semiconductor industry observers are quick to note that the chip market, which on average grew 17% a year over the past two decades, is notoriously volatile. To be sure, the industry has experienced periods of slow, and even negative growth in the past, intermingled with boom periods. Over the past 23 years, the industry has posted year-over-year sales declines on three different occasions (1975, 1985, and 1996). The years 1989 through 1992 represented the longest period during which semiconductor industry sales grew less than 10% in each year.

In this historical context, the current semiconductor industry downturn appears to be more protracted than those of the past. In 1975 and 1985, for example, when revenues declined by 17% and 12% respectively, the industry subsequently rebounded sharply. In fact, each down year was followed by a three- to five-year period of above-trend growth.

Following the most recent down year in 1996, however, the chip market has proven to be less resilient than in the past. After dropping 8% in 1996, industry revenues rebounded by only 4% in 1997, and year-to-date sales through July 1998 were down 11%. Thus, 1998 is likely to be the second year of negative semiconductor industry growth within three years.

## ASIAN CRISIS CRIMPS DEMAND

In our view, the global economic slowdown continues to be the primary hurdle to a semiconductor industry recovery. **Chips are merely components used in a myriad of other goods, ranging from personal computers to automobiles. Therefore, to the degree that sales of these and other semiconductor-rich final products are economically sensitive, so too are sales of semiconductors.**

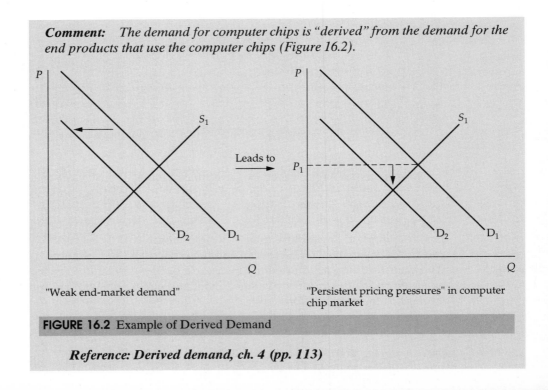

*Comment:* *The demand for computer chips is "derived" from the demand for the end products that use the computer chips (Figure 16.2).*

"Weak end-market demand"

"Persistent pricing pressures" in computer chip market

**FIGURE 16.2** Example of Derived Demand

*Reference: Derived demand, ch. 4 (pp. 113)*

While still generally healthy, the growth rates of some of the world's top original equipment makers (OEMs)—including PC manufacturers, telecommunications firms, and data networking companies—have slowed because of deteriorating economic conditions. For example, International Data Corporation (IDC), an independent research firm, estimates that year-to-year PC sales growth in the third quarter of 1998 tapered off to 11%, down sharply from 20% in the third quarter of 1997. This slower growth, in conjunction with continued OEM inventory reductions, has resulted in the recent flat semiconductor unit sales growth. **While unit sales have remained steady, revenues have fallen as a result of continuously declining prices.**

***Comment:*** *The increase in supply causes an increase in the quantity sold. The decrease in demand causes a decrease in the quantity sold. The two changes can offset each other, resulting in little or no change in the market quantity (Figure 16.3).*

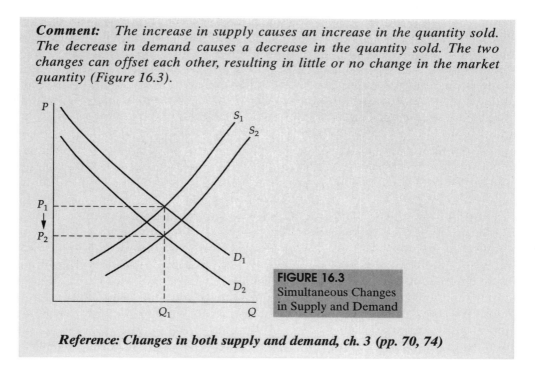

**FIGURE 16.3**
Simultaneous Changes in Supply and Demand

***Reference: Changes in both supply and demand, ch. 3 (pp. 70, 74)***

The well-documented Asian financial crisis has been a primary factor in the semiconductor industry downturn. From 1990 to 1997, the Asia/Pacific region (excluding Japan) was the world's fastest growing chip market. Driven by average annual expansion of 26%, the region's share of the semiconductor market grew from 14% to 22% during that seven-year time frame. Although Japan has seen much slower growth than the rest of the Asian region in recent years, it still accounted for 23% of global semiconductor consumption in 1997.

Clearly, Asia's economic meltdown is hurting end-market demand for semiconductor-rich electronic goods. Across the board, producers of PCs, cellular phones, communications equipment and other electronic goods are reporting weak demand from the region. Accordingly, OEM semiconductor order patterns have slowed.

An analysis of World Semiconductor Trade Statistics (WSTS) data underscores the depth of Asia's recent weakness. In the three months ended July 1998, chip sales to

Asia (excluding Japan) fell 10% from the immediately preceding three months and were down 14% from the three-month period ended July 1997. During the same time period, sales in Japan fell 10% from the preceding three months, and 30% from the year-earlier period.

### ECONOMICS 101: OVERSUPPLY + WEAK DEMAND = FALLING PRICES

According to Integrated Circuit Engineering Corp., an independent research firm based in Scottsdale, Arizona, the average selling price (ASP) per semiconductor unit fell to an all-time low of $1.79 in the first quarter of 1998, down almost 40% from the 1995 peak. **Chip prices generally fall as manufacturers pass cost savings on to customers in an attempt to stimulate unit demand.** Recent price erosion has been steeper than normal, however, largely reflecting a precipitous drop in commodity memory chip prices.

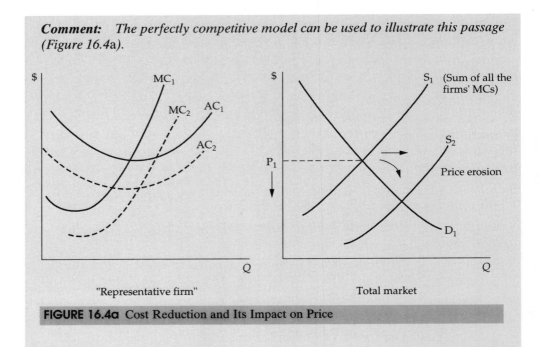

*Comment:* *The perfectly competitive model can be used to illustrate this passage (Figure 16.4a).*

"Representative firm"          Total market

**FIGURE 16.4a** Cost Reduction and Its Impact on Price

 *Each firm's reduction in cost (left graph) leads to an increase in the total market supply,* decreasing market price (right graph).

 *The model of imperfect competition can also be used (Figure 16.4b). Suppose the "price leader" follows the MR = MC rule in establishing the market price $P_1$ for itself and the other firms in the market. A decrease in the leader's cost (noted in the diagram by $AC_2$ and $MC_2$) would cause it to lower its price to $P_2$, assuming it continues to follow the MR = MC rule.*

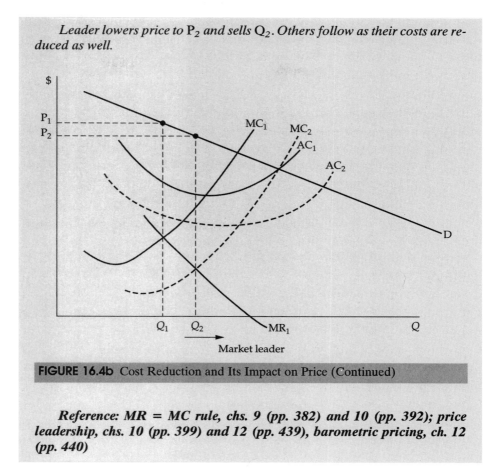

*Leader lowers price to* $P_2$ *and sells* $Q_2$. *Others follow as their costs are reduced as well.*

**FIGURE 16.4b** Cost Reduction and Its Impact on Price (Continued)

*Reference: MR = MC rule, chs. 9 (pp. 382) and 10 (pp. 392); price leadership, chs. 10 (pp. 399) and 12 (pp. 439), barometric pricing, ch. 12 (pp. 440)*

This rapid reduction in average selling prices is a function of both oversupply and slower unit growth. **Chip makers, tempted by prospects of strong profitability, invested heavily in manufacturing capacity between 1994 and 1997. This aggressive investment, coupled with enormous advances in productivity, has led to the oversupply condition that currently prevails in the marketplace.**

*Comment:* *The concept of "short-run" and "long-run" market changes is very useful in helping to understand this passage. Assume the short run is 1994 and the long run effects take place three years later, in 1997. In 1994 we can imagine that the "typical firm" earns an economic profit at the current market price, as shown in Figure 16.5a:*

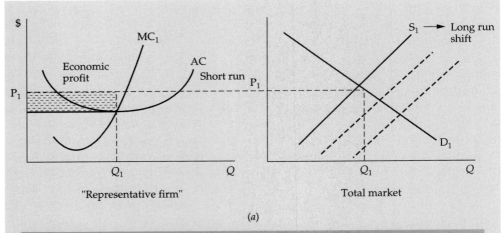

(a)

**FIGURE 16.5a** Short- and Long-Run Changes

Seeing this economic profit, this firm and all others like it begin to make investments to increase their capacity. This increase in capacity causes their average
and marginal cost curves to shift to the right. The increase in productivity would
cause the curves to shift downward and to the right, as we see in Figure 16.5b.

Although the firm's AC drops, it still has trouble earning economic profit because the market price also drops considerably.

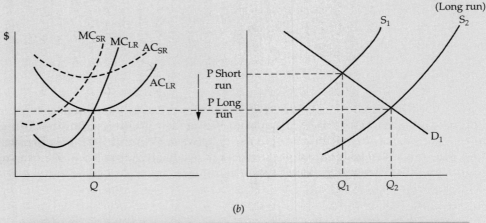

(b)

**FIGURE 16.5b** Cost Reduction and Increasing Supply

**Reference: Long-run market changes, ch. 3 (pp. 80–81); changes in the cost
curves, ch. 8 (pp. 309–310)**

Recent productivity gains have been characterized by the shrinking of device sizes, which in turn enables manufacturers to cram more chips on the same square inch of silicon. As chipmakers have rapidly accelerated to .25 micron processing and below, a glut of semiconductor supply has ensued. **Compounding the oversupply condition is the recent slowdown in semiconductor unit demand. From the peak in 1995 to the first quarter of 1998, the 28% increase in chip unit volume sales was not enough to offset the 40% decline in selling prices. This slower-than-expected unit expansion has significantly hampered chipmakers' capacity utilization rates.** According to SIA data, metal-oxide semiconductor (MOS) fabrication plants ("fabs" in industry parlance) were running at 86.4% of capacity in the second quarter of 1998, compared with 90.2% in the first quarter. At the peak of the cycle in the second half of 1995, MOS IC makers were running their fabs at 96.9% capacity.

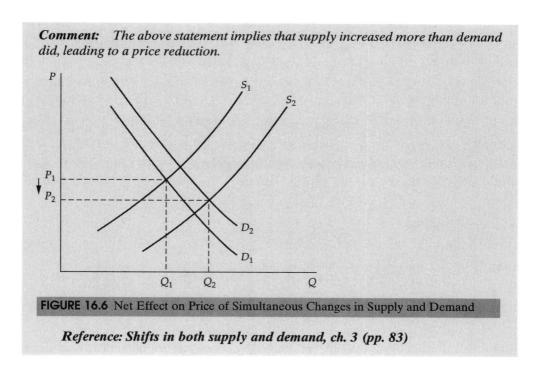

**Comment:** *The above statement implies that supply increased more than demand did, leading to a price reduction.*

**FIGURE 16.6** Net Effect on Price of Simultaneous Changes in Supply and Demand

*Reference: Shifts in both supply and demand, ch. 3 (pp. 83)*

As the economic environment has deteriorated, recent unit sales growth has fallen even further, to virtually zero. **Since semiconductor manufacturing costs are largely fixed in nature, the lower capacity utilization rates have resulted in significant deterioration of industry profits.**

*Comment:* This passage brings to mind the concepts of break-even and operating leverage. The high fixed cost means that computer chip manufacturers
have a high operating leverage. Any reduction in volume reduces their ability to
earn a high contribution margin. Moreover, if the volume falls below the break-
even point, the high operating leverage implies serious losses for these firms
(Figure 16.7).

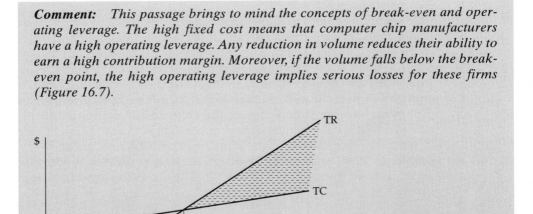

Large amounts of profits are lost as volume is pushed down
closer to break even point.

**FIGURE 16.7** Reduction
in Quantity and High
Operating Leverage:
Impact on Profit

*Reference: Operating leverage, ch. 11 (pp. 421 and 426)*

## DRAM MARKET SHAKEUP

Without question, the market for dynamic random access memory (DRAM) chips
has been the hardest hit sector during the semiconductor market slide. DRAMS are
commodity chips used extensively in PCs to store data. Despite continued solid demand from the PC sector, DRAM prices fell dramatically over the past three years,
reflecting the industry's overcapacity. A recent study by Sematech, an industry
trade group, concluded that the chip industry has roughly 15 more 200-millimeter
fabs than it needs to support memory market demand. According to Micron Technology, the largest U.S. DRAM company, per-megabit prices declined approximately 45% in the fiscal year ended August 1996, 75% in fiscal 1997, and 60% in
fiscal 1998.

**With even the leanest of manufacturers operating in the red, some DRAM indus-
try participants have begun to reexamine their commitment to the struggling sector.
Other companies are going the merger route, in the hope that consolidation will restore
rationality to the chaotic market.**

> **Comment:** *This passage points out how difficult it is to make money in a competitive market because firms are unable to exert market power and can only make a profit by continually lowering costs. It then points out that by merging, price takers hope to attain a certain amount of market power (i.e., price-making power).*
> **Reference: Perfect competition, ch. 9 (pp. 357); monopolistic competition and oligopoly, ch. 10 (pp. 412)**

## MICRON, TEXAS INSTRUMENTS TIE THE KNOT

In June 1998, Micron Technology agreed to acquire the semiconductor memory assets of Texas Instruments (TI) for a combination of common stock and the assumption of debt totaling approximately $800 million. This complex transaction, which closed in October 1998, included TI's share in two DRAM manufacturing joint ventures.

**For TI, the move is one of many strategic divestitures of non-core businesses over the last several years. The company's focus is now squarely on the digital signal processing (DSP) market, where it holds a commanding 45% share.**

**For Micron, the transaction will allow the firm to acquire manufacturing capacity at very favorable financial terms. According to the agreement, Micron will receive $750 million in financing from TI, facilitating the deployment of Micron's superior manufacturing technology in the plants. Micron will gain market share, without a significant increase in research and development or in operating costs.**

> **Comment:** *This move by TI can be seen as an effort to secure the role of price leader in the DSP market. At the very least, by focusing on a market in which it has a 45 percent share, it has a better chance of exercising some degree of market power, regardless of whether it is the clear-cut price leader. By the same token, Micron may see itself as having a better chance of controlling the price in the chip market by increasing its market share. We can also imagine that Micron's financial help from TI and the avoidance of additional R&D and operating costs would make the capital budgeting results very attractive, if Micron actually conducted such an analysis.*
> **Reference: Oligopoly pricing and price leadership, chs. 10 (pp. 396) and 12 (pp. 439); capital budgeting, ch. 13 (pp. 475)**

## KOREAN MEGAMERGER FURTHER CONCENTRATES MARKET

Under pressure from the Korean government, semiconductor giants Hyundai Electronics Co. and LG Semicon Co. agreed to merge in September 1998. The transaction was part of a massive swap of *chaebol* (a Korean word for conglomerate) subsidiaries in the aerospace, petrochemical, railroad, rolling stock, and power generation industries. As of this writing, important details regarding the agreement, including management control and shareholding levels, had yet to be decided.

**This merger, in conjunction with the TI/Micron agreement, will concentrate roughly two-thirds of DRAM industry market share in the hands of four suppliers.**

> *Comment:* *According to the rule of thumb, the "four-firm concentration ratio,"*
> *this makes this market an oligopoly. Will Samsung be the leader?*
> *Reference: Oligopoly and firm-firm concentration ration, ch. 10 (pp. 395)*

According to Dataquest, a market research firm, Korea's Samsung remains the largest DRAM producer, with 19% market share, followed by Hyundai/LG Semicon (16% market share), Micron/Texas Instruments (14%) and Japan's NEC Corp. (12%).

**This fundamental shift in the balance of DRAM power could lead to a shake-out among second- and third-tier suppliers, which may find it difficult to compete with the resources of the "big four." In recent months, some smaller DRAM makers have opted to scale back production, particularly for older-generation chips.** For example, Hitachi Ltd. closed its four-megabit (Mb) fab in Irving, Texas, and Matsushita Electric Industrial Co. Ltd. announced in September that it would close its U.S. fab in Puyallup, Washington. Fujitsu Ltd. also reported that it was closing its U.K. fab, which manufactured 16-Mb devices.

> *Comment:* *This is an interesting variation in the perfectly competitive and oli-*
> *gopoly models. We discussed an industry shake-out as part of the long-run adjust-*
> *ment process in a perfectly competitive market. However, as this passage indicates,*
> *the shake-out can also occur in imperfect competition. We can imagine that the*
> *"second- and third-tier firms" that may be shaken out of the market are the price*
> *followers. They must in fact take the prices that are either set by the forces of supply*
> *and demand or that the larger leaders set, given whatever supply and demand con-*
> *ditions exist in the market.*
> *Reference: Long-term industry adjustment, chs. 3 (pp. 80–81) and 9 (pp. 371);*
> *price leadership, ch. 12 (pp. 439).*

## HAVE DRAM PRICES HIT BOTTOM?

Although a full-fledged recovery in the beleaguered DRAM market has not yet occurred, some positive signs have emerged. After bottoming out in June 1998, prices for 64-Mb DRAMs ticked higher in July and were relatively stable in August and September. **The price comeback has been fueled by production cutbacks, coupled with continued increases in memory content per PC.**

It remains to be seen, however, if the recent price stabilization is sustainable. In part, current demand trends reflect seasonal strength, as PC makers order components in advance of the holiday selling season. Furthermore, any near-term uptick in price may result in additional supply being brought to the market, thereby causing prices to retreat again.

*Comment:*   *This passage is a good illustration of the on-going adjustment process that takes place in a competitive market, even one that is less than perfect. In the text, we have tried to show this adjustment in terms of "short run" versus "long run." But as this passage shows, industry analysts do not usually make this distinction.*
     *Reference: Long-run adjustment, chs. 3 (pp. 80–81) and 9 (pp. 371)*

## OUTLOOK FOR MODERATE RECOVERY IN 1999

In June 1998, the Semiconductor Industry Association (SIA) issued a forecast calling for chip industry sales to fall 1.8% in 1998, followed by 17.2% growth in 1999. **The SIA indicated that economic turbulence in Asia would limit expansion in 1998, but predicted that explosive growth in Internet usage would likely push chip industry growth to near historic levels in 1999.** We believe this forecast is overly optimistic. Semiconductor sales were down approximately 11% through July 1998, and recent data suggest that the pace of the decline is accelerating. **On a positive note, reports suggest that OEM component inventory levels are very low, hinting that chip demand, particularly for microprocessors, should be firm as we enter the seasonally strong fourth quarter.** Consequently, we expect total chip industry sales to be down roughly 10% to 12% for full-year 1998.

The outlook for 1999 remains clouded by many of the issues presented in this section—namely economic malaise in Asia, continued overcapacity, and the resultant weak pricing environment. The SIA forecast for 17.2% growth in 1999 is predicated in part on a quick improvement in DRAM supply/demand dynamics, and nearly 27% sales growth in this sector.

**The recent sharp capital-spending cutback by chip manufacturers in every geographic market will help to alleviate the oversupply problem;** but we believe overcapacity will linger at least through the first half of 1999. The relentless shrinking of device sizes and aggressive moves to below .25 micron processing continue to reveal "hidden capacity" in manufacturing facilites, to the detriment of the supply/demand equation.

**Still, we believe the chip market will rebound by roughly 10% in 1999. Despite the weak economic environment in Asia, prosperity in key end-markets for semiconductors, including PCs and communications equipment, should drive demand for microprocessors, DRAMs, and digital signal processors. In addition, the emergence of new consumer products, such as digital cameras and digital video disks, should help to expand chip industry opportunities.**

*Comment:*   *All the passages marked in this concluding section are good examples of how various factors can be used in qualitative forecasting (i.e., forecasting the direction and relative strength of the change in demand and supply rather than the numerical magnitude). For this type of analysis, a thorough understanding of the nonprice determinants of demand and supply is essential.*
     *Reference: Nonprice determinants of demand and supply, ch. 3 (pp. 71–72, 75); forecasting techniques, ch. 6 (pp. 206)*

# The Case of Standard Microsystems Corporation (SMSC)

We now look at a specific company operating within the turbulent semiconductor industry. We selected a relatively small company, Standard Microsystems Corporation (SMSC), because its recent trials and tribulations present a fascinating example of the challenges facing the managers of a company that must deal with the economic pressures of the highly competitive market for computer chips. Standard Microsystems Corporation describes itself in the following way:

> *SMSC is a worldwide supplier of metal-oxide-semiconductor/very-large-scale-integrated (MOS/VLSI) circuits (ICs) for the personal computer industry and is also a foundry supplier of MicroElectroMechanical Systems (MEMS) devices. The Company is most prominent as one of the world's leading suppliers of input/output (I/O) circuits for personal computers. I/O circuits perform many of the basic input/output functions required in every personal computer, including floppy disk control, keyboard control and BIOS, parallel port control, and serial port control. The Company also supplies ICs for local area network applications, connectivity applications and embedded control systems. While most of the Company's IC products are manufactured by world-class semiconductor foundries and assemblers, the Company's MEMS devices are produced in the Company's own wafer foundry, which specializes in MEMS manufacturing.*
>
> *Standard Microsystems Corporation sells its ICs worldwide and counts most of the world's leading personal computer and personal computer motherboard manufacturers as customers for its I/O circuits. The company's I/O circuits reside on the motherboards of personal computer products made by Compaq Computer Corporation, Dell Computer Corporation, IBM, Intel Corporation, Hewlett-Packard Company and most other leading personal computer manufacturers.*
>
> *The company is based in Hauppauge, New York and maintains offices in the United States, Europe and Asia. The Company conducts its business in the Japanese market through its majority-owned subsidiary, Toyo Microsystems Corporation.[2]*

For its fiscal year ending February 28, 1998, SCSM incurred an operating loss of $5.8 million and a net loss of $18.9 million on revenues of about $155.7 million. It also lost money in the previous fiscal year. The size of its revenue indicates that it is one of the smaller players in the semiconductor market. (1997 revenues for Intel and Texas Instruments, in contrast, were about $25 billion and $10 billion, respectively.) In the first six months of its new fiscal year, it managed to earn an operating profit of $.73 million and a net income of about $1 million on revenue of $78.5 million.

---

[2]Standard Microsystems Corporation, *Annual Report, 1998,* Hauppauge, NY: SMSC, 1998, p. 13. More information about the company can be found on the World Wide Web at www.smsc.com.

As indicated by its bottom-line results over the past several years, the company suffered serious setbacks, some of which are directly related to the soft semiconductor market. Readers will see in the next section that SMSC's CEO took a number of steps to restore the profitability of the company. Ample illustrations of the challenges facing SMSC in the volatile semiconductor market are provided in its 1997 annual report, particularly in the section, "Management's Discussion and Analysis of Financial Conditions and Results of Operations." Every company's annual report contains such a section. It provides valuable information for current or would-be investors in a company as well as interesting real-world examples for students of managerial economics. In particular, we will take passages from the subsection, "Other Factors That May Affect Future Operating Results." As we did with Standard & Poor's industry report, the passages in the subsection most relevant to managerial economics are highlighted, followed by our comments.

## OTHER FACTORS THAT MAY AFFECT FUTURE OPERATING RESULTS[3]

Certain statements and information contained in this annual report constitute "forward-looking statements" within the meaning of the Federal Securities laws. These forward-looking statements involve **risks and uncertainties** which may cause actual results and performance to be different from those expressed or implied in such statements.

> **Comment:** *Not only do companies have to consider risks and uncertainties when they make certain internal decisions about long-term investment in various projects, but they also have to disclose their beliefs about these risks to those who are external to the company, such as stockholders. As you will see, many of these risks pertain directly to the economics of their business.*
> *Reference: Risk factors, ch. 14 (pp. 517)*

### The Semiconductor Industry

The Company competes in the semiconductor industry, which has historically been characterized by **intense competition, rapid technological change, cyclical market patterns, price erosion, and periods of mismatched supply and demand.** The semiconductor industry has experienced significant economic downturns at various times in the past, characterized by diminished product demand and accelerated erosion of selling prices. In addition, **many of the Company's competitors in the semiconductor industry are larger and have significantly greater financial and other resources than the Company.**

---

[3]Ibid., pp. 18–19.

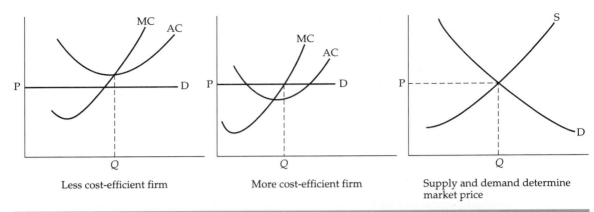

Less cost-efficient firm        More cost-efficient firm        Supply and demand determine market price

**FIGURE 16.8** Different Levels of Success at Given Market Price

> **Comment:**   *In Standard & Poor's industry survey reprinted earlier in this chapter, you had a sort of "bird's-eye view" of the turbulent semiconductor industry. With this passage, you get a sense of what it must be like to be in the center of the storm. This is particularly rough, given the fact that SMSC is a relatively small company without the resources or economies of scale that are afforded the dominant computer chip manufacturers.*
> *Economic theory generally refers to a "representative" or "typical" firm. From this passage you are reminded that with a given market price, some firms fare better than others because they are not all alike. Figure 16.8 uses the model of perfect competition to illustrate this.*
> **Reference: Cost structure and competition, ch. 9 (pp. 368–70)**

### The Personal Computer Industry

**Sales of most of the Company's products depend largely on sales of personal computers.** Reductions in the rate of growth in the PC market could adversely affect the Company's operating results. In addition, **as a component supplier to PCX manufacturers, the Company often experiences a greater magnitude of demand fluctuation than its customers themselves experience. Also, some of the Company's products are used in the PCs for the consumer market,** which, in recent years, has tended to be a more volatile market than other segments of the PC marketplace.

> **Comment:**   *As indicated earlier, the demand for semiconductors is derived from the demand for personal computers. When the demand for PCs falls, so does the demand for the computer chips.*
> **Reference: Derived demand, ch. 4 (pp. 113)**

## Product Development and Technological Change

The Company's success is highly dependent upon the successful development and timely introduction of new products at competitive prices and performance levels. The success of new products depends on various factors, including timely completion of product development programs, **market acceptance of the Company's and its customers' new products, securing sufficient foundry capacity for volume manufacturing of wafers, achieving acceptable wafer fabrication yield by the Company's independent foundries** and the Company's ability to offer new products at competitive prices. **In order to succeed** in having the Company's products incorporated into new products being designed by its customers, **the Company must anticipate market trends and meet performance, quality and functionalist requirement of such customers and must successfully develop and manufacture products that adhere to these requirements.** In addition, the Company must meet the timing and price requirements of its customers and must make such products available in sufficient quantities. **In order to help accomplish these goals, the Company has considered in the past and will continue to consider in the future the acquisition of other companies or the products and technologies of other companies. Such acquisitions carry additional risks such as a lack of integration with existing products and corporate culture, the potential for large write-offs, and the diversion of management attention.**

> **Comment:**  *In economic theory, it is assumed that whatever the demand and price, firms have the ability to meet the demand with an adequate quantity supplied. Here we see that in the real world, this is not always the case and in fact, for smaller firms, providing adequate supply can be serious problem. Small firms may link up with other firms or use the production capacity of other firms to ease this problem, but as indicated in this passage, this implies certain downside risks.*

There can be no assurance that the Company will be able to identify market trends or new product opportunities, develop and market new products, achieve design wins or respond effectively to new technological changes or product announcements by others.

> **Comment:**  *As in the previous passages, this passage gives a good idea of the difference between theory and reality. In economic theory, it is assumed that firms will respond to changes in market conditions, following the dictates of profit maximization and the MR = MC rule. But in reality, it is not always clear which particular product market will offer the best chance to maximize economic profit.*

## Price Erosion

The semiconductor industry is characterized by intense competition. Historically, average selling prices in the semiconductor industry generally, and for the Company's products in particular, have declined significantly over the life of each product. While the company expects to reduce the average selling prices of its products over time as it achieves manufacturing cost reductions, competitive pressures may require the reduction of selling prices more quickly than such cost reductions can be achieved. In addition, the Company sometimes approves price reductions on specific sales opportunities to meet competition. If not offset by reductions in manufacturing costs or by a shift in the mix of products sold toward higher-margined products, declines in the average selling prices can reduce gross margin.

> **Comment:** *This whole section is a great example of what it means to be a firm operating as a price follower or price taker in a highly competitive market. The challenges of trying to earn a profit solely by keeping costs down are very real. If a firm cannot earn a profit by lowering its costs, it has to try to exercise some degree of price-making power by differentiating its products. The passage's reference to the need to shift to "higher-margined products" indicates to us that the managers of this company understand this point quite well. This idea is the basis for Porter's generic strategies of differentiation and cost leadership.*
>     *Reference: **Monopolistic competition and Porter's ideas on strategy, ch. 10 (pp. 408–9)***

### Reliance upon Subcontract Manufacturing

The vast majority of the Company's products are manufactured, assembled, and tested by independent foundries and subcontract manufacturers. **This reliance upon foundries and subcontractors involves certain risks, including potential lack of manufacturing availability, reduced control over delivery schedules, the availability of advanced process technologies, changes in manufacturing yields, and potential cost fluctuations.**

> **Comment:** *To reduce costs and the capital investment, companies such as SMSC have resorted to outsourcing of manufacturing (part of the "deverticalization" of manufacturing discussed in the text). Another advantage of outsourcing manufacturing is the reduction in factory overhead costs (e.g., fixed manufacturing costs) and hence the reduction in the operating leverage of the company. As you know, this helps to reduce its risk. As this statement shows, there are other downside risks associated with this effort to reduce operating costs and investment in fixed assets. In an effort to reduce the risk of high operating leverage, these risks must be taken into account.*
>     *Reference: **Operating leverage, ch. 11 (pp. 426) and Outsourcing, ch. 2 (p. 25), ch. 8 (p. 302)***

### Forecasts of Product Demand

The Company generally must order inventory to be built by its foundries and subcontract manufacturers well in advance of product shipments. Production is often based upon either internal or customer-supplied forecasts of demand, which can be highly unpredictable and subject to substantial fluctuations. Because of the volatility in the Company's markets, there is risk that the Company may forecast incorrectly and produce excess or insufficient inventories. This inventory risk is increased by the trend for customers to place orders with increasingly shorter lead times.

> **Comment:** *Forecasting is not just an academic exercise. An accurate forecast is vital to this company's financial health.*
> *Reference: Forecasting, ch. 6 (pp. 204); three stages of production, ch. 7 (pp. 269)*

## Business Concentration in Asia

A significant number of the company's foundries and subcontractors are located in Asia. Many of the Company's customers also manufacture in Asia or subcontract their manufacturing to Asian companies. **This concentration of manufacturing and selling activity in Asia poses risks that could affect demand for and supply of the Company's products, including currency exchange rate fluctuations, economic and trade policies, and the political environment within Asian communities.**

> **Comment:** *Global and international activity is now an important part of American business—it has the advantages of expanding product markets and reducing product costs, but also carries with it certain risks. This is a good example of the kinds of risks involved in global operations. We have illustrated this risk in the "International Application" at the end of most of the chapters.*

## Protection of Intellectual Property

The Company has historically devoted significant resources to research and development activities and believes that the intellectual property derived from such research and development is a valuable asset that has been and will continue to be important to the Company's success. The Company relies upon nondisclosure agreements, contractual provisions, and patent and copyright laws to protect its proprietary rights. No assurance can be given that the steps taken by the Company will adequately protect its proprietary rights.

## Customer Concentration

**A limited number of customers account for a significant portion of the Company's revenues.** The Company's revenues from any one customer can fluctuate from period to period depending upon market demand for that customer's products, the customer's inventory management of the Company's products, and the overall financial condition of the customer.

> **Comment:** *The company is in a* monopsonistic *market, one in which relatively few buyers exercise considerable power in setting the market price. (A market that has only one buyer is called a* monopsony.*)*
> *Reference: Monopsony power of the federal government, ch. 15 (pp. 557)*

## Dependence on Key Personnel

The success of the Company is dependent in large part on the continued service of its key management, engineering, marketing, sales, and support employees. Competition for qualified personnel is intense in the semiconductor industry, and the loss of current key employees, or the inability of the Company to attract other qualified personnel, could hinder the Company's product development and ability to manufacture, market, and sell its products.

> *Comment:*  *The economic theory of the firm assumes that inputs of a particular type (e.g., labor) are equally qualified (e.g., homogeneous labor inputs). Clearly in the real world this is not true, and this is particularly important to keep in mind in knowledge-intensive industries such as semiconductors.*
> *Reference: Assumptions made in establishing the production function, ch. 7 (pp. 248)*

### Volatility of Stock Price

**The market price of the Company's common stock can fluctuate significantly** on the basis of such factors as the Company's or its competitors' announcements of new products, quarterly fluctuations in the Company's financial results or in the financial results of other semiconductor companies, or general conditions in the semiconductor industry or in the financial markets. In addition, stock markets in general have recently experienced extreme price and volume volatility. This volatility has had a significant impact on the stock price of high technology companies, at times for reasons unrelated to the performance of the specific companies.

> *Comment:*  *As pointed out in chapter 2, the creation of shareholder wealth is an important objective of any publicly held company. This section reminds the reader that a company in the semiconductor industry is subject to many short-run changes in market value.*
> *Reference: Shareholder wealth, ch. 2 (pp. 32)*

# Managerial Economics and the Job of the Chief Executive Officer

The economic theory of the firm tends to talk about the "representative firm" as an abstract entity. It does not make specific references to the people in the firm. There is no mention of hierarchy and organization, the leadership ability of its managers, or the differences in the quality among its inputs. Ironically, it was economist Peter Drucker who gave the firm a more human dimension by developing the modern study of management and important roles that managers play in running the firm.

*Who actually makes MR = MC decisions in large firms?* In many cases middle managers do, with approval from top managers. *Who makes the decisions about whether the firm should be in the business? Whether it should enter a new market, whether it should leave?* In most instances, the top management makes these decisions. *What are the long-run goals and objectives of the company? What is its strategy for achieving these objectives?* These questions must be ultimately answered by the firm's chief executive officer, or CEO.

Following is the 1998 farewell message of the CEO of SMSC, who stepped down that year to resume his position as chairman of the board. It provides an excellent example of how important are leadership and management for the economic success of a company.

To the Employees and Shareholders of Standard Microsystems Corporation:[4]

As you may know, over twenty-seven years ago, I had the honor of being one of the founders of Standard Microsystems Corporation (SMSC) and actually was the company's first employee. Since then, I have served the company in a number of executive positions, namely Vice President of Research & Development, President, Chief Executive Officer and Chairman of the Board. During that period, Standard Microsystems Corporation has grown from a small, embryonic startup operation, with just a few employees and virtually no assets, to where it is today a profitable, growing international supplier of integrated circuit components that is currently the world's leading supplier of input/output circuits to the personal computer industry, with total assets of over $215 million, including over $60 million in cash and no bank debt. SMSC is well-known for its leading-edge technology, enjoys strategic alliances with some of the largest and most prestigious electronics manufacturers in the world (including Intel Corporation) and has what we believe to be one of the most powerful intellectual property portfolios in the semiconductor industry.

However, just a few years ago, things certainly did not look as bright as they do today. In particular, in July of 1995, when Standard Microsystems was experiencing some very significant problems, the Board of Directors asked me, after having served as the Company's Chairman for many years, to, once again, assume the additional position of Chief Executive Officer. I agreed to do so reluctantly. Nevertheless, I accepted this additional challenge mainly because of the heavy responsibility I felt, as a founder of the Company, to see SMSC overcome its problems and succeed. The Company, indeed, had some very substantial problems at that time. **For the quarter ended May 31, 1995, SMSC had reported substantial losses, resulting primarily from major problems in its System Products Division.** The losses were increasing rapidly. Cash flow was highly negative. **SMSC was losing market share in its core businesses.** A number of lawsuits were pending against the company. Inventories, both within the company and at its distributors, were at very high levels. In addition, because of these problems, **the Company was technically in default of its bank covenants.** With all this as a background, I agreed to come back as CEO, even though my responsibilities necessitated sometimes working six and seven days a week in order to deal with SMSC's many problems in a timely fashion.

Since July of 1995, in my opinion, our Company has made considerable progress. . . . In particular, since then, among many other positive accomplishments:

- *We solidified Standard Microsystems' business relationships with its semiconductor foundries, greatly strengthening those relationships and, in the process, providing SMSC with sufficient high-level, cost-effective manufacturing capacity to service its worldwide customer bases.*

- *We exited the unprofitable Local Area Network systems business . . .*

---

[4]Company news release, December 1, 1998. Highlights added. This letter is not reprinted in its entirety. Sections omitted are indicated by ellipses.

- *We negotiated agreements with Intel Corporation . . . which were executed and announced in March of 1997. As a result, Intel Corporation is currently Standard Microsystems Corporation's largest shareholder and a valued partner in developing next-generation input/output integrated circuit components for the personal computer industry.*

- *With Intel's help, we effected substantial improvements in our overall product quality levels. . . . SCSM is consistently rated as the top quality supplier in our peer group by most of the world's largest personal computer manufacturers.*

- *We negotiated modifications to the royalty-bearing intellectual property licensing agreements each of SMSC's three major Taiwanese competitors (Winbond Electronics Corporation, Acer Laboratories Inc. and United Microelectronics Corp.) has with the Company and, in doing so, tightened restrictions on their coming out with pin-compatible versions of SMSC's integrated circuit component products. (We subsequently announced a comprehensive strategic alliance with Winbond, which gave SMSC exclusive rights to market Winbond's personal computer peripheral integrated circuit product line in North America, Europe and Japan and, going forward, providing for Winbond to serve as an additional semiconductor foundry for SMSC.)*

- *We settled all the major litigation pending against the Company . . .*

- *We substantially increased our research and new product development efforts and introduced a broad range of new, advanced integrated circuit components which were enthusiastically received by our customers. As a result, Standard Microsystems is now the leading supplier of input/output circuits to the worldwide personal computer industry.*

- *We restored the Company's operations to profitability . . .*

- *As a result of these actions, we greatly strengthened Standard Microsystems Corporation's financial position. The Company was able to pay off all of its bank debt and, in addition, SMSC's cash position has increased from about $12 million, as of August 31, 1995, to approximately $61 million, as of August 31, 1998.*

Looking back and realizing how much we have accomplished since July of 1995, I would like to tell you how proud I am of the job that our executive staff, management team and employees did. With the Company now operating profitably and its financial resources stronger than they have ever been in its twenty-seven year history, I feel that is time for me to return to my position as Chairman of the Board and to focus on the long-term strategic issues that Standard Microsystems Corporation will be facing over the years ahead. . . . I would like to thank Standard Microsystems Corporation's shareholders, its loyal employees, its dedicated management team, my fellow directors, SMSC's valued customers and the Company's trusted suppliers for all the friendship, cooperation and support that I have received over the years.

Sincerely yours,

Paul Richman /s/
Chairman of the Board and
Chief Executive Officer

## Question for Further Study

**1.** The highly volatile nature of the semiconductor industry means that whatever is written for a textbook will have changed by the time it is published. As we were completing the final draft of this edition, the semiconductor industry had started to show signs of turning around. An article in *BusinessWeek* talked about how companies that made chip manufacturing equipment as well as the chip makers themselves were experiencing increasing orders.[5] However, there were some continuing soft spots, particularly in the market for dynamic memory (DRAM) chips. The main problem is that chip makers generally tend to add too much capacity when they see demand increasing. An industry analyst quoted in the *BusinessWeek* article stated, "While demand for memory chips should catch up to capacity in 2000, for instance, new plants will drive capacity ahead of demand again in 2002."

Conduct a current analysis of the semiconductor industry. In particular, what is the relationship between supply and demand in the industry? Is there overcapacity once again as predicted by the industry analyst? What are the main factors affecting demand? How are industry conditions affecting the various types of computer chips (e.g., memory chips and specialty chips that are used in computers, networking equipment, consumer electronics, and automobiles)?

---

## Take It to the Net

We invite you to visit the Keat/Young page on the Prentice Hall Web site at:

**http://www.prenhall.com/keat**

for additional resources.

---

[5]See "Chipmakers: At Last, An Upturn," *BusinessWeek,* May 10, 1999, p. 35.

# Appendix A
# Linear Programming[1]

## Introduction

The Maximus Computer Company (MCC) has three basic computers it sells to students and small businesspeople. The first, called the Starter, is a basic, no-frills computer. It has most of the amenities that a new user or a buyer on a strict budget could want, including CD-ROM with sound, an entry-level processor, a small hard disk, a modem for Internet access, and a 15-inch monitor. The second model, called the Midrange, is for more demanding users, offering a faster processor, larger hard disk, more RAM, a DVD player, and a 15-inch monitor. The third model, the Super, gives most of the computing power a user could want. It offers even more RAM, a very fast processor, large hard disk, DVD player with hardware decoder, and 17-inch monitor. All but the most demanding users would be very happy with this model. However, for those who want the "very best," the company offers the Extreme, with state-of-the-art processor, huge hard disk, the best multimedia package (the latest generation DVD-ROM with a five-piece speaker system), 19-inch monitor, and more.

Thus, the company offers only four models, but feels there is enough flexibility to cover most of the target computer audience. It is a small start-up company and management knows it has to compete against the heavily entrenched products from Dell, IBM, Compaq, Hewlett-Packard, and Gateway.

The company philosophy is to ship computers with known-brand components and offer superior service, all at a lower cost to consumers than that of the competition. The person in charge of manufacturing and production, Silas Barnaby, is a veteran who has been in the business for many years. MCC recently hired him because of his background and knowledge of production techniques. Also recently hired was Wendy Levin, who had just earned her MBA in quantitative methods from a local university. Management assigned Wendy to work with Silas, whose knowledge of the

[1]This appendix was written by Jack Yurkiewicz, Professor of Management Science, Lubin School of Business, Pace University. The authors are very grateful for Professor Yurkiewicz's contribution.

business was based on "hands-on" experience and who was also a bit leery of using quantitative methods to improve the process (probably because he had a weak background in the subject). After several days of learning about the company in general, upper management asked Wendy to work specifically with Silas on forecasting production of its computer line.

# The Challenge of Forecasting Production

WENDY: Hi, Silas. Well, I think I know a bit about the philosophy of the company and its immediate goals. Can you please tell me a little more about the four models of computers we offer?

SILAS: Hello, Wendy, and welcome aboard. As you know, we make four models with different levels of features, all with the same customer support. We believe that whatever the sophistication of the machine, customer support should be "top notch" and not be skimped. In the long run, that will generate customer good will and promote our growth in the market.

WENDY: I agree wholeheartedly. Tell me a bit more about the computers themselves.

## THE PROBLEM IS DESCRIBED

SILAS: Well, as you know, the computer industry is currently very competitive, and profit margins are low for each model. The net profit on a Starter is $50, for a Midrange it is $120, for a Super it is $250, and for an Extreme it is $300. These figures already take into account material, labor, depreciation, taxes, shipping, and so on. In other words, these are the *net* profits to the company for each computer sold.

WENDY: Eventually we can delve into how these values are determined and perhaps how we can increase them, but for now, let's assume that they are sacrosanct. What else can you tell me about the operation?

SILAS: Well, we basically have three operations that make a computer. We call the first operation "manufacture." This includes taking the customer's phone call, determining which computer and options he or she wants and getting that information to the management of the production staff. They in turn will get the necessary components and make them available to the workers on the assembly line. We call the second operation "assembly," in which the assembly line workers actually put together the computer, according to the order's specifications. These are skilled workers who take pride in their work, and even though they work on an assembly line, they don't have an "assembly line mentality." They are making custom products for specific customers. We call our last operation "inspection." Here we install the software, run various diagnostics tests, and generally check out and pack up the computer before we send it to the customer.

WENDY: I see. Do you have approximate time figures on how long it takes to do these operations?

SILAS: Well, it does vary by computer. However, we have been doing this for some time now and so the time values don't vary all that much from machine to machine. So, for instance, for a Starter, we figure 0.1 hours for manufacture, 0.2 hours for assembly, and 0.1 hours for inspection. Our units are always in hours and I hope that doesn't confuse you.

WENDY: Not at all. Actually, I'm used to minutes, so I'm making mental transformations, but since the "company units" are always measured in hours, I will use them, too. Tell me the corresponding values for the other computers.

SILAS: For a Midrange, we use 0.2 hours to manufacture, 0.5 hours to assemble, and 0.2 hours for inspection. Each Super requires 0.7 hours to manufacture, 0.25 hours to assemble, and 0.3 hours inspection and testing. Finally, the Extreme gets 0.8 hours to manufacture, 0.2 hours to assemble, and 0.5 hours for inspection. As I said, these numbers really don't vary all that much from machine to machine, but as you can see, they do differ from model to model.

WENDY: OK. What about your resources? How many people, or even better, how many people-hours are available to do those three operations?

SILAS: On a daily basis, you can figure that the company has 250 hours available for manufacture, 350 hours available for assembly, and 150 hours to do the inspection and testing. Do you need to know anything more?

WENDY: Not really. It sounds like we can model the entire production process as a linear program. We'll get the information into the computer, and that should tell us how . . .

SILAS: I'm afraid that leaves me out. I did have a course in linear programming years ago, and I spent a frustrating term trying to learn the subject. We did many hand calculations involving things called "tableaus." I was working with equations and doing operations called "elementary row operations." Believe me, there was nothing "elementary" about them. I got a "B" in the course, but I'll be darned if I remember a thing.

WENDY: I commiserate with you, but can tell you that things have changed. Unless you are a specialist who needs to know how the algorithm works that solves these kinds of problems, you really don't make "hand calculations" anymore. In fact, you can solve these problems in Excel. Excel comes with an add-on package called Solver that is easy to use and yet powerful enough to solve most mathematical programming problems. All we have to do is make a spreadsheet model of the problem and Solver will do the rest.

SILAS: Well, that certainly is good news. I use Excel and I have made many models. But how do you make a linear program model in Excel?

Wendy opened her notebook computer, started Excel, and in just several minutes came up with model of MCC's computer problem.

## MODELING THE PROBLEM IN EXCEL

WENDY: Here, let me show you. I will also show you how Solver can be used to get the answer for us. Look at my spreadsheet model for our problem. Cells B1, C1, D1, and E1 give the labels of our computers, which in linear programming terminology are called **decision variables.** We want the values of these variables to appear in cells B2, C2, D2, and E2. Excel's Solver will call these cells the **changing cells.** We put the per-unit profit of each computer into cells B4 through D4. These numbers are traditionally called the **objective function coefficients.** We have to put a formula into cell I2 (which we labeled as the Profit in cell I1) that will give the net profit for all the computer's made.

SILAS: I know how to do that. We would type in cell I2 the formula:

```
=B2 × B4 + C2 × C4 + D2 × D4 + E2 × E4
```

Algebraically, we are saying, with this formula:

```
50(Starters) + 120(Midrange) + 250(Super) + 300(Extreme)
```

Of course, the value in cell I2 is zero because we have zero values for the number of computers made in cells B2 through E2.

WENDY: Exactly. We can use a shortcut to this rather tedious formula. Excel has the built-in function =SUMPRODUCT that will save us much typing. That is, in cell J2 we can simply type

```
=SUMPRODUCT(B2:E2,B4:E4)
```

That says: multiply the values in cells B2 through E2 by the corresponding values in the cells B4 through E4 respectively, and then add up the results. That gives us the same result as your formula. However, it is easier to input, since we need just type in the =SUMPRODUCT, highlight the ranges, and type the parentheses. The result is our total profit, and Solver calls this our *target cell.*

|   | A | B | C | D | E | F | G | H | I |
|---|---|---|---|---|---|---|---|---|---|
| 1 |   | Starter | Midrange | Super | Extreme |   |   |   | Profit |
| 2 |   | 0 | 0 | 0 | 0 |   |   |   | 0 |
| 3 |   |   |   |   |   |   |   |   |   |
| 4 | max | 50 | 120 | 250 | 300 |   |   |   |   |
| 5 |   |   |   |   |   | Available | Used | Slack |   |
| 6 | manufacture | 0.1 | 0.2 | 0.7 | 0.8 | 250 | 0 | 250 |   |
| 7 | assembly | 0.2 | 0.5 | 0.25 | 0.2 | 350 | 0 | 350 |   |
| 8 | inspection | 0.1 | 0.2 | 0.3 | 0.5 | 150 | 0 | 150 |   |

SILAS: I suspect that we will be using that =SUMPRODUCT function again. Tell me about the other stuff I see in the spreadsheet.

WENDY: Our model is incomplete. We need to specify the *constraints.* These account for the technological, economic, or other limitations of the system, and restrict the values of the decision variables to some feasible set. We have three constraints in our problem: manufacturing, assembly, and inspection. Our manufacturing constraint is

```
0.1(Starter) + 0.2(Midrange) + 0.7(Super) + 0.8(Extreme) 250
```

SILAS: That makes sense. The 250 represents the number of people-hours available daily. The expression on the left must represent the total number of manufacturing hours used by the four models of computers. In short, the number of manufacturing hours used by the company is less than or equal to the number of manufacturing hours available from the labor.

WENDY: Exactly so.

SILAS: Let me see if I can figure out what you entered in the spreadsheet. I see the manufacturing values in the cells B6 through E6. The number of hours of manufacturing available is the 250, in cell F6. I'll bet the formula in cell G6 is

```
=SUMPRODUCT(B2:E2,B6:E6)
```

WENDY: Nice going. That's exactly what I entered.

SILAS: I assume we need similar constraints for assembly and inspection.

WENDY: Absolutely. Thus, the assembly constraint says

```
0.2(Starter) + 0.5(Midrange) + 0.25(Super) + 0.2(Extreme) 350
```

and this translates as the number of hours used for assembly is less than or equal to the number of hours available for assembly, or 350.

SILAS: Right, and that's why the formula in cell G7 is

```
=SUMPRODUCT(B2:E2,B7:E7)
```

This gives us the number of hours used to assemble the computers. Finally, the last constraint should indicate that the number of inspection hours used is less than or equal to 150 inspection hours available:

```
0.1(Starter) + 0.2(Midrange) + 0.3(Super) + 0.5(Extreme) 150
```

And the formula in cell G8 is

```
=SUMPRODUCT(B2:E2,B8:E8)
```

represents the number of inspection hours that are used for the computers.

WENDY: Right again, Silas. Let's look at the spreadsheet with the formulas showing instead of the values. You'll notice that the formulas in the G column have dollar signs. That's because I copied the formula from cell G6 to cells G7 and G8, and I needed the Excel concept of absolute addressing. The only other thing I've added is a column called "Slack." A slack variable for a less than or equal constraint is the difference between the number of units of the resource *available* minus the number of units of the resource actually *used*. It tells us how many units of each resource we have left over in a less than or equal constraint.

| | A | B | C | D | E | F | G | H | I |
|---|---|---|---|---|---|---|---|---|---|
| 1 | | Starter | Midrange | Super | Extreme | | | | Profit |
| 2 | | 0 | 0 | 0 | 0 | | | | =SUMPRODUCT(B2:E2,B4:E4) |
| 3 | | | | | | | | | |
| 4 | max | 50 | 120 | 250 | 300 | | | | |
| 5 | | | | | | Avail | Used | Slack | |
| 6 | Man | 0.1 | 0.2 | 0.7 | 0.8 | 250 | =SUMPRODUCT($B$2:$E$2,B6:E6) | =F6-G6 | |
| 7 | Asm | 0.2 | 0.5 | 0.25 | 0.2 | 350 | =SUMPRODUCT($B$2:$E$2,B7:E7) | =F7-G7 | |
| 8 | Insp | 0.1 | 0.2 | 0.3 | 0.5 | 150 | =SUMPRODUCT($B$2:$E$2,B8:E8) | =F8-G8 | |

SILAS: I remember you said that we can get an answer using a technique called linear programming. What I would do is just try different values for the computer models in the cells B2 through E2, all the time monitoring the profit in cell I2. Eventually, I would just pick a product mix that would give me the highest profit I obtained. What does linear programming do?

WENDY: It will find the optimal product mix. That is, it will give me the product mix that yields the highest profit and still not violate any constraints. This is called the *optimal solution*.

## USING SOLVER TO GET THE OPTIMAL SOLUTION

SILAS: And you said that Excel had a feature called Solver that can do that? I never even knew about it, and I have been using Excel for years. How does it work?

WENDY: We go to the Tools section on Excel's main menu. There you will see Solver. (*Note to the reader: Wendy at this point gives Silas a complete set of instructions on how to enter a linear programming problem into Solver. This discussion will not be repeated here. If you want help with Solver, try the Help system in Excel for details.*)

WENDY: Do you see that Solver got the optimal solution to appear in our specified cells, B2 through E2? (This is shown in Table A.1.)

| | A | B | C | D | E | F | G | H | I |
|---|---|---|---|---|---|---|---|---|---|
| 1 | | Starter | Midrange | Super | Extreme | | | | Profit |
| 2 | | 0 | 375 | 250 | 0 | | | | 107500 |
| 3 | | | | | | | | | |
| 4 | max | 50 | 120 | 250 | 300 | | | | |
| 5 | | | | | | Available | Used | Slack | |
| 6 | manufacture | 0.1 | 0.2 | 0.7 | 0.8 | 250 | 250 | 0 | |
| 7 | assembly | 0.2 | 0.5 | 0.25 | 0.2 | 350 | 250 | 100 | |
| 8 | inspection | 0.1 | 0.2 | 0.3 | 0.5 | 150 | 150 | 0 | |

## THE SOLUTION IS REVEALED

SILAS: Well, I see the optimal solution. Solver tells us to make no Starters, 375 Midranges, 250 Supers, and no Extremes on a daily basis. I must admit that is not what we are currently doing, but Solver says that if we make that daily product mix, our daily profit will be $107,500, which is considerably more than we are currently making. It is interesting that

**TABLE A.1   Solver's Answer Report**

### Target Cell (Max)

| Cell | Name | Original Value | Final Value |
|------|------|----------------|-------------|
| $I$2 | Profit | 107,500 | 107,500 |

### Adjustable Cells

| Cell | Name | Original Value | Final Value |
|------|------|----------------|-------------|
| $B$2 | Starter | 0 | 0 |
| $C$2 | Midrange | 0 | 375 |
| $D$2 | Super | 0 | 250 |
| $E$2 | Extreme | 0 | 0 |

### Constraints

| Cell | Name | Cell Value | Formula | Status | Slack |
|------|------|------------|---------|--------|-------|
| $G$6 | manufacture | 250 | $G$6 <= $F$6 | Binding | 0 |
| $G$7 | assembly | 250 | $G$7 <= $F$7 | Not Binding | 100 |
| $G$8 | inspection | 150 | $G$8 < = $F$8 | Binding | 0 |

Solver is telling us that we should abandon the "low end" and "high end" of the market as compared to offering a "complete product line" for the entire spectrum of customers. We will have to take that up with upper management at our next weekly meeting.

WENDY: I can tell you that I could have predicted something like this. It is a fact of "linear programming life" that the optimal solution would tell us not to make at least one of our computer styles. The reason is that our model had only three constraints, and therefore it is impossible that we will end up making more than three products. In other words, the number of positive decision variables can never be more than the number of constraints in a linear programming optimal solution. Thus, I knew that because we had just three constraints, at least one of our four products should not be made. I didn't know which. The fact that Solver tells us not to make two of these products is a slight surprise, but quite reasonable.

SILAS: Well, as I said, we can take up the solution with upper management. But what does the rest of the output tell us? Is it important?

WENDY: Yes, but before we get into that, I should point out to you that Solver gave us integer optimal values for the number of computer models to make. That will not always happen. That is, the solution may not be integers. If we want integer solutions, we need to use another technique called *integer programming*, which Solver can do. However, we will not discuss it now.

SILAS: OK, I guess I'll ask your help on that in the future when I need it. Let's get back to all that additional output. Tell me if I need to understand or worry about it.

WENDY: The additional output is what makes linear programming such a rich topic. It is all related to the concept of sensitivity analysis, which tells us how sensitive is our solution to any changes in the data.

## SHADOW PRICES ARE DISCUSSED

SILAS: OK, then let me try asking *you* a question. I overheard a conversation among some upper management people last week. The gist was that they wanted to achieve a daily profit of $130,000 per day. If we follow the computer's advice and implement the optimal solution, we would achieve a daily profit of $107,500. We are still about $22,500 short. If we relax some constraints, could we do it?

WENDY: By "relaxing" the constraints, I assume you mean we get additional resources, such as more hours of manufacture, or assembly, or inspection. Right?

SILAS: Exactly. Well, could we come up with the additional $22,500?

WENDY: That brings up the notion of a *shadow price* for a constraint. A shadow price for a particular constraint refers to how much the objective function changes for a unit increase in the right-hand value of that constraint. You can see that Solver lists these values in the Sensitivity Report. For example, look at the manufacture constraint. (This is shown in Table A.2.)

SILAS: I see that the shadow price for that constraint is 175, or I assume $175.

WENDY: What that tells us is this: for each additional hour of manufacturing the company obtains above the already available 250 daily hours, its profit will increase by $175. The shadow price is sometimes called the constraint's *marginal value,* because it tells us the most the company would be willing to pay, above and beyond what it currently does pay, for an additional unit of the resource.

SILAS: So, let me see if I get this straight. We would like to have the company pick up an additional $22,500 per day. For each hour of manufacturing

### TABLE A.2   Solver's Sensitivity Report

| Cell | Name | Final Value | Reduced Cost | Objective Coefficient | Allowable Increase | Allowable Decrease |
|------|------|-------------|--------------|-----------------------|--------------------|--------------------|
| $B$2 | Starter | 0 | −10 | 50 | 10 | 1E + 30 |
| $C$2 | Midrange | 375 | 0 | 120 | 46.67 | 20 |
| $D$2 | Super | 250 | 0 | 250 | 170 | 70.00 |
| $E$2 | Extreme | 0 | −52.50 | 300 | 52.50 | 1E + 30 |

| Cell | Name | Final Value | Shadow Price | Constraint R.H.Side | Allowable Increase | Allowable Decrease |
|------|------|-------------|--------------|---------------------|--------------------|--------------------|
| $G$6 | manufacture | 250 | 175 | 250 | 100 | 80 |
| $G$7 | assembly | 250 | 0 | 350 | 1E + 30 | 100 |
| $G$8 | inspection | 150 | 425 | 150 | 26.67 | 42.86 |

WENDY:   time we hire, the company gets a $175 profit. So if the company could hire an additional 22,500/175, or 128.57, hours of manufacturing time, we would achieve our profit goal.

WENDY:   Almost. The calculation is correct except for one thing. These shadow prices are valid only over some limited range of the available value. The Sensitivity Report gives that range.

SILAS:   I see it. The allowable increase for manufacturing is 100 and the allowable decrease is 80. Please be specific. Just what do these numbers tell us?

WENDY:   The shadow prices for the constraints, as given in the Sensitivity Report, will remain constant as long as the range for the available resource stays between those two values. Thus, if the number of daily manufacturing hours is between 170 (250 − 80) and 350 (250 + 100), then the shadow prices are fixed. Because your calculation called for getting an additional 128.57 hours of manufacturing time, which is above the allowable increase of 100 hours for that constraint, we cannot be certain that the shadow prices are as given. Thus, your calculation is wrong.

SILAS:   OK, I get it. Let me try another one. I see that the shadow price for inspection is $425. If I got an additional $22,500/425, or 52.94, hours, we would get to the profit's goal. But because the allowable increase for inspection is only 26.67 hours, our calculation is wrong because 52.94 is more than the allowable increase of 26.67. I've answered my own question. We can't get the additional $22,500 that way either, right?

WENDY:   Unfortunately, no. Your analysis is totally correct.

SILAS:   How about this. What if we got some additional hours of manufacture *and* inspection? Enough to get us the additional $22,500, but still not going outside the allowable range. That should do it.

WENDY:   Almost. Unfortunately, our discussion of sensitivity analysis of an available resource infers that we change just *one* resource amount. You are changing two. There is something called the *100% Rule,* which tells us how to analyze making changes to more than one data item, but we will save that for another time.

SILAS:   OK, you're right. Let me try to understand what linear programming says and then change our production schedule to get the $107,500 daily profit. That will be enough for now, and will certainly please upper management. But it does look like we are not going to get the additional $22,500 from our current linear programming model, right?

WENDY:   That's about it.

SILAS:   OK, let me ask you another question. The shadow price for assembly is zero. I don't get that. Can you explain it, please?

WENDY:   Remember that the shadow price of a constraint tells us how much more we would be willing to pay for an additional unit of that resource. Let me ask you something. Did we use up all of our available 350 hours of assembly?

SILAS:   No, because if we make the number of computer models Solver says, we would only use up 250 daily hours of assembly. In fact, we would have 100 hours left over, and the slack value of 100 tells me that, right?

WENDY: Right, indeed. So if you have 100 such hours not used, why would you want to buy additional assembly hours? Let me rephrase that. What's the most you would pay for an additional hour of assembly?

SILAS: I wouldn't pay anything for it, because I don't need it.

WENDY: Precisely. Assembly time is an example of a *nonbinding* constraint. That means that we do not use all the available resources of that constraint at the optimal solution. The shadow price of a nonbinding constraint is zero. On the other hand, if a constraint is *binding,* or *tight,* then we are using up all the available resource for that constraint. If you look at Solver's Answer Report, it will tell you which constraints are binding and which are not binding.

SILAS: I get it. Then we would be willing to pay for some more of that resource, because that resource was all used up at the optimal solution. So the shadow price for a tight constraint would not be zero.

WENDY: Bingo. You just stated a key theorem in the subject of linear programming, called the *Complementary Slackness Theorem.* Generally stated, if a constraint is tight, then its slack value is zero, and its shadow price will not be zero. If a constraint is not tight, its slack variable is positive and its shadow price is zero. This is true if the problem is not "degenerate."

SILAS: I don't like the tone of that word. What is a degenerate problem?

WENDY: It's not as bad as the term sounds. I'll get into its definition later, but I can tell you now that you don't have to worry about it.

SILAS: OK, that's a relief. Let me just go over this concept of shadow price another time to confirm I got it right.

WENDY: Fire away.

SILAS: OK. Suppose a person comes into my office looking for employment. She says she is skilled in manufacturing. She is willing to work 10 hours a day, and she wants $50 an hour in salary. I normally pay manufacturing workers $30 an hour (which we don't see *explicitly* in our model, but it *is* there *implicitly,* as part of the net profit coefficients of the objective function), so she really wants $20 more than I ordinarily pay my workers. Still, I would hire her because for each hour she works, the firm gets an additional $175, which is what the shadow price tells me. So the net profit for the company would be 175 minus the $20 of her extra salary, or $155. We are still ahead and I would hire her.

WENDY: Your analysis is correct. Notice that you can hire her to work the 10 hours, because the additional 10 daily hours is less than the allowable increase of 100 hours.

SILAS: I think I've got it. However, another thing just jumped out at me. What good is hiring her to do just manufacturing? To build any computer, don't we need manufacturing, assembly, and inspection, all three?

WENDY: You've just hit on something. When you change the amount of available resource to a different value, even if you are in the allowable range, *the optimal solution to the problem will change.* All that stays the same are the shadow prices. We generally don't know what the new optimal solution would be, and would have to rerun the problem in

Solver to get the new optimal solution. But I can tell you for a fact that the product mix will be different. The computer sees that you have increased just *one* available resource, manufacturing for instance, and will come up with a new and different product mix based on the available resources.

SILAS: OK, let me continue with my example. If I hire this hypothetical person to work an additional 10 hours in manufacturing at $50 per hour, which is $20 more than the $30 per hour I ordinarily pay for manufacturing time, the company would achieve an additional daily profit of $175 − $20, or $155 per hour. So for the 10 additional hours she works, the company would gain an additional $1,550. However, the product mix, zero Starters, 375 Midranges, 250 Supers, and zero Extremes would no longer be the optimal solution. And if I wanted to know what that new solution is, I would have to rerun the problem in Solver to get it.

WENDY: Correct. However, I can tell you something about the new solution, even if I don't run the problem again on Solver. If we change the value of an available resource, and we stay within the allowable range, the shadow prices stay the same. What also stays the same is the make-up of the product mix. Without getting too technical, what that says is we would still make the same product before we made the change of the resource, although in different amounts. Also, we do not make any products that Solver told us not to make. In other words, without rerunning this problem, if you hire this woman to work the additional 10 manufacturing hours, I can tell you for a fact that we should still make Midrange and Super models, but no Starters and Extremes. However, the number of Midranges and Supers will indeed be different from the original optimal values of 375 and 250 respectively, and if we want those amounts, we would have to run the problem again in Solver.

SILAS: That is useful to know. What about the slack for our assembly constraint? Will there still be slack there?

WENDY: Yes. The "optimal solution" means the values of the original variables and any slack variables. Once again, if we make a change in the amount of available resource, and that change is within the allowable range, the optimal solution values will be different. However, those that were positive before will still be positive, and those that were zero before will still be zero.

SILAS: I understand. Can you tell me what the rest of the output is all about?

## OBJECTIVE FUNCTION SENSITIVITY ANALYSIS

WENDY: Certainly. Consider the Midrange computer for a moment. According to our model, its current profit is $120 per machine. Would you not agree that if that profit were actually lower than the $120, perhaps we should not make 375 machines per day that Solver tells us to?

SILAS: That makes sense. If the profit on a Midrange fell low enough, perhaps we shouldn't make any at all, but use our resources to make some other model or more of another model.

WENDY: And if the profit were actually something higher than the $120, wouldn't it make sense perhaps to make more of these Midrange models instead of the 375 per day?

SILAS: Sure.

WENDY: To summarize, if the per-unit profit of the Midrange computer were high enough, or low enough, the optimal solution, which says to make 375 Midranges, would no longer be correct.

SILAS: I'll buy that.

WENDY: In other words, there must be a range of values for the per-unit profit of Midrange computers over which the optimal solution would not change. Solver gives us that range, for each model or variable, in the Sensitivity Report.

SILAS: I see it. Let me try this to see if I understand it. Let me consider a hypothetical story. Let's suppose management, after some consultation, realizes that the per-unit profit of a Super computer, which was originally deemed to be $250, was really $200. Because this $50 "loss" is less than the allowable decrease of $70 for the Super computer, the entire optimal solution (zero Starters, 375 Midranges, 250 Supers, and zero Extremes) is still the same. However, the profit is not $107,500, because although we are still making the same number of Super computers (250), we are getting only $200 profit on each, instead of the assumed $250. So the actual profit can be calculated to be $107,500 − 250($50), or $95,000. Well, how did I do?

WENDY: I couldn't have said it better myself. Do you see how really useful the objective function sensitivity analysis is? Once we run the problem on Solver, we can change values on the per-unit profit, and if our new values are within the allowable range, we know that we should make the same number of computer models that Solver found before we made the change. And we didn't have to rerun the problem to get this information.

SILAS: I agree, this is all very useful. Let me take the discussion on a different tack. If I understand this correctly, Solver tells us not to make the Starter and Extreme computers. I assume that this is because the per-unit profits of these models are just too low. The optimal solution will stay the same as long as the profit coefficients, or as you call them, the objective function coefficients, stay within the allowable range given. If I look at the allowable increase for the Starter, I see $10. Is this telling me that if the Starter profit were just $10 more than the current $50, then it would pay to make either of these models?

WENDY: Precisely. If the Starter profit were $60 ($50 + $10) or higher, it would pay to produce Starters. Similarly, if the per unit profit of an Extreme was $52.50 higher than it is now, or at least $352.50, then it would pay to make Extremes.

SILAS: What would happen if the profit of a Starter were really *precisely* $60?

WENDY: At $60, we may or may not produce Starters. That is, we would be indifferent, for the profit would be identical in either case. We would have a situation called *alternative optima*. That means there is another optimal solution to the problem (another product mix, if you will) with the same profit. Both sets of answers are equally "good."

## REDUCED COSTS ARE EXPLAINED AT LAST

SILAS: Well, Wendy, I must admit the analysis is not so complicated as I had originally thought. The only item that remains left unexplained is the Reduced Cost column in the Sensitivity Report. What are these values all about?

WENDY: If you look at the Sensitivity Report (see Table A.2), you may notice that the reduced cost of a variable is a number other than zero whenever the value of that variable itself is zero. Also, the reduced cost is zero whenever the value of a variable is not zero.

SILAS: Yes, I do see that. Will that always be the case, or is it a coincidence?

WENDY: No, this is not a coincidence.

SILAS: So?

WENDY: The *reduced cost* of a "zero" variable tells us how much the profit would change for a unit increase of that variable.

SILAS: Could you say that in English, please?

WENDY: Sorry. It simply tells us that if we want to make a product that Solver told us not to make (gave a zero as the optimal value for that variable), then that is how much our profit would decrease.

SILAS: I think I get it. Are you saying that if I insist on producing an Extreme computer line, for each one I make and sell, the company would be losing $52.50?

WENDY: Right. Of course, the company doesn't "lose" money if it made an Extreme. It would be making $52.50 less than it could if it had not made and sold the Extreme computer.

SILAS: I was wondering about that. Often, companies would not want to drop a product line as it might alienate customers or send a negative message to the marketplace. In particular, I'm not so sure upper management would want to eliminate the Extreme computer line, despite what the optimal solution says.

WENDY: Fine. Then they should know that for every Extreme they sell at the current profit of $300, they are making $52.50 less than the optimal daily profit of $107,500. That is quite common in business, for a company to implement a *sub-optimal* solution instead of the optimal one.

SILAS: Well, this has been very useful and productive, Wendy. Thanks for spending all this time explaining linear programming to me. Welcome aboard to our team. What do you say we meet again next week and you tell me all about that 100% Rule?[2]

---

[2]If you want to know about the 100% Rule now, Wendy highly recommends the textbook that originally introduced the topic, and which is an excellent text on linear programming, integer programming, and other advanced mathematical programming topics. Stephen Bradley, Arnoldo Hax, and Thomas Magnanti, *Applied Mathematical Programming,* Reading, MA: Addison-Wesley, 1977.

# Appendix B
# Statistical and
# Financial Tables

**TABLE B.1a  Future Value of $1 at the End of *n* Periods**

| Period | 1% | 2% | 3% | 4% | 5% | 6% | 7% | 8% | 9% | 10% |
|---|---|---|---|---|---|---|---|---|---|---|
| 1 | 1.0100 | 1.0200 | 1.0300 | 1.0400 | 1.0500 | 1.0600 | 1.0700 | 1.0800 | 1.0900 | 1.1000 |
| 2 | 1.0201 | 1.0404 | 1.0609 | 1.0816 | 1.1025 | 1.1236 | 1.1449 | 1.1664 | 1.1881 | 1.2100 |
| 3 | 1.0303 | 1.0612 | 1.0927 | 1.1249 | 1.1576 | 1.1910 | 1.2250 | 1.2597 | 1.2950 | 1.3310 |
| 4 | 1.0406 | 1.0824 | 1.1255 | 1.1699 | 1.2155 | 1.2625 | 1.3108 | 1.3605 | 1.4116 | 1.4641 |
| 5 | 1.0510 | 1.1041 | 1.1593 | 1.2167 | 1.2763 | 1.3382 | 1.4026 | 1.4693 | 1.5386 | 1.6105 |
| 6 | 1.0615 | 1.1262 | 1.1941 | 1.2653 | 1.3401 | 1.4185 | 1.5007 | 1.5869 | 1.6771 | 1.7716 |
| 7 | 1.0721 | 1.1487 | 1.2299 | 1.3159 | 1.4071 | 1.5036 | 1.6058 | 1.7138 | 1.8280 | 1.9487 |
| 8 | 1.0829 | 1.1717 | 1.2668 | 1.3686 | 1.4775 | 1.5938 | 1.7182 | 1.8509 | 1.9926 | 2.1436 |
| 9 | 1.0937 | 1.1951 | 1.3048 | 1.4233 | 1.5513 | 1.6895 | 1.8385 | 1.9990 | 2.1719 | 2.3579 |
| 10 | 1.1046 | 1.2190 | 1.3439 | 1.4802 | 1.6289 | 1.7908 | 1.9672 | 2.1589 | 2.3674 | 2.5937 |
| 11 | 1.1157 | 1.2434 | 1.3842 | 1.5395 | 1.7103 | 1.8983 | 2.1049 | 2.3316 | 2.5804 | 2.8531 |
| 12 | 1.1268 | 1.2682 | 1.4258 | 1.6010 | 1.7959 | 2.0122 | 2.2522 | 2.5182 | 2.8127 | 3.1384 |
| 13 | 1.1381 | 1.2936 | 1.4685 | 1.6651 | 1.8856 | 2.1329 | 2.4098 | 2.7196 | 3.0658 | 3.4523 |
| 14 | 1.1495 | 1.3195 | 1.5126 | 1.7317 | 1.9799 | 2.2609 | 2.5785 | 2.9372 | 3.3417 | 3.7975 |
| 15 | 1.1610 | 1.3459 | 1.5580 | 1.8009 | 2.0789 | 2.3966 | 2.7590 | 3.1722 | 3.6425 | 4.1772 |
| 16 | 1.1726 | 1.3728 | 1.6047 | 1.8730 | 2.1829 | 2.5404 | 2.9522 | 3.4259 | 3.9703 | 4.5950 |
| 17 | 1.1843 | 1.4002 | 1.6528 | 1.9479 | 2.2920 | 2.6928 | 3.1588 | 3.7000 | 4.3276 | 5.0545 |
| 18 | 1.1961 | 1.4282 | 1.7024 | 2.0258 | 2.4066 | 2.8543 | 3.3799 | 3.9960 | 4.7171 | 5.5599 |
| 19 | 1.2081 | 1.4568 | 1.7535 | 2.1068 | 2.5270 | 3.0256 | 3.6165 | 4.3157 | 5.1417 | 6.1159 |
| 20 | 1.2202 | 1.4859 | 1.8061 | 2.1911 | 2.6533 | 3.2071 | 3.8697 | 4.6610 | 5.6044 | 6.7275 |
| 21 | 1.2324 | 1.5157 | 1.8603 | 2.2788 | 2.7860 | 3.3996 | 4.1406 | 5.0338 | 6.1088 | 7.4002 |
| 22 | 1.2447 | 1.5460 | 1.9161 | 2.3699 | 2.9253 | 3.6035 | 4.4304 | 5.4365 | 6.6586 | 8.1403 |
| 23 | 1.2572 | 1.5769 | 1.9736 | 2.4647 | 3.0715 | 3.8197 | 4.7405 | 5.8715 | 7.2579 | 8.9543 |
| 24 | 1.2697 | 1.6084 | 2.0328 | 2.5633 | 3.2251 | 4.0489 | 5.0724 | 6.3412 | 7.9111 | 9.8497 |
| 25 | 1.2824 | 1.6406 | 2.0938 | 2.6658 | 3.3864 | 4.2919 | 5.4274 | 6.8485 | 8.6231 | 10.835 |
| 26 | 1.2953 | 1.6734 | 2.1566 | 2.7725 | 3.5557 | 4.5494 | 5.8074 | 7.3964 | 9.3992 | 11.918 |
| 27 | 1.3082 | 1.7069 | 2.2213 | 2.8834 | 3.7335 | 4.8223 | 6.2139 | 7.9881 | 10.245 | 13.110 |
| 28 | 1.3213 | 1.7410 | 2.2879 | 2.9987 | 3.9201 | 5.1117 | 6.6488 | 8.6271 | 11.167 | 14.421 |
| 29 | 1.3345 | 1.7758 | 2.3566 | 3.1187 | 4.1161 | 5.4184 | 7.1143 | 9.3173 | 12.172 | 15.863 |
| 30 | 1.3478 | 1.8114 | 2.4273 | 3.2434 | 4.3219 | 5.7435 | 7.6123 | 10.063 | 13.268 | 17.449 |
| 40 | 1.4889 | 2.2080 | 3.2620 | 4.8010 | 7.0400 | 10.286 | 14.974 | 21.725 | 31.409 | 45.259 |
| 50 | 1.6446 | 2.6916 | 4.3839 | 7.1067 | 11.467 | 18.420 | 29.457 | 46.902 | 74.358 | 117.39 |
| 60 | 1.8167 | 3.2810 | 5.8916 | 10.520 | 18.679 | 32.988 | 57.946 | 101.26 | 176.03 | 304.48 |

**TABLE B.1*a*   (*continued*)**

| Period | 12% | 14% | 15% | 16% | 18% | 20% | 24% | 28% | 32% | 36% |
|--------|------|------|------|------|------|------|------|------|------|------|
| 1  | 1.1200 | 1.1400 | 1.1500 | 1.1600 | 1.1800 | 1.2000 | 1.2400 | 1.2800 | 1.3200 | 1.3600 |
| 2  | 1.2544 | 1.2996 | 1.3225 | 1.3456 | 1.3924 | 1.4400 | 1.5376 | 1.6384 | 1.7424 | 1.8496 |
| 3  | 1.4049 | 1.4815 | 1.5209 | 1.5609 | 1.6430 | 1.7280 | 1.9066 | 2.0972 | 2.3000 | 2.5155 |
| 4  | 1.5735 | 1.6890 | 1.7490 | 1.8106 | 1.9388 | 2.0736 | 2.3642 | 2.6844 | 3.0360 | 3.4210 |
| 5  | 1.7623 | 1.9254 | 2.0114 | 2.1003 | 2.2878 | 2.4883 | 2.9316 | 3.4360 | 4.0075 | 4.6526 |
| 6  | 1.9738 | 2.1950 | 2.3131 | 2.4364 | 2.6996 | 2.9860 | 3.6352 | 4.3980 | 5.2899 | 6.3275 |
| 7  | 2.2107 | 2.5023 | 2.6600 | 2.8262 | 3.1855 | 3.5832 | 4.5077 | 5.6295 | 6.9826 | 8.6054 |
| 8  | 2.4760 | 2.8526 | 3.0590 | 3.2784 | 3.7589 | 4.2998 | 5.5895 | 7.2058 | 9.2170 | 11.703 |
| 9  | 2.7731 | 3.2519 | 3.5179 | 3.8030 | 4.4355 | 5.1598 | 6.9310 | 9.2234 | 12.166 | 15.917 |
| 10 | 3.1058 | 3.7072 | 4.0456 | 4.4114 | 5.2338 | 6.1917 | 8.5944 | 11.806 | 16.060 | 21.647 |
| 11 | 3.4785 | 4.2262 | 4.6524 | 5.1173 | 6.1759 | 7.4301 | 10.657 | 15.112 | 21.199 | 29.439 |
| 12 | 3.8960 | 4.8179 | 5.3502 | 5.9360 | 7.2876 | 8.9161 | 13.215 | 19.343 | 27.982 | 40.037 |
| 13 | 4.3635 | 5.4924 | 6.1528 | 6.8858 | 8.5994 | 10.699 | 16.386 | 24.759 | 36.937 | 54.451 |
| 14 | 4.8871 | 6.2613 | 7.0757 | 7.9875 | 10.147 | 12.839 | 20.319 | 31.691 | 48.756 | 74.053 |
| 15 | 5.4736 | 7.1379 | 8.1371 | 9.2655 | 11.974 | 15.407 | 25.196 | 40.565 | 64.359 | 100.71 |
| 16 | 6.1304 | 8.1372 | 9.3576 | 10.748 | 14.129 | 18.488 | 31.243 | 51.923 | 84.954 | 136.97 |
| 17 | 6.8660 | 9.2765 | 10.761 | 12.468 | 16.672 | 22.186 | 38.741 | 66.461 | 112.14 | 186.28 |
| 18 | 7.6900 | 10.575 | 12.375 | 14.463 | 19.673 | 26.623 | 48.039 | 85.071 | 148.02 | 253.34 |
| 19 | 8.6128 | 12.056 | 14.232 | 16.777 | 23.214 | 31.948 | 59.568 | 108.89 | 195.39 | 344.54 |
| 20 | 9.6463 | 13.743 | 16.367 | 19.461 | 27.393 | 38.338 | 73.864 | 139.38 | 257.92 | 468.57 |
| 21 | 10.804 | 15.668 | 18.822 | 22.574 | 32.324 | 46.005 | 91.592 | 178.41 | 340.45 | 637.26 |
| 22 | 12.100 | 17.861 | 21.645 | 26.186 | 38.142 | 55.206 | 113.57 | 228.36 | 449.39 | 866.67 |
| 23 | 13.552 | 20.362 | 24.891 | 30.376 | 45.008 | 66.247 | 140.83 | 292.30 | 593.20 | 1178.7 |
| 24 | 15.179 | 23.212 | 28.625 | 35.236 | 53.109 | 79.497 | 174.63 | 374.14 | 783.02 | 1603.0 |
| 25 | 17.000 | 26.462 | 32.919 | 40.874 | 62.669 | 95.396 | 216.54 | 478.90 | 1033.6 | 2180.1 |
| 26 | 19.040 | 30.167 | 37.857 | 47.414 | 73.949 | 114.48 | 268.51 | 613.00 | 1364.3 | 2964.9 |
| 27 | 21.325 | 34.390 | 43.535 | 55.000 | 87.260 | 137.37 | 332.95 | 784.64 | 1800.9 | 4032.3 |
| 28 | 23.884 | 39.204 | 50.066 | 63.800 | 102.97 | 164.84 | 412.86 | 1004.3 | 2377.2 | 5483.9 |
| 29 | 26.750 | 44.693 | 57.575 | 74.009 | 121.50 | 197.81 | 511.95 | 1285.6 | 3137.9 | 7458.1 |
| 30 | 29.960 | 50.950 | 66.212 | 85.850 | 143.37 | 237.38 | 634.82 | 1645.5 | 4142.1 | 10143 |
| 40 | 93.051 | 188.88 | 267.86 | 378.72 | 750.38 | 1469.8 | 5455.9 | 19427 | 66521 | * |
| 50 | 289.00 | 700.23 | 1083.7 | 1670.7 | 3927.4 | 9100.4 | 46890 | * | * | * |
| 60 | 897.60 | 2595.9 | 4384.0 | 7370.2 | 20555 | 56348 | * | * | * | * |

* > 99,999

## TABLE B.1b  Sum of an Annuity of $1 per Period for *n* Periods

| Number of Periods | 1% | 2% | 3% | 4% | 5% | 6% | 7% | 8% | 9% | 10% |
|---|---|---|---|---|---|---|---|---|---|---|
| 1 | 1.0000 | 1.0000 | 1.0000 | 1.0000 | 1.0000 | 1.0000 | 1.0000 | 1.0000 | 1.0000 | 1.0000 |
| 2 | 2.0100 | 2.0200 | 2.0300 | 2.0400 | 2.0500 | 2.0600 | 2.0700 | 2.0800 | 2.0900 | 2.1000 |
| 3 | 3.0301 | 3.0604 | 3.0909 | 3.1216 | 3.1525 | 3.1836 | 3.2149 | 3.2464 | 3.2781 | 3.3100 |
| 4 | 4.0604 | 4.1216 | 4.1836 | 4.2465 | 4.3101 | 4.3746 | 4.4399 | 4.5061 | 4.5731 | 4.6410 |
| 5 | 5.1010 | 5.2040 | 5.3091 | 5.4163 | 5.5256 | 5.6371 | 5.7507 | 5.8666 | 5.9847 | 6.1051 |
| 6 | 6.1520 | 6.3081 | 6.4684 | 6.6330 | 6.8019 | 6.9753 | 7.1533 | 7.3359 | 7.5233 | 7.7156 |
| 7 | 7.2135 | 7.4343 | 7.6625 | 7.8983 | 8.1420 | 8.3938 | 8.6540 | 8.9228 | 9.2004 | 9.4872 |
| 8 | 8.2857 | 8.5830 | 8.8923 | 9.2142 | 9.5491 | 9.8975 | 10.260 | 10.637 | 11.028 | 11.436 |
| 9 | 9.3685 | 9.7546 | 10.159 | 10.583 | 11.027 | 11.491 | 11.978 | 12.488 | 13.021 | 13.579 |
| 10 | 10.462 | 10.950 | 11.464 | 12.006 | 12.578 | 13.181 | 13.816 | 14.487 | 15.193 | 15.937 |
| 11 | 11.567 | 12.169 | 12.808 | 13.486 | 14.207 | 14.972 | 15.784 | 16.645 | 17.560 | 18.531 |
| 12 | 12.683 | 13.412 | 14.192 | 15.026 | 15.917 | 16.870 | 17.888 | 18.977 | 20.141 | 21.384 |
| 13 | 13.809 | 14.680 | 15.618 | 16.627 | 17.713 | 18.882 | 20.141 | 21.495 | 22.953 | 24.523 |
| 14 | 14.947 | 15.974 | 17.086 | 18.292 | 19.599 | 21.015 | 22.550 | 24.215 | 26.019 | 27.975 |
| 15 | 16.097 | 17.293 | 18.599 | 20.024 | 21.579 | 23.276 | 25.129 | 27.152 | 29.361 | 31.772 |
| 16 | 17.258 | 18.639 | 20.157 | 21.825 | 23.657 | 25.673 | 27.888 | 30.324 | 33.003 | 35.950 |
| 17 | 18.430 | 20.012 | 21.762 | 23.698 | 25.840 | 28.213 | 30.840 | 33.750 | 36.974 | 40.545 |
| 18 | 19.615 | 21.412 | 23.414 | 25.645 | 28.132 | 30.906 | 33.999 | 37.450 | 41.301 | 45.599 |
| 19 | 20.811 | 22.841 | 25.117 | 27.671 | 30.539 | 33.760 | 37.379 | 41.446 | 46.018 | 51.159 |
| 20 | 22.019 | 24.297 | 26.870 | 29.778 | 33.066 | 36.786 | 40.995 | 45.762 | 51.160 | 57.275 |
| 21 | 23.239 | 25.783 | 28.676 | 31.969 | 35.719 | 39.993 | 44.865 | 50.423 | 56.765 | 64.002 |
| 22 | 24.472 | 27.299 | 30.537 | 34.248 | 38.505 | 43.392 | 49.006 | 55.457 | 62.873 | 71.403 |
| 23 | 25.716 | 28.845 | 32.453 | 36.618 | 41.430 | 46.996 | 53.436 | 60.893 | 69.532 | 79.543 |
| 24 | 26.973 | 30.422 | 34.426 | 39.083 | 44.502 | 50.816 | 58.177 | 66.765 | 76.790 | 88.497 |
| 25 | 28.243 | 32.030 | 36.459 | 41.646 | 47.727 | 54.865 | 63.249 | 73.106 | 84.701 | 98.347 |
| 26 | 29.526 | 33.671 | 38.553 | 44.312 | 51.113 | 59.156 | 68.676 | 79.954 | 93.324 | 109.18 |
| 27 | 30.821 | 35.344 | 40.710 | 47.084 | 54.669 | 63.706 | 74.484 | 87.351 | 102.72 | 121.10 |
| 28 | 32.129 | 37.051 | 42.931 | 49.968 | 58.403 | 68.528 | 80.698 | 95.339 | 112.97 | 134.21 |
| 29 | 33.450 | 38.792 | 45.219 | 52.966 | 62.323 | 73.640 | 87.347 | 103.97 | 124.14 | 148.63 |
| 30 | 34.785 | 40.568 | 47.575 | 56.085 | 66.439 | 79.058 | 94.461 | 113.28 | 136.31 | 164.49 |
| 40 | 48.886 | 60.402 | 75.401 | 95.026 | 120.80 | 154.76 | 199.64 | 259.06 | 337.88 | 442.59 |
| 50 | 64.463 | 84.579 | 112.80 | 152.67 | 209.35 | 290.34 | 406.53 | 573.77 | 815.08 | 1163.9 |
| 60 | 81.670 | 114.05 | 163.05 | 237.99 | 353.58 | 533.13 | 813.52 | 1253.2 | 1944.8 | 3034.8 |

**TABLE B.1b**   *(continued)*

| Number of Periods | 12% | 14% | 15% | 16% | 18% | 20% | 24% | 28% | 32% | 36% |
|---|---|---|---|---|---|---|---|---|---|---|
| 1 | 1.0000 | 1.0000 | 1.0000 | 1.0000 | 1.0000 | 1.0000 | 1.0000 | 1.0000 | 1.0000 | 1.0000 |
| 2 | 2.1200 | 2.1400 | 2.1500 | 2.1600 | 2.1800 | 2.2000 | 2.2400 | 2.2800 | 2.3200 | 2.3600 |
| 3 | 3.3744 | 3.4396 | 3.4725 | 3.5056 | 3.5724 | 3.6400 | 3.7776 | 3.9184 | 4.0624 | 4.2096 |
| 4 | 4.7793 | 4.9211 | 4.9934 | 5.0665 | 5.2154 | 5.3680 | 5.6842 | 6.0156 | 6.3624 | 6.7251 |
| 5 | 6.3528 | 6.6101 | 6.7424 | 6.8771 | 7.1542 | 7.4416 | 8.0484 | 8.6999 | 9.3983 | 10.146 |
| 6 | 8.1152 | 8.5355 | 8.7537 | 8.9775 | 9.4420 | 9.9299 | 10.980 | 12.136 | 13.406 | 14.799 |
| 7 | 10.089 | 10.730 | 11.067 | 11.414 | 12.142 | 12.916 | 14.615 | 16.534 | 18.696 | 21.126 |
| 8 | 12.300 | 13.233 | 13.727 | 14.240 | 15.327 | 16.499 | 19.123 | 22.163 | 25.678 | 29.732 |
| 9 | 14.776 | 16.085 | 16.786 | 17.519 | 19.086 | 20.799 | 24.712 | 29.369 | 34.895 | 41.435 |
| 10 | 17.549 | 19.337 | 20.304 | 21.321 | 23.521 | 25.959 | 31.643 | 38.593 | 47.062 | 57.352 |
| 11 | 20.655 | 23.045 | 24.349 | 25.733 | 28.755 | 32.150 | 40.238 | 50.398 | 63.122 | 78.998 |
| 12 | 24.133 | 27.271 | 29.002 | 30.850 | 34.931 | 39.581 | 50.895 | 65.510 | 84.320 | 108.44 |
| 13 | 28.029 | 32.089 | 34.352 | 36.786 | 42.219 | 48.497 | 64.110 | 84.853 | 112.30 | 148.47 |
| 14 | 32.393 | 37.581 | 40.505 | 43.672 | 50.818 | 59.196 | 80.496 | 109.61 | 149.24 | 202.93 |
| 15 | 37.280 | 43.842 | 47.580 | 51.660 | 60.965 | 72.035 | 100.82 | 141.30 | 198.00 | 276.98 |
| 16 | 42.753 | 50.980 | 55.717 | 60.925 | 72.939 | 87.442 | 126.01 | 181.87 | 262.36 | 377.69 |
| 17 | 48.884 | 59.118 | 65.075 | 71.673 | 87.068 | 105.93 | 157.25 | 233.79 | 347.31 | 514.66 |
| 18 | 55.750 | 68.394 | 75.836 | 84.141 | 103.74 | 128.11 | 195.99 | 300.25 | 459.45 | 700.94 |
| 19 | 63.440 | 78.969 | 88.212 | 98.603 | 123.41 | 154.74 | 244.03 | 385.32 | 607.47 | 954.28 |
| 20 | 72.052 | 91.025 | 102.44 | 115.38 | 146.63 | 186.69 | 303.60 | 494.21 | 802.86 | 1298.8 |
| 21 | 81.699 | 104.77 | 118.81 | 134.84 | 174.02 | 225.03 | 377.46 | 633.59 | 1060.8 | 1767.4 |
| 22 | 92.503 | 120.44 | 137.63 | 157.41 | 206.34 | 271.03 | 469.06 | 812.00 | 1401.2 | 2404.7 |
| 23 | 104.60 | 138.30 | 159.28 | 183.60 | 244.49 | 326.24 | 582.63 | 1040.4 | 1850.6 | 3271.3 |
| 24 | 118.16 | 158.66 | 184.17 | 213.98 | 289.49 | 392.48 | 723.46 | 1332.7 | 2443.8 | 4450.0 |
| 25 | 133.33 | 181.87 | 212.79 | 249.21 | 342.60 | 471.98 | 898.09 | 1706.8 | 3226.8 | 6053.0 |
| 26 | 150.33 | 208.33 | 245.71 | 290.09 | 405.27 | 567.38 | 1114.6 | 2185.7 | 4260.4 | 8233.1 |
| 27 | 169.37 | 238.50 | 283.57 | 337.50 | 479.22 | 681.85 | 1383.1 | 2798.7 | 5624.8 | 11198.0 |
| 28 | 190.70 | 272.89 | 327.10 | 392.50 | 566.48 | 819.22 | 1716.1 | 3583.3 | 7425.7 | 15230.3 |
| 29 | 214.58 | 312.09 | 377.17 | 456.30 | 669.45 | 984.07 | 2129.0 | 4587.7 | 9802.9 | 20714.2 |
| 30 | 241.33 | 356.79 | 434.75 | 530.31 | 790.95 | 1181.9 | 2640.9 | 5873.2 | 12941 | 28172.3 |
| 40 | 767.09 | 1342.0 | 1779.1 | 2360.8 | 4163.2 | 7343.9 | 22729 | 69377 | * | * |
| 50 | 2400.0 | 4994.5 | 7217.7 | 10436 | 21813 | 45497 | * | * | * | * |
| 60 | 7471.6 | 18535 | 29220 | 46058 | * | * | * | * | * | * |

\* > 99,999

## TABLE B.1c  Present Value of $1 Received at the End of *n* Periods

| Period | 1% | 2% | 3% | 4% | 5% | 6% | 7% | 8% | 9% | 10% |
|--------|------|------|------|------|------|------|------|------|------|------|
| 1 | .9901 | .9804 | .9709 | .9615 | .9524 | .9434 | .9346 | .9259 | .9174 | .9091 |
| 2 | .9803 | .9612 | .9426 | .9246 | .9070 | .8900 | .8734 | .8573 | .8417 | .8264 |
| 3 | .9706 | .9423 | .9151 | .8890 | .8638 | .8396 | .8163 | .7938 | .7722 | .7513 |
| 4 | .9610 | .9238 | .8885 | .8548 | .8227 | .7921 | .7629 | .7350 | .7084 | .6830 |
| 5 | .9515 | .9057 | .8626 | .8219 | .7835 | .7473 | .7130 | .6806 | .6499 | .6209 |
| 6 | .9420 | .8880 | .8375 | .7903 | .7462 | .7050 | .6663 | .6302 | .5963 | .5645 |
| 7 | .9327 | .8706 | .8131 | .7599 | .7107 | .6651 | .6227 | .5835 | .5470 | .5132 |
| 8 | .9235 | .8535 | .7894 | .7307 | .6768 | .6274 | .5820 | .5403 | .5019 | .4665 |
| 9 | .9143 | .8368 | .7664 | .7026 | .6446 | .5919 | .5439 | .5002 | .4604 | .4241 |
| 10 | .9053 | .8203 | .7441 | .6756 | .6139 | .5584 | .5083 | .4632 | .4224 | .3855 |
| 11 | .8963 | .8043 | .7224 | .6496 | .5847 | .5268 | .4751 | .4289 | .3875 | .3505 |
| 12 | .8874 | .7885 | .7014 | .6246 | .5568 | .4970 | .4440 | .3971 | .3555 | .3186 |
| 13 | .8787 | .7730 | .6810 | .6006 | .5303 | .4688 | .4150 | .3677 | .3262 | .2897 |
| 14 | .8700 | .7579 | .6611 | .5775 | .5051 | .4423 | .3878 | .3405 | .2992 | .2633 |
| 15 | .8613 | .7430 | .6419 | .5553 | .4810 | .4173 | .3624 | .3152 | .2745 | .2394 |
| 16 | .8528 | .7284 | .6232 | .5339 | .4581 | .3936 | .3387 | .2919 | .2519 | .2176 |
| 17 | .8444 | .7142 | .6050 | .5134 | .4363 | .3714 | .3166 | .2703 | .2311 | .1978 |
| 18 | .8360 | .7002 | .5874 | .4936 | .4155 | .3503 | .2959 | .2502 | .2120 | .1799 |
| 19 | .8277 | .6864 | .5703 | .4746 | .3957 | .3305 | .2765 | .2317 | .1945 | .1635 |
| 20 | .8195 | .6730 | .5537 | .4564 | .3769 | .3118 | .2584 | .2145 | .1784 | .1486 |
| 25 | .7798 | .6095 | .4776 | .3751 | .2953 | .2330 | .1842 | .1460 | .1160 | .0923 |
| 30 | .7419 | .5521 | .4120 | .3083 | .2314 | .1741 | .1314 | .0994 | .0754 | .0573 |
| 40 | .6717 | .4529 | .3066 | .2083 | .1420 | .0972 | .0668 | .0460 | .0318 | .0221 |
| 50 | .6080 | .3715 | .2281 | .1407 | .0872 | .0543 | .0339 | .0213 | .0134 | .0085 |
| 60 | .5504 | .3048 | .1697 | .0951 | .0535 | .0303 | .0173 | .0099 | .0057 | .0033 |

**TABLE B.1c** *(continued)*

| Period | 12% | 14% | 15% | 16% | 18% | 20% | 24% | 28% | 32% | 36% |
|--------|-----|-----|-----|-----|-----|-----|-----|-----|-----|-----|
| 1 | .8929 | .8772 | .8696 | .8621 | .8475 | .8333 | .8065 | .7813 | .7576 | .7353 |
| 2 | .7972 | .7695 | .7561 | .7432 | .7182 | .6944 | .6504 | .6104 | .5739 | .5407 |
| 3 | .7118 | .6750 | .6575 | .6407 | .6086 | .5787 | .5245 | .4768 | .4348 | .3975 |
| 4 | .6355 | .5921 | .5718 | .5523 | .5158 | .4823 | .4230 | .3725 | .3294 | .2923 |
| 5 | .5674 | .5194 | .4972 | .4761 | .4371 | .4019 | .3411 | .2910 | .2495 | .2149 |
| 6 | .5066 | .4556 | .4323 | .4104 | .3704 | .3349 | .2751 | .2274 | .1890 | .1580 |
| 7 | .4523 | .3996 | .3759 | .3538 | .3139 | .2791 | .2218 | .1776 | .1432 | .1162 |
| 8 | .4039 | .3506 | .3269 | .3050 | .2660 | .2326 | .1789 | .1388 | .1085 | .0854 |
| 9 | .3606 | .3075 | .2843 | .2630 | .2255 | .1938 | .1443 | .1084 | .0822 | .0628 |
| 10 | .3220 | .2697 | .2472 | .2267 | .1911 | .1615 | .1164 | .0847 | .0623 | .0462 |
| 11 | .2875 | .2366 | .2149 | .1954 | .1619 | .1346 | .0938 | .0662 | .0472 | .0340 |
| 12 | .2567 | .2076 | .1869 | .1685 | .1372 | .1122 | .0757 | .0517 | .0357 | .0250 |
| 13 | .2292 | .1821 | .1625 | .1452 | .1163 | .0935 | .0610 | .0404 | .0271 | .0184 |
| 14 | .2046 | .1597 | .1413 | .1252 | .0985 | .0779 | .0492 | .0316 | .0205 | .0135 |
| 15 | .1827 | .1401 | .1229 | .1079 | .0835 | .0649 | .0397 | .0247 | .0155 | .0099 |
| 16 | .1631 | .1229 | .1069 | .0930 | .0708 | .0541 | .0320 | .0193 | .0118 | .0073 |
| 17 | .1456 | .1078 | .0929 | .0802 | .0600 | .0451 | .0258 | .0150 | .0089 | .0054 |
| 18 | .1300 | .0946 | .0808 | .0691 | .0508 | .0376 | .0208 | .0118 | .0068 | .0039 |
| 19 | .1161 | .0829 | .0703 | .0596 | .0431 | .0313 | .0168 | .0092 | .0051 | .0029 |
| 20 | .1037 | .0728 | .0611 | .0514 | .0365 | .0261 | .0135 | .0072 | .0039 | .0021 |
| 25 | .0588 | .0378 | .0304 | .0245 | .0160 | .0105 | .0046 | .0021 | .0010 | .0005 |
| 30 | .0334 | .0196 | .0151 | .0116 | .0070 | .0042 | .0016 | .0006 | .0002 | .0001 |
| 40 | .0107 | .0053 | .0037 | .0026 | .0013 | .0007 | .0002 | .0001 | * | * |
| 50 | .0035 | .0014 | .0009 | .0006 | .0003 | .0001 | * | * | * | * |
| 60 | .0011 | .0004 | .0002 | .0001 | * | * | * | * | * | * |

*The factor is zero to four decimal places.

**TABLE B.1d   Present Value of an Annuity of $1 per Period for *n* Periods**

| Number of Payments | 1% | 2% | 3% | 4% | 5% | 6% | 7% | 8% | 9% |
|---|---|---|---|---|---|---|---|---|---|
| 1 | 0.9901 | 0.9804 | 0.9709 | 0.9615 | 0.9524 | 0.9434 | 0.9346 | 0.9259 | 0.9174 |
| 2 | 1.9704 | 1.9416 | 1.9135 | 1.8861 | 1.8594 | 1.8334 | 1.8080 | 1.7833 | 1.7591 |
| 3 | 2.9410 | 2.8839 | 2.8286 | 2.7751 | 2.7232 | 2.6730 | 2.6243 | 2.5771 | 2.5313 |
| 4 | 3.9020 | 3.8077 | 3.7171 | 3.6299 | 3.5460 | 3.4651 | 3.3872 | 3.3121 | 3.2397 |
| 5 | 4.8534 | 4.7135 | 4.5797 | 4.4518 | 4.3295 | 4.2124 | 4.1002 | 3.9927 | 3.8897 |
| 6 | 5.7955 | 5.6014 | 5.4172 | 5.2421 | 5.0757 | 4.9173 | 4.7665 | 4.6229 | 4.4859 |
| 7 | 6.7282 | 6.4720 | 6.2303 | 6.0021 | 5.7864 | 5.5824 | 5.3893 | 5.2064 | 5.0330 |
| 8 | 7.6517 | 7.3255 | 7.0197 | 6.7327 | 6.4632 | 6.2098 | 5.9713 | 5.7466 | 5.5348 |
| 9 | 8.5660 | 8.1622 | 7.7861 | 7.4353 | 7.1078 | 6.8017 | 6.5152 | 6.2469 | 5.9952 |
| 10 | 9.4713 | 8.9826 | 8.5302 | 8.1109 | 7.7217 | 7.3601 | 7.0236 | 6.7101 | 6.4177 |
| 11 | 10.3676 | 9.7868 | 9.2526 | 8.7605 | 8.3064 | 7.8869 | 7.4987 | 7.1390 | 6.8052 |
| 12 | 11.2551 | 10.5753 | 9.9540 | 9.3851 | 8.8633 | 8.3838 | 7.9427 | 7.5361 | 7.1607 |
| 13 | 12.1337 | 11.3484 | 10.6350 | 9.9856 | 9.3936 | 8.8527 | 8.3577 | 7.9038 | 7.4869 |
| 14 | 13.0037 | 12.1062 | 11.2961 | 10.5631 | 9.8986 | 9.2950 | 8.7455 | 8.2442 | 7.7862 |
| 15 | 13.8651 | 12.8493 | 11.9379 | 11.1184 | 10.3797 | 9.7122 | 9.1079 | 8.5595 | 8.0607 |
| 16 | 14.7179 | 13.5777 | 12.5611 | 11.6523 | 10.8378 | 10.1059 | 9.4466 | 8.8514 | 8.3126 |
| 17 | 15.5623 | 14.2919 | 13.1661 | 12.1657 | 11.2741 | 10.4773 | 9.7632 | 9.1216 | 8.5436 |
| 18 | 16.3983 | 14.9920 | 13.7535 | 12.6593 | 11.6896 | 10.8276 | 10.0591 | 9.3719 | 8.7556 |
| 19 | 17.2260 | 15.6785 | 14.3238 | 13.1339 | 12.0853 | 11.1581 | 10.3356 | 9.6036 | 8.9501 |
| 20 | 18.0456 | 16.3514 | 14.8775 | 13.5903 | 12.4622 | 11.4699 | 10.5940 | 9.8181 | 9.1285 |
| 25 | 22.0232 | 19.5235 | 17.4131 | 15.6221 | 14.0939 | 12.7834 | 11.6536 | 10.6748 | 9.8226 |
| 30 | 25.8077 | 22.3965 | 19.6004 | 17.2920 | 15.3725 | 13.7648 | 12.4090 | 11.2578 | 10.2737 |
| 40 | 32.8347 | 27.3555 | 23.1148 | 19.7928 | 17.1591 | 15.0463 | 13.3317 | 11.9246 | 10.7574 |
| 50 | 39.1961 | 31.4236 | 25.7298 | 21.4822 | 18.2559 | 15.7619 | 13.8007 | 12.2335 | 10.9617 |
| 60 | 44.9550 | 34.7609 | 27.6756 | 22.6235 | 18.9293 | 16.1614 | 14.0392 | 12.3766 | 11.0480 |

**TABLE B.1d** *(continued)*

| Number of Payments | 10% | 12% | 14% | 15% | 16% | 18% | 20% | 24% | 28% | 32% | 36% |
|---|---|---|---|---|---|---|---|---|---|---|---|
| 1 | 0.9091 | 0.8929 | 0.8772 | 0.8696 | 0.8621 | 0.8475 | 0.8333 | 0.8065 | 0.7813 | 0.7576 | 0.7353 |
| 2 | 1.7355 | 1.6901 | 1.6467 | 1.6257 | 1.6052 | 1.5656 | 1.5278 | 1.4568 | 1.3916 | 1.3315 | 1.2760 |
| 3 | 2.4869 | 2.4018 | 2.3216 | 2.2832 | 2.2459 | 2.1743 | 2.1065 | 1.9813 | 1.8684 | 1.7663 | 1.6735 |
| 4 | 3.1699 | 3.0373 | 2.9137 | 2.8550 | 2.7982 | 2.6901 | 2.5887 | 2.4043 | 2.2410 | 2.0957 | 1.9658 |
| 5 | 3.7908 | 3.6048 | 3.4331 | 3.3522 | 3.2743 | 3.1272 | 2.9906 | 2.7454 | 2.5320 | 2.3452 | 2.1807 |
| 6 | 4.3553 | 4.1114 | 3.8887 | 3.7845 | 3.6847 | 3.4976 | 3.3255 | 3.0205 | 2.7594 | 2.5342 | 2.3388 |
| 7 | 4.8684 | 4.5638 | 4.2883 | 4.1604 | 4.0386 | 3.8115 | 3.6046 | 3.2423 | 2.9370 | 2.6775 | 2.4550 |
| 8 | 5.3349 | 4.9676 | 4.6389 | 4.4873 | 4.3436 | 4.0776 | 3.8372 | 3.4212 | 3.0758 | 2.7860 | 2.5404 |
| 9 | 5.7590 | 5.3282 | 4.9464 | 4.7716 | 4.6065 | 4.3030 | 4.0310 | 3.5655 | 3.1842 | 2.8681 | 2.6033 |
| 10 | 6.1446 | 5.6502 | 5.2161 | 5.0188 | 4.8332 | 4.4941 | 4.1925 | 3.6819 | 3.2689 | 2.9304 | 2.6495 |
| 11 | 6.4951 | 5.9377 | 5.4527 | 5.2337 | 5.0286 | 4.6560 | 4.3271 | 3.7757 | 3.3351 | 2.9776 | 2.6834 |
| 12 | 6.8137 | 6.1944 | 5.6603 | 5.4206 | 5.1971 | 4.7932 | 4.4392 | 3.8514 | 3.3868 | 3.0133 | 2.7084 |
| 13 | 7.1034 | 6.4235 | 5.8424 | 5.5831 | 5.3423 | 4.9095 | 4.5327 | 3.9124 | 3.4272 | 3.0404 | 2.7268 |
| 14 | 7.3667 | 6.6282 | 6.0021 | 5.7245 | 5.4675 | 5.0081 | 4.6106 | 3.9616 | 3.4587 | 3.0609 | 2.7403 |
| 15 | 7.6061 | 6.8109 | 6.1422 | 5.8474 | 5.5755 | 5.0916 | 4.6755 | 4.0013 | 3.4834 | 3.0764 | 2.7502 |
| 16 | 7.8237 | 6.9740 | 6.2651 | 5.9542 | 5.6685 | 5.1624 | 4.7296 | 4.0333 | 3.5026 | 3.0882 | 2.7575 |
| 17 | 8.0216 | 7.1196 | 6.3729 | 6.0472 | 5.7487 | 5.2223 | 4.7746 | 4.0591 | 3.5177 | 3.0971 | 2.7629 |
| 18 | 8.2014 | 7.2497 | 6.4674 | 6.1280 | 5.8178 | 5.2732 | 4.8122 | 4.0799 | 3.5294 | 3.1039 | 2.7668 |
| 19 | 8.3649 | 7.3658 | 6.5504 | 6.1982 | 5.8775 | 5.3162 | 4.8435 | 4.0967 | 3.5386 | 3.1090 | 2.7697 |
| 20 | 8.5136 | 7.4694 | 6.6231 | 6.2593 | 5.9288 | 5.3527 | 4.8696 | 4.1103 | 3.5458 | 3.1129 | 2.7718 |
| 25 | 9.0770 | 7.8431 | 6.8729 | 6.4641 | 6.0971 | 5.4669 | 4.9476 | 4.1474 | 3.5640 | 3.1220 | 2.7765 |
| 30 | 9.4269 | 8.0552 | 7.0027 | 6.5660 | 6.1772 | 5.5168 | 4.9789 | 4.1601 | 3.5693 | 3.1242 | 2.7775 |
| 40 | 9.7791 | 8.2438 | 7.1050 | 6.6418 | 6.2335 | 5.5482 | 4.9966 | 4.1659 | 3.5712 | 3.1250 | 2.7778 |
| 50 | 9.9148 | 8.3045 | 7.1327 | 6.6605 | 6.2463 | 5.5541 | 4.9995 | 4.1666 | 3.5714 | 3.1250 | 2.7778 |
| 60 | 9.9672 | 8.3240 | 7.1401 | 6.6651 | 6.2492 | 5.5553 | 4.9999 | 4.1667 | 3.5714 | 3.1250 | 2.7778 |

**TABLE B.2 Areas Under the Normal Curve**

| Z | .00 | .01 | .02 | .03 | .04 | .05 | .06 | .07 | .08 | .09 |
|---|-----|-----|-----|-----|-----|-----|-----|-----|-----|-----|
| 0.0 | .0000 | .0040 | .0080 | .0120 | .0160 | .0199 | .0239 | .0279 | .0319 | .0359 |
| 0.1 | .0398 | .0438 | .0478 | .0517 | .0557 | .0596 | .0636 | .0675 | .0714 | .0753 |
| 0.2 | .0793 | .0832 | .0871 | .0910 | .0948 | .0987 | .1026 | .1064 | .1103 | .1141 |
| 0.3 | .1179 | .1217 | .1255 | .1293 | .1331 | .1368 | .1406 | .1443 | .1480 | .1517 |
| 0.4 | .1554 | .1591 | .1628 | .1664 | .1700 | .1736 | .1772 | .1808 | .1844 | .1879 |
| 0.5 | .1915 | .1950 | .1985 | .2019 | .2054 | .2088 | .2123 | .2157 | .2190 | .2224 |
| 0.6 | .2257 | .2291 | .2324 | .2357 | .2389 | .2422 | .2454 | .2486 | .2517 | .2549 |
| 0.7 | .2580 | .2611 | .2642 | .2673 | .2704 | .2734 | .2764 | .2794 | .2823 | .2852 |
| 0.8 | .2881 | .2910 | .2939 | .2967 | .2995 | .3023 | .3051 | .3078 | .3106 | .3133 |
| 0.9 | .3159 | .3186 | .3212 | .3238 | .3264 | .3289 | .3315 | .3340 | .3365 | .3389 |
| 1.0 | .3413 | .3438 | .3461 | .3485 | .3508 | .3531 | .3554 | .3577 | .3599 | .3621 |
| 1.1 | .3643 | .3665 | .3686 | .3708 | .3729 | .3749 | .3770 | .3790 | .3810 | .3830 |
| 1.2 | .3849 | .3869 | .3888 | .3907 | .3925 | .3944 | .3962 | .3980 | .3997 | .4015 |
| 1.3 | .4032 | .4049 | .4066 | .4082 | .4099 | .4115 | .4131 | .4147 | .4162 | .4177 |
| 1.4 | .4192 | .4207 | .4222 | .4236 | .4251 | .4265 | .4279 | .4292 | .4306 | .4319 |
| 1.5 | .4332 | .4345 | .4357 | .4370 | .4382 | .4394 | .4406 | .4418 | .4429 | .4441 |
| 1.6 | .4452 | .4463 | .4474 | .4484 | .4495 | .4505 | .4515 | .4525 | .4535 | .4545 |
| 1.7 | .4554 | .4564 | .4573 | .4582 | .4591 | .4599 | .4608 | .4616 | .4625 | .4633 |
| 1.8 | .4641 | .4649 | .4656 | .4664 | .4671 | .4678 | .4686 | .4693 | .4699 | .4706 |
| 1.9 | .4713 | .4719 | .4726 | .4732 | .4738 | .4744 | .4750 | .4756 | .4761 | .4767 |
| 2.0 | .4772 | .4778 | .4783 | .4788 | .4793 | .4798 | .4803 | .4808 | .4812 | .4817 |
| 2.1 | .4821 | .4826 | .4830 | .4834 | .4838 | .4842 | .4846 | .4850 | .4854 | .4857 |
| 2.2 | .4861 | .4864 | .4868 | .4871 | .4875 | .4878 | .4881 | .4884 | .4887 | .4890 |
| 2.3 | .4893 | .4896 | .4898 | .4901 | .4904 | .4906 | .4909 | .4911 | .4913 | .4916 |
| 2.4 | .4918 | .4920 | .4922 | .4925 | .4927 | .4929 | .4931 | .4932 | .4934 | .4936 |
| 2.5 | .4938 | .4940 | .4941 | .4943 | .4945 | .4946 | .4948 | .4949 | .4951 | .4952 |
| 2.6 | .4953 | .4955 | .4956 | .4957 | .4959 | .4960 | .4961 | .4962 | .4963 | .4964 |
| 2.7 | .4965 | .4966 | .4967 | .4968 | .4969 | .4970 | .4971 | .4972 | .4973 | .4974 |
| 2.8 | .4974 | .4975 | .4976 | .4977 | .4977 | .4978 | .4979 | .4979 | .4980 | .4981 |
| 2.9 | .4981 | .4982 | .4982 | .4983 | .4984 | .4984 | .4985 | .4985 | .4986 | .4986 |
| 3.0 | .4987 | .4987 | .4987 | .4988 | .4988 | .4989 | .4989 | .4989 | .4990 | .4990 |

**TABLE B.3*a*  Critical Values for the *F*-Distribution ($\alpha = .05$)**

| Degrees of Freedom for Denominator | Degrees of Freedom for Numerator | | | | | | | | |
|---|---|---|---|---|---|---|---|---|---|
| | *1* | *2* | *3* | *4* | *5* | *6* | *8* | *10* | *15* |
| 1 | 161.4 | 199.5 | 215.7 | 224.6 | 230.2 | 234.0 | 238.9 | 241.9 | 245.9 |
| 2 | 18.51 | 19.00 | 19.16 | 19.25 | 19.30 | 19.33 | 19.37 | 19.40 | 19.43 |
| 3 | 10.13 | 9.55 | 9.28 | 9.12 | 9.01 | 8.94 | 8.85 | 8.79 | 8.70 |
| 4 | 7.71 | 6.94 | 6.59 | 6.39 | 6.26 | 6.16 | 6.04 | 5.96 | 5.86 |
| 5 | 6.61 | 5.79 | 5.41 | 5.19 | 5.05 | 4.95 | 4.82 | 4.74 | 4.62 |
| 6 | 5.99 | 5.14 | 4.76 | 4.53 | 4.39 | 4.28 | 4.15 | 4.06 | 3.94 |
| 7 | 5.59 | 4.74 | 4.35 | 4.12 | 3.97 | 3.87 | 3.73 | 3.64 | 3.51 |
| 8 | 5.32 | 4.46 | 4.07 | 3.84 | 3.69 | 3.58 | 3.44 | 3.35 | 3.22 |
| 9 | 5.12 | 4.26 | 3.86 | 3.63 | 3.48 | 3.37 | 3.23 | 3.14 | 3.01 |
| 10 | 4.96 | 4.10 | 3.71 | 3.48 | 3.33 | 3.22 | 3.07 | 2.98 | 2.85 |
| 11 | 4.84 | 3.98 | 3.59 | 3.36 | 3.20 | 3.09 | 2.95 | 2.85 | 2.72 |
| 12 | 4.75 | 3.89 | 3.49 | 3.26 | 3.11 | 3.00 | 2.85 | 2.75 | 2.62 |
| 13 | 4.67 | 3.81 | 3.41 | 3.18 | 3.03 | 2.92 | 2.77 | 2.67 | 2.53 |
| 14 | 4.60 | 3.74 | 3.34 | 3.11 | 2.96 | 2.85 | 2.70 | 2.60 | 2.46 |
| 15 | 4.54 | 3.68 | 3.29 | 3.06 | 2.90 | 2.79 | 2.64 | 2.54 | 2.40 |
| 16 | 4.49 | 3.63 | 3.24 | 3.01 | 2.85 | 2.74 | 2.59 | 2.49 | 2.35 |
| 17 | 4.45 | 3.59 | 3.20 | 2.96 | 2.81 | 2.70 | 2.55 | 2.45 | 2.31 |
| 18 | 4.41 | 3.55 | 3.16 | 2.93 | 2.77 | 2.66 | 2.51 | 2.41 | 2.27 |
| 19 | 4.38 | 3.52 | 3.13 | 2.90 | 2.74 | 2.63 | 2.48 | 2.38 | 2.23 |
| 20 | 4.35 | 3.49 | 3.10 | 2.87 | 2.71 | 2.60 | 2.45 | 2.35 | 2.20 |
| 21 | 4.32 | 3.47 | 3.07 | 2.84 | 2.68 | 2.57 | 2.42 | 2.32 | 2.18 |
| 22 | 4.30 | 3.44 | 3.05 | 2.82 | 2.66 | 2.55 | 2.40 | 2.30 | 2.15 |
| 23 | 4.28 | 3.42 | 3.03 | 2.80 | 2.64 | 2.53 | 2.37 | 2.27 | 2.13 |
| 24 | 4.26 | 3.40 | 3.01 | 2.78 | 2.62 | 2.51 | 2.36 | 2.25 | 2.11 |
| 25 | 4.24 | 3.39 | 2.99 | 2.76 | 2.60 | 2.49 | 2.34 | 2.24 | 2.09 |
| 26 | 4.23 | 3.37 | 2.98 | 2.74 | 2.59 | 2.47 | 2.32 | 2.22 | 2.07 |
| 27 | 4.21 | 3.35 | 2.96 | 2.73 | 2.57 | 2.46 | 2.31 | 2.20 | 2.06 |
| 28 | 4.20 | 3.34 | 2.95 | 2.71 | 2.56 | 2.45 | 2.29 | 2.19 | 2.04 |
| 29 | 4.18 | 3.33 | 2.93 | 2.70 | 2.55 | 2.43 | 2.28 | 2.18 | 2.03 |
| 30 | 4.17 | 3.32 | 2.92 | 2.69 | 2.53 | 2.42 | 2.27 | 2.16 | 2.01 |
| 40 | 4.08 | 3.23 | 2.84 | 2.61 | 2.45 | 2.34 | 2.18 | 2.08 | 1.92 |
| 50 | 4.03 | 3.18 | 2.79 | 2.56 | 2.40 | 2.29 | 2.13 | 2.03 | 1.87 |
| 60 | 4.00 | 3.15 | 2.76 | 2.53 | 2.37 | 2.25 | 2.10 | 1.99 | 1.84 |
| 70 | 3.98 | 3.13 | 2.74 | 2.50 | 2.35 | 2.23 | 2.07 | 1.97 | 1.81 |
| 80 | 3.96 | 3.11 | 2.72 | 2.49 | 2.33 | 2.21 | 2.06 | 1.95 | 1.79 |
| 90 | 3.95 | 3.10 | 2.71 | 2.47 | 2.32 | 2.20 | 2.04 | 1.94 | 1.78 |
| 100 | 3.94 | 3.09 | 2.70 | 2.46 | 2.31 | 2.19 | 2.03 | 1.93 | 1.77 |
| 125 | 3.92 | 3.07 | 2.68 | 2.44 | 2.29 | 2.17 | 2.01 | 1.91 | 1.75 |
| 150 | 3.90 | 3.06 | 2.66 | 2.43 | 2.27 | 2.16 | 2.00 | 1.89 | 1.73 |
| 200 | 3.89 | 3.04 | 2.65 | 2.42 | 2.26 | 2.14 | 1.98 | 1.88 | 1.72 |
| $\infty$ | 3.84 | 3.00 | 2.60 | 2.37 | 2.21 | 2.10 | 1.94 | 1.83 | 1.67 |

**TABLE B.3b** Critical Values for the *F*-Distribution ($\alpha = .01$)

| Degrees of Freedom for Denominator | Degrees of Freedom for Numerator | | | | | | | | |
|---|---|---|---|---|---|---|---|---|---|
| | *1* | *2* | *3* | *4* | *5* | *6* | *8* | *10* | *15* |
| 1 | 4052 | 4999 | 5403 | 5625 | 5764 | 5859 | 5981 | 6056 | 6157 |
| 2 | 98.50 | 99.00 | 99.17 | 99.25 | 99.30 | 99.33 | 99.37 | 99.40 | 99.43 |
| 3 | 34.12 | 30.82 | 29.46 | 28.71 | 28.24 | 27.91 | 27.49 | 27.23 | 26.87 |
| 4 | 21.20 | 18.00 | 16.69 | 15.98 | 15.52 | 15.21 | 14.80 | 14.55 | 14.20 |
| 5 | 16.26 | 13.27 | 12.06 | 11.39 | 10.97 | 10.67 | 10.29 | 10.05 | 9.72 |
| 6 | 13.75 | 10.92 | 9.78 | 9.15 | 8.75 | 8.47 | 8.10 | 7.87 | 7.56 |
| 7 | 12.25 | 9.55 | 8.45 | 7.85 | 7.46 | 7.19 | 6.84 | 6.62 | 6.31 |
| 8 | 11.26 | 8.65 | 7.59 | 7.01 | 6.63 | 6.37 | 6.03 | 5.81 | 5.52 |
| 9 | 10.56 | 8.02 | 6.99 | 6.42 | 6.06 | 5.80 | 5.47 | 5.26 | 4.96 |
| 10 | 10.04 | 7.56 | 6.55 | 5.99 | 5.64 | 5.39 | 5.06 | 4.85 | 4.56 |
| 11 | 9.65 | 7.21 | 6.22 | 5.67 | 5.32 | 5.07 | 4.74 | 4.54 | 4.25 |
| 12 | 9.33 | 6.93 | 5.95 | 5.41 | 5.06 | 4.82 | 4.50 | 4.30 | 4.01 |
| 13 | 9.07 | 6.70 | 5.74 | 5.21 | 4.86 | 4.62 | 4.30 | 4.10 | 3.82 |
| 14 | 8.86 | 6.51 | 5.56 | 5.04 | 4.69 | 4.46 | 4.14 | 3.94 | 3.66 |
| 15 | 8.68 | 6.36 | 5.42 | 4.89 | 4.56 | 4.32 | 4.00 | 3.80 | 3.52 |
| 16 | 8.53 | 6.23 | 5.29 | 4.77 | 4.44 | 4.20 | 3.89 | 3.69 | 3.41 |
| 17 | 8.40 | 6.11 | 5.19 | 4.67 | 4.34 | 4.10 | 3.79 | 3.59 | 3.31 |
| 18 | 8.29 | 6.01 | 5.09 | 4.58 | 4.25 | 4.01 | 3.71 | 3.51 | 3.23 |
| 19 | 8.18 | 5.93 | 5.01 | 4.50 | 4.17 | 3.94 | 3.63 | 3.43 | 3.15 |
| 20 | 8.10 | 5.85 | 4.94 | 4.43 | 4.10 | 3.87 | 3.56 | 3.37 | 3.09 |
| 21 | 8.02 | 5.78 | 4.87 | 4.37 | 4.04 | 3.81 | 3.51 | 3.31 | 3.03 |
| 22 | 7.95 | 5.72 | 4.82 | 4.31 | 3.99 | 3.76 | 3.45 | 3.26 | 2.98 |
| 23 | 7.88 | 5.66 | 4.76 | 4.26 | 3.94 | 3.71 | 3.41 | 3.21 | 2.93 |
| 24 | 7.82 | 5.61 | 4.72 | 4.22 | 3.90 | 3.67 | 3.36 | 3.17 | 2.89 |
| 25 | 7.77 | 5.57 | 4.68 | 4.18 | 3.85 | 3.63 | 3.32 | 3.13 | 2.85 |
| 26 | 7.72 | 5.53 | 4.64 | 4.14 | 3.82 | 3.59 | 3.29 | 3.09 | 2.81 |
| 27 | 7.68 | 5.49 | 4.60 | 4.11 | 3.78 | 3.56 | 3.26 | 3.06 | 2.78 |
| 28 | 7.64 | 5.45 | 4.57 | 4.07 | 3.75 | 3.53 | 3.23 | 3.03 | 2.75 |
| 29 | 7.60 | 5.42 | 4.54 | 4.04 | 3.73 | 3.50 | 3.20 | 3.00 | 2.73 |
| 30 | 7.56 | 5.39 | 4.51 | 4.02 | 3.70 | 3.47 | 3.17 | 2.98 | 2.70 |
| 40 | 7.31 | 5.18 | 4.31 | 3.83 | 3.51 | 3.29 | 2.99 | 2.80 | 2.52 |
| 50 | 7.17 | 5.06 | 4.20 | 3.72 | 3.41 | 3.19 | 2.89 | 2.70 | 2.42 |
| 60 | 7.08 | 4.98 | 4.13 | 3.65 | 3.34 | 3.12 | 2.82 | 2.63 | 2.35 |
| 70 | 7.01 | 4.92 | 4.07 | 3.60 | 3.29 | 3.07 | 2.78 | 2.59 | 2.31 |
| 80 | 6.96 | 4.88 | 4.04 | 3.56 | 3.26 | 3.04 | 2.74 | 2.55 | 2.27 |
| 90 | 6.93 | 4.85 | 4.01 | 3.53 | 3.23 | 3.01 | 2.72 | 2.52 | 2.24 |
| 100 | 6.90 | 4.82 | 3.98 | 3.51 | 3.21 | 2.99 | 2.69 | 2.50 | 2.22 |
| 125 | 6.84 | 4.78 | 3.94 | 3.47 | 3.17 | 2.95 | 2.66 | 2.47 | 2.19 |
| 150 | 6.81 | 4.75 | 3.91 | 3.45 | 3.14 | 2.92 | 2.63 | 2.44 | 2.16 |
| 200 | 6.76 | 4.71 | 3.88 | 3.41 | 3.11 | 2.89 | 2.60 | 2.41 | 2.13 |
| ∞ | 6.63 | 4.61 | 3.78 | 3.32 | 3.02 | 2.80 | 2.51 | 2.32 | 2.04 |

**TABLE B.4   Critical Values for the *t*-Distribution**

| One-Tail α = | .10 | .05 | .025 | .01 | .005 |
|---|---|---|---|---|---|
| Two-Tail α = | .20 | .10 | .05 | .02 | .01 |
| df = 1 | 3.078 | 6.314 | 12.706 | 31.821 | 63.657 |
| 2 | 1.886 | 2.920 | 4.303 | 6.965 | 9.925 |
| 3 | 1.638 | 2.353 | 3.182 | 4.541 | 5.841 |
| 4 | 1.533 | 2.132 | 2.776 | 3.747 | 4.604 |
| 5 | 1.476 | 2.015 | 2.571 | 3.365 | 4.032 |
| 6 | 1.440 | 1.943 | 2.447 | 3.143 | 3.707 |
| 7 | 1.415 | 1.895 | 2.365 | 2.998 | 3.499 |
| 8 | 1.397 | 1.860 | 2.306 | 2.896 | 3.355 |
| 9 | 1.383 | 1.833 | 2.262 | 2.821 | 3.250 |
| 10 | 1.372 | 1.812 | 2.228 | 2.764 | 3.169 |
| 11 | 1.363 | 1.796 | 2.201 | 2.718 | 3.106 |
| 12 | 1.356 | 1.782 | 2.179 | 2.681 | 3.055 |
| 13 | 1.350 | 1.771 | 2.160 | 2.650 | 3.012 |
| 14 | 1.345 | 1.761 | 2.145 | 2.624 | 2.977 |
| 15 | 1.341 | 1.753 | 2.131 | 2.602 | 2.947 |
| 16 | 1.337 | 1.746 | 2.120 | 2.583 | 2.921 |
| 17 | 1.333 | 1.740 | 2.110 | 2.567 | 2.898 |
| 18 | 1.330 | 1.734 | 2.101 | 2.552 | 2.878 |
| 19 | 1.328 | 1.729 | 2.093 | 2.539 | 2.861 |
| 20 | 1.325 | 1.725 | 2.086 | 2.528 | 2.845 |
| 21 | 1.323 | 1.721 | 2.080 | 2.518 | 2.831 |
| 22 | 1.321 | 1.717 | 2.074 | 2.508 | 2.819 |
| 23 | 1.319 | 1.714 | 2.069 | 2.500 | 2.807 |
| 24 | 1.318 | 1.711 | 2.064 | 2.492 | 2.797 |
| 25 | 1.316 | 1.708 | 2.060 | 2.485 | 2.787 |
| 26 | 1.315 | 1.706 | 2.056 | 2.479 | 2.779 |
| 27 | 1.314 | 1.703 | 2.052 | 2.473 | 2.771 |
| 28 | 1.313 | 1.701 | 2.048 | 2.467 | 2.763 |
| 29 | 1.311 | 1.699 | 2.045 | 2.462 | 2.756 |
| 30 | 1.310 | 1.697 | 2.042 | 2.457 | 2.750 |
| 40 | 1.303 | 1.684 | 2.021 | 2.423 | 2.704 |
| 50 | 1.299 | 1.676 | 2.009 | 2.403 | 2.678 |
| 60 | 1.296 | 1.671 | 2.000 | 2.390 | 2.660 |
| 70 | 1.294 | 1.667 | 1.994 | 2.381 | 2.648 |
| 80 | 1.292 | 1.664 | 1.990 | 2.374 | 2.639 |
| 90 | 1.291 | 1.662 | 1.987 | 2.368 | 2.632 |
| 100 | 1.290 | 1.660 | 1.984 | 2.364 | 2.626 |
| 125 | 1.288 | 1.657 | 1.979 | 2.357 | 2.616 |
| 150 | 1.287 | 1.655 | 1.976 | 2.351 | 2.609 |
| 200 | 1.286 | 1.653 | 1.972 | 2.345 | 2.601 |
| ∞ | 1.282 | 1.645 | 1.960 | 2.326 | 2.576 |

**TABLE B.5a** Durbin-Watson Statistic: Significance Points for $d_l$ and $d_u$ (One-Tail Test, $\alpha$ = .05)

| | k = 1 | | k = 2 | | k = 3 | | k = 4 | | k = 5 | |
|---|---|---|---|---|---|---|---|---|---|---|
| *n* | $d_l$ | $d_u$ | $d_l$ | $d_u$ | $d_l$ | $d_u$ | $d_l$ | $d_u$ | $d_l$ | $d_u$ |
| 15 | 1.08 | 1.36 | 0.95 | 1.54 | 0.82 | 1.75 | 0.69 | 1.97 | 0.56 | 2.21 |
| 16 | 1.10 | 1.37 | 0.98 | 1.54 | 0.86 | 1.73 | 0.74 | 1.93 | 0.62 | 2.15 |
| 17 | 1.13 | 1.38 | 1.02 | 1.54 | 0.90 | 1.71 | 0.78 | 1.90 | 0.67 | 2.10 |
| 18 | 1.16 | 1.39 | 1.05 | 1.53 | 0.93 | 1.69 | 0.82 | 1.87 | 0.71 | 2.06 |
| 19 | 1.18 | 1.40 | 1.08 | 1.53 | 0.97 | 1.68 | 0.86 | 1.85 | 0.75 | 2.02 |
| 20 | 1.20 | 1.41 | 1.10 | 1.54 | 1.00 | 1.68 | 0.90 | 1.83 | 0.79 | 1.99 |
| 21 | 1.22 | 1.42 | 1.13 | 1.54 | 1.03 | 1.67 | 0.93 | 1.81 | 0.83 | 1.96 |
| 22 | 1.24 | 1.43 | 1.15 | 1.54 | 1.05 | 1.66 | 0.96 | 1.80 | 0.86 | 1.94 |
| 23 | 1.26 | 1.44 | 1.17 | 1.54 | 1.08 | 1.66 | 0.99 | 1.79 | 0.90 | 1.92 |
| 24 | 1.27 | 1.45 | 1.19 | 1.55 | 1.10 | 1.66 | 1.01 | 1.78 | 0.93 | 1.90 |
| 25 | 1.29 | 1.45 | 1.21 | 1.55 | 1.12 | 1.66 | 1.04 | 1.77 | 0.95 | 1.89 |
| 26 | 1.30 | 1.46 | 1.22 | 1.55 | 1.14 | 1.65 | 1.06 | 1.76 | 0.98 | 1.88 |
| 27 | 1.32 | 1.47 | 1.24 | 1.56 | 1.16 | 1.65 | 1.08 | 1.76 | 1.01 | 1.86 |
| 28 | 1.33 | 1.48 | 1.26 | 1.56 | 1.18 | 1.65 | 1.10 | 1.75 | 1.03 | 1.85 |
| 29 | 1.34 | 1.48 | 1.27 | 1.56 | 1.20 | 1.65 | 1.12 | 1.74 | 1.05 | 1.84 |
| 30 | 1.35 | 1.49 | 1.28 | 1.57 | 1.21 | 1.65 | 1.14 | 1.74 | 1.07 | 1.83 |
| 31 | 1.36 | 1.50 | 1.30 | 1.57 | 1.23 | 1.65 | 1.16 | 1.74 | 1.09 | 1.83 |
| 32 | 1.37 | 1.50 | 1.31 | 1.57 | 1.24 | 1.65 | 1.18 | 1.73 | 1.11 | 1.82 |
| 33 | 1.38 | 1.51 | 1.32 | 1.58 | 1.26 | 1.65 | 1.19 | 1.73 | 1.13 | 1.81 |
| 34 | 1.39 | 1.51 | 1.33 | 1.58 | 1.27 | 1.65 | 1.21 | 1.73 | 1.15 | 1.81 |
| 35 | 1.40 | 1.52 | 1.34 | 1.58 | 1.28 | 1.65 | 1.22 | 1.73 | 1.16 | 1.80 |
| 36 | 1.41 | 1.52 | 1.35 | 1.59 | 1.29 | 1.65 | 1.24 | 1.73 | 1.18 | 1.80 |
| 37 | 1.42 | 1.53 | 1.36 | 1.59 | 1.31 | 1.66 | 1.25 | 1.72 | 1.19 | 1.80 |
| 38 | 1.43 | 1.54 | 1.37 | 1.59 | 1.32 | 1.66 | 1.26 | 1.72 | 1.21 | 1.79 |
| 39 | 1.43 | 1.54 | 1.38 | 1.60 | 1.33 | 1.66 | 1.27 | 1.72 | 1.22 | 1.79 |
| 40 | 1.44 | 1.54 | 1.39 | 1.60 | 1.34 | 1.66 | 1.29 | 1.72 | 1.23 | 1.79 |
| 45 | 1.48 | 1.57 | 1.43 | 1.62 | 1.38 | 1.67 | 1.34 | 1.72 | 1.29 | 1.78 |
| 50 | 1.50 | 1.59 | 1.46 | 1.63 | 1.42 | 1.67 | 1.38 | 1.72 | 1.34 | 1.77 |
| 55 | 1.53 | 1.60 | 1.49 | 1.64 | 1.45 | 1.68 | 1.41 | 1.72 | 1.38 | 1.77 |
| 60 | 1.55 | 1.62 | 1.51 | 1.65 | 1.48 | 1.69 | 1.44 | 1.73 | 1.41 | 1.77 |
| 65 | 1.57 | 1.63 | 1.54 | 1.66 | 1.50 | 1.70 | 1.47 | 1.73 | 1.44 | 1.77 |
| 70 | 1.58 | 1.64 | 1.55 | 1.67 | 1.52 | 1.70 | 1.49 | 1.74 | 1.46 | 1.77 |
| 75 | 1.60 | 1.65 | 1.57 | 1.68 | 1.54 | 1.71 | 1.51 | 1.74 | 1.49 | 1.77 |
| 80 | 1.61 | 1.66 | 1.59 | 1.69 | 1.56 | 1.72 | 1.53 | 1.74 | 1.51 | 1.77 |
| 85 | 1.62 | 1.67 | 1.60 | 1.70 | 1.57 | 1.72 | 1.55 | 1.75 | 1.52 | 1.77 |
| 90 | 1.63 | 1.68 | 1.61 | 1.70 | 1.59 | 1.73 | 1.57 | 1.75 | 1.54 | 1.78 |
| 95 | 1.64 | 1.69 | 1.62 | 1.71 | 1.60 | 1.73 | 1.58 | 1.75 | 1.56 | 1.78 |
| 100 | 1.65 | 1.69 | 1.63 | 1.72 | 1.61 | 1.74 | 1.59 | 1.76 | 1.57 | 1.78 |

*Note: n* = number of observations, *k* = number of regressors.

**TABLE B.5*b*   Durbin-Watson Statistic: Significance Points for $d_l$ and $d_u$ (Two-Tail Test, $\alpha = .05$)**

| | k = 1 | | k = 2 | | k = 3 | | k = 4 | | k = 5 | |
|---|---|---|---|---|---|---|---|---|---|---|
| *n* | $d_l$ | $d_u$ | $d_l$ | $d_u$ | $d_l$ | $d_u$ | $d_l$ | $d_u$ | $d_l$ | $d_u$ |
| 15 | 0.95 | 1.23 | 0.83 | 1.40 | 0.71 | 1.61 | 0.59 | 1.84 | 0.48 | 2.09 |
| 16 | 0.98 | 1.24 | 0.86 | 1.40 | 0.75 | 1.59 | 0.64 | 1.80 | 0.53 | 2.03 |
| 17 | 1.01 | 1.25 | 0.90 | 1.40 | 0.79 | 1.58 | 0.68 | 1.77 | 0.57 | 1.98 |
| 18 | 1.03 | 1.26 | 0.93 | 1.40 | 0.82 | 1.56 | 0.72 | 1.74 | 0.62 | 1.93 |
| 19 | 1.06 | 1.28 | 0.96 | 1.41 | 0.86 | 1.55 | 0.76 | 1.72 | 0.66 | 1.90 |
| 20 | 1.08 | 1.28 | 0.99 | 1.41 | 0.89 | 1.55 | 0.79 | 1.70 | 0.70 | 1.87 |
| 21 | 1.10 | 1.30 | 1.01 | 1.41 | 0.92 | 1.54 | 0.83 | 1.69 | 0.73 | 1.84 |
| 22 | 1.12 | 1.31 | 1.04 | 1.42 | 0.95 | 1.54 | 0.86 | 1.68 | 0.77 | 1.82 |
| 23 | 1.14 | 1.32 | 1.06 | 1.42 | 0.97 | 1.54 | 0.89 | 1.67 | 0.80 | 1.80 |
| 24 | 1.16 | 1.33 | 1.08 | 1.43 | 1.00 | 1.54 | 0.91 | 1.66 | 0.83 | 1.79 |
| 25 | 1.18 | 1.34 | 1.10 | 1.43 | 1.02 | 1.54 | 0.94 | 1.65 | 0.86 | 1.77 |
| 26 | 1.19 | 1.35 | 1.12 | 1.44 | 1.04 | 1.54 | 0.96 | 1.65 | 0.88 | 1.76 |
| 27 | 1.21 | 1.36 | 1.13 | 1.44 | 1.06 | 1.54 | 0.99 | 1.64 | 0.91 | 1.75 |
| 28 | 1.22 | 1.37 | 1.15 | 1.45 | 1.08 | 1.54 | 1.01 | 1.64 | 0.93 | 1.74 |
| 29 | 1.24 | 1.38 | 1.17 | 1.45 | 1.10 | 1.54 | 1.03 | 1.63 | 0.96 | 1.73 |
| 30 | 1.25 | 1.38 | 1.18 | 1.46 | 1.12 | 1.54 | 1.05 | 1.63 | 0.98 | 1.73 |
| 31 | 1.26 | 1.39 | 1.20 | 1.47 | 1.13 | 1.55 | 1.07 | 1.63 | 1.00 | 1.72 |
| 32 | 1.27 | 1.40 | 1.21 | 1.47 | 1.15 | 1.55 | 1.08 | 1.63 | 1.02 | 1.71 |
| 33 | 1.28 | 1.41 | 1.22 | 1.48 | 1.16 | 1.55 | 1.10 | 1.63 | 1.04 | 1.71 |
| 34 | 1.29 | 1.41 | 1.24 | 1.48 | 1.17 | 1.55 | 1.12 | 1.63 | 1.06 | 1.70 |
| 35 | 1.30 | 1.42 | 1.25 | 1.48 | 1.19 | 1.55 | 1.13 | 1.63 | 1.07 | 1.70 |
| 36 | 1.31 | 1.43 | 1.26 | 1.49 | 1.20 | 1.56 | 1.15 | 1.63 | 1.09 | 1.70 |
| 37 | 1.32 | 1.43 | 1.27 | 1.49 | 1.21 | 1.56 | 1.16 | 1.62 | 1.10 | 1.70 |
| 38 | 1.33 | 1.44 | 1.28 | 1.50 | 1.23 | 1.56 | 1.17 | 1.62 | 1.12 | 1.70 |
| 39 | 1.34 | 1.44 | 1.29 | 1.50 | 1.24 | 1.56 | 1.19 | 1.63 | 1.13 | 1.69 |
| 40 | 1.35 | 1.45 | 1.30 | 1.51 | 1.25 | 1.57 | 1.20 | 1.63 | 1.15 | 1.69 |
| 45 | 1.39 | 1.48 | 1.34 | 1.53 | 1.30 | 1.58 | 1.25 | 1.63 | 1.21 | 1.69 |
| 50 | 1.42 | 1.50 | 1.38 | 1.54 | 1.34 | 1.59 | 1.30 | 1.64 | 1.26 | 1.69 |
| 55 | 1.45 | 1.52 | 1.41 | 1.56 | 1.37 | 1.60 | 1.33 | 1.64 | 1.30 | 1.69 |
| 60 | 1.47 | 1.54 | 1.44 | 1.57 | 1.40 | 1.61 | 1.37 | 1.65 | 1.33 | 1.69 |
| 65 | 1.49 | 1.55 | 1.46 | 1.59 | 1.43 | 1.62 | 1.40 | 1.66 | 1.36 | 1.69 |
| 70 | 1.51 | 1.57 | 1.48 | 1.60 | 1.45 | 1.63 | 1.42 | 1.66 | 1.39 | 1.70 |
| 75 | 1.53 | 1.58 | 1.50 | 1.61 | 1.47 | 1.64 | 1.45 | 1.67 | 1.42 | 1.70 |
| 80 | 1.54 | 1.59 | 1.52 | 1.62 | 1.49 | 1.65 | 1.47 | 1.67 | 1.44 | 1.70 |
| 85 | 1.56 | 1.60 | 1.53 | 1.63 | 1.51 | 1.65 | 1.49 | 1.68 | 1.46 | 1.71 |
| 90 | 1.57 | 1.61 | 1.55 | 1.64 | 1.53 | 1.66 | 1.50 | 1.69 | 1.48 | 1.71 |
| 95 | 1.58 | 1.62 | 1.56 | 1.65 | 1.54 | 1.67 | 1.52 | 1.69 | 1.50 | 1.71 |
| 100 | 1.59 | 1.63 | 1.57 | 1.65 | 1.55 | 1.67 | 1.53 | 1.70 | 1.51 | 1.72 |

*Note: n* = number of observations, *k* = number of regressors.

# Appendix C
## Solutions to Odd-Numbered Problems

**Chapter 2 Appendix**

**1. a.** $Q = 75 - 0.5P$    **b.** $P = 150 - 2Q$

**3. a.** $AVC = 300 - 25Q + 1.5Q^2$
$\quad\quad AC = 1,500/Q + 300 - 25Q + 1.5Q^2$
$\quad\quad MC = 300 - 50Q + 4.5Q^2$
$\quad AVC = 300 + 25Q$
$\quad\quad AC = 1,500/Q + 300 + 25Q^2$
$\quad\quad MC = 300 + 50Q$
$\quad AVC = 300$
$\quad\quad AC = Q + 300$
$\quad\quad MC = 300$

**Chapter 3**

**1. a.** 800 caps

$\quad$ **b.** $10

$\quad$ **c.** $20

**3. b.** $P = $4.00$

**5. a.** $Q_D = 61,000 - 200P$

$\quad$ **b.** $0, 26,000, 31,000, 36,000$

$\quad$ **c.** $80

**7.** Supply curve shifts to right and demand curve shifts to left. The combined shifts drastically reduced the world market price of sugar.

**9. a.** No, because point elasticity is $-.625$.

$\quad$ **b.** Yes, although the number of units sold would drop from 12,000 to 10,000, the combined impact of an inelastic demand and the increase in advertising would raise total revenue from $36,000 to $40,000. Moreover the incremental revenue is far greater than the $100 increase in advertising expenses.

**11. a.** $P = 25 - 0.1Q$

$\quad$ **b.** $P = 9.29 - 0.007Q$

$\quad$ **c.** $P = 90 - 2Q$

## Chapter 4

**1.** $0.2/-0.1 = -2$

**3.** **b.** Point $-1.27$; arc $-1.08$

   **c.** Point $0.45$; arc $0.48$

   **d.** Point $-1.45$; arc $-1.25$

**5.** Quantity 5,212; revenue increases.

**7.** Price $26.73; elasticity $-1.73$

**9.** At price $= \$5.00$; arc $-2.33$, point $-2$, MR $3.00; at price $= \$4.00$; arc $-1.31$, point $-1.14$, MR $1.00; at price $= \$2.50$; arc $-0.58$, point $-0.5$; MR $-\$2.00$

**11.** **a.** Elasticity for Brown's shoes may be greater than elasticity for all shoes in general. If elasticity for Brown's shoes is $> /1/$, then price decrease could lead to revenue increase.

   **b.** Increase 9 percent.

**13.** **a.** $-1.4$

   **b.** Complementary good; cross elasticity $-0.7$.

   **c.** Yes, revenues for ice cream and syrup rise, and probably so does profit.

**15.** **a.** 1,800

   **b.** $0, $100, $25

   **c.** $TR = 100Q - 0.05Q^2$; $MR = 100 - 0.1Q$

   **d.** $TR = \$42,000$; $MR = \$40$

   **e.** $\epsilon = 2.33$

   **f.** $TR = \$48,000$; $MR = \$20$; $\epsilon = 1.5$

   **g.** 1,000

## Chapter 5

**1.** **a.** Focus groups, telephone surveys, or historical data on similar products such as VCRs.

   **b.** Price, advertising expenditures, per capita GDP, price of competing products (e.g., VCRs), or complementary products (e.g., CDs)

**3.** **a.** $Q = 91.32 - 0.006P$; (SE 11.4) (SE 0.0009)

   **b.** Interest rates, advertising promotional rebates.

**5.** **a.** $E_p = -1.74$, $E_A = 0.69$, $E_{PC} = 0.10$, $E_M = 0.47$, $E_C = 0.14$

   **b.** One-tail test could be used for each variable.

   **c.** Interest rates would be more appropriate for time series analysis.

**7.** **a.** Exponents of $P_a$ and $P_j$ indicate a higher degree of substitution between European and Japanese luxury cars than between European and American luxury cars.

   **b.** Yes, coefficient 1.6 is greater than unity, thereby indicating a luxury product.

   **c.** Not surprising. Prices of cars could be low relative to the high incomes of those who buy them.

## Chapter 6

**1.** 16 percent; $1,691,277

**3.** **a.** 16 percent (exact answer is 15.98 percent)   **b.** $1,012,680; $1,174,709

   **c.** 14 percent (exact answer is 14.02 percent)   **d.** $995,220; $1,134,551

   **e.** Growth rate decreases about 1 percentage point each year.

**5.** **a.** $176.667 + 20.5879t$, $176.667 + 20.5879\,(11) = \$403$; Past ten years describe straight line; thus, some confidence that trend will continue.

   **b.** $382 \times 0.7 + 353 \times 0.3 = 373$. Upward trend makes exponential smoothing an inferior forecasting tool; it underestimates.

**7. a.** $Q = 17,350$
   **b.** $Q = 17,200$; $Q = 17,400$
   **c.** $Q = 17,500$
   **d.** $Q$ decreases by 1,200
**9.** January $55.4 million; April $104.3 million; July $87.5 million; October $109.6 million.
**11. a.** (1)  $703.0381 + 743.7536 \times t$
   (2)  $2241.0639 \times (1.1274)^t$
   (3)  $-6820.91 + 2.359605 \times \text{GDP}$
   **b.** Exponential trend, 15,265

## Chapter 7

**1. a.** False   **b.** True   **c.** True   **d.** False
**3. a.** 4 units   **b.** 1–6, 6–11, 11 and above units of labor.
   **c.** 9 workers, reduce to 8, no change because still in Stage II.
**5. a.** more to Mexico or possibly Taiwan
   **b.** either Mexico or Taiwan (Taiwan has lower MP/P but also lower overhead)
**7. a.** and **b.**

| Variable Factor | Quantity | Average Product | Marginal Product |
|---|---|---|---|
| 0 | 0.0 | | |
| 1 | 7.5 | 7.5 | 7.5 |
| 2 | 15.6 | 7.8 | 8.1 |
| 3 | 23.7 | 7.9 | 8.1 |
| 4 | 31.2 | 7.8 | 7.5 |
| 5 | 37.5 | 7.5 | 6.3 |
| 6 | 42.0 | 7.0 | 4.5 |
| 7 | 44.1 | 6.3 | 2.1 |
| 8 | 43.2 | 5.4 | −0.9 |
| 9 | 38.7 | 4.3 | −4.5 |
| 10 | 30.0 | 3.0 | −8.7 |

**9. a.** $\log Q = 1.889 + .414 \log M$
   **b.** Fairly satisfactory, could improve if additional independent variables are included.
   **c.** 2.91, 2.66, 2.51, 2.46, 2.37, 2.22, 2.16
**11. a.** budget line shifts to right
   **b.** budget line becomes steeper (from X)
   **c.** budget line becomes flatter (from Y)
   **d.** budget line rotates and becomes steeper
   **e.** isoquant shifts to right with bias towards Y
   **f.** parallel shift of isoquant to the left
**13. a.** CRTS   **b.** CRTS   **c.** IRTS   **d.** DRTS   **e.** IRTS   **f.** IRTS
   **g.** If exponents sum to unity, CRTS. If they are less than unity, DRTS. If they are greater than unity, IRTS.

**15. a.** $0.75 + 0.3 = 1.05.$ Increasing

**b.**

| Labor | Capital | Quantity |
|-------|---------|----------|
| 100 | 50 | 132.9 |
| 150 | 75 | 203.5 |
| 300 | 150 | 421.3 |

**c.** 10.9 percent

**d.** 7.4 percent; decreasing marginal product     **e.** 2.9 percent     **f.** Constant returns to scale

## Chapter 8

**1.**

| Q | TC | TFC | TVC | AC | AFC | AVC | MC |
|---|-----|-----|-----|------|------|-----|-----|
| 0 | <u>120</u> | 120 | 0 | X | X | X | |
| 1 | 265 | 120 | 145 | <u>265</u> | 120 | 145 | 145 |
| 2 | 384 | 120 | <u>264</u> | 192 | 60 | 132 | 119 |
| 3 | 483 | 120 | 363 | <u>161</u> | 40 | 121 | 99 |
| 4 | 568 | 120 | 448 | 142 | 30 | 112 | <u>85</u> |
| 5 | 645 | 120 | <u>525</u> | 129 | 24 | 105 | 77 |
| 6 | 720 | 120 | 600 | <u>120</u> | 20 | 100 | 75 |
| 7 | 799 | 120 | 679 | 114.1 | 17.1 | <u>97</u> | 79 |
| 8 | 888 | 120 | <u>768</u> | 111 | 15 | 96 | 89 |
| 9 | 993 | 120 | 873 | 110.3 | 13.3 | <u>97</u> | 105 |
| 10 | 1120 | 120 | 1000 | 112 | 12 | 100 | <u>127</u> |

**3.** If only relevant costs are included, it would be $188 or $9.40 per fish.

**5. a.** False, decisions are future oriented so managers should use the replacement, not the historical costs of raw materials.

**b.** True, this can be explained by the mathematical relationship between marginal and average.

**c.** True, declining long run AC means economies of scale and increasing long run AC means diseconomies of scale.

**d.** False, marginal cost can also be used in long run analysis because even the "fixed" cost varies in the long run.

**e.** False, the rational firm will operate where profit is maximized. This may not coincide with the point of minimum average cost because per unit revenue must also be taken into account.

**7. a.** $LRAC = 160 - 20Q + 1.2Q^2$

$LR\ MC = 160 - 40Q + 3.6Q^2$

**b.** Because of the particular functional form of the LRAC, we know that this firm experiences economies of scale at about 8 units of output (8.3 to be exact).

**9. b & c.**   Straight line:     $TC = 94.93 + 0.46$

$R^2 = 0.91 \qquad t = 8.96$

Quadratic:     $TC = 106.68 - 0.13Q + 0.005Q^2$

$R^2 = 0.99 \qquad t_b = -1.41; t_c = 6.70$

Cubic:     $TC = 99.5 + 0.51Q - 0.009Q^2 + 0.00008Q^3$

$R^2 = 0.999 \qquad t_b = 6.30; t_c = -5.07; t_d = 8.36$

Cubic function gives best fit.

**11. c.** (1) Straight-line function; AVC and MC are constant. (2) TC increases at increasing rate; MC rises. (3) TC increases at decreasing rate; MC, AVC, and AC decrease.

**13. a. & b.**

| QUANTITY | TOTAL COST | AVERAGE TOTAL COST | AVERAGE VARIABLE COST | MARGINAL COST |
|----------|-----------|--------------------|-----------------------|---------------|
| 1 | 193.5 | 193.50 | 23.50 | 23.50 |
| 4 | 282.0 | 70.50 | 28.00 | 32.50 |
| 7 | 397.5 | 56.79 | 32.50 | 41.50 |
| 10 | 540.0 | 54.00 | 37.00 | 50.50 |
| 13 | 709.5 | 54.58 | 41.50 | 59.50 |

**c.** Marginal cost rises throughout.

## Chapter 9

**1.** The graph indicates the firm is losing money but is earning enough revenue to cover all of its fixed cost and contributes the rest to its variable cost. In the long run, it would have to drop out of the market unless the market price increased or the firm is able to reduce its costs.

**3. a.** Implies a quadratic total cost function (i.e., law of diminishing returns occurs at outset of production).
   **b.** At $Q = 1,500$, MC $= \$157.50$; At $Q = 2,000$, MC $= \$160.00$; At $Q = 3,500$, MC $= \$167.50$
   **c.** MC $= \$150 + 0.005$, $Q = \$175$, $Q^* = 5,000$
   **d.** Supply curve is the portion of the firm's marginal cost that lies above the shutdown point.

**5. b.** Yes   **c.** Produce 14 units because loss would be less than total fixed cost.

**7. a.** $63   **b.** $50

**9.** Setting the derivative of the total cost function equal to the derivative of the total revenue function and solving for $Q$ yields the same result as setting the total profit function equal to 0 and solving for $Q$.

## Chapter 10

**1. a.** At 50-cent intervals starting from $12.50 and decreasing to $8.00, the arc elasticities are $-1.96, -1.74, -1.55, -1.38, -1.24, -1.11, -1, -0.9, -0.8$.
   **b.** $8.75 would be too low for the students. Optimal price is between $12 and $11.50.
   **c.** Students would suffer a loss if the opportunity cost of their venture were included in the total cost.
   **d.** $8.75 may help to increase the store's revenue. It could even be offered to customers as a loss leader.

**3. b.** The first firm will have the following MR (starting from $10.00 and decreasing to $3.00 at one dollar intervals): $8.75, $6.75, $4.75, $2.75, $0.75, $-\$1.25$, and $-\$3.25$. The second firms comparable data are $4.33, $2.33, $.033, $-\$1.67, -\$3.67, -\$5.67, -\$7.67$.
   **e.** Range would be at where the MR line is vertical.

**5. a.** Although prices are lower, the costs of goods sold are proportionately even lower and so profit margins are often higher for private label goods than for brand name items.
   **b.** Very often the manufacturers of the private products are the very same ones that manufacture the brand names. By selling them as private label products, they save on the marketing expenses.

**7. a.** $P = \$22$   **b.** Demand would fall, economic profit would approach zero.   **c.** $P = \$12$.

9. Assume that you have decided $250,000 to be the maximum amount that you could spend for the new product, leaving the rest for the other products. You will probably end up spending this maximum amount (this is the equivalent of a firm charging the lowest possible price).

## Chapter 11

1. **a.** 2,000   **b.** $50,000   **c.** $15,000   **d.** 2,500
   **e.** 2,500 = (37,500 + 15,000) / (P − 10); P = $31
3. AVC = $77; TFC = $120,000
   **a.** 120,000/(100 − 77) = 5,217   **b.** $521,700
   **c.**

   | Q | PROFIT |
   |---|---|
   | 2,000 | $−74,000 |
   | 4,000 | −28,000 |
   | 6,000 | 18,000 |
   | 8,000 | 64,000 |
   | 10,000 | 110,000 |

5. **a.** 20,000   **b.** (60,000 + 15,000) / (9 − 6) = 25,000   **c.** Undefined (denominator = 0); 5   **d.** 3
7. **a.** 70,000   **b.** (1) 80,000   (2) 70,000 = 1,200,000 / (P − 5); P = $22.14
   **c.** (1) (Q × 12) − 840,000 = (Q × 14) − 1,200,000   Q = 180,000   Profit = $1,320,000
   (2) 1.64; 1.91   (3) No; equal profit reached at 180,000 units.
9. **a.** 80,000
   **b.** $100,000
   **c.** 125,000
   **d.** $9.50
   **e.** $3.50
   **f.** 125,000

## Chapter 12

1. TC = 6 + 10Q; TR = 15X − 0.5Q²; Profit = −0.5Q² + 5Q −6; Maximum profit = 6.5, at Q = 5 and P = 12.5
3. **a.** (1) Schedule: Q = 7−8, P = $340−360; Equation: Q = 7.5, P = $350 (2) Schedule: Q = 12−13, P = $240−260; Equation: Q = 12.5, P = $250 (3) Schedule: Q = 10, P = $300
   **b.** (1) Same as above.   (2) Same as above. (3) Q = 9, P = $320
   **c.** In the Baumol model, a change in TFC affects price and quantity.
5. $67.50
7. When TC = $15,000: profit = $21,000, peaches = 400 bushels, apples = 600 bushels. When TC = $25,000: profit = $29,000, peaches = 600 bushels, apples = 900 bushels.
9. Charge high transfer prices when shipping products from low tax country to high tax country, and vice-versa. Use the following example: Company ships 1,000 units from operation in A to operation in B. Transfer price is 100/unit. A's cost of sales if 65,000 and operating expenses 15,000. B's operating expenses are 10,000. Income tax in A is 20%, in B 40%. Profit in A is 16,000, in B 18,000. Now change transfer price to 120/unit. Profit in A is 32,000, in B 6,000.

## Chapter 13

1. Buyer must make monthly payments, thus decreasing balance in savings account, and interest earnings will be lower.
3. Sell at the end of year 4. NPV decreases in year 5.

**5.** Operating cash flows (after taxes)

| | |
|---|---:|
| Year 1 | $27,000 |
| Years 2, 3, and 4, each | 36,000 |
| Year 5 | 24,000 |

| | |
|---|---:|
| PV of operating cash flows | $114,927 |
| PV of salvage (after taxes) | 3,404 |
| Additional working capital | −15,000 |
| PV of returned working capital | 8,511 |
| Original investment | −150,000 |
| NPV | $−38,158 |

Do not make investment.

**7.** Net present value cost of furnishing car is $13,402. Net present value cost of paying mileage is $11,982. Company should pay mileage.

**9.** Cost of retained earnings is 14.4%. Cost of new equity is 14.6%.

**11.**

| | | |
|---|---|---|
| Bonds | 0.28 × 0.066 | 0.0185 |
| Equity | 0.72 × 0.14 | 0.1008 |
| Weighted cost | | 0.1193 = 11.9% |

**13. a.**

| | NPV | IRR |
|---|---|---|
| Project C | $10,355 | 23.0% |
| Project D | 9,237 | 25.0 |

**b.** Select C; NPV is higher.

## Chapter 14

**1. a.** $320 **b.** $30.98 **c.** 0.097

**3.**

| | Book A | Book B |
|---|---|---|
| Expected profit | $2,450 | $1,800 |
| Variance | 94,500 | 26,000 |
| Standard deviation | 307.4 | 161.2 |
| Coefficient of variation | 0.125 | 0.090 |

Depends on attitude toward risk. A has higher profit and higher relative risk.

**5. a.** NPV = 295; $\sigma$ = 115; CV = 0.3898

**b.** Relative risk is about equal, but B's NPV is higher; thus, B could be selected.

**7. a.** NPV = $6,729 **b.** NPV = $6,729

**9. b.** $Z = (12 - 16.7)/6.2 = -0.76$; 77.6%

**c.** $Z = (0 - 16.7)/6.2 = -2.69$; 99.6%

**11.** Large: NPV $58,100; $\sigma$ $81,270; CV 1.4

Small: NPV $52,300; $\sigma$ $32,090; CV 0.6

**13. a.** NPV = −$51,737; not acceptable

**b.** NPV = $21,671; acceptable

Value of option = $73,408.

# Index

Note: Page entries in *italics* refer to figures; entries followed by *n* refer to footnotes; entries followed by *t* refer to tables.

# ECONOMIC RESOURCES ON THE WEB

*Search Engines*

| Web Site Name | Web Address | Description |
|---|---|---|
| Alta Vista | www.altavista.com | Largest Web Index |
| Deja News | www.dejanews.com | Searches Usnet Newsgroups |
| Beaucoup | www.beaucoup.com | Searches over 2,500 other search engines |
| The Electronic Library | www.elibrary.com | 1000 newspapers, magazines and academic journals |
| Excite | www.excite.com | Concept Base Navigation |
| Global Online Directory (G.O.D) | www.god.co.uk | Global Search Engine |
| Hot Bot | www.hotbot.com | Personal robot for searching the web |
| IBM InfoMarket | www.infomarket.com | Serious searchers - Web searching, Commercial resources, 66 news wires, 300 newspapers, 770 News Letters, 63 journals and 11 million companies |
| InfoSeek Guide | www.infoseek.com | #1 Search engine by PC Week |
| Lycos | www.lycos.com | Internet Catalog Search |
| Web Crawler | www.webcrawler.com | "search for unusual sites" |
| What's New | www.whatsnu.com | List of best new sites on the Web |
| WhoWhere | www.whowhere.lycos.com | Fast and easy way to find who and where |
| Yahoo | www.yahoo.com | Pioneer of searching |

*Useful Financial Services Reference Sites*

| Web Site Name | Web Address | Description |
|---|---|---|
| The Finance Net | www.financenet.gov | Financial resource list, newsgroups, libraries and searchables |
| CNNfn | www.cnnfn.com | Central directory of resources and financial information |
| The Edgar Report | edgar.stern.nyu.edu | Get Corporate SEC filings. Search corporate profiles |
| The Corporate Finance Network | www.corpfinet.com | Directory of all matters relating to corporate finance |
| Wall Street Net | www.netsource.com/wsn | Investment bankers and issuers |
| American Bankers Association | www.inter.net/aba/cbihorne/cbiinfo.htm | The center for banking information |
| Corporate Finance Newsletter | www.corpfinet.com/newsform.html | Published monthly and sent to you via e-mail |
| Financial World Virtual Yellow pages | www.imsworld.com/yo/finance.html | Search sites related to finance, banking and stocks |
| Internet Banking Index | www.ddsi.corn/banking/ | Searchable list of banks, mortgage companies and Internet banking technologies |
| Insurance Web | www.insweb.com | Contains industry, regulatory, broker and consumer information |
| ˙rs Daily News ˙lines | www.yahoo.com/headlines/current/business/ | Reuters news printed online |